Grounded in the most recent research on language, writing, and literary culture in premodern sinographic East Asia, David C. S. Li et al.'s exciting new Brush Conversation in the Sinographic Cosmopolis *breaks new ground in this heretofore neglected field of study at the intersection of Literary Sinitic, sinography, diplomatic history, and East Asian cultural and intellectual exchange. The first book-length collection in English on the topic, this volume mobilizes an impressive range of East Asian brush talk scholars and covers numerous pre- and early modern East Asian polities. The results force us to take seriously pre- and early modern East Asian 'synchronous writing-mediated cross-border face-to-face communication' and the multi-faceted written records that this unique cultural practice produced.*

– **Ross King,** Professor of Korean, Department of Asian Studies, University of British Columbia Asian Centre, 1871 West Mall Vancouver, BC V6T 1Z2

Everybody working on East Asia knows what brush talk is, the use of Sinitic (literary Chinese) to conduct a silent conversation, and everybody knows how useful it was (and still can be) for communication between speakers of different languages, such as Chinese, Japanese, Korean and Vietnamese. But that is the limit of what everybody knows, for brush talk has been extraordinarily neglected by historians, in spite of the fact that plenty of records of these written conversations survive today. This enthralling collection of essays redresses the balance by focusing on the phenomenon of brush talk in all its extraordinary variety. Koreans, Japanese and Ryukyuans shipwrecked on the Chinese coast had no alternative but to resort to brush talk to explain who they were and to find out where they had landed, so long as at least one member of the crew had some command of Sinitic. Vietnamese diplomats, like most diplomats in premodern East Asia, had little or no knowledge of any form of spoken Chinese and were forced to rely on interpreters, but for social interactions as well as for more intellectual exchanges they turned to brush talk. The essays in this pathbreaking book explore the uses of brush talk in different contexts and between speakers of various languages, they consider the value of the written records of brush conversations that survive and they weigh up the implications for attitudes towards spoken languages in premodern East Asia. This is a stimulating and fascinating book, and one that rightly draws attention to a crucially important means of communication between peoples in East Asia.

–**Peter Kornicki,** Professor

Brush Conversation in the Sinographic Cosmopolis *presents a fascinating, in-depth view of an under-studied mode of written communication that was once widely employed across East Asia. Through "brush talk", conversational interactions in written Classical Chinese, people from various parts of the "sinographic" world were able to communicate in real time despite their inability to speak or understand each other's languages. Brush talk conversations ranged from the simple communication of basic information — as in the interrogation of "boat drifters" washed ashore after maritime accidents — to formalized and emotionally rich exchanges of poetry. Brush talk was sometimes preferred to spoken conversation even when interpreters were readily available, indicating its power and attraction as an expression of erudition and cultural status.*

In this ground-breaking volume, scholars specializing in the languages and cultures of Japan, Korea, Vietnam, China, and the Ryukyus (Okinawa) plumb the historical record to reveal and analyze the fascinating array of written conversations that survive in the historical record. These conversations provide insights into the worlds of diplomacy, travel, espionage, and war, bringing to life a now-vanished cross-national culture with a shared foundation in Classical Chinese language and texts. At the same time, these historical records reveal to us that while a common written language could successfully bridge linguistic divides, they also throw into sharp relief vast cultural differences that were not always so easy to overcome.

The different book chapters, despite their separate authorship, are unified by a sophisticated theoretical framework. Combining scholarly rigor with dramatic storytelling, this book is the only scholarly investigation of brush talk that looks at the phenomenon with such a wide lens. As part of the current interest in the "Sinographic Cosmopolis" prior to the 20th century, this book is sure to be of interest to scholars of East Asian history, culture, language, and texts.
– **Zev Handel**

Brush Conversation in the Sinographic Cosmopolis

For hundreds of years until the 1900s, in today's China, Japan, North and South Korea, and Vietnam, literati of Classical Chinese or Literary Sinitic (*wényán* 文言) could communicate in writing interactively, despite not speaking each other's languages.

This book outlines the historical background of, and the material conditions that led to, widespread literacy development in premodern and early modern East Asia, where reading and writing for formal purposes was conducted in Literary Sinitic. To exemplify how 'silent conversation' or 'brush-assisted conversation' is possible through writing-mediated brushed interaction, synchronously face-to-face, this book presents contextualized examples from recurrent contexts involving (i) boat drifters; (ii) traveling literati; and (iii) diplomatic envoys. Where profound knowledge of classical canons and literary works in Sinitic was a shared attribute of the brush-talkers concerned, their brush-talk would characteristically be intertwined with poetic improvisation.

Being the first monograph in English to address this fascinating lingua-cultural practice and cross-border communication phenomenon, which was possibly *sui generis* in Sinographic East Asia, it will be of interest to students of not only East Asian languages and linguistics, history, international relations, and diplomacy, but also (historical) pragmatics, sociolinguistics, sociology of language, scripts and writing systems, and cultural and linguistic anthropology.

David C. S. Li (李楚成) is Professor and Head of the Department of Chinese and Bilingual Studies (中文及雙語學系), The Hong Kong Polytechnic University (香港理工大學). He received his BA in English (Hong Kong), MA in Applied Linguistics (France), and PhD in Linguistics (Germany). He has published widely in multilingualism in Greater China, World Englishes, Hong Kong English, China English, bilingual education and language policy, bilingual interaction and code-switching (translanguaging), Cantonese as an additional language, and South Asian Hongkongers' needs for written Chinese. He speaks Cantonese, English and Mandarin fluently, is conversant in German and French, and is learning Japanese and Korean. More recent interests focus on the historical spread of written Chinese (Sinitic) and its use as a scripta franca until the early twentieth century in Sinographic East Asia (China, Japan, Korea, and Vietnam).

Reijiro Aoyama's (青山玲二郎) research is concerned with transnational and global processes mediated by migration and the movement of information, symbols, capital and cultural commodities. His research interests include anthropology of work and mobility, narratives of migration, and material and non-material culture of cross-border interactions. He has conducted several long-term ethnographies of the Japanese presence in East Asia, and has published on Japanese diaspora, craftsmanship, and emotional work in service industries, Sino-Japanese animation, and historical cross-border interactions mediated by Sinitic writing. Before taking up his post at The Hong Kong Polytechnic University, he taught at Fudan University, Tsinghua University, and City University of Hong Kong.

Wong Tak-sum (黃得森) is a post-doctoral fellow in the Department of Chinese and Bilingual Studies at The Hong Kong Polytechnic University. He received his BEng in Computer Science from Hong Kong University of Science and Technology (2004), and PhD in Linguistics from City University of Hong Kong (2018). He has built a treebank of the Tripiṭaka Koreana during his doctoral study and has been working on the quantitative study of historical syntax. His research expertise covers Chinese historical linguistics, Cantonese linguistics, corpus linguistics, computer-assisted language learning, Chinese dialectology and Chinese paleography.

Routledge Studies in the Early History of Asia

1. **Imperial Tombs in Tang China, 618–907**
   The politics of paradise
   Tonia Eckfeld

2. **Elite Theatre in Ming China, 1368–1644**
   Grant Guangren Shen

3. **Marco Polo's China**
   A Venetian in the realm of Khubilai Khan
   Stephen G Haw

4. **The Diary of a Manchu Soldier in Seventeenth-Century China**
   "My service in the army", by Dzengeo
   Introduction, Translation and Notes by Nicola Di Cosmo

5. **Past Human Migrations in East Asia**
   Matching archaeology, linguistics and genetics
   Edited by Alicia Sanchez-Mazas, Roger Blench, Malcolm D. Ross, Ilia Peiros and Marie Lin

6. **Rethinking the Prehistory of Japan**
   Language, genes and civilisation
   Ann Kumar

7. **Ancient Chinese Encyclopedia of Technology**
   Jun Wenren

8. **Women and the Literary World in Early Modern China, 1580–1700**
   Daria Berg

9. **Asian Expansions**
   The historical experiences of polity expansion in Asia
   Edited by Geoff Wade

10. **The Emergence of Civilizational Consciousness in Early China**
    History Word by Word
    Uffe Bergeton

11. **Cultural Astronomy of the Japanese Archipelago**
    Exploring the Japanese Skyscape
    Akira Goto

12. **The Birth of Japanese Historiography**
    John Bentley

13. **The Imperial Network in Ancient China**
    The Foundation of Sinitic Empire in Southern East Asia
    Maxim Korolkov

14. **Brush Conversation in the Sinographic Cosmopolis**
    Interactional Cross-border Communication Using Literary Sinitic in Early Modern East Asia
    Edited by David C. S. Li, Reijiro Aoyama and Wong Tak-sum

Brush Conversation in the Sinographic Cosmopolis

Interactional Cross-border Communication Using Literary Sinitic in Early Modern East Asia

Edited by
David C. S. Li, Reijiro Aoyama and Wong Tak-sum

LONDON AND NEW YORK

First published 2022
by Routledge
4 Park Square, Milton Park, Abingdon, Oxon OX14 4RN

and by Routledge
605 Third Avenue, New York, NY 10158

Routledge is an imprint of the Taylor & Francis Group, an Informa business

© 2022 selection and editorial matter, David C. S. Li, Reijiro Aoyama and Wong Tak-sum; individual chapters, the contributors

The right of David C. S. Li, Reijiro Aoyama and Wong Tak-sum to be identified as the authors of the editorial material, and of the authors for their individual chapters, has been asserted in accordance with sections 77 and 78 of the Copyright, Designs and Patents Act 1988.

All rights reserved. No part of this book may be reprinted or reproduced or utilised in any form or by any electronic, mechanical, or other means, now known or hereafter invented, including photocopying and recording, or in any information storage or retrieval system, without permission in writing from the publishers.

Trademark notice: Product or corporate names may be trademarks or registered trademarks and are used only for identification and explanation without intent to infringe.

British Library Cataloguing-in-Publication Data
A catalogue record for this book is available from the British Library

Library of Congress Cataloguing-in-Publication Data
A catalog record for this book has been requested

ISBN: 978-0-367-49940-2 (hbk)
ISBN: 978-0-367-49942-6 (pbk)
ISBN: 978-1-003-04817-6 (ebk)

DOI: 10.4324/9781003048176

Typeset in Times New Roman
by Apex CoVantage, LLC

Contents

Frontispiece 1   x
Frontispiece 2   x
List of Figures   xi
List of Tables   xii
List of Contributors   xiii
Foreword to Brush Conversation in the Sinographic
   Cosmopolis: *the second miracle*   xvii
Preface   xxiii
Epigraph   xxix
Map   xxx

1 **Writing-mediated cross-border communication face-to-face: from Sinitic brush-talk (漢文筆談) to pen-assisted conversation**   1
   DAVID C. S. LI, REIJIRO AOYAMA AND WONG TAK-SUM

2 **East Asian brush-talk literature: introduction and proposed classification**   46
   WANG YONG

PART 1
Brush-talk involving traveling literati and boat drifters in East Asia   87

3 **Brush conversation between maritime officials and foreign seafarers in drifting records in eighteenth- and nineteenth-century East Asia**   89
   MATSUURA AKIRA AND REIJIRO AOYAMA

4 Senzaimaru's maiden voyage to Shanghai in 1862: brush conversation between Japanese travelers and people they encountered in Qing China 111
DAVID C. S. LI AND REIJIRO AOYAMA

5 Identity verification and negotiation through Sinitic brush-talk in Ming China and Japan: drifting accounts by Ch'oe Pu (1488) and Yi Chi-hang (1696–1697) 127
HUR KYOUNG-JIN

6 A study of salient linguistic features of two Ryukyuan brush conversations in Sinitic, 1611 and 1803 153
WONG TAK-SUM

PART 2
Brush-talk involving diplomatic envoys in East Asia 179

7 Sinitic brush-talk between Vietnam and China in the eighteenth century: a study of vice-envoy Lê Quý Đôn's mission to Qing China 181
NGUYỄN TUẤN-CƯỜNG AND NGUYỄN THỊ-TUYẾT

8 Lingua-cultural characteristics of brush-talk: insights from *Ōkōchi Documents* 大河內文書 199
WANG BAOPING

9 The charm and pitfalls of Sinitic brush-talk: a study of brush conversation records involving the first legation staff of Late Qing China in Japan (1870s–1880s) 217
LIU YUZHEN

10 Japanese-Korean brush-talk during the early Edo period, 1603–1711 243
KOO JEA-HYOUN AND JOO IAN

11 Brush-talk between Chosŏn envoys and Tokugawa literati: contesting cultural superiority and 'central efflorescence' 中華, 1711–1811 257
JANG JIN-YOUP

PART 3
Script-specific communication in Sinitic: significance for historical pragmatics, cultural anthropology, and East Asian studies   281

12 Sociocultural functions of Chinese characters and writing: transnational brush-talk encounters in mid-nineteenth- and early-twentieth-century East Asia   283
   REIJIRO AOYAMA

13 Discussion paper   309
   REBEKAH CLEMENTS

   Index   319

Figures

1.1	Example of morphographic sinograms pronounceable in different Sinitic languages	29
3.1	Early nineteenth-century Japanese painting of local officials questioning the Chinese crew from the stranded trading vessel Wansheng 萬勝	92
3.2a	Early nineteenth-century Japanese drawing of the stranded Chinese trading ship Yongmao 永茂	95
3.2b	Schematic description of the types of information on the drawing of the trading ship Yongmao	96
6.1	Sample digitalized image of the brush-talk record in 'A record of exchange of poetic verses with Ryukyu ambassadors'	159
6.2	Screenshot showing an edited version of the original text, its translation in modern Korean, and a photocopy of the typeset brush-talk record in 'A record of exchange of poetic verses with Ryukyu ambassadors'	159
6.3	Sample digitalized image of the first page of *Ryukan hitsudan* 琉館筆談, the Hawley version	162
6.4	Digitalized image of the first page of *Ryukan hitsudan* 琉館筆談, the Tsukuba version	163
6.5	An excerpt of *Hakusei Kanwa* 白姓官話 ('Haku's Mandarin')	168
8.1	*Ōkōchi Documents*, Luó yuán tiě 羅源帖, vol. 4, p. 37	211
8.2	*Ōkōchi Documents*, Luó yuán tiě 羅源帖, vol. 8, p. 406	211
12.1	*Chōsen no kozōzu* 朝鮮小童図 or 'Calligraphy of a Korean boy'	304

Tables

1.1	Ming tributaries as of 1587	19
2.1	Details of twenty *t'ongsinsa* missions to Japan	69
2.2	'Collection of information on the drifting of Tang ships during the Edo Period', no. 1–10 (江戸時代飄着唐船資料集一至十)	77
3.1	Interpreting service for communication with distressed Chinese seafarers during the early modern era	105
4.1	Some examples of sinograms in Literary Sinitic pronounced in Chinese, Korean, and Japanese	115
6.1	A comparison of the basic statistics in *Cungtaplok* and the *Ryukan hitsudan*	169
7.1	Basic information about 20 (brush) conversations in question-and-answer mode as documented in 'A complete record of an embassy to the North' 北使通錄 (vol. 4)	183
8.1	Japanese-flavored Sinitic expressions and their corresponding meanings in Chinese	214

Contributors

Matsuura Akira (松浦章) specializes in the economic history of Ming and Qing dynasties, Sino-Japanese relations, and East Asian shipping and cultural exchanges. He obtained a Doctor of Letters in 1989, and a Doctor of Cultural Interactions in 2011. He was appointed as Professor at Kansai University in 1988, and Honorary Professor in 2017. He served as the director of the East-West Academic Research Institute and the Asian Cultural Research Center from 2011 to 2013. The focus of his research began with sailing ships along the coast of China and gradually expanded to East Asian waters, including the movement of people, commodities, and funds. He has published 22 books including 'Cultural exchange between Japan and China through a study of Chinese junks during the Edo period' and 'A compilation of drifting records of Chinese ships collected during the Edo period' (in Japanese); and 'Research on the history of overseas trade during the Qing dynasty' (in Chinese). Email: songpuzh@gmail.com.

Reijiro Aoyama's (青山玲二郎) research is concerned with transnational and global processes mediated by migration and the movement of information, symbols, capital and cultural commodities. His research interests include anthropology of work and mobility, narratives of migration, and material and non-material culture of cross-border interactions. He has conducted several long-term ethnographies of the Japanese presence in East Asia, and has published on Japanese diaspora, craftsmanship, and emotional work in service industries, Sino-Japanese animation, and historical cross-border interactions mediated by Sinitic writing. Before taking up his post at The Hong Kong Polytechnic University, he taught at Fudan University, Tsinghua University, and City University of Hong Kong. Email: reijirou2000@gmail.com.

Wang Baoping (王寶平) is a professor of the Faculty of Literature, Nishōgakusha University (二松學舍大學). He received his BA in Japanese Language from Hangzhou University; MA from Beijing Foreign Studies University; and DLitt from Kansai University. Before joining Nishōgakusha University, he had served as professor at Zhejiang University and Zhejiang Gongshang University. He has published extensively in the history of Sino-Japanese cultural exchange and philology. His major publications include 'Research in

xiv *Contributors*

China-Japan academic exchange during the Qing dynasty' (清代中日學術交流之研究, in Japanese), 'A collection of Japanese Books with prefaces and postscripts written by Qing Chinese' (日本典籍清人序跋集), and 'Late Qing brushtalk interaction data between Chinese, Japanese, and Koreans in Japan – the Ōkōchi documents' (日本蔵晚清中日朝筆談資料: 大河內文書, in Chinese). The last-mentioned was awarded the top National Outstanding Ancient Books Prize in 2016. Email: ouhouhei@163.com.

Rebekah Clements is an ICREA (Catalan Institution for Research and Advanced Studies) Research Professor at the Autonomous University of Barcelona, Spain. She is a cultural historian of Japan, specializing in the Tokugawa period, and was trained at the Australian National University, Waseda University, and the University of Cambridge. Her research focuses on language, society, and the characteristics of Japanese early modernity, as understood in the broader context of East Asia. She is currently the Principal Investigator and director of the European Research Council-funded project 'Aftermath of the East Asian War of 1592–1598' (https://aftermath.uab.cat/). Her previous publications include *A cultural history of translation in early modern Japan* (Cambridge University Press, 2015); 'Brush talk as the 'lingua franca' of East Asian diplomacy in Japanese-Korean encounters, c. 1600–1868', *The Historical Journal* (2019); and 'Speaking in tongues? Daimyo, Zen monks, and spoken Chinese in Japan, 1661–1711', *The Journal of Asian Studies* (2017). Email: rebekah.clements@icrea.cat.

Joo Ian (朱易安) is a doctoral student at the Department of Chinese and Bilingual Studies, The Hong Kong Polytechnic University. He has studied at Université Laval (Canada) for his bachelor's degree in literary studies and at National Chiao Tung University (Taiwan) for his master's degree in linguistics. He specializes in language typology. His areas of interest include language contact, language change, and linguistic iconicity. Currently, he is mainly working on his doctoral project of identifying linguistic areas in East Asia. He is from South Korea. Email: ian.joo@connect.polyu.hk.

Koo Jeah-youn (具智賢) is a Professor at the Department of Korean Language and Literature at Sunmoon University, South Korea. She received her undergraduate, master, and doctorate degrees in Korean Language and Literature at Yonsei University, focusing on Sino-Korean literature, a well-defined literary branch within the vast body of Korean classics. Specifically, she examines the brush-talk or silent conversations between Korean and Japanese literati of Literary Sinitic, their shared written language. She has written multiple articles on the travelogues of Koreans in foreign countries during the premodern era and is currently researching the (mis)understandings between Koreans and foreigners as shown in their intercultural encounters during the transition from early modernity to the modern era. Email: kokoroatari@gmail.com.

Jang Jin-youp (張眞熀) is an assistant professor at Department of Classical Chinese Education of Sungshin Women's University in Seoul. She received her BA in Korean Language and Literature, MA and PhD in Classical Korean Literature from Yonsei University in Seoul. The primary focus of her recent research interest is the search for a valid methodology for the study of Chosŏn's Sino-Korean literature (韓國漢文學). She has published books and articles mainly on the cultural exchange between Chosŏn Korea and Tokugawa Japan as gauged through written records of Chosŏn envoys (*t'ongsinsa* 通信使) to Japan. Recently, she started examining the wide-ranging literature bequeathed by Chosŏn people's brush-talk records when interacting with literati of Sinitic from Japan and China. Email: apricity@sungshin.ac.kr.

Hur Kyung-jin (許敬震) is Professor Emeritus of the Department of Korean Language and Literature, Yonsei University in Seoul, Korea. He has made significant contributions to the popularization of classical Sino-Korean literature in modern Korean through translation and commentaries. Among his more recent endeavors is the creation of a digital database consisting of letters written by Christian missionaries who came to Korea toward the end of the nineteenth century. Email: hur@yonsei.ac.kr.

David C. S. Li (李楚成) is Professor and Head of the Department of Chinese and Bilingual Studies (中文及雙語學系), The Hong Kong Polytechnic University (香港理工大學). He received his BA in English (Hong Kong), MA in Applied Linguistics (France), and PhD in Linguistics (Germany). He has published widely in multilingualism in Greater China, World Englishes, Hong Kong English, China English, bilingual education and language policy, bilingual interaction and code-switching (translanguaging), Cantonese as an additional language, and South Asian Hongkongers' needs for written Chinese. He speaks Cantonese, English, and Mandarin fluently, is conversant in German and French, and is learning Japanese and Korean. More recent interests focus on the historical spread of written Chinese (Sinitic) and its use as a scripta franca until the early twentieth century in Sinographic East Asia (China, Japan, Korea, and Vietnam). Email: david.cs.li@polyu.edu.hk.

Wong Tak-sum (黃得森) is a post-doctoral fellow in the Department of Chinese and Bilingual Studies at The Hong Kong Polytechnic University. He received his BEng in Computer Science from Hong Kong University of Science and Technology (2004), and PhD in Linguistics from City University of Hong Kong (2018). He has built a treebank of the Tripiṭaka Koreana during his doctoral study and has been working on the quantitative study of historical syntax. His research expertise covers Chinese historical linguistics, Cantonese linguistics, corpus linguistics, computer-assisted language learning, Chinese dialectology, and Chinese paleography. Email: wong_taksum@hotmail.com.

Nguyễn Thị-Tuyết (阮氏雪) is a researcher at the Institute of Sino-Nom Studies at the Vietnam Academy of Social Sciences (VASS), Hanoi, Vietnam. She is currently a PhD candidate in literature at Guangxi University for Nationalities (中國廣西民族大學) in China. She concentrates on Vietnamese Sino-Nom historiographic documentation and Vietnamese classical literature. She has published several journal articles and conference papers in Vietnamese and Chinese. Her Vietnamese-language translation of Lê Quý Đôn's 'Complete accounts of north-bound envoys' 北使通錄 was published in Vietnam in 2018. Email: nguyenthanhtuyet@gmail.com.

Nguyễn Tuấn-Cường (阮俊強) obtained his PhD in Sino-Nom Studies (Vietnamese Sinology). He is currently Associate Professor and director of the Institute of Sino-Nom Studies at the Vietnam Academy of Social Sciences (VASS), Hanoi, Vietnam. He is also Adjunct Professor of Sino-Nom Studies at Vietnam National University, Hanoi. His research focuses on Vietnamese Sinology, classical philology, Confucianism, and traditional education in Vietnam. He has authored publications in Vietnamese, English, Chinese, and Japanese, including two co-edited books with HE Huazhen (何華珍) published in Chinese: 'Research on East Asian Sinographic texts and Vietnamese classical dictionaries' (東亞漢籍與越南漢喃古辭書研究, 2017); and 'Research on Vietnamese classical texts and East Asian sinographs' (越南漢喃文獻與東亞漢字整理研究, 2019). Email: cuonghannom@gmail.com.

Liu Yuzhen (劉雨珍) is a professor at the College of Foreign Languages and an adjunct professor at the Japan Institute of Nankai University. He received his first PhD in Human Cultural Studies from Kobe University in 1997 and the second PhD in Cultural Interaction from Kansai University in 2020. He is also the chairman of the China chapter of the International Conference of East Asian Comparative Cultures (東亞比較文化國際會議中國分會會長), the Associate Director of the China Japanese Language Teaching Association (中國日語教學研究會), and an executive member of the Chinese Association for Japanese Studies (中華日本學會). He has published widely in Sino-Japonic comparative literature and the history of Sino-Japanese cultural interchange. His major publications include 'Notes on investigation of political and legal systems in Japan: collection of travel diaries in Japan during late Qing' (日本政法考察記—晚清東游日記彙編, 2001), 'A Collection of brush conversations by the staff of the first Qing embassy to Japan' (清朝首屆駐日公使館員筆談資料彙編, 2010), and 'Studies in the Sino-Japanese history of literature and cultural interchange' (中日文學與文化交流史研究, 2019). Email: liuyzhth@163.com.

Foreword to *Brush Conversation in the Sinographic Cosmopolis*: the second miracle

The great Galileo once expressed his awe at the invention of writing in these words:

> But of all other stupendous inventions, what sublimity of mind must have been his who conceived how to communicate his most secret thoughts to any other person, though very far distant, either in time or place? And with no greater difficulty than the various arrangement of two dozen little signs upon paper? Let this be the seal of all the admirable inventions of man.

However, without the prior invention of spoken language, there would be no way of arranging '*little signs upon paper*'. Speaking indeed was the first miracle that firmly set us upon the trajectory which made our species unique, though that invention happened too long ago to allow for a clear understanding of how it happened. However, the sounds of speech do not travel far or last long. They vanish the instant after they are spoken. The second miracle was to inscribe spoken language in visible symbols that can last for millennia, and that can be carried over great distances.

The earliest samples of such symbols date back not much beyond six millennia from Western Asia, inscribed variously on tablets, pottery, or animal bones. These symbols became increasingly refined over the centuries, and their use grew from an elite few in the community toward ever greater mass literacy. Although there still remain millions of people today who lack the foundational skills to read and write, the growth of literacy in the world over the past 60 years has been a fundamental transformation of our species.

But in the world's thousands of languages, not all symbols work the same way as Galileo's '*two dozen little signs*'. It is true that the Latin alphabet and its several historically related alphabets, which all trace back to the Phoenicians, have spread over much of the world, especially as a product of European expansions in recent centuries. But there are other ways of writing language down, such as the system invented in ancient China, which is the subject matter of this volume. While alphabetic writing is based exclusively on how a language sounds, the system of symbols invented in China, or sinograms, are mostly based on a hybrid combination of both the sounds and the meanings of the language, where individual meanings may be represented by various methods. These methods were explained in the first major Chinese dictionary, 'Explaining Graphs and Analyzing Characters' (說文解字, *Shuowen Jiezi*), which was compiled by Xu Shen 許慎 some two thousand years ago (c. 100 CE).

Sinograms – more commonly known as Chinese characters – are a great deal more numerous than the letters of an alphabet; so they require more time to learn. For more than a century starting in the mid-1840s, when China's self-esteem was almost wiped out by wars with the Western powers and Japan, sinograms were blamed to be a cause of illiteracy. Many well-known writers even advocated abolishing sinograms altogether, and to adopt alphabetic writing. Fortunately, such surreal moments have all passed. Recent studies in psycholinguistics and neurolinguistics have greatly increased our understanding of the subtle relations among sound, sense, and script. Many factors enter into the question as to what an optimal script is – how best to write a language down. These include the amount of homophony in the language, how many affixes there are and how frequently they are used, and so on. At any rate, learning several hundred sinograms is not a serious problem for young children – they are remarkable learning machines. Such learning presumably nurtures the growth of their memory as well.

An early report in this area of research was published by Rozin et al. (1971) in the prestigious journal *Science*, with the intriguing title: '*American children with reading problems can easily learn to read English represented by Chinese characters*'. For dyslexic children in Philadelphia to learn to read English written in sinograms must have been an exhilarating experience. Many of the problems in dyslexia arise because of sequential ordering of the letters. A typical dyslexic child has difficulty distinguishing WAS from SAW or DOES from DOSE. Although individual sinograms can get graphically very complex, their recognition does not critically depend on such left/right decisions.

Perhaps more important, for some children it just seems more natural to look for meaningful parts in a holistic sinogram, than to attend to meaningless letters in an alphabetic word. This was the case with my daughter. We lived in California then, and our home language was English. But we tried to give her an early start learning sinograms, by treating English as though it was written in sinograms. So she learned that *Mama* was written with the sinogram 媽, and *Sister* with the sinogram 姐, without any accompanying explanations.

When she was about fifteen months old, we got her a female puppy, named *Xiaobaijin*. The name means *little white gold*, because it was colored like a mixed collie, brown with patches of white; in sinograms, the name was 小白金. The surprise came when she raised the question shortly after the puppy came. Why, she asked, since 小白金 was a girl, wasn't there the 'girl' part in her written name? At fifteen months, she had independently factored out the female radical on the left side of the 媽, and 姐, and was asking why this feature was not in the name of her puppy? The human mind is constantly searching for meanings, especially when it is young.

Turning now to *Brush Conversation in the Sinographic Cosmopolis*, sinograms are of course the underlying theme in this fascinating volume, but it is so much more! While illustrating profusely the communicative power of a writing system that is based on meaning rather than sound, it also brings to life vivid aspects of the cultural history of East Asia over several centuries. Although sinograms were invented in China, her neighbors adopted them extensively at times, especially Japan, Korea, and Vietnam, even as the sociopolitical backgrounds underwent major changes as the world's powers waxed and waned over a half millennium. At times these neighbors were proud to be joint inheritors of this great Sinographic tradition, gateway to centuries of the best moral and political philosophies as well as time-honored novels and poetry. Now, however, a combination of national pride and European domination has led to the virtual abandonment of sinograms in Korea and Vietnam, though thousands are still being actively used in Japan.

An interesting observation I gleaned from these pages is that in certain contexts, brush conversations were actually preferred over spoken language on certain occasions of international diplomacy, even when official interpreters were present. Perhaps intangible values of the sinograms, their associated heritage of Confucian learning, poetic tradition, and the art of calligraphy, were all in the psychological background to lead to such a preference. More generally, writing seems to bestow an added dimension of sharing.

This calls to mind a passage from *Anna Karenina* that I found particularly romantic and touching. It was when Levin and Kitty finally professed their love for each other by writing in chalk on a tablecloth. Their minds were so closely set that they were able to communicate with just the first letters of the words. The story became all the more moving when I learned later from reading Lev Vygotsky that "*In just this way, Tolstoy told his future wife of his love for her*" (1962: 141, 2012: 252). Instead of merely representing sounds that vanish instantly from the ear, writing has taken on an added dimension of sharing meaning by communicating to the eye.

A few months ago, I was reading *Zhai Zi Zhongguo* 宅茲中國, authored by Ge Zhaoguang 葛兆光 (2011, cf. Ge 2017). Ge mentioned that China, with her prestigious culture widely spread and highly appreciated in neighboring countries, used to view herself as equivalent to the East. He argued that starting from the mid-seventeenth century, however, the three nations (China, Chosŏn, and Japan) underwent a process from 本是一家 (we are family) to 互不相認 (non-recognition of each other), which reflects the collapse of a common cultural identity in East Asia. These remarks are thought-provoking, given that conflicts arising from territorial dispute or trade war among these nations are getting increasingly common. On what ground can we claim that for centuries, there did exist a relatively homogeneous East Asian culture historically? This is one main theme explored in *Brush Conversation in the Sinographic Cosmopolis*.

As the epigraph of the volume ingeniously makes the point: 'At the tip of the brush is a tongue, what to expect from speech?' (筆端有舌 何待言語). In fact, this phenomenon of brush conversation was early noted by the Italian Jesuit Matteo Ricci, as WANG Yong mentioned in Chapter 2. There is one crucial requirement for the use and spread of sinograms: the 'phonetic intersubjectivity' as Li and Aoyama characterize it in Chapter 4. In other words, sinograms can function as a scripta franca because they can be pronounced differently by speakers of various regions. A simple example for illustration: the surname 林 is read *Lin* in Mandarin, *Im* in Korean and *Lâm* in Vietnamese, but *Hayashi* in Japanese, not to mention multiple other readings in the diverse Chinese dialects.

One may get the impression that brush conversations, being something done spontaneously, must be short in duration and simple in content. Chapter 7 by Nguyễn and Nguyễn tells us that brush-talks involving conversational routines or poetic improvisation are indeed shorter in length, but those concerning academic exchange of viewpoints tend to be longer and more elaborate. In fact, such a mode of communication can last for hours, as Liu quoted from *Miyajima Documents* 宮島文書 in Chapter 9: 'the literary talents well-versed in Sinitic . . . drank jubilantly and wielded their writing brush generously, meeting up at noon and breaking up late at night'.

Although there have been numerous written brush conversations published so far, the editors cautioned in their introductory Chapter 1 that we must not be deceived to think the original notes are as tidy and orderly as what they appear to be. As a matter of fact, many of the notes are polished and edited before publication, with unavoidable addition or deletion. Jang addressed the competing attitudes between Chosŏn envoys or *t'ongsinsa* 通信使 and Tokugawa literati in Chapter 11. The Japanese Confucianist Arai Hakuseki 新井白石 challenged Chosŏn's status as the guardian of Chinese civilization, but he did not express his derogatory thoughts in the face of the Chosŏn Chief-Envoy. There are two published versions of his brush-talk records with the Chosŏn diplomats, one edited by the Chosŏn Vice-Envoy and the other compiled by Hakuseki himself. As Jang noted,

> Hakuseki's deprecating remarks are found . . . not in the Korean version, suggesting that such remarks were subsequently inserted while the Japanese edition was edited. . . . It was through those post-*t'ongsinsa* exchange remarks that we learned about the critical stance of Japanese intellectuals for the first time in 1711.

Chapter 10 by Koo and Joo also deals with the Japanese-Korean brushed exchange. They mentioned that even if many Tsushima islanders spoke fluent Korean and often acted as interpreters for the Korean envoys, 'brush-talk was preferred probably because it was an opportunity for both sides to showcase their erudition as well as membership within the Sinosphere'. This idea is echoed in WANG Baoping's Chapter 8, and Clements' Chapter 13. In Wang's investigation of the *Ōkōchi Documents* 大河內文書, he explained that 'for Ōkōchi, engaging a go-between for speech-based interpretation was no match for the direct heart-to-heart communication mediated by a talking brush'. Clements, in her final chapter that concludes this volume, also maintains that 'as well as being a necessary expedient, brush-talk could also be a deliberate choice'.

This monograph is full of captivating anecdotes. Thumbing through the pages, one not only learns about the historical and diplomatic relationships between several nations but also gains linguistic insights. For example, two foreign languages, Chinese and Dutch, played a significant role in the nineteenth-century USA-Japan negotiations. In Chapter 12, Aoyama calls our attention to an essential figure in Japan's diplomatic event with the Americans. A Cantonese businessman by the name Luo Sen 羅森 was recruited to act as the assistant translator to the chief interpreter Samuel Wells Williams in the Black Ships expedition led by the American naval commander Matthew C. Perry, who ended Japan's seclusion policy for more than 200 years. As Aoyama commented,

> Luo Sen's ability to compose erudite phrases . . . helped more than just to overcome a language barrier; . . . his agility and literary flair in Sinitic brush-talk provided the wherewithal to earn goodwill from the Japanese side, and helped to allay latent suspicion of the samurai officials and extenuate some of the tension that inevitably afflicted the initial negotiations.

In addition to such accounts, which give us glimpses of debates on cultural superiority and political confrontations between bureaucrats and scholars of different origins, brush-talk records are usually characterized by a mixture of written and spoken elements, which is of particular interest. For instance, Matsuura and Aoyama in Chapter 3 gave examples of both Classical Chinese and vernacular or topolect expressions from brush conversation between Korean maritime officials on Cheju Island and Chinese seafarers. The former includes sentence-final particles like 耳 and 矣, or the question marker 耶, and the latter includes first-person plural pronouns 俺等 and interrogative pronouns 多少. A similar mix of Classical Chinese and vernacular elements is also attested in Wong's study of Sinitic brush-talk between Ryukyuan, Japanese and Korean literati in Chapter 6.

I was also fascinated by a reconstructed fifteenth-century brush-talk record by Ch'oe Pu 崔溥 from Chapter 5 by Hur Kyoung-Jin. Ch'oe served as an official at Cheju and was supposed to return home on the Korean Peninsula from the island for a period of mourning after hearing of his father's death. The ship was blown off course and ended up on the Zhejiang shores, where he began a five-month travel in China along the Peking-Hangzhou Grand Canal before finally reaching home. In his travelogue, Ch'oe mentioned how he was warmly received by some Liaodong merchants. Because of geographical proximity, these merchants came to visit him with some gifts, and remarked that they were like a single family, since Liaodong was adjacent to Chosŏn. Upon hearing these friendly words, Ch'oe responded that Liaodong used to be the capital of Old Koguryŏ, and Koguryŏ now belonged to the land of Chosŏn, so they were indeed one and the same country. I was especially interested in this account, because there was once an immensely popular Korean TV series, which depicts the story of *Chumong* 朱蒙, the founder of the Koguryŏ Kingdom. This drama series caused some controversy in China, since the whole screenplay is written from a Korean perspective, where *Chumong*'s father was hailed as a hero fighting against the tyrannic rule of the Han dynasty. From the Chinese viewpoint, however, *Chumong* was a member of a Chinese ethnic minority and Koguryŏ was never an independent state, but simply a local regime of China. With such diverse conceptions between the two nations, I cannot help but wonder how mutual respect and tolerance would contribute to a more fruitful and reciprocal cross-border relationship, just like Ch'oe's pleasant encounter with those amicable businessmen from Liaodong.

This volume is a valuable contribution to linguistics to be sure; in contrast to the abundant studies on spoken language, there is a dearth of attention paid to written language as a medium of communication *per se*. As the world gets increasingly wired up for communicating via the screen, WeChat, WhatsApp, Line, etc., as well as its numerous emojis, we are grateful that this volume offers us a look back at past centuries, at how sinograms served communication in East Asia within a rich tapestry of cultural history of an important region of the world.

As I was writing this foreword for this volume, one of its editors, Professor David C. S. Li, told me that a follow-up project of the same topic is in the works. It will be a penta-lingual manga project (Chinese, Japanese, Korean, and Vietnamese, in addition to English), featuring at least two (possibly three) stories, one each involving the three recurrent contexts in which 漢文筆談 was commonplace historically in East Asia, involving boat drifters, diplomats, and traveling literati. I am elated that the editors have initiated a new paradigm of linguistic research, one that takes into consideration not only historically preserved texts but also promotes a multidisciplinary approach.

In the evolution of our species, cooperation, rather than competition, has been a critical feature for our success, as discussed by Edward O. Wilson in *The Social Conquest of Earth* (2012). As the eighteenth-century Vietnamese scholar-official Lê Quý Đôn 黎貴惇 (Chapter 7) remarked: '*to get to know each other through writing, then we are all brothers within the four seas*' (以文字相知，即四海皆兄弟也). Let us hope that academically and geopolitically, kindness and collaboration will soon return to displace rivalry and conflict, and lead us back to a more united East Asia, building upon the time-honored cultural values of harmony carried across millennia by the shared sinograms.

William Shiyuan Wang
The Hong Kong Polytechnic University

References

Ge, Zhaoguang [葛兆光]. (2011). Zhai Zi Zhongguo 宅茲中國 ('Here in 'China' I dwell: Reconstructing historical discourses of China for our time'). Taipei: Linking Publishing.

Ge, Zhaoguang. (2017). *Here in 'China' I dwell: Reconstructing historical discourses of China for our time* (Jesse Field & Qin Fang, Trans.). Leiden & Boston: Brill.

Rozin, P., Poritsky, S., & Sotsky, R. (1971). American children with reading problems can easily learn to read English represented by Chinese characters. *Science* 171: 1264–1267.

Vygotsky, L. S. (1962/2012). *Thought and language* (Eugenia Hanfmann & Gertrude Vakar trans., ed. by Alex Kozulin). Cambridge, MA: MIT Press.

Wilson, E. O. (2012). *The social conquest of earth*. New York: Liveright Pub. Corp.

Preface

For well over a millennium until the early twentieth century, Sinitic brush-talk 漢文筆談 was a salient lingua-cultural communication pattern in Sinographic East Asia 漢字文化圈, which is also known as the Sinographic cosmopolis (Koh & King 2014). Being writing-mediated, 'silent conversation' using brush, ink, and paper could take place in cross-border communication contexts between literati of Classical Chinese or Literary Sinitic (文言 *wényán*, hereafter Sinitic) with no shared spoken language.[1] Instead of vocalized speech, there is ample documented evidence of brush-talkers relying on the semiotic potential and sociopragmatic affordance of Sinitic, which was written orthographically with morphographic, non-phonographic characters or sinograms 漢字, and lexico-grammatically with sparse and simplex morphologies. Its Han Chinese heritage being rooted in the Middle Kingdom, Sinitic was functionally designed not for speaking but for formal writing purposes.

For historical reasons, since the Tang dynasty (618–907 CE) large quantities of Sinitic texts produced in dynastic China were successively imported via different means into neighboring polities that correspond geographically with today's North Korea, South Korea, Japan and Vietnam. Acquired and used by the politically influential elites and socioeconomically affluent aristocrats, literacy in Sinitic was also a hallmark of social standing as well as the extent of being educated. Before the emergence of indigenous phonographic scripts for writing their respective national languages (i.e., Korean *hangŭl* 한글; Vietnamese the *chữ Quốc ngữ* script; and Japanese *hiragana* ひらがな and *katakana* カタカナ, which are mixed with non-phonographic kanji), Sinitic had been adapted locally for writing purposes (Handel 2019; Kornicki 2018; cf. Clements 2015). This is by and large the historical background, how literati of Sinitic from different parts of Sinographic East Asia were able to get around the modality of speech-based communication

---

1 In this book, the terms 'sinogram' and 'Sinitic' will be used when reference is made to the historical, transnational and transcultural use of Chinese characters and Literary Chinese, respectively, which are distinct from the contemporary use of Chinese characters in China and kanji in Japan. For terminological differences between Literary Sinitic and Classical Chinese, see Kornicki (2018: 19) and Handel (2019).

and make meaning through writing synchronously, interactively and face-to-face (i.e., Sinitic brush-talk 漢文筆談; for historical background, recurrent cross-border contexts, and the variety of data in the brush-talk literature, see Chapters 1 and 2). The epigraph captures a slice of life involving a brush encounter of two literati of Sinitic – one from China, the other from Japan in 1862 Shanghai. More details may be found in Chapter 4 (Li & Aoyama, this volume).

The papers in this volume were conceived shortly after the *Two-day International Symposium on Cultural and Linguistic Interactions across Sinographic East Asia* 東亞漢字文化圈中的語言文化交流國際研討會 at The Hong Kong Polytechnic University in June 2019 (http://wongtaksum.no-ip.info:81/brush-talksymposium.htm). About two dozen experts from China, Japan, South Korea, and Vietnam came together to share their research insights. The participants were plurilingual to different extents. They each gave a presentation in their preferred language – Japanese, Korean, or Mandarin Chinese – which were translated into the other two East Asian languages through simultaneous interpretation. Interestingly, 'pen-talk' in Sinitic – the twenty-first-century equivalent of sinogram-based brush-talk – was found useful to overcome the language barrier occasionally. Contributions for this volume were then solicited from the participants; for various reasons, not all invitations to contribute were accepted. Except for Chapter 2 (WANG Yong), which is adapted from his (Wang 2018) book in Chinese, the rest of the twelve papers in this volume represent original work that has not been published before. English being the target language, most of the original drafts were first written in the authors' preferred language before being edited and/or rewritten in English by the editors.

Each of the papers has gone through successive drafts interactively with the authors not only for 'fact check', but also to address miscellaneous questions related to coherence, consistency, filling information gaps, keeping to stylistic preferences, and so forth. Li assumes primary responsibility for rendering the following chapters from Chinese into English: Chapter 2 (WANG Yong), Chapter 8 (WANG Baoping), and Chapter 9 (LIU Yuzhen). Despite rigorous cross-checking with the authors in the drafting process, responsibility for any inadequacies that remain in these three chapters rests with the editors.

Whereas the editors of this book were organizers of the aforementioned International Symposium, none of us was professionally trained in East Asian studies. Our expertise by training is, respectively, linguistics and sociolinguistics (Li), cultural anthropology (Aoyama), and historical and corpus linguistics (Wong). The inspiration to conduct research in Sinitic brush-talk that culminated in the compilation of this volume was derived somewhat accidentally in summer 2017, when Li was reading into late-nineteenth-century Vietnamese anti-colonial history (*Vietnamese anticolonialism 1885–1925*, Marr 1971; *Colonialism and language policy in Viet Nam*, DeFrancis 1977; see Li et al. 2020 for details). There, brush conversations between politicians from Japan, monarchists and revolutionaries from Qing China and Vietnam were outlined in some detail. That their primarily writing-mediated brush conversations on topics of considerable complexity was described as seamless was linguistically and pragmatically intriguing. After being briefed about this fascinating lingua-cultural phenomenon, Aoyama and Wong accepted Li's invitation to probe more deeply into such a unique, apparently script-specific modality of communication. This was followed by regular meetings to update and learn from what we found, leading to ideas for journal papers and a research project. Looking back, we are pleased to see our collective efforts bear fruit as our submissions to international journals and conferences, a proposal for a competitive research grant (General Research Fund, Hong Kong Research Grants Council), including the proposal for the present book, were mostly successful. What is presented within the covers of this volume represents the fruit of our joint intellectual endeavor in the last four years, which would not have been possible without the fine contributions and patience of all the contributors. Their input, critique, trust, and cooperation are hereby gratefully acknowledged.

Like other works on East Asian studies, we had to decide upon a number of typographic conventions. Regardless of the number of syllables, personal names in East Asia generally begin with a family name followed by a given name. Such an order is the opposite of the general practice in English and other European languages, where the first name precedes the last (family) name. In this book, we will follow the *East Asian order*: family name – given name.[2] Where ambiguity may arise, the family name will be romanized in upper case. This order is maintained for not just the historical figures and protagonists of Sinitic brush-talk, but also for the East Asian researchers cited, except when a Western-style author name is preferred (e.g., WONG Tak-sum, Reijiro AOYAMA). Wherever possible, the original sinogram-based names appearing in the data sources will be provided when first mentioned. The same applies to dynasties and rulers, and the duration of their reign will also be indicated. Likewise for names of places that are likely to be obscure to the reader, which will appear in both romanization and sinograms, if available. Where specific dates are mentioned, most of the chapters follow the Gregorian calendar. There are several exceptions, however. Where the dates are recorded according to the lunar calendar, for convenience's sake, the lunar months and days will be presented in digits, with the month preceding the day separated by a colon. Thus, '10:05' would mean 'the 5th day of the 10th lunar month'.

Regarding the in-text citation of literary works or publications written in Sinitic, a free translation of their titles into English will be introduced, followed by the original titles in sinograms. In terms of typeface, the English translation of such titles will be put within single quotes when first mentioned. In the subsequent citation of the same works or publications in the chapter, the titles in English translation will appear in *italics* but the original titles in sinograms will be spared.[3]

---

2 Except when preference for the opposite 'given name – family name' order was conveyed to us explicitly.
3 For instance, the idiomatic translation of the book 'A complete record of an embassy to the North' will appear before the original title in Sinitic 北使通錄. Subsequently, the book will be referred to in italics as *A complete record of an embassy to the North*.

As for romanization of lexical items in East Asian languages, although historically most sinograms were pronounceable across East Asian languages, their regional pronunciation was usually unintelligible to people who were unfamiliar with the speaker's native language. Such an intelligibility problem in cross-border communication is partly reflected in the romanization of the same characters (e.g., consider the bisyllabic word meaning 'Chinese character' or 'sinogram', 漢字: Mand: *hànzì*; Jap: *kanji*; Kor: *hanja*; Viet: *chữ Hán* 字漢). In this book, pinyin will be used for romanizing the names of Chinese people and places, historical terms, book titles, and so forth. Those in Japanese and Korean will follow the romanization convention of Modified Hepburn and McCune-Reischauer, respectively. Vietnamese historical figures and places will be romanized using the Roman script *chữ Quốc ngữ*, which was widely used in Vietnamese society since the early twentieth century. As for Chinese topolects mentioned occasionally, sinograms pronounced in Cantonese 粵語 will be romanized using Jyutping 粵拼 devised by the Linguistic Society of Hong Kong,[4] while those in Southern Min (Minnanhua 閩南話) will follow the romanization system proposed by the Ministry of Education in Taiwan.[5]

As is different from earlier scholarly works in East Asian studies, rather than displaying sinograms in the end matters (e.g., presented as a glossary in an appendix), wherever possible Chinese characters or sinograms will be displayed *in situ* for quick reference. For the sake of convenience, sinograms meant to be read in Chinese will be printed in traditional (as opposed to simplified) Chinese characters, while those in Japanese *kanji*, Korean *hanja* and Vietnamese *chữ Nôm* (字喃, literally 'southern characters') will follow the actual written forms as shown in the historical data sources or reference works as closely as possible.

We are grateful to the following copyright holders for granting us permission to reproduce digital images of artwork or the inside pages of old book manuscripts in their collections:

- Osaka Museum of History: digital image of the scroll painting by Hanabusa Itchō 英一蝶 (1652–1724).
- Waseda University Library: 'Yugu sasin chŭngdamnok' (琉球使臣贈答錄, 1633), *Kotenseki Sōgō database of Japanese and Chinese classics*.
- Institute for the Translation of Korean Classics 韓國古典翻譯院: 'Yugu sasin chŭngdamnok' (琉球使臣贈答錄, 1633), *Comprehensive Database of Korean Classics* 韓國古典綜合 DB.

---

4 LSHK, see www.lshk.org/jyutping. Instead of using a single digit 1–6 to represent the tone marks of six distinctive tones in Cantonese, we will use two digits in superscript to indicate the tone contours: 'high level tone' (55), 'mid level tone' (33), 'low level tone' (22), 'high rising tone' (35), 'low rising tone' (23), and 'low falling tone' (21). For instance, 漢文筆談 ('Sinitic brush-talk') will be romanized as hon[33] man[21] bat[55] taam[21].

5 See 臺灣閩南語羅馬字拼音方案 [簡稱臺羅], https://twblg.dict.edu.tw/holodict_new/compile1_3_9_3.jsp.

- University of Hawai'i at Manoa Library: the first page of 'Ryukan hitsudan' 琉館筆譚, the Hawley version, *Ryūkyū/Okinawa Special Collection Digital Archives*.
- University of Tsukuba Library: the first page of 'Ryukan hitsudan' 琉舘筆談, the Tsukuba version.

Every effort has been made to trace copyright, but in the event of any accidental infringement where it has proved untraceable, we shall be pleased to come to a suitable arrangement with the owner.

Who will benefit from reading this collection of papers? This book was conceived to introduce the semiotic affordance and interactional dynamics of writing-mediated cross-border communication between literati of Sinitic in premodern and early modern Sinographic East Asia, interactively and face-to-face. It is the first monograph written in English to address this salient lingua-cultural practice and phenomenon. As such, the book will be of interest to students of East Asian languages and linguistics, especially (historical) pragmatics, sociolinguistics, sociology of language, scripts and writing systems, cultural anthropology, linguistic anthropology, recorded history, and of course East Asian history, international relations and diplomacy.

In the process of editing the papers for this volume, we have received generous assistance from many colleagues. First and foremost, we are grateful to the two anonymous reviewers of our book proposal and the most helpful suggestions they provided, which we believe have been acted upon. A number of contributors have provided kind assistance by serving as reviewers of multiple draft chapters. In particular, special thanks are due to Jang Jin-youp 張眞熀 (author of Chapter 10) and NGUYỄN Tuấn Cường 阮俊強 (first author of Chapter 7) for their critical comments and constructive suggestions for improvement. We are also indebted to a few colleagues who similarly have provided insightful feedback to our questions and selected earlier drafts, including Han Xiaorong 韓孝榮, Hartmut Haberland, Jens Høyrup, and Oh Sunyoung 吳宣榮. We would like to thank their timely feedback and insightful response to our questions. Special thanks are due to Hartmut Haberland and John Whelpton, who helped us translate excerpts of Latin into English in Chapter 1. Our heartfelt gratitude is also extended to Fuma Susumu 夫馬進 of Kyoto University, who took the trouble to meet with Li and Aoyama at his residence, and to LIN Shaoyang 林少陽 and Iwatsuki Jun'ichi 岩月純一 in their Tokyo University office at the formative stage of our Sinitic brush-talk project. As we were new to 'brush conversation' in premodern and early modern East Asia, several colleagues' sharing of insights at the aforementioned two-day symposium in 2019 has greatly enriched our understanding of Sinitic brush-talk as a writing-mediated transcultural communication phenomenon in cross-border contexts. They include NGUYỄN Hữu Tâm 阮友心, ZHANG Bowei 張伯偉, CHAN Shui-Duen 陳瑞端, Machi Senjūrō 町泉寿郎, and XU Yuji 徐雨霽. To our student helpers, HO Ka Lun Harry and LAU Sze-ming, we thank them for their efficient and unfailing completion of tasks. To Ms. WONG Chi Man 黃芷汶, we are indebted to her calligraphy that she improvised so elegantly with an artistic brush for our epigraph. Also, throughout the 18-month editing and writing process, we are immensely grateful to Mr. Simon Bates, editor of Routledge, whose encouragement and trust meant a great deal to us – indeed instrumental for keeping us focused and on track to meet the deadline, which had to be postponed three times due to extraneous circumstances beyond our control. Simon's kind understanding, patience, and trust are much appreciated. Finally, the work described in this collection of papers was partially supported by a General Research Fund (GRF) award from the Research Grants Council (RGC) of the Hong Kong Special Administrative Region, China (15603420, 2021–2022). The RGC support is hereby gratefully acknowledged.

David C. S. Li (李楚成), Reijiro Aoyama (青山玲二郎),
and Wong Tak-sum (黃得森)
Hong Kong

References

Clements, R. (2015). *A cultural history of translation in early modern Japan.* Cambridge: Cambridge University Press.

DeFrancis, J. (1977). *Colonialism and language policy in Viet Nam.* The Hague: Mouton.

Handel, Z. (2019). *Sinography: The borrowing and adaptation of the Chinese script.* Leiden: Brill.

Koh, J., & King, R. (2014). *Infected Korean language: Purity versus hybridity.* Amherst, New York: Cambria Press.

Kornicki, P. F. (2018). *Languages, scripts, and Chinese texts in East Asia.* Oxford: Oxford University Press.

Li, D. C. S., Aoyama, R., & Wong, T.-S. (2020). Silent conversation through brushtalk (筆談): The use of Sinitic as a scripta franca in early modern East Asia. *Global Chinese* 6(1): 1–23.

Marr, D. G. (1971). *Vietnamese anticolonialism 1885–1925.* Berkeley, CA: University of California Press.

Wang, Y. [王勇] (2018). 東亞筆談文獻經眼錄 ('A survey of the East Asian Sinitic brushtalk literature: An annotated bibliography'). Shanghai: Shanghai Jiao Tong University Press.

Epigraph

惜乎言語兩不會意
筆端有舌何待言語

'*Regrettably, our respective spoken languages would not be able to get across our meanings.*'
'*At the tip of the brush is a tongue, what to expect from speech?*'

1862, Shanghai

Map

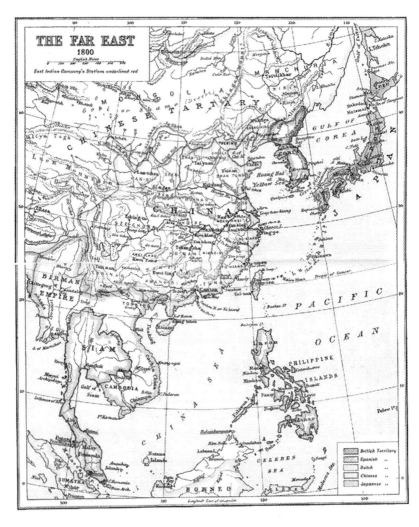

Map 1 A map of East Asia dated 1800.

1 Writing-mediated cross-border communication face-to-face

From Sinitic brush-talk (漢文筆談) to pen-assisted conversation

David C. S. Li, Reijiro Aoyama and Wong Tak-sum

Synchronous writing-mediated communication before the advent of the Internet

The last decade of the twentieth century ushered in the age of the Internet. Advances in computing technologies along with the popularization of personal computers (PCs) since then have revolutionized the way people communicate and the speed with which information is sent and received. Today, subject to the only constraint of the quality of Internet connection, especially high-speed Wi-Fi, real-time synchronous communication over a long distance can take place instantly using e-gadgets such as a mobile phone, laptop, or a tablet like an iPad. By eliminating the space barrier to synchronous telecommunication, be it in audio-visual mode, voice-only telephone mode, or entirely writing-mediated, e-applications (apps) like Skype, Microsoft Teams, Zoom, WhatsApp, and WeChat have made the world literally smaller. To digital natives, especially millennials and members of Generation Z born and growing up with such a barrier-free telecommunication landscape, it is hard to imagine a world in which physical distance would impose such a big constraint for people wishing to stay connected, not to mention that old, asynchronous communication technologies like telegram or telegraph – a speedier alternative to regular postal service – was not widely available and only accessible at a considerable cost. Today, given the convenience and popularity of emails, messaging systems, and sundry social media e-platforms like Facebook, TikTok, and Twitter that are accessible at one's fingertips, sending stamped postcards or personal letters to loved ones is probably still practiced by people in their 50s or above, if not already a thing of the past.

For talking humans, writing is in general secondary to speaking and would normally be adopted when speech is not an option, for example, due to separation by a physical distance. In face-to-face encounters, on the other hand, writing as a mode of synchronous social interaction would normally not be considered by talking humans as an alternative to speech, even though anecdotes of impatient parents sending a WhatsApp or email reminder like 'dinner's ready!' (French: 'à table!') to family members hooked to their respective e-devices at home are not

DOI: 10.4324/9781003048176-1

uncommon. Still, relative to uttering those same words in speech – pitch level likely varying with the degree of impatience – the writing mode would be perceived as unusual or marked, for the general unmarked perception among talking humans is: if we can talk face-to-face, why write?

Speaking, however, is premised on the speakers having at least one shared spoken language. What happens when none is available, as in cross-border communication contexts? And, when speech is not an option in face-to-face interaction, would writing be able to function as a substitute modality of communication by helping the writers 'speak' their mind, interactively in real time? To our knowledge, this does not seem to be so common in Anglo-American and European cultures.[1] The same is not true of speakers whose linguistic repertoire includes literacy knowledge of Chinese characters or 'sinograms' (Wang & Tsai 2011). For instance, speakers of Chinese and Japanese may use written Chinese or kanji to facilitate meaning-making, synchronously and face-to-face. To date, there has been a dearth of empirical research on this communication pattern (Hwang 2009 being a rare exception, see later in this section), but there is ample anecdotal evidence showing how East Asians with no or limited knowledge of each other's spoken language could resort to writing for effective communication. Following are a few instructive examples of East Asians composing sinograms to make meaning interactively and effectively in face-to-face encounters, sometimes making it serve as an auxiliary communication tool.

The first example, adapted from a Korean blog (Kim 2008), involves two separate situations in which a Korean equipped with a certain level of literacy in Sinitic wrote sinograms (i) to buy medicine while traveling in China; and (ii) to alert some Vietnamese villagers to run for their lives in the face of an imminent US air raid during the Vietnam War (1955–1975):

> During a trip to China, I visited a pharmacy after consuming unfamiliar food. I handed a note to the pharmacist written with 腹痛 ('abdominal pain') and 消化不良 ('indigestion'), and the Chinese pharmacist understood and prescribed the medicine. There is also a true story from the Vietnam War [attributed to Song Yŏng-ho, also known by the blog name 燒燻 So-hun]. Accordingly, a Korean platoon leader wrote a few Chinese characters to a Vietnamese village headman alerting him to an imminent US air raid, which helped save the lives of many innocent villagers at a critical moment.
>
> (Kim 2008, original in Korean, our translation)[2]

---

1 Consider a typical if not universal example of a kidnappee scribbling a word like 'Help!' or its equivalent in other languages on a piece of paper, hoping that someone would pick it up and inform the police for assistance, but that is unilateral, delayed, and asynchronous communication (compare the 'bank hold-up' example in the following).

2 Original blog in Korean: "중국 여행중, 익숙지 않은 음식 때문에 약국에 들른 적이 있다. '복통 (腹痛) 소화불량 (消化不良)'이라고 적은 쪽지를 약사에게 건넸더니 중국인 약사가 약을 처방해 주었다. 베트남전 때의 실화도 있다. 미군기의 공습이 예정된 지역의 베트남인 촌장과 한국인 소대장은 긴급한 순간에 한자로 필담을 나눴고, 그 덕분에 무고한 베트남인들

In both cross-border communication contexts the interactants had no shared spoken language, but Sinitic-based writing turned out to be very effective in getting the speaker's meaning across. While it is unclear what Chinese characters or sinograms the Korean platoon leader wrote in that life-and-death situation that alerted the innocent Vietnamese villagers to flee, the blogger Song indicates that he wrote down '腹痛' ('stomach ache') and '消化不良' ('indigestion') when buying medicine from a Chinese pharmacist, which successfully helped him procure the medicine he needed.

The next example, also an anecdote, is adapted from a battlefield report written by an acclaimed Japanese novelist Kunikida Doppo 國木田獨步 (1871–1908),[3] reminiscing an event that he had witnessed while working as a war correspondent during the early stage of the First Sino-Japanese War (1894–1895). According to his recollection (1966: 31–33), after assaulting a village on the northeastern part of Liaodong Peninsula in the early morning of October 24, 1894, the Japanese lieutenant Asano 淺野, leader of some fifty troops, conducted a Sinitic-based 'brush conversation' (筆談, *hitsudan*) with the oldest civilian that he singled out from the frightened and curious villagers for investigation. Writing was attempted because they did not have a shared spoken language. Following is a verbatim reconstructed version of what the two men had purportedly written, interlaced with Kunikida's own sarcastic comments (English translation on the right adapted from Morris 1989):

Writing-mediated conversation reconstructed and interlaced with comments by Kunikida	Free translation adapted from Morris (1989: 275)
少尉先づ問ふて曰く…『官人は何れにあるか』	'Where are your officials?' asked Lt. Asano first of all.
『無し』然るに渠問ふて曰く『何國の人なるや』	'There are none.' The man then asked in turn, 'what country are you from?'
少尉反問して曰く『爾、之れを知らざるか』	Lt. Asano asked, 'You don't know?'
『知らず』（見よ、彼れ日清戰争を知らざるに似たり）	'No, we don't.' (Look at that – as though not knowing about the Sino-Japanese War!)
少尉乃ち答えて曰く『吾はこれ大日本帝國の人なり』（意氣堂々！）	'We are men from the Great Empire of Japan.' (And with that magnificent spirit!)
彼れ問ふて曰く『此地に來る、何事を為すぞ』	Then the man asked, 'What have you come here to do?'

(*Continued*)

의 생명을 구했다는 이야기다." (金榮旭, 2008, retrieved October 6, 2020, http://m.blog.daum.net/thddudgh7/16510273).

3 Based on one of Kunikida's field reports for 国民新聞 'Citizen times' or *Kokumin Shimbun*. As a war correspondent, he wrote those reports in a frank and intimate manner as if he had written to his own sick younger brother. They were compiled under 'Correspondence with my beloved brother' (愛弟通信 *Aitei tsūshin*), which were published posthumously (see Kunikida 1966).

Writing-mediated conversation reconstructed and interlaced with comments by Kunikida	Free translation adapted from Morris (1989: 275)
是に於てか、少尉筆を執て、大いに氣焰を吐く、曰く『清國われと兵端を開らく、吾れ今来りて之れを討たんとす。然れども安ぜよ。吾れ猥りに無辜の民を害する者に非ず』	At which point the lieutenant grabbed the brush and, spitting forth his anger, said, 'The Qing nation had opened hostilities with us; we have come to punish it. Yet, be at ease – we would not bring harm to innocent people.'
...	...
『此処に来る、誰れと戦んと欲するか』(愚！)	'Now that you are here, who do you intend to fight?' (Stupid!)
『此地に於ては戦争せず』	'We shall not do battle here.'
『然らば此に到る何事をかなす』	'If that is so, what, now that you are here, will you do?'
少尉少しく窮す、誤魔化して曰く『吾兵を休養せんが為めなり』	The lieutenant, somewhat perplexed, prevaricated: 'We shall give our troops a rest.'

Given that the elderly civilian had no knowledge of Japanese literacy, his input in the original silent conversation was most certainly written in Chinese consisting of sinograms only. On the other hand, it is unclear whether the Japanese lieutenant had interspersed his kanji input with kana; in any case, no literacy problem on the part of the Chinese conversation partner was reported. Kunikida's (1966: 31–33) version adapted verbatim earlier is thus a Japanese reconstruction re-written using *kanbun kundoku* 漢文訓讀, or Japanese reading of a passage in Sinitic. Still, we can get a taste of what that original Sinitic-based writing-mediated conversation might have looked like by cleansing the narrative and comments, as follows:

Writing-mediated conversation in Sinitic, reconstructed in modern Japanese (Kunikida 1966: 31–33; translation in English based on Morris 1989: 275)

少尉:	官人は何れにあるか	Lieutenant:	'Where are your officials?'
長者:	無し	Old man:	'There are none.'
	何國の人なるや		'What country are you from?'
少尉:	爾、之れを知らざるか	Lieutenant:	'You don't know?'
長者:	知らず	Old man:	'No, we don't.'
少尉:	吾はこれ大日本帝國の人なり	Lieutenant:	'We are men from the Great Empire of Japan.'
長者:	此地に来る、何事を為すぞ	Old man:	'What have you come here to do?'
少尉:	清國われと兵端を開らく、吾れ今来りて之れを討たんとす。然れども安ぜよ。吾れ猥りに無辜の民を害する者に非ず	Lieutenant:	'The Qing nation had opened hostilities with us; we have come to punish it. Yet, be at ease – we would not bring harm to innocent people.'
	...		...

長者:	此処に来る、誰れと戦んと欲するか	Old man:	'Now that you are here, who do you intend to fight?'
少尉:	此地に於ては戦争せず	Lieutenant:	'We shall not do battle here.'
長者:	然らば此に到る何事をかなす	Old man:	'If that is so, what, now that you are here, will you do?'
少尉:	吾兵を休養せんが為めなり	Lieutenant:	'We shall give our troops a rest.'

While it is impossible to reconstruct the original writing-based exchange entirely in Sinitic, it seems safe to assume that most of the sinograms in the Japanese text were derived from the original writing-mediated conversation. Notice that apart from the fact that it is writing-mediated, the question-and-answer turn-taking or mode of interaction is not so different from that in speech-based dyadic conversation.

The third example is derived from Hwang (2009), an empirical study of partly writing-assisted conversation which the researcher refers to as 'brush-talk' 筆談, in keeping with that age-old traditional lingua-cultural practice in Sinographic East Asia 漢字文化圏. It was the topic of a doctoral dissertation[4] that adopted the standard methodologies and analytical framework in conversation analysis (CA) research. Hwang (2009) is to our knowledge the only empirical study of Sinitic brush-talk (or 'pen-talk') to date, which was characterized as communicating via writing morphographic, non-phonographic characters, 'a unique and effective repair mechanism to facilitate interactions between Chinese and Japanese users' (p. 48). Based on 28 hours of audio and video recordings of writing-assisted conversational interaction in small groups between Mandarin-L1 speakers (n=25) and Japanese-L1, Chinese-L2 speakers (n=36) collected at different universities in the USA, mainland China, and Taiwan, Hwang (2009) demonstrates how Chinese and Japanese speakers who are trilingual to different extents in Chinese, Japanese, and English would spontaneously resort to writing sinograms for clarification or disambiguation purposes.[5] This happened frequently and spontaneously when speech – in Mandarin, Japanese, or English, or in any combination – failed to get across their intended meanings. For instance, the Japanese word *kaimono* was obscure to Chinese interlocutors, but its meaning was instantly recognized as soon as they saw 買物 written on paper (compare Mandarin *mǎi dōngxi* 買東西, 'to buy thing', i.e., 'shopping', Hwang 2009: 52). In a similar vein, Mandarin *guì*, 'expensive' created an intelligibility problem to the Japanese interlocutors, but its meaning became clearer in context (talking about prices) after the Chinese character 貴 was written down, as evidenced by the Japanese interlocutor's remark that the corresponding meaning in Japanese was expressed by the sinogram 高 (i.e.,

---

4 Dissertation title: 'Brush talk at the conversation table: Interaction between L1 and L2 speakers of Chinese'.
5 Writing is usually done on paper, but when no paper is available, it may also be performed by finger-dancing in the air or finger-drawing on a flat surface like a table using tea or water.

高い, *takai*, pp. 61–63). In other cases, lexical items using identical sinograms but in a different order was unproblematic (e.g., Mand. 介紹 *jièshào*; Jap. 紹介 *shōkai*, both 'introduce', p. 167). Improvising sinograms did not always resolve the intelligibility problem instantly, however. Thus, it took considerably more conversational repair and clarification to sort out the meaning of 手紙 (*tegami*, Jap. 'letter', p. 10) and 面倒 (*mendō*, 'troublesome', pp. 110–119). The former is commonly understood as 'toilet paper' in Mandarin, while the latter is not used in Chinese but is interpretable as a semantically awkward expression 'face – fall' (cf. Jap. 地元, *jimoto*, 'local' or 'hometown', which is likewise incomprehensible to Mandarin speakers, pp. 120–126). Hwang (2009) concludes as follows:

> Brush-talk worked as one device by which novices used repair devices during their turns of speaking [when conducting] word search. Both novices and language experts used brush-talk to clarify their prior utterances in Chinese, Japanese, or English when their interlocutors displayed problems of understanding following the failure of other repair devices. . . . Brush-talk was also used by novices to identify names of people, objects, songs, and places, while proficient speakers were able to explain characters vocally by paraphrasing or drawing references from common knowledge shared among the interactants.
>
> (Hwang 2009: 225)

In Hwang's (2009) study, writing-assisted conversational interaction or pen-talk was commonly found between plurilingual Chinese and Japanese interlocutors. Writing was not used exclusively; instead, it played an auxiliary role in that it helped clarify or disambiguate any intelligibility problem arising in their speech-based social interaction. Similar pen-assisted conversational exchange has been reported in a couple of other studies (Miyazoe Wong 1996; Fan 1992), albeit incidental to the main findings. Miyazoe Wong (1996) conducted a study of the impact of study-abroad experience on fifteen Hong Kong Chinese university students' interactive competence after their nine-week stay in Japan. Being proficient in both Cantonese and English, they participated in a work/study plus home stay program after receiving about 460 hours of classroom instruction in Japanese. Among the interesting findings is the subjects' spontaneous use of writing-mediated sinograms when intelligibility problems arose in their interaction with Japanese interlocutors:

> In order to solve language/communication problems during their stay in Japan, the subjects often requested clarification and/or repetition from Japanese participants. One of the most interesting points reported by all the subjects was that they communicated with the Japanese participants by writing Chinese characters (*hitsudan*) when they could not understand each other. This is one of the unique features in Chinese-Japanese contact situations, which needs to be explored more in details in the future.
>
> (Miyazoe Wong 1996: 95)

Miyazoe Wong (1996) further cited an earlier study (Fan 1992: 293) in which 'the participants' shared knowledge of Chinese characters (*kanji*) plays an important role in Chinese-Japanese interaction' (p. 95).

As we will see in the contributions to this volume, most of the examples of Sinitic brush-talk are derived from historical sources featuring brush conversation involving literati of Sinitic from different parts of the Sinographic cosmopolis (Koh & King 2014) who had little or no knowledge of their conversation partners' native spoken languages. For this reason, the historically salient lingua-cultural practice of Sinitic-based brush conversation is also commonly referred to as 'silent conversation' (Wang & Xie 2015; Li et al. 2020).

Writing-mediated communication face-to-face: who and why?

As a biologically endowed capacity that comes with birth, the ability to communicate is by no means restricted to humans, but communicating in any natural language(s), more characteristically spoken than written between *talking* humans, is what sets them apart from other known species. In face-to-face encounters with people who share the same language(s), speech is naturally the unmarked modality of communication unless it is physically impossible or socially undesirable to do so. This happens, for example, when the interactants find themselves skydiving or under water, being inconvenienced by a surgical mask while performing surgery, in an extremely noisy environment, or in the middle of a solemn ceremony like a mass or funeral. In such contexts, writing or signing with hand gestures would likely be improvised as a contingent substitute modality, which may or may not be effective. There are other circumstances where writing may be consciously preferred even though speaking is unhindered. Consider a bank hold-up, a recurrent scene in gangster movies. An armed robber, panicky or composed, would typically pass a piece of paper written with a parsimoniously worded instruction to a teller, often nervously and always surreptitiously. If speech is deliberately avoided or suppressed, it is because the equivalent directive, if uttered, might attract undue attention that would jeopardize the hold-up plan. In an envisioned scenario rehearsed many times in the robber's mind before execution, from subtly getting the paper slip across to swiftly collecting stacks of banknotes surrendered by the teller to fleeing, few if any words need to be verbalized.

In everyday life, interaction between talking humans is premised on the sharing of at least one language. What happens in situations where no shared spoken language could be found? That would seem to be the limit of speech as an innate human faculty. If there is a dire need to communicate, like in emergency situations, one would still struggle verbally to convey the message, most probably in a lingua franca – global or regional – if there is one within the interlocutors' repertoire. To increase the odds of being understood, grammatical morphemes and function words would be radically simplified or deleted while complex structures would give way to broken syntax, thereby reducing what one wants to say to its bare bones – the content keywords. Amidst all this frustrating experience, the pidginized verbiage would typically be accompanied by hand gestures and other body language including facial expressions.

Could writing be of any help? In the literature of cross-border communication involving the use of a regional lingua franca like Latin and Arabic, to our knowledge, there is little evidence of writing serving a similar real-time interactional function in like circumstances. This is especially intriguing given that for national languages written with a shared writing system (e.g., the Roman alphabet in Romance languages of Western Europe; abjad in languages of the Arabic-speaking world from North Africa to the Middle East; see, e.g., Daniels & Bright 1996), there is no shortage of orthographically recognizable cognates and loanwords. Would writing as a substitute modality for speech be a convenient solution in those transactional communication contexts (Brown & Yule 1983) between strangers where no shared spoken language could be found? Cross-linguistically, it remains an open question whether writing is resorted to as a substitute modality to compensate for the absence of a shared spoken language and, if so, how frequently or characteristically this is done when speech fails to get one's meaning across.

In short, writing-mediated exchange of information – interactively, synchronously, and face-to-face – is uncommon between talking humans without a shared spoken language. If this is likened to a rule, a notable exception may be found in Sinographic East Asia for well over a thousand years until the 1900s. In cross-border communication involving Chinese and Japanese speakers who have no knowledge of each other's native language, there is plenty of historical evidence suggesting that composing *hànzì* 漢字 (Jap: *kanji*, Kor: *hanja*, Viet: *chữ Hán* ෮漢, *chữ nho* ෮儒, or *Hán tự* 漢字) on paper is one efficient and effective way to clarify what one wants to say. Today, as a script, *hànzì* continues to be taught and used in Greater China (China mainland, Taiwan, the two SARs Hong Kong and Macau) and Japan, less so in South Korea and North Korea (C.-W. Kim 1978; J.-S. Lee 2018; Song 2001), and not in the formal Vietnamese education curriculum. If foreign travelers and the locals literate in Sinitic are able to make meaning interactively in their pen-assisted conversation or 'pen-talk' (see, e.g., Hwang 2009), it may be explained by the fact that the majority of characters or sinograms in Chinese *hànzì* and Japanese *kanji* are semantically close even though they may not be identical in meaning (cf. Shen 2019). As we have seen, this was exactly how in face-to-face encounters the communication barrier of no shared spoken language was successfully overcome, as evidenced by writing-mediated interaction between (i) the Japanese soldier and Chinese villager in Manchuria during the First Sino-Japanese War (1894–1895), (ii) the Korean blogger's procurement of medicine from a Chinese pharmacist when traveling in China, and (iii) the Korean platoon leader and Vietnamese villagers during the Vietnam War. Paradoxically, for interlocutors with no knowledge of each other's spoken language, the same sinograms would hardly be intelligible if uttered in speech because they are pronounced very differently (e.g., '漢字' mentioned previously). We will refer to this morphographically mediated orthographic–phonetic interface as '*intersubjective* subvocalized speech' – the modus operandi of 'silent conversation' through brush-talk or pen-talk (cf. 'Sinitic as semantic interface', Aoyama, this volume).

What is Sinitic brush-talk (漢文筆談)?

Literary Sinitic (Kornicki 2018; cf. *wényán* 文言, Classical Chinese) is a 'cosmopolitan' language comparable to Latin in the 'medieval West' (Whitman 2011) and Sanskrit in ancient South Asia (Pollock 1998, 2000; the 'Sanskrit cosmopolis', Pollock 2006). For hundreds of years until the late nineteenth century, written Chinese was learned and used in East Asia both formally for record-keeping purposes and informally for meeting practical literacy needs in daily life. In the 'Sinographic cosmopolis' (Koh & King 2014), reading and writing were largely mediated by morphographic sinograms (cf. 'Sinitic', Mair 1994; Handel 2019). In cross-border communication, literati without a shared spoken language were able to 'speak' their mind through 'brush conversation' or 'brush-talk' (筆談 *bitán*; Jap: *hitsudan* ひつだん; Kor: *p'iltam* 필담; Viet: *bút đàm*) – the East Asian response to the need for a regional lingua franca, albeit written rather than spoken, hence 'scripta franca' (Denecke 2014; cf. Clements 2019; Li et al. 2020).

For centuries, cross-border encounters in East Asia have yielded plenty of brush-talk artifacts. Multiple volumes featuring face-to-face brush conversation have been compiled (e.g., Chi-Jap, Jap-Kor, Chi-Viet, Ryu-Chi). Four recurrent types of brush-talk with fairly predictable *topical foci* and *participant roles* have been identified: 'political brush-talk' 政情筆談 and/or 'poetic brush-talk' 詩文筆談 (i.e., literary improvisation) between diplomatic envoys and scholar-officials; 'boat drifting brush-talk' 漂流筆談 between maritime officials and foreign seafarers (e.g., Chi-Ryu, Chi-Kor, Chi-Jap); and 'travelogue brush-talk' 遊歷筆談 between foreign travelers soliciting information or service from local strangers or new acquaintances (Li 2020; Li et al. 2020; Wong & Li 2020). Following WANG Yong (Chapter 2), in this book we will categorize the brush-talk literature according to the *typical agents* (or brush-talkers) involved in three principal cross-border communication contexts, viz.: 'brush-talk involving diplomatic envoys' 外交官筆談, 'brush-talk involving boat drifters' 漂流民筆談, and 'brush-talk involving traveling literati' 遊歷者筆談 (cf. Lan 2020).

Being morphographic and non-phonographic, the Sinitic script provides very little clue to the pronunciation of individual sinograms (see the next section for illustrations). In the centuries-old process of script borrowing into Korean, Japanese, and Vietnamese, phonetic and/or semantic adaptation was necessary to domesticate sinograms for local use (Handel 2019), be it modeling on the monosyllabic pronunciation of Chinese speakers or mapping local pronunciation (typically polysyllabic) onto discrete sinograms. Literacy in hundreds of phonetically intersubjective sinograms that are semantically stable and mutually intelligible in writing thus provided the semiotic potential and pragma-linguistic affordance for people with no shared spoken language to compose sinograms to make meaning in cross-border communication, synchronously and face-to-face. Unlike speech-based lingua francas, reliance on writing between literati of Sinitic within the

Sinographic cosmopolis obviated the need for them to ask 'How do you say this in your language?'. This helps explain why for hundreds of years, despite a lack of a shared spoken language, East Asian literati of Sinitic were able to engage in 'silent conversation' through brush-talk.

Researching 'brush conversation' in Sinitic: a brief literature review

What scientific interests and intellectual merits can be gained from researching Sinitic-based brush conversation? Linguistically, brush-talk holds the key to understanding the interactional dynamics of writing-based meaning-making as the third or fourth known and once vibrant modality of face-to-face communication – after **speech** between 'normal' hearing/speaking interlocutors, and *(tactile)* ***sign language*** between hearing-impaired and/or sight-impaired persons (see, e.g., Pfau et al. 2012). This book introduces and exemplifies this as yet little understood modality of communication between humans. For hundreds of years, brush-talk functioned as a scripta franca for literati of Sinitic who were inconvenienced by a lack of a shared spoken language. Early documented records go as far back as the eighth and ninth centuries (e.g., in the diary and travelogue of Japanese monk Ennin 円仁 in China, 794–864 CE), among many others (Li 2020; Wong & Li 2020). Kornicki (2018: 101–102) notes that brush-talk was 'an effective substitute for oral communication' until the late nineteenth century, and that 'the history of brush conversation in East Asia is yet to be written'.

Since the new millennium, research on brush-talk has attracted increasing attention in East Asia. Commenting on topically diverse brush-talk datasets that survived in different parts of East Asia, ZHANG Bowei 張伯偉 likens them to fieldwork reports, with good potential for uncovering interdisciplinary scholarly insights from political studies, economics, law, intellectual currents 學術思想, ethics, education, literature, art, history, geography, encyclopedic knowledge 博物, agriculture, medicine, environmental studies, customs and traditions 風俗 (B. Zhang 2017: 289, 2018). GE Zhaoguang 葛兆光 (2005, 2018) extrapolates from diary-like narratives of Korean envoys to China, interactional brush-talk data included, and argues that after the Ming dynasty gave way to Qing 'barbarian rule', people in Chosŏn regarded themselves as staunch adherents and guardians of fine Confucianist cultural traditions since the Han (206 BCE – 220 CE) and Tang (618–907 CE) dynasties. Such a widely shared perception is reflected, among other sources, in the renaming of Chosŏn envoys' routine missions to the Chinese capital: from 'tributes to heaven' (朝天, Ming) to 'business travel to the Chinese capital' (燕行, Qing). Ge (2015) also shows how Sinitic brush-talk was commonly used by Korean and Japanese literati in their face-to-face interaction to assert their cultural superiority and claim to be truer-than-thou adherents of bona fide Chinese traditions and culture. One instructive example may be found in a 1748 brush conversation between Korean envoy Cho Myŏngch'ae 曹命采 (1700–1764) and Japanese courtier Fujiwara Akitō 藤原明遠 (1697–1761). When asked by the latter about Korean customs and traditions, the former responded by composing a poem, a pentasyllabic octave 五言律詩, which reportedly made the Japanese questioner blush with shame (Ge 2015: 34):

欲識吾邦事	[You] want to be acquainted with our national characteristics.
何難說與聽	What difficulty is there [for me] to tell you?
人皆從古禮	[Our] people all adhere to ancient rituals.
家自誦遺經	At home we chant [Chinese] canons [we] inherited.
衣尚殷時白	[We Koreans] favor white color, a tradition [we] inherited since the Shang dynasty.
山連岱岫青	[Our] blue mountains are connected with Mount Tai [in China].
文明盡在此	[Korea now] preserves [Han-Tang-Song-Ming] civilization.
方夏遜華名	China no longer deserves the name Hua.' (Cho Myŏngch'ae, our free translation)

Intended or otherwise, the Korean envoy apparently interpreted that question as a challenge and appeared to spare no effort to assert Korea's cultural superiority vis-à-vis Japanese culture (compare Jang, this volume).

The last decade has witnessed a large number of scholarly works on Sinitic brush-talk written in Chinese. Lan (2020) provides a succinct historical overview of East Asian cultural exchange 東亞文化交流 through Sinitic brush-talk, and explicates how its semiotic potential and pragma-linguistic affordance was made possible by the use of the shared sinogram-based script in cross-border encounters between literati of Sinitic whose respective spoken languages were mutually unintelligible 同文異音. ZHANG Bowei (2017, 2018) gives a bird's eye view of key brush-talk research outputs and critiques them for inaccurate documentation, misattribution of brush-talkers, above all an ill-informed analytical framework whereby isolated datasets are analyzed locally, with little attempt to connect or make reference to broader historical contexts 見樹不見林. In China, collecting brush-talk literature from 'foreign Sinographic texts' 域外文獻 written by non-Chinese scholars was part of an important *12th Five-Year Publication Plan of National Key Books Project* 十二五國家重點圖書出版規劃項目 (2011–2015). Prominent among such outputs is a compilation of original brush-talk manuscripts in colored, high-resolution photocopies of 'Ōkōchi Documents' 大河內文書 in Japan (8 volumes, WANG Baoping 2016, see also Wang, this volume). Similar multivolume works have also been made available through collaboration with Vietnamese and Korean research institutes (edited by GE Zhaoguang). The rationale is strategically well grounded. As Ge (2015, 2018) explains, up until the Song dynasty (960–1279 CE), imperial China's world view was largely characterized by an imagination of the Middle Kingdom being located at the center 中原 of a nebulous cosmos under Heaven 天下, a center-periphery mindset reinforced by a nationwide belief that the Empire was bordered in the four cardinal directions by uncivilized savages (viz. 四夷: 東夷、南蠻、西戎、北狄).[6] To the emperor

---

6 'The term 四夷 (*siyí*, lit. "Four barbarians") is a collective term for the various barbarians dwelling in the four quadrants of the compass on the periphery of the civilized world of which China was the

and his scholar-officials, a simple way to live peacefully with them was to persuade them to accept the status of tributaries by obliging them to send a mission to the imperial capital periodically as a symbol of their vassalage in exchange for imperial gifts, but also to acquaint themselves with refined Chinese culture and more civilized lifestyles. According to Ge, such a deep-seated imagination 想像 only changed gradually during the Ming dynasty in the late sixteenth century following the arrival of Western scholars/missionaries like Matteo Ricci 利瑪竇 (1552–1610). The scientific know-how from astronomy to geometry plus maps and other images of world geography that they brought to China, to use Ge's (2015, 2018) metaphor, is like a mirror, making Chinese intellectuals see themselves more clearly. By the same token, from today's perspective, the ways in which Ming and Qing China's history, politics, culture, and social life were perceived by her East Asian neighbors represent another invaluable mirror, all the more because most of those foreign Sinographic texts are composed in China's heritage written language, Literary Sinitic, which functioned as the shared scripta franca for all literati in a de facto 'transnational literary community' (文人共和國, B. Zhang 2017: 295) in premodern East Asia (cf. the 'Sinographic cosmopolis', Koh & King 2014). Of interest to us is that a significant body of that Sinitic literature is constituted by social interaction, enacted through brush-talk synchronously face-to-face, between prominent political figures (e.g., ambassadors or envoys during their extended missions) and their local literati hosts, especially courtiers, scholar-officials, aristocrats, and acquaintances.

Another important contribution is LIU Yuzhen's (2010) 712-page compilation of brush-talk between Qing diplomatic personnel in Japan and Japanese scholars and friends. And, thanks to careful documentation and annotation by brush-talkers like Ōkōchi Teruna 大河內輝聲 (1848–1882) and Miyajima Seiichirō 宮島誠一郎 (1838–1911), the manuscripts are still decipherable despite occasional legibility problems. Original brush-talk manuscripts were enthusiastically collected. Among the best-known records of 'silent' interactions and debates are 'Ōkōchi Documents' 大河內文書 (Nakamura 2018; Shima 2017) and 'Miyajima Documents' 宮島家文書 (W. Zhang 2000; Y. Zhang 2004). *Ōkōchi Documents* contains hundreds of brush conversation records involving 132 brush-talkers (69 Japanese, 58 Chinese, 5 Korean) from 1875 to 1881 (B. Wang 2016, this volume). One study thematizes espionage showing how brush-talk was consciously exploited by a 'spy' (Miyajima) to gather state intelligence from the Qing embassy staffer HUANG Zunxian 黃遵憲 (1848–1905) (Y. Zhang 2004; compare Liu, this volume).

More recently, editing and annotating important Sinitic brush-talk texts as preserved in Korea and Japan (including Okinawa, the former Ryukyu Kingdom) was the goal of the 'East Asian Brush-talk Research Series' 東亞筆談文獻研究叢書, which was one of the big national book publication projects under *The 13th*

---

center. It therefore indicates the barbarians in general – all the barbarians, not those of any particular place' (Fairbank & Teng 1941: 137; slightly amended).

Five-Year Publication Plan of National Key Books Project 十三五國家重點圖書出版規劃項目 (2016–2020) in China. Under the supervision of WANG Yong 王勇, Director of the Japanese Cultural Institute 日本文化研究所所長 at Zhejiang University 浙江大學, this important project has already led to the publication of a number of hefty volumes, each containing analyses and commentaries on thoroughly proofread and typeset brush-talk texts arising from brush conversations involving personages with particular historical significance, complete with annotations and high-resolution photocopies of original manuscripts:

Editor	Year	Book title
ZHOU Yan 周妍. ZHANG Xinpeng 張新朋	2016	內藤湖南筆談文獻研究 'Studies in Naitō Torajirō's brush-talk interaction documents'
CHEN Xiaofa 陳小法. WANG Yong 王勇	2018	《朝鮮漂流日記》研究 'Studies in *Chosŏn boat drifters' diaries*'
WANG Lianwang 王連旺	2018	朝鮮通信使筆談文獻研究 'Studies in Chosŏn envoys' brush-talk interaction documents'
WANG Yong 王勇	2018	東亞筆談文獻經眼錄 'A survey of the East Asian Sinitic brush-talk literature: An annotated bibliography'
WANG Yong 王勇. XIE Yong 謝詠	2018	名倉予何人筆談文獻研究 'Studies in Nakura Anato's brush-talk interaction documents'
WANG Yong 王勇. ZHU Zihao 朱子昊	2018	朱舜水筆談文獻研究 'Studies in Zhu Shunshui's brush-talk interaction documents'
ZHU Zihao 朱子昊. GUO Xiumei 郭秀梅	2018	東亞醫學筆談文獻研究 'Studies in East Asian medical brush-talk interaction documents'

Of these works, one is related to a late Ming Confucian scholar, ZHU Shunshui 朱舜水 (1600–1682), who fled the sociopolitical turmoil in China during the transition years to Qing reign (1644–1912) and who spent over two decades of his twilight years from 1660 until his death in Japan (Wang & Zhu 2018). During this period, ZHU Shunshui left behind sizable amounts of brush conversation data, especially surviving brush-talk records when responding to questions put to him by a variety of Japanese interlocutors. For several decades now, the compilation and publication of rather well-preserved manuscripts of Zhu's brushed encounters with others has spawned considerable research interest, including his huge contributions and highly valued legacies to Edo and even Meiji Japan (e.g., Qian 2008; Q. Zhu 1981; Z. Zhu 2018; see Li 2020 for more discussion).

Wang and Xie's (2015) edited volume contains 17 chapters, covering varied data sources and contexts (e.g., Chi-Jap, Chi-Kor, Jap-Kor) with rather different topical foci. Other published works include reports of Vietnamese envoys to China (Y.-J. Liu 2007; J. Zhang 2012); brush conversation between Korean and

Vietnamese envoys (WANG Yong 2013); records of SUN Yat-sen 孫逸仙 (a.k.a. SUN Zhongshan 孫中山 and SUN Wen 孫文, 1866–1925) brush-talking with Vietnamese revolutionaries (Yu & Liang 2013) and Miyazaki Tōten 宮崎滔天 (1871–1922) (He et al. 2010; ZSJYZ 2016). A few other studies focus on Japanese and Korean medical doctors' exchange of information or views on Chinese medicine (M. Li 2017; compare Trambaiolo 2014); and between distressed foreign boat drifters and maritime officials in Japanese waters (Liang 2015) and Korean waters (Jin 2018).

Research outputs written in Japanese and Korean involve two main contexts: shipwreck incidents documented in 'drifting records' from the seventeenth to nineteenth centuries (brush-talk involving boat drifters 漂流民筆談); and encounters between diplomats and scholar-officials and their foreign counterparts (brush-talk involving diplomatic envoys 外交官筆談). Kansai University Press has published a series of ten books recording Japanese maritime officials' interrogation of Chinese seafarers during the mid-Edo and late Edo period (1603–1868) (e.g., Ōba 1985; Matsuura 2007, 2009, 2011, 2014; Cen 2014; cf. Fuma 2015, 2016; see also Matsuura 2015; Matsuura & Aoyama, this volume).[7] For instance, Cen (2014) shows how, from 1750 to 1882, 'conversation' between distressed Ryukyuan boat drifters and Chinese rescuers was conducted exclusively in Sinitic brush-talk, until an interpreter provided verbal interpretation at a Ryukyuan trading outpost in Fuzhou (cf. Kornicki 2018: 98). Chosŏn diplomatic and trade missions to Japan during the seventeenth and eighteenth centuries also gave rise to many brush-talk records (Yi 1997; Ogawa 2012), including trilateral interaction between Korean envoys, the feudal lord of Tsushima, and Tokugawa officials in 1607 (Moon 2018). Interestingly, brush-talk was often preferred to multistep interpreting because what transpired through brush and ink on paper was felt to be more direct and accurate. Apart from being unequivocal evidence of Sinitic brush-talk's scripta franca function, it also illustrates the semiotic potential and pragma-linguistic affordance of that written mode of meaning-making in the hands of creative and aesthetically minded brush-talkers who were eager to showcase their scholarship, poetic flair, and calligraphy.

Sinitic brush-talk research published in English to date is relatively scanty (for a brief review, see Li 2020). Brush-talk data tends to be ancillary to a main theme such as Sino-Japanese cultural exchange, sometimes supplemented with poetic improvisation. In his 342-page treatise on *Borders of Chinese Civilization*, Howland (1996: 43–53) includes 'silent conversation' through brush-talking to exemplify literary exchange between Qing Chinese diplomats and Japanese scholars during the 1870s–1880s. Their poetic verses, presented in English translation rather than in sinograms, illustrate how Literary Sinitic served as a written

---

7 For data sources on 'brush-talk involving boat drifters' 漂流民筆談, see *Pipyŏnsa Tŭngnok* 備邊司謄錄 (1706a, 1706b, retrievable online: http://db.history.go.kr/item/level.do?itemId=bb), which consists of 39 brush-talk records between Korean maritime officials and Chinese 'boat drifters' during the period 1687–1880.

nexus for both sides to engage intellectually, performatively, but also strategically when making subtle identity claims. Similarly, in Keaveney's (2009) discussion of Sino-Japanese literary exchange in the interwar period (1919–1937), brush-talk is characterized as an interactive mode of 'traditional cultural communication . . . among literate individuals in the Sinitic world' (p. 3).

Kelley (2005) critiques the 'nationalist inventions of a Vietnamese past' by Western scholars after the Second World War (p. 10). Driven by an 'autonomous history' perspective, they denied the French colonialists' characterization of Vietnam (then Annam) as a replica of China. Kelley believed that such a blanket denial of the 'little China' theory was going too far. With the help of Sinitic poems composed by Vietnamese envoys to Peking from the sixteenth to nineteenth centuries, including those they exchanged with fellow Korean envoys on similar tributary missions there, Kelley (2005) shows that such Vietnamese scholar-officials clearly demonstrated erudite knowledge of Classical Chinese canons and traditional Chinese culture plus an unmistakable sense of identification with Confucianist values as well as strong emotional attachment to a shared Sinitic-based literary heritage. According to Kelley (2005), such an intellectual orientation and affective disposition were due in no small measure to the institutionalization of the Confucian civil service examination system for over 800 years (科舉制度, *kējǔ zhìdù*; Viet: chế độ khoa cử, 1075–1913). This is clearly evidenced by the famous poetic exchange between the Vietnamese envoy Phùng Khắc Khoan 馮克寬 (1528–1613) and Korean envoy Yi Su-kwang 李睟光 (1563–1628) at several brush conversations that Kelley analyzes in some detail (Kelley 2005: 182–192; for more discussion of their brush conversations, see Pore 2008; cf. Li 2020: 200). For centuries after this event, the Sinitic poems arising from the Phùng-Yi poetic improvisation and exchange became fine models for Vietnamese literati to emulate.

Trambaiolo (2014) analyzes surviving records of brush conversation between Korean and Japanese medical practitioners in Japan from 1607 to 1811. During this Tokugawa period, a total of twelve Korean missions visited Japan, each lasting for about six months. For each of these missions, included in the four hundred odd entourage were several Korean doctors whose job was to look after the physical well-being of their envoys. With effect from 1682, an additional medical expert was selected to join the mission for the explicit purpose of strengthening intellectual exchange of medical knowledge and new clinical practices with their Japanese counterparts. According to Trambaiolo, such Korean missions were greatly valued by Japanese medical practitioners, who considered them a golden opportunity for an update of their knowledge base and sharing of advanced practices for treating thorny illnesses. Since neither side knew the other's spoken language well enough, and interpreters were few in number, the majority had to rely on Sinitic brush-talk as the principal method for meaning-making as well as poetic improvisation and socializing chanting 漢詩酬唱. Interestingly, such brushed encounters were not always convivial, as when one side's question or response was interpreted as asserting superiority, expressing doubt or disbelief, or even a challenge to one's authority. Such confrontations and cultural conflicts arising from complex identity claims were not rare. While no Sinitic-based brush conversation examples were cited by Trambaiolo (2014), there is no doubt that the brush-talk datasets are rich and enlightening in many ways. In such slippery transcultural brushed encounters, miscommunication partly induced by inadequate understanding of cross-cultural values and mismatch of expectations could not be ruled out. As pointed out and exemplified by Nguyễn and Nguyễn (2019), Chinese–Vietnamese communication during the premodern and early modern period was anything but obvious, for the lack-luster performance of interpreters (*tōngyán* 通言) was a matter of perennial concern.

Based on the *Peking Memoir* (Ledyard 1982), a 'diplomatic travel diary' written by Korean envoy Hong Tae-yong 洪大容 (1731–1783) consisting of detailed notes and observations he took while participating in the winter solstice embassy to Peking 燕行 in 1765–1766, Ledyard (1982) gives a succinct account of the brush conversations that Hong had with three Chinese scholars from Hangzhou in central China during the expedition that lasted for over five months. Intriguing is not only the content of their intellectual exchange enacted through Sinitic brush-talk but also many fine details of the brush-talking process (see Li 2020: 221–224; for a treatise on this *Kanjŏng p'iltam* 乾淨筆譚 in Japanese, see Fuma 2016). Published brush-talk records, being edited works, give the impression of being clean, tidy, and orderly. Such an impression is deceptive, however. Based on Hong Taeyong's description in his diary, this is a far cry from the messy spread of loose sheets scattered around when the brush-talkers' attention was focused entirely on the content of intellectual or poetic exchange in the heat of the moment. Instances of sheets of paper misplaced, containing corrections of wrong sinograms, false start, and non-sequitur were not rare:

> In our 'talks' we would each hold on to paper and brush, writing on this piece or that, our hands hardly stopping. In one day we would surely have written more than ten thousand words . . . both sides at any given moment were mainly concerned with exchanging remarks, so that much of what we wrote got mixed up or fell out of order. For this reason, even the notes I still have contain questions with no answers, or answers with no questions, or remarks with no beginning or end. If in such cases I could no longer recall the conversation, I discarded the notes. When I could still remember, I added a few words to the remarks of the three friends to fill them out . . . Where there was no obstacle, we tried to preserve the original wording, but places can also be found where we did not hesitate to polish the prose in the interests of truth or sincerity.
> (Ledyard 1982: 95–96; also cited in Li 2020: 223)

As for the use of Sinitic in international diplomacy involving a Western power, negotiation between Tokugawa Japan and the USA led by Commodore Perry's 'black ships' in 1854 was perhaps the least expected. Tao (2005) gives an informative account of the significant role played by written Chinese in early Japanese–US diplomatic negotiations (compare Aoyama, this volume). Since few Japanese were conversant in English while the American side could not find anyone well versed in Japanese, a Chinese merchant of Hong Kong origin called LUO Sen 羅

森 was appointed by Perry as translator. Since the beginning of the Tokugawa period in the early seventeenth century, Dutch was the dominant foreign language in Japan, the window to the outside world (cf. *rangaku*, 蘭學, 'Dutch studies'). Hence, it is not surprising that Dutch was selected for verbal communication with US negotiators, while formal records were written in Classical Chinese or Sinitic. Although Luo did not speak any Japanese, his fluent English and sound knowledge of Classical Chinese and literary works enabled him to communicate with the Japanese negotiators effectively, albeit indirectly in writing mode. Beyond his normal duties, wherever he went Luo's improvisation of Chinese poetic verses was also widely sought after by Japanese admirers and amateurs of Sinitic art forms such as paper fans adorned with elegantly written Sinitic words of wisdom or poetic verses (Aoyama 2020; see also Aoyama, this volume).

Clements (2019) analyzes brush-talk data, personal diaries, and official records arising from the Chosŏn missions to Japan from the seventeenth to nineteenth centuries, and argues that while ritual-like, brush-talk allows literati on both sides to 'speak' their minds and to engage in literary improvisation interactively, making subtle shifts in their identities in the process. Given that what is improvised in brush-talk is neither pidginized nor spoken, however, Clements (2019: 21) questions the suitability of the term 'lingua franca' for the bridging function of Literary Sinitic; instead, she finds Denecke's (2014: 209) characterization of 'scripta franca' more appropriate (cf. 'written linguistic code', Howland 1996: 45). Denecke (2014) critiques the traditional view of written Chinese being inferior to Eurocentric alphabetic writing systems and points to the time-honored function of 'character scripts' in turning premodern East Asian Sinosphere into 'worlds without translation' through glossing (Whitman 2011; cf. Handel 2019; Lurie 2011).

In terms of the script selected for representing brush-talk interaction in English publications, however, whether the genre in question is poetic or otherwise, the original brush-talk data in sinograms is seldom reproduced. There appears to be little interest in the script-specific interaction carried out through brush conversation, as is evidenced by brush-talk content being translated into English rather than displaying the Sinitic original (see, e.g., brush-talk between Ōkōchi Teruna 大河内輝聲 and Qing Chinese officials, Howland 1996: 48–49; Ledyard 1982: 74–75). English translation is also the unmarked citation practice in treatises written in English when poetic verses in Sinitic are excerpted for illustration (see, e.g., Chapter 4, 'The Historiographical Use of Poetry', Howland 1996: 108–156; Kelley 2005: 182–192).

In his study of vernacularization and the historical role played by the language of learning in East Asia, Kornicki (2018: 100–102) observes that writing-based Sinitic brush-talk played a key role complementary to oral communication in that it facilitated intellectual exchange between literati speakers who had no shared spoken language. He also appeals for systematic research on the history of Sinitic brush-talk in Sinographic East Asia, which has yet to be written. Given the historical nature of Sinitic brush-talk and the instrumental role it played for centuries as a nexus linking literati of Sinitic when they were engaged in cross-border communication, research on brush conversation clearly has significant contributions to make in early modern East Asian history, notably politics and international diplomacy, among other things presenting a personal touch, indexed by brush-talk interaction patterns, that complement standard standpoints at the national policy level (see 'Discussion paper', Clements, this volume).

Sinosphere 漢字文化圈: the 'center' and its 'peripheries'

For centuries since the Han dynasty (202 BCE–220 CE), imperial China institutionalized a loose network of inter-state or cross-border relations with the polities in the four cardinal directions of the Middle Kingdom. Such a network was characterized by Fairbank and Teng (1941) as the 'tributary system' (cf. Fairbank 1968). For neighbors of the Middle Kingdom big and small, recognition of the mandate and suzerainty of the Chinese emperor as the 'Son of Heaven' 天子 was enough to receive, in return, a guarantee of peaceful co-existence, conferment of the king or prince status through the bestowal of a formal investiture (often along with a crown and a seal) and, above all, lucrative trading opportunities. Such loose diplomatic relations were formalized during the Ming dynasty (1368–1644), with more rigorous protocols governing rituals and ceremonies to be observed by embassies when brought in front of Chinese dignitaries of different ranks from provincial officials to the emperor's audience (e.g., varying kowtow 叩頭 and prostration rituals, Fairbank & Teng 1941: 138–139). To symbolize acceptance of the Middle Kingdom's suzerainty, tributaries were under obligation to send an embassy to the celestial capital periodically, bringing with them precious gifts to please the Son of Heaven (see Table 1.1 for a list of tributaries from East Asia during the Ming dynasty in 1587).[8] In return, the embassies would be rewarded with imperial gifts which, in pecuniary value, would normally exceed that of their aggregate tribute items.[9] In addition, tributaries would be allowed to conduct trading activities through permits, which was widely looked upon as a lucrative and attractive source of revenue. For instance, after establishing initial contact with the Ming dynasty in the late 1360s and securing formal tributary status from Emperor Hongwu 明太祖 洪武帝 in 1372, the Ryukyu Kingdom was pleased because '[f]ormal submission meant official license to trade with the largest and most powerful nation in the Far East' and that '[w]ithin the next two decades at least nine official missions crossed to the Chinese capital' (Kerr 1958/2000: 65–66).[10]

---

8 For details of the composition of an embassy, pre-departure preparation and the route of Chosŏn missions, see Chun (1968: 95–98).
9 Chun (1968) contends that in the case of the 'model tributary', Korea (p. 90), 'the value of the tributary goods from Korea and the Korean gifts to Chinese embassies far exceeded what Korea received' (only about one-tenth, pp. 105, 109).
10 The Ryukyu Kingdom practiced dual subordination as a tributary to both dynastic China and Japan for over 260 years (1609–1872). From 1611 to 1850, '[e]ighteen embassies made their solemn way to Edo. . . . Leading members of the Shuri government were made ambassadors, who traveled with a large suite. Scholars and craftsmen, administrative officers and merchants went overland

Table 1.1 Ming tributaries as of 1587

Country	Tribute Embassies	Periodicity	Route via
Korea (Chosŏn)	1369 ff.	1372. every 3 yrs. or 1 yr.: after 1403. annual	Yalu River. Liaoyang. Shanhaiguan
Japan	1374 refused. accepted 1381. 1403–1551 occasional	10 yrs.	Ningbo
Ryukyu	1368 ff.	2 yrs.	Fuzhou
Annam	1369 ff.	3 yrs.	Pingyangzhou. Guangxi
Cambodia (Zhenla 真臘)	1371 ff.	Court tribute indefinite	Guangdong
Siam	1371 ff.	3 yrs.	Guangdong
Champa	1369 ff.	3 yrs.	Guangdong
Java (Zhaowa 爪哇)	1372. 1381. 1404. 1407	1443 every 3 yrs.. later indefinite	

Source: Adapted from Fairbank and Teng (1941: 151)

As noted by many scholars, the mutually beneficial center-peripheries relationship enacted through the tributary system was more symbolic than demeaning, for, not only did the tributaries get a nominal promise of protection (if attacked), but also because hardly any aspect of their political independence would be compromised by such a Confucianist Chinese World Order (Fairbank 1968). As noted by WANG Gungwu (1968), the tributary system 'was the result of both "majesty and power" and the extension of Chinese principles of government' (G.-W. Wang 1968: 62), which was largely based on 'the idea of the emperor's moral superiority and rule-by-virtue (*dé* 德), as exemplified preeminently during the Tang [dynasty] (618–907)' (Fairbank 1968: 15). According to GE Sun (2000) and Hamashita (2008), the tributary system had its own organizing principles and connections, which differed significantly from the contemporary nation-state relations in the Western world:

> The tribute system constitutes an ordered region with an inherent logic completely different from modern Europe. That is, in contrast to the 'state' as a unit, there is the regional mechanism of the 'center to its periphery' and the corresponding relationships of paying tributes and conferring titles.
> (S. Ge 2000: 333)

The tributary system was an organic network of relations linking the center and its peripheries, including the provinces and dependencies of the empire, rulers of native tribes and districts, tributary states and even trading partners.

---

to Edo through the Japanese countryside. accompanied by an armed escort from Satsuma. They returned . . . ladened with ideas as well as with material things of importance to the Ryukyuan economy' (Kerr 1958/2000: 168).

> This tributary system, broadly understood, constituted the arena in which the states and other entities of southeast, northeast, central and northwest Asia operated and defined their multiple relations with China and other regions of Asia.
>
> (Hamashita 2008: 13)

Part and parcel of the acceptance of the tributary status was recognition of the cultural superiority of the Middle Kingdom and, at least in theory, a willingness to learn to read and write the Chinese language. According to Fairbank and Teng (1941) and Fairbank (1968), the 'center-peripheries' Chinese World Order had been sustained by the tributary system for nearly two millennia; it only started to crumble after Qing China had to put up with one humiliating defeat after another by Western powers and rapidly modernizing Japan beginning from the 1840s. The cultural superiority of the Middle Kingdom, reinforced by novelties brought back by not only envoys to the celestial capital but also merchants, students and monks periodically, made books and other printed materials from China particularly attractive to the wealthy and elite classes. This was especially the case with regard to China's land-bound or sea-borne neighbors to the east (Korea and Japan) and to the south and southeast (Vietnam and the Ryukyu Kingdom). What follows is a brief outline of the history of the 'periphery' states or polities within Sinographic East Asia.

Korea (Chosŏn)

Formerly the Kingdom of Old Chosŏn, Korea is located on the Korean Peninsula facing Japan across the East Sea 東海 (a.k.a. Sea of Japan 日本海). The ancient kingdom had also been ruled by invadors from China, namely Kija 箕子 (Kija Chosŏn 箕子朝鮮, 1120–195 BCE), who allegedly fled Shang China in 1122 BCE, and Wiman 衛滿 (Wiman Chosŏn 衛滿朝鮮, 195–108 BCE). Conquered by Han China in 108 BCE, the Chosŏn Kingdom gradually evolved into Three Kingdoms: Silla 新羅, Koguryŏ 高句麗, and Paekche 百濟. For several hundred years, Paekche acquired Chinese culture and advanced know-how through maritime contacts with the Southern dynasties (南朝 420–589) and played a fundamental role in transmitting Chinese culture such as written Chinese and Buddhism to the Japanese archipelago, while Koguryŏ adopted Chinese institutions, laws and culture and had many military confrontations with China. Linguistically, the Korean language has been mutually unintelligible with Sinitic languages although its vocabulary was sinicized to a large extent after intensive contact with Sinitic civilization and Classical Chinese for well over two millennia (Yurayong & Szeto 2021). Sinitic literature was first spread to Korea after the Han dynasty established the four commanderies 漢四郡 during the first century BCE.

In 668, Silla conquered the other two kingdoms and ruled until 935. The learning and use of Literary Chinese were institutionalized and expanded soon after unification. A national institute, called *Kukhak* 國學, was set up in 682 to teach Confucian classics. Places and administrative positions were given Chinese names using Sino-Korean pronunciation. After the founding of Koryŏ (918), the use of Chinese characters became more widespread. The civil service examination was introduced in 958. During this period, interlinear annotation and glossing techniques called *kugyŏl* 口訣 were added to Chinese texts to facilitate reading. All formal writing was done in Classical Chinese until the late nineteenth century. After withstanding the Mongolian invasions for four decades until the 1270s, the Koryŏ dynasty continued to rule until 1392 despite interference from Yuan China. During the Yuan-Ming transition period, the unstable political situation in Koryŏ was overcome with the founding of the Kingdom of Chosŏn, which lasted for over 500 years (1392–1910). Throughout the Koryŏ dynasty and Chosŏn dynasty, the level of Chinese writing gradually increased, and all formal writing was done in Classical Chinese until the late nineteenth century.'

Before the promulgation of the Korean alphabet called *Hunminjŏng'ŭm* (訓民正音, 'The Correct Sounds for the Instruction of the People') by King Sejong 世宗大王 in 1446 and the gradual spread of *hangŭl* (*yŏnmun* 諺文) in Korean society, early attempts had been made to write the Korean language using sinograms with their meanings and pronunciations domesticated, plus a complex process of glossing involving morphosyntactic adjustment and marking (*Idu* 吏讀). One consequence is that over half of the Korean lexicon is made up of Sino-Korean words. For centuries, the use of *hangŭl* was limited to vernacular and informal writing until 1894, when the civil service examination was abolished and all government documents were required by law to be written in *hangŭl* mixed with *hanja* 漢字.

In 1876, Korea was forced to open ports to Meiji Japan. Rivalry over Korea triggered the Russo-Japanese War (1904–1905), after which Korea became a Japanese protectorate and was subsequently colonized for 35 years (1910–1945). In 1948 it was partitioned into the Democratic People's Republic of Korea 朝鮮民主主義人民共和國 (North Korea) and the Republic of Korea 大韓民國 (South Korea). Extensive Sinitic influence for centuries helps explain why Koreans who were literate in Sinitic could engage in writing-mediated brush conversation with other literati of Sinitic elsewhere from Sinographic East Asia. Today, *hanja* is still taught in school in both North and South Korea to different extents (Handel 2019; Kim 1978; Jeon 2019: 115–116; Lee 2018; Song 2001, 2019). According to Song (2019: 132–133):

> Chinese characters have been taught at the secondary and tertiary levels since 1968. . . . North Korean students learn more Chinese characters (i.e. 1,500 characters at the secondary level, and 500 or 1,000 additional ones at the technical-college or university level, respectively) than South Korean students (i.e. 1,800 characters in total). Moreover, Hanja is only an elective subject in South Korea, while this is not the case in North Korea.

Japan

Among the earliest mentions of the Japanese archipelago and its inhabitants were *Wa* 倭 and *Wajin* 倭人 that appeared in the 'Treatise on Geography' 地理志 in 'The Book of Han' 漢書 in 111 CE. To elude the pejorative connotation of the sinogram 倭, the Japanese gradually started to refer to their own country as *Nippon* 日本 during their missions to Sui (遣隋使, 607–614) and Tang (遣唐使, 630–894) China. Although Japan's status as China's tributary remained in place until the ninth century, China accepted the change of the name as evidenced in 'The Old Book of Tang' 舊唐書:

日本國者　倭國之別種也　以其國在日邊　故以日本爲名
(Liu et al. 1945/1975: 5340)

The country *Nippon* was another name for the country *Wa*. Because the country is close to the Sun, it is named *Nippon*.

(Our translation)

The meaning of the compound word 日本 ('rooted in the Sun', or 'rising Sun') reflects Japan's geographical location to the east of the Middle Kingdom and the Korean Peninsula, which is clearly indexical of the Japanese positioning of their own country vis-à-vis its awesome neighbor, China. Through successive generations of settlers from Korea and the west-bound missions to China, Japan absorbed advanced sociopolitical practices and cultural knowledge including the bureaucratic system of everyday administration, city planning, architecture, clothing, Buddhist teachings, and above all, Sinitic writing.

The inhabitants of the Japanese archipelago did not have any writing until the introduction of sinograms by Korean and Chinese immigrants around the third century, who later settled and held various positions in the hereditary Japanese court. Around the seventh century, the Japanese began adapting the sinograms for their own use, including composing poems and literary works. Earliest historiographies including 'The records of ancient matters' 古事記 (712) and 'The chronicles of Japan' 日本書紀 (720) were all written in a form of literary Chinese with a heavy admixture of Japanese vernacular elements (e.g., subject-object-verb word order and *man'yōgana* 萬葉仮名, a set of sinograms representing the sounds of Japanese). As a way of negotiating the significant typological differences between the two languages, the Japanese gradually simplified sinograms over time and developed two phonographic scripts: square form *katakana* 片仮名 and cursive form *hiragana* 平仮名 (Habein 1984; Seeley 2000; Igarashi 2007; cf. Handel 2019). As a result of growing enthusiasm for learning Buddhism, Japanese monks developed simplified versions of the *man'yōgana* and inserted them as reading aids for deciphering ritual texts written in Classical and literary Chinese. This new simplified script functioned as mnemonic signs that were, however, considered imperfect compared with *man'yōgana*, hence they came to be called *katakana*, literally 'deformed characters'. The other set of phonographic script, *hiragana*, was developed from the cursive forms of *man'yōgana* and often used to satisfy the aesthetic demands of calligraphy and facilitate the continuous flow of short poems called *waka* 和歌. With two phonetic scripts and one logographic script (written with sinograms or *kanji* 漢字) at their disposal, the Japanese have been able to either choose one or mix and match any or all of the three to lend expression to their ideas depending on the genres and types and purposes of their writing. Besides China, Japan remains one of the few countries where sinograms continue to be actively used today.

Kanbun (漢文, literally 'Chinese writing'), one type of Japanese classical writing, is entirely written in sinograms but typically read in vernacular Japanese with the visual aid of *kunten* 訓點 glosses. This technique of translating literary Chinese into vernacular Japanese is called *kundoku* (訓読, 'reading by gloss') and it allows Japanese readers to rearrange the word order from verb-medial to verb-final with the help of morphosyntactic annotations, and to connect words by grammatical markers necessitated by agglutinating morphologies. Following the *kundoku* practice, the Japanese managed to translate literary Chinese texts into vernacular Japanese while preserving the original text with inserted glosses (Clements 2015). *Kanbun* is not only one of the most significant literary styles for official and intellectual writing in the past, but it continues to be taught in Japanese schools as part of compulsory education. As recently as 2021, *Kanbun* figured in the Japanese language paper of the National University Entrance Examinations.

The Ryukyu Kingdom

Before becoming a Japanese prefecture in 1879 and being formally renamed as Okinawa, the Ryukyu Kingdom enjoyed relative political independence for several hundred years. Okinawa 沖繩 means literally a 'rope in the offing' as the island chain resembles 'a knotted rope tossed carelessly upon the sea' on the map (Kerr 1958/2000: 22). From north to south, the island chain stretches about 1,100 kilometers (700 miles) from the northernmost island south of Kyushu to the southernmost island that is within sight of Taiwan on a fine day. About three dozen of the islands are inhabited, while over a hundred of the rest are not. As a kingdom, Ryukyu accepted the suzerainty of Ming China in 1372, and remained a tributary for 500 years until late Qing in 1872 when it was transformed into the Ryukyu domain and renamed Okinawa seven years later. Back in the early seventeenth century, the Satsuma domain 薩摩藩 had invaded Ryukyu in 1609 out of apprehension for the increasing presence of Western vessels including warships coming up from the south to menace the Japanese archipelago. One consequence is that Ryukyu also accepted to be a tributary of Tokugawa Japan, in effect practicing dual subordination to China and Japan for over 260 years.

Natural resources being meager, plus harsh climatic conditions especially typhoons in the summer months, successive generations of Ryukyuans relied on entrepot trade as their lifeline, especially the trading of luxury goods with China, Japan, and the Southeast Asian nations as far south as Java, Sumatra, and Malacca (Kerr 1958/2000: 63). Over time, trade with China became so voluminous that a Ryukyuan outpost, Ryukyu-kan 琉球館, serving as a liaison office cum 'trading depot with a permanent staff in residence' was set up in 1493 in Fuzhou, which remained in use for 436 years until 1875 (Kerr 1958/2000: 93).

Linguistically, early Ryukyuans spoke a language similar to those in southern Kyushu. Until the thirteenth century, prior to regular trading relations and sustained contact with China, the Ryukyuans had been using a simple phonetic syllabary developed in Japan for writing the Ryukyuan language, not only formal records but also poetry (Kerr 1958/2000: 52). This changed gradually after a sizable number of Chinese immigrants settled in Kume Village (Kumemura 久米村) of the Ryukyu kingdom upon the Ming emperor's order in 1393. Since then, written Chinese texts gradually spread on the island kingdom while the Chinese administrative system in a modified form was progressively adapted to meet Ryukyuan needs. By the late eighteenth century, the extent to which the Ryukyu Kingdom was sinicized may be gauged by the scholarships awarded periodically to the best-performing students in two rigorous examinations to study in Peking for three years, following a curriculum designed specifically for students from tributary states (Kerr 1958/2000: 225). All this helps explain why many Ryukyuans were literate in Sinitic and able to engage literati of Sinitic from other polities in brush conversation.

Vietnam

Vietnam, also called Annam historically, is a maritime country on the Indochina Peninsula facing the South China Sea. While the Red River crisscrosses the northern plains, the delta area of southern Vietnam is irrigated by the Mekong. The north is rich in mineral resources, while crops like rice, sugarcane, coffee, tea, and banana are grown throughout the country. In 207 BCE, the Qin Emperor of China 秦始皇 sent General ZHAO Tuo 趙佗 to conquer present-day northern Vietnam, Guangdong Province and Guangxi Province (Âu Lạc 甌雒). Following the demise of the short-lived Qin Empire (221–206 BCE), Zhao proclaimed himself Emperor Wu 武王 and established the Kingdom of Nam Việt 南越 in 204 BCE, which was later annexed by Han dynasty in 111 BCE. For over a millennium, the Vietnamese people were subjected to Chinese rule until 938 CE. During this period, the governors and top officials were Chinese while the Vietnamese elites were educated in Chinese.

Having declared independence, the administration and governance of Vietnam during the Monarchical period (938–1858) was carried out by mandarins who were trained very much like their Chinese counterparts by pursuing a rigorous study of Confucian canons and other literary works in Classical Chinese. Confucian influence kept expanding, with a Confucian Temple of Literature (Văn Miếu 文廟) being erected in the capital in 1070. The civil service examination, following the Chinese model, began in 1075 while a college was also established for training sons of the ruling elite in Confucian classics. It was implemented for over 800 years without interruption until being abolished by the French colonial government in 1913. The shared Sinitic-based written language made it possible for Vietnamese scholars to communicate with literati elsewhere in East Asia through writing. For centuries, the Vietnamese sent their best scholars as envoys to the Chinese capital on tributary missions, where they would purchase the latest Chinese books and routinely participate in poetry-writing competitions with Chinese and Korean scholars, among others.

Linguistically, being an Austro-Asiatic language, Vietnamese is mutually unintelligible with Sinitic languages. Sinitic-based literacy, read with Sino-Vietnamese pronunciation, was a privilege of the upper classes who were acquainted with Classical Chinese (*chữ Hán* 𡨸漢, *chữ nho* 𡨸儒) as the medium of administration for writing official documents but also producing scholarship from literature to medicine. From the eleventh century onwards, the emergence of indigenized *chữ nôm* 𡨸喃, a set of 'demotic characters' (Lo Bianco 2001: 161) created to lend expression to local meanings, allowed native Vietnamese words to be recorded, but they were notoriously cumbersome and difficult to learn. From the fifteenth to nineteenth centuries, *chữ nôm* was widely used by the elites for their popular vernacular works, mainly in the form of verses. As for the influence of the Chinese language, Sinitic words were imported wholesale into the Vietnamese language ever since the Qin dynasty. This helps explain why the Sino-Vietnamese vocabulary accounts for over half of the modern Vietnamese lexicon (Handel 2019). The Sinitic literacy landscape outlined earlier lasted well into the early twentieth century (Lo Bianco 2001).

For about 120 years until the 1970s, Vietnam went through one political turbulence after another. It was under colonial rule first by France (1858–1940), then by Japan (1940–1945). This was followed by over two decades of bitter fighting and devastation during the Vietnam War (1955–1975). In 1976, North and South Vietnam were reunited as the Socialist Republic of Vietnam. The teaching and use of *chữ nôm* and *chữ Hán* in society gradually came to a halt between the two world wars and were completely discontinued after reunification in 1945. The romanized *Quốc Ngữ* alphabet, which had been created by the Portuguese missionaries in the early seventeenth century, was adopted as the national script – *chữ Quốc Ngữ* – to write the Vietnamese language (Lo Bianco 2001: 161). Parallel to that development was the gradual loss of the Vietnamese people's ability to converse through brush-talk with other literati of Sinitic elsewhere in East Asia.

Historical spread of written Chinese and Sinitic-based literacy in Sinographic East Asia

For over 1,500 years until the early twentieth century, Classical Chinese (*wényán* 文言) – the formal writing genre of dynastic China – has exerted tremendous lingua-cultural influence on her East Asian neighbors. Prior to the emergence of their own scripts for writing their respective national languages, Classical Chinese or Literary Sinitic was the only written language accessible to small numbers of sociopolitically and economically privileged elites in successive generations. Despite being written in Chinese, a language that is typologically very different from their respective vernaculars, massive numbers of Classical Chinese canons and a great variety of other literary works in poetic and other genres were imported from China and studied avidly, resulting in a de facto virtual 'transnational literary community' (文人共和國, B. Zhang 2017: 295) across time (from Tang dynasty to the 1900s) and space (Sinographic East Asia, 漢字文化圈 or the Sinographic cosmopolis 漢字大都會, Koh & King 2014). What these literati of Sinitic had in common is that notwithstanding their deficient knowledge of spoken Chinese, they were profoundly influenced by Chinese language and culture after acquiring (sometimes erudite) knowledge of extant Classical Chinese canons and literary works. As a result of heavy reliance on Sinitic texts and successive borrowing of massive numbers of Sinitic vocabulary into Korean, Vietnamese, and Japanese in multiple layers depending on the historical periods, a deep substratum of Sinitic influence continues to be found in all of the modern East Asian languages (Japanese and Vietnamese: over 50 percent; Korean: over 60 percent, Handel 2019).

Assisted to different extents by bilinguals with literacy in Chinese and the local vernacular(s), the educated elites in modern-day Koreas, Japan and (northern) Vietnam would imitate the (partly imagined) pronunciation of individual graphic units called characters or sinograms while trying to express their local vernacular meanings. Given the relatively small number of bilingual speakers of Chinese (except in certain parts of Old Korea and northern Vietnam at the early stage of language contact) and the diversity of dialectal variation in Chinese, how did they learn to read Classical Chinese and, more challenging still, refashion Chinese characters and turn them into their own language by making them serve their own vernacular writing purposes, from producing official documents required for administration and governance to meeting the practical needs of daily chores like keeping miscellaneous records of business transactions and herbs with healing effects?

To answer this question, we need to understand the basic characteristics of the way Chinese is written, in particular how it relates to speech. The absolute majority of the world's written languages are phonographic. In a phonographic language, a finite set of basic units (graphs) carry one or more distinctive sound values of a spoken language. If the graphs encode both consonant and vowel sounds of a language, the writing system is said to be made up of an alphabet.[11] For instance, *USSR*, an English abbreviation made up of four letters, stands for the now defunct political entity, the '**U**nion of **S**oviet **S**ocialist **R**epublics' ('Soviet Union' in popular parlance). The Russian counterpart is also spelled with four letters, *CCCP* (**С**оюз **С**оветских **С**оциалистических **Р**еспублик), where <С> has the sound value of /s/ while <Р> is pronounced as /r/. Both English and Russian are thus phonographic languages: English is spelled with letters of the Roman alphabet, while Russian is written in the Cyrillic script.

By contrast, written Chinese is not phonographic but logographic or morphographic. Individual units are known as *hànzì* (漢字, 'Chinese characters' or 'sinograms'). A sinogram encapsulates pronunciation 音 and meaning 義 in addition to written form 形 – all in one, with sound and meaning tightly conjoined. For example, that which we call a flower in Chinese is pronounced as *huā* in Mandarin, *faa⁵⁵* in Cantonese – also pronounceable in many other Chinese topolects or 'dialects', and written as 花. There is no direct connection between its pronunciation and the way it is written. More experienced Chinese readers may be able to deduce that the embedded sinogram 化 (Mand: *huà*; Cant: *faa³³*; Min: *huà*), which is also shared in another sinogram like (simplified character) 华 (Mand: *huá*; Cant: *waa²¹*; Min: *huâ*), provides some clue to pronunciation, but the connection

---

11 In some Semitic languages like Arabic and Hebrew, words are traditionally spelled with only consonants and very few vowels are represented in writing. Their writing system, only partially alphabetical, is generally referred to as an abjad (Daniels & Bright 1996).

is opaque and apparent only after the reader has developed literacy of at least several hundred sinograms (Erbaugh 2002: 47):

> Understanding phonetics in characters is difficult. If you don't speak Chinese, the phonetics are invisible. . . . For students, phonetic cues are little help until one has already memorized hundreds of characters.

Further, when uttered in isolation by speakers of different Chinese topolects each insisting on using their own, there is no guarantee for intelligibility in their inter-dialectal communication.

Before avid readers in Sinographic East Asia beyond the Middle Kingdom were able to appreciate what the sinograms meant and how they contributed to the meanings of the sentence and text at hand, first they needed to read them out loud by imitating the pronunciation of a bilingual teacher of Chinese (if present) or based on what in their imagination was their normative pronunciation as a scholarly literatus would pronounce them. There is some indication that primers from China played a crucial role in the spread of Chinese and Sinitic-based literacy in Sinographic East Asia. Historically, there is ample evidence showing massive importation of Sinitic texts to these polities (Clements 2015; Lurie 2011), including primers used for teaching literacy in Sinitic to young learners. Given that native-speaking Chinese teachers might not be available, there was no reliable information regarding how reading pronunciation of sinograms was taught systematically. What we do know is that Sinitic texts were domesticated and learned through reading techniques known as glossing (Whitman 2014) as well as indigenized and partly imagined pronunciation introduced by local teachers. For instance, one such primer which became enormously popular in Japan was called 蒙求 (Mand: *Méngqiú*; Jap: *Mōgyū*), which was originally authored by a Tang dynasty official Li Han 李翰, and subsequently adapted by a Song scholar Hsü Tzu-kuang 徐子光 (Li & Hsü 1189/1979). The book title, which literally means 'the seeking of the unenlightened', was adapted from the fourth hexagram in the *Book of Changes* 易經. *Méngqiú* consisted of 'historical allusions culled from a wide variety of sources, cast in rhymed form and supplied with notes to explain the events to which they referred' (Burton Watson, translator of Li & Hsü 1189/1979: 7). Stylistically, it made use of over 600 quadri-syllabic phrases, each referring to a historical or legendary personage before the Tang dynasty (618–907). For example:

諸 葛 顧 廬
> (Mand: *zhūgé gù lú*, 'Zhuge visits cottage', Li & Hsü 1189/1979: 162)

This four-sinogram phrase alludes to a famous event during the Three Kingdom 三國 period (220–280): Just before dying, the King of the state of Shu (蜀國, in today's Sichuan) LIU Bei 劉備 (161–223) entrusted his son to the Prime Minister ZHUGE Liang 諸葛亮 (181–234), prompting the latter to write a widely acclaimed soul-searching plea and plan, 'Pre-battle memorandum to his majesty' 出師表 that subsequently immortalized him for posterity. The former two sinograms make reference to a name (here surname: 諸葛), while the latter captures an action or characteristic for which the person is renowned (here: 顧廬). By design, the primer was intended to facilitate easy memorization by young learners. According to the translator, Burton Watson, this primer was very popular in China until the Yuan dynasty (1271–1368), but its repute was 'on the wane' during the Ming and Qing dynasties (p. 10). By contrast, the primer became highly popular in Korea and Japan for centuries. Known as *Mōgyū* in Japan, it was used as a textbook for educating Prince Sadayasu 貞保親王 (870–924) and later used throughout the Heian period (794–1185) for members of the aristocracy to acquire basic Chinese literacy (p. 11). Of particular interest is one detail concerning collective reading-aloud practice as an integral part of the pronunciation teaching method. According to Watson, there was a proverb in Japanese making reference to sparrows' chirping of *Mōgyū* phrases:

> An oft-quoted proverb of the period declares that 'The sparrows of the *Kangaku-in* chirp the *Mōgyū*' [蒙求]. The *Kangaku-in* was a school in Kyoto set up for the education of sons of the powerful Fujiwara clan. The proverb has customarily been interpreted to mean that even the sparrows living in the vicinity of the school have learned the text of the *Mōgyū* by heart, so often have they heard it recited. It is possible, however, that the sparrows are the students themselves, whose piping recitations of the text in Chinese pronunciation would have been unintelligible to ordinary Japanese ears of the time as the language of the birds.
>
> (Watson, translator of Li & Hsü 1189/1979: 11)

There is thus some evidence of Sinitic literacy being learned by those who could afford it – an important detail concerning the background against which a Sinosphere of literate readers and writers of Sinitic gradually emerged. The Sinosphere may be characterized as a space that existed for well over a millennium from at least the Tang dynasty (618–907) until the early twentieth century, in which Sinitic-based writing was regularly consumed and produced, such that texts generated by literati in one polity are intelligible to their peers in others, despite the fact that the texts, pronounced in their respective local languages, would be mutually unintelligible when uttered in speech. One implication for cross-border communication is that to make sense of a Sinitic text, there is no need to ask the foreign writer, 'How do you pronounce this in your language?'. Such an intersubjective reading literacy phenomenon and experience may be illustrated with a relatively recent example.

In January 2020, in the wake of the global spread of the novel coronavirus and the pandemic (subsequently termed COVID-19) that it unleashed in Hubei Province, China, leading to the total lockdown of the provincial capital Wuhan, a Japanese office in charge of administering the 'Chinese Proficiency Test' (*Hanyu Shuiping Kaoshi*, HSK, 漢語水平考試)[12] donated dozens of cartons of medical

---

12 The donor of the medical supplies is attributed to '日本汉语水平考试 HSK 事务局支援湖北高校物资'. Although HSK is a standardized Chinese language examination designed for non-Chinese test takers, the donor was an official Japanese organization staffed entirely by Japanese employees (www.dcdapp.com/ugc/article/1657396077170695).

Figure 1.1 Example of morphographic sinograms pronounceable in different Sinitic languages.
Source: Pictures circulated widely and downloadable conveniently from the Internet

supplies including masks to the higher education institutions in Hubei Province (see Figure 1.1).

Except for 'HSK', the marking on the cartons is in Chinese or Sinitic. Of interest to us are eight sinograms printed in a smaller font at the bottom of the cartons and highlighted in Figure 1.1:

山川異域，風月同天[13]	
Japanese	*Sansen iiki, fūgetsu dōten*
Mandarin/Putonghua	*Shānchuān yìyù, fēngyuè tóng tiān*
Cantonese[14]	*Saan³⁵ cyun⁵⁵ ji²² wik²², fung⁵⁵ jyut²² tung²¹ tin⁵⁵*
Minnanhua[15]	*San tshuan ī ik, hong ú tông thian*
	Literally 'Mountains and rivers differ, wind and moon under the same sky', which may be glossed as 'Lands apart, sky shared'. Or, more idiomatically and poetically, 'Though we are oceans apart, a shared moon connects hearts'.

13 The modern Chinese sinograms printed on the cartons are written in simplified script 简化字, including the eight sinograms enlarged in a rectangular box for attracting attention (Figure 1.1). Those eight sinograms at the bottom, however, are written in traditional script 繁體字 (compare simplified script: 山川异域，风月同天).
14 For details of the romanization system, see www.lshk.org/jyutping, retrieved April 16, 2021.
15 For details of the romanization system, see 「臺灣閩南語羅馬字拼音方案」(簡稱臺羅), https://twblg.dict.edu.tw/holodict_new/compile1_3_9_3.jsp, retrieved April 16, 2021.

30   David C. S. Li et al.

Without solid literacy training in traditional Sinitic literature, Japanese readers today may only appreciate the meaning of these two Sinitic idioms through translation using mixed-script kanji 漢字 and hiragana 平仮名 such as the following[16]:

別の場所に暮らしていても、自然の風物はつながっている。

These two quadrisyllabic idioms 四字詞 may be traced back to a Buddhist poem during the Tang dynasty (618–907). In 742, Prince Nagaya 長屋王 wanted to entice a famous Buddhist monk 鑒真 (Mand: Jianzhen; Jap: Ganjin) to visit Japan. The two idioms were knitted on a patchwork-style robe ('kasaya', 袈裟, Mand: *jiāshā*, borrowed from Sanskrit: काषाय, *kāṣāya*) presented to him as a gift. Jianzhen was reportedly deeply moved and decided to lead a Buddhist delegation of about two dozen followers on a perilous journey across the sea to Japan. Of interest here is that despite its historical origin dating back to the eighth century, these eight sinograms are still comprehensible and pronounceable in Japanese and Chinese (Mandarin, Cantonese, Shanghainese, Minnanhua, among many other Chinese topolects). What is remarkable is that, in speech, a speaker of Japanese would have been unable to get across the meaning of this well-intentioned Buddhist wisdom (*Sansen iiki, fūgetsu dōten*), which over a millennium later was invoked – in writing – by a Japanese organization as a comforting spirit-lifter for the Chinese who were battling an invisible coronavirus and the deadly pandemic disease COVID-19 that it unleashed.

Thanks to this shared lingua-cultural heritage, for over a millennium until the early twentieth century, knowledge of Classical Chinese or Literary Sinitic allowed its literati to make meaning interactively, albeit not in speech but in writing – a modality of communication that apparently was unique to Sinographic East Asia 漢字文化圈 or the Sinographic cosmopolis 漢字大都會 (Koh & King 2014; cf. Li et al. 2020; Wong 2019).

Overcoming typological differences: phonetic, semantic, and syntactic adaptations in the indigenization process

For centuries, there is one linguistic complication that made the reading and comprehension of Classical Chinese texts an arduous task for East Asian readers: differences in language typology. Chinese, like Vietnamese, is typologically an isolating language with scanty morphology and normative subject-verb-object (SVO) word order. Morphologically, there is no indication of tense and aspect (past, present, perfect, continuous, etc.) as in the verbs of English and other

---

16 While the kanji-kana mixed-script writing has been used for a long time, the exclusive use of kanji as a mode of written communication was more common up until the end of the Meiji Restoration (1868–1912) period; see, for example, the Sinitic-based novels written by Mori Ōgai 森鷗外 (1862–1922). Owing to the post-Meiji vernacularization movement 言文一致運動 requiring close alignment between speech and writing (Lin 2019), the teaching and exclusive use of kanji in society gradually declined and gave way to mixed-script writing in Japan.

European languages like French and German, but also Japanese and Korean; nor are syntactic relationships such as 'subject case' and '(in)direct object case' marked in their nouns and pronouns using grammatical particles or suffixes, which are rich in the aforementioned inflectional and agglutinating languages. Unlike the isolating languages Chinese and Vietnamese, Japanese and Korean are agglutinating languages characterized by morphological features in their verbs and nouns, and they follow the normative SOV (subject-object-verb) word order.

Owing to marked typological differences in word order and morphological types, while reading or consuming texts in Classical Chinese, Japanese and Korean readers would have to make syntactic adjustment (glossing) in what is virtually a decoding cum translation process (Clements 2015). Once the students of Classical Chinese have developed a sense of how the sinograms are structured and 'hang together' syntactically speaking, they would need to provide conventional marks as hints for instructing – as a kind of mnemonic to oneself or the reader – how the sinograms should be re-structured syntactically in order to produce a corresponding sentence in the local vernacular with more or less equivalent meaning. Such a laborious process is known as glossing (Whitman 2011), which makes the reading or consumption of Classical Chinese texts as much a comprehension exercise as a translation task. Over time, through institutional encouragement and support from the court and the hard work of designated members of the officialdom, scholar-officials and erudite literati of Sinitic were able to crack the code and to make sense of the Classical Chinese texts by progressively evolving and refining a set of conventionalized glossing techniques, which for centuries were used in premodern Korea and Japan for composing Sinitic texts in their own languages respectively. Sinogram-based Literary Sinitic in these East Asian languages served a variety of formal functions, from national governance and regional administration to the writing of history and poetry uninterruptedly until the late nineteenth century. What is interesting is that despite being authored by non-Chinese literati intended primarily for local readers, such Sinitic texts created beyond China proper were by and large comprehensible to literati elsewhere within Sinographic East Asia, thanks to the fact that reading – silently or aloud – does not require any knowledge of how the sinograms are pronounced in the writer's own native language or vernacular.

Is Sinitic brush-talk 漢文筆談 sui generis *and unique to Sinographic East Asia?*

Beyond the Sinographic cosmopolis where Literary Sinitic prevailed traditionally, writing-based face-to-face communication in other phonographic languages seems rare. According to two scholars we consulted (Jens Høyrup, a historian of science on medieval and Renaissance learning, and Hartmut Haberland, Emeritus Professor, Roskilde University, Denmark, personal communication, July 2018), interactive meaning-making through writing as an alternative to speech by literate readers of Latin – for centuries the regional lingua franca in medieval Europe – was 'unheard of'. Likewise, Qur'ān-based Standard Arabic, written with a consonant-only abjad script, is phonetically and morphosyntactically obscure to L2 speakers, who 'needed much more guidance as to how the words should be pronounced'; and 'even native speakers of Arabic might have dialectal disagreements as to the correct pronunciation of words' (Gnanadesikan 2009: 163; cf. Collin 2011: 18; Rogers 2005: 133).

In an attempt to confirm the Latinist experts' view, we consulted a few scholarly works on Latin, including a highly informative biography of Erasmus (c. 1469–1536) (Halkin 1987), the Renaissance humanist of Dutch origin who spent his whole life promoting the learning, teaching, and use of Classical Latin, including multiple volumes exalting and illustrating the exemplary epistolary styles in Latin using selected personal letters that he received from others. In this 360-page coverage of Erasmus's life from infancy to his death, there is only one mention of writing-mediated synchronous interaction between him and his teenage friend, Fausto Andrelini. That happened most likely in the middle of a dull lecture, as they 'exchanged short notes under the noses of their teachers' in Latin as follows (Halkin 1987: 27)[17]:

Fausto to Erasmus:	FRVGALEM omnino mihi coenam postulo; nihil volo praeter muscas et formicas. Bene vale.	'I want my dinner to be quite a simple one. I ask for nothing but flies and ants. Farewell.'
Erasmus to Fausto:	QVAE, malum, tu mihi obiicis aenigmata? Num me Oedipum putas, aut Sphingem mihi esse domi? Quanquam equidem somnio tuas muscas auiculas, formicas cuniculos velle. Verum alias iocabimur, nunc coena emenda est; quare aenigmatista esse desinas oportet. Vale.	'Confound it, what are these riddles you sent me? Do you think I am an Oedipus, or the owner of a Sphinx? Still, I imagine that your 'flies' are fowls, your 'ants' rabbits. But shall we put off joking to another time? We have to buy our supper now; so you should stop talking in riddles. Farewell.'
Fausto to Erasmus:	NVNC plane intelligo te Oedipum esse. Nihil volo praeter auiculas, et quidem paruulas; de cuniculis absit. Vale, optime aenigmatum interpres.	'I can see clearly now that you are an Oedipus. I want nothing but fowls – small ones will do. Not a word about rabbits, please! Farewell, you first-rate solver of puzzles.'
Erasmus to Fausto:	VT tu, iocosissime Fauste, eadem opera et mihi ruborem et theologo illi stomachum excitabas; aderat enim in eodem auditorio. Verum non expedit, opinor, irritare crabrones. Bene vale.	'My most witty Fausto, how at one and the same time you have made me blush and that theologian rage! For he was in the same lecture hall as ourselves. But I do not believe that it serves any purpose to stir up a nest of hornets. Farewell.'

17 Original Latin and English translation based on two works: (i) *The Collected Works of Erasmus* (1974), pp. 99–100, vol. 1, University of Toronto Press; and (ii) P. S. Allen, (Ed.) (1906). *Opus Epistolarum Desiderius Erasmi Roterodami*, Ep. 96–100, vol. 1 (1484–1514), pp. 235–236 (ca. year 1499). See also 'Works by Desiderius Erasmus Roterodamus', Oxford Scholarly Editions Online (www.oxfordscholarlyeditions.com/view/10.1093/oseo/person.00005652).

Fausto to Erasmus:	FAVSTVM pro suo Erasmo vel emori audacter posse quis nescit? Blaterones istos tanti omnino faciamus quanti culicem elephantus Indicus. Vale. Faustus inuito liuore tuus.	'Everyone knows that Fausto is capable of dying boldly for his friend Erasmus. As for those prattlers, let us take no more notice of them than an Indian elephant does of a gnat. Farewell. Yours, whatever envious tongues may say.'

Notice that the writing mode was chosen because both Erasmus and Fausto considered it socially inappropriate to talk in the middle of a lecture. In other words, exchanging short notes in writing, synchronously in face-to-face interaction, was a negative choice, given that situationally talking in class in front of the teacher would be seen as a grave offence.

Unlike Classical Chinese or Literary Sinitic, which is written with a logographic script, Latin is written with an alphabetic script. Much like knowledge of the de facto global lingua franca English today, back in the fifteenth and sixteenth centuries, knowledge of Latin was a *sine qua non* when considering recruiting non-Danish-speaking teaching staff at higher education institutions like Copenhagen University, where Latin was functioning as an academic lingua franca (Haberland & Mortensen 2012: 3). The exact sound values of specific Roman letter combinations may vary from place to place, resulting in variation in pronunciation leading to more or less discrete and mutually intelligible accents. Allen (1978: 107) provides an instructive example adapted from Erasmus's *Dialogue* in the sixteenth century, where speeches addressed to Emperor Maximilian in Latin by speakers from different European countries were spoken with rather different regional accents:

> A Frenchman read his speech 'adeo Gallice' that some present thought he was speaking in French; such was the laughter that the Frenchman broke off his speech in embarrassment, but even greater ridicule greeted the German accent of the next speaker; a Dane who followed 'sounded like a Scotsman', and next came a Zeelander – but, as Erasmus remarks, 'dejerasses neutrum loqui Latine'. Ursus here asks Leo, who tells the story, whether the emperor himself was able to refrain from laughter; and Leo assures that he was, since 'assueverat huiusmodi fabulis'.
>
> (Allen 1978:107; Latin-English translation courtesy of Hartmut Haberland and John Whelpton)[18]

Laughter, it would seem, suggests that despite accented pronunciations that sounded so amusing to all present, they could by and large make sense of one

---

18 *adeo Gallice*: 'so Frenchly, i.e., in such a French way'; *dejerasses neutrum loqui Latine*: 'you would have (solemnly) sworn that neither of them was speaking in Latin'; *assueverat huiusmodi fabulis*: 'he had got used to this kind of (ridiculous) events'.

another's spoken Latin, and that intelligibility appeared not to be a major issue in their speech-based communication. According to Jens Høyrup (personal communication 16/07/2018, courtesy Hartmut Haberland), there was neither compelling need nor basis for writing-mediated interaction like Sinitic brush-talk for Latin in Europe across the three phases of its historical development: the Middle Ages, Renaissance and Reformation, and Enlightenment and the Modern Era. Summarizing Høyrup's input, Haberland further affirmed that 'the idea of using written Latin to bridge oral understanding problems would not have occurred to European scholars. And it is not mentioned anywhere in the literature, not even anecdotally' (personal communication 16/07/2018). For interlocutors with a comparable level of competence in Classical Latin, could it be that their shared knowledge of the alphabetically based academic lingua franca made it unnecessary for them to turn to writing as an alternative to speech, unlike morphographic, non-phonographic Sinitic in Sinographic East Asia? In the absence of empirical data that would help us ascertain the validity of this claim, this is at best an intelligent guess, pending fine-grained research in future.

Despite the aphorism, 'the absence of evidence is no evidence of its absence', prima facie (lack of parallel) evidence seems to suggest that the scripta franca function of Literary Sinitic might be *sui generis* or script-specific (Li et al. 2020), hence the 'morphographic hypothesis', which predicts that under normal circumstances (excluding situations where speech is banned or not a feasible option situationally or biologically), a morphographic script is a necessary condition for writing-based communication to take place interactively face-to-face (Li 2020: 228). Such a null hypothesis is falsifiable, however, pending evidence of writing-mediated face-to-face interaction in other classical languages. It is our wish that by 'tossing bricks in the hope of getting jade in return' 拋磚引玉, we would be able to attract scholarly interest in the question, whether writing-mediated interaction, synchronously and face-to-face, was similarly enacted by a scripta franca in some other civilization, ancient or modern.

Synopsis of the book

In Chapter 2, WANG Yong introduces the Sinitic brush-talk literature by providing an annotated overview of the better-known surviving brush-talk records in different parts of Sinographic East Asia. As a historically salient lingua-cultural phenomenon, Sinitic brush-talk is known to take place between acquaintances but also strangers in cross-border communication contexts, covering topics from intellectually perplexing and aesthetically poetic to playfully frivolous and prosaically mundane. Wang begins with the question: how should the vast array of brush-talk literature be categorized? After discussing several options, he considers it more convincing and productive to categorize brush-talk data according to the identities of the typical agents engaged in context-specific brush conversation. To give the reader an overview of the variety of Sinitic brush-talk records collected from different geographical locations but also the polities where the brush-talkers originated as well as the primary purpose of their writing-mediated brush conversation, we find it useful to follow Wang's classification. Accordingly, the chapters in this book will be divided into three parts. **Part 1** consists of four chapters (3–6), featuring brush-talk involving traveling literati and boat drifters who are typically strangers caught in chance encounters. **Part 2**, covering five chapters (7–11), focuses on brush-talk involving diplomatic envoys visiting a foreign country on a state-level mission. As such, their brushed encounters are usually pre-arranged, which either form part of the official scheduled activities or are initiated by enthusiastic literati in their private capacities to deliberate on some topic(s) of shared interest. The book will end with two chapters (12–13) in **Part 3**, where the cross-cultural import of Sinitic brush-talk as a social practice in Sinographic East Asia and implications for further research in historical pragmatics, cultural anthropology, and East Asian studies will be discussed.

In Chapter 3, by analyzing the records of shipwreck incidents in the eighteenth and nineteenth centuries, Matsuura and Aoyama investigate how and to what extent East Asian nationals with no shared spoken language relied on brush-talking in impromptu transcultural encounters. Although interpreting service was available at the national level in the political center of the state capital (e.g., Seoul) or the seaport with sizable trading volumes and capacities (e.g., Nagasaki), transcultural communication was made possible by the use of writing-mediated brush conversation at the site where the vessels were stranded. For security and humanitarian reasons, officials of the local authorities were duty-bound to interrogate the surviving foreign 'boat drifters'. Extant drifting brush-talk records show that the maritime officials usually wanted specific answers to a fairly long list of wh-questions pertaining to who, what, why, and how, among other reasons to quickly determine whether there were any security or health-risk issues at stake. Content analysis of such records shows that the literacy level of the foreign seafarer(s) affects the quality and depth of interactional communication.

In Chapter 4, Li and Aoyama explore the sociocultural significance of brush-talking as a modality of cross-border communication that facilitated historical Chinese-Japanese encounters. After an over 200-year suspension of the official contact between China and Japan resulting from Japan's self-imposed isolationist policy, Japanese samurais and merchants on board the Senzaimaru 千歳丸 set sail for a two-month visit to Shanghai in 1862. Rich anecdotes and verbatim records of brush-talking in their travelogues exemplify patterned writing-mediated face-to-face communication between Chinese and Japanese people, despite the absence of a shared spoken language. In addition to the sharing and exchange of information, Sinitic was also used to improvise aesthetically pleasing poetic verses, express deep personal feelings, and cement friendship that might be genuine and intimate but destined to be short-lived. The intersubjective nature of Sinitic brush-talk will be elucidated and illustrated with the help of instructive examples.

In Chapter 5, Hur Kyoung-Jin analyzes the boat drifting records produced by two prominent Korean boat drifters: Ch'oe Pu 崔溥 (1454–1504) drifting to Zhejiang Province of Ming China in 1488, and Yi Chi-hang 李志恒 (1647–?) to Hokkaido, Japan in 1696–1697. In both drifting incidents, without a shared spoken language, Sinitic brush-talk played a crucial role for the respective maritime officials to find out the answers to a list of questions concerning the identities of the alien 'boat drifters', their place of origin, original destination, circumstances leading to their boats drifting ashore, and the like. For Ch'oe Pu and his men, who were suspected of being Japanese pirates in disguise, the investigation took the form of cross-examination, again through brush-talk, by different investigators that lasted for over a month. Once the boat drifters' Korean identities were ascertained, however, their shared knowledge of Sinitic was put to meaningful use by shifting to rapport-building via intellectual and/or poetic exchange. In particular, through brush-talk, Ch'oe Pu was able to confirm the position and identity of Chosŏn within the Sinosphere and obtained various information on politics, society, and culture of Ming China, especially the region south of the Yangtze River. His precious first-hand experiences and eye-witness accounts, described in elaborate detail in his formal report to the king of Chosŏn and subsequently wider dissemination through wood block printing, were shared with his countrymen for many generations. Regarding different types of writing-mediated accounts, Hur distinguishes between one-sided stories typical of travel diaries, two-sided co-constructed brush conversation and, intermediate between these two genres, the testimonies produced by boat drifters whose vessels were swept ashore in alien land due to stormy weather. In all of these accounts, authentication of content accuracy would be difficult, as the inputs by the other brush-talkers tend to be unavailable. Ch'oe Pu's and Yi Chi-hang's reports suggest that for brush-talk to be smooth and effective, a certain level of literacy in Sinitic was a must.

In Chapter 6, WONG Tak-sum studies the salient linguistic features of two surviving brush-talk records – one Ryukyuan-Korean (1611), the other Ryukyuan-Japanese (1803). He shows that lexico-grammatical markers of Old Chinese (first millennium, BCE), Middle Chinese (ca. 1–750 CE), and Early Mandarin (ca. 750–1800 CE) are all attested, suggesting that the brush-talkers engaged in cross-border communication had a reasonably good grasp of Classical Chinese or Literary Sinitic, but were also rather familiar with Chinese vernacular literature. Elements proper to Classical and vernacular Chinese were well within their linguistic resources as evidenced in their writing-mediated brush-talk interaction. For instance, for self-address and other-referencing, canonical personal pronouns characteristic of speech were used infrequently. Rather, out of concern to mark politeness, a variety of honorific terms like 貴國 'your esteemed country' and 本國 'my own country' were used instead.

In Chapter 7, NGUYỄN Tuấn Cường and NGUYỄN Thị Tuyết analyze the brush conversations as documented in 'A complete record of an embassy to the North' 北使通錄 by the Vietnamese envoy Lê Quý Đôn 黎貴惇 (1726–1784) during his two-year mission to Peking (1760–1762). The document was compiled essentially based on his travel diary, but elaborate details dating from his appointment as Vice-Envoy in 1758 were also included. It consisted of four volumes, but only volumes 1 and 4 have survived. The analysis shows that writing-mediated brush conversation, with or without the presence of an interpreter, lent itself very well to Vietnamese-Chinese cross-border communication, from simple exchange of practical information to deference-loaded expressions of compliments, but also deep conversation on a variety of intellectually demanding topics. There is also evidence of brush-talk being used for the purpose of socializing chanting 筆談唱和.

In Chapter 8, based on brush-talk data involving cross-border, transcultural communication between Chinese, Japanese, and Koreans during the early Meiji period as documented in the 'Ōkōchi Documents' 大河內文書, WANG Baoping outlines and illustrates the key interactional characteristics of this mode of writing-mediated communication which, as a semiotic meaning-making system that clearly draws its linguistic resources from Classical Chinese or Literary Sinitic, is comparable to speech-based verbal communication in many ways. He distinguishes between three types of motivation for engaging in brush conversation: involuntary brush-talk 被動筆談, cultural brush-talk 文化筆談, and espionage brush-talk 情報筆談. Wang highlights the heuristic value of such special historiographic data sources, which have attracted a lot of attention and interest among scholars working on humanities-related research areas in different parts of East Asia since the new millennium.

In Chapter 9, drawing on brush conversation records between the staff of the first Qing Chinese embassy to Japan and their Japanese hosts and acquaintances during the 1870s and 1880s, LIU Yuzhen shows how the semiotic potential and pragma-linguistic affordance of brush conversation in meaning-making allowed literati well versed in Sinitic to tap into the charm of poetic improvisation and socializing chanting 漢詩酬唱 and other aesthetically pleasing literary expressions. In addition, brush-talk being a common lingua-cultural practice between literati of Sinitic from diverse ethnolinguistic backgrounds to deepen their intellectual and emotional bond, Liu illustrates how it was exploited by brush-talkers with ulterior motives to elicit state secrets. Such a pitfall of espionage was clearly evidenced by the conscious efforts of Miyajima Seiichirō 宮島誠一郎 to collect politically sensitive intelligence when he was engaged in casual brush conversation with Chinese embassy staff by posing as a personal acquaintance and collecting brush-talk artifacts with diplomatic value for the Meiji government.

In Chapter 10, KOO Jea-hyoun and Ian JOO examine the brush-talk interactions between Korean envoys to Japan during the Edo period (1603–1868) and identify systematic differences between both sides' contrastive motivations, objectives, and expectations for entering into brush conversation. Being trained to attain scholar-official positions in the bureaucratic hierarchy within the Chosŏn government, the Korean envoys were keen on maintaining good diplomatic relations with their Japanese hosts while collecting politically useful intelligence from them. On the other hand, the Japanese literati were more interested in upgrading and updating their knowledge base of various academic, cultural, and technical issues with the help of the Korean visitors' sharing through brush conversation. The authors attribute such diverged expectations to the role of the study of Sinitic literature in Japanese and Korean societies: whereas a firm grasp through deep study of Confucian classics was a stepping stone to a career in the state bureaucracy through success in the civil service examination in Korea, in Japan the absence of such a career ladder via a comparable examination system helps explain why the Japanese Confucianists were interested in more practical and cultural aspects of everyday life.

In Chapter 11, based on in-depth analysis of extensive brush-talk interactions between Chosŏn envoys and Japanese literati of Sinitic during successive *t'ongsinsa* 通信使 missions to Japan from 1607 to 1811, JANG Jin-youp provides ample evidence of Japanese-Korean dueling and contestation for cultural superiority enacted through writing-mediated brush-talk. At stake was the question, whether Chosŏn's self-complacent cultural superiority vis-à-vis Japan could live up to the stature and attribute of 'central efflorescence' 中華 after the Ming dynasty gave way to 'barbarian' rule in Qing China. As speech-based communication was not an option, brush-talking in Sinitic became the site of assertion, critique, defense, and counterattack. Whereas Japanese Confucianists criticized the quality of Chosŏn envoys' poetic improvisation and took pride in adhering to ancient Chinese culture as shown in their clothing style and musical compositions reminiscent of the finest Qin-Han period, the Korean envoys countered that they had never stopped learning and infusing the good teachings of Confucius into everyday life, as shown in the implementation of Confucian rites and rituals and collective respect for Confucian values and cultural practices in Korean society. One consequence of such writing-mediated contestation and dueling was Japanese literati's significantly enhanced self-confidence of membership in the Confucianist Sinocentric World Order, and Korean literati's gradual recognition and acceptance of Japan's position in it.

In Chapter 12, focusing on cross-border interactions of historical figures from China, Vietnam, and Japan in the mid-nineteenth and early twentieth century, Reijiro AOYAMA explores the manners in which actors involved in such encounters assigned sociocultural values to Chinese characters, or sinograms, that transcended their linguistic functions, and how they made the most of Sinitic writing as a resource for establishing rapport with foreigners in transcultural communication settings. Thanks to their rich potential to convey both linguistic and cultural meanings, sinograms and Sinitic writing allowed strangers with no shared spoken language to forge meaningful relationships centered on interactive, face-to-face inscriptions in Chinese characters, thus furthering their embeddedness in the literary and cultural tradition of Sinographic East Asia.

In the last chapter (Chapter 13), the discussion paper, Rebekah Clements delineates the historical practice of brush-talk by examining abundant and complex brush-talk events as shown in the preceding chapters. She points out that despite the availability of interpreters, the persistence of brush-talk epitomizes the diplomats' preference for using written Sinitic in face-to-face encounters in place of any of the speech-based East Asian languages at the disposal of the brush-talkers. Drawing attention to the recurrent function of brush-talk in private, non-official encounters, Clements considers such linguistic records as compelling cultural artefacts that are instrumental for analyzing the interpersonal relations of not only official representatives of East Asian states, but also other 'interested observers' such as literati, medics, and even passers-by who eagerly sought opportunities to engage foreign literati of Sinitic in 'silent conversation'.

Coda

With this book, we hope to make a convincing case that writing down what one wants to say, interactively face-to-face, has been historically an effective substitute for speech in cross-border communication contexts within Sinographic East Asia. There is ample evidence showing how literati of Sinitic were able to conduct silent conversation not only to solicit and convey information, articulate their thoughts and exchange ideas but also to build rapport through sinogram-based, aesthetically pleasing poetic improvisation and sharing. To this day, there are signs that such a time-honored tradition of using writing to overcome oral communication barriers continues to be relevant and observable between literati of morphographic sinograms (i.e., 漢字), including in Chinese–Chinese social interaction. The only difference is that brush and ink have yielded to more convenient and handy writing instruments, hence brush-talk has given way to pen-talk. We would like to end this chapter with an instructive quotation from WANG Guohua 王國華 (2015), who recalls brush-talking with the late centenarian Sinologist, JAO Tsung-I 饒宗頤 (1917–2018) in their periodical intellectual exchange (also cited in Wong & Li 2020: 78):

> 我與饒公交流的最大障礙是語言。我是山東口音，饒公是潮州口音。年齡上又是兩代人，百歲饒公是國學大師，語言與學問上的落差，使我們交流時經常借助於筆談。一次交流談話，一般要寫滿一個本子。這也留下了許多珍貴資料。

> In my academic exchange with Master Jao, language was the greatest barrier. My spoken Chinese carries a Shandong accent, while Master Jao was a speaker of Chaozhou (Teochew) dialect. Age-wise we belong to different generations. Master Jao was a centenarian guru in Sinology. The gaps in our language and scholarship made it necessary for us to resort to pen-talk to facilitate academic exchange. Every time we were engaged in pen-talk, in general an entire notebook would be filled with scribbles. Plenty of valuable materials were left behind for this reason.
>
> (G. Wang 2015: 50, our translation)

Sinitic brush-talk, a vibrant substitute for oral communication for ages until the late nineteenth century and possibly a *sui generis* modality of lingua-cultural communication in Sinographic East Asia, remains little understood. The history of brush conversation has yet to be written (Kornicki 2018: 101–102). We hope this book will provide the impetus needed to stimulate more collaborative research in this direction.

References

Allen, W. S. (1978). *Vox Latina: A guide to the pronunciation of classical Latin* (2nd ed.). Cambridge: Cambridge University Press.

Aoyama, R. (2020). Writing-mediated interaction face-to-face: Sinitic brushtalk in the Japanese missions' transnational encounters with foreigners during the mid-nineteenth Century. *China and Asia* 2(2): 234–269.

Brown, G., & Yule, G. (1983). *Discourse analysis*. Cambridge: Cambridge University Press.

Cen, L. [岑玲] (2014). Language contact with crew of Ryukyu's drifting ships in the Qing dynasty 清朝中國に漂著した琉球船乘員の言語接觸. *Journal of East Asian Cultural Interaction Studies* 東アジア文化交渉研究 7: 449–461.

Chun, H.-J. (1968). Sino-Korean tributary relations in the Qing period. In J. K. Fairbank (Ed.), *The Chinese world order: Traditional China's foreign relations* (pp. 90–111). Cambridge, MA: Harvard University Press.

Clements, R. (2015). *A cultural history of translation in early modern Japan*. Cambridge: Cambridge University Press.

Clements, R. (2019). Brush talk as the 'lingua franca' of East Asian diplomacy in Japanese-Korean encounters (17th-19th centuries). *The Historical Journal* 62(2): 289–309.

Collin, R. (2011). Revolutionary scripts: The politics of writing systems. In M. A. Morris (Ed.), *Culture and language: Multidisciplinary case studies* (pp. 29–68). Frankfurt: Peter Lang.

Daniels, P. T., & Bright, W. (1996). *The world's writing systems*. New York: Oxford University Press.

Denecke, W. (2014). Worlds without translation: Premodern East Asia and the power of character scripts. In S. Bermann & C. Porter (Eds.), *A companion to translation studies* (pp. 204–216). Chichester: Wiley-Blackwell.

Erbaugh, M. (2002). How the ideographic myth alienates Asian studies from psychology and linguistics. In M. Erbaugh (Ed.), *Difficult characters. Interdisciplinary studies of Chinese and Japanese* (pp. 21–51). Columbus, Ohio: The Ohio State University, National East Asian Language Resource Centre.

Fairbank, J. K. (Ed.). (1968). *The Chinese world order: Traditional China's foreign relations*. Cambridge: Harvard University Press.

Fairbank, J. K., & Teng, S.-Y. (1941). On the Ch'ing tributary system. *Harvard Journal of Asiatic Studies* VI(2): 135–246.

Fan, S.-K. (1992). *Language management in contact situations between Japanese and Chinese*. Unpublished PhD dissertation, Monash University, Australia.

Fuma, S. [夫馬進] (2015). 朝鮮燕行使と朝鮮通信使 ('Chosŏn envoys to Peking and Chosŏn envoys to Japan'). Nagoya: The University of Nagoya Press.

Fuma, S. [夫馬進] (2016). 乾淨筆譚──朝鮮燕行使の北京筆談錄 ('*Kanchŏng p'iltam*: The brush-talk record of Chosŏn envoys travelling to Peking'). Tokyo: Heibonsha.

Ge, S. (2000). How does Asia mean? (Part II). *Inter-Asia Cultural Studies* 1(2): 319–341.

Ge, Z. [葛兆光] (2005). 大明衣冠今何在 ('Where are the hats and clothes of Ming dynasty nowadays?'). *Journal of Historical Science* 史學月刊 10: 41–48.

Ge, Z. [葛兆光] (2015). 導言: 朝鮮赴日通信使文獻的意義 ('Significance of documents written by Chosŏn envoys to Japan: Introduction'). In 復旦大學文史研究院, 朝鮮通信使文獻選編 第一冊 ('An anthology of Chosŏn *t'ongsinsa* literature') (vol. 1, pp. 3–46). Shanghai: Fudan University Press.

Ge, Z. [葛兆光] (2018). *What is China? Territory, ethnicity, culture, and history* (M. G. Hill, Trans.). Harvard: Harvard University Press.

Gnanadesikan, A. E. (2009). *The writing revolution: Cuneiform to the internet*. Hoboken, NJ: Wiley-Blackwell.

Habein, Y. S. (1984). *The history of the Japanese written language*. Tokyo: University of Tokyo Press.

Haberland, H., & Mortensen, J. (2012). Language variety, language hierarchy, and language choice in the international university. *International Journal of the Sociology of Language* 216: 1–6.

Halkin, L. (1987). *Erasmus: A critical biography* (J. Tonkin, Trans.). Oxford: Blackwell.
Hamashita, T. (2008). *China, East Asia and the global economy: Regional and historical perspectives*. London & New York: Routledge.
Handel, Z. (2019). *Sinography: The borrowing and adaptation of the Chinese script*. Leiden: Brill.
He, D., Shao, Q., Li, P., Tag, Q., & Zhao, B. [何大章、邵群、李朋、唐詮、趙波] (Eds.). (2010). 宮崎滔天家藏—來自日本的中國革命文獻 ('Miyazaki Tōten's family collection: Documents on Chinese October Revolution from Japan'). Peking: People's Fine Arts Publishing House.
Howland, D. R. (1996). *Borders of Chinese civilization: Geography and history at empire's end*. Durham & London: Duke University Press.
Hwang, M. (2009). *Brush talk at the conversation table: Interaction between L1 and L2 speakers of Chinese*. Unpublished PhD dissertation, University of Hawai'i at Manoa.
Igarashi, Y. (2007). *The changing role of katakana in the Japanese writing system*. Unpublished PhD dissertation, University of Victoria, Canada.
Jeon, J.-H. (2019). Language education policies in South Korea. In A. Kirkpatrick & A. J. Liddicoat (Eds.), *The Routledge international handbook of language education policy in Asia* (pp. 111–123). Abingdon, Oxon & New York: Routledge.
Jin, X. [金秀慧] (2018). 《朝鮮漂流日記》研究 ('Studies in Chosŏn boat drifters' diaries'). Unpublished MA thesis, Zhejiang Gongshang University.
Keaveney, C. T. (2009). *Beyond brushtalk: Sino-Japanese literary exchange in the interwar period*. Hong Kong: Hong Kong University Press.
Kelley, L. C. (2005). *Beyond the bronze pillars: Envoy poetry and the Sino-Vietnamese relationship*. Honolulu: Association for Asian Studies and University of Hawai'i Press.
Kerr, G. (1958/2000). *Okinawa: The history of an island people*. North Clarendon, VT: Tuttle Publishing.
Kim, C.-W. (1978). Linguistics and language policies in North Korea. *Korean Studies* 2: 159–175.
Kim, Y.-U. [김영욱, 金榮旭] (2008). '漢字盲' 방치해서는 안된다 ('Illiteracy in *hanja* [Chinese characters] should not be neglected'). Retrieved October 6, 2020, from http://m.blog.daum.net/thddudgh7/16510273.
Koh, J., & King, R. (2014). *Infected Korean language: Purity versus hybridity*. Amherst, New York: Cambria Press.
Kornicki, P. F. (2018). *Languages, scripts, and Chinese texts in East Asia*. Oxford: Oxford University Press.
Kunikida, D [國木田獨步]. (1966). *Kunikida Doppo zenshū* ('Compilation of writings by Kunikida Doppo') (vol. 5, pp. 31–33). Tokyo: Gakushū Kenkyūsha.
Lan, J.-C. [藍日昌]. (2020). 筆談: 同文異音下的東亞文化交流 (Pen talk: East Asian cultural exchange under the same words). 中正漢學研究 (Chung Cheng Chinese Studies) 35(1): 189–208.
Ledyard, G. (1982). Hong Taeyong and his 'Peking Memoir'. *Korean Studies* 6: 63–103.
Lee, J.-S. (2018). *State ideology and language policy in North Korea: An analysis of North Korea's public discourse*. Unpublished PhD thesis, East Asian Language & Literature, University of Hawai'i at Manoa.
Li, D. C. S. (2020). Writing-mediated interaction face-to-face: Sinitic brushtalk (漢文筆談) as an age-old lingua-cultural practice in premodern East Asian cross-border communication. *China and Asia* 2(2): 193–233.
Li, D. C. S., Aoyama, R., & Wong, T.-S. (2020). Silent conversation through brushtalk (筆談): The use of Sinitic as a scripta franca in early modern East Asia. *Global Chinese* 6(1): 1–23.

Li, H., & Hsü, T. [李翰、徐子光] (1189/1979). *Meng Ch'iu* (蒙求)*: Famous episodes from Chinese history and legend* (B. Watson, Trans.). Toyko, New York & San Francisco: Kodansha International Ltd.

Li, M. [李敏] (2017). 18世紀日朝筆談的醫學史料研究 ('A study of the source materials in Japanese- Korean brush-talk on medicine during the 18th century'). Unpublished PhD dissertation, Beijing University of Chinese Medicine.

Liang, J. [梁佳麗] (2015). 寶曆三年八丈島漂著南京船研究 ('A study of the Nanking ship drifting to Hachijou Island in 1753'). Unpublished MA thesis, Zhejiang Gongshang University.

Lin, S. [林少陽] (2019). 章炳麟とその周辺の「文學」概念: 漢字圏の言文一致運動と清末という二つの文脈 ('The concept of literature in the works of Zhang Taiyan and his contemporaries in the context of the *genbun itchi* movement and late Qing China'). 中國 21 (China 21) 50: 29−52.

Liu, X. [劉昫] (Ed.). (1975). 舊唐書 ('The old book of Tang'). Peking: Zhonghua Book Company (Original work published 1945).

Liu, Y.-J. [劉玉珺] (2007). 越南漢喃古籍的文獻學研究 ('A philological study of Hán nôm antique books in Vietnam'). Peking: Zhonghua Book Company.

Liu, Y.-Z. [劉雨珍] (2010). 清代首屆駐日公使館員筆談資料彙編 ('A collection of brush-talks by the staff of the first Qing Embassy to Japan'). Tianjin: Tianjin Renmin Press.

Lo Bianco, J. (2001). Viet Nam: Quoc Ngu, colonialism and language policy. In N. Gottlieb & P. Chen (Eds.), *Language planning and language policy: East Asian perspectives* (pp. 159–206). Richmond, UK: Curzon Press.

Lurie, D. B. (2011). *Realms of literacy. Early Japan and the history of writing.* Cambridge, MA: Harvard University Press.

Mair, V. H. (1994). Buddhism and the rise of the written vernacular in East Asia: The making of National Languages. *Journal of Asian Studies* 53(3): 707−751.

Matsuura, A. [松浦章] (2007). 近世東アジア海域諸國における海難救助形態 ('Aspects of salvaging seafarers in early modern East China coastal nations'). 関西大學東西學術研究所紀要 (The Bulletins of the Institute of Oriental and Occidental Studies, Kansai University) 40: 1−20.

Matsuura, A. [松浦章] (2009). 近世東アジア海域における中國船の漂著筆談記錄 ('The record of brush conversation of drifting ship from China in early modern of the East China Sea surrounding nations'). 韓國學論集 *The Journal of Korean Studies* 45: 181−243.

Matsuura, A. [松浦章] (2011). 江戸時代後期における天草崎津漂著唐船の筆談記錄 ('Brush-talk in drifting records of Chinese ships on Amakusa Islands during the late Edo period'). In K. Aratake, H. Noma & Y. Yabuta [荒武賢一朗、野間晴雄、藪田貫] (Eds.), 天草諸島の文化交渉學研究 周緣の文化交渉學シリーズ ('Cultural interaction studies on the Amakusa Islands') (pp. 115–138). Osaka, Japan: Institute for Cultural Interaction Studies, Kansai University.

Matsuura, A. [松浦章] (2014). 朝鮮國漂著中國船の筆談記錄にみる諸相 ('Observations in records of written dialogues concerning Chinese shipwreck in Chosŏn'). 関西大學東西學術研究所紀要 ('The Bulletins of the Institute of Oriental and Occidental Studies, Kansai University') 47: 57−69. Retrieved October 21, 2019, from https://kuir.jm.kansai-u.ac.jp/dspace/handle/10112/8430.

Matsuura, A. [松浦章] (2015). 前近代東亞海域的筆談形態 ('Forms of Sinitic brush-talk in pre- and early modern East Asian waters'). In Y. Wang & Y. Xie [王勇、謝詠] (Eds.), 東亞的筆談研究 ('Studies on brush-talk in East Asia') (pp. 19−32). Hangzhou, China: Zhejiang Gongshang University Press.

Miyazoe Wong, Y. (1996). The impact of a study/work programme in Japan on interactive competence in contact situations. *Japanese Language Education around the Globe* 6: 83–100.

Moon, K. [文慶喆] (2018). 筆談による日韓のコミュニケーション ('Communication of Japan and Korea by a conversation by means of writing'). 総合政策論集 *Policy Management Studies* 17(1): 73–88.

Morris, M. (1989). Review of *The fracture of meaning: Japan's synthesis of China from the eighth through eighteenth centuries*. by D. Pollack (1986). Princeton University Press. *The Journal of Japanese Studies* 15(1): 275–284.

Nakamura, S. [中村史朗] (2018). 「大河内文書」にみる明治期の日中書法交流―楊守敬來日前後の事情をめぐって ('Sino-Japanese calligraphic exchange during the Meiji era as seen in Ōkōchi documents: Yáng Shǒujìng's visit to Japan'). *Calligraphic Studies* 書學書道史研究 18: 31–41.

Nguyễn, H.-T., & Nguyễn T.-C. [阮黃申、阮俊強] (2019). 越南與諸國筆談概論 ('An outline of brush-talk between Vietnam and other countries'). In H. He [何華珍] & T.-C. Nguyễn [阮俊強] (Eds.). 越南漢喃文獻與東亞漢字整理研究 ('Research on Vietnamese classical texts and East Asian sinograms') (pp. 101–117). Peking: China Social Sciences Press.

Ōba, O. [大庭脩] (1985). 寶曆三年八丈島漂著南京船資料 ('A study of Nanking boat drifting to Hachijou Island in 1753'). Osaka, Japan: Institute of Oriental and Occidental Studies, Kansai University.

Ogawa, K. [小川和也] (2012). 天和度朝鮮通信使と大老・堀田正俊の「筆談唱和」 ('"Brush-talk and poetry exchange" between Tenwado Korean envoys and the Tairou Hotta Masatoshi'). 日韓相互認識 ('Mutual Understanding between Japan and Korea') 5: 1–53.

Pfau, R., Steinbach, M., & Woll, B. (Eds.). (2012). *Sign language: An international handbook*. Berlin: Walter de Gruyter.

Pibyŏnsa Tŭngnok 備邊司謄錄. 奎章閣原文檢索서비스 ('Kyujanggak Original Text Searching Service'). Kyujanggak Institute for Korean Studies 奎章閣韓國學研究會. Retrieved March 20, 2021, from http://kyudb.snu.ac.kr/pf01/rendererImg.do?item_cd=VBS&book_cd=GK15044_00&vol_no=0001&page_no=079a.

Pollock, S. (1998). The cosmopolitan vernacular. *The Journal of Asian Studies* 57(1): 6–37.

Pollock, S. (2000). Cosmopolitan and vernacular in history. *Public Culture* 12(3): 591–625.

Pollock, S. (2006). *The language of the gods in the world of men: Sanskrit, culture, and power in premodern India*. Berkeley: University of California Press.

Pore, W. (2008). The inquiring literatus: Yi Su-gwang's 'brushtalks' with Phung Khac Khoan in Beijing in 1598. *Transactions of the Royal Asiatic Society – Korea Branch* 83: 1–26.

Qian, M. [錢明] (2008). 勝國賓師 – 朱舜水傳 ('Guest teacher of a vanquished nation: A biography of Zhu Shunshui'). Hangzhou, China: Zhejiang People's Publishing House.

Rogers, H. (2005). *Writing systems: A linguistic approach*. Oxford: Blackwell.

Seeley, C. (2000). *A history of writing in Japan*. Hawai'i: University of Hawai'i Press.

Shen, G. [沈國威] (2019). 漢語近代二字詞研究――語言接觸與漢語的近代演化 ('A study on Chinese bisyllabic words in modern times: Language contact and recent evolution of Chinese'). Shanghai: East China Normal University Press.

Shima, Y. [島善高] (2017). 『日本蔵晚清中日朝筆談資料 大河内文書』の出版 ('Publication of *Late Qing brush-talk data between Chinese, Japanese and Koreans in Japan – Ōkōchi Documents*'). ふみくら: 早稲田大學図書館報 ('Fumikura: Waseda University Library Bulletin') 92: 5–6.

Song, J.-J. (2001). North and South Korea: Language policies of divergence and convergence. In N. Gottlieb & P. Chen (Eds.), *Language planning and language policy: East Asian perspectives* (pp. 129–157). Richmond, UK: Curzon Press.

Song, J.-J. (2019). Language education policy in North Korea. In A. Kirkpatrick & A. J. Liddicoat (Eds.), *The Routledge international handbook of language education policy in Asia* (pp. 124–136). Abingdon, Oxon & New York: Routledge.

Tao, D. [陶德民] (2005). Negotiating language in the opening of Japan: Luo Sen's journal of Perry's 1854 expedition. *Japan Review* 17: 91–119.

Trambaiolo, D. (2014). Diplomatic journeys and medical brush talks: Eighteenth-century dialogues between Korean and Japanese medicine. In O. Gal & Y. Zheng (Eds.), *Motion and knowledge in the changing early modern world: Orbits, routes and vessels* (pp. 93–113). Dordrecht: Springer Verlag.

Wang, B. [王寶平] (Ed.). (2016). 日本藏晚清中日朝筆談資料——大河內文書 ('Late Qing brush-talk data between Chinese, Japanese and Koreans in Japan: Ōkōchi Documents'). Hangzhou, China: Zhejiang Ancient Books Publishing House.

Wang, G.-H. [王國華] (2015). 心經簡林: 饒宗頤的書法藝術 ('Wisdom Path: Jao Tsung-I's calligraphic art'). Hong Kong: Chung Hwa Book Company.

Wang, G.-W. [王賡武] (1968). Early Ming relations with Southeast Asia: A background essay. In J. K. Fairbank (Ed.), *The Chinese world order: Traditional China's foreign relations* (pp. 34–62). Cambridge, MA: Harvard University Press.

Wang, W. S.-Y. [王士元] & Tsai, Y. [蔡雅菁] (2011). The alphabet and the sinogram: Setting the stage for a look across orthographies. In P. D. McCardle, B. Miller, J. Lee & O. Tzeng (Eds.), *Dyslexia across languages: Orthography and the brain-gene-behavior link* (pp. 1–16). Baltimore, MD: Brookes Publishing.

Wang, Y. [王勇] (2013). 燕行使筆談文獻概述——東亞筆談文獻研究之一 ('Review on written documents of travelers to Peking in Ming and Qing Dynasties: A study of East Asian written documents'). *Foreign Studies* 外文研究 1(2): 37–42.

Wang, Y., & Xie, Y. [王勇、謝詠] (Eds.). (2015). 東亞的筆談研究 ('Studies on brush-talk in East Asia'). Hangzhou, China: Zhejiang Gongshang University Press.

Whitman, J. (2011). The ubiquity of the gloss. *Scripta: International Journal of Writing Systems* 3: 95–121.

Wong, T.-S. [黃得森] (2019). 漢文筆談文獻於中日韓越之整理匯編概況 ('An overview of the collocation and compilation of Sinitic brushtalk documents in Sinographic East Asia'). *Journal of the Classical Literature Association of Yon Min* 淵民學志 32: 285–319.

Wong, T.-S., & Li, D. C. S. [黃得森、李楚成] (2020). 漢文筆談——一個盛行東亞以紙筆作緘默交談的近古傳意模式 ('Sinitic brushtalk as a once vibrant mode of communication: Conducting silent conversation using brush, ink, and paper in early modern East Asia'). *Lexicographical Studies* 辭書研究 2020(1): 81–89.

Yi, W.-S. [李元植] (1997). 朝鮮通信使の研究 ('Studies of Chosŏn envoys to Japan'). Kyōto: Shibunkaku.

Yu, X., & Liang, M. [于向東、梁茂華] (2013). 歷史上中越兩國人士的交流方式：筆談 ('Brush conversation: Mode of communication between Chinese and Vietnamese in history'). 中國邊疆史地研究 (China's Borderland History and Geography Studies) 23(4): 108–116.

Yurayong, C., & Szeto, P.-Y. [司徒沛嶢] (2021). Altaicization and de-Altaicization of Japonic and Koreanic. *International Journal of Eurasian Linguistics* 2(1): 108–148. doi: 10.1163/25898833-12340026.

Zhang, B. [張伯偉] (2017). 東亞漢文學研究的方法與實踐 ('The methods and practice in research on East Asian Sinitic literature'). Peking: Zhonghua Book Company.

Zhang, B. [張伯偉]. (2018). Preface to Korean edition of "The methods and practice in research on East Asian Sinitic literature". *Journal of Cultural Interaction in East Asia* 9: 23–30.

Zhang, J. [張京華] (2012). 三夷相會: 以越南漢文燕行文獻爲中心 ('Meeting of three barbarians: Focusing on the *Yanxing* literatures of Vietnam written in Chinese'). *Foreign Literature Review* 外國文學評論 1: 5–44.

Zhang, W. [張偉雄] (2000). 文酒唯須らく舊好を修むべし: 宮島誠一郎と清國公使団員との筆談考(一) ('A Study of brush conversations between Miyajima Seiichirō and his Chinese friends (I)'). *The Sapporo University Journal* 札幌大學總合論叢 9: 19–30.

Zhang, Y. [張應斌] (2004). 黃遵憲與中日文人筆話 ('Brush conversations between Huáng Zūnxiàn and intellectuals from China and Japan'). *Journal of Jiaying University* 嘉應學院學報 22(5): 69–73.

Zhu, Q. [朱謙之] (Ed.). (1981). 朱舜水集 ('A collection of Zhu Shunshui's writings'). Peking: Zhonghua Book Company.

Zhu, Z. [朱子吳] (2018). 朱舜水 '筆談' 資料芻議 ('My humble opinion on Zhu Shunshui's brush conversation material'). In P. Zha 查屏球 (Ed.). 梯航集: 日藏漢籍中日學術對話錄 ('Tihang collection: Kanji-based Sino-Japanese academic dialogue in Japan') (pp. 382–392). Shanghai: Shanghai Classics Publishing House.

ZSJYZ (*Zhōngguó Sòng Qìnglíng Jījīnhuì Yánjīu Zhōngxīn*) 中國宋慶齡基金會研究中心. (2016). 宮崎滔天家藏民國人物書札手迹 ('Collection of letters and original handwriting of Chinese Republican figures stored at Miyazaki Tōten's family'). Peking: Sino-Culture Press.

2 East Asian brush-talk literature

Introduction and proposed classification[1]

Wang Yong

Introduction

Brush conversation, also called 'silent conversation', involved two or more brush-talkers who were literate in Sinitic, typically in cross-border contexts where speech was not an option due to a lack of a shared spoken language. Historically, plenty of brush-talk records make up a body of literature, giving living testimony of brush-talkers imparting knowledge or engaged in exchanging information, ideas, and thoughts through Sinitic-based writing-mediated communication, that is, by improvising Chinese characters or sinograms (cf. 漢字 Mand: *hànzì*, Jap: *kanji*, Kor: *hanja*, Viet: *chữ Hán, chữ nho, Hán tự*) using brush, ink, and paper. Brush conversation, therefore, typically involved border-crossing, giving rise to opportunities for spontaneous encounters between people from two or more regions or nations within the Sinosphere. As such, brushed encounters are necessarily characterized by features indexical of inter-ethnic, cross-linguistic, and intercultural communication.

In Sinographic East Asia, over an extended historical period, brush conversation occurred in various regions, on various occasions, involving people pertaining to more or less distinctive groups. Such records of brush-talk interaction do not lend themselves to convenient classification, be it by countries, content, or interaction patterns. Why?

First of all, as a cross-border communication phenomenon, although brush conversation may be traced back to the Tang (618–906) and Song (960–1279) dynasties, there are very few surviving brush-talk records during that historical period. Most brush-talk data sources were produced during the Ming and Qing dynasties for a number of reasons. Following the emergence of regional market economy and international trade, coupled with advances in navigation and shipbuilding technologies in response to growing maritime traffic in East Asian waters, the scale of cross-border movements of people as well as commodities, land-bound or sea-borne, gradually expanded. For those engaged in these activities, notably

---

1 This chapter is an abridged version adapted from WANG Yong [王勇] (2018), 東亞筆談文獻經眼錄 ('A survey of the East Asian Sinitic brush-talk literature: An annotated bibliography'), 總論 ('General overview'), pp. 1–36.

DOI: 10.4324/9781003048176-2

merchants and seafarers from different East Asian polities, cross-border transcultural communication became routine, day in day out. In the absence of a shared vernacular, sinogram-based writing-mediated 'silent conversation' using brush, ink, and paper turned out to be a productive way of meaning-making, interactively and face-to-face. This was possible thanks largely to the emergence of a class of literate users of written Chinese or Sinitic with foundational knowledge of a shared body of Classical Chinese canons and literary works, which in turn was a logical sequel of growing numbers of learners of written Chinese in East Asian states.

Following the spread of Western influence at the dawn of modernity, however, such a mode of interstate communication gradually discontinued. In the last decades of the nineteenth century, as the age-old Confucianist culture and shared Sinographic tradition gave way to Western thoughts, institutions, and sociocultural practices characteristic of modernism along with rising nationalistic sentiments in East Asia, admiration of ancient Chinese philosophy, and dependency on written Chinese started waning. Over time, literacy in Sinitic in China's neighboring East Asian states declined; as a result, the foundation and capacity for brush-talkers to conduct silent conversation in Sinitic were lost. Such a historical development spelled doom for Sinitic brush-talk as a commonplace modality of transcultural communication between East Asian peoples engaged in cross-border encounters.

In view of the historical development outlined earlier, one question pertaining to the epistemology of Sinitic brush-talk research is: what is the most reasonable and productive way to categorize the body of literature constituted by scattered surviving brush-talk interaction data sources? A chronological approach subdividing brush-talk records by dynasties (e.g., 'Ming brush-talk', 'Qing brush-talk') would make little sense, all the more because large amounts of Sinitic brush-talk data were produced and preserved in the former 'periphery' states of imperial China, the proverbial 'center' according to the Chinese World Order characterized by diplomatic obligations of and relations between the suzerain state and its tributaries (Fairbank 1968).

Secondly, from the point of view of genre, brush-talk interaction does not lend itself to convenient classification either. Given that the brush-talkers from two or more distinct polities relied on sinograms for visual, writing-mediated communication, nation-based labels such as 'Chinese brush-talk' or 'Japanese brush-talk', 'Korean brush-talk', 'Vietnamese brush-talk', 'Ryukyuan brush-talk' would hardly do justice to the diversity and mix of individual brush-talkers' ethnic backgrounds, cultural identities, and native languages in any cross-border brushed encounter. Furthermore, even though brush conversation is writing-mediated, as a modality of communication it exhibits many characteristics of speech-based conversation, including spontaneous improvisation and unplanned digressions, words selected based on impulse, lack of coherence, topical diversity and unpredictability, and so forth. All this makes it difficult and unrealistic to use content as the basis for classifying brush-talk datasets.

Finally, surviving brush-talk records are preserved in a variety of physical forms. Some exist as stand-alone records, kept privately or accessible in some public (online) space, but they are not easily identifiable as no 'brush-talk' labels are attached to them. Instead, they are commonly embedded in other types of historiographic data. Tracking them down is therefore anything but obvious. Prominent examples include the collections of brush conversations by Naitō Konan 內藤湖南 (1866–1934), Morohashi Tetsuji 諸橋轍次 (1883–1982), Kang Youwei 康有爲 (1858–1927), and Liang Qichao 梁啓超 (1873–1929). Other brush conversations may be scattered in various travelogues or personal journals, collections of poetry and essays, or book series, for example, 'Travelogues to Peking' (*Yŏnhaengnok* 燕行錄), 'Collection of Chinese envoys' poetry' 皇華集, 'Total collection of travel by sea' 海行總載, 'Full record of sea traffic' 通航一覽, etc. A third category consists of collections of brush-talk records compiled by enthusiastic brush-talkers themselves or their descendants, such as 'Ōkōchi documents' 大河內文書 and 'A brush-talk record at the Ryūkyū residence' 琉館筆談. Particularly rich and well documented are those embedded in handwritten manuscripts which were subsequently copied, collated, and compiled by Chosŏn envoys (*t'ongsinsa* 通信使) to Japan from the seventeenth to nineteenth centuries. Finally, many brush-talk datasets are original manuscripts appearing in loose sheets, for instance, those involving Sun Yat-sen 孫中山 (1866–1925) and Naitō Konan, while others like those edited and compiled by Chosŏn envoys exist in bound volumes. The physical forms of brush-talk manuscripts varied considerably; as a method for classifying brush-talk records, that does not seem appropriate either.

In view of the aforementioned observations, we propose to divide brush-talk records into three categories according to the key agents involved in brush conversation. First, diplomats and envoys, a group of brush-talkers who were entrusted with a national mission. In the process of executing their official duties in foreign land, the spoken language barrier obliged them to conduct sinogram-based brush conversation, a writing-mediated mode of communication which was expected of them and known to be effective within the Sinographic cosmopolis (Koh & King 2014). The second group refers to 'boat people' whose vessels were blown off course after succumbing to extreme weather conditions at sea and subsequently drifted ashore in alien waters. Unlike the case of scholar-officials on cross-border diplomatic missions who could count on bilingual interpreters to resolve the language barrier problem, for such unwanted guests getting lost in a foreign country, brush-talk was probably the only hope and means for them to communicate their plight to the locals.

The third group is made up of East Asian intellectuals who, by definition, were proficient users of Sinitic with a solid foundation in Classical Chinese canons and literary works, including poetic genres. They were those who purposely went abroad to extend their knowledge horizons and were eager to exchange views with the locals and other foreigners. To overcome the language barrier, Sinitic brush-talk gave them the best chance and greatest mileage to make themselves understood – interactively, synchronously, and face-to-face. For well over a thousand years of interstate communication within Sinographic East Asia, the above three groups have produced and left behind sizable clusters of Sinitic brush-talk datasets, which have great historical value thanks to their immensely rich content (cf. Lan 2020). In the following, we will briefly outline the clusters of brush-talk literature collected from key agents involved in these three recurrent contexts.

(1) Diplomatic envoys. Most of these brush-talk records are collected in various Sinitic-based personal accounts in the form of journals or travelogues, such as Korean 'Travelogues to Peking' (*Yŏnhaengnok* 燕行錄), Japanese 'Ennin's diary: The record of a pilgrimage to China in search of the law' 入唐求法巡禮行記, Vietnamese 'North-bound envoys' accounts' 北使錄, Chosŏn envoys' 'Records of missions to Japan' 使行錄, Qing Chinese envoys' *Collection of Chinese envoys' poetry* 皇華集, and records of diplomatic exchange between Ryukyu and her neighboring states. Also included are brush-talk records produced by ambassadors in a foreign state, of which the most famous is probably *Ōkōchi documents*, in which elaborate records of brush conversation between the staff of the first Qing legation to Japan and their Japanese acquaintances are collected (see WANG Baoping, this volume).

(2) Boat drifters. In the history of people movements between East Asian countries, unlike government-dispatched envoys, boat drifters arriving by sea were 'unsolicited guests'. With the emergence of an East Asian economic zone and trading region during the Ming and Qing dynasties, boat drifting incidents along the coasts of adjacent states became more and more common. As there was no expectation that the junks would land on alien shores, usually no interpreters were present. To make meaning interactively, writing-mediated brush conversation proved to be the only means of communication with the local officials and other literati of Sinitic. In one instructive example, explicit mention of writing as a surrogate of speech was stated:

問答須憑筆 言談在此書

For question and response, [we] need to use a brush; to conduct conversation, write here.

(Source: 'Copy of *Brush-talk of the Tokutai Ship*' 得泰船筆語抄; see Matsuura & Aoyama, this volume)

Boat drifting incidents being so frequent, there is no shortage of brush-talk records or, where the stakes were high, detailed official reports written by local maritime officials to their king or emperor. Such records were virtually investigation reports of 'boat people' incidents, whose provenance included China, Japan, Korea, Vietnam, Ryukyu, and even Western countries.

(3) Traveling literati well versed in Sinitic. Cross-border ventures of intellectuals were motivated primarily by the pursuit of truth, knowledge, information, or some tangible benefits. Through question-and-response enacted by writing-mediated brush-talk, they were eager to inquire and exchange views with local elites who were equally well versed in Sinitic. According to brush-talk records in this category, a wide range of topics were covered in the give-and-take of such intellectuals, from Buddhism, Confucianism, and the classics to sundry other topics such as medicine, customs, trade, and the like. Such brush-talk records were

mostly compiled by the traveling literati themselves; compared with other types of brush-talk literature, they constitute a fairly compact and systematic set.

On top of the three clusters of brush-talk literature outlined earlier, there are also miscellaneous brush-talk records that are difficult to categorize. For instance, many Chinese students studying in Japan during the late Qing period also relied on brush-talk before getting over the language barrier. Another example was a manual entitled 'Japanese-Qing Chinese conversation for military use: pen-talk made easy' 軍用日清會話: 筆談自在, which was compiled for Japanese soldiers' use during the First Sino-Japanese War (1894–1895).[2] It contained a contrastive word list and instructions on how to conduct writing-mediated 'silent conversation'. From the point of view of Chinese republican history, there are also extremely precious brush-talk records left by politically influential figures like Sun Yat-sen, Kang Youwei, Liang Qichao during their exile in Japan. Being unsystematic and produced ad hoc, such brush-talk materials are temporarily classified as the fourth category 'Other East Asian brush-talk literature'.

Brush-talk literature: East Asian diplomatic envoys (Part 1)

Chinese-Japanese brush-talk concerning the Japanese invasions of Korea during the reign of Ming Emperor Wanli

First, let us examine the brush-talk materials of Chinese envoys abroad. According to available data sources, the earliest records may be traced back to the reign of Ming emperor Wanli 萬曆 (Ming Shenzong 明神宗, r. 1572–1619). In 1592, Toyotomi no Hideyoshi 豊臣秀吉 (1537–1598) invaded Chosŏn as a prelude of a mega plan to bring the whole of East Asia under his control and influence. Supported by 160,000 troops, this military venture resulted in one victory after another, capturing Seoul, Pyongyang, and all the eight provinces of Chosŏn within a month. King Sŏnjo 宣祖 (Yi Yŏn 李昖, r. 1567–1608), who fled to Ŭiju 義州 near the Chinese border for his life, entreated Ming China, the suzerain state, for assistance to fend off the invaders. His plea was granted. Thereupon about 10,000 Ming troops were dispatched to rescue Chosŏn, thus setting the scene for a six-year regional war.[3]

In the tenth lunar month of 1592, Ming China put Song Yingchang 宋應昌 (1536–1606) as the chief administrator of military affairs against Japanese forces 經略備倭軍務, and appointed Yi Rusong 李如松 (1549–1598) as the commander-in-chief of all armies in Korea 防海禦倭總兵官. On 12:25,[4] Yi

---

2 By Suzuki Dōu 鈴木道宇 (1895), published by Yamanaka Kanjirō 山中勘次郎 in Kyoto; available at the National Diet Library of Japan 日本国会図書館 (see also Lan 2020: 192; Suzuki 1895/2015).
3 This is known in Korea as the 'Japanese Invasion of Korea' (1592–1598, 'Imjin War' 壬辰倭亂). In China, this six-year war is called 'Wanli Japanese infestation' 萬曆倭患. In Japan, the two main battles are referred to as the 'Bunroku 文禄 battle' (1592) and 'Keichō 慶長 battle' (1597).
4 The dates are all recorded according to the lunar calendar. For convenience's sake, all lunar months and days will be presented in digits, with the month preceding the day separated by a colon. Thus, '12:25' would mean 'the 25th day of the 12th lunar month'.

Rusong led an army of more than 43,000 troops into Chosŏn. In the first lunar month of 1593, the Ming army recaptured Pyongyang and chased the enemies all the way to Pyŏkchegwan 碧蹄館 in the vicinity of Seoul, where massive numbers of Japanese troops several times the Ming army were encountered. The war then entered a protracted stalemate and hints for armistice were heard on both sides. On 03:15, Shen Weijing 沈惟敬 (1537–1599) went to Seoul for diplomatic talks with Konishi Yukinaga 小西行長 (1558–1600). The Japanese side demanded the Ming to send envoys to Japan to negotiate with Toyotomi in person. After careful consideration, Song Yingchang dispatched two aides-de-camp Xie Yongzi 謝用梓 (1559–1600) and Xu Yiguan 徐一貫 as special envoys to Japan.

The Ming envoys arrived at Kyushu on 05:13 and reached the Japanese military base Nagoya 名護屋 on 05:15. One week later, on 05:23, Toyotomi received the envoys and engaged in the first formal brush-talk with them, with the monk Keitetsu Genso 景轍玄蘇 (1537–1611) of Rinzai school of Zen Buddhism 臨濟宗 serving as a brush-assisted interpreter 通事. A second official brush-talk with the Ming envoys took place on 06:21, which was facilitated by another Rinzai monk, Genhō Reisan 玄圃霊三 (1535–1608) appointed by Toyotomi. The Japanese side laid out several conditions, which were disputed by the Ming envoys. The next day (06:22), after consulting Toyotomi, Genpo Reisan held a third formal brush-talk with the Ming envoys. Both sides had heated verbal exchanges and failed to reach any consensus. While in Nagoya, the envoys also met with Fujiwara Seika 藤原惺窩 (1561–1619), among other Japanese literati, and had brush conversations with them. One of the original manuscripts featuring a brush-talk between Xie Yongzi and 'a certain nobleman' 某侯 has been preserved to this day.

On 06:28, the Ming envoys returned to Chosŏn after more than 40 days of brush-assisted negotiations in Japan. Particularly noteworthy is the fact that the Chinese-Japanese negotiations were carried out entirely through brush conversation, which is no doubt unique in the history of international diplomacy conducted synchronously face-to-face. The historical value of this body of brush-talk records is extremely high.

Brush-talks between the first Qīng legation to Japan and Japanese personalities

In 1877, the first Qīng Embassy led by He Ruzhang 何如璋 (1838–1891) was dispatched to Japan. The sixth article of the 'Sino-Japanese Friendship and Trade Treaty' 中日修好條規 (1871) stipulated that:

> 嗣後兩國往來公文，中國用漢文，日本國用日本文，須副以譯漢文，或只用漢文，亦從其便。(《同治條約》卷二十)
>
> Hereinafter, for official diplomatic documents exchanged between the two nations, China will use Classical Chinese while Japan will use Japanese, the

latter to be accompanied by a translation in Classical Chinese. Japanese documents may also be written in Classical Chinese only.

(Source: Scroll 20, Tongzhi Treaty; see National Archives of Japan 2021 for the Japanese version)[5]

Accordingly, the Qing Court did not find it necessary to appoint too many interpreters among the legation staff. Consequently, for interactive communication with the locals, they had to rely on writing-mediated brush-talk. The Japanese Sinologist Ishikawa Kōsai 石川鴻斎 (1833–1918), an active brush-talk participant, described the situation of the brush-talk as follows:

默對禮終嗤啞然, 寒暄無語共俱憐

How laughable to remain silent and dumb when expressing courtesy face-to-face, speechless greetings make us all pitiable.

To this unusual mode of communication, Oka Senjin 岡千仞 (1833–1914) commented:

凡舌所欲言, 出以筆墨, 縱橫自在, 不窮其說則不止

Whatever the tongue wants to say can be expressed freely and comfortably with brush and ink, boundlessly until the very end.

(Source: 'Shizan Isshō' 芝山一笑)

Ōkōchi Documents 大河内文書

Originally the last feudal lord of the Takasaki clan 高崎藩 in Japan, Minamoto no Teruna's 源輝聲 (1848–1882) ancestral home was in Ōkōchi 大河内. His appellation being Keikaku 桂閣, he was also known as Ōkōchi Teruna 大河内輝聲 or Minamoto no Keikaku 源桂閣. As part of the Meiji reforms, the government converted all the feudal clans into prefectures, Ōkōchi was re-appointed as the governor of Takasaki Prefecture 高崎県. Unhappy with the government's thoroughgoing westernization policy measures, he resigned and moved to a house on the banks of the Sumie River 墨江 in Tokyo. An amateur and enthusiast of writing and painting, Ōkōchi loved to befriend acquaintances with a high level of literacy in Sinitic, especially enjoying the outpouring of emotions through brush-talking with his Chinese and Korean friends. He was a frequent visitor of the Qing embassy; before his visit, he would bring with him a stack of paper and be fully prepared for elaborate brush-talking. Encountering the interpreter of the

---

5 JACAR (Japan Center for Asian Historical Records), '大日本國大清國修好條規 通商章程及兩國海關関税則 (C1)', 外務省外交史料館 (Diplomatic Archives of the Ministry of Foreign Affairs of Japan), Ref. B13090891200. Retrieved March 30, 2021, from www.jacar.archives.go.jp/aj/meta/image_B13090891200.

embassy would make no difference, as he would rather 'exchange a brush for tons of verbiage in speech' 以一枝筆換千萬語言, and prefer brush-talking so that 'inked treasures' could be collected. After each brush-talk, he would bring all of the inked treasures home, and have them sorted, framed, and bound into retrievable volumes, a valuable heirloom to be passed on for posterity within the family.

Professor Sanetō Keishū 実藤恵秀 (1896–1985) of Waseda University 早稲田大学 first discovered these precious materials at Hirabayashi Temple in Saitama Prefecture 埼玉県 平林寺 in 1943, and named them 'Ōkōchi Documents' 大河内文書. There were originally 95 volumes in this batch of brush-talk materials, of which 78 have survived. They are housed separately at various locations, including the libraries of Waseda University and Daito Bunka University 大東文化大學, but also Yorimasa Shrine in Saitama Prefecture 埼玉県 賴政神社. Details of the 78 volumes are as follows:

1	*Ra-Gen Chō*: Document between Luo Xuegu 羅雪谷 and Minamoto no Teruna 源輝聲	羅源帖	16 volumes
2	*Teichō hitsuwa*: 1877 brush-talk	丁丑筆話	7 volumes
3	*Bo'in hitsuwa*: 1878 brush-talk	戊寅筆話	25 volumes saved
4	*Kibō hitsuwa*: 1879 brush-talk	己卯筆話	2 volumes saved
5	*Kōshin hitsuwa*: 1880 brush-talk	庚辰筆話	9 volumes saved
6	*Shitsuen hitsuwa*: brush-talk with Wang Qiyuan	漆園筆話	17 volumes
7	*Kanjin hitsuwa*: brush-talk with Koreans	韓人筆話	1 volume
8	*Shoga hitsuwa*: brush-talk on painting and calligraphy	書畫筆話	1 volume

The 78 surviving volumes of *Ōkōchi Documents* contain about 1,500 brush-talks from the eighth (1875) to the fourteenth year (1882) of the Meiji era, with a relatively fixed person, time, and location being counted as one brush-talk event. Apart from Ōkōchi himself, other Japanese Sinologists participating in miscellaneous brush-talk events included Miyajima Seiichirō 宮島誠一郎 (1838–1911), Ishikawa Kōsai, Oka Senjin, Aoyama Nobutoshi 青山延寿 (1820–1906), Masuda Mitsugu 増田貢 (1825–1899), Mori Shuntō 森春濤 (1819–1889), and Katō Ōrō 加藤櫻老 (1811–1884). The Chinese side was represented by several legation staff, notably He Ruzhang 何如璋, Zhang Sigui 張斯桂 (1817–1888), Huang Zunxian 黃遵憲 (1848–1905), and Shen Wenying 沈文熒 (1833–1886). They were often joined by a few Chinese literati residing in Japan, including Liao Xien 廖錫恩 (1839–1887), Yang Shoujing 楊守敬 (1839–1915), Wei Limen 魏梨門 (1860–1933), He Qiyi 何其毅 (1866–1921), and other diplomats and their families in Japan, in addition to Wang Zhiben 王治本 (1835–1908), Wang Tizhai 王惕齋 (1839–1911), Wang Fanqing 王藩清 (1847–1898), Zhang Zifang 張滋昉 (1839–1900), Feng Xueqing 馮雪卿 (1844–1926), Chen Manshou 陳曼壽 (1825–1884), Wang Tao 王韜 (1828–1897), Li Xiaopu 李筱圃 (1893–1930), and Luo Xuegu 羅雪谷 (1862–?), among others. Their brush conversations were occasionally also joined by a few literati from Chosŏn Korea (see B. Wang 2016 for more details).

Original brush-talk manuscripts are preserved intact in the *Ōkōchi documents*, a huge compilation of precious brush-talk materials which are immensely rich in content, comprising not only fine details of formal diplomatic exchange at a more personal level, but also spontaneous improvisation of sinogram-based poetry and socializing chanting 詩歌酬唱. In short, as a yet untapped primary data source regarding the diplomatic history of Sino-Japanese relations, the *Ōkōchi Documents* is extremely valuable indeed.

Brush-talk by Yang Shoujing

As an attaché, Yang Shoujing 楊守敬 accompanied the first Qīng legation to Japan in 1880. He was frequently engaged in Sinitic brush-talk with the Japanese Sinologist Mori Risshi 森立之 (1807–1885). Among the best-known brush-talk materials arising from their brushed encounters was 'Brush-talk with Qing guests' 清客筆話, which was collated by Chen (1997). In addition, Yang brought tens of thousands of calligraphic inscriptions with him to Japan, creating a stir among local amateurs and interest groups of calligraphy. He then bought or exchanged ancient Chinese classics with enthusiasts, creating tremendous influence among local literati circles. Yang's intellectual exchange with leading Japanese calligraphers and scholars was conducted exclusively through brush-talk, resulting in huge quantities of brush-talk materials. Unfortunately, fine-grained research still awaits Chinese scholars as a systematic review of such materials has barely started.

(1) 'Brush-talk with Qing guests' 清客筆話. It is a record of Yang's brush-talk with Mori, who integrated the original brush conversations with related personal letters in 10 volumes, the last two being brush-talk and other materials produced in Mori's exchange with Li Shuchang 黎庶昌 (1837–1898) and Yao Wendong 姚文棟 (1853–1929). The brush-talk part accounted for 66 *folia* or leaves of paper and is accessible from Keio University's Stow Library 慶応大学斯道文庫. Dated 1881–1882, this body of brush-talk materials is content-wise concerned with various activities related to ancient books from collecting, trading to copy-editing.

(2) Yang's brush-talk with Miyajima Seiichirō. Separately stored in the National Diet Library of Japan 日本国会図書館 and Waseda University Library, this set of brush-talk records contains several tens of thousands of characters. It covers recommendations for improving the wording of poetic verses, but also current affairs concerning Ryukyu and Chosŏn (for a systematic study, see Chen 1998).

(3) Yang's brush-talk with Kusakabe Meikaku 日下部鳴鶴 (1838–1922). It consists of an exchange of views on calligraphy as an art form, spanning over 16 *folia*, representing a selection by Kusakabe himself. A photocopy of this brush-talk may be found in 'Hachiryō Kensai's catalogue essay' 八稜研斎随録.

(4) Yang's brush-talk with Iwatani Ichiroku 岩谷一六 (1834–1905). Copied on 36 pages of letter paper, this set of brush-talk records covers topics such as calligraphy and engraving. A photocopy was reproduced and appeared in

volumes 1–3 of the magazine, *Shogei* 書藝, after Yang's original handwriting was authenticated.

(5) Brush-talk between Yang Xingwu 楊惺吾 (1839–1915) and Matsuda Sekka 松田雪柯 (1823–1881). Collated version with free translation was published in volume 4 of the magazine, *Shogei* 書藝.

(6) 'Eloquent discussion by Xingwu' 惺吾談屑. This is a hand-written copy of the brush-talk record between Yang and his Japanese acquaintances (1880–1881). Other than the excerpts from *Hachiryō Kensai's catalogue essay*, its content remained obscure, until this precious hand-written copy figured in the list of items to be auctioned in Shanghai in April 2010, where it was sold for RMB 168,000.[6] *Eloquent discussion by Xingwu* consists of two volumes in 288 folia, amounting to more than 50,000 characters. Content-wise it mainly involves personnel disputes at the Qīng Embassy, evaluation of visiting scholars in Japan such as Wang Tao 王韜 (1828–1897), and other issues like appreciation and critique of Japanese calligraphy.

Brush-talk by Miyajima Seiichirō

Miyajima Seiichirō 宮島誠一郎 (1838–1911) was very fond of poetry and literary works. Having worked at the Office of Historical Documentation 修史館 before, he was keen on befriending Chinese literati, in so doing leaving behind a lot of brush-talk materials. The Waseda University Library alone holds a collection of about 40 items; their dates and titles are exemplified here:

Item no. and name	Date
1 Brush-talk by Li Shuchang 黎庶昌筆談	Oct 8, 1876
2 Brush-talk in the tenth year of Meiji 明治十年筆談	1877
3 Brush-talk by Qing ambassadors 清國公使筆談	Feb 13, 1878
4 Brush-talk by Qing Ambassador He Ruzhang, and Counselor Huang Zunxian 清國公使何如璋參贊黃遵憲筆談	1878
5 Brush-talk by Qing ambassadors (Sinology Section) 清國公使筆談(漢學之部)	Feb 15, 1878
6 Questions and Answers between Lord Kurika and Chinese people 栗香大人與支那人問答錄	Feb 1878, Jan 1879, Jan 1880
7 Brush-talk before Shen Wenying's departure 沈文熒臨別筆談	1879
8 The volume of Shen-Huang 沈黃之卷	Mar 2, 1879
9 Brush-talk by He Ruzhang 何如璋筆談	Unknown
10 Brush-talk by Huang Zunxian, etc. 黃遵憲筆談等	1880–1890
11 Brush-talk by Qing ambassadors 清國公使筆談	1880–1881
12 Brush-talk by embassy officials He and Huang in the 14th Year of Meiji 明治十四年何黃二使談	1880

(*Continued*)

---

6 For background details of the auction, see https://auction.artron.net/paimai-art64130074/.

Item no. and name	Date
13 Document presented to His Excellency Mister He 奉贈何君閣下書	Dec 1880
14 Brush-talk by Li Shuchang 黎庶昌筆談	1881
15 Brush-talk records at Kurika Study 栗香齋筆談錄, including brush-talks by Li Shuchang and others 黎庶昌等筆話	May 14, 1881 – Jul 21, 1886
Brush-talk records by Li Shuchang and others 黎庶昌等筆談錄	Aug 4, 1888 – Jan 3, 1889 (10 days)
16 Brush-talk by Zhang Daomin 張導岷筆談	1881
17 Brush-talk by Yao Wendong 姚文棟筆談	Jul 1881
18 Brush-talk occasioned by Yao Wendong's visit 姚文棟來訪筆談	Unknown
19 Brush-talk by Li Shuchang, etc. 黎庶昌筆談等	about 1881
20 Brush-talk by Yao Wendong 姚文棟筆談	July 19, 1883
21 Brush-talk record (Yao Wendong, etc.) 筆談錄 (姚文棟等)	1884
22 Brush-talk by Li Shuchang 黎庶昌筆談	Unknown
23 Brush-talk records (Zhang Zifang, Huang Xiquan, etc.) 筆談錄 (張滋昉, 黃錫銓等)	Unknown
24 Letters and brush-talk by Huang Zunxian, Wang Fengzao, and others 黃遵憲, 汪鳳藻等書函及筆談	1886
25 Brush-talk by Ambassador Li Shuchang 黎庶昌公使筆談	Feb 9, 1887
26 Brush-talk by Qing envoys He-Huang-Shen 清國使節何黃沈筆談	Unknown
27 Brush-talk by Zhang Daomin 張導岷筆談	1886
28 Xingwu brush-talk by Yang Shoujing 楊守敬惺吾筆談	Unknown
29 Brush-talk by Ambassador He Zie before departure 何子峨公使臨別筆談	Unknown
30 Brush-talk by Qing ambassadors He Zie and Huang Zunxian 清國使節何子峨黃遵憲筆談	Unknown
31 Brush-talk records 筆談錄	Unknown
32 Brush-talk by Qing ambassadors 清使筆談	Jun 1888
33 Brush-talk records 筆談錄	1889
34 Brush-talk occasioned by Qing ambassador Yu Geng's visit 清使裕庚來談	Jul 1894
35 Brush-talk by Huang Zunxian 黃遵憲筆談	Unknown

In addition to Waseda University, the National Diet Library of Japan, the Miyajima family, among other institutions, also hold some materials on Miyajima's brush conversations with Chinese people.

Brush-talk literature: East Asian diplomatic envoys (Part 2)

The bulk of research on 'Envoys to Peking' 燕行使 to date focuses on the envoys of Chosŏn 朝鮮燕行使, while those of Vietnam 越南燕行使 during more or less the same period were relatively neglected. This is largely because historiographic compilation and collation of original 燕行錄 (Kor: *Yŏnhaengnok*; Mand: *Yanxinglu*) texts in Korea had an early start, making it possible for scholars to conduct fine-grained, detailed analysis. Particularly noteworthy was the publication of the 'Complete collection of travel journals of Chosŏn envoys to Peking' 燕行錄全集 by Lim Key-zung 林基中 (2001). In contrast, basic documentation of similar travelogues in Vietnam appeared to be lagging behind.

This situation changed in 2010, however, with the publication of the 'Collection of literature on Vietnamese envoys' Sinitic travelogues to Peking' 越南漢文燕行文獻集成, which was jointly published by the Institute for Advanced Humanistic Studies 文史研究院 of Fudan University and the Institute of Sino-Nom Studies 院研究漢喃 (Chi: 漢喃研究院) of Vietnam.[7] Included in this compilation are original manuscripts of 79 works by 53 'envoys visiting Qing China' 如清使. This work has laid a solid foundation for research on Vietnamese envoys' missions to Peking.

Travelogues to Peking: nomenclature

The envoys from Chosŏn on tributary missions to Ming and Qing China are generally referred to as 'envoys to Peking' 燕行使, and the records they left behind 'Travelogues to Peking' 燕行錄. Although these terms have very much become a convention, strictly speaking such a nomenclature is not so accurate. Yanjing 燕京 was the capital of the Ming and Qing dynasties; missions to Yanjing represented an obligation of tributary states like Chosŏn Korea (Fairbank 1968). From the points of view of identity as well as Confucianist etiquette, the naming of such missions as 'travel to Peking' 燕行 obscures Qing China's status as the sovereign state.

This is in stark contrast with earlier references of similar missions to mainland China. According to the *Complete works of travelogues to Peking*, earlier travelogue records were given more venerable titles, for example, 'Records of missions to Celestial Empire' 朝天錄 (Kor: *Choch'ŏnnok*, Mand: *Chaotianlu*; compare: 'Chronicles of missions to Celestial Empire' 朝天紀, 'Diaries of missions to Celestial Empire' 朝天日記/朝天日乘, 'Poetry composed during missions to Celestial Empire' 朝天詩, etc.). 'Travel to Peking' 燕行 was thus very much a parallel shift from the earlier naming of travelogues to Shenyang 瀋陽 (e.g., 'Shenyang diary' 瀋陽日記/瀋陽日錄), the capital of the Manchus before they became the master of China.[8]

What does the change in naming practice tell us about the Korean attitudes to China? Chosŏn looked to Ming dynasty as a suzerain or 'Celestial Empire' 天朝, and revered it as 'central efflorescence' 中華 (Mand: *zhōnghuá*, Jap: *chūka*, Kor: *chunghwa*, Viet: *trung hoa*). Such an attitude was fully reflected in the naming of their mission as 'to make a pilgrimage to the Celestial Empire' 朝天. By contrast,

---

7 Published by Fudan University Press, 2010.
8 Compare: 瀋陽日錄, 瀋陽日乘, 瀋館錄. Such a shift results in the use of 燕行 in a host of other similar records, e.g., 燕行記, 燕行詩, 燕行日錄, 燕行雜志, 燕行記事, 燕行別錄, etc.

although Koreans succumbed to the Manchus' military prowess, deep down the new Qing ruler was dismissed as 'barbarians' 夷, who did not deserve their reverence. The regime change from Ming to Qing is thus the background to the shift in attitudes among China's East Asian neighbors Korea and Japan, where the Confucians were convinced that Qing China had degenerated into a 'barbarian' state. A logical sequel of this line of thinking is that thenceforth, they should look elsewhere for the new center of 'efflorescence' (cf. the Japanese stance of 'reversal of efflorescence-barbarian relations' 華夷變態, see Jang, this volume). Such attitudinal changes are reflected not only in the naming of Korean missions to Peking but also in Korean envoys' brush-talk records when conducting silent conversations with envoys from other countries.

Therefore, without a solid understanding of the transformation of *Hua-yi* 華夷 ideology of East Asian countries towards China as the Ming dynasty yielded to the Qing, it would be difficult to see a tremendous change in the forms and contents of Chosŏn envoys' records of their missions to China. This is why it would seem inappropriate to label the body of literature related to Korean missions to China collectively as 'missions to Peking' 燕行. Instead, it seems more reasonable to keep the two separate bodies of literature distinct: 'Travelogues to Peking' 燕行錄 on one hand, and 'Records of missions to Celestial Empire' 朝天錄 on the other.

Travelogues to Peking: content

Content-wise, there are two types of 'Travelogues to Peking'. The first one consisted of official reports on the completed missions submitted to the Chosŏn government by the officer(s) in charge of writing. The format was fixed and well defined, comprising various types of sensitive information, from political and economic to military and diplomatic. Such reports were usually brief, with no traces of personal views embedded in brush conversation. The other type resembled personal diaries in genre, detailing personal experiences and reflections, and for this reason much richer and variegated in content, and also more elaborate and reliable. Often embedded in this second type of travelogues was a wealth of brush-talk records, including original manuscripts. This latter type of personalized 'Travelogues to Peking' was mostly included in private literary collections and circulated in the form of printed books and manuscripts. In recent years, there is a general consensus among Korean, Chinese, and Japanese scholars ascertaining the historical value of 'Travelogues to Peking'. Some scholars started conducting in-depth research from multiple angles and vantage points, in effect challenging some traditional views regarding the diplomatic history of interstate relations in premodern and early modern East Asia during the Ming and Qing dynasties.

Bae Younghee 裴英姬 (2009) summarized the research findings on 'Travelogues to Peking' in China, Chosŏn Korea, and Japan to date, and identified four directions of scholarly attention: (i) relations between the suzerain state (the 'Center') and tributaries (the 'peripheries') 朝貢關係; (ii) tributary missions' trading activities 朝貢貿易; (iii) conceptual distinction between efflorescence-barbarian states (respecting Zhou dynasty while reminiscing Ming) 華夷觀念 (尊周思明); and (iv) intercultural exchange and dissemination 文化交流及傳播. Clearly, brush-talk materials embedded in *Travelogue to Peking* have not been fully utilized; rare are those scholars who regard Sinitic brush-talk as a separate research area of scholarly inquiry in its own right.

Travelogues to Peking: types of texts

In July 2011, 'Selected works of Korean envoys' Sinitic travelogues to Peking' 韓國漢文燕行文獻選集, jointly compiled by the Institute for Advanced Humanistic Studies 文史研究院 of Fudan University 復旦大學 and the Academy of East Asian Studies 東亞學術院 of Sungkyunkwan University 成均館大學 in Korea, was formally published and launched by Fudan University Press. That event instantly became a hot topic within academia and public media alike. Included are 33 types of 'Travelogues to Peking' from Ming to Qing dynasties, spanning over 30 volumes. Even so, this covers only a tiny part of the extant *yanxinglu* literature.

Prior to this (June 2010), Guangxi Normal University Press had launched the 'Complete collection of travelogues to Peking' (the first series) edited by Hong Huawen 弘華文, covering 147 books in 12 volumes. The scope of this series ranged from the Song to Qing dynasties, which gives the impression of being a mixed bag and relatively not as prestigious.

How many records of 'Travelogues to Peking' are there? Currently, the most authoritative catalogue may be found in the 'Complete collection of travel journals of Chosŏn envoys' travelogues to Peking' 燕行錄全集 (Lim 2001). Altogether there are 100 volumes, including 380 distinct records. In 2008, Lim further published 107 travelogues in 50 volumes in a new sequel (燕行錄續集), thus bringing the total number of travelogues to 487.

The Daedong Institute for Korean Studies 大東文化研究院 at Sungkyunkwan University 成均館大學 in Korea was a pioneer in this research area. In 1960, two volumes of 'Selected travelogues of Chosŏn envoys to Peking' 燕行錄選集 were published; this was followed by a sequel of three additional volumes in 2008. In addition, in 2001, Fuma Susumu 夫馬進 of Kyoto University teamed up with Lim Key-zung to launch 'The complete works of *Travelogues to Peking* collected in Japan' 燕行錄全集日本所藏編. According to Bae Younghee, altogether 568 distinct travelogues of Chosŏn envoys to China have been published.

'Oral talk' and 'brush-talk'

As mentioned earlier, 'Travelogues to Peking' are first-hand recollections of proceedings of Chosŏn envoys' tributary missions to China. In addition to formal reports that followed specific genre requirements, they also contained a lot of brush-talk records, poetic improvisation, and socializing chanting, etc. Although the Chosŏn envoys were accompanied by interpreters, formal interpretation was limited to ceremonies and deliberation of state affairs attended by high-level scholar-officials when tribute rites and rituals were performed. In most private activities involving large numbers of people, the majority of members of the Chosŏn mission had too little spoken Chinese to be able to converse with their Chinese hosts interactively. For interpersonal exchange with Chinese and other foreign envoys, they had to rely on Sinitic brush-talk. This is why in Chosŏn-Chinese interaction and intellectual exchange, a distinction was made between 'oral conversation' 口談 and 'brush conversation' 筆談, although a mixed mode of both oral and written communication was not uncommon.

In 1881, King Kojong 高宗 (r. 1863–1907) of Chosŏn appointed Kim Yun-sik 金允植 (1835–1922) as the Chief-Envoy to lead a delegation of about 100 to Tianjin, the purpose being to study equipment manufacturing. Kim stayed in China for nearly a year; his personal observations and experiences were detailed in the 'History of the ups and downs' 陰晴史 and 'Brief discussions in Tianjin' 天津談草, which contains a total of 43 brush conversation records, namely 10 with Li Hongzhang 李鴻章 (1823–1901), 14 with Zhou Fu 周馥 (1837–1921). The rest of the brush conversation was conducted with other political and literary figures individually, including You Zhikai 游智開 (1816–1899), Ma Jianzhong 馬建忠 (1845–1900), Zhang Shusheng 張樹聲 (1853–1862), Yuan Shikai 袁世凱 (1859–1916), Tang Tingshu 唐廷樞 (1832–1892), Liu Hanfang 劉含芳 (1840–1898), Luo Fenglu 羅豐禄 (1850–1901), and Paul Georg von Möllendorff 穆麟德 (1847–1901). The opening parts of the first four brush-talks with Li Hongzhang are particularly instructive regarding when and how brush-talk was preferred to speech:

(1) 《辛巳(1881),十一月二十八日保定省署談草》 'Initial talk on 11:28, 1881 at the Baoding Provincial Office'	中堂問國王安寧及行中安否,各人出身年紀,令從事官弁先出,留余及別遣,乃開筆談。	'Li Hongzhang inquired whether the king was in peace and whether all was well with him during his journey; [Li also asked about] the accompanying persons' backgrounds and ages. [Then] he ordered the official to go out and leave us alone, and started the brush-talk.'
(2) 《是月三十日督署談草》 'Initial talk on the 30th of the lunar month at the Governer-general's Office'	中堂先使通詞傳言:"國王禮物,使臣所送,不必番番有之. 彼此貽弊,不如省事. 此後置之爲好." 仍始筆談.	'Li Hongzhang first asked the interpreter to convey the message: "Regarding the king's gift conveyed by the envoy, there is no need to do that every time. It is too troublesome to exchange gifts; let's skip this. It is better to do it afterwards." Only then did [we] start the brush-talk.'
(3) 《十二月初一日督署邀飲時使通詞傳語口談》 'Oral discussion on 12:01 upon the invitation of the Governor-general's office for a drink, [I asked] the interpreter to convey my request through verbal exchange'	中堂使通詞問:"貴國有何土産否?"答:"土陋民貧,別無所産,惟衣食所需,僅支自給而已."	'Li Hongzhang asked the interpreter to inquire: "Are there any native products in your country?" Answer [orally]: "The soil [of our country] is infertile and [our] people are poor; [we have] nothing else to produce. But we can subsist on food and clothing needed for everyday life".'

East Asian brush-talk literature 61

| (4) 《十二月十九日再至督署談草》 'Brief discussion on 12:19 at the Governor's Office' | 李中堂以筆談問曰:"游道示貴國主書意并閔公書稿.均閱悉.何以公等出境時未先商定.不久又有此信?" | 'Li Hongzhang asked through brush-talk: "You Dao shared the idea with your esteemed country's official in charge of writing, and showed [him] Mister Min's manuscript; [I] have read [them] all. Why did [you] not agree before leaving the country, and then came up with this letter so soon?"' |

In (1) and (2), their interaction began with orally based greetings, while substantive deliberations were conducted in 'brush-talk'. In (3), the interaction was carried out in 'oral exchange' entirely, while (4) was conducted completely through brush-talk. Judging from the 43 brush(-assisted) conversations collected in *Brief discussions in Tianjin*, those between China and Chosŏn were mainly conducted through brush-talk, supplemented with a speech-based verbal exchange. Given the important role assigned to Sinitic brush-talk in official interstate deliberations, it is understandable why as a mode of communication, brush-talk figured so prominently in private encounters and intellectual exchange between officials from different polities, synchronously and face-to-face.

Brush-talks by Chosŏn envoys

The brush-talk materials preserved in 'Travelogues to Peking' mainly fall into the following categories:

(1) *Complete brush-talk records*. Following are some examples:

Min Chŏng-chung 閔鼎重 (1628–1692)	'Questions and answers with Scholar Mr. Wang' 王秀才問答 'Questions and answers with County Magistrate Mr. Yan' 顏知縣問答
Hong Tae-yong 洪大容 (1731–1783)	'Tamhŏn's travelogue to Peking' 湛軒燕記 'Questions and Answers with Wu Peng' 吳彭問答 'Questions and Answers with Jiang Zhou' 蔣周問答 'Questions and Answers with Hallerstein and Gogeisl' 劉鮑問答 'Brush-talk at Kanjŏng Alley' 乾淨衕筆譚
Pak Chi-wŏn 朴趾源 (1737–1805), all included in 'Jehol diary' 熱河日記	'Brush-talk at Suzhai' 粟齋筆談 'Brush-talk at Shanglou' 商樓筆談 'Questions and answers about Lamaism' 黃教問答 'Full story of Panchen Lama' 班禪始末 'Forgotten Goat Record' 忘羊錄 'Brush-talk with Huding' 鵠汀筆談

(2) *Poetic improvisation and chanting by Chosŏn envoys and people from China.* Such materials are ubiquitous in 'Travelogues to Peking', but mostly scattered and incomplete. More complete ones are those by Nam Ku-man 南九萬 (1629–1711), such as 'Miscellaneous records of mission to Peking' in 1686

丙寅燕行雜錄. Poetic exchange and socializing chanting were not necessarily conducted face-to-face. For instance, 'Collection of intimate friendship' 縞紵集 (6 volumes in 2 sets) by Pak Che-ka 朴齊家 (1750–1815) is a written record of his exchange of poetic verses, including some appearing in letters between him and the Qing literati he encountered. This suggests that poetic exchange via letter correspondence was another viable mode of Sinitic brush-talk communication in Sinographic East Asia.

(3) *Brush-talk records mixed in diary writing.* This type of material is scattered but massive, mostly isolated phrases or short passages. *P'yohae'nok* 漂海錄 by Ch'oe Pu 崔溥 (1454–1504) contains relatively more elaborate and complete brush-talk records. Although research on 'Travelogues to Peking' seems to be getting popular, relatively little effort is devoted to brush-talk (Pak 2011, 2015 being rare exceptions). The book 'A study of the Northern School's collection of Chosŏn envoys' brush-talk records in their travelogues to Peking' 北學派燕行錄所載筆談研究 (Pak 2015) is a treatise on the brush-talks produced by Hong Tae-yong, Pak Chi-wŏn, Pak Che-ka, and Yu Tŭk-kong 柳得恭 (1748–1807) when interacting with Qing literati they encountered, with specific reference to the forms and writing characteristics of Sinitic brush-talks. Compared with earlier research from the perspectives of epistemology and new cultural experiences, this book focuses on the meanings of mutual communication 相互溝通的涵義. The focus was the brush-talk records of four celebrated Chosŏn literati, such as *Brush-talk at Kanjŏng Alley* (by Hong Tae-yong); *Brush-talk at Suzhai, Shanglou brush-talk, Brush-talk with Huding, Questions and answers about Lamaism,* and *Forgotten Goat Record* (by Pak Chi-wŏn); 'Revisiting Peking: Traveling Records' 燕臺再游錄 (by Yu Tŭk-kong), and 'Collection of intimate friendship' 縞紵集 (by Pak Che-ka). Pak (2015) gives an account of the high literary values of their brush-talks, explicates their writing styles, motivation for engaging in creative works, and topical development. Rather than interpreting brush-talk texts, it compares the respective stances of the literati in China and Chosŏn. Which factors accounted for the smooth proceeding of brush-talk interactions between the literati of the two countries, resulting in huge amounts of brush-talk records? That is the key research question addressed in his book. Pak (2015) approaches this question by (i) outlining the historical background and characteristics of brush-talk, (ii) extracting basic information of the brush-talk participants, and (iii) analyzing the level of recognition of mutual identities.

Vietnam's Travelogues to Peking

Vietnamese envoys who paid tribute to Qing China traveled from south to north, and so they are generally called 'north-bound envoys' 北使, and their travelogues are generally called 'North-bound envoys' records' 北使錄. Since the destination of their tribute journey had been formerly called Yanjing 燕京 (ancient name of

East Asian brush-talk literature 63

Peking, which was also the capital of the Yan state of the Warring States period), the character *Yan* 燕 was commonly used in the envoys' formal reports. For example, in 1868, Nguyễn Tư Giản 阮思僩 (1823–1890) served as the Second commissioner visiting Qing 如清甲副使 with the title 'Vice-president of the Court of Ceremonies' 鴻臚寺少卿. Nguyễn wrote prolifically during his mission to China; many of his writings were included in multiple collections of poetry and essays authored by him, including 'Written records of the journey to Yan by carriage' 燕軺筆錄, 'Draft poems on the journey to Peking by carriage' 燕軺詩草, 'Poetry collection on the journey to Peking by carriage' 燕軺詩集, 'Poetry and essays on the journey to Peking by carriage' 燕軺詩文集. In general, such collections of essays were written and compiled by Vietnamese ambassadors to China and, like similar works produced by Korean envoys to Peking, they are generally referred to as Vietnamese 'Travelogues to Peking'.

Poetic improvisation and chanting of Vietnamese north-bound envoys

There are about 80 odd collections of poetry and essays in Vietnam based on 'Travelogues to Peking' to date, the earliest being 'Giới Hiên's poems' 介軒詩稿 by Nguyễn Trung Ngạn 阮忠彥 of Trần Dynasty 陳朝 (1225–1400), with 81 poems written during his mission to Yuan China in 1315. The most widely circulated is 'Collection of poems during diplomatic mission to China' 使華叢詠 (1742) by Nguyễn Tông Khuê 阮宗奎 of the Latter Lê dynasty 後黎, which exists in 17 hand-copied versions. Of these, two versions were quite well acclaimed among scholar-officials of Qing China: one prefaced by Zhang Hanzhao 張漢昭 of Jinling 金陵 (Nanjing) dated 1743, the other prefaced by Li Bancun 李半村 of Huaiyin 淮陰 (1748), which won praise among the literati in China. The poetic works collected included those improvised (i) at banquets before the embassies' departure from Peking, (ii) during north-bound envoys' journey out of admiration of China's scenic spots and historical sites, and (iii) the poetic exchange between Nguyễn Tông Khuê and Chief-Envoy Nguyễn Kiều 阮翹, among others. The poetic improvisation and socializing chanting 唱和 (Mand: *changhe*, Jap: *shōwa*, Kor: *changhwa*, Viet: *xướng hoạ*) with Chinese scholar-officials and Korean envoys constituted the main substance of the collections of poetic works by Vietnamese north-bound envoys.

Some collections employ 'socializing chanting' 唱酬 or 'social exchange' 酬應 in their book titles directly, for example, 'Central Plain social exchange collection' 中州酬應集, 'Dazhushibu social-intercourse chanting' 大珠使部唱酬. These works also attracted the attention of Chinese literati. In 1877, Bùi Văn Dị 裴文禩 was appointed as Chief-Envoy to China. He and the Qing official in charge of reception, Yang Enshou 楊恩壽, were engaged in extended poetry composition and socializing chanting. Their poetic works were subsequently included in Yang's edited volume 'Collection of socializing chanting on the envoy boat' 雉舟酬唱集 (also appeared in 'The complete works of Tanyuan' 坦園全集).

Brush-talk of Vietnamese envoys to Peking

Like their Korean counterparts, most Vietnamese envoys to Peking were non-conversant in spoken Chinese and had to rely mainly on brush-talking as the default mode of communication with Chinese officials and acquaintances. In the 26th year of emperor Qianlong (1761), Vietnam dispatched a tribute mission to the Qing court. During this mission, many rounds of brush-talk and poetic improvisation were held by the Vice-Envoy Lê Quý Đôn 黎貴惇 (1726–1784) and an official from the Qing Ministry of Rites 禮部 Qin Chaoyu 秦朝釪, the latter being charged with escorting the Vietnamese envoys and their retinues on their return journey from Jiujiang 九江, Jiangxi Province 江西省 to Darongjiang 大榕江, Xing'an 興安. There were also other participants who left behind a lot of precious brush-talk materials, which Lê took with him back to Vietnam and included in his book 'Complete accounts of north-bound envoys' 北使通錄 (see Nguyễn & Nguyễn, this volume).

Lê and Qin's brush-talk records were embedded with poetic improvisation and chanting 詩歌酬唱, exchange of viewpoints and reflections on specific books of shared interests, but also the soliciting of the second parts of rhyming couplets. For instance, on arrival at Wuchang on 09:08, Qin gave Lê a poem as a gift. Thereupon Lê reciprocated with a poem entitled 'Response to Huzhai 岵齋 at Wuchang following the second rhyme while climbing up Yellow Crane Tower on the day before the Double Ninth Festival' 駐武昌城次韻答岵齋重九前一日登黃鶴樓. At Yuezhou 岳州 on 09:25, Qin wrote a preface for two books authored by Lê, 'A review and criticism of books' 群書考辨 and 'Records of model sages and nobles' 聖模賢範錄, and signed off with 'Written on a boat at Dongting Lake' 書於洞庭舟次 (see Nguyễn & Nguyễn, this volume, for more details). Some rejoinders by Qin may also be found in 'Quế Đường collection of poems' 桂堂詩集.

Cross currents: cross-border encounters between East Asian literati

As shown in 'Travelogues to Peking', Chosŏn envoys frequently encountered their counterparts from Vietnam and Ryukyu and had close contacts with them during their journey to Peking. Given that speech-based communication was not an option due to a lack of a shared spoken language, they had to rely on writing-mediated Sinitic brush-talk for conducting 'silent conversation'.

In 1868, Vietnam dispatched a mission to China. Nguyễn Tư Giản 阮思僩 was appointed as the Second commissioner with the title 'Vice-president of the Court of Ceremonies' 鴻臚寺少卿. In his travelogues all bearing the expression 燕軺 ('on the journey to Yan by carriage'), some brushed encounters with Chosŏn envoys were recorded, providing valuable data concerning Vietnamese-Korean diplomatic and poetic exchange through brush conversation. In the following year (1869), the day when Nguyễn and his entourage arrived at Peking, they came across a few Chosŏn envoys on the street. After recording fine details of their attire meticulously, Nguyễn felt inspired and improvised two poetic verses (compare Jang, this volume):

却喜朝鮮門館近　Delightful to know the lodging is so close to where Chosŏn envoys stay,
相逢略識古衣冠　Ancient clothes and hats seem familiar despite [our] chance encounter.

The clothing style of the Ming dynasty differed from that of the Qing drastically. Both Vietnamese and Korean literati were more strongly emotionally attached to Ming clothing style; no wonder the Vietnamese envoys perceived a sense of intimacy and felt affectionately close to their Korean peers. The next day, three Chosŏn envoys Kim Yu-yŏn 金有淵 (1819–1887), Nam Chŏng-sun 南廷順, and Cho Pyŏng-ho 趙秉鎬 (1847–1910) paid a formal visit at the lodging of the Vietnamese envoys by writing a letter that contained several poems as a gift. Nguyễn responded gratefully with a pentasyllabic quatrain as follows:

邈爾東南海	Between [your] East Sea and [my] South Sea is a great distance.
相逢燕薊中	[Such a] chance encounter [we had] in Peking.
候門未半面	Never before have [we] met in court.
問俗本三同	Conversing shows three things [we have] in common.[9]

In his written reply, Nguyễn further noted that:

僕昨日進館，於紅塵陌上邂逅相遇，車馳馬驟，不及通揖，而衣裳古制，金玉盛儀，獲我心矣。... 未能投帖請見，不謂先施之雅，紅帖忽來。

I was entering the lodge yesterday and happened to meet [you] on a flourishing street. The traffic was so busy, leaving no time for greeting. Yet [your] clothing style indicative of the ancient [Han Chinese] model, ornamented with jade and gold, has captured my heart.... [I] regretted missing the chance to request meeting [you] with a formal invitation. Such a pleasant surprise [to see your] red invitation note; what an elegant move [on your part]!

Before the Chosŏn envoys returned home, Nguyễn composed a heptasyllabic octave to commemorate their encounter and separation:

傾蓋燕臺樂未終	Though the joy of first encounter in Peking is not over yet.
泥鴻去影已匆匆	Departure footprints and shadows have hurried by.
歸心鴨綠花開外	Beholding Yalu River [your] home-coming hearts bloom with flowers.
清夢龍池柳色中	The court of Qing China is covered in green willows.
萬里關山難送客	Visitors from afar, so hard to see them off.
四洲人物幾同風	So close are people from four nations sharing similar cultural roots.
別君更憶·蚪髯傳·	[Your] departure evokes memories of the 'Qiuranke legend'.
西海如今漸向東	West Sea is now heading east.

Nguyễn further added:

萍蹤偶合，藉翰墨通殷勤，喜可知也。 顧此旬日間，纔得霎時晤對，今又永言別矣。客中送客，情何可喻！

---

[9] That they were born in the same year, passed the civil service examination in the same year, and worked in a similar office.

[In our] chance encounters, wanderers got to know one another through brush and ink. How delightful! Looking back our fleeting rendezvous over the last ten days, the time has come for permanent separation. Seeing guests off in a foreign country, what complex emotions!

This prompted all three envoys to respond by composing poetic verses. Kim Yu-yŏn wrote a pentasyllabic quatrain:

海濱各有國	Both our countries border on the sea,
但識輿圖中	[We] know [them] only on the map.
證契奇緣合	United in [our] fateful encounter is harmony,
論詩逸格同	How gracefully sublime and similar is [our] poetry.

Nam Chŏng-sun then composed a rejoinder:

山河應有異	Mountains and rivers should be different,
翰墨自相同	But brush and ink are essentially the same.

Zhao Binghao echoed:

交契三生重	Friendship is important for [our] past, present and future existence,
車書四海同	Tracks of chariots and how we write are the same in [our] universe.

All this illustrates nicely the affordance of writing-mediated brush conversation, including the improvisation of calligraphically aesthetic and emotionally appealing poetic verses.

Brush-talk literature: East Asian diplomatic envoys (Part 3)

From the East Asian perspective, 'Travelogues to Peking' 燕行錄 is no isolated dataset. There is a parallel dataset consisting of brush-talk records produced by Chosŏn envoys dispatched to Japan during the same period, which are generally referred to as 'travelogues of *t'ongsinsa* missions' 使行錄. In the same period, Korean envoys to Japan were called 'messengers' (*t'ongsinsa* 通信使), among other titles. Like 'Travelogues to Peking', 'travelogues of *t'ongsinsa* missions' also contain a large number of brush-talk interactions. In China, these two types of literature have been neglected; there is plenty of room for making new discoveries in historiographic research.

T'ongsinsa: *rectification of the name*

According to the 'National History Dictionary (of Japan)' 国史大辞典, *t'ongsinsa* 通信使 refers to a diplomatic mission dispatched by the king of Chosŏn to present a letter of credence 書契 (國書) and a list of gifts to the Tokugawa General, hence it was also called *Chosŏn t'ongsinsa* 朝鮮通信使, *Chosŏn sinsa* 朝鮮信使, among other titles. The earliest mention of *t'ongsinsa* appeared in volume 30 of 'An abridged history of Koryŏ' 高麗史節要 edited by Kim Chong-sŏ et al. 金宗瑞等 (1452): 'Dispatch of *t'ongsinsa* Na Hŭng-yu [羅興儒] to Japan' 送通信使興儒於倭. He was dispatched to Japan in 1375 to persuade the Japanese government to thwart piracy, which was rampant along the southern coast of Korea.[10] To manage international relations, the Chosŏn dynasty (1392–1910) adopted a two-tier principle: 'serve the great, and befriend the neighbors' 事大交鄰, whereby they looked to Ming dynasty as the superior suzerain, while maintaining good neighborly relations with surrounding states on an equal footing. Ming dynasty being the suzerain, the missions to Peking were led by 'envoys to Celestial Empire' 朝天使; after Ming gave way to Qing 'barbarians', the missions were renamed as 'journeys to Peking' 燕行使. Since the Sui (581–618) and Tang (618–907) dynasties, successive kingdoms on the Korean Peninsula succumbed to Japanese military prowess, and so the envoys dispatched to Japan were called 'tribute envoys' 調貢使. But this changed under the Chosŏn dynasty, who wished to emphasize parity in political status. The term *t'ongsinsa* 通信使, with its intended meaning of 'cultivating friendly relations' 通好, was used to reinforce this point.

The official Korean title of the first three missions to Edo Japan (1607, 1617, 1624) was called 'Respond-cum-Return Envoy' 回答兼刷還使, clearly in reference to Toyotomi's invasions of Chosŏn in 1592 and 1597, which did much to destabilize the international order of East Asia. Afterward, whereas Japan was keen on demanding Chosŏn to resume sending tributary missions 朝貢, Chosŏn insisted on using the word 'respond' 回答, while at the same time urging Japan to 'return' 刷還 Korean war prisoners, hence a *double entente* built into the title of the 'Respond-cum-Return Envoy'. The third mission (1624) was occasioned by Japan's request to send envoys to commemorate the accession of Tokugawa Iemitsu 德川家光 to the rank of General. Thereafter, in subsequent appointments of Generals in the Japanese military, the Chosŏn would send envoys to commemorate the events, hence the alternative title of the envoys as 'Messengers acting on the King's behalf' 御代替信使, or *t'ongsinsa* 通信使 in general.

Number of t'ongsinsa *missions*

How many *t'ongsinsa* missions did Chosŏn dispatch to Japan? Existing records are inconsistent, mainly because *t'ongsinsa* may be defined differently, in a broad or narrow sense. Broadly speaking, there were 19 or 20 missions (1412–1811), depending on whether the first one (1412) should be considered as a stand-alone mission. Interpreted in a narrow sense, *t'ongsinsa* missions referred to those which took place

---

10 "判典客寺事羅興儒上書, 請行成日本. 乃以興儒爲通信使. 遣之." (Cited from 高麗史節要. 卷 30: 辛禑一: 禑王元年 (1375): 二月.) The author is grateful to JANG Jin-youp 張眞熀 of Sungshin Women's University for this quotation and source.

during the Edo period, altogether 12 times (1607–1811, see Jang; and Koo & Joo, this volume). The periodization in Japan was different. There were six *t'ongsinsa* missions during the Muromachi period (室町時代 1336–1573), twice the Sengoku period (戦国時代 1467–1568), and 12 times the Edo period (江戸時代 1603–1868).

Whereas the Japanese side asked Chosŏn to send envoys to commemorate the inauguration of Japanese generals, the Chosŏn side demanded Japan to thwart or stop Japanese piracy. During the Sengoku period, Toyotomi no Hideyoshi invaded Chosŏn and ordered Chosŏn to subordinate to Japan as part of his ambition and plan to become the hegemon of East Asia. Chosŏn, on the other hand, was mindful of Japan's further assault, and so they sent envoys to Japan to gather intelligence and to better understand Japan's intention (Clements 2019). The Edo period saw 12 *t'ongsinsa* missions, the first three times trying to deal with postwar problems, the remaining nine missions were motivated by transcultural exchange. Details of the 20 missions are listed in Table 2.1.

Overview of Chosŏn t'ongsinsa *visits to Japan*

A Chosŏn mission to Japan generally consisted of a retinue of about 500 led by three envoys (*t'ongsinsa* 通信使): the Chief-Envoy (正使), Vice-Envoy (副使), and the Third-Envoy (從事官 or 書狀官).[11] Other members would include general secretaries, an 'official in charge of writing' (*chesulgwan* 製述官), painters, medical doctors, military officers, and interpreters (for more details about the ranks and files of initial Chosŏn missions, see WANG Yong 2018: 20). Of particular interest is that the official in charge of writing was added upon the request of the Japanese side beginning from the third Chosŏn mission to Edo Japan (1624), the stipulated purpose being to strengthen academic exchange, in effect re-defining the official role of Chosŏn envoys from diplomats to cultural ambassadors.

In terms of transport arrangements, in general six vessels were deployed, with one being assigned to each of the three envoys, the rest to be loaded with gifts. The mission would normally depart from Seoul for Pusan 釜山, then set sail to Tsushima 対馬 of Kyushu before crossing the Seto Inland Sea 瀬戸内海 toward Ōsaka and then the final destination Edo (today's Tokyo). Some members of the mission would attend the formal welcome ceremony at Nikkō 日光 upon the request of the Bakufu. Toward the end of 2006, major newspapers in South Korea published an advertisement with the heading 'Yokoso! Japan' placed by Japanese Prime Minister Abe Shinzo 安倍晋三 and his wife, in which the last paragraph made explicit reference to *t'ongsinsa* visits from Chosŏn:

> 2007年將迎來'朝鮮通信使四百周年'.朝鮮通信使是江戶時代朝鮮派往德川幕府的外交使節團, 從九州的對馬登陸, 沿途經過許多城市, 最終抵達江戶及日光, 當時的江戶幕府舉國上下予以歡迎. (Original in Japanese, translated by author into Chinese)

---

11 The title 從事官 (Third-Envoy) was used during the twelve *t'ongsinsa* missions to Edo Japan. The corresponding title used for missions before the Imjin war (1592–1598) was 書狀官.

East Asian brush-talk literature 69

Table 2.1 Details of twenty *t'ongsinsa* missions to Japan

No.	Year according to Japanese reign	Year according to Korean reign	Common era	Reigning monarch	Chief-Envoy	Japan's stipulated reason(s) of visit	Chosŏn's stipulated reasons(s) of visit	No. of people in a mission
01	Ōei 20 應永20年	T'aejong 13 太宗13年	1412	Ashikaga Yoshimochi 足利義持	Pak Pun 朴賁	–	Urge Japan to stop piracy, collect intelligence	Aborted
02	Eikyō 1 永享元年	Sejong 11 世宗十一年	1429	Ashikaga Yoshinori 足利義教	Pak Sŏ-saeng 朴瑞生	Celebrate the appointment of the new shogun, mourn the passing of the former shogun	Celebrate the appointment of the new shogun, mourn the passing of the former shogun	–
03	Eikyō 11 永享十一年	Sejong 21 世宗廿一年	1439	Ibid.	Ko Tŭk-chong 高得宗	Restore diplomatic relations	Restore dispatch of envoys bilaterally, urge Japan to stop piracy	–
04	Kakitsu 3 嘉吉三年	Sejong 25 世宗廿五年	1443	Ashikaga Yoshikatsu 足利義勝	Pyŏn Hyo-mun 卞孝文	Celebrate the appointment of the new shogun, mourn the passing of the former shogun	Celebrate the appointment of the new shogun, mourn the passing of the former shogun	approx. 50
05	Kanshō 1 寬正元年	Sejo 5 世祖五年	1460	Ashikaga Yoshimasa 足利義政	Song Ch'ŏ-kŏm 宋處儉	Request for the Chinese *Buddhist Canon* 大藏經	Send envoy to reply to the king of Japan, present gifts including *Chinese Buddhist Canon*	approx. 100
06	Bunmei 11 文明十一年	Sŏngjong 10 成宗十年	1479	Ashikaga Yoshinao 足利義尚	Yi Hyŏng-wŏn 李亨元	?	Restore diplomatic relations	–

(Continued)

Table 2.1 (Continued)

No.	Year according to Japanese reign	Year according to Korean reign	Common era	Reigning monarch	Chief-Envoy	Japan's stipulated reasons(s) of visit	Chosŏn's stipulated reasons(s) of visit	No. of people in a mission
07	Tenshō 18 天正十八年	Sŏnjo 23 宣祖廿三年	1590	Toyotomi no Hideyoshi 豊臣秀吉	Hwang Yun-kil 黃允吉	Urge Chosŏn to accept the status of being Japan's tributary	Celebrate unity under Heaven, find out whether Japan intends to invade Chosŏn	–
08	Keichō 1 慶長元年	Sŏnjo 29 宣祖廿九年	1596	ibid	Hwang Sin 黃愼	Urge Chosŏn to surrender and sign an armistice	Cultivate friendship, request Japan to withdraw troops	309
09	Keichō 12 慶長十二年	Sŏnjo 40 宣祖四十年	1607	Tokugawa Hidetada 德川秀忠	Yŏ U-kil 呂祐吉	Restore diplomatic relations	Maintain amicable relations with Japan, repatriate prisoners of war, collect intelligence	504
10	Genna 3 元和三年	Kwanghaegun 9 光海君九年	1617	ibid	O Yun-kyŏm 吳允謙	Celebrate the quelling of uprising in Osaka and unification of the country	Collect intelligence, repatriate prisoners of war, contain the Tsushima domain	428
11	Kan'ei 1 寛永元年	Injo 2 仁祖二年	1624	Tokugawa Iemitsu 德川家光	Chŏng Rip 鄭岦	Celebrate Iemitsu's appointment as the new shogun	Celebrate the appointment of the new shogun, repatriate prisoners of war, collect intelligence	460
12	Kan'ei 13 寛永十三年	Injo 14 仁祖十四年	1636	ibid	Im Kwang 任絖	Celebrate peace	Affirm Japan's policies toward Chosŏn, support Lord of Tsushima domain, discuss strategies dealing with China	478
13	Kan'ei 20 寛永二十年	Injo 21 仁祖二十一年	1643	ibid	Yun Sun-chi 尹順之	Celebrate the birth of Ietsuna and extension of Nikkō Temple	Maintain amicable relations, contain Qing China, collect intelligence	477

14	Meireki 1 明暦元年	Hyojong 6 孝宗六年	1655	Tokugawa Ietsuna 德川家綱	Cho Hyŏng 趙珩	Celebrate Ietsuna's appointment as the new shogun	Celebrate the appointment of the new shogun	478
15	Tenna 2 天和二年	Sukjong 8 肅宗八年	1682	Tokugawa Tsunayoshi 德川綱吉	Yun Chi-wan 尹趾完	Celebrate Tsunayoshi's appointment as the new shogun	Celebrate the appointment of the new shogun	473
16	Shōtoku 1 正德元年	Sukjong 37 肅宗三十七年	1711	Tokugawa Ienobu 德川家宣	Cho T'ae-ŏk 趙泰億	Celebrate Ienobu's appointment as the new shogun	Celebrate the appointment of the new shogun	500
17	Kyōhō 4 享保四年	Sukjong 45 肅宗四十五年	1719	Tokugawa Yoshimune 德川吉宗	Hong Ch'i-chung 洪致中	Celebrate Yoshimune's appointment as the new shogun	Celebrate the appointment of the new shogun	475
18	Kan'en 1 寬延元年	Yŏngjo 24 英祖二十四年	1748	Tokugawa Ieshige 德川家重	Hong Kye-hŭi 洪啟禧	Celebrate Ieshige's appointment as the new shogun	Celebrate the appointment of the new shogun	477
19	Meiwa 1 明和元年	Yŏngjo 40 英祖四十年	1764	Tokugawa Ieharu 德川家治	Cho Ŏm 趙曮	Celebrate Ieharu's appointment as the new shogun	Celebrate the appointment of the new shogun	477
20	Bunka 8 文化八年	Sunjo 11 順祖十一年	1811	Tokugawa Ienari 德川家齊	Kim I-kyo 金履喬	Celebrate Ienari's appointment as the new shogun	Celebrate the appointment of the new shogun	327

2007 will usher in the '400th anniversary of Chosŏn *t'ongsinsa* visits to Japan'. Chosŏn envoys and their retinue were dispatched by the Chosŏn government to Tokugawa Japan on diplomatic missions during the Edo period. They landed at Tsushima of Kyushu, passing through many cities before finally arriving at Edo and Nikkō. They would then be officially welcomed by the Tokugawa government at Edo nation-wide.

Just as Japanese ambassadors to Tang China were regarded as a symbol of Sino-Japanese friendship, so the *t'ongsinsa* visits were seen as a symbol of friendly relations between Chosŏn and Japan in addition to their role as cultural ambassadors. This helps explain why the history of *t'ongsinsa* visits is such a popular research topic within the academic circles in Japan and Korea.

'Battle of writing' 文戰 *or 'brush battle'* 筆戰 between Chosŏn and Japan

At that time, diplomatic relations between Chosŏn and Japan were delicate. Japan prided itself as a 'bukoku' 武國 unsurpassed in military prowess, while Chosŏn was conceited about her flair in classical writing 文邦, whose literary and cultural superiority was believed to be unparalleled. As bemoaned by Nakai Chikuzan 中井竹山 in *Sōbōkigen* 草茅危言 regarding the 1764 *t'ongsinsa* visit that he witnessed:

> 朝鮮既不能以武力勝我，遂欲以文事淩駕於我，誠如新筑州之《五事略》所論。因乘我邦學疏，欺我無知，道中鹵簿建"巡視""清道""令"之旗，無禮之極。

> Chosŏn could not defeat us by force, so it wanted to dominate us through literary writing and culture. Like Shin Chikushu's 'Five Events' (*Gojiryaku*), the Koreans took advantage of our ignorance and lack of book knowledge. On the way, the imperial procession used flags and banners with words like 'inspection tour' 巡視, 'clear way for passage' 清道, 'command or order' 令. That was extremely impudent.

The way the Koreans referred to the Japanese – 'dwarf' (*wae* 倭) or 'barbarian' (*man* 蠻) – was reminiscent of the Korean king talking 'down' to them. By contrast, the Koreans were addressed or referred to by the Japanese as 'Tang people' 唐人 or 'efflorescence' 華, reflecting their respect by talking 'up' to the Koreans. One instructive example may be found in the brush-talk interaction between Sin Yu-han 申維翰 (1681–1752) and Amenomori Hōshu 雨森芳洲 (1668–1755) as follows:

> 余又問：貴國人呼我曰'唐人'，題我人筆帖曰'唐人筆跡'，亦何意？

> I then asked: People in your esteemed country [Japan] call us 'Tang people' and describe our writing as 'Tang people's handwriting'. What does that mean?

> 東曰：國令則使稱客人，或稱朝鮮人。而日本大小民俗，自古謂貴國文物與中華同，故指以唐人，是慕之也。（青泉集續集 卷八）

Amenomori said: [Our] state policy is to address Chosŏn envoys as guests or Koreans. Since ancient times Japanese folk customs, big and small, recognize the culture and things in your esteemed country as the same as those of 'central efflorescence', China. This is why we refer to you as 'Tang people', as an act of admiration.[12]

('Sequel to the collected works of Ch'ŏngch'ŏn' 青泉集續集, vol. 8)[13]

Early *t'ongsinsa* envoys, on the other hand, generally had a very low opinion of Japan.[14] For this reason, whenever Chosŏn envoys arrived in Japan, the Tokugawa court would select the most talented Confucianists to receive them, suggesting subtly that culturally Japan was not at all inferior. This is thus the background to the extended 'battle of writing' or 'brush battle' between Chosŏn Korea and Edo Japan (see Jang, this volume).

Brush conversation, poetic improvisation, and chanting

There is plenty of evidence that brush conversation and poetic improvisation and chanting 唱和 was a common interactional practice between Japanese and Korean literati of Sinitic. In volume 108 of 'Full record of sea traffic' 通航一覽, Hayashi Fukusai 林復齋 (1850) wrote:

> 彼使者每來聘，必有筆談唱和。天和（1682年）、正德（1711年）之頃，其事益盛，故其成書冊者至百有數十卷。

> Every time the Chosŏn envoy comes to visit us, brush conversation, poetic improvisation and chanting will take place. The scale was especially large during the Chosŏn missions to Japan in 1682 (the 2nd year of the Tenna 天和 era) and 1711 (the 1st year of the Shōtoku 正德 era); the number of compilations of brush-talk records amounted to well over one hundred volumes.

In 'Submission to the Secretary of Chosŏn Vice-Envoy Wŏn Hyŏn-ch'ŏn' 呈朝鮮國副使書記元玄川, Ishikawa Kinkoku 石川金谷 (1737–1779) wrote in volume 1, 'Resonances after meeting Chosŏn envoys' 問槎餘響卷上:

> 不愁相值方言異，清興熟時揮彩毫。

> No concern at all about diverse vernacular languages during our encounters, wielding the brush of colors lends expression to enthusiasm of the sober mind.

---

12 This may reflect Amenomori's own personal opinion. In the late Tokugawa period, the term '唐人' was used as a general term to refer to 'Chinese' or 'foreigners'.
13 Ch'ŏngch'ŏn 青泉 was the pen name of Sin Yu-han 申維翰. This is also cited in his travelogue to Japan 'Record of sea travel' 海遊錄, which was later compiled into his collected works: See 海遊錄[下], 附聞見雜錄.
14 See, e.g., the commentary by Nam Yong-ik 南龍翼 (1628–1692) during the sixth *t'ongsinsa* mission to Japan in 1655 (WANG Yong 2018: 21).

Many brush-talk records by Chosŏn envoys point to Japanese literati's addiction to collecting brush-talk artifacts containing Chinese characters 漢字 or *kanji* as they are known in Japan. Soliciting poetry from Chosŏn travelers during their mission to Japan was a very common scene indeed (see Aoyama, this volume). Take Sin Yu-han's account as an example. In volume one of 'Miscellaneous observations and notes of travel by sea' 海遊錄(附)聞見雜錄, under the section 'Customs' 風俗, he wrote:

日本人求得我國詩文者，勿論貴賤賢愚，莫不仰之如神仙，貨之如珠玉。即舁人、廝卒目不知書者，得朝鮮楷草數字，皆以手攢頂而謝。所謂文士，或不遠千里而來待於站館。一宿之間，或費紙數百幅。求詩而不得，則雖半行筆談，珍感無已。蓋其人生長於精華之地，素知文字之可貴。而與中華絕遠，生不見衣冠盛儀，居常仰慕朝鮮。故其大官、貴遊則得我人筆語為誇耀之資，書生則為聲名之路，下賤則為觀瞻之地。書贈之後，必押圖章以為真跡。每過名州巨府，應接不暇。(青泉集續集 卷七)

The Japanese who solicit and obtain poetry from our nation, be they noble or ignoble, wise or foolish, would deem it as worthy of the fairies, precious like pearls or jade. Sedan porters and coolies alike, they may not know what the writing is about; upon receiving several brushed characters from a Chosŏn literatus, they would place their hands above their heads to express gratitude. Those who are literate would travel from afar and wait patiently at the travel lodge. The whole night, paper lined with scribbles may stack up to hundreds of pieces. If a person's entreaty for poetry is futile, half a line of brushed response would make him feel gratified. People growing up in an elitist environment know how precious Chinese characters are. Central efflorescence of China being so remote, civilized clothing including proper headdresses, and lavish ceremonies are nowhere to be seen. This makes Chosŏn people so admirable. Senior officials and nobles will cherish our brushed artifacts for the convenience of bragging in front of others; students will find them useful for their future road to fame; while the lowly will display them as objects of appreciation. For authentication, brushed artifacts must be impregnated with a seal before being gifted. When passing through affluent places and sizable residences, I was terribly busy serving [i.e. writing for] them).

(cited from 'Sequel to the collected works of Ch'ŏngch'ŏn', vol. 7)

Likewise, according to the record of Chief-Envoy Cho Ŏm 趙曮 (1719–1777) dated 10:06, 1763 in 'Diary of travel by sea' 海槎日記:

前後信使，毋論使臣員役，多有日記者。洪尚書啟禧廣加搜集，名以《海行總載》，徐副學命膺翻謄之，題以《息波錄》，合為六十一編，以為行中考閱之資。... 余固未及詳覽，而概見之。

Most of the envoys on a Chosŏn mission and others in the retinue, regardless of their official ranks and responsibilities, would keep a diary. These were collected extensively by Hong Kye-hŭi 洪啟禧, and the compilation was given the title 'Total collection of travel by sea' 海行總載. The content was then adapted by Sŏ Myŏng-ŭng 徐命膺 into 61 volumes and renamed as 'Calming waves' [*Sikp'a'nok* 息波錄, metaphorically meaning 'making peace between Korea and Japan'], the purpose being to make it easier for the reader to examine every voyage in detail. . . . But I did not read it in detail.

The 1763–64 Chosŏn mission yielded plenty of diary-like recollections of brush-talk and/or poetic improvisations produced during the envoys' writing-mediated interaction with their Japanese hosts, including 'Diary of travel by sea' 海槎日記 by Chief-Envoy Cho Ŏm 趙曮; 'Sights of Japan' 日觀記 and 'Sights and socializing poetic chanting in Japan' 日觀唱酬 by *chesulgwan* Nam Ok 南玉 (1722–1770); 'Record of Japan' 日本錄 by Chief-Envoy's secretary Sŏng Tae-chung 成大中 (1732–1812); 'Record of sailing' 乘槎錄 and 'Record of Japan' 和國志 by Vice-Envoy's secretary Wŏn Chung-kŏ 元重擧 (1719–1790), the latter being an encyclopedic treatise on Japan.

The extent and scale of the Japanese literati's enthusiasm may be gauged by Wŏn's observation in 'Writing after Naba Kyōkei's *Journey to the East*' 書那波孝卿東遊卷後, as follows:

> 築之東，武之西，三四月之間，揖讓一千餘人，酬唱二千餘篇。
>
> From the east of Chikuzen to the west of Musashi, between the third and fourth lunar months [of 1764], [we] greeted well over one thousand people; [the number of poems we] improvised and chanted amounted to well over 2,000.

Statistically, according to the official in charge of writing and the three secretaries, the total number of poems improvised in Japan during the Chosŏn mission of 1763–64 amounted to 4,000 (see also Jang, this volume).

Brush-talk literature involving Chosŏn envoys to Japan (t'ongsinsa *missions*)

Chosŏn envoys to Japan and their Japanese hosts were regularly engaged in brush conversation as well as poetic improvisation and exchange. Some of these artifacts have survived intact in Japan and are accessible in public or private libraries, while others are preserved in temples and shrines. Careful selection, editing, and compilation have yielded several large-scale book series and scholarly works.[15]

---

15 These include: the eight-volume 'Collection of Chosŏn envoys to Japan' 大系朝鮮通信使 (Sin Ki-su & Nakao Hiroshi [辛基秀、仲尾宏], published by Akashi Bookstore, 1994); 'A manuscript on the catalogue of Chosŏn envoys' poetic improvisation and chanting' 朝鮮通信使唱和集目錄稿 (Takahashi Masahiko [高橋昌彦], published by Fukuoka University, 2007, 2009); and 'Research on Chosŏn envoys to Japan' 朝鮮通信使之研究 (Yi Wŏn-sik [李元植], published by Shibunkaku, 1997).

Judging from existing records and materials, brush conversation intertwined with poetic improvisation and exchange first emerged during the *t'ongsinsa* mission in 1636 and became very popular in 1711. A total of 169 sets of such materials collected from 1636 to 1811 have survived. Two long lists of brush-talk titles produced during the *t'ongsinsa* missions of 1711 (n=31) and 1719 (n=26) may be found in WANG Yong (2018: 23–25).

Of course, these brush-talk titles represent only the body of *t'ongsinsa* literature that has been preserved in Japan. There exists a separate collection of *t'ongsinsa* literature in Korea. But even in Japan, there are brush-talk materials scattered in other works awaiting scholarly research. For instance, Hayashi Razan 林羅山, a great Edo Confucian scholar, is known to have engaged in brush-talk with Chosŏn envoys many times in 1607, 1617, 1624, 1636, and 1643. These brush-talk records have been incorporated into his anthology under 'Brush-talk with Korean guests' 韓客筆語.

Brush-talk literature involving boat drifters in East Asia

Of the different types of brush-talk literature, those involving boat drifters resulting from shipwreck are huge and extremely diverse, making it difficult to identify, defying research efforts of systematic categorization. The exchange of people and materials between East Asian countries mainly relied on maritime trading routes extending in all directions. During the premodern era when shipbuilding technologies and navigation know-how were still underdeveloped, it was quite common, even routine, to find boats drifting ashore in alien waters after being blown off course by strong winds under extreme weather conditions at sea. Whenever such shipwreck incidents occurred, out of administrative need or coastal defense protocol depending on the location, the maritime officials in charge would interrogate the boat drifters meticulously, in most cases with interpreting being unavailable to either side. Writing-mediated brush conversation was basically the mode of communication by default, thence sizable amounts of brush-talk records were generated periodically.

Judging from observable trends in academia, the Chinese and Japanese boat drifters, especially those who drifted from China to Japan, have attracted more scholarly attention, as shown in the compilations of original brush-talk materials by Ōba Osamu 大庭脩 and Matsuura Akira 松浦章 in Japan, Meng Xiaoxu 孟曉旭 and Liu Xufeng 劉序楓 in China, among others. By contrast, there is not much research concerning Japanese boat drifters in China and South Asia, Chinese boat drifters in Chosŏn and Ryukyu, not to mention those from Western countries whose vessels ended up in various East Asian waters unexpectedly.

Brush-talk records involving Chinese boat drifters in Japan

Ōba Osamu of Kansai University was among the first scholars to recognize the value of historical materials involving boat drifters whose ships wrecked and were blown ashore in alien land. He collated the written records and compiled

East Asian brush-talk literature 77

them into the 'Collections of information on the drifting of Tang ships during the Edo Period' 江戶時代漂着唐船資料集, which appeared in a series beginning from 1985. Ōba's research endeavor was further pursued by his student, Matsuura Akira 松浦章. A total of nine titles under the series 'Sources and materials series, Institute of Oriental and Occidental Studies, Kansai University' 関西大學東西學術研究所資料集刊 have been published (see Table 2.2).

The compilations listed in Table 2.2 contain large numbers of (i) transcripts of original interrogations in the form of questions and answers by local maritime and central government officials in Japan, and (ii) brush conversations and spontaneous poetic improvisation and chanting between foreign boat drifters and Japanese literati from different parts of the country.

Brush-talk records involving Chinese boat drifters in Korea

During the Ming and Qing dynasties, China's commercial and economic activities were already burgeoning, unlike neighboring countries which basically adopted a

Table 2.2 'Collection of information on the drifting of Tang ships during the Edo Period', no. 1–10 (江戶時代漂着唐船資料集一至十)

No.	Editor	Title (Japanese)	Title (English)
13–1	Ōba Osamu 大庭脩	寶曆三年八丈島漂着南京船資料	'Materials on the drifting of Nanking ships on Hachijō Island in 1753 (no. 1)'
13–2	Tanaka Kenji & Matsuura Akira 田中謙二、松浦章	文政九年遠州漂着得泰船資料	'Materials on the drifting Detai boat in Shizuoka Prefecture 1826 (no. 2)'
13–3	Matsuura Akira 松浦章	寬政元年土佐漂着安利船資料	'Materials on the drifting of the Anli boat at Kochi Prefecture in 1789 (no. 3)'
13–4	Matsuura Akira 松浦章	文化五年土佐漂着江南商船郁長發資料	'Materials on the drifting of the Jiangnan merchant ship Yuchangfa at Kochi Prefecture in 1808 (no. 4)'
13–5	Ōba Osamu 大庭脩	安永九年安房千倉漂着南京船元順號資料	'Materials on the drifting of the Nanking ship Yuanshun at Chikura (Awa) in 1780 (no. 5)'
13–6	Yabuda Yutaka 藪田貫	寬政十二年遠州漂着唐船萬勝號資料	'Materials on the drifting of the Tang ship Wansheng at Enshu (Shizuoka) in 1800 (no. 6)'
13–7	Matsuura Akira 松浦章	文政十年土佐浦戶漂着江南商船蔣元利資料	'Materials on the drifting of the Jiangnan merchant ship Jiang Yuanli at Kochi Prefecture in 1827 (no. 7)'
13–8	Matsuura Akira 松浦章	安政二・三年漂流小唐船資料	'Materials on the small drifting Chinese boats in 1855, 1856 (no. 8)'
13–9	Matsuura Akira 松浦章	文化十二年豆州漂着南京永茂船資料	'Materials on the Nanjing ship Yongmao in Shizuoka Prefecture in 1815 (no. 9)'
13–10	Matsuura Akira 松浦章	天保七年薩摩片浦南京船全勝號資料	'Materials on the Nanking ship Quansheng in Tatsuma Kataura in 1836 (no. 10)'

closed-door policy out of various concerns such as piracy. Compared with Japan and Chosŏn, therefore, Chinese merchant ships were much more visible and active at sea. One consequence is that large numbers of Chinese junks drifted ashore in Japan or Chosŏn after succumbing to extreme weather conditions in the coastal waters of East Asia. Mentions of Chinese boat drifters stranded in Chosŏn may be found, if scattered, in both public archives and private documents in Chosŏn. These materials were collocated and published recently: 'Chinese historical materials in the records of Chosŏn dynasty' 朝鮮李朝實錄中的中國史料 by Wu Han 吳晗, and 'Ming dynasty historical materials in the Korean collection of essays' 韓國文集中的明代史料 and 'Qing dynasty historical materials in the Korean collection of essays' 韓國文集中的清代史料 by Du Honggang 杜宏剛.

In addition, from the mid-sixteenth century to the mid-nineteenth century, the chronicles involving foreign affairs entitled 'Records of the Border Defense Council of Chosŏn' 備邊司謄錄 compiled by Chosŏn government officials contain a total of 273 volumes, giving details of how various issues of national import were discussed and handled, including decision-making processes. Of these, the transcripts of original official interrogations of boat drifters from China were reproduced intact. In Matsuura's 'Compilation of history materials in East Asian shipping during the Qing dynasty' 清代帆船東亞航運史料彙編,[16] details of 40 entries of drifting incidents involving Chinese boat drifters in *Records of the Border Defense Council of Chosŏn* 備邊司謄錄 were extracted (see Wong 2021; Matsuura & Aoyama, this volume).

Brush-talk records involving Chinese boat drifters in Vietnam

On 12:15, 1832, a junk loaded with rice from Guangdong was blown off course and drifted to Sơn Trà 山茶, Vietnam. The 70 crew members were rescued by local officials and residents. In the seventh lunar month of the following year, Vietnam sent envoys to escort the junk back to Humen 虎門 of the Pearl River estuary. The Vietnamese escort mission consisted of Lý Văn Phức 李文馥, Nguyễn Văn Chương 阮文章, Lê Văn Khiêm 黎文謙, Huỳnh Quýnh 黃炯, Nhữ Bá Sĩ 汝伯仕, among others. Nguyễn had visited Guangdong four years earlier in 1829 and was acquainted with Liu Wenlan 劉文瀾, a local literary figure. On that trip, he acquired ten copies of 'Literary composition game' 文章遊戲 written by Liu's friend Miao Gen 繆艮. After the Vietnamese mission in Guangdong had arrived, Liu prepared wine and delicacies to pay Nguyễn a visit and engaged in poetic improvisation and chanting together with Lý Văn Phức and Huỳnh Quýnh. While feasting, Nguyễn expressed his admiration of and obsession with the 'Literary composition game', and the wish to consult the author Miao Gen directly in person. Liu agreed to organize a gathering with not only Miao but also other local literary figures. The banquet attended by leading literary figures from Guangdong and Vietnam took place on 07:05, 1833 at Haizhu Temple 海珠寺. Apart from

---

16 Published by Lexis Book Company 樂學書店, Taipei, 2007.

six Vietnamese envoys, the Chinese side was represented by Liu, Miao, Liu's son Liu Boyang 劉伯陽 and Liu Boyang's teacher Liang Nanming 梁南溟. While the guests and hosts were inconvenienced by a lack of a shared spoken language, Sinitic brush-talk allowed all ten banquet participants to 'speak their mind' and lend expression to their emotions seamlessly through brush-talk, together yielding a total of 25 poems.

In the seventh lunar month of 1834, another Guangdong junk drifted to Vietnam. Again, an escort mission was formed by the Vietnamese government to repatriate the Chinese 'boat people' back to Guangdong. Entrusted in this mission were Lý Văn Phức 李文馥, Lê Bác Tú 黎伯秀, Nguyễn Đăng Uẩn 阮登蘊, Nguyễn Lạc Thiện 阮樂善, Lê Văn Hào 黎文豪, among others. Lý led the other envoys to visit Miao Gen; thereupon another Vietnamese-Chinese gathering of leading literary figures was arranged. Huỳnh Quýnh, who participated in the gathering in the previous year but could not make it this time, requested Lý to forward his poetic work entitled 'Delivering feelings' 寄懷 to Miao, to which he improvised rejoinders one by one.

Regarding the poetic encounters between Chinese and Vietnamese literary figures, the Qing literatus Chen Jiacan 陳家璨 wrote a preface for 'Miscellaneous notes on missions to Guangdong' 粵行雜草, which consisted of a collection of poems by Vietnamese north-bound envoys 北使詩集. There, Chen recalled that the Vietnamese escort envoys arrived at Guangdong:

與我粵名流唱酬屬和，或呼雲喝月，對酒當歌；或使墨驅煙，登高能賦	'[They] were engaged in poetic improvisation and chanting with Guangdong celebrities. [In the process, they] would summon the clouds and sing to the moon while sipping wine, or drive the fumes, climb high to compose verses with their ink-brush.'

Similarly, in the preface he wrote for Lý Văn Phức's 'Enchanting notes on the mission to Guangdong: A sequel' 粵行續吟草, Miao Gen portrayed the magnanimous gatherings of Chinese and Vietnamese literati as follows:

癸巳秋，越南國使李君隣芝，偕同官護送師船來粵。友人劉君墨池邀余，與隣芝諸君作中外群英會。觴詠之後，因得往來唱和，閱數月而別。	During the autumn of 1833, esteemed Vietnamese envoy Lý Lân Chi [= Lý Văn Phức] and his fellow officials escorted the vessel to Guangdong. My friend Liu Mochi [= Liu Wenlan] invited leading local literary figures to meet with foreign elites. Drinking wine and composing poems at the first meeting was followed by more invitational poetic improvisation and chanting, lasting for several months before [we] bid farewell.

A total of 88 poems were composed during the two gatherings of leading literary figures from China and Vietnam. Other artifacts produced included book prefaces, invitation letters, brief notes of brushed encounters, etc. Miao

Gen cherished the convergence of literary talents so much that he hand-copied them all as a personal souvenir. Later, Miao's friend Lu Ji 陸吉 compiled them into two volumes and published them with the title 'A record of encounters between Chinese and foreign literary figures' 中外群英會錄 to commemorate both enchanting occasions. The existing copy of *A record of encounters between Chinese and foreign literary figures* (also called 'Collection of poems arising from encounters between Chinese and foreign literary figures' 群英會詩) was a hand-copied version dated the eighth year of Qing emperor Guangxu (1882), now housed in the Institute of Sino-Nom Studies in Vietnam 院研究漢喃 (Chi: 漢喃研究院; call number A.2039). Three distinct calligraphic scripts – regular, running and cursive (楷、行、草) – are discernible, all marked with periods and commas.

Brush-talk records involving Japanese boat drifters

Japan being an island state surrounded by the sea, marine transportation was naturally crucial for communication with the outside world, but internal waterways were also important conduits for domestic transportation. This is why vessels of all kinds drifting to alien waters after being blown off course by strong winds were not uncommon. The boat-drifting literature 漂流記 constituted by this body of historical materials first attracted the attention of Japanese scholars. Among the published edited works are the following:

Ishii Kendō 石井研堂	'Complete collection of drifting tales (revised)' 校訂漂流奇談全集 (1900, published by Hakubunkan 博文館)
	'A collection of exotic drifting tales' 異國漂流奇譚集 (1927, Fukunaga Shoten 福永書店)
Arakawa Toshihide 荒川俊秀	'Historical materials of vessels drifting ashore in Japan' 日本漂流漂着史料 (1962, Yoshikawa Kōbunkan 吉川弘文館)
	'Collection of exotic drifting tales' 異國漂流記集 (1962, Yoshikawa Kōbunkan 吉川弘文館)
	'Collection of modern drifting tales' 近世漂流記集 (1969, Hosei University Press 法政大学出版局)

In addition, the 79 volumes of 'New knowledge learnt overseas' 海表異聞 compiled by Tetsusō Dojin 徹桑土人 also contain a large number of records involving boat drifting incidents and drifters. In the drifting records literature, there is no shortage of precious historical materials, including the poetic improvisation and chanting between Japanese boat drifters and Chinese and Chosŏn officials and gentry, as well as official documents and letters issued by the Chinese government. The 'Poems gifted to Japanese refugees' 贈倭國難民詩 included in the appendix of WANG Yong 王勇 (2018) is one such example. The aforementioned drifting records cover only those preserved in Japan. In fact, smaller amounts of drifting records are also found in China and Korea, awaiting discovery and careful research.

Brush-talk records involving Korean boat drifters

The datasets of Korean boat drifters to date have yet to be categorized and researched systematically. Based on my observation, more drifting records are preserved in Japan than in China and Korea. One instructive example is 'A record of drifting across the sea' 漂海錄 written by Chosŏn official Ch'oe Pu 崔溥 (1454–1504). In 1488, while returning to his hometown to attend a funeral, Ch'oe encountered a fierce storm at sea and drifted to the Taizhou Prefecture, Zhejiang Province 浙江台州府 bordering Linhai County 臨海縣 in China. After he was rescued, it took him four and a half months to travel north from Hangzhou along the Peking-Hangzhou Grand Canal to Peking, and then from Peking back to Chosŏn via the Amnok River (see Hur, this volume). It happened to be a time when Japanese pirates 倭寇 were rampant along the coasts of China. While the vessel was drifting at sea, Ch'oe Pu and his entourage encountered pirates. Interestingly, both sides resorted to brush conversation for negotiation. Later, upon being apprehended by Ming maritime officials, the Chosŏn seafarers were suspected to be Japanese pirates in disguise. Every passenger on board had to undergo interrogation, which was also conducted essentially through writing-mediated brush-talk.

A record of drifting across the sea is a travelogue of more than 50,000 characters. A wide range of topics are covered, including politics, military, economy, culture, transportation, landscape, and social customs as seen through the eyes of Ch'oe Pu during the late fifteenth century. The book thus has high reference value, especially in the historical study of Ming China's coastal defense, political and legal systems, various aspects of culture, geography but also landscape from canals and cities to general topography and, above all, interstate diplomatic relations between Chosŏn Korea and Ming China. Originally this detailed record was reserved as a 'secret report' for the Chosŏn King's reference exclusively. Subsequently published in 1571 after being declassified, it was reprinted several times in 1573, 1676, 1724, and 1896 in Korea (see Hur, this volume).

In 1769, this book was translated by Seita Kiminishiki 清田君錦 into Japanese and given the title 'Tang China Journey' 唐土行程記. Nearly two centuries later, an English version translated by John Meskill was published in 1965 (reprinted in 1994 as *Choe Pu's diary: a record of drifting across the sea*). In 1979, Ch'oe Ki-hong 崔基泓, a descendant of Ch'oe Pu, translated the original in Sinitic into contemporary Korean. Then in 1992, a version with Chinese commentaries by Ge Zhenjia 葛振家 of Peking University was published by the China Social Sciences Archives Press.

Drifting brush-talk records involving Western boat drifters

Christopher Columbus's ventures at sea and the opening up of new navigation routes to Asia in the fifteenth century enticed more and more Western missionaries, explorers, and merchants to the Far East. Although many would work very hard to learn the local languages, any attempt to master all the Asian languages of interest would be unrealistic and futile. That is one important reason why and how, when traveling within Sinographic East Asia, Westerners with literacy in written Chinese tended to find Sinitic brush-talk useful for understanding the locals and getting their meanings across. Brush conversation data involving Westerners is relatively scarce, but not without a trace. For example, in 1543, a Portuguese merchant ship setting off from South Asia for Ningbo 寧波, China was blown off course unexpectedly and drifted ashore on Tanegashima Island 種子島 in Japan. Due to language barriers, tension and hostility prevailed and skirmishes were about to break out between the seafarers and islanders. It was at this point that a Ming Chinese passenger on board the Portuguese vessel called Wufeng 五峰 tried to communicate with the chief of the island community by writing with a stick on sand 以杖書於沙上 as follows:

島主問: 舡中之客，不知何國人也。何其形之異哉！	Island chief asked: 'The passengers on board, [I] wonder what their nationality is. How come they look so queer!'
五峰答: 此是西南蠻種之賈胡也。粗雖知君臣之義，未知禮貌之在其中。... 以其所有易其所需而已，非可怪者矣。	Wufeng responded: 'They are a barbarian tribe from the southwest. Although they have some idea of the obligations binding the king and his ministers, they are hardly aware of rites and rituals . . . They just exchange what they have with what they need, not so strange.'

While it was clearly not brush conversation, this anecdote shows how an international crisis was defused through writing-mediated communication in Sinitic. More details may be found in 'The matchlock gun incident' (鉄砲記, Jap: *Teppōki*, Mand: *Tiepaoji*; see also WANG Baoping, this volume). Wufeng was the appellation of WANG Zhi 汪直, a merchant cum Confucian scholar whose mediation successfully turned hostility into friendship. Less well known is the fact that after this incident the Japanese islanders started buying cannons from the Portuguese, imitating and successfully manufacturing modern artillery firearms, then spreading them to different parts of the island. The historical significance of this incident can hardly be underestimated, for it accelerated the process of political unification across the Japanese archipelago. In addition, the 'Records of an envoy traveling by wagon to Peking' 燕轅直指 compiled by the Korean Kim Kyŏngsŏn 金景善 (1788–1853) is accompanied by 'A drifting ship from England' 英吉利國漂船記, where the plight of distressed British seafarers whose vessel drifted in East Asian waters was described in some detail. There, too, some writing-mediated brush-talk interactions may be found.

Brush-talk literature involving East Asian intellectuals

The aforementioned classification of brush-talk records is based on the types of brush-talkers conducting brush conversation in more or less well-defined historical contexts. Apart from diplomatic envoys and 'boat people' whose vessels drifted ashore in alien land, literati of Sinitic from different countries within Sinographic East Asia were also avid brush-talkers. Their salient characteristics are: well versed in written Chinese (Classical Chinese or Literary Sinitic), well informed about traditional Chinese culture, intellectually curious, and very eager to learn.

Brush conversations between Oka Senjin and Chinese people

Many examples may be cited here, but we will focus on a couple of better-known historical figures. Oka Senjin 岡千仞 (1833–1914) was a Sinologist whose name was relatively familiar to Chinese readers because he had published a travelogue entitled 'Diary on a sightseeing tour' 觀光紀遊 (1886), documenting his reflections during his China tour in 1884. While in Japan and traveling in China, he was engaged in brush conversation with a large number of Chinese literary figures and left behind a considerable amount of brush-talk records.

(1) 'Lotus pond brush-talk' 蓮池筆談, 1 Aug 1878, 11 folia in total. Brush-talk with Huang Zunxian 黃遵憲, Shen Wenying 沈文熒, and Wang Zhiben 王治本. Their deliberations centered on customs in China and Japan, reviews of and commentaries on Chinese poetry, and the current state of Sinology research, and so forth.[17]

(2) 'Banquet brush conversation' 清讌筆話, 20 Sep 1878, six folia in total. Oka Senjin's brush-talk with Shen Wenying on the relocation of the Chinese embassy, the compilation of 'History of the World' 萬國史, Japanese Sinologists, etc.[18]

(3) 'Brush-talk with Huang Zunxian' 與黃遵憲筆談, content-wise focusing on Confucius temples in Japan, contrast between Chinese and Western scholarship, etc.[19]

(4) 'Brush-talk between Sheng Xuanhuai and Oka Senjin' 盛宣懷與岡千仞筆談, autumn-winter in 1884.[20]

(5) 'Brush-talk between Sheng Xuanhuai, Oka Senjin and Oka Sentaku' 盛宣懷與岡千仞、岡千濯筆談. Same time frame as in (4).[21]

(6) 'Brush conversation' 筆話. Oka Senjin came to China in May 1884. His brush conversations with Shanghai literati on the 9th and 15th of June were serialized on July 9–11 in Japan's newspaper 'Yūbin Hōchi Shinbun' 郵便報知新聞.

---

17 This brush-talk is accessible from Special Collection 岡鹿門雜輯 ('Okarokumon Miscellaneous Series'), vol. 294, Tokyo Metropolitan Library.
18 Ibid.
19 Ibid., vol. 292.
20 For details, see Wang Erh-min [王爾敏] et al. (1993). 清季外交因應函電資料 ('Diplomatic response letters and telegrams in the Qing Dynasty'). Hong Kong: The Chinese University of Hong Kong Press.
21 Ibid.

Brush-talk between Chinese and Japanese civilians may be traced back to a long time ago. It took various forms involving people from different walks of life. For example, 'Keiho Brush-talk' 瓊浦筆語 is a record of brush conversations between Japanese literary figures and Chinese merchant shipowner Jiang Yunge 江芸閣. Similarly, Zhu Shunshui 朱舜水 (1600–1682), the late Ming Confucian scholar who spent 20 twilight years in Japan, was regarded as a great sage and teacher by many Japanese admirers and students. He left behind a huge amount of brush-talk materials (see Li 2020). Such a trend continued till the early twentieth century, as evidenced by brush-talk records involving the Japanese Sinologist Morohashi Tetsuji 諸橋轍次 (1883–1982) and Chinese intellectuals Hu Shi 胡適 (1891–1962), Zeng Guangjun 曾廣鈞 (1866–1929), Ye Dehui 葉德輝 (1864–1927), Chen Baochen 陳寶琛 (1848–1935), etc.

Sinitic brush-talk was naturally not limited to intellectuals from China and Japan; it was also commonly found between literati from China, Korea, Ryukyu, and Vietnam, and certainly not restricted to two countries. In some brush-talk records, officials and members of the gentry class from three or more nationalities were represented. The esteemed Jesuit missionary, Matteo Ricci's 利瑪竇 *De Christiana expeditione apud Sinas* (1615/1983) captures the following scene[22]:

> Japanese, Koreans, Cochinchina [today's Vietnam] and Ryukyuan people share a number of literary works, but their spoken languages are so different that no one can understand the others. However, they can all understand written language with the same meaning, but each ethnic group speaks its own vernacular.

Although the languages of East Asian countries are so different, they can 'express heartfelt feelings through brush and ink' 藉翰墨通殷勤, a telling description of the essence of writing-mediated brush-talk interaction.

References

Bae, Y.-H. [裴英姬] (2009). History of the *Yeon Haeng Rok*: A review article 《燕行錄》的研究史回顧 (1933–2008). *Historical Inquiry* 臺大歷史學報 43: 219–256.

Chen, J. [陳捷] (1997). 楊守敬集 ('Collected works of Yang Shoujing'). Wuhan, China: Hubei Education Press.

Chen, J. [陳捷] (1998). 楊守敬與宮島誠一郎的筆談記錄 ('Brushtalk records between Yang Shoujing and Miyajima Seiichirō'). 中國哲學研究 (Chinese Philosophical Studies) 12: 96–158.

Ch'oe, P. [崔溥] (1965). *Choe Pu's diary: A record of drifting across the sea* (John Meskill, Trans.). Tucson: The University of Arizona Press.

---

22 Source: Matteo Ricci (1615, 1615/1983). 利瑪竇中國札記 ('Matteo Ricci's notes on China,' trans. by He Gaoji et al. [何高濟等]), vol. 1, chapter 5, 關於中國人的人文科學, 自然科學及學位的運用 ('On the use of Chinese humanities, natural sciences and academic degree titles'). Peking: Zhonghua Book Company.

Clements, R. (2019). Brush talk as the 'lingua franca' of East Asian diplomacy in Japanese-Korean encounters, c. 1600–1868. *The Historical Journal* 62(2): 289–309.

Fairbank, J. K. (Ed.). (1968). *The Chinese world order: Traditional China's foreign relations*. Cambridge, MA: Harvard University Press.

Fuma, S., & Lim, K.-Z. [夫馬進、林基中] (2001). 燕行録全集日本所蔵編 ('The complete works of *Yanxinglu* collected by Japan'). Seoul: Research Institute of Korean Literature Studies, Dongguk University Press.

Koh, C.-S., & King, R. (2014). *Infected Korean language, purity versus hybridity: From the Sinographic Cosmopolis to Japanese colonialism to global English*. New York: Cambria Press.

Lan, J.-C. [藍日昌]. (2020). 筆談: 同文異音下的東亞文化交流 ('Pen talk: East Asian cultural exchange under the same words'). 中正漢學研究 (Chung Cheng Chinese Studies) 35(1): 189–208.

Li, D. C. S. (2020). Writing-mediated interaction face-to-face: Sinitic brushtalk (漢文筆談) as an age-old lingua-cultural practice in premodern East Asian cross-border communication. *China and Asia* 2(2): 193–233.

Lim, K.-Z. [林基中] (2001). 燕行録全集 ('Complete collection of travel journals of Chosŏn envoys to Peking'). Seoul: Dongguk University Press.

Pak, H.-R. [朴香蘭] (2011). 燕行録所載筆談的文学形式研究—以洪大容與朴趾源爲中心 ('A study of forms of brush-talk literature as seen in Travelogues to Peking, with special reference to Hong Tae-yong and Pak Chi-wŏn'). 世界文學評論 (World Literature Review) 2: 221–229.

Pak, H.-R. [朴香蘭] (2015). 北學派燕行録所載筆談研究 ('A study of the Northern School's collection of Chosŏn envoys' brushtalk records in their travelogues to Peking'). Changchun, China: Yanbian University Press.

Ricci, M. [利瑪竇] (1615). *De Christiana expeditione apud Sinas suscepta ab Societate Jesu: ex P. Matthaei Ricij eiusdem societatis comentarijs libri V: Ad S.D.N. Paulum V. in quibus Sinensis Regni mores leges atq. instituta & nouae illius ecclesiae difficillima primordia accurate & summa fide describuntur* (N. Trigault 金尼閣, Trans.). Augustae Vind: Apud Christoph Mangium.

Ricci, M. [利瑪竇] (1615/1983). 利瑪竇中國劄記 ('Matteo Ricci's notes on China'. G. He, Z. Wang & S. Li [何高濟、王遵仲、李申], Trans.). Peking: Zhonghua Book Company.

Suzuki, D. [鈴木道字] (1895/2015). 筆談自在：軍用日清會話 ('Japanese-Qing Chinese conversation for military use: pen-talk made easy'). In W. Li 李無未 (Ed.). 日本漢語教科書匯刊－江戸明治編 ('A collection of Chinese textbooks in Japan' – published in Edo and Meiji periods', pp. 13995–14177). Peking: Zhonghua Book Company.

Wang, B.-P. [王寶平] (Ed.). (2016). 日本藏晚清中日朝筆談資料：大河内文書 ('Late Qīng brush-talk materials in Japan – Collection of brush conversations between Chinese, Japanese and Koreans in Ōkōchi Documents'). Hangzhou, China: Zhejiang Ancient Books Publishing House.

Wang, E.-M. [王爾敏] et al. (1993). 清季外交因應函電資料 ('Diplomatic response letters and telegrams in the Qing Dynasty'). Hong Kong: The Chinese University of Hong Kong Press.

Wang, Y. [王勇] (2018). 東亞筆談文獻經眼録 ('A survey of the East Asian Sinitic brush-talk literature: An annotated bibliography'). Shanghai: Shanghai Jiaotong University Press.

Wong, T.-S. [黃得森] (2022). Chosŏn Border Defense Council's drifting records of Chinese vessels in early modern East Asia: A quantitative analysis of statistically salient place names and common nouns in the conversation records from Pibyŏnsa Tŭngnok (1687–1880). *China and Asia* 3(1).

Part 1
Brush-talk involving traveling literati and boat drifters in East Asia

3 Brush conversation between maritime officials and foreign seafarers in drifting records in eighteenth- and nineteenth-century East Asia

Matsuura Akira and Reijiro Aoyama

Introduction

During the summer months, East Asian waters from the South China Sea to the Sea of Japan are frequently struck by rough weather and, as the case may be, devastating typhoons. Historical records of the growing trade and cross-border visits between East Asian countries during the early modern era, notably during the late Qing period in the eighteenth and nineteenth centuries, provide a rich body of written accounts of distressed seafarers from Qing China, Tokugawa Japan, Chosŏn Korea, and Ryukyu Kingdom, whose vessels were stranded in the coastal waters of another polity after being blown off course. Given that bilingualism in speech was uncommon in the region at the time, how did the maritime officials collect baseline information from the distressed seafarers in the absence of an interpreter? Before deciding what to do with the stranded aliens, fairly elaborate information had to be obtained to assess the circumstances of the case in hand, for instance, the place of origin and destination of the ship, the numbers and identities of passengers and the kinds and volumes of commodities on board, the presence of any public health concerns such as passengers with symptoms of a contagious disease or in need of emergency treatment, details of the arrangements of the group's homeward-bound journey, and so forth. Many of these records, invariably written in Sinitic, contain evidence of brush conversation or brush-talk 漢文筆談. That is, except when written information was readily available for quick reference (e.g., in the form of a list showing passengers' names, ages, and places of origin, plus details of commodities on board), the two sides would communicate in Sinitic using brush and ink to make meaning interactively on paper, hence 'brush conversation'. In terms of genre, the formal records of 'drifting brush-talk' 漂流民筆談 were composed like reports to a senior official, sometimes to the Emperor, and generally demonstrated a high Chinese literary standard. There is however relatively little clue about the literacy level of the distressed seafarer(s) responding to questions. This chapter exemplifies sociolinguistic evidence of the 'Question and Answer' mode of sinogram-based brush conversation in Japanese and Korean records and analyzes brush(-assisted) conversation between local maritime officials and Chinese boat drifters conducted in Sinitic.

DOI: 10.4324/9781003048176-4

Historical background

After successfully containing and defeating anti-Qing forces in Taiwan in 1683, the Qing government lifted the preemptive coastal evacuation policy whereby residents of the littoral areas of Guangdong, Fujian, Zhejiang, and Shandong were required to retreat inland. The subjects were once again allowed to build vessels to engage in maritime trading activities with foreigners (Shi 2006; Matsuura 2011; Matsuura & Pien 2007). Permitted to venture out into the ocean, Chinese merchants began transporting passengers across the Yellow Sea, loading vessels with sizable volumes of goods, and sailed back and forth between the ports in the East and South China Seas. Tianjin-bound vessels from Ningbo, for instance, routinely carried rice, medicine, paper, bamboo, and wood produced in the south, and returned to Ningbo with soybeans, peanuts, and jujube mainly produced in the north.

Chinese merchants, in particular those from the south, extended their sailing routes to foreign ports in Tokugawa Japan, Chosŏn Korea and Southeast Asian polities utilizing vessels called Fujian junks 福建船 and Guangdong junks 廣東船. The marine routes crisscrossing the Yellow Sea and East China Sea surrounded by China, the Korean Peninsula, the Japanese archipelago, Ryukyu Islands, and Taiwan played an important role in international trade among East Asian countries. The goods carried by Chinese vessels to Japan, for example, included food products, high-grade silk, and traditional medicinal materials such as ginseng. Before the eighth Tokugawa Shogun Yoshimune 徳川吉宗 (1684–1751) gave impetus for farming improvements resulting in domestic cultivation of sugar cane, Japan had been largely relying on imported sugar produced in China's eastern Guangdong and southern Fujian. It was the advancement in Chinese shipbuilding and navigation techniques that made these long-distance voyages possible, greatly contributing to the development of inter-regional trade. As a consequence of the isolationist policies adopted by Chosŏn Korea and Tokugawa Japan which forbade outbound sailing and outlawed the construction of floating vessels for non-domestic use, Chinese merchants and their junks dominated international maritime activities in the waters of East and South China Seas from the late seventeenth to mid-nineteenth centuries, before western steamers became active in the region.

Travel by sea was not always safe, in particular owing to hazardous weather conditions which made sailing perilous during the summer monsoon season. It was not unusual for vessels to disappear without a trace, while some were stranded after being blown off course or drifted ashore in foreign lands, giving rise to a substantial body of Sinitic-based written records of distressed seafarers and their vessels stranded in the coastal areas of today's China, Japan, Korea, and Okinawa. By the eighteenth and nineteenth centuries, fairly standardized protocols emerged to provide humanitarian rescue to the boat drifters and to salvage the damaged vessels found adrift, typically in response to sighting reports by local villagers or mariners (Kanezashi 1965; Matsuura 2007). Recovery operations in Qing China were highly regulated in terms of the provision of basic supplies and treatment of the injured. The Qing salvage and rescue protocol became increasingly regimented during the successive reigns of Emperors Kangxi 康熙 (1661–1722), Yongzheng 雍正 (1722–1735), and Qianlong 乾隆 (1735–1795). Given a shipwreck incident involving a foreign vessel, the maritime official had to write a detailed report complete with a proposed repatriation plan to the Emperor for approval. Apart from humanitarian grounds, the repatriation policy was also a calculated diplomatic strategy to lend credence to the authority, benevolence, and generosity of the Middle Kingdom.

Qing dynasty's salvation and repatriation protocols were not only directed at the boat drifters from tributary countries such as Korea and Ryukyu but also extended to those from Japan, with which China had no official diplomatic relations until 1871.[1] The stranded vessels and distressed seafarers originating from China's tributary countries were routinely sent back along the tribute-trading routes. They would normally be escorted by officials to Beijing, where they had to wait for tributary envoys from their home country to arrange for their homeward-bound journey. Although the tributary status was not recognized by the Japanese shogunate, stranded Japanese seafarers would be similarly rescued and sent back to Japan on Chinese trading junks bound for Nagasaki.

Aspiring to be seen as respectable political equals, the governments of the Chosŏn dynasty, the Ryukyu Kingdom, and the Tokugawa shogunate emulated the generous salvage policy of the Qing, repatriating distressed seafarers to their home countries either through the tribute routes (Korea and Ryukyu) or the customary trading routes (Japan). Since the governments in East Asia regarded the rescue operations of stranded foreign vessels and their seafarers as an integral part of trans-national diplomacy, an official document recording each rescue case would usually contain a detailed account of the process of salvation and a repatriation plan. Of interest is that the opening section of such a document often includes some record of brush-talk that took place between local officials and one or more distressed seamen or passengers with Sinitic literacy. This chapter examines a few shipwreck incidents involving distressed Chinese seafarers whose vessels were stranded in Tokugawa Japan and Chosŏn Korea during the eighteenth and nineteenth centuries. Our goal is to cast some light on how brush-talk was utilized as an extemporaneous means of soliciting and providing information in impromptu transcultural encounters between East Asian nationals with no shared spoken language.

Records of brush-talk between Japanese officials and Chinese seafarers

During the Edo or Tokugawa period (1603–1868), Japan embarked on a policy of national seclusion whereby foreign vessels were only allowed to cast their anchors

---

1 The Sino-Japanese Friendship and Trade Treaty between Japan and Qing China was signed on 13 September 1871 in Tianjin by Date Munenari 伊達宗城 (1818–1892) and Plenipotentiary Li Hongzhang 李鴻章 (1823–1901).

in the port of Nagasaki. In accordance with the law, the shogunate would tow any stranded Chinese vessels along the Japanese coast to Nagasaki and, from there, repatriate them to China. The general protocol required that regional functionaries at the point of rescue investigate and record the conditions of the stranded vessels and the passengers on board before making arrangements to have them escorted to Nagasaki, where they would have a better chance of coming into contact with Japanese merchants and officials with experience in conducting business with foreigners and interpreting skills between Japanese and Chinese or Dutch. Given the fact that the officials at the point of rescue along the coast spoke hardly any Chinese, they would try to communicate with the boat drifters in writing using brush, ink, and paper.

One such instructive incident is depicted in a painting showing two Japanese officials distinguished by their long swords and, at the bottom, two Qing Chinese traders whose hair was bundled in a queue (Yabuta 1997, see Figure 3.1). In 1800, the twelfth year of the Kansei 寛政 era, Wansheng 萬勝, a Chinese trading vessel plying international waters, drifted ashore in Enshu 遠州 (today's Shizuoka Prefecture) on the southern coast of Honshu Island, about one thousand kilometers to the east of Nagasaki. Depicted on the bottom left of Figure 3.1 is Liu Ranyi 劉然乙, Wansheng's captain. Holding a brush in his hand, Liu seems busy writing something on paper, possibly explaining the origin and destination of their stranded vessel, the number and identities of those on board, how they ended up

Figure 3.1 Early nineteenth-century Japanese painting of local officials questioning the Chinese crew from the stranded trading vessel Wansheng 萬勝 (Yabuta 1997: 73).

being stranded in Japan, and so forth. All this information was expected of him by the investigator, the official identified as Honma Shunpaku 本間春伯, whose name is clearly visible on the top left. With his gaze directed toward Liu, he seems to be observing what Liu is writing, which is possibly a response to one of those questions put to him on paper. To Honma's left is another Japanese official (apparently also surnamed Honma 本間), who seems absorbed in reading a sheet of paper dotted symbolically with lines of sinograms written vertically from top to bottom and who, being visibly less senior, appears to be a scribe dictating questions raised by his superior. Of further interest are, (i) in the middle, a tray-like black container holding ink and a small black bar that resembles an ink stone; (ii) on bottom left, a clay pot, possibly dispensing tea for the brush-talkers; and (iii) six sinograms across on top:

事之對應中舩

which, reading from right to left as was customary during the premodern and early modern era, gives the meaning 'scene of interaction on the ship'. These visual cues, impressionistic though they are, provide clear evidence as well as rich contextual details of Japanese maritime officials and Chinese seafarers being engaged in 'drifting brush-talk', which in all likelihood was a standing Japanese administrative practice handling distressed seafarers with literacy in Sinitic.

A similar encounter is documented in 'Jiangnan Conversation on Commerce' 江南商話 written in 1808, which includes the record of a shipwreck incident involving a Chinese domestic trading junk headed to Shandong province from the Yangtze River Delta (Matsuura 1989). On its way north, the junk got blown away off course toward the east, eventually landing in Tosa 土佐 in the south of Shikoku Island in Japan. The account begins as follows (ibid. p. 5):

文化五年戊辰（嘉慶十三） 十一月念七日 江南商船遭遇風難、飄到于 吾土佐國安藝郡奈良志津 浦、 ... 臣亦以楮墨換舌、 及其餘裔、每會往復探 討 ...	Bunka 5th year (Jiaqing 13th year. 1808) 27th day. 11th lunar month[2] Jiangnan trading junk was seriously damaged after encountering strong winds and drifted to the seaport of Narashitsuura of Aki county in Tosa. ... Also. instead of exchanging information with our tongues. I used brush and ink when meeting with the survivors repeatedly to clarify things.

The expression 以楮墨換舌 (literally 'to substitute paper and ink for [our] tongues') testifies to the interlocutors' effective use of ink and mulberry paper in place of speech for the purpose of establishing factual details about the junk,

---

2 The dates are all recorded according to the lunar calendar. For convenience's sake, all lunar months and days will be presented in digits, with the month preceding the day separated by a colon. Thus, '03:05' would mean 'the 5th day of the 3rd lunar month'.

its passengers and commodities on board. Unlike the Wansheng shipwreck incident discussed earlier, Japan was not the destination of the domestic trading junk; nor did those on board have any knowledge of it. Despite mounting intercultural unease and a lack of a shared spoken language, both sides managed to communicate and make themselves understood through brush-talking in Sinitic.

Further indubitable evidence of brush-talking as a standing Japanese administrative practice may be found in the 1826 compilation 'Brush-talk of the Tokutai Ship' 得泰船筆語. This brush-talk record documents the rescue of the Chinese crew on board the Tokutai (Mand. Detai), a Hangzhou vessel, after it drifted ashore in Enshu, the same location where Wansheng was stranded 26 years earlier. Upon hearing the Chinese seafarers' plight, the Tokugawa shogunate dispatched Noda Tekiho 野田笛浦 (1799–1859), a *kangaku* scholar, to the port of Shimizu 清水 and ordered him to escort the seafarers to Nagasaki. Clear evidence of Chinese-Japanese brush conversation between Noda and Liu Shengfu 劉聖孚, a Chinese passenger of the ship, is discernible as follows (Tanaka & Matsuura 1986: 137):

野田笛浦: (Noda)	問答須憑筆	Jap: *mondō su hyō hitsu*[3] Chi: *wen da xu ping bi*	'For question and response, [we] need to use a brush.'
劉聖孚: (Liu)	言談在此書	Chi: *yan tan zai ci shu* Jap: *gen dan zai shi sho*[4]	'To conduct conversation, write here.'

To exchange question and response, Noda hinted at the need for using a brush (and implicitly, writing on paper). To this suggested mode of communication, Liu, a literatus himself, readily agreed and pointed to the spot where the 'writing' of their conversation should begin. That it is a bona fide conversation is clearly evidenced by the semantic coherence of the five sinograms produced by each side. What makes it different from speech-based conversation is that here, no attempt is made for the interlocutor to 'hear' how the sinograms are pronounced in the

---

3 While the romanization is based on contemporary Japanese *on* pronunciation (*on'yomi*, 音読み) and Chinese pinyin, we make no claims about how the sinograms in this verbal exchange were actually pronounced in this historical context. By displaying the pronunciation of individual sinograms improvised interactively, we wish to highlight the phonetically intersubjective nature of sinogram-based brush-talking, in that at the level of mental representation, the same sinogram was typically associated with completely different pronunciations. The romanized transcription merely foregrounds the fact that successful comprehension was achieved entirely in abstraction of verbalized speech. Paradoxically, given the absence of a shared vernacular, communication would have been blocked if uttered in speech.

4 When engaging in synchronous face-to-face communication via brush-talk, whether the Japanese interlocutor would rearrange the word order from verb-medial (VO) to verb-final (OV) in his mind is another pertinent yet unanswerable question. Following the conventional morphosyntactic techniques called *kundoku* 訓読, which was required for reading or translating Sinitic into the Japanese vernacular (Saito 2021; Aoyama 2020), the contemporary reading of the ten sinograms in this brush-talk exchange could be rendered as: *mondō subekaraku fude ni yorubeshi gendan wa konosho ni ari* (問答スベカラク筆ニ憑ルベシ 言談ハコノ書ニ在リ).

brush-talker's language, and yet they convey the exact meanings all the same thanks to their morphographic nature: unlike phonographic languages written with an alphabet or a syllabary, each of the sinograms is vested with more or less stable semantic content that can be independently discerned or comprehended by literati of Chinese or Sinitic, regardless of how they are pronounced intersubjectively in their respective vernaculars.

Successful brush-talking was contingent on one condition: literacy in Sinitic. What follows is an example of a diary-style record constructed by a Japanese author apparently based on brush-assisted conversation rather than a verbatim record of two-way brush-talk between Chinese seafarers and the Japanese author (see Appendix). On 11:20, 1815, a Chinese trading junk Yongmao 永茂 left the port of Zhapu 乍浦 heading to Nagasaki with 86 passengers on board (Matsuura 2011). For a few days, the junk was blown off course; five weeks later, it drifted ashore at the Izu Peninsula 伊豆半島 in Japan. The supercargo Yang Qiutang 楊秋棠 wrote a letter to local officials explaining their situation and pleading for food, firewood, and water. Apparently unhindered by any intelligibility problem, the governor Egawa Tarozaemon 江川太郎左衛門 swiftly provided the requested supplies and towed the junk to a nearby port for repairs. Then, following standard protocol, the shogunate engaged a ship to escort Yongmao and its crew to Nagasaki, where it became the object of a detailed drawing by a Japanese illustrator, who gave a brief description of Yongmao's plight and outlined its loading capacity, the names of all those on board plus other details (see Figures 3.2a and 3.2b).

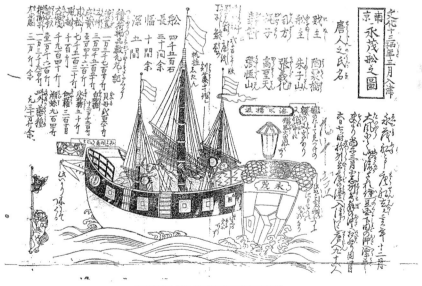

南京永茂船之圖 （大阪府立中之島図書館蔵）

Figure 3.2a Early nineteenth-century Japanese drawing of the stranded Chinese trading ship Yongmao 永茂 (Matsuura 2011: illustrated pages 2 and 347).

VIII Commodities: types and quantities	VI Tonnage and Measures of Yongmao	V Description of the mast 帆柱, canvass, and other structures	III Names of Chinese passengers	I Date and title of drawing
IX Description of the anchor	VII Indicative sketch of Yongmao's appearance as seen from the port side of the ship 茂永		IV 波揚不海[5]	II Brief narrative of the Yongmao incident

Figure 3.2b Schematic description of the types of information on the drawing of the trading ship Yongmao.

Yongmao eventually arrived in Nagasaki in the fifth lunar month and left for China in the eighth lunar month in 1816 after successfully concluding trading business with the Japanese merchants. Asakawa Zenan 朝川善庵 (1781–1849), a Japanese Confucian scholar who came to Shimoda from Edo to meet the Chinese seafarers, later published 'Qing-Ship Brush-talk' 清舶筆話, a series of five books containing his brush-talk conversations with the Chinese traders.

Asakawa referred to his face-to-face writing exchange with the passengers of Yongmao as 'Issues of talking by brush' 以掌筆話之事, his diary-style compilation being based on paper records of their silent conversations. There are plenty of points of linguistic interest in his compilation. In the following, we will analyze the first brush-talk with the Chinese distressed seafarers documented, featuring interaction between Asakawa and a couple of the Yongmao crew after the ship drifted to the port of Shimoda (see Appendix).

Linguistically, there is no shortage of quasi-forensic evidence of the brush-talk record being penned (or more accurately 'brushed') by a Japanese author, with hardly any input from the Chinese seafarers. Structurally, within the space of about 1,500 sinograms, the record provides the following information:

i   One-paragraph description of the shipwreck incident, and the circumstances under which the author decided to compile a record based on his observations for future reference;
ii Indication of year (according to *gengō* 元号, the Japanese era name) and month (3rd lunar calendar), plus the record keeper's name;
iii Five bisyllabic Chinese keywords and their Japanese 'equivalents';

---

5 Traditional Sinitic texts are written from top-to-bottom and right-to-left, be it vertically or horizontally. Apart from the name of the ship 永茂 (Yongmao, displayed in the drawing as 茂永), there is a quadrisyllabic expression 波揚不海 in the drawing which appears to be framed within a plaque. Read in today's left-to-right order, 海不揚波 (*hǎi bù yáng bō*, literarily 'The sea raises no waves') is a traditional expression wishing seafarers a calm and peaceful journey.

iv   A metalinguistic comment reminding the reader of Chinese-Japanese semantic divergence with regard to a few sinograms;
v   A long appendix consisting apparently of a verbatim record of several brush-talk interactions (question-and-answer; requests for food items, permission to repatriate, and assistance in their return journey; and expression of gratitude), albeit composed almost entirely by the Japanese brush-talker.

The one-paragraph description of the shipwreck incident contains important clues to the mode of interaction between Asakawa and the Chinese seafarers (see Appendix):

文化乙亥十二月廿九日南京永茂舩漂到豆州下田港余不佞以文墨承乏爲属吏於韮山以掌筆話之事但恨漂商無文字其所應對率皆公務除公務外絶無風流文雅之語欲一一皆存之乎言渉忌諱事係機密者間或有之不可以存乎亦是人世奇遇書生孔筆、豈忍弁髦視之乎因令取舍斟酌存十一於千百以寓鷄肋之意云 　　　文化丙子春三月善菴朝川鼎撰	On 12:29 in Bunka 12th year (1815), the Nanking ship Yongmao drifted to Shimoda seaport in Zu Prefecture. Despite my limited competence in Sinitic, in the absence of a suitable official, I was tasked with collecting information through brush conversation at Nirayama. Regrettably, the drifting merchants had little knowledge of written Chinese. Our exchange was limited to official business, with no mention of anything of literary interest at all. Occasionally we touched upon taboo topics or sensitive issues, which were not suitable for recording. Still, in view of such an unusual encounter, it would be a great pity not to leave any trace of our written records behind, hence the compilation of a short selection of our interaction for what it is worth. 　　　3rd lunar month, Bunka 13th year (1816). 　　　　　　　　　　　　Asakawa Zenan

From the previous description, we can sense Asakawa's expectation of engaging in literary improvisation or poetic exchange with Chinese seafarers, only to be utterly disappointed due to their very limited knowledge of written Chinese (但恨漂商無文字), not to mention familiarity with Classical Chinese canons, literary and poetic works. This point is nicely corroborated by the five putative equivalents of five Chinese-Japanese bisyllabic words in (iii), most of which being lexically as well as orthographically inaccurate. For example, neither 目侶 nor 随使 appeared to be Chinese job titles in reference to workers on board the Yongmao in Qing China, while 摠管 reflects Japanese orthographic preference (Qing Chi: 總管), even though both are attested in contemporary Chinese writing from Song dynasty (960–1279) to Qing dynasty (1644–1911). The metalinguistic notes in (iv), such as the grammatical functions of the sinograms 湏 (an 'auxiliary word' 助語), 故 and 而 (必故二次、而已現在) reflect Asakawa's linguistic observations of Chinese-Japanese contrastive differences. The Annex 附録 contains excerpts of selected brush-assisted conversations with the Chinese seafarers on four to five separate days. While it is obvious that the information concerning the

Chinese seafarers must have been obtained interactively through brush conversation, many other lexical and stylistic choices suggest that the content was authored by the Japanese brush-talker, even though the byline refers explicitly to the ship's captain or owner 南京舩主楊秋棠印; 財副陶粟橋印. Such lexical and stylistic choices include:

- Chinese self-reference as 'Great Tang (country)' (大唐, 大唐國), which is identical to Asakawa's reference to China (大唐國), rather than 'Great Qing' (大清, 大清國);
- The use of the adverb 大 pre-modifying a verb (e.g., 洋中大遇惡風), including its reduplicated form 大大 (e.g., 諸事大大費心), reflects Japanese Sinitic rather than Chinese usage;
- In one excerpt attributed to the owner of Yongmao (文化十三年正月 南京舩主楊秋棠印), the captain was said to be referring to a Japanese leader using a term of address 大頭目 *daitōmoku* (top leader), which had/has very negative connotation in Chinese. For a Chinese user, 大頭目 would contradict the use of the politeness marker 貴地 'your esteemed place' in the same collocation, viz.: 貴地大頭目; compare 即請各位大頭目. ('now invite all top leaders'). Such a negative connotation and collocational constraint in Chinese did not seem to be shared in Sinitic usage in Tokugawa Japan.
- Japanese-specific lexical usages using kana 洋紙外國ノ紙ヲ云美濃紙ニ充ル四刀 ('Western paper is foreign in origin, the size of the paper is equivalent to four folds of mino paper', the term 洋紙 means foreign paper, corresponding to four sets of Japanese paper *minoshi*).

All this shows that, while the brush was manifestly the instrument used for recording factual, albeit fragmentary, information obtained from Chinese distressed seafarers, there was very little brush-talk in the sense of two-way conversation, making one doubt the reliability of Asakawa's written record. How much of it was based on Asakawa's own conjecture based on what he made out from the barely literate seafarers during their interaction, we do not know. What the record does show is that knowledge of Sinitic, however limited, allowed for basic sense-making between speakers with no shared spoken language in a particular context like interrogation of survivors of a shipwreck, whereby identity checking of the boat drifters plus the probing of other ancillary information pertaining to the vessel and all those on board was urgently needed. Unlike other drifting brush-talk events where brush-talking took place more or less interactively, what we saw in the record of the Yongmao incident is one extreme case of a 'brush-assisted conversation' resulting from a markedly uneven distribution of literacy in Chinese or Sinitic.

In short, as exemplified in the Sinitic-based written records, brush-talking was the standard means and mode of communication between Chinese and Japanese in chance encounters occasioned by shipwreck incidents along the coasts of the Japanese archipelago. How successful and reliable the records were would depend crucially on the literacy level of the brush-talkers, especially the surviving seafarers. Further, there is substantial evidence ascertaining that marine salvage and rescue practices in Tokugawa Japan were guided by well-defined protocols laid down by the Shogun.

Records of brush-talk between Korean officials and Chinese seafarers

This section presents brush-talk records produced during encounters between Korean maritime officials and Chinese seafarers as documented in 'Records of Chosŏn Border Defense Council' (*Pibyŏnsa Tŭngnok* 備邊司謄錄). Chosŏn dynasty first established the Border Defense Council 備邊司 in 1517 as a response to an increasing number of Japanese settlers in the Samp'o 三浦 area to resolve conflicts between new immigrants and local residents. It was Chosŏn Korea's highest administrative office charged with national border defense. The council records contain materials that are indispensable for the informed study of Chosŏn Korea's relations with Japan and China, including numerous instances of stranded Chinese and Japanese vessels. The maritime rescue operations were handled by Korean maritime officials with great care given Chosŏn Korea's tributary status vis-à-vis Qing China, and that national security and interests were clearly at stake. This is probably why records of the stranded vessels were maintained up to the highest standard. Meticulous record-keeping resulted in well-structured documentation of detailed exchanges between Korean border officials and foreign crew members, including the exact locations of the stranded vessels, duties and origins of the crews and passengers, destinations and chains of events leading to shipwreck, types and tonnage of cargo on board, and so forth. In *Pibyŏnsa Tŭngnok*, a total of 40 shipwreck incidents involving Chinese vessels from 1617 to 1880 were documented, including three vessels engaged in international trade (foreign trading ships) and 37 junks trading domestically along the China coast (Matsuura 2014).

Following is an excerpt of one record of Chosŏn maritime officials interrogating Chinese seafarers.[6] The event took place in 1706, after a Chinese domestic trading junk that took off from Laiyang 萊陽 heading to Suzhou 蘇州 with thirteen people onboard encountered strong wind and drifted ashore on Cheju Island between the Yellow Sea and the East China Sea. This sample report, clearly structured in question-and-answer (問、答) format, is rather long giving elaborate details. Linguistically it provides interesting features of language use in Sinitic-based transcultural communication between the Chosŏn maritime official(s) – likely one or more literati of Sinitic who were bilingual in Korean and Chinese working as

---

6 The entire record of the dialogue is accessible at http://db.history.go.kr/item/level.do?itemId=bb&l evelId=bb_057_001_04_0110&types=o
while the scanned images are also accessible at http://kyudb.snu.ac.kr/pf01/rendererImg.do?item_cd=VBS&book_cd=GK15044_00&vol_no=0057&page_no=053a

interpreter(s) – and Chinese seafarers in the early eighteenth century. Such linguistic features are illustrated in the following excerpt.

丙戌四月十三日　　濟州漂到人問情別單		04:13, 1706. Interrogation record of the boat drifters stranded on Cheju Island
問	你等居在何地、而姓甚名誰耶。	Question: [All of] you, where are your hometowns, and what are your names?
答曰	俺等十三人姓名。管帳車琯、年三十九歲、山東省登州府萊陽縣人。管買賣柴米崔凌雲、年五十二歲、山東省登州府文登縣人。...	Answer: There are thirteen of us; our names are: Bookkeeper Che Guan, age 39, resident of Laiyang County of Dengzhou Prefecture, Shandong Province. Merchandizer Cui Lingyun, age 52, Wendang County of Dengzhou Prefecture, Shandong Province. ...
問	你等、因何事往何地方、緣何漂到我國耶。	Question: Where were you heading, for what reason, and how come your junk drifted to our country?
答	俺等、以買賣事、往蘇州地方、洋中遇風、漂到貴國耳。...	Answer: We were heading for Suzhou on trading business; on the way, our junk encountered strong wind and drifted to your esteemed country....
問	你等、離發山東萊陽縣時、作伴向蘇州者、幾船耶。	Question: When you departed Laiyang County of Shandong Province for Suzhou, how many junks were involved?
答	俺等、萊陽縣開船時、無作伴船矣。...	Answer: When our junk took off from Laiyang County, there were no accompanying vessels.
問	你等大船所載物種、多少幾許耶。	Question: Your junk-load of commodities, what are they and in what quantities?
答	黃豆二百四十擔、白蠟二百四十斤、紅花二百四十斤、繭紬三疋、紫草三百九十八包、防風一包、杏仁一小包、鹽猪十二口耳。	Answer: Soya beans 240 piculs, white wax 240 catties, safflower 240 catties, pongee three rolls, purple gromwell 398 packs, saposhnikovia one pack, almond one small pack, and 12 salted pigs.

Unlike the Yongmao record discussed earlier, which was more like one enthusiastic Japanese literatus's brush-assisted compilation of information collected from barely literate Chinese seafarers whose vessel was stranded in Japanese waters, the sample record produced by his Korean counterpart looks more like a transcript of a standard question-and-answer report for handling Chinese boat drifters stranded in Korean waters. Content-wise the lexico-grammatical expressions are perfectly intelligible to literate Chinese readers even today, which lends considerable support to the conjecture that the interrogation was conducted orally in a vernacular peculiar to central or northern China. Vernacular-specific examples include the consistent use of personal pronouns (second person plural 你等 'you' and 俺等 'we', the latter being characteristic of the Shandong topolect); the bisyllabic nouns for 地方 'place' and 買賣 'trading, literally buying and selling'; the adsentential subordinate clause marker of time 時 'when'; the interrogative pronouns 多少 and 幾 'how much' or 'how many'; the verb phrase 開船 'start sailing'; the resultative verb 漂到 'drift to'; and miscellaneous classifiers of nouns (e.g., for persons 箇[7] and for pigs 口, as in 鹽猪十二口 'twelve salted pigs').

At the same time, there is no shortage of elements that are more characteristic of Classical Chinese or Sinitic, such as the interrogative pronoun 'which' or 'what' 何; sentence-final particles such as the marker of statement 耳 or 矣, and the question marker 耶. In terms of linguistic resources, therefore, the Korean report clearly drew on both vernacular as well as Classical elements. And, compared with the Japanese record excerpted earlier, one finds far fewer idiosyncratic usages characteristic of Korean users of Chinese; among the more eye-catching ones are the collocation for the meaning 'depart' 離發[8]; the juxtaposition of two bisyllabic expressions – 多少幾許 – from different registers with essentially the same meaning ('how many'), the first one characteristic of the vernacular (多少), the second from Classical Chinese (幾許)[9]; and the non-use of a classifier where one is expected (e.g., 'how many vessels?' 幾[x]船耶).[10]

The aforementioned analysis points toward the active use of speech in the question-and-answer sequences, with the give-and-take being written up in a highly structured and formulaic report. This in turn suggests that both sides had no need to rely on brush-talking, at least not exclusively. In other words, although numerous records of questions and answers are found in *Pibyŏnsa Tŭngnok*, Koreans did not necessarily resort to brush-talk when interrogating shipwreck survivors as extensively as the Japanese did, probably because professionally trained Chinese-speaking interpreters were more readily available to assist with the interrogation on most occasions (Okumura 2016: 27–32). The following record, for example, clearly shows that the Chosŏn official promptly summoned a professional interpreter to investigate stranded Chinese seafarers immediately after their rescue in 1713 (Okumura 2016: 25). Additionally, Korean interpreters always accompanied Chinese seafarers from the port of rescue to Seoul, the Korean capital, assisting the officials in soliciting information using spoken Chinese. We can thus safely conclude that most of the question-and-answer dialogues in *Pibyŏnsa Tŭngnok* are edited written transcripts of *spoken* conversations conducted between Korean officials and Chinese seafarers mediated by Korean interpreters.

---

7 As in 登州府、有幾箇官人耶。 'In Dengzhou Prefecture, how many officials are there?'
8 Compare contemporary Mandarin: 'leave' 離開, and 'depart' 出發.
9 Compare the use of 幾何 for this same meaning 'how many' in: 山東所屬州縣、共幾何耶。 'Those counties that belong to Shandong Province, how many are they?'
10 Normative usage of the vernacular would predict the use of a classifier for vessels 艘 or 條: 幾艘船耶? or 幾條船耶? By contrast, Classical Chinese or Sinitic usage would favor a topic-comment structure: 船幾艘耶?

司 啓辭，即接濟州漂人領來譯官李樞手本，則十月二十八日領率漂人自於蘭鎭離發，今月十一日到公州十六日當爲進京，...且其入京後，本司郎廳一員，解語譯官數人...其漂到情實更加盤問...	Minister hereby reports, interpreter Yi Ch'u's handwritten record of drifting seafarers whose junk was stranded on Cheju Island was just received. On 10:28, I escorted the seafarers to depart from Ŏran for Kongju, arriving on 11:11 and expecting to reach the capital on 11:16.... After arriving at the capital, one officer of this ministry and a few interpreters... would conduct detailed interrogation of the drifting incident.

However, a drifting record of a Chinese ship stranded near the Korean shore in 1791, which is part of the 1,893-volume annual records of the Chosŏn dynasty kept from 1413 to 1865, indicates explicitly that the conversation between the Koreans and Chinese in this instance was conducted in writing (pp. 78–80, volume 33, 'Veritable Records of King Chŏngjo' 正祖大王實錄):

忠清道水軍節度使金明遇狀啓言。水軍虞候金守基牒呈。異樣船漂到洪州地、言語不通、以書問之。答云、大清國山東登州府福山縣人民、船戶安永和、因奉天省裝糧一載、運往山東、交結糧客、在山東因遭風患到此、現有船票一俗爲正云。...[11]	Ch'ungch'ŏng Province Regional Navy Commander Kim Myŏng'u hereby presents: naval official Kim Suki submitted a report respectfully. A strange-looking ship drifted to the land of Hongju. Since speech communication was not possible, questions were raised in writing. In the response, Great Qing ship owner An Yonghe, a resident of Fushan County of Dengzhou Prefecture in Shandong Province, said they had departed from Fengtian Province and were bound for Shandong, transporting and delivering a ship-load of foodstuff to a client there, but encountered strong winds near Shandong and got stranded here. He claimed to have a bag of tickets as evidence.

The Chinese junk carrying five passengers and 16 crew left the port of Fushan 福山 in the Shandong Peninsula for a Yellow Sea crossing to the port of Jinzhou 金州 in Liaodong Peninsula. On its way, it encountered a storm in the coastal area of Shandong and drifted eastwards to the western coast of the Korean Peninsula. As mentioned in the excerpt, 言語不通，以書問之 'Since speech communication was not possible, questions were raised in writing'. Given that interrogation in speech was not an option, the Korean officials had to resort to brush-talking.

Further, despite the availability of interpreting, there is evidence that Korean-Chinese interpreters would need the assistance of literate Chinese speakers. One such instructive example may be found in the brush-talk record involving a Chinese junk with 30 odd passengers stranded on Korean waters in 1774 (*Pibyŏnsa Tŭngnok*, vol. 156):

---

11 Adapted from http://sillok.history.go.kr/id/wva_11512018_002.

靈光漂人問情別單 'Interrogation record of the boat drifters at Yŏnggwang County (영광)'

問	你們漂蕩辛苦事情.既已聞知.近日天氣寒冷.我國路上好來否?	Question: About your suffering while drifting at sea. we heard about it. The weather is getting cold. did you have a good journey on the road of our country?
答	幸蒙 貴國恩典.飽飯騎馬.路上好 ㄹ 來。	Answer: Thanks to the gracious generosity of your esteemed country. we were given horses to ride on after full meals: the journey on the road was wonderful.
問	你們中識字人誰也?	Question: Among all of you. who can read and write?
答	只有兩箇人.利君一于小。	Answer: Only two persons: Li Junyi and Yu Xiao.
問	你們漢人耶.滿洲人耶?	Question: Are you Chinese or Manchu people?
答	俱是漢人。	Answer: All Chinese.
問	你們幾箇人.姓甚名誰.年紀幾何.原住何處?	Question: How many are you? What are your names and ages? Where is your hometown?
答	小的們共二十五人.俱是山東省登州府福山縣人.曲欽一.年五十九.夏喜.年三十三.曲乃直.年三十三...	Answer: Our humble group consists of 25 people. all come from Fushan County. Dengzhou Prefecture of Shandong Province. Qu Qinyi. age 59: Xia Xi. age 33: Qu Naizhi. age 33...

問: Question raised by Korean maritime official. 答: Chinese seafarer's response.

Unlike other interactions between maritime officials and seafarers, this one did not take place at the waterfront. Instead, it is a dialogue between a Korean-Chinese interpreter and a literate seafarer at a port where limited interpreting service was available. This is because after the seafarers' identity was established, they would normally be transferred by land to a port where professionally trained Korean-Chinese interpreters were on duty, hence the first question about the journey 'on the road'. Assuming a shared vernacular that allowed both sides to communicate more or less effectively in speech was available – more likely a Chinese variety than Korean, there remains the question of Chinese homophones, which would be unpredictable when putting down the names of individual passengers on board. That is probably why among the first things the Chosŏn official asked was whether one or more persons with literacy in Sinitic could be identified. In this particular case, two literate passengers were identified who could be counted upon to assist the Chosŏn official to resolve any ambiguity arising. Unlike the Chinese-Japanese interaction pattern, the Korean-Chinese interaction pattern is clearly structured, with the question 問 and answer 答 turn-taking being flagged systematically.

Further, from the linguistic point of view, it is interesting that elements of Classical Chinese (Sinitic) and vernacular Chinese were mixed. Chinese vernacular elements include the second-person plural pronoun 你們 and the classifier 箇, while from Classical Chinese, the sentence-final particle 耶 and the interrogative pronoun 何 ('what', 'how many', 'how much') are used to express a yes-no question and the meaning 'what age' or 'how old', respectively.

Discussion and conclusion

The three polities in East Asia – China, Japan, and Korea – all have very long coastlines. While geographically close to one another, rough weather and typhoons that commonly strike the region during the summer months make navigating the waters separating the three countries a risky endeavor. For that reason, fatalities arising from sunken vessels were not uncommon in the premodern and early modern era, while in less disastrous cases, vessels would be stranded in an alien territory after being blown off course and/or having run aground or drifted ashore. Such shipwreck incidents were not uncommon during the eighteenth and nineteenth centuries. For security and humanitarian reasons, local maritime officials (coastguards in modern terminology) were duty-bound to interrogate the surviving crew and passengers. Extant drifting brush-talk records show that the maritime officials usually wanted specific answers to a fairly long list of wh-questions pertaining to who, what, why, and how, among other reasons to quickly determine whether there were any security or health-risk issues at stake. Such encounters between strangers were already administratively rather complex (e.g., from providing humanitarian assistance to the survivors and taking care of those who had deceased or fallen ill, to identifying a suitable vessel and making repatriation arrangements for their return journey). Without a shared spoken language, however, such interrogations were anything but obvious.

Interpreting service was of course available at the national, diplomatic level, in the political center of the state capital and one or more seaports with sizable trading volumes and capacities. To handle shipwreck incidents, maritime officials in Qing China, Chosŏn Korea, and Tokugawa Japan appeared to follow a prescribed protocol to gather all the required information needed for a formal report, often complete with detailed support measures and a repatriation plan. Depending on how serious the cases were, such reports might need to be submitted to a senior official in the (state or regional) capital or, in the case of China, even the Emperor for approval. Owing to the recurring nature of shipwreck incidents, interpreting service from or into Chinese was made available at maritime offices in Nagasaki and Seoul.[12] If the site of the shipwreck was a distance away, a routine procedure would be to escort the alien seafarers to the (nearest) office where in-depth interrogation could take place in the presence of one or more interpreters on duty. But between the spot where the vessel adrift was stranded and the office where verbal

---

12 Chosŏn Korean protocol was to send interpreters from Seoul or the nearest coastal offices to the exact location of stranded vessels and take distressed seafarers to Seoul before repatriating them to Peking. On the other hand, the Japanese authorities would send one or more scholar officials with literacy of Sinitic from the nearest offices to the location of stranded vessels and escort them to Nagasaki, where verbal interpreting service could be arranged (Matsuura 2014; Okumura 2016).

Table 3.1 Interpreting service for communication with distressed Chinese seafarers during the early modern era

	Japan	Korea
Mode of interaction at the site of the stranded vessel	Brush-talk	Oral interpretation or brush-talk
Language used	Sinitic (written)	Chinese topolect (spoken) or Sinitic (written)
Location where interpreting service was available	Nagasaki	Seoul and coastal offices

interpreting service could be arranged, the maritime officials and the distressed seafarers would need to mobilize all linguistic and paralinguistic resources at their disposal to improvise and get their meanings across. Table 3.1 shows the availability of Japanese-Chinese and Korean-Chinese interpreting service, the language used, and the location where interpreting service was available.

Where the seafarers' vernaculars were unintelligible to the interpreter(s), brush-talking was looked upon as an alternative mode of communication for information gathering, albeit with no guarantee of success. For brush-talking to yield the desired communicative effect, it was imperative that at least one seafarer with a certain level of Sinitic literacy be identified. We have seen in Asakawa Zenan's diary-like account of the Chinese vessel Yongmao, that details as presented in the 'Qing-Ship Brush-talk' 清舶筆話 were essentially filtered through the Japanese literatus's brush-assisted interaction with a couple of literate persons on board the Chinese vessel. There was very little two-way brush-talk exchange so to speak, which Asakawa found disappointing as he manifestly had high hopes of engaging in spontaneous improvisation of literary verses and poetic exchange with literati of Chinese on board that ship from Qing China even though they were total strangers.[13] So, while the affordance of morphographic Sinitic allowed for writing-mediated communication more or less effectively, dyadic or otherwise, it was premised on one important condition, namely a certain level of Sinitic literacy was required of brush-talkers who wished to make sense of each other's intended meanings. On one extreme, rich and nuanced substance from topically the most practical to the literary could be displayed and exchanged using brush and ink on paper; on the other extreme, imbalanced levels of Sinitic literacy in dyadic interaction would render the give-and-take more like a brush-assisted interrogation, the content of which would tend to be colored with subjective guessing, making its reliability open to doubt.

In terms of linguistic resources, we have seen that even in those brush-talk records compiled by or in the presence of an interpreter, Classical Chinese or Sinitic elements which by design were traditionally intended for reading and writing,

---

13 "但恨漂商無文字、其所應對、率皆公務、除公務外、絶無風流文雅之語" ('Regrettably, the drifting merchants had little knowledge of written Chinese. Our give-and-take was limited to official business, with no mention of anything of literary interest at all.' See Appendix.)

were improvised spontaneously to serve transactional communication purposes (Brown & Yule 1983) between strangers, namely maritime officials and foreign seafarers. Neither side had any prior knowledge of the other; the only reason why they were engaged in communication was to go through the prescribed question-and-response routine, with a view to co-constructing a coherent account of the sequence of events leading to the shipwreck incident and, in the process, ascertaining the foreigners' identities and authenticating their stories before deciding what humanitarian support measures to provide and how to repatriate them, taking into account whether there was any security or health risk at stake. Amidst the meaning-making through brush(-assisted) conversation in writing, however, elements characteristically associated with individual brush-talkers' vernaculars might also surface, resulting in an admixture of lexico-grammatical elements from both written and spoken registers. Depending on the target reader, such reports might be written formally by a maritime official if intended to be read by someone in the upper echelons of the government (typically in Qing China and Chosŏn Korea), or loosely structured and informal, giving a summary of the main points of interest if the best that could be done was to engage an enthusiastic literatus of Sinitic to compile a record for the local archives (more characteristic of Edo Japan). In either case, the absence of a shared spoken language did little to prevent eager brush-talkers from making themselves understood using the morphographically intelligible and semantically more or less stable sinograms, an affordance of the Sinitic script apparently unparalleled by phonographic scripts like Latin or Arabic. As for writing technology, brush-talkers used brush, ink, and paper as a substitute for their tongues and, in so doing, they were able to get around an impediment in transcultural communication in speech, namely the annoying question 'How do you say this in X?', thanks to the intersubjective pronunciation of morphographic sinograms (Li 2020).

In terms of research outputs, in Japan and Korea, there is no shortage of compilations of records of 'drifting brush-talk' between maritime officials and distressed seafarers, varying in the extent to which the question-and-answer mode of interaction was, on one extreme, constructed single-handedly by one literatus (usually a maritime official or a scholar) based on fragmentary information gathered from illiterate seafarers or, on the other extreme, a near-verbatim record of brush conversations conducted interactively. The analysis of 'drifting brush-talk' as a recurrent sociolinguistic phenomenon during the eighteenth and nineteenth centuries in this chapter has barely scratched the surface. Much remains to be done with a view to better understanding the semiotic affordance of Sinitic and the functional role of brush-talking as a substitute modality of communication for speech in the maritime history of Sinographic East Asia.

References

Aoyama, R. (2020). Writing-mediated interaction face-to-face: Sinitic brushtalk in the Japanese missions' transnational encounters with foreigners during the mid-nineteenth Century. *China and Asia* 2(2): 234–269.

Brown, G., & Yule, G. (1983). *Discourse analysis*. Cambridge: Cambridge University Press.

Kanezashi, S. [金指正三] (1965). 近世海難救助制度の研究 ('Research on maritime salvage system in the early modern era'). Tokyo: Yoshikawa Kōbunkan [吉川弘文館].

Li, D. C. S. (2020). Writing-mediated interaction face-to-face: Sinitic brush-talk (漢文筆談) as an age-old lingua-cultural practice in premodern East Asian cross-border communication. *China and Asia* 2(2): 193–233.

Matsuura, A. [松浦章] (Ed.). (1989). 文化五年土佐漂着江南商船郁長發資料 ('Bunka 5th year document of drifting Jiangnan trading ship Yu Chang Fa in Tosa Prefecture'). Osaka, Japan: Institute of Oriental and Occidental Studies, Kansai University Press.

Matsuura, A. [松浦章] (2007). 近世東アジア海域諸国における海難救助形態 ('Rescue and salvage practices of East China Sea maritime nations in the early modern era'). *Institute of Oriental and Occidental Studies, Departmental Bulletin Paper, Kansai University* 40: 1–20.

Matsuura, A. [松浦章] (Ed.). (2011). 文化十二年豆州漂着南京永茂船資料 ('Bunka 12th year document of drifting Nanking ship Yongmao in Zu Prefecture'). Osaka, Japan: Institute of Oriental and Occidental Studies, Kansai University Press.

Matsuura, A. [松浦章] (2014). 朝鮮国漂着中国船の筆談記録にみる諸相 ('Observations of brush-talk records concerning Chinese shipwrecks in Chosŏn-dynasty Korea'). *Institute of Oriental and Occidental Studies, Departmental Bulletin Paper, Kansai University* 47: 57–69.

Matsuura, A., & Pien, F.-K. [松浦章、卞鳳奎] (2007). 清代帆船東亞航運史料彙編 ('Compilation of history materials on junks in East Asian shipping during the Ching dynasty'). 關西大學亞洲文化交流研究中心海外論叢 第三輯 *CSAC Overseas Publication Series 3, Kansai University*. Taipei: Lexis Books Ltd. [樂學書局有限公司].

Okumura, K. [奥村佳代子] (2016). 非漢語圏における中国語問答記録 — 『備邊司謄錄』「問情別単」の「問」の言葉 ('Records of dialogues in Chinese in non-Chinese speaking regions: An investigation of the surveys of shipwrecked Chinese sailors in the *Records of the Border Defense Council of Chosŏn*, with a focus on their linguistic significance'). *Institute of Oriental and Occidental Studies, Departmental Bulletin Paper, Kansai University* 49: 21–36.

Pibyŏnsa Tŭngnok [備邊司謄錄] ('A collection of the Record of the Border Defense Command of Chosŏn'). (1706a). 奎章閣原文檢索서비스 'Kyujanggak Original Text Searching Service'. 奎章閣韓國學研究會 Kyujanggak Institute for Korean Studies. Retrieved from http://kyudb.snu.ac.kr/pf01/rendererImg.do?item_cd=VBS&book_cd=GK15044_00&vol_no=0001&page_no=079a.

Pibyŏnsa Tŭngnok [備邊司謄錄] ('A collection of the Record of the Border Defense Command of Chosŏn'). (1706b). 韓國史데이터베이스 ('Database of Korean History'). National Institute of Korean History 國史編纂委員會. Retrieved March 4, 2021, from http://db.history.go.kr/item/level.do?itemId=bb&levelId=bb_057_001_04_0110&types=o.

Saito, M. (2021). *Kanbunmyaku: The literary Sinitic context and the birth of modern Japanese language and literature*. Leiden: Brill.

Shi, Z. [史志宏] (2006). China's overseas trade policy and its historical results: 1522–1840. In A. J. H. Latham & H. Kawakatsu (Eds.), *Intra-Asian trade and the world market* (pp. 24–43). London & New York: Routledge.

Tanaka, K., & Matsuura, A. [田中謙二、松浦章] (Ed.). (1986). 文政九年遠州漂着得泰船資料 ('Bunsei 9th year document of the drifting Tokutai ship in Enshu Prefecture'). Osaka, Japan: Institute of Oriental and Occidental Studies, Kansai University Press.

Yabuta, Y. [薮田貫] (Ed.). (1997). 寛政十二年遠州漂着唐船萬勝號資料 ('Kansei 12th year document of drifting Chinese ship Wansheng in Enshu Prefecture'). Osaka, Japan: Institute of Oriental and Occidental Studies, Kansai University Press.

Appendix: The first drifting record documented in Asakawa Zenan's 'Qing-Ship Brush-talk' 清舶筆話 (1815) (Matsuura 2011: 4–10)

清舶筆話叙

文化乙亥十二月廿九日南京永茂舩漂到豆州下田港余不佞以文墨承之爲属吏於韮山以掌筆話之事但恨漂商無文字其所應對率皆公務除公務外絶無風流文雅之語欲一一皆存之乎言渉忌諱事係機密者間或有之不可以存乎亦是人世奇遇書生孔筆豈忍弁髦視之乎因令取舍斟酌存十一於千百以寓鷄肋之意云

文化丙子春三月善菴朝川鼎撰

舩主　　舩主
夥長　　財副
摠管　　舵工
目侶　　目侶
随使　　隋使

唐商單子上有必故字乃一定之義故而者預先之義鷄鷄倍輕湏重湏起湏活湏等湏字乃助語全意義讀者勿誤其義

附録

卒啓
舩是何國住人將行長﨑貿易或将行佗邦洋中值惡風漂流于此哉意旨如何貴國王太守二書之可通于此郷次舩中衆人幾人詳誌之可呈

　本舩大唐于十一月二十日由乍地開駕行長﨑貿易在洋中遇暴風漂收貴地外港但此舩在外寄碇因風甚大即早催小舩㨨進内港以便通舩人衆平安放心爲感
　正月初一日　　南京舩主楊秋棠印

昨通折簡已審本舩大唐國往長﨑貿易洋中遇暴惡風漂泊于此地即請㨨入港内茲諾奈属日遇風緊外港泛張不任小舩力㨨大舩渡故遅澁也俟風色稍穏時速催便通舩㨨而入内港宜使君等心得平安必勿忡忡矣

　孟正二日　　豆州下田津　　出役
　　上

具禀人楊秋棠本舩舩名永茂向来往日本長﨑貿易于十一月二十日在大唐開行洋中大遇惡風槓棋傷損漂到貴地外港寄碇因風甚大不能放

心恐怕走碇即速催追小舩捧進内港、感不淺矣亦不知地名往長崎港門又不知來去有求貴地衆人即禀
貴地大頭目恩准上舩細細禀明貴國牌照爲憑所求勲感不淺矣

　　文化十三年正月　　南京舩主楊秋棠印
　　本舩在洋中遇惡風檣根損傷斷去篷擔漂收

貴國外港因風浪甚大恐傍碇地不好即速催小舩捧進内港但此舩往長崎貿易現在通舩水手九十人在洋日久柴水米俱已用完通舩人衆驚惶速請
通事老爹下舩細細商酌再行詳禀

　　正月初一日　　南京舩主楊秋棠印

再見投尺素茲審本舩大唐國開行之際所配柴米水等在洋中日久漂蕩今已欠缺通舩九十人難以度日活命茲承請求即命小舩米九斗柴百束水等聊送給一日之用耳其佗乏用之物不日入津時更寫字報知本舩長崎護送之事佗日承蒙日本南海之濱名伊豆州下田津

大頭目駕遇我等之舩細細再以申明我等之舩未知㝎在何月何可以開行往入長崎有求即發令諭以免昏悶所求恩准則感不淺矣
　　正月初九日　　財副陶粟橋印

本舩需用米粉芋艿麪粉洋紙祈照後開禀准爲感
計開
一　米粉　　　二十斤
一　芋艿　　　五十斤
一　麪粉　　　三十斤
一　洋紙外國ノ紙ヲ云美濃紙ニ充ル四刀
　　　以上今日給付是感
　　正月初九日　南京舩主楊秋棠印
　　　　計開
一　炭

以上銀額祈向長崎會所給付是感本舩昨日捧来　　尊諭承
江都王之好聖之德恩舜之心本舩衆人等感恩之致有勞各位委員大人諸事大大費心辦理之事感不淺矣本舩駕駛護送長崎之事有求各位大人即要趕緊議定送入長崎舩上人等一路日久在舩一切苦楚難以細細申明現在本舩目侣人等往長崎之路一一不知況且本舩大篷傷損不堪不能可用本舩交托貴地人等駕駛舩上大篷索路一切請貴地人上船細細看明應該添用早日端整配好所求恩准則感不淺矣

正月初八日　南京財副陶粟橋印

承
賜獸肉申謝恩念之致即請各位大頭目前均已問安矣我等昨日禀上一啓諒必收閲諸事一切有求恩典趕緊議定我等之舩即請王令早日駕送長崎感激不淺矣我等在舩一路漂泊苦楚明日請

一　豆腐
一　蘿卜
一　活鷄
一　蕃茹
以上之物不俱多少祈即付下是感
　　　正月初八日　　南京舡主楊秋棠印

本舡昨日付下魚菜等但通舡九十人必故二次而已現在用完祈日付下以便應用是感

正月初八日　　同

4 Senzaimaru's maiden voyage to Shanghai in 1862

Brush conversation between Japanese travelers and people they encountered in Qing China

David C. S. Li and Reijiro Aoyama

> Few Japanese learned to speak Chinese, but many travelers could read *Kanbun* (Literary Chinese), for centuries the *lingua franca* among all educated men and women in East Asia. This alone enabled a level of communication with the Chinese, particularly intellectuals and officials, that few Westerners ever attained. Even a Japanese visitor to China who knew little or effectively no Literary Chinese could still make some sense of the great majority of sights observed because of the proximity of meaning between the Chinese characters seen and their usually equivalent meaning in Japanese. For those who knew Literary Chinese well enough to communicate in it, communication took place through the medium of the 'brush conversation' in which the participants wrote in Literary Chinese on a piece of paper passed between them, just as they had for centuries. Their instinctive closeness was often referred to as *Kanji bunka*, the shared 'culture of Chinese characters'.
>
> (Joshua A. Fogel 1995: 80, slightly modified)

> The greatest advantage of the Chinese script . . . is that it enabled literate people in premodern East Asia to communicate directly in the absence of a common spoken language. Chinese-style writing was the East Asian lingua franca, or we should rather say scripta franca, because unlike elites who wrote and conversed in Latin in medieval and early modern Europe, Chinese-style writing was written language, a grapholect. When reading a Chinese text, Koreans, Japanese, and Vietnamese would voice them in their own vernaculars.
>
> (Wiebke Denecke 2014: 209)

Introduction

1862 was an auspicious year in the history of Sino-Japanese relations (Fogel 2014). After imposing restrictions on travel and trade – inbound as well as outbound – for over 200 years, the Tokugawa government dispatched a ship to Qing China with the express purpose of getting firsthand information about the Middle Kingdom, which for centuries was admired and looked upon as a source of inspiration by people on the Japanese archipelago. In the face of external

DOI: 10.4324/9781003048176-5

pressure demanding the opening of ports to facilitate trade and commerce, plus disturbing rumors that the Qing government had suffered a humiliating defeat in the hands of the British in the First Opium War (1839–1842), followed by the Taiping Rebellion (1851–1865) that preoccupied the Qing army for over a decade, the Tokugawa government desperately needed to weigh various options when dealing with Western powers whose demands were backed by ghastly gunboats and horrific firepower. There was thus an urgent need to find out what policy lines China adopted when dealing with Western aggression, how effective they were, with what particular outcomes as a result of those policy decisions. Above all, to avoid the unenviable fate of what befell Qing China, a good understanding of various sociopolitical institutions that had or had not worked well was a must. That was the background against which the Senzaimaru 千歳丸, acquired from the British, purpose-refitted and manned by a European crew of 16 headed by a British captain, set sail to Shanghai on 2 June 1862. On board were fifty-one Japanese passengers who were carefully selected by the Tokugawa government, including eight samurais and their 13 servants, six officials and six merchants from Nagasaki, four interpreters of Chinese and two interpreters of Dutch, two doctors, six cooks, and four sailors (Nōtomi 1862/1997: 24). Some were tasked with specific duties. For instance, the 'secret itinerary' of Godai Saisuke 五代才助 (1836–1885) was to chart shipping routes from Satsuma to Shanghai and to observe trading activities and conditions (Fogel 1995: 85).

As a historical event, the 'maiden voyage' (Fogel 2014) of Senzaimaru to Shanghai has been the object of study in a number of book-length treatises (e.g., Feng 2001/2017; Fogel 2014) and several journal articles and book chapters (Feng 1999, 2000; Fogel 1995, 2002, 2008; Sheng 2016). From the point of view of documentation, researchers of the Senzaimaru voyage are blessed with elaborate records of the Japanese travelers' personal experiences, keen observations, and reflective insights they gained during their two-month venture in the most modern metropolis of the time in East Asia. Altogether a total of 17 texts were produced: 16 travelogues or diary accounts by the samurais, plus one by a merchant from Nagasaki, including verbatim records of brush-talk artifacts. Two extended series of brushed encounters were compiled: 'No cause brush-talk' (*Botsubi hitsugo* 没鼻筆語) by Hibino Teruhiro 日比野輝寛 (1838–1912), and 'Brush-talk' (*Hitsudan* 筆談) by Takasugi Shinsaku 高杉晋作 (1839–1867). Such records suggest that from the outset, artifacts produced through brush-talking were consciously collected for record-keeping and subsequent dissemination through publication. Written essentially in *kanji*, a form of Literary Sinitic comprehensible to literati speaking different languages elsewhere in Sinographic East Asia (Kornicki 2018; Handel 2019; cf. Clements 2019), these written outputs provide elaborate details on the sociopolitical and econo-cultural realities of Qing China, which were shocking and thought-provoking in many ways. The Japanese travelers did not just rely on their eyes; much of the information and detailed descriptions pertaining to people, sociopolitical institutions, rituals and customs, livelihood of the locals, and social practices (ways of doing and seeing things) were gathered by communicating with the people they met, mainly Chinese but also some westerners. But how? From the language profile of the Japanese travelers, few except four interpreters had any working knowledge of spoken Chinese, not to mention varieties of the Wu topolect 吳語 widely spoken in and around Shanghai. In a similar vein, with few exceptions (a few merchants whose cross-border trading activities had taken them to Nagasaki on short-term stays) the Chinese people they met spoke hardly any Japanese. Bilingualism being uncommon, how did Chinese and Japanese communicate? Not having a shared spoken language was indeed an inconvenience, but it did little to prevent both sides from making meaning, synchronously and interactively face-to-face.

Morphographic script: phonetic intersubjectivity of written Chinese

Whatever the writing system, phonographic or otherwise, the graphic units in writing are mediated by speech (DeFrancis 1984, 1989). On the other hand, in many parts of the world, the language used for writing may diverge lexico-grammatically from the language in speech considerably. There are many communities where the local vernaculars are used alongside a divergent, highly codified, and superposed written language associated with a strong cultural heritage and prestige (i.e., 'diglossia', Ferguson 1959; Fishman 1967; Snow 2010, 2013). In effect, in a diglossic community, a standardized, high (H) variety is used in writing while a colloquial, low (L) variety is used for communication in speech. Classical examples of such communities include different parts of medieval Europe, where the H variety Latin was used for formal writing purposes while the local vernaculars diverged lexico-grammatically from Latin considerably. A contemporary parallel may be found in different parts of Germany, Austria, and Switzerland. In German-speaking Switzerland, for instance, Standard German (H) is reserved for formal functions (e.g., education, printed media, news broadcast) while a colloquial (L) variety of Swiss German is used for informal communication purposes (compare also the functional division of labor between Classical Arabic and regional colloquial varieties of Arabic in the Middle East).

China is another frequently cited classical example of diglossia. Until the 1910s, before the vernacularization or 'plain language' movement caught on in early republican China, for over a thousand years Literary Sinitic or Classical Chinese (*wenyan* 文言) had been used for all formal communication purposes from imperial decrees to commercial agreements (Handel 2019). Since the Sui dynasty (581–618 CE), familiarity with a prescribed body of Classical Chinese canons was also a *sine qua non* for gaining access to officialdom via the civil service examination system (*kējǔ* 科舉), which was implemented for well over a millennium before being abolished in 1905 (Elman 2014). With its highly condensed lexico-grammar that deviates from the regional vernaculars of practically all Han Chinese speakers, Classical Chinese was taught and learned through reading aloud in the local topolect. This is why whatever the topolect of the literati, they were able to pronounce individual graphic units – Chinese characters or sinograms – according to local pronunciation norms, even though in speech, a completely different set of lexico-grammatical and stylistic norms were followed. Unlike speakers of alphabetic languages like Classical Greek and Classical Latin, whose word pronunciation is guided by more or less systematic correspondence between the phonetic values of discrete letters and their combinations resulting in regional accents or dialects of the same language, the phonetic value of non-alphabetic sinograms varies intersubjectively, subject to the preferred pronunciation of speakers of different regional topolects, which may not be mutually intelligible.

What happened when Classical Chinese texts were disseminated and learned in Korean- and Japanese-speaking communities, whose languages are typologically very different from Chinese? For instance, Chinese sinograms are essentially morpho-syllabic, have little morphology, and follow a verb-medial normative word order (SVO); by contrast, Japanese and Korean are morphologically agglutinating and verb-final (SOV). Prior to the emergence of their scripts for writing their respective national languages, since the seventh century, Classical Chinese texts had been devoured – acquired through Chinese primers and imitated in their use – through complex reading and writing processes of *kundoku* (訓讀, Kor: *hundok*; Mand: *xùndú*, Lurie 2011) and *idu* 吏讀, the latter being 'a method of writing that was widely employed in [Korean] official documents, memoranda, and textual annotations up until the early twentieth century' (Lurie 2011: 202). In terms of linguistic resources, Handel (2019: 110–111) regards *idu* as 'a highly stylized form of written Korean employing a large amount of Sino-Korean vocabulary' and, as such, it may be seen as 'a natural extension of the glossing of Literary Sinitic texts' (cf. 'cleric writing', Taylor & Taylor 2014). There is some evidence that the reading and writing practices of *kundoku* were spread from the Korean peninsula to the Japanese archipelago[1] via Korean scribes employed by their Japanese hosts from as early as the fifth or sixth century (Lurie 2011; cf. Handel 2019).

Like their Han Chinese counterparts, when reading aloud, Korean and Japanese literati would assign their local vernacular pronunciation to individual sinograms, while adjusting the syntax and word order to make them conform to the grammatical norms of their own language (Clements 2015). As a result of very similar literacy training processes and practices, the same sinograms – be they monosyllabic or polysyllabic words – would take on rather different phonetic values when used (i.e., pronounced in their own language) by literati from different parts of Sinographic East Asia (Denecke 2014; see Table 4.1 for illustrations).

While engaged in transcultural, cross-border communication, such literati would each be guided by the pronunciation of their respective languages when invoking specific sinograms, which have a good chance of being intelligible if they were selected from a shared inventory of literary canons, thanks to the divergent phonetic incarnations of written Chinese, a non-alphabetic script. In short,

---

1 Including the kingdom of Ryukyu, see Wong, this volume.

Table 4.1 Some examples of sinograms in Literary Sinitic pronounced in Chinese, Korean, and Japanese

Sinograms	Meaning (English)	Chinese (e.g., Mandarin)	Korean	Japanese
孔子	Confucius	kǒngzǐ	kongja	kōshi
學生	pupil, student	xuésheng	haksaeng	gakusei
中國	China	zhōngguó	chung-guk	chūgoku
筆談	brush-talk	bǐtán	p'iltam	hitsudan

this is how, despite a lack of a shared spoken language, for hundreds of years educated literati of Literary Chinese were able to make themselves understood in cross-border communication through brush-talk, without knowing or having to ask how the sinograms they improvised were actually pronounced in their fellow brush-talkers' own language (Kornicki 2018). We will characterize this feature as 'phonetic intersubjectivity', which is a crucial writing condition for the use and spread of Classical Chinese or Sinitic as a written lingua franca or 'scripta franca' (Denecke 2014: 209; cf. Clements 2017, 2019).

Use of Sinitic as a scripta franca: brush conversation in Sino-Japanese encounters

Some of the instances of Sinitic brush-talk involved transactional communication, of which the most commonly cited contexts are buying and selling, and requesting factual information, but there were also interactional 'chats' from inquiries and responses to deep intellectual exchange of views on matters of shared literary or sociopolitical interest. The latter was clearly possible only after rapport had been built and friendship cemented in previous encounters.

To illustrate the scripta franca function of Sinitic (Li et al. 2020), let us begin with one instructive example of brush conversation showing how a Senzaimaru traveler was pleasantly surprised by the communicative potential of his improvisation in writing when buying ink from a proprietor-seller in Shanghai, as noted in his diary account (Hibino 1862b/1997: 65).[2]

---

2 An idiomatic translation of this brush conversation episode in English may be found in Fogel (1995: 81, quoted with slight modification): 'When I would go to a market, I could not communicate orally there. Replacing the tongue with the brush, though, enabled rapid communication. . . . If I wrote [in *kanbun*], "How much is this ink?" [the proprietor-seller] might respond, "One yuan". If I wrote, "You're overcharging me", he might respond, "That's the genuine, true price" or "That's the real price, none other". Suppose I wrote, "I don't like the color of the ink, and it has no aroma. I think it was produced recently", He might respond, "All of these goods are aged, and the aroma is within"'. (Source: Hibino Teruhiro (1862b/1997), 贅尤録 ['Boredom Notes'] (entry for 5/10), in *Bunkyū ninen Shanhai nikki*, p. 65)

	Brush conversation[3]	Idiomatic translation
HT:	此墨價若干	'This ink costs how much?'
P-S:	一元	'One yuan'
HT:	虛價	'Not the real price'
P-S:	真正實價/實價不二	'That's the genuine, true price'/'That's the real price, none other'
HT:	墨色不好，且不香，想近製	'Ink color not good, not fragrant either, I think it was made only recently'
P-S:	都是陳貨，香在內	'All aged products, aroma inside'

HT: Hibino Teruhiro (日比野輝寛); P-S: Proprietor-seller in Shanghai

At this point, Hibino urged the proprietor-seller to offer a more favorable price, but gave no indication how that speech act of bargaining was expressed in sinograms. That brush-talk episode ended with two sinograms written by the proprietor-seller: 遵命, which was understood intersubjectively to mean 'As [you] wish'.

Likewise, having discovered the communicative potential of brush conversation when communicating with Chinese where no interpreting was needed, Takasugi was overcome with joy (Fogel 1995: 91). A similar exhilarating discovery was reported in the diary account of Nakura Anato 名倉予何人 (1822–1901): 'Travel observations in China' 支那見聞錄. Encouraged by a shared written language, he initiated to express himself in writing, only to be pleasantly surprised that the sinograms he brushed on paper managed to get his meanings across more or less successfully, as evidenced by the meaningful responses he received from fellow Chinese brush-talkers. What is more, he noted that the same sinograms, if articulated in speech, would sound very strange and funny:

和漢ノ字義同フテ音訓殊ニ言語不通深クアヤシムモノアリ或ハ余ニ請フテ筆語ノ文字ヲ讀マレム余シ乃チ邦讀從テ朗カニ讀起セバ且ツ怪シミ且ツ笑テ掌ヲ撫スルモノアリ(名倉予何人 Nakura Anato 1862/1997: 208)

---

[3] As mentioned, in principle a sinogram is pronounceable in any Chinese or Japanese topolect. This is further complicated by the fact that a sinogram may have multiple reading pronunciations depending on the historical periods when the words they were associated with were imported into Japan, not to mention regional and individual variations of reading preferences or practices. There is no way for us to tell how the sinograms were actually pronounced or heard by individual brush-talkers. For this reason, no attempt will be made to transcribe sinogram-based brush-talk content into Chinese (e.g., Shanghainese or Mandarin) or Japanese (e.g., *on* reading vs. *kun* reading). What is important is to bear in mind that successful meaning-making in transcultural communication through brush-talking was warranted by literacy of writing-mediated sinograms rather than their pronunciation. Put differently, mutual intelligibility would have been blocked if the sinograms were uttered in speech due to phonetic intersubjectivity. For example, 此墨 ('this ink') in Hibino's first question was instantly understood by the Chinese proprietor-seller despite tremendous diversity in their respective pronunciations: *shi boku* (Jap: *on* reading), *kono sumi* (Jap: *kun* reading), *cĭ mò* (Mandarin Chinese), ci^{35} mak^{22} (Cantonese), not to mention many other dialectal variations in China. In the rest of the brush-talk examples, the pronunciation of specific sinograms will only be provided if deemed relevant and important.

Sinograms in Japanese and Chinese are identical [but] are pronounced very differently, hence not mutually intelligible in speech, something that [we] found very strange. Sometimes I invited my counterpart to engage in brush conversation, and requested that the sinograms be read out loud in Chinese [before] I pronounced the same sinograms in Japanese. As we each read [them] out loud, we were both struck by how strange the other side's reading sounded, which was marvelous and gave us a good laugh.[4]

That awareness later led Nakura to conduct brush conversations with refugees he came across near the Qing-Taiping battlefield. Many refugees reportedly wanted to 'talk' to him using brush, ink, and paper, but it was not always possible partly due to literacy problems (Fogel 1995: 89). While the intended meaning of whatever transpired on paper might be missed and that miscommunication could not be avoided, Nakura's observation as mentioned earlier provides strong evidence that in Chinese-Japanese cross-border communication, each side's speech sounded strange or hilarious to the other, and was therefore not an option for interactional meaning-making. This is in stark contrast with the communicative potential of a body of shared but phonetically intersubjective written sinograms in their respective linguistic repertoire. Indeed, in response to a Qing Chinese official, Zhejiang Inspector Fang Yaoqing 浙江巡察 方瑤卿, who expressed regret for not being able to engage in deep talk owing to a lack of a shared spoken language, Hibino (1862a/1997: 141) remarked that the brush is a good-enough substitute:

	Brush conversation	Idiomatic translation
FYQ:	接閱來字，可謂一見如故。如不相棄，容日定當面領教言也。惜乎，言語兩不會意。	'Your message was well received, as if we were old friends in our first encounter. If our friendship is not relinquished, I would definitely receive good teaching from your Good Self someday. Regrettably, our respective spoken languages would not be able to get across our meanings.'
HT:	筆端有舌，何待言語。	'At the tip of the brush is a tongue, what to expect from speech?'

FYQ: Fang Yaoqing (方瑤卿); HT: Hibino Teruhiro (日比野輝寬)

A total of 17 diary accounts were produced by Senzaimaru passengers (Takasugi contributed five). In their portrayal of communication with Qing Chinese people they encountered, brush-talk was the most frequently mentioned modality of communication, which was made possible by the fact that Chinese and Japanese

---

4 Our translation; compare Chinese translation by Feng (2001/2017: 198): '和漢字同，音訓殊，言語不通，深以爲怪。有時我請對方筆語，又請對方將漢字讀出，我用邦讀。彼此朗朗讀出，互相以爲怪異，都撫掌而笑。'

shared the same written language, and that face-to-face interaction between them could take place through writing. This point is nicely captured by one instructive observation of Nōtomi Kaijirō 納富介次郎 (1844–1918) in his diary account:

> 皇邦ハ諸外夷ト異ニ聖教ヲ崇ビ文字明ラカナリト聞イテ、楽ミテ我 輩ヲ来リ訪ヒ、詩画筆語等ニテ自ラ親シクナリ (納富介次郎 Nōtomi 1862/1997: 20)
>
> They [the Chinese] heard that unlike westerners, people from the Japanese kingdom respected and followed the teaching of the sages, and both sides could communicate using the same written words, so many people would take pleasure in visiting [us], indulging in an outpouring of [our] inner feelings through exchange of poetic verses in our brush conversation.[5]

Regarding the salience of Sinitic brush-talk as a viable lingua-cultural practice in the history of Chinese-Japanese cross-border communication, Feng (2001/2017: 198–201) points out that extensive brush-talk records were produced by the celebrated Ming Chinese scholar Zhu Shunshui 朱舜水 (1600–1682) during his visits to Nagasaki.[6] Being highly respected by his hosts, including many daimyōs 大名,[7] Zhu was able to give lectures on Chinese classics and responded to their questions, interactively and apparently seamlessly using brush, ink, and paper. Plenty of evidence of such a prolific mode of communication, often exuding deep intellectual exchange, may be found in the contextualized examples of brush-talk plus personal notes that were edited and published in 'Posthumous notes of Zhu Shunshui' (舜水遺書, cf. Matsuura 2011; 'Collected works of Zhu Shunshui' 朱舜水集, edited by Zhu Qianzhi 朱謙之 1981; extensive records of brush conversation may be found on pp. 381–424. For more details, see Li 2020).

For brush-talk to take place more or less effectively, however, the brush-talkers must be able to read and write hundreds if not thousands of sinograms. While the majority of sinograms are semantically stable and intelligible in cross-border communication, given marked cultural differences in Qing China and Japan, it is not surprising that Senzaimaru visitors would encounter literacy problems occasionally. For instance, upon arrival in Shanghai and shortly after settling down, Hibino recalled being struck by the sinograms displayed in a shop sign, Kroes & Co. 點耶洋行, a Dutch company which was named after the Vice-Consul of the

---

5 Our translation; compare translation into Chinese by Feng (2001/2017: 195): '他們聽說皇邦與諸洋人不同，崇聖教，彼此文字相通，故有不少人樂於來訪，詩話筆語，交流感情。'
6 Zhu Shunshui 朱舜水 visited Nagasaki six times for short periods in 1645, 1647, 1652, 1653, 1654, and 1658, before staying there for almost seven years from 1659 to 1665. In the next seventeen years until his death in 1682, Zhu was invited to serve as a guest teacher 賓師 of the daimyō of the Mito domain 水戶 and an advisor to Tokugawa Mitsukuni 德川光圀 (1628–1701).
7 For example, Tokugawa Mitsukuni 德川光圀 (1628–1701), Andō Morinari 安東守約 (1622–1701), Asaka Kaku 安積覺 (1656–1738) and Oyake Seijun 小宅生順 (1638–1674).

Dutch Consulate, Theodorus Kroes.[8] Through brush-talk, Hibino was 'told' that the first two sinograms 點耶 was the name of the business, while 洋行 denoted a company whose lexical equivalent in modern Japanese was 商社 (Jap: *shōsha*; compare modern Mandarin Chinese: *shāng shè*).

In the diary accounts of some Senzaimaru travelers, the collecting of information through brush-talk was sometimes inconvenienced by the target respondents' lack of literacy in Sinitic (e.g., refugees who wanted to 'talk' to Nakura Anato but could not). On one such occasion, Hibino reported a wish to find out what the Taiping Rebellion leader Hong Xiuquan 洪秀全 (1814–1864) was like as a person. Upon learning that a servant 從僕 of Jiangsu merchant Jia Chunling 賈春舲 had been captured by Taiping troops, and had seen Hong Xiuquan before escaping from Suzhou to Shanghai, Hibino requested brush-talking with that servant, only to give up upon learning that it would be impracticable. Coming from a socioeconomically underprivileged background, the servant simply did not have enough literacy in Sinitic to engage in brush conversation (Hibino 1862a/1997: 166):

	Brush conversation	Idiomatic translation
HT:	欲與從僕筆語,可乎?	'[I] wanted to engage your servant in brush conversation, is that possible?'
JCL:	彼不知一丁字	'He hardly knew any sinograms.'

HT: Hibino Teruhiro (日比野輝寬); JCL: Jia Chunling (賈春舲)

All this shows that brush-talk was premised on a sufficiently high level of literacy in Literary Sinitic, which was sometimes mixed with some vernacular elements.

In terms of topics, the diary accounts of brush-talk with Qing Chinese locals encountered cover a wide range. Following is a short list of those salient ones mentioned in two or more diary accounts by Senzaimaru travelers:

- military organization, leadership and training (how drills were conducted)
- how Shanghai's defense against Taiping rebels was carried out by the British and French army
- adverse social impact of opium and why it was so popular among men and so difficult to curb
- refugees' place of origin and livelihood
- religion, spread of Christianity, and missionaries' curing and nursing activities in Qing China compared with strict prohibition of Christianity in Japan
- education system and schooling practice in Qing China
- values of antique Chinese books and paintings

---

8 See http://godaidon.com/2018/01/31/.

Interestingly, some topics were apparently sociopolitically too sensitive for the brush-talk artifacts to be kept for record and had to be destroyed (Feng 2001/2017: 201). One instructive remark may be found in Takasugi's diary account:

> 六月廿日訪陳汝欽，告別，筆話。此日予與陳汝欽談素志，不可記之事甚多，因不錄。

> On June 20, I visited Chen Ruqin to bid farewell through brush conversation. On this day Chen Ruqin and I spoke our minds candidly, and so plenty of topics in our brush-talk could not be kept, and so they were not retained.
>
> (Takasugi 1862/1916: 117)

Apart from diary accounts involving Qing Chinese brush-talkers, brush-talk was also conducted with American and British consulate personnel. For instance, in a diary account focusing on intelligence collected from foreigners (Takasugi 1862/1916), Takasugi mentioned one such 'conversation' he had with a few Chinese employees hired by the Dutch at the aforementioned Kroes & Co. (Feng 2001/2017: 167). As he was about to get his brush and writing kit ready to inquire why Russia was such a formidable power, the brush conversation was abruptly called off due to some urgent matter relayed by a consulate staffer (Takasugi 1862/1916: 106). According to Takasugi, he and Godai Saisuke were engaged in a few other brush conversations in a publishing house *Mohai shuguan* 墨海書館; one of the brush-talkers was William Muirhead (adopted Chinese name Mu Weilian 慕維廉), an American priest well versed in Chinese and English working as an interpreter there.

Sociocultural significance of brush conversation as a modality of cross-border communication

The Senzaimaru diary accounts also contain ancillary evidence of brush-talk being a regular lingua-cultural activity of the Japanese adventurers during their visit. Before departing for Shanghai, paper was among various necessities loaded onto the Senzaimaru (e.g., '5,000 sheets of paper' 形付紙 5000 枚, Matsudaya 松田屋伴吉1862/1997: 48; cf. Feng 2001/2017: 60). Two months later, paper was among a list of items purchased by Japanese travelers shortly before setting sail for their homeward-bound journey (Feng 2001/2017: 185). While we have no evidence of what sort of purpose that amount of paper was used for (e.g., commodity versus personal use), it is conceivable that clean paper was needed for personal diary writing and other forms of record-keeping. Whether or not the instrumental role of paper in sustaining a 'brush conversation' was discovered accidentally by the Japanese travelers after arriving in Shanghai, the paper purchased before their return trip might well serve to tidy up and consolidate the loose sheets and other artifacts arising from their brushed encounters in Shanghai.

One of the indispensable stationery items in the writing kit is an ink stone (硯, Jap: *suzuri*; Mand: *yàn*). Whereas brush, ink, and paper are all consumables, an ink stone is more durable and may last a sufficiently long time for personal emotional attachment to develop. It comes as no surprise, therefore, that when bidding farewell, an ink stone would be considered a meaningful gift for someone whose friendship was treasured and whom one would possibly never see again. This happened to Takasugi, who had developed deep intellectual communion with Chen Ruqin 陳汝欽 during his visit to Shanghai. To express his profound gratitude to Chen, he offered him his own personal Japanese-polished ink stone, which was accepted, if reluctantly (Takasugi 1862/1916: 117):

	Brush conversation	*Idiomatic translation*
TS:	固古硯一具呈於足下，是弟所常用之硯。石固疏，然是亦東洋之產，乃贈兄報知己之恩而己。	'This old ink stone presented in front of your Esteemed Self, is an ink stone used by Younger Brother [my humble self]. The quality of the stone is admittedly not so good, yet given that it is a product of Japan, I would like to offer it to Elder Brother [you] as a token of your favorable recognition of me as a true friend.'
CRQ:	此物諒亦甚珍，賜送與弟恐不得其人也。然卻之，恐蹈不恭之誚。謹拜謝，登受。	'This object must be extremely precious, not sure if Younger Brother [my humble self] is the right person to receive it as a gift. But to decline it would render me disrespectful. Hence I accept it with sincere gratitude.'

TS: Takasugi Shinsaku (高杉晋作); CRQ: Chen Ruqin (陳汝欽)

In addition to the sharing and exchange of views, Sinitic was also commonly used for literati to improvise aesthetically pleasing poetic verses, which was one affectively loaded genre that allowed for an outpouring of deep emotions and personal feelings triggered by the brush-talk context (see Liu, this volume). Indeed, there is plenty of evidence that in transcultural, cross-border communication, poetry, being a popular genre of choice among literati of Classical Chinese canons and literature in Sinographic East Asia, would be composed for a variety of purposes. As pointed out by Howland (1996: 48): 'the quintessential practice of this common [brush-talking] discourse was poetry writing, the purpose of which was to concretize past and present in a self-perpetuating and universal Civilization'. Being terse and sublime, poetry allowed such literati to express deep emotions and personal sentiments, or make thoughtful connections with the interactional context at large such as signaling admiration and agreement of intellectual sharing made by the fellow brush-talker, spiritual communion by alluding to works or deeds of prominent literary figures, comparison with well-known historical events in the past, or simply appreciation of colorful aromatic flowers in the vicinity, and the like. Thus, given the emotional bonding with Chen Ruqin which evolved after several rounds of intellectually deep brush conversation, it is not surprising that Takasugi would offer to write him a poem – a heptasyllabic quatrain[9] – among other things to register his mixed feelings while bidding farewell, knowing full well that their personal bond would likely be severed forever (Takasugi 1862/1916: 85):

臨敵練磨武與文	'Keep up your martial arts and literary flair in the face of adversaries;
他年應有建功勳	You can expect to win recognition for your achievements and merits.
孤生千里歸鄉後	Upon my lonesome return to my hometown thousands of *li* away;
每遇患難又思君	My thoughts will be with you whenever my life is imperiled.' (Our translation)

In return, Chen requested Takasugi to offer him to autograph, as a souvenir, a calligraphic token of his newly adopted appellation 默生,[10] which was purposely modeled on that of Chen (勉生). Then, beholding Takasugi's calligraphy, Chen could not help remarking (Takasugi 1862/1916: 118):

書更妙，字亦以英氣建之。	'Your writing looks even more ingenious, and the characters are permeated with charm and valor.' (Our translation)

All this attests to the sociocultural significance of brush conversation as a lingua-cultural practice as well as a viable means of cross-border communication between Chinese and Japanese literati of Literary Sinitic, synchronously and interactively face-to-face.

Coda

The Senzaimaru expedition to Shanghai in 1862 gave the Japanese travelers firsthand information about the Qing Empire. The seventeen eye-witness diary accounts contain rich details of the sorry state of Qing China some two decades after her humiliating defeat by British 'red-haired barbarians' armed with lethal gunboats and formidable weaponry. Among the eyesores was the dire state of sanitation in the densely populated areas, where clean water was hard to come by largely because untreated sewage including human feces were disposed directly into the river and the sea. One consequence of such appalling sanitary conditions

---

9 In Mandarin Chinese, 七言絕句 *qī yán juéjù*: verses made up of four seven-syllable lines.
10 According to Takasugi Shinsaku, the appellation 默生 was inspired by a philosophical treatise of the celebrated Ming Confucianist Wang Yangming 王陽明 (Feng 2001/2017: 214).

was that three of the fifty-one Japanese travelers died in Shanghai after contracting a disease. Such observations and experiences as reported by Senzaimaru adventurers had a huge and lasting impact among intellectuals in Japan. Thenceforth, the Middle Kingdom ceased to be a role model to emulate. Above all, the centuries-old Tokugawan diplomacy of strictly controlling foreign trade and residents gave way to a more enlightened open-door policy and learning from the West (Toby 1984; Arano et al. 2012). There was near consensus, especially among the lower social strata of samurais, that such a strategic re-orientation was absolutely necessary and urgently needed if Japan were to avoid being caught in a quagmire like what her once-venerable neighbor across the Sea of Japan had to put up with.

In the Senzaimaru travelogues, eye-witness accounts and commentaries are complemented with plenty of information gathered from locals they met in the heart and periphery of China's most modern metropolis Shanghai, not only commoners and people doing business in the street but also a few Qing government officials and Westerners. A lack of a shared spoken language made it difficult for Chinese-Japanese encounters and interactive meaning-making to take place in speech, and yet communication did not seem to be a big problem, thanks largely to the option of writing or composing sinograms in Literary Sinitic. Such an option appeared to be functioning well from day one of the Senzaimaru ventures in Shanghai (recall that Hibino Teruhiro found out through brush-talk what the four sinograms that made up the name of a shop near the lodging meant). By far brush conversation facilitated by the use of brush, ink, and paper was the most popular modality of communication with locals, despite the presence of interpreters conversant in Chinese and Dutch.

Brush-talking between Chinese and Japanese literati was possible because Literary Sinitic that they shared was written with the same script, which was morphographic or non-alphabetic (Handel 2019; cf. Clements 2017, 2019; Denecke 2014; Kornicki 2018). As the hundreds or even thousands of sinograms were semantically more or less stable when invoked in Chinese-Japanese cross-border communication, a certain level of literacy in Literary Sinitic allowed them to make meaning directly and interactively in writing while a question in speech like 'How do you say this in your language?' would be obviated. Such a sinogram-based, writing-mediated modality of cross-border communication, synchronously and interactively face-to-face, seemed to be script-specific and unparalleled in other phonographic languages written with an alphabetic script (cf. the 'morphographic hypothesis', Li 2020).

This brings to mind a remark by Masao Miyoshi 三好将夫 (1928–2009), how frustrating it was for the 1860 Japanese diplomatic mission to the USA to communicate in English (Fogel 1995: 94), a problem that Japanese travelers in China – like those visiting Shanghai on board the Senzaimaru in 1862 – could mitigate or even get around by resorting to writing as a substitute modality for speech, thanks to the phonetic intersubjectivity of a shared morphographic, non-alphabetic script. According to recollections of Japanese participants in the 1860 mission to the USA, those communication problems and frustrations they encountered when communicating with Americans in English were in stark contrast with their brush-talk experiences when interacting and exchanging views with the Chinese diasporas in the USA as well as others they met during their return journey at trading ports like Batavia and Hong Kong. Like the Senzaimaru passengers' fruitful brush-talk experiences exemplified earlier, recollections of the literate participants in the 1860 Japanese mission to the USA show that writing-mediated, sinogram-based improvisation using brush, ink, and paper allowed them to engage in 'silent conversation' with literate members of the Chinese diasporas effectively (see Aoyama 2020; also this volume).

References

Aoyama, R. (2020). Writing-mediated interaction face-to-face: Sinitic brushtalk in the Japanese missions' transnational encounters with foreigners during the mid-nineteenth century. *China and Asia* 2(2): 234–269.

Arano, Y., Ishii, M., & Murai, Shōsuke [荒野泰典、石井正敏、村井章介] (2012). 近代化する日本 ('Modernizing Japan'). Tokyo: Yoshikawa Kōbunkan.

Clements, R. (2015). *A cultural history of translation in early modern Japan*. Cambridge: Cambridge University Press.

Clements, R. (2017). Speaking in tongues? Daimyo, Zen monks, and spoken Chinese in Japan, 1661–1711. *The Journal of Asian Studies* 76(3): 603–626.

Clements, R. (2019). Brush talk as the 'lingua franca' of diplomacy in Japanese-Korean encounters, c. 1600–1868. *The Historical Journal* 62(2): 289–309.

DeFrancis, J. (1984). *The Chinese language: Fact and fantasy*. Honolulu: University of Hawai'i Press.

DeFrancis, J. (1989). *Visible speech: The diverse oneness of writing systems*. Honolulu: University of Hawai'i Press.

Denecke, W. (2014). Worlds without translation: Premodern East Asia and the power of character scripts. In S. Bermann & C. Porter (Eds.), *A companion to translation studies* (pp. 204–216). Chichester: Wiley-Blackwell.

Elman, B. A. (2014). Unintended consequences of classical literacies for the Early Modern Chinese civil examinations. In E. A. Elman (Ed.), *Rethinking East Asian languages, vernaculars, and literacy, 1000–1919* (pp. 198–219). Leiden and Boston: Brill.

Feng, T. [馮天瑜] (1999). 千歲丸上海行：日本幕末期の中國觀察を評す ('The Shanghai voyage of the Senzaimaru: Evaluating the observations of China in late-Edo Japan'). *Chūgoku* 中国 21(7): 169–198.

Feng, T. [馮天瑜] (2000). 千歲丸：日本鎖國 二百年後使清第一船 ('Senzaimaru: The first ship to visit China following two hundred years of Japan's closed country'). *The Qing History Journal* 清史研究 3: 86–93.

Feng, T. [馮天瑜] (2001/2017). 千歲丸上海行日本人 1862 年的中國觀察（第二版）('The Senzaimaru's trip to Shanghai: Japanese views of China in 1862') (2nd ed.). Wuhan: Hubei People's Press.

Ferguson, C. (1959). Diglossia. *Word* 15: 325–340.

Fishman, J. (1967). Bilingualism with and without diglossia; Diglossia with and without bilingualism. *Journal of Social Issues* 23(2): 29–38.

Fogel, J. A. (1995). The voyage of the Senzaimaru to Shanghai: Early Sino-Japanese contacts in the modern era. In J. A. Fogel (Ed.), *The cultural dimension of Sino-Japanese relations: Essays on the nineteenth and twentieth centuries* (pp. 79–94). New York: M. E. Sharpe.

Fogel. J. A. (2002). Japanese travelers to Shanghai in the 1860s. In J. A. Fogel & J. C. Baxter (Eds.). *Historiography and Japanese consciousness of values and norms* (pp. 79–99). Kyoto: International Research Center for Japanese Studies.

Fogel. J. A. (2008). A decisive turning point in Sino-Japanese relations: The Senzaimaru voyage to Shanghai of 1862. *Late Imperial China* 29.1 Supplement: 104–124.

Fogel. J. A. (2014). *Maiden voyage: The Senzaimaru and the creation of modern Sino-Japanese relations*. Oakland. CA: University of California Press.

Handel. Z. (2019). *Sinography: The borrowing and adaptation of the Chinese script*. Leiden & Boston: Brill.

Hibino. T. [日比野輝寛] (1862a/1997). 沒鼻筆語 ('No cause brush-talk'). In S. Kojima [小島晋治] (Ed.). 幕末明治中国見聞録集成第1巻 ('Collection of travel accounts of China from the late Edo and Meiji periods') (vol. 1. pp. 137–177). Tokyo: Yumani shobo.

Hibino. T. [日比野輝寛] (1862b/1997). 贅尤録 ('Boredom notes'). In S. Kojima [小島晋治] (Ed.). 幕末明治中国見聞録集成第1巻 ('Collection of travel accounts of China from the late Edo and Meiji periods') (vol. 1. pp. 47–135). Tokyo: Yumani shobo.

Howland. D. R. (1996). *Borders of Chinese civilization: Geography and history at empire's end*. Durham & London: Duke University Press.

Kornicki. P. F. (2018). *Languages. scripts. and Chinese texts in East Asia*. Oxford: Oxford University Press.

Li. D. C. S. (2020). Writing-mediated interaction face-to-face: Sinitic brushtalk (漢文筆談) as an age-old lingua-cultural practice in premodern East Asian cross-border communication. *China and Asia* 2(2): 193–233.

Li. D. C. S.. Aoyama. R.. Wong. T.-S. (2020). Sinitic brushtalk (漢文筆談): Literary Chinese as a scripta franca in early modern East Asia. *Global Chinese* 6(1): 1–23.

Lurie. D. B. (2011). *Realms of literacy. Early Japan and the history of writing*. Cambridge. MA: Harvard University Press.

Matsudaya. H. [松川屋伴吉] (1862/1997). 唐國渡海日記 ('Diary of a sea voyage to China'). In S. Kojima [小島晋治] (Ed.). 幕末明治中国見聞録集成第11巻 ('Collection of travel accounts of China from the late Edo and Meiji periods') (vol. 11. pp. 39–86). Tokyo: Yumani shobo.

Matsuura. A. [松浦章] (2011). 朱舜水日本来航時の日中文化交流 ('Sino-Japanese relations during Zhu Shunshui's visits to Japan'). 東アジア文化交渉研究 *Journal of East Asian Cultural Interaction Studies* 4: 345–371.

Nakura. A. [名倉予何人] (1862/1997). 支那見聞録 ('Travel observations in China'). In S. Kojima [小島晋治] (Ed.). 幕末明治中国見聞録集成第11巻 ('Collection of travel accounts of China from the late Edo and Meiji periods') (vol. 11. pp. 165–218). Tokyo: Yumani shobo.

Nōtomi. K. [納富介次郎] (1862/1997). 上海雑記 ('Miscellaneous notes on Shanghai'). In S. Kojima [小島晋治] (Ed.). 幕末明治中国見聞録集成第1巻 ('Collection of travel accounts of China from the late Edo and Meiji periods') (vol. 1. pp. 7–45). Tokyo: Yumani shobo.

Sheng. B. (2016). The Senzai Maru's visit to Shanghai and its understanding of China. *Chinese Studies in History* 49(1): 19–27. doi: 10.1080/00094633.2016.1085764.

Snow. D. (2010). Diglossia in East Asia. *Journal of Asian Pacific Communication* 20(1): 124–151. doi: 10.1075/japc.20.1.10sno.

Snow. D. (2013). Towards a theory of vernacularisation: Insights from written Chinese vernaculars. *Journal of Multilingual and Multicultural Development* 34(6): 597–610. doi: 10.1080/01434632.2013.786082.

Takasugi, S. [高杉晋作] (1862/1916). 游清五録 ('Five records of a trip to China'). In T. Kido [木戸孝正] (Ed.), 東行先生遺文 ('Posthumous writings of Takasugi Shinsaku') (pp. 72–124). Tokyo: Minyūsha.

Taylor, I., & Taylor, M. M. (2014). *Writing and literacy in Chinese, Korean and Japanese* (2nd ed.). Amsterdam/Philadelphia: John Benjamins.

Toby, R. P. (1984). *State and diplomacy in early modern Japan: Asia in the development of the Tokugawa bakufu*. Princeton, NJ: Princeton University Press.

Zhu, Q. [朱謙之] (Ed.). (1981). 朱舜水集 ('A collection of Zhu Shunshui's writing'). Hong Kong: Chunghua Book Company.

5 Identity verification and negotiation through Sinitic brush-talk in Ming China and Japan

Drifting accounts by Ch'oe Pu (1488) and Yi Chi-hang (1696–1697)

Hur Kyoung-jin

Introduction

Up until the early twentieth century, East Asian countries – Korea, China, Japan, Vietnam, among others – belonged to the Sinosphere 漢字文化圈. The elites of all these countries were by definition literati of Classical Chinese or Literary Sinitic (Kornicki 2018, hereafter Sinitic), yet their spoken languages differed drastically. In each of these countries, the relationship between Sinitic-based literature and sociopolitical power depended crucially on the extent of influence that Confucianism had exerted on their respective institutions. Of the countries that embraced Confucianism, access to officialdom depended crucially on one's knowledge of a body of Confucian classics and literary works, in addition to writing skills in Sinitic which was absolutely essential. Academic talents were selected through civil service examinations (Kor: 科擧, 과거, *kwagŏ*; Mand: *kējǔ*, 科擧). In Koryŏ 高麗, for instance, there are two subjects in the primary test 小科: a test on Sinitic writing skills and another test on the interpretation of Confucian classics. In the final examination 大科, a very high level of writing skills in Sinitic was a *sine qua non* for success.

As an artifact of Confucian teachings, Korean kings considered effective communication as instrumental in politics, be it conveying the will of the governing to the governed 上意下達 or conveying the will of the governed to the governing 下意上達. For this reason, most of the examination subjects were concerned with and directed toward testing the examinees' writing skills. When King Sejong 世宗 created and promulgated 'The right sound to educate the people' 訓民正音 (i.e., *hangŭl*, 'Korean alphabet') in 1443, it was stated in the introduction that 'many people, uneducated, are unable to express their thoughts when they wish to'. This shows how important it was to be able to convey the will of the governed to the governing properly and efficiently. That was also an important reason why *hangŭl* was conceived and invented as an auxiliary writing system for the Korean people who lacked the literacy skills to understand or express themselves in Chinese

DOI: 10.4324/9781003048176-6

characters (漢字, Mand: *hànzì*; Jap: *kanji*; Kor: *hanja*; Viet: *chữ Hán* 字漢, *chữ nho* 字儒, *Hán tự* 漢字). Crucially, the main reason for the Chosŏn government to designate Sinitic as its official written language was to meet the need for formal written communication with China.

Very early on, leaders of Chosŏn's literary circle – including chief scholar (*taejehak* 大提學) of the Hall of Worthies (*Chip'yŏnjŏn* 集賢殿), Yi Maeng-kyun 李孟畇 (1371–1440) – argued vehemently for the need to study the poems of celebrated Tang and Song poets such as Li Bai 李白, Du Fu 杜甫, Han Yu 韓愈, Liu Zongyuan 柳宗元, Ouyang Xiu 歐陽修, Wang Anshi 王安石, Su Shi 蘇軾, and Huang Tingjian 黃庭堅. Since then, for nearly half a century most of the literati elites studied their poems painstakingly, with the ultimate goal of accessing the pinnacle of the career awaiting all aspiring scholar-officials at court. On average, it would take around twenty to thirty years for a regular male person to pass the civil service examination (Kim 1986). While the literati of Chosŏn generally lacked proficiency in spoken Chinese vernaculars, they were in general very skillful in reading and writing Sinitic. This ability allowed them to engage in brush conversation or brush-talk 漢文筆談 with other fellow literati of Sinitic in cross-border communication contexts using brush, ink, and paper. Those who studied and made a serious attempt to prepare for the civil service examination for over a decade were usually adept at Sinitic writing, which would allow them to display their high-level writing skills or even erudition through brush-talk. An average person literate in Sinitic would be able to respond to a Chinese person's factual inquiry; well-read elites, on the other hand, could draw on their extensive reading to explain things coherently and raise intellectually challenging questions pertaining to their own fields of interest.

Three recurrent brush-talk contexts: diplomatic encounters and beyond

That the civil service examination heavily favored writing skills development was not without opposition. The main objection was that the study of the Confucian and other literary classics should receive priority over training in writing. But since the fundamental principle of diplomacy for successive Chosŏn governments was to 'serve the great, and befriend the neighbors' 事大交隣, the examination continued to prioritize writing for practical diplomatic reasons. While the countries within Sinographic East Asia relied on Sinitic as their 'scripta franca' until the early twentieth century (Denecke 2014: 209; cf. Clements 2019: 308), their spoken languages varied tremendously. Cross-border communication between Koreans, Chinese, and Japanese in speech thus had to rely on translation and interpreting. For official events, translators were routinely dispatched alongside the envoys, but in private, personal interactions between the envoy and fellow literati in the host country, Sinitic brush-talk was the preferred mode of communication almost by default. Not unlike natural speech-based conversation, brush conversation covered a great variety of topics ranging from mundane to serious, including intellectual exchange of views on academic issues of shared interest.

When Korean envoys traveled to China, Korean literati would explore and cherish opportunities to engage in brush-talk with Chinese literati. Upon their return to Chosŏn, the contents of their brush-talk would be embedded in their 'Travelogues to Peking' (*Yŏnhaengnok* 燕行錄), which they would circulate among their literati peers in bounded volumes but were rarely published. By contrast, when Korean literati traveled to Japan, Japanese literati would visit them in their lodgings and invite them to engage in brush conversation. The contents of their brushed encounters would almost immediately be made publicly available. While commercial publishing was not so widespread in Chosŏn, the opposite was true in Japan. Such a trend was largely sustained by an emerging book market for brush-talk interactions with or by foreigners, which appeared to have mass appeal among growing numbers of readers who were literate in Sinitic (Clements 2015).

In premodern and early modern East Asia, Japanese-Korean encounters were quite frequent. Sinitic was typically used to write up accounts of their brush conversations. In terms of context-specific genres, Sinitic was commonly used to write three types of texts: (i) travel journal or travelogue 紀行文, (ii) brush conversation or brush-talk, and (iii) poetic chanting and exchange 漢詩唱和. A travelogue is a diary-like one-sided account, which was typically compiled and edited after one had returned to one's homeland. Brush-talk records, with or without poetic chanting and exchange embedded, were accounts co-produced by two or more brush-talkers actively communicating their thoughts in writing. In Japan, most records were edited and published by Japanese brush conversation participants, which would take some time to edit, compile, and print. Since the Korean literati were often unable to check the published versions before they returned to Chosŏn, the accounts of their brush-talk communication would typically be modified, sometimes misrepresented subject to the editor's interpretation and/or ulterior intent. While it would be unwise to label a published Japanese account as 'false' or 'distorted' just because its contents had been altered, there is a need to probe just how far the editing process adhered to the proceedings of the original brush-talk interaction. When examining the records of Korean-Japanese relations, therefore, their authenticity must be cross-checked and verified carefully, but this is by no means easy.

One-sided accounts: records of diplomatic missions

Records of diplomatic missions 使行錄, often quoted as primary sources in studies of historical international relations, are accounts of Chosŏn envoys who traveled to China or Japan on official missions. With the dates and duration clearly marked, such records were usually published and filed chronologically. Some of the records contain Sinitic poetry or brush-talk. As these records are personal accounts, in general, there is no way to verify their authenticity unless they are matched by corresponding accounts produced by the other brush-talker(s). The schedule of diplomatic missions tended to be very hectic, thus the brush-talk artifacts produced during the trip were usually kept as drafts. For Chinese-Korean brush-talk, mostly the Korean envoys would request taking the brush-talk manuscripts with them, which was usually granted. If they had time, they would tidy up and compile them into bound volumes after completing their mission. In the process of copy-editing the contents of the brush-talk, words or acts that did not comply with the national law were most likely deleted or altered. The 'Diary of Jehol' 熱河日記 by Pak Chi-wŏn 朴趾源 (1737–1805) is one instructive example; multiple drafts and different versions of the same brush-talk records appeared because the author kept revising the content. In such cases, scrutinizing and determining the 'designated copy' 定本 is a crucial step before in-depth study.

Two-sided accounts: brush-talk

Unlike diary-like records of diplomatic missions, brush-talk records were based on writing-mediated interactions involving two or more brush-talkers, who were typically seated face to face, offering their respective viewpoints on a topic of shared interest. Interestingly, those who were more curious about their counterpart would initiate a brush-talk request and name a topic of interest, sometimes accompanied by fairly specific questions, and the initiator would tacitly assume having the right to collect the brush-talk manuscripts produced afterward. In this regard, Chosŏn envoys had very different experiences on their respective missions to China and Japan. As they usually were the ones to initiate brush conversation requests with their Chinese hosts, they tended to assume having the right to request the brush-talk manuscripts, which was usually granted. On the other hand, in Japan, Chosŏn envoys were usually requested by their Japanese hosts to engage in brush conversation on one or more rather specific topics, and so it was generally assumed that the right to collect the brush-talk manuscripts rested with the Japanese side. Bound volumes of such manuscripts would then be kept or circulated like books in the modern sense; printed copies for commercialized distribution did occur, but they belonged to the minority (e.g., only about 40 percent of existing Chosŏn *t'ongsinsa* brush-talk records in Japan were published in printed form).

Likewise, in Japanese-Korean brush-talk interaction, the Japanese who requested to meet with Chosŏn envoys would typically edit the brush-talk manuscripts by himself. To my knowledge, there are no known published compilations of Korean-Chinese brush-talk records before the twentieth century, probably because there was no market for their commercial publication in Chosŏn Korea.

Pak Chi-wŏn had included the records of his brush conversations with Chinese literati in his work, *Diary of Jehol*, which was subsumed with the following brush-talk records: 'Brush-talk at Suzhai' 粟齋筆談, 'Brush-talk at Shanglou' 商樓筆談, 'Forgotten goat record' 忘羊錄, 'Brush-talk with Huding' 鵠汀筆談, 'Brush-talk about Lamaism' 黃教問答, and 'Record at Chengde resort' 避暑錄. Pak's personal views permeated those brush-talk records, but they were never formally published. Take *Brush-talk with Huding* as an example. There are traces of improvised words crossed out by Huding (i.e., erased with ink); where Huding's words were felt to be imprecise, Pak would fill in the 'missing words' following his own recollection or guess. Where the content was felt to be too sensitive (e.g., how much Huding missed Ming China), he would insist on taking the brush-talk manuscripts with him. Pak, on the other hand, wanted to include all the conversations they shared as he had no problem including such content deemed politically sensitive by Huding for Korean readers, so he decided to fill in those gaps. In the process of performing editing tasks, Pak would recall from memory what he believed had actually transpired during their brushed encounter, or even improvise anew if need be.

Japanese literati, on the other hand, would typically come to a brushed encounter well prepared. Before they visited the Korean envoys and made a formal request for conducting brush conversation, they would normally raise specific inquiries beforehand. The accounts arising from Japanese-Korean brushed encounters were usually compiled, edited, and published right away. Such compilations or collections of brush-talk records, typically embedded with poetic chanting and exchange, amounted to about 170 in Korea and Japan in total. Of these, many were published commercially.

One exceptional case was 'Brush-talk at the feast' 坐間筆語, which was an account of the brush conversations that took place in 1711 between the Chosŏn envoys – Cho T'ae-ŏk 趙泰億 (1675–1728), Im Su-kan 任守幹 and Yi Pang-ŏn 李邦彥 – and the Japanese official in charge of hospitality Arai Hakuseki 新井白石 (1657–1725). It was the only *t'ongsinsa* 通信使 brush-talk record that was separately compiled in Chosŏn (in the form of a manuscript) and Japan (printed and published), resulting in two different versions. Neither side consulted each other in the editing process, partly because communication or contact over a distance was not as convenient. One consequence is that misrepresentation of ideas or fabrication of content was not uncommon. In the case of *Brush-talk at the feast*, we can compare the contents of two books and judge the validity of how the brush conversations were presented, but this is only possible if corresponding editions of Japanese-Korean brush-talk records exist. Thus, even though the brush-talk records gave the impression of being primary sources created or co-produced seemingly interactively involving two or more parties, great care is needed to ascertain whether the actual proceedings had been altered in the editing or publication process resulting in false or distorted representation.

The boat drifter's testimony

Intermediate between private, one-sided diary-like accounts of envoys traveling on a diplomatic mission and multiparty brushed encounters between two or more brush-talkers is the testimony 供招 of a boat drifter 漂流民 whose vessel was blown off course and landed in the waters of an alien country. While diplomatic encounters would usually be formal events with the brush-talkers' official capacities mutually recognized, a maritime official's interrogation of the boat drifter(s) would follow a less stringent structure. In general, boat drifters were expected to answer the local official's interrogation on the spot where their vessel was washed ashore. Interpretation was sometimes possible if bilingual speakers such as merchants happened to be on board. In most cases, however, few boat drifters were able to speak the local language fluently, and so local literati of Sinitic were often called upon to engage them in brush conversation, interactively and face-to-face. The purpose was to try to find out the answers to a host of more or less standard questions prepared by the maritime official (see Matsuura & Aoyama, this volume; Wong, this volume). Success in this give-and-take would depend crucially on whether a boat drifter with sufficient literacy in Sinitic could be identified. Where none was available, brush conversation could hardly proceed, and the maritime official would be unable to learn anything beyond individual boat drifters' basic personal information such as their names and places of origin.

Where the stake was felt to be high, and the national identity of the boat drifters evoked suspicion, maritime officials would carry out interrogations multiple times in order to ascertain the validity of their claims, especially their national identity, destination, merchandise on board and their values if relevant, and the circumstances leading to shipwreck and/or boat drifting. One such famous case was Ch'oe Pu 崔溥 (1454–1504), a Chosŏn official whose boat was adrift in the waters of Linhai County 臨海縣, Taizhou Prefecture 台州府, China in 1488. According to his diary-like report 'A record of drifting across the sea' 漂海錄, he was interrogated multiple times by Chinese military officials Xu Qing 許清 of Haimen-wei 海門衛, Chen Hua 陳華 of Taozhu-suo 桃渚所, and Liu Ze 劉澤 of Songmen 松門. Their methods of questioning and cross-examining were very similar; only after Ch'oe Pu's replies were deemed consistent was he allowed to travel back to his homeland in Chosŏn (Meskill 1965: 19). *A record of drifting across the sea* is thus a personal account of Ch'oe Pu's experiences and observations, the accuracy of which could not be verified in the absence of corresponding accounts produced by the Chinese officials (for Ch'oe Pu's writing process, see Hur 2010a).[1] In the following, I will illustrate the functional role of Sinitic brush-talk and poetic chanting and exchange in two drifting accounts as reported by Yi Chi-hang and Ch'oe Pu, respectively.

Two different drifting records of Yi Chi-hang, a Korean boat drifter to Hokkaido, Japan (1696–1697)

A Chosŏn military officer Yi Chi-hang 李志恒 (1647–?, appellation Sŏndal 先達),[2] who resided in Tongnae 東萊, drifted to Japan in the spring of 1696. Upon his return to Pusan 釜山 in the spring of 1697, he wrote up an account of his drifting experience with the title 'Record of the drifting ship' 漂舟錄. Yi and his men

---

1 Hur (2010a) made an attempt to track down the source materials at Taozhu-suo and Huanghua building 皇華館, but in vain.
2 *Sŏndal* 先達 refers to a person who had passed the civil service examination (martial arts) but was not (yet) given a governmental post. Yi Chi-hang referred to himself as a *sŏndal* probably because he felt guilty for being unable to fulfill his official duties while drifting in Japan.

landed on the northwestern islands of Hokkaido 北海道 inhabited by the Ainu people (Jap: アイヌ; Chi: 阿伊努族), and could only communicate with them using body language. Later they met some Japanese, with whom they tried to communicate in speech or conducted brush(-assisted) conversation. Despite being a military officer, Yi was well versed in Sinitic and capable of writing Chinese poetry (*hanshi* 漢詩), and so he communicated his ideas with Japanese officials and monks, of which a few were also well versed in composing *hanshi*. Although the official record in the Chosŏn government office – *Record of the drifting ship* – does not contain much poetry, many poems were included in the official record produced by the Japanese government office, 'Submission of the Chosŏn boat drifter Ri Sendatsu' 漂流朝鮮人李先達呈辭 (Hur 2010b, hereafter *Submission*).

By the end of the seventeenth century, Japanese-Korean poetic exchange and chanting was getting popular in Japan and many brush-talk records obtainable in the book market were circulated among Japanese readers. In 1696, when Yi Chi-hang and his men drifted to Japan, about 25 collections of Korean brush-talk records had been circulated in Japan, of which five books were published and sold, the most representative being volume 7 of 'Record of poetic chanting and exchange between Japan and Korea' 和韓唱酬集 (1682) and 'Collection of Chosŏn brush-talk in 1636' 朝鮮筆談集 1636 (1682). Clearly, many Japanese readers literate in Sinitic were interested in reading about Chosŏn culture. *Submission* contained Yi's poetry and brush-talk, but it was not published. This is probably because the Japanese government office merely wanted to ascertain the sequence of events leading to the boat drifting and to welcome Yi, rather than to commercialize the brush-talk and poetry he composed.

Yi Chi-hang's drifting incident has yielded at least two separate accounts. The record from the Chosŏn side – *Record of the drifting ship* – was included in the book series *All records of sea travels* 海行摠載 as found in the revised edition compiled by 'Chosŏn's Old Books Publishing Association' 朝鮮古書刊行會 in 1914. By contrast, the other record *Submission* produced in Japan was obscure to Korean readers. The Japanese official who discovered Yi Chi-hang produced the official account after escorting him to Matsumae domain 松前藩. Being an earlier account chronologically speaking, the Japanese record included dozens of *hanshi* exchanged with Japanese officials and monks, amounting to 20 pages. It is currently kept and accessible at Hokkaido University library (Hur 2010b: 59). After Yi Chi-hang and his men returned to Chosŏn, he wrote another testimony, *Record of the drifting ship*, at the government office in the port of Pusan. As the purpose was to give a detailed account of the entire drifting event complete with the choice of return route from Japan, with few exceptions the poetic exchange with his Japanese brush-talkers was mostly excluded[3] (for a comparative study of the Japanese and Korean versions, see Hur 2010b).

---

3 Whereas Yi Chi-hang's own poems were omitted, seven poems received from the Japanese brush-talkers were included: one being authored by the monk Zuiryū 瑞流, six were written by the governor-general of Matsumae, the latter plausibly aided by the monk.

According to the *Record of the drifting ship*, Yi Chi-hang's boat was adrift after encountering northwesterly 'horizontal wind' 橫風 on 04:28,[4] and subsequently swept ashore on a beach in Hokkaido on 05:12. They soon found themselves in an Ainu community who had little knowledge of spoken Japanese, nor did they have any knowledge of sinograms or *kanji* characters. Speech-based communication being a big problem, Yi Chi-hang then decided to travel south, where they finally met some speakers of Japanese. Proficiency in spoken Japanese being limited, Yi Chi-hang's men tried to write in Hiragana, but soon realized that the officials they encountered could understand and write Chinese characters. At this point, brush conversation began. To explain their identity and the sequence of events leading to their drifting in Japan, Yi Chi-hang was instructed to write a testimony, which was very formal, as shown in the *Submission*. For instance, even though the informal first-person pronoun 我 or 余 is used throughout, which follows the typical style of a diary or travel journal of the time, the date and writer are marked formally:

文禄九年夏五月漂着朝鮮人先達手啓

Bunroku 9th year summer, the 5th lunar month, hand-written and submitted by the boat drifter Sendatsu from Chosŏn

The addressee and the undersigned in the formal *Submission of the Chosŏn boat drifter Ri Sendatsu* also followed the formal genre of a testimony:

Addressee	日本國松前州太守閣下	'Honorable Governor of Japan's Matsumae Precinct'
Undersigned	朝鮮國漂人李志恒呈辭	'Boat drifter from Chosŏn, Yi Chi-hang respectfully submitted'
Signature 1	朝鮮漂人李先達	'Boat drifter from Chosŏn, Yi Sŏndal'
Signature 2	朝鮮漂人李志恒先達	'Boat drifter from Chosŏn, Yi Chi-hang Sŏndal'

By contrast, there were less formal brush conversations in *Record of the drifting ship*. One such surviving brush-talk record was dated 07:23:

邊將者盛設鋪陳, 迎余上拜.... 金白善及他船人等, 別坐外廳, 令人待之. 出置筆硯, 以毛綿紙, 取書問情. 余盡記以進, 則卽爲堅封, 馳送報知于松前太守前.

The border patrol official welcomed me with a majestic banquet, and politely bowed to me. . . . Kim Paek-sŏn and other sailors were seated separately

---

4 The dates are all recorded according to the lunar calendar. For convenience's sake, all lunar months and days will be presented in digits, with the month preceding the day separated by a colon. Thus, '03:05' would mean 'the 5th day of the 3rd lunar month'.

Identity verification and negotiation 135

and were asked to wait outside. The official brought along brushes and an ink stone, then inquired about my circumstances by writing on a piece of *maomian* paper 毛綿紙 imported from China. I recast my story in full there; then he sealed the paper securely and ordered to have it quickly sent to the governor-general of Matsumae Precinct for notification.

Up until that point, communications took place via Kim Paek-sŏn – a man from Tongnae – because he spoke basic Japanese. But from the point when the border patrol official took out the brushes and an ink stone, brush-talk with Yi Chi-hang began after discovering that he was literate in Sinitic. The Chosŏn seafarers stayed there for three days and were then transported to Matsumae, where further brush-talk with the governor-general began on 07:27:

招入白善傳語曰太守設酌送慰云. 又傳一章, 開視其文曰: 是行也吾丈等, 爲何發船? 欲到何境而漂流于海瀛耶? 有幾日漂着我境耶? 海上有逢日本商舶耶? 朝鮮發船者, 何月何日乎?

Kim Paek-sŏn was summoned to pass the message that a consolation banquet was being prepared by the governor-general. Then he delivered another page, which I opened and saw the following words: 'On this trip, for what purpose did you board the ship? Where were you headed and how did you end up adrift in Japanese waters? For how many days were you adrift before reaching our shores? Have you encountered any Japanese merchant ships while drifting at sea? On which day of which month did the ship depart Chosŏn?'

(*Record of the drifting ship*)

The first words were spoken to Kim Paek-sŏn in Japanese, but the rest of the quoted words were notes written down and directed to Yi Chi-hang, who began to reply and make a formal testimony in the form of a letter. The next day he received a reply from the governor-general along with another letter. Questions and answers concerning the drifting experiences of Yi and his men were continuously exchanged via brush-talk and letters. Yi's command of Literary Sinitic must have impressed the governor-general a great deal. Soon they started exchanging poetry in Sinitic. Whereas brush-talk and letters concerned mundane factual information, poetic verses conveyed sublime personal feelings. Poetic exchange was initiated by the governor-general of Matsumae Precinct. On 07:28, upon receiving Yi's response to queries on his testimony, the governor-general offered gifts and requested Yi to engage in poetic exchange a few days later:

一日太守送侍倭問安, 兼送唐紙十張. 令白善傳語曰: "尊自曳沙峙, 旣陸行觀覽本州形概, 題詩以送如何." 不得已來路所思詩六首. 聯書以呈.

One day, the governor-general ordered a Japanese servant to send his regards and bring along ten sheets of Chinese paper. He then asked Kim Paek-sŏn to convey a request: 'Your esteemed self have observed the scenery of this town

while walking on land from Esashi 曳沙峙 – would you like to grace us with a poem?' Feeling obliged, I sent them six poems conceived on my way here.
(*Record of the drifting ship*)

It was the first time in three months for Yi Chi-hang to engage in poetic exchange after his boat ended up in Japan.[5] Soon, the governor-general reciprocated with rejoinders signed off by a monk from Edo by the name Zuiryū 瑞流, following the rhyming scheme in Yi's poems:

莫言春到雪蒙頭	Don't say your hair has frosted when spring is here,
羈旅憐君鄉路悠	I feel pity for your long return journey.
蘇李分裳難再遇	Su Wu [蘇武] and Li Ling [李陵] shall not meet once they part their sleeves,
河梁一別已千秋	A good millennium has elapsed, their farewell at the bridge.
...	
諦澳人間萬事非	Worldly matters of human existence all in vain,
豈圖相遇又相違	What chance is there to meet and separate again?
春風縱今掛帆去	Now that we sail with the spring breeze,
莫忘雲山伴衲衣	Don't forget meeting this monk at the clouded mountain.

(*Record of the drifting ship*)

Whereas the *Record of the drifting ship* contains six poems composed by the governor-general, *Submission* only included the poems written by Yi Chi-hang, while excluding the afore-mentioned poems written by the governor-general – presumably because it was meant to be a compilation of Yi's records. Yi and the governor-general did not exchange poetry interactively. The governor-general first requested poetry from Yi and reciprocated with poetry following the same rhyming scheme, albeit written by a monk from Edo. This suggests that the governor-general was not sufficiently well versed in poetry composition in Sinitic. Composing poetic verses in Sinitic while adhering to a particular rhyming scheme, spontaneously and interactively, required highly sophisticated literary skills available only to well-read and talented scholar-poets.

After Yi, the boat drifter was apprehended by maritime officials in Hokkaido and upon his return to Tongnae, Korea, the government office in both countries required him to produce a formal testimony. Being an official account, a testimony is very different from personal stories based on one's travel diaries, which tended to be one-sided accounts submitted by the boat drifter, with little trace of verbal exchange or interaction. But in the *Record of the drifting ship*, after the first question, only the responses were recorded, with no indication of the questions that triggered them. This characteristic makes the record look more like a diary or

---

5 According to *Record of the drifting ship*, Yi only mentioned being engaged in poetry composition but did not include the poems in the *Record*.

Identity verification and negotiation 137

travel journal. Although the *Record of the drifting ship* was written to report on the circumstances of the author's drifting experiences to the government office, it may be seen as a travel journal to Japan considering the way it was written. This is probably why the *Record of the drifting ship* was included in *All records of sea travels*, which was mainly composed of travel journals. By contrast, *Submission* is divided into several documents, each with a title and signature may be out of a concern that it should follow the structure of an official testimony.

Apart from marked differences in the choice of sinograms or Sinitic characters and the writing style of the testimonies, another major difference between the two reports is that in *Submission*, there are no records of any events beyond 08:15. Since Yi Chi-hang and his men left the Matsumae Domain on 08:15, it is only natural that events beyond that day are only found in the *Record of the drifting ship*. What seems puzzling is the reason why the Sinitic poems were excluded in the *Record of the drifting ship*. More specifically, Yi included the poems that the governor-general of Matsumae sent him in *Record of the drifting ship*, but did not include his own. A poet who was used to composing a lot of poetry would usually be able to memorize his own poems at ease. Given his ability to recall from memory the Japanese governor-general's poems that followed the same rhyming scheme he initiated in his own poems, it did not seem possible that Yi had failed to do the same with his own poetry. So, was he oblivious of his own poetic improvisation? Possibly not. In my view, it was deliberately omitted because he considered it inappropriate to include poetry in a formal drifting record submitted to his own government. This is probably why he withheld his own poetic improvisation on purpose. More fine-grained research is needed to ascertain this point.

Brush-talk records reconstructed from memory: Ch'oe Pu's account of his drifting experience in Ming China (1488)

A record of drifting across the sea 漂海錄, an earlier account of his six-month drifting ordeal in Ming China which was far more famous than those produced by Yi Chi-hang, was written and submitted by Ch'oe Pu (崔溥, 1454–1504) to King Sŏngjong 成宗 (1457–1495; r. 1469–1495) upon his command. It was conceived as a candid, legally binding, and meticulous record based on his travel journals including his testimony in response to formal interrogation by Chinese officials, supplemented with personal observations and commentaries. However, since Ch'oe Pu did not have access to the brush conversation artifacts produced by his Chinese interlocutors, it was a 'reconstructed' brush-talk record at best. His ordeal began in 1488 when returning home to the Korean Peninsula by boat from Cheju Island 濟州 upon hearing the passing of his father, but the boat was blown off course by a storm and drifted to the shores of Zhejiang Province in China. Being well versed in Sinitic, he was able to explain the plight that befell him and his 42 men by writing 'two long, written depositions on the whole incident, his own background, and on Korean geography, history, customs, and institutions' (Meskill 1965: 19). Only after producing these elaborate statements, plus intelligent answers to Chinese officials' questions through brush-talk during a prolonged process of interrogation, that Ch'oe Pu and his men were able to embark on a four-month homeward journey escorted by Chinese officials, first on the waterborne route via the Peking-Hangzhou Grand Canal 京杭大運河, then on a landbound route from Peking to Ŭiju 義州, the Korean frontier town on the Amnok (a.k.a. Yalu) River.[6] As soon as he returned to Chosŏn, he received the king's order for a comprehensive account of his observations and experiences in China that eventually culminated in that formal report. Given that it was a command that he could not resist, he had to start writing on the very day he returned, which was no easy task because he had gotten ill in Peking and was carriage-bound during the rest of his homeward journey.

According to the 'Family rites of Zhuzi' 朱子家禮, a fundamental Confucian principle in Chosŏn governing the son's mourning of his father's passing, being the chief mourner, he was supposed to head to his hometown Naju 羅州 to keep vigil for three years. That undertaking was complicated by the king's order, however, in that he felt obliged to finish writing the report at the Ch'ŏngp'a Station 青坡驛 before returning to Naju. That delay turned out to be a curse, as he was later accused of committing a crime by missing the three-year mourning ritual expected of a dutiful son immediately upon arriving in Chosŏn. This incrimination cost him the appointment as a fifth rank official (*kyoli* 校理) of the Office of Special Advisors (*Hongmun'gwan* 弘文館) for which he was highly eligible.

Chosŏn literati who had read Chinese books their entire lives wished to learn more about China. King Sŏngjong, who had to rule his people and serve China, the suzerain state, had an even more intense desire to do so. Whereas opinion was divided at court, 'between filial piety 孝 and loyalty 忠, which one should come first?' Sŏngjong had no problem seeing Ch'oe Pu's submission of a comprehensive first-hand eye-witness account of his entire journey as a higher priority. In terms of its lasting impact, after Ch'oe Pu was executed during the purge of scholars in 1504, for a long time *A record of drifting across the sea* did not appear in the king's *Annals* 實錄, suggesting that there was no mention of it among the vassals and kings at court. But after the ruling clique changed following the revolt of Chungjong 中宗反正, popular support for its publication prevailed, with the justification well documented in the *Annals of King Chungjong* in 1511:

> 崔溥 《漂海錄》, 自金陵至帝都, 山川風土習俗, 無不備記. 吾東方人, 雖不目覩中原, 因此可知, 請并開刊傳播.
>
> (中宗實錄 6年 3月 14日)

Ch'oe Pu's *A record of drifting across the sea* contains a comprehensive documentation of China, including its climate, customs, mountains, rivers and the landscape from Jinling [Nanjing] to the capital [Peking]. From this book,

---

6 Ch'oe Pu departed Hangzhou on 02:13, arrived at Peking on 03:28. He came back to Chosŏn after crossing the Amnok River (Yalu River 鴨綠江) on 06:04, arriving at Seoul on 06:14.

our people could learn about China without visiting the country. Please let this book be published and disseminated.

(*Annals of King Chungjong*, Year 6 (1511), 03:14)

After the book was published using a bronze metal type, *A record of drifting across the sea* was reproduced through wood block printing for wider dissemination (Meskill 1965: 23). As long as the desire to learn about China persisted, its reference value sustained by popular interest did not subside. Ch'oe Pu had a hard time defending that he and his men were no Japanese pirates (Meskill 1965: 18–19). After that suspicion was lifted, he then switched his attention to investigating and recording details of China that people in Chosŏn would be interested in or concerned about.

Officials' probe into the Sinosphere identity of Ch'oe Pu and his men via Sinitic brush-talk

Chinese people living in the southern part of the country had less chance to encounter people from Chosŏn. From Liaodong 遼東 to Peking, envoys from Chosŏn would visit a few times each year; but they could not encounter any foreign envoys in Zhejiang province. Foreigners they met were Japanese envoys coming to China via the port of Ningbo on a tributary mission once a decade, or Japanese pirates who often plundered their land, no wonder among the first encounters of Ch'oe Pu and his men at sea were Japanese pirates. After surviving the threat of Japanese pirates, Ch'oe Pu and his men were interrogated by Liu Ze, commander-in-chief against Japanese forces 備倭指揮 把摠官 of Songmen 松門 at Huanghua building 皇華館. Liu Ze first asked about their identities and the size of Chosŏn before getting more specific with the following questions:

汝國與日本琉球高麗相通乎?	Does your country have diplomatic relations with Japan, Ryukyu and Koryŏ?
汝國亦朝貢我朝廷否?	Does your country, too, pay tribute to our Court?
汝國用何法度? 別有年號乎?	In your country, what regulations does your country have? Do you have your own reign titles?[7]

After asking these questions, Liu waited for Ch'oe Pu's response, and said:

汝邦屢歲朝貢, 義有君臣之好. 既無侵逆之情, 當遇以禮.

Your state has paid tributes; you have acted as a good subject state. Since there is nothing to indicate seditious intent, you shall be treated courteously.[8]

---

7 English translation adapted, with minor modification, from Meskill (1965: 60).
8 English translation adapted, with minor modification, from Meskill (1965: 60).

The Chinese official was asking those questions not because he was ignorant, but because he wanted to cross-check if Ch'oe Pu was indeed an official from Chosŏn as claimed. Other Chinese officials who Ch'oe Pu met later asked similar questions. A question like 'does Chosŏn adhere to Confucianism?' was intended to probe if Ch'oe Pu's country of origin belonged to the Sinosphere and to ascertain their cultural knowledge and affinity. As it turned out, the interrogators were sometimes surprised by the fact that people from Chosŏn appeared to be even more deeply influenced by Confucian teachings than people in Ming China. When Ch'oe Pu was staying at Wulin Station 武林驛 in Hangzhou 杭州, a station worker called Gu Bi 顧壁 conveyed to him:

> 我杭城西山八般嶺有古刹, 名高麗寺. 寺前有二碑記古跡, 距此十五里, 即趙宋時, 高麗使來貢而建也. 你國人越境, 尚且造寺, 則其崇佛之意可知矣.

> On Baban Range in the mountains west of Hangzhou is an old monastery named Koryŏ Temple. In front of the temple are two stone tablets that commemorate the old ruins. They are about fifteen *li* from here. It was built by a Koryŏ envoy who was on a tributary mission during the Song dynasty. That your countrymen build temples even beyond their own borders must mean that they revere the Buddha.[9]

Such an assumption about Chosŏn people's interest in Buddhism and reverence of the Buddha was fiercely contested by Ch'oe Pu, who argued that:

> 此則高麗人所建也. 今我朝鮮, 闢異端尊儒道.... 若有髡首者則並令充軍.

> It could be that this [Koryŏ temple] was built by the people of Koryŏ, but today, in Chosŏn, we are utterly opposed to such heresy and adhere to the Confucian Way instead. . . . Anyone who shaves his head is banished and condemned to forced labor.[10]

Ch'oe Pu was at pains to explain to Liu why Chosŏn was a veritable Confucian state and how closely Koreans adhered to the teachings of Confucius. A similar example may be found in a separate brush conversation on 01:19, the leap first month of 1488. Ch'oe Pu met a student 書生 called Lu Furong 盧夫容 in Taozhusuo, who asked why Chosŏn and China did not share the same language:

| 盧夫容: 車同軌, 書同文, 獨你語音, 不同中國, 何也? | Lu Furong: 'When [your] carriages have the same axle-width and [your] books the same writing as those of China, why is your speech not the same?' |

---

9 English translation adapted, with minor modification, from Meskill (1965: 83).
10 English translation adapted, with minor modification, from Meskill (1965: 83).

臣答曰: 千里不同風, 百里不同俗. 足下怪聽我言, 我亦怪聽足下之言. 習俗然也. 然同得天所賦之性, 則我之性, 亦堯舜孔顏之性, 豈嫌於語音之有異哉?	I, your servant, responded: 'Just as the same wind does not blow over a thousand *li*, so customs vary over a hundred. If you wonder at the sound of my words, me too I wonder at the sound of yours. It is a matter of customs. But if we share the nature given by Heaven, my nature, too, is the nature of Yao and Shun, Confucius and Yan Hui. How can one object to a difference in speech?'
其人撫掌曰: 你奔喪, 可行朱文公家禮乎?	The man applauded and said: 'When you are bereaved and go into mourning, do you observe [the rules of] the *Family rites of Zhuzi*?'[11]

Lu's question here clearly reflected a Sinocentric perspective. To the query 'why are you different from us?', Ch'oe Pu audaciously replied that 'I also find your speech strange'. By the response 'Heaven has bestowed us with the same human nature', he implied that they are all followers of Yao 堯, Shun 舜, Kongzi (Confucius 孔子), and Yan Hui 顏回, and thus fostered a sense of solidarity and oneness with them. Ch'oe Pu's projection and assertion of a Confucianist identity may also be discerned in his eloquent remark when gratefully bidding farewell to Li Ang 李昂, who escorted him to Jiantiao-suo 健跳所 on the 25th day of the leap 1st month, 1488:

蓋我朝鮮, 地雖海外, 衣冠文物, 悉同中國, 則不可以外國視也, 況今大明一統, 胡越爲家, 則一天之下, 皆吾兄弟, 豈以地之遠近, 分內外哉?

Although my Korea is beyond the sea, its clothing and culture being the same as China's, she cannot be considered a foreign country. That is especially so now, with Great Ming's unification, the barbarians have been incorporated into one family. Therefore, being unified under Heaven, [they are] all my brothers; how can we discriminate among people because of distance?[12]

Ch'oe Pu's reasoning was grounded in the pronouncement of Ming Emperor Taizu 太祖 (r. 1368–1398) that emphasized the strong bond between efflorescence and barbarian 華夷. After the founder of the Ming Empire re-unified China following the disintegration of the Mongolian Empire, Ch'oe Pu believed that culturally China and Chosŏn were sufficiently close to be considered belonging to the same country, sharing not only the same attire but also Confucian values and cultural practices.

Despite the same cultural roots within the Sinosphere, the Chinese people that Ch'oe Pu encountered kept asking how Chosŏn was different from China. On

---

11 English translation adapted, with minor modification, from Meskill (1965: 53–54).
12 English translation adapted, with minor modification, from Meskill (1965: 15).

02:17, two eminent officials surnamed Wang and Song received Ch'oe Pu at the Gusu 姑蘇 Station. Through brush-talk, they asked Ch'oe Pu:

又問曰: 箕子封朝鮮, 今有後否? 且有廟墓祀事不廢否?	Wang and Song asked: 'Kija having been enfeoffed in Chosŏn, are there now descendants of Kija today? And, are his shrine, graves, and rites still kept up?'
臣對曰: 箕子之後, 箕準爲衛滿所逐, 奔馬韓以立都. 後爲百濟所滅, 今無嗣. 箕子廟在平壤, 國家每歲春秋, 降香祝牲幣以致祭.	I, your servant, responded: 'Ki Chun, Kija's successor, was expelled by Wi Man. He fled to Mahan and founded a new capital. But he was later defeated by Paekche and left no living descendants. Kija's Shrine is in P'yŏngyang; every year in spring and fall, the state honors him by burning incense, sacrificing animals and making other offerings.'
又問曰: 你國有何長技, 能却隋唐之兵乎?	They further asked: 'What great technique did your country have, that helped repel the armies of Sui and Tang?'[13]

Chinese literati tended to associate the history of Chosŏn with Kija in part to substantiate their claim that Chosŏn was a country that Kija had been enfeoffed. According to this Sinocentric perspective, Chosŏn being merely a tributary state, how could Koguryŏ defeat the armies of Sui and Tang? That made Wang curious and asked about Koreans' secret talent. To this Ch'oe Pu replied:

謀臣猛將, 用兵有道, 爲兵卒者率皆親上死長

The ministers, who planned well, and the generals, who were bold, knew the ready way to wage war. All the soldiers cherished their leaders and died for them.[14]

Then he further explained that Silla, Paekche, and Koguryŏ were united to become one country, to emphasize that Chosŏn had inherited the legitimacy of Koguryŏ, which defeated the invading armies of Sui and Tang. By virtue of physical proximity, residents of Shandong or Liaodong – the regions closer to Chosŏn – would naturally feel emotionally more closely attached to the people of Chosŏn. On 03:15, Liaodong merchants who Ch'oe Pu met at Qingyuan Station 清源驛, Linqing Prefecture 臨清州, came to visit him and hosted a banquet:

---

13 English translation adapted, with minor modification, from Meskill (1965: 93).
14 English translation adapted, with minor modification, from Meskill (1965: 93).

有遼東人陳玘王鑽張景張昇王用何
玉劉傑等. 以商販事. 先到于此. 聞
臣等之至. 以清酒三壺. 糖餳一盤.
荳腐一盤. 大餠一盤來饋臣及從
者. 且曰:·我遼東城. 地隣貴國. 義
同一家. 今日幸得相見於客旅之中.
敢將薄物. 以爲禮耳.·

臣曰:·貴地卽古高句麗故都. 高句麗.
今爲我朝鮮之地. 地之沿革. 雖因
時有異. 其實同一國也.·

Liaodong man Chen Qi. Wang Zuan. Zhang Jing. Zhang Sheng. Wang Yong. He Yu. Liu Jie. among others. had arrived earlier for business. Upon hearing of us. they brought three pots of refined wine. one plate of sweetmeats. one plate of tofu. and one plate of large pancakes and served them to me and my staff. One of them said: 'The site of our city of Liaodong is adjacent to your country. and we are like a single family. We are fortunate today to have met you on our journey and venture to offer these crude things to you only as tokens of courtesy.'

I. your servant. said. 'your esteemed land is where the capital of Old Koguryŏ used to be. and Koguryŏ is now the land of my Chosŏn. Though the conditions of rule of the land have changed with the times. it is really the same country'.[15]

The Liaodong merchants said to Ch'oe Pu and his entourage that they felt like members of the same family given the proximity between Chosŏn and their homeland, which prompted Ch'oe Pu to point out that where they met, it used to be the capital of Old Koguryŏ. In this sense, it was one and the same country, be it Chosŏn or Old Koguryŏ. Ch'oe Pu actually met a monk called Jiemian 戒勉 at Liaoyang Station 遼陽驛 on 05:24, who happened to be Korean by descent:

僧系本朝鮮人. 僧祖父逃來于此, 今已三世矣. 此方地近本國界, 故本國
人來住者甚夥. 中國人最怯懦無勇, 若遇賊, 皆投戈奔竄. 且無善射者, 必
抄本國人向化者, 以謂精兵, 以爲先鋒. 我本國一人, 可以當中國人什百
矣. 此方卽古我高句麗之都, 奪屬中國千有餘載. 我高句麗流風遺俗, 猶
有未殄. 立高麗祠以爲根本, 敬祀不怠, 不忘本也.

Originally my ancestors were Koreans, but my grandfather fled to this place. It has been three generations now. Since this region is near the border of the Old Koguryŏ, many of us come here to live. Chinese people being extremely cowardly and lacking in courage, [they] would all throw away [their] spears and flee if [they] meet bandits. [They] have no good bowmen, so [they] would seize immigrants from Old Koguryŏ and use them as vanguards of the army, calling them picked troops. One man from our country is worth ten, or even a hundred Chinese. This region was the capital of Old Koguryŏ. It was annexed by China over a thousand years ago, but the traditional rites and customs of Koguryŏ have not yet all died out. We have built a Koryŏ temple and use it

---

15 English translation adapted. with minor modification. from Meskill (1965: 111).

as a center. We sacrifice regularly and our ancestral rituals have never ceased, because [we] have not forgotten our origins and roots, and [we] never will.[16]

Jiemian, a speaker of Korean, clearly projected an identity that differed significantly from other Chinese people encountered by Ch'oe Pu. While they must have conversed in spoken Korean, there is no indication whether the report in Sinitic was extracted from their brush-talk interaction or based on Ch'oe Pu's recollection entirely. What is clear is that a strong sense of communion was in evidence when the topic of common Korean ancestry was brought up. Their conversation then switched to Buddhism; there again, we can see that Ch'oe Pu perceived Old Koguryŏ to be their shared lineage through the eyes of the Chinese people.

Among Chinese people, there were officials who knew Chosŏn well. The eunuch commander 鎭守太監, Zhang Qing 張慶, ordered an official to let him know which position Chosŏn men held, including Chŏng In-chi 鄭麟趾, Sin Suk-chu 申叔舟, Sŏng Sam-mun 成三問, Kim Wan-chi 金浣之, Cho Hye 趙惠, Yi Sa-ch'ŏl 李思哲, Yi Pyŏn 李邊, and Yi Kyŏn 李堅. Among these, Yi Pyŏn, Kim Wan-chi, Cho Hye, and Yi Kyŏn were men who even Ch'oe Pu had not heard about. It is most likely that Zhang Qing read 'Accounts of Chosŏn' 朝鮮紀事 written by Ni Qian 倪謙, who was among the Ming Chinese envoys on a mission to Chosŏn (Park 2006: 222–223). That travelogue account must have been rather influential among the scholar-officials and literati in China at the time while Ch'oe Pu drifted to China. On 02:08, another official in Hangzhou asked Ch'oe Pu[17]:

景泰年間, 我國給事中官張寧奉使你國, 做却金亭詩, 皇華集. 你曉得否?	During the Jingtai (1450–1456) reign, our country's Supervising Secretary, Zhang Ning, went to your country on a mission and wrote 'A poem on Kŭm Pavilion', as well as 'Collection of Chinese envoys' poetry' 皇華集; are you aware of that?
臣對曰: 張給事到我國, 著皇華集. 其中題漢江樓詩, . . . 尤稱籍.	I, your servant, replied: 'Supervising Secretary Zhang came to our country and wrote 'Collection of Chinese envoys' poetry'. Among its poems, 'A poem on Han River pavilion' . . . is particularly acclaimed'

The official knew about the poetry included in *Collection of Chinese envoys' poetry* because Zhang Ning happened to live in the region, but the book was known in other areas as well. Zheng and his men, who interrogated Ch'oe Pu at Wulin Station in Hangzhou, commented after reading Ch'oe Pu's brush-talk responses in its entirety. He praised Ch'oe Pu, telling him that 'you seem like a scholar who is truly well read; people here just didn't realize that' 你實讀書士, 此地人固不識

---

16 English translation adapted, with minor modification, from Meskill (1965: 145–146).
17 English translation adapted, with minor modification, from Meskill (1965: 80).

也. Ch'oe Pu, like Sŏ Kŏ-chŏng 徐居正 (1420–1488), came to be recognized for his erudition. While it is difficult to generalize this impression to the entire Chinese population based on brush-talk interactions between Ch'oe Pu and regional elites of China, it seems safe to say that some people in Ming China came to have a more balanced view of Chosŏn thanks to their brush-talk interaction with Ch'oe Pu.

Ch'oe Pu introduced facets of Ming China unbeknown to Chosŏn envoys

When the capital of Ming China was located in Jinling (today's Nanjing), Chosŏn envoys traveled by sea for their tributary mission to the Celestial Empire. After the capital was relocated to Peking in 1421, Chosŏn envoys' tributary journey was re-routed by land, whereby the opportunity to visit the regions south of Peking was removed. As a result, little was known about southern China, which is why Ch'oe Pu's detailed first-hand eye-witness account evoked so much curiosity among the literati class in Chosŏn Korea.

When his boat drifted to the waters of Ningbo Prefecture 寧波府 after drifting for thirteen days, Ch'oe Pu came across some Chinese people at sea:

人皆穿黑襻袴芒鞋, 有以手帕裹頭者, 有着竹葉笠棕皮蓑者. 喧豗叫噪, 渾是漢語, 臣度其乃是中國人.

The men were all wearing black, padded trousers and straw boots. Some had towels wrapped around their heads, and some wore bamboo-leaf rain hats and coir-bark raincoats. They clamored and shouted loudly. What they uttered was all in Chinese, and I judged them to be men of China.[18]

Based on the boatmen's hollering and language use, Ch'oe Pu had no problem concluding that they were from China. With no knowledge of spoken Chinese, however, Ch'oe Pu began to communicate with them through brush-talk:

令程保書紙以遺曰: 朝鮮國臣崔溥奉王命, 往海島, 犇父喪過海, 遇風漂到. 不知是何國邑地也.

[I] ordered Chŏng Po to write [a message] on a piece of paper and pass it to them. It said, 'I, Ch'oe Pu, an official from Chosŏn, received the king's order to go to an island in the sea [Cheju]. I was in a hurry rushing to mourn for my father and, crossing the sea, encountered a storm and drifted here. I do not know what land or district this is'.[19]

Such a succinct statement of the Chosŏn identity of Ch'oe Pu and his men and the circumstances leading to their plight at sea was well understood by the Chinese

---

18 English translation adapted, with minor modification, from Meskill (1965: 40).
19 English translation adapted, with minor modification, from Meskill (1965: 40).

boatmen, who responded that they had entered Ningbo Prefecture of Zhejiang Province. So, through Sinitic brush-talk, both sides managed to make out each other's identity smoothly. On the same day, Ch'oe Pu soon encountered another boat. There were seven or eight men on board who were clad in a similar outfit as those on the previous boat, which gave Ch'oe Pu and his men the illusion that they were similarly Chinese boatmen, whereas in reality, they were Japanese pirates who wanted to extort valuables, in particular gold and silver from them. They disguised themselves as Chinese; one of them approached Ch'oe Pu's ship and, through brush-talk, attracted Ch'oe Pu and his crew to an island. Then a group of pirates showed up and revealed their true colors. While they were unresponsive to Ch'oe Pu's brush-talk, their interest in objects of pecuniary value backed by the threat of brute force was unmistakable, as Ch'oe Pu noted:

| 以杖杖臣左臂七八下曰: "你若愛生, 便出金銀." | [The pirates] beat my left arm with a stick seven or eight times and said, 'if you love [your] life, better bring out [all your] gold and silver.' |
| 臣大號曰: "身可齏骨可碎, 何所得金銀乎." 賊不曉臣言, 解臣縛, 許以寫意. 臣卽寫之. 賊魁怒, 瞋目張喙, 指程保而叫, 指臣而叫. | 'I, your servant, shouted: '[You can] cut [my] body and break [my] bones, but where am I to get gold and silver?' The pirates did not understand what I said, [so they] untied my bonds to let me write what I meant, and I wrote it. The pirate chief was enraged, stared at me ferociously, his mouth wide open. He started screaming while pointing at Chŏng Po and me.[20] |

Ch'oe Pu's initial attempt to clarify his identity as a Chosŏn official and the drifting incident that befell him and his entourage through Sinitic brush-talk was driven by the assumption that the alien seafarers they were facing came from China. That is why emphasis was placed on his obligation to attend his father's funeral, which he believed to be universally acknowledged as a cultural practice of utmost importance within the Sinosphere. As it turned out, those black-clad boatmen were actually Japanese pirates in disguise. It is unclear whether Ch'oe Pu's brushed plea was intelligible to the pirates. What we do know is that one of the pirates revealed their true intention through writing in Sinitic: All they were interested in was valuables, especially gold and silver from Ch'oe Pu and his crew, but not who they were and why their boat was adrift. Once Ch'oe Pu made it clear in writing that they possessed neither gold nor silver, the assault began. Here, the role of Sinitic brush-talk was ancillary to the foregrounded action, namely piracy enacted through physical violence and abusive language.

By contrast, subsequent encounters with the Chinese that he met after drifting at sea for another thirteen days gave Ch'oe Pu a totally different impression. Having been deceived and robbed a few times, Ch'oe Pu made careful observations

---

20 English translation adapted, with minor modification, from Meskill (1965: 42).

of the speech and behaviors of his interlocutors. Gradually, he formulated a more positive impression of people from southern China (*Jiangnan*)[21]:

> 下山之盜不殺臣等, 且有遺物. 仙岩之人, 不隱所劫, 竟還奪鞍. 可以觀風氣柔弱, 人心不甚暴惡之驗也.

> Robbers from Xiashan Island did not kill us and pass us some daily necessity. People from Xianyan Li [仙岩里] did not hide what they took and surprisingly gave us back our saddles. All this is proof that their culture is characterized by gentility and sensitivity, and that their hearts are free from brutality and malice.[22]

> 姓尹老官人引程保等, 詣私第飲食之. 因見其妻妾子女以展禮. 其人心淳厖如此.

> An old official surnamed Yin took Chŏng Po and others to his own house, treated him with food and drinks, and instructed his wives and children to show respect to him. What a kind and generous person he is.[23]

Many other encounters with Chinese people he met left Ch'oe Pu a deep impression. For instance, Chen Hua of Taozhu-suo asked him how the hat he was wearing was called; other officials asked him if he ate pork; they even addressed the Chosŏn king as emperor. A lot of eager brush-talkers approached him with paper and brush, but Ch'oe Pu could not respond to them all. Then an official surreptitiously showed Ch'oe Pu a note that said, 'The people here are a bad lot. Do not talk with them' 此處人輕薄, 休與閑講 (Meskill 1965: 57). For Ch'oe Pu, even ordinary expressions used by Chinese people were interesting and impressive.

When Ch'oe Pu was making his way across the Chinese mainland on his homeward journey, it happened to be the first year of the Hongzhi 弘治 era (1488) under the reign of the new Ming Emperor Xiaozong 孝宗. When a new emperor acceded to the throne, he was expected to rectify the misrule of the previous regime and promulgate new benevolent policies. At Luqiao Station 魯橋驛 on 03:08, Ch'oe Pu heard from two convoy men Fu Rong 傅榮 and Chen Xuan 陳萱 that, according to a decree of the new emperor, Buddhism would be banned. As a Confucian scholar, Ch'oe Pu welcomed this policy and could not help sharing his view in his brush-talk with them that such a decree augured well in a new political era 弘治新政.

> 萱曰: 成化皇帝最重道佛二法. 今新皇帝一切禁之.

> Xuan said, 'Emperor Chenghua revered Taoism and Buddhism, but the new emperor has banned them strictly'.

---

21 Such a positive impression was in stark contrast with Ch'oe Pu's subsequent impression of people in northern China (*Jiangbei*) during his land-bound return journey from Peking to Korea.
22 English translation adapted, with minor modification, from Meskill (1965: 63).
23 English translation adapted, with minor modification, from Meskill (1965: 64).

Chen Xuan's remark reinforced Ch'oe Pu's belief that Chinese people did not revere Confucianism as much as Koreans did in Chosŏn. Before the reign of the new emperor Hongzhi in 1488, it had been well over a century since the Ming dynasty was founded. Many social and economic problems were already observable, suggesting a gradual decline in national vigor was in evidence. At the ideological level, Neo-Confucianism was giving way to studies of the heart and mind 心學 (Elman 2001). Such keen observations and reflections may be found in Ch'oe Pu's diary account. Through the brush-talk between Ch'oe Pu and Fu Rong while he was passing by Cangzhou 滄州 on 03:21, one sees how much Ch'oe Pu was interested in the new era of Hongzhi:

河邊有望竿上懸人頭以示衆. 傅榮謂臣曰: 彼乃强盜首也....	At the edge of the river, a man's head fastened on top of a pole was displayed to all. Fu Rong said to me, 'That is the head of a notorious bandit...'
臣問諸傅榮曰: 自過淮河以後, 若兵部, 刑部, 吏部等各司之官之舡, 絡繹不絶, 何也?	I, your servant, asked Fu Rong, 'Ever since we passed the Huai River, there has been a steady line of boats of officials from the various bureaus of the Ministries of War, Punishments, and Personnel. Why?'
榮曰: 今天子聖明, 朝臣以舊日所爲, 或致小過者, 皆降貶之. 河路中帶錫牌而歸者, 皆見貶下鄉朝士也....	Fu Rong said, 'Because some of the ministers of the Court may have made small errors in what they did in former days, the present Emperor in his wisdom is dismissing them all. All those who are carrying pewter tablets and going the other way in the river are ministers of the Court who have been dismissed and are going to their homes.'...
臣曰: 朝臣貶秩者多, 何以不斥宦寺之徒, 使得意以行....	I, your servant, said 'If many court ministers are being degraded, why does [the Emperor] not dismiss the eunuchs instead of letting them have their way?'...
臣曰: 當今天下再得堯舜之君, 舉元凱黜四凶, 朝廷肅淸, 四海妥帖, 不亦賀乎.	I, your servant, said 'Now the Empire under Heaven has got again a ruler like Yao and Shun. He elevates good men and dismissed wicked ones. The Court is calm, and the Four Seas are steady. Shall we not give praise?'[24]

After getting over a prolonged period of interrogation by the Chinese, Ch'oe Pu finally gained their trust, which allowed him to make careful observations of various issues of interest that came to his attention. His brush conversation with Fu Rong exemplified earlier is an instructive example. Ch'oe Pu's conscious gathering of information on China during his return journey suggests that he had intended to keep a travel journal in preparation for writing up his observations and

---

24 English translation adapted, with minor modification, from Meskill (1965: 114).

experiences in China after returning home, even without being commanded by the king to do so. Later, as he was finishing his account crossing the Amnok River (a.k.a. Yalu River 鴨綠江), he outlined the differences in the regions between the north (*Jiangbei* 江北) and south (*Jiangnan* 江南) of Yangtze River. Such differences are captured succinctly by Meskill's summary of Ch'oe Pu's description of China, as follows (Meskill 1965: 15; see also 154–157):

> The South . . . prospers far more than the North. In the Yangtze Valley, Ch'oe finds rich fields, luxuriant fruit trees, and fair scenery. Villages cluster across the countryside. Most remarkable of all, the great cities of the South contain magnificent houses, a multitude of markets, wine shops and music halls, and crowds of ornamented and splendidly dressed people. Large numbers of ships gather at Hangzhou, Suzhou, and the junction of the Grand Canal and the Yangtze, indicating a flourishing waterborne commerce. The great gates and other architectural monuments of the cities defy his attempt to record them all.
>
> The North, on the other hand, conveys a feeling of poverty and desolation. Sand storms begin to discomfort the travelers. The fields are less bountiful, the villages fewer and more squalid. Though the major cities appear to be thriving, they lack the atmosphere of brilliant prosperity of the southern ones. So it is even for Peking, which receives most of its supplies from the South. The farther north Ch'oe goes, the more desolate the land becomes.

On one hand, such differences and stark contrasts appeared to be characteristic of other regions in China; on the other hand, they revealed how different China was from Chosŏn. For instance, toward the end of his report, after laying out the major differences north and south of the Yangtze river, Ch'oe Pu remarked that in China, 'everyone does business' 人皆以商賈爲業, which is strongly suggestive of his conviction and contempt that per orthodox Confucianism, commerce and profit were valued much less in Chosŏn:

> 其所同者, 尚鬼神崇道佛, 言必搖手, 怒必蹙口唾沫.... 人皆以商賈爲業, 雖達官巨家, 或親袖稱錘, 分析錙銖之利.

> As to similarities, [Chinese people] honor gods and demons and revere the Taoist gods and the Buddha. When they talk, they always wave their hands. When they are angry, they always purse their lips and slaver.... Everyone does business; even some senior scholar-officials, men from well-to-do clans and powerful families carry balances in their sleeves and will not hesitate quibbling over profits.[25]

The first draft of Ch'oe Pu's diary that he submitted was written up in China. It was full of keen observations, complete with precise information about the day's

---

25 English translation adapted, with minor modification, from Meskill (1965: 157).

weather. In reality, however, the report actually submitted to King Sŏngjong had been checked and modified by several co-editors. In the last paragraph of that report, it is stated that:

臣之歷覽, 千載難又. 然在衰経之中, 不敢觀望遊賞, 採取勝槩, 秪令陪吏四人逐日觀標榜, 問地方. 掛一漏萬, 記其大畧耳.

> What this vassal [me] has seen and experienced was an opportunity that will not come again for another thousand years. As [I was] in a state of mourning, [I] was disinclined to enjoy the splendid scenery on the way and to depict it from memory. [I] could only order my four subordinates to observe the road signs and notices on the wall, and ask about the sites in the region. Yet for every single point noted, a thousand details must have been missed – [this report] can only offer a glimpse.
>
> (compare Meskill 1965: 157)

The concern for fine details suggests a desire to enhance self-awareness through the lens of others. This seemed to have been the shared duty or responsibility of not only Ch'oe Pu, but also the other men in the Chosŏn entourage. No wonder the other officials like Chŏng Po, Kim Chung 金重, Yi Chŏng 李楨, and Son Hyo-cha 孫孝子 all took meticulous notes throughout the journey including at times when their own lives were under threat, resulting in elaborate accounts that Ch'oe Pu could draw on to corroborate fine details of individual events. Some names were lost or missed, be it due to oversight or oblivion, but their desire and attitude to document thousands of names of people and regions, all following their natural time sequence during their journey, shows how important they perceived the task of informing their peers in Chosŏn by portraying China properly through their first-hand eye-witness accounts. Clearly, such a goal could only be achieved if the narratives in their co-constructed travelogue report were accurate and reliable.

At a more macro, sociopolitical level, all the boat drifters who underwent the same ordeal that Ch'oe Pu had to put up with seemed to be duty-bound to help their literati peers in Chosŏn to gain a better view of China, their suzerain state. But that is not all, for, through China, people in Chosŏn could also get a better understanding of their own nation. Whether this was intended by the author(s) of *A record of drifting across the sea*, we may never know, but at least this may be regarded as a long-term goal towards developing a more accurate mutual understanding at the personal level, which in turn is the foundation for proper mutual recognition at the inter-state level.

Coda

While Korea, Japan, and China were members of the Sinosphere in the premodern and early modern East Asia, the relative social status of the literati of Sinitic and the relationship between their literacy in Sinitic and political power, economic standing, social mobility were rather different, despite the fact that the

Identity verification and negotiation 151

civil service examination was adopted in both China and Chosŏn Korea. In Ming China, literacy was a privilege of the powerful and affluent and, for this reason, very unevenly distributed, not to mention women who were not encouraged to learn how to read and write. Familiarity with Classical Chinese canons and literary works was a prerequisite for acceding to officialdom within the government through success in the civil service examination. In Korea, literati of Sinitic were similarly encouraged to join the elite class of high-ranking scholar-officials in the bureaucratic hierarchy through success in the national civil service examination that tested the examinees' familiarity and profundity of knowledge in the 'four books and three classics' 四書三經 (Chen 2014), among many other literary works. By contrast, since no such examination existed in Japan, knowledge of literacy in Sinitic was not directly related to socioeconomic status in society or political power at court. Such a difference – the absence versus the presence of a national civil service examination system – may help explain varying levels of motivation, interest and ability on the part of literati of Sinitic in these three polities to engage in silent conversation with others.

Thanks to the shared knowledge of the same body of Sinitic classics and literature, literati of Sinitic were able to 'speak' their mind by conducting 'silent conversation' with other fellow literati in cross-border transcultural communication contexts. Where speech-based interaction had failed them due to the absence of a shared spoken language, writing-mediated brush-talk in Sinitic turned out to be a viable mode of communication. As shown in Yi Chi-hang's testimonies as a boat drifter in Japan and Ch'oe Pu's detailed account of his personal observations and experiences of his drifting ordeal in China, brush conversation allowed them to respond to maritime officials' tough questions regarding the circumstances under which they were stranded in alien land, explicate or negotiate their national identities in part by demonstrating their membership within the Sinosphere through literacy-focused interaction in Sinitic, including intellectual and poetic exchange with others for rapport-building purposes or simply showing civility and appreciation.

Of course, smooth and seamless brush-talking is premised on one condition, namely the participants must possess a certain level of literacy in Sinitic. Supporting evidence for this may be found in surviving documentation of both drifting incidents. For instance, members of the Ainu community were those whom Yi Chi-hang and his men tried to talk to after their boat drifted to the waters of Hokkaido. Since the Ainu had very limited literacy in Sinitic, the boat drifters failed to communicate their plight through brush-talking to them. Likewise, the Japanese pirates encountered by Ch'oe Pu and his crew had only a basic understanding of written Chinese, so communication between them was anything but smooth, and it proceeded clumsily given the absence of a shared spoken language.

Finally, travelogue accounts like Ch'oe Pu's (1488) *A record of drifting across the sea* 漂海錄 proved to be attractive among successive generations of Korean literati largely because it contained rich details about southern China (*Jiangnan*) that few Korean readers had a chance to visit. That has no doubt enhanced their understanding of China beyond the Celestial Capital, which in turn helps explain its strong market appeal, as reflected in new editions as recently as 1896 (see WANG Yong, this volume), and it came to be read widely and avidly by successive generations of literati in Korea.

References

Chen, Y. [陳亦伶] (2014). 從「四書五經」到「四書三經」– 對韓國經學研究的影響與展望 ('From "Four books, five classics" to "Four books, three classics" – Impact on and prospect of classical studies in Korea'). 中國文哲研究通訊 (Newsletter of the Institute of Chinese Literature and Philosophy) 24(1): 55–72.

Ch'oe Pu [崔溥] (1488). 漂海錄 ('*A record of drifting across the sea*'). Unpublished manuscript, 韓國 國立中央圖書館 (National Library of Korea). 韓國古典綜合DB (Comprehensive Database of Korean Classics). Retrieved July 25, 2021, from https://db.itkc.or.kr/dir/item?itemId=GO#/dir/node?dataId=ITKC_GO_1410A.

Clements, R. (2015). *A cultural history of translation in early modern Japan*. Cambridge: Cambridge University Press.

Clements, R. (2019). Brush talk as the 'lingua franca' of East Asian diplomacy in Japanese-Korean encounters, c. 1600–1868. *The Historical Journal* 62(2): 289–309.

Denecke, W. (2014). Worlds without translation: Premodern East Asia and the power of character scripts. In S. Bermann & C. Porter (Eds.), *A companion to translation studies* (pp. 204–216). Chichester, UK: Wiley-Blackwell.

Elman, B. A. (Ed.). (2001). *From philosophy to philology: Intellectual and social aspects of change in Late imperial China*. Los Angeles: Asia-Pacific Institute, California.

Hur, K.-J. [許敬震] (2010a). 『漂海錄』體現的朝中兩國人的相互認识 ('Mutual understanding between Chosun and China from the perspective of *P'yohaenok*'), 中國研究 (*Journal of Sinology and China Studies*) 48: 219–230.

Hur, K.-J. [許敬震] (2010b). 漂流民 李志恒과 아이누人, 日本人 사이의 意思 疏通 (Wrecked Lee Ji-hang and Ainus, the Communication with Japanese), 洌上古典研究 (*Yeol-sang Journal of Classical Studies*) 32: 53–82.

Kim, Y.-M. [金泳謨] (1986). 朝鮮支配層研究 ('Studies on elites of Yi-dynasty'). Seoul: Ilchogak.

Kornicki, P. F. (2018). *Languages, scripts, and Chinese texts in East Asia*. Oxford: Oxford University Press.

Meskill, J. T. (1965). *Choe Pu's diary: A record of drifting across the sea*. Ann Arbor, MI: University Microfilms International.

Park, W.-H. [朴元熇] (2006). 崔溥漂海錄研究 ('Studies on the *Accounts of the drift* by Ch'oe Pu'). Seoul: Korea University Press.

6 A study of salient linguistic features of two Ryukyuan brush conversations in Sinitic, 1611 and 1803

Wong Tak-sum

Introduction

The Okinawa Prefecture of Japan is located on the Ryukyu Archipelago to the southwest of Kagoshima 鹿兒島. It was ruled by the royal clan, the Shoo 尚 family, of the former Ryukyu Kingdom before its transformation into the Ryukyu domain in 1872 and Japanese annexation in 1879. During this period, some original historical documents were transferred to the Ministry of Home Affairs in Tokyo while the rest were housed in the Okinawa Prefectural Library (1924; see 琉球史料目録 'A catalogue of the historical documents of Ryukyu'). The former batch was consumed by fire during the Great Kantō Earthquake in 1923 while the latter batch was entirely destroyed during the Battle of Okinawa in 1945. Fortunately, copies of a number of these documents had been made by some institutions and individuals before the disasters struck, which paved the way for the systematic study of the archipelago's premodern history.[1] Recently, photocopies of quite a number of these surviving documents have been compiled and published in China (see, e.g., Takatsu & J. Chen 2013; Y.-F. Wang 2012; Zhai 2015).

Mention of language contact between Ryukyuans and people from other parts of the Sinosphere is not uncommon, for example, in the official records of the Qing court, which was published in 1993 by the First Historical Archives of China 中國第一歷史檔案館 as 'Selected Records from Sino-Ryukyu Relation Archive of Qīng Dynasty' 清代中琉關係檔案選編 (See also Cen 2014a, 2014b). Since the Ryukyuan languages, which belong to the Japonic language family (cf. Heinrich et al. 2015) are mutually unintelligible with Sinitic languages, which belong to the Sino-Tibetan family, Sinitic brush-talk proved to be the most effective mode of communication in such Sino-Ryukyu language contact situations. Today, some surviving records of brush conversations involving Ryukyuans may be found in inherited documents in Japan and Korea, but not in China. In this

---

1 Today, copies of such documents may be accessed at Okinawa Prefectural Arts University Library, Okinawa Prefectural Library, the Institute of Okinawan Studies of the Hosei University, Naha Municipal Library, the National Taiwan University Library, and the Historiographical Institute of the University of Tokyo (see also Okinawa Prefectural Library 1924; Higa 1962).

DOI: 10.4324/9781003048176-7

154 *Wong Tak-sum*

chapter, we will focus on two such records, namely 'A record of exchange of poetic verses with Ryukyu ambassadors' (*Yugu sasin chŭngdamnok* 琉球使臣贈答錄) and 'A brush-talk record at the Ryukyu residence' (*Ryukan hitsudan* 琉館筆談). We will first give a brief overview of the history of Ryukyu before outlining the key characteristics of these two brush-talk records. This will set the scene for a study of some of the most salient linguistic and discourse-pragmatic features there.

A brief history of Ryukyu

The Ryukyu Kingdom got its name from the Ryukyu Islands where it flourished.[2] Before the unification of the Okinawa Island by Shō Hashi (also spelled Shoo Hashii, 尚巴志1372–1439, r. 1422–1439) in 1429, historical records of this premodern period are fragmentary while conflicting and inconsistent accounts of historical events are not uncommon. During this Sanzan period 三山時代, three polities competed for ascendency, namely, Hokuzan 北山 (*Fukuuzan* in Northern Okinawan language), Chūzan 中山, and Nanzan 南山.[3] For their respective rulers, diplomatic relations with China were paramount given lucrative profits derived from regional maritime trade, which became a bone of contention in Ryukyuan politics. Nevertheless, the lineage of Chūzan kings was officially recognized by successive Ming emperors as the rightful rulers of the island state. In fact, the family name of the Chūzan monarchy, Shoo 尚, was conferred by Ming Chengzu 明成祖, the Yongle Emperor 永樂皇帝 in 1421.

Having defeated the other two archrivals in 1429, the Chūzan monarch unified the Ryukyu Kingdom, whereupon sinicization gradually took root on an unprecedented scale. For instance, Shō Hashi adapted the Ming Chinese hierarchical court system complete with its nomenclature as the principal political institution. In fact, a Ryukyuan Chinese community had been formed in Kume Village (Kumemura 久米村, *Kuninda* in Okinawan language; Chi. 唐營, 唐榮) already as early as in 1392 after Ming Emperor Hongwu 洪武 sent 'thirty-six' families of people from Fujian Province to Ryukyu.[4] Among them were professional translators and clerks, but also craftsmen, shipbuilders and sailors engaged in the nuts and bolts of the tribute system (Kerr 1958/2000: 75). The Chinese immigrants in Kume Village played a key role in assisting the Okinawans to learn advanced methods of shipbuilding and 'the civilizing arts of Chinese administration' (Kerr

---

2 Ryukyu (variously spelt as Ruuchuu, Liu-chiu, Luchu, Loochoo, Loo-choo, and Lewchew) is written as 琉求 and 瑠求 in Chinese historical documents. It used to refer to a much wider region that also included Formosa (present-day Taiwan) before the Ryukyu Kingdom joined the Ming tribute system (Akamine 2017: 23; see also Kerr 1958/2000: xvii, 54–55). For a detailed study of Ryukyuan personal and place names, see Sakamaki 1964).
3 After the three principalities were united as Ryukyu Kingdom, they were referred to as 国頭 Kunigami (Hokuzan), Nakagami 中頭 (Chūzan), and 島尻 Shimajiri (Nanzan).
4 Thirty-six is not an exact figure; rather, it is most likely a 'figure of speech which merely meant a widely representative group' (Kerr 1958/2000: 76; cf. Akamine 2004).

1958/2000: 75). Some members in this community subsequently dominated the important positions in the royal government, helped set up key political and sociocultural institutions, disseminated skills of governance as well as knowledge of the Chinese language to the Ryukyu officials.[5] The Ryukyu Kingdom then thrived, thanks to maritime trade, until the late sixteenth century when the emergence of Japanese pirates (*wakō* 倭寇) and intense competition arising from the increasing presence of Portuguese traders among other factors gradually took its toll. In 1609, out of apprehension of possible invasion by adventurous and militant Europeans such as the Spanish coming from the south, Tokugawa Ieyasu 德川家康 (1543–1616) authorized the Satsuma domain 薩摩藩, present-day Kagoshima Prefecture 鹿兒島縣 to send an expeditionary force to conquer the Ryukyu Kingdom on the pretext of her refusal to meet the demand of Toyotomi no Hideyoshi 豐臣秀吉 (1537–1598) for providing sufficient military support to assist Satsuma's invasion of Chosŏn (Kerr 1958/2000: 3; Akamine 2017: 63). Consequently, the Ryukyu Kingdom became a vassal state of Satsuma. In the next 260 years until 1872, the Ryukyu Kingdom entered into tributary relations with both Japan and China. Such a dual subordination was obscure to the Qing government, however, who had no idea that the Ryukyu government had already compromised their allegiance by becoming a tributary of the Japanese shogunate, a strategy that allowed the Ryukyu Kingdom to preserve its tenuous national identity (Kerr 1958/2000: 166–169, 564–565; T.-T. Chen 1968; Akamine 2017: 82). For successive envoys from Qing China to Ryukyu on their investiture missions,[6] Japanese influence was keenly felt as shown in different editions of Chinese classics bearing Japanese reading marks of individual characters and the reign title of the Japanese emperor (T.-T. Chen 1968: 163). As T.-T. Chen (1968) further observes, hiding tributary relations with Satsuma from the Chinese was no easy task; dual subordination was possible 'only when the East Asian world was isolated and while Japan remained in seclusion', a condition that no longer obtained by the late nineteenth century (T.-T. Chen 1968: 164).

---

5 For a brief overview of the historical ties binding Ryūkyū and China, see Mansfield (2017). 'Disputatious legacies: examining the historic ties that bind Okinawa and China' in *Japan Times*. Retrieved March 1, 2021, from www.japantimes.co.jp/life/2017/04/08/lifestyle/disputatious-legacies-examining-historic-ties-bind-okinawa-china/.

6 From 1663 to 1866, altogether eight missions were dispatched by the Qing court to the Ryukyu kingdom. Most Chinese envoys kept detailed travel notes in their personal journals, of which eight were published. Of these, seven were of very high quality, so good that the Ryukyuans 'relied on these Chinese sources in compiling their own national history, and the Japanese also used them' (T.-T. Chen 1968: 158). Two of these journals were translated into English (see Sakamaki 1963: 78–81): 'Memoirs of Ryukyu' 中山傳信錄 and 'Brief gazetteer of the Kingdom of Liu-Chiu' 琉球國志略. According to T.-T. Chen (1968: 158), these journals were

> equivalent to detailed travel accounts plus background of the kind found in a Chinese Gazetteer, with historical, economic, geographic, social, and cultural information illustrated by drawings by artist members of the mission and maps made on the scene – not only invaluable historical sources but monuments to the cultural relations between the two countries.

To resist the onslaught of the shogunate and Satsuma, and avoid complete absorption into the Japanese political system, the Ryukyu Kingdom tried to speed up the pace of sinicization to create a pseudo-Chinese national identity and autonomy with the support of the élite families from Kume Village. For instance, the Chinese ritual ceremony was introduced, *fengshui* cosmology was incorporated when the Shuri Castle 首里城 was rebuilt. In addition, in the late eighteenth century, Confucian education was spread in Ryukyu. Elementary schools teaching Chinese classics started at academies in Shuri 首里, Naha 那覇, Tomari 泊, etc. 'Three Character Classic' 三字經 and 'Twenty-Four Filial Exemplars' 二十四孝 were used as primers for teaching elementary *kanbun* 漢文 knowledge using Ryukyuan-style *kundoku* (*gōon kundoku* 合音訓読). In national schools, apart from spoken Mandarin Chinese, Confucian classics like the 'Four Books and Five Classics' 四書五經 at mid- and advanced levels were also taught following the *kaion kundoku* 開音訓読 method (Takahashi 2002). Consequently, the study of Confucian classics became the foundation of the national curriculum while Confucian philosophy permeated every level of Ryukyuan society although only the aristocratic class had the opportunity to receive formal education in the kingdom.

In 1686, the practice of sending students to China to study was resumed after the power base of the Qing court became stable. These students, known as *government students* (官生 *kanshō*),[7] normally studied for three years at the Imperial Academy 國子監, which was the training center for academic elites in China. Upon returning to Ryukyu, they would assume superior positions within the Confucian education hierarchy of the kingdom. In addition to these government students, many people from Kume Village also crossed to China by serving in the crew of an envoy ship, the purpose being to absorb as much knowledge of Chinese as possible stealthily while in Fuzhou 福州 (a.k.a. Foochow). These are recognized as *working students* (勤學, Jap: *kingaku*), which was one way to improve their life chances. While some of them would focus on studying the Chinese classics and Confucian rituals, many of them studied other disciplines like calendar making, medicine, the codes of law, and so forth. Since only long-term government-sponsored students were allowed to stay and study in China, the Qing court remained uninformed of the purpose and presence of these working students. Nonetheless, these government students and working students have made great contributions in spreading Confucian knowledge and values from China to Ryukyu.

In 1701, *Chūzan seikan* 中山世鑑, a genealogy of the royal family, was translated from Japanese into Chinese by the Kume scholar, Shitahaku Ueekata Tensho 志方伯親方天將 (Chinese name: 蔡鐸 *Sai Taku*). Subsequently, a chronologically ordered history of the kingdom, *Kyūyō* 球陽 (*Chuuyuu* in Okinawan language) was also translated into Chinese. As reflected in the revised genealogies

---

7 A government student, Han Sō 潘相, has recorded his study experience in China in 'An eye-witness account of Ryukyuans entering school' 琉球入学見聞 (Han 1768). Retrieved March 1, 2020/21, from https://shimuchi.lib.u-ryukyu.ac.jp/collection/sakamaki/hw79001.

compiled by the Ryukyu royal government in 1690, the official genealogies started taking on the style of Chinese genealogy while members of the elite families also adopted Chinese family names.

During the short reign of the precocious young king Shō On 尚溫 (1784–1802, r. 1795–1802), the royal education policy was revamped and the basis of training for government offices was broadened. A national academy was founded within the palace complex while elementary schools were established for children of the gentry in Shuri but also for children of the farmers in the countryside. Henceforth, eligibility for the Peking scholarships was gradually extended to young men beyond the Kume Village community. Such a reform sparked a rebellion, which was quickly put down, resulting in the abolition of some of the exclusive privileges of the villagers of Kume Village (Kerr 1958/2000: 226–227).

Notwithstanding the royal clan's tremendous efforts in sinicization, the shogunate's military expansion and eventual annexation of the Ryukyu kingdom proved unstoppable. After being renamed the Ryukyu Domain by Emperor Meiji in 1872, the Ryukyu Kingdom was dissolved and retitled as the Okinawa Prefecture on 27 March 1879. The last king of Ryukyu Kingdom, Shoo Tee 尚泰 (Jap: *Shō Tai*, 1843–1901, r. 1848–1879), was forced to relocate to Edo 江戶 (present-day Tokyo). He was conferred the title of a Marquess, the second tier of the *kazoku* 華族 peerage system as a consolation. A number of the royal supporters of the kingdom fled to China (for more historical details, see Higaonna 1950; Kerr 1958/2000; and Akamine 2004). For over 450 years until the late nineteenth century, the Ryukyu Kingdom's political frailty was largely attributable to her lack of natural resources, but also the geopolitical predicament of the tiny island state being caught between maritime powers, notably China and Japan, among others. As Kerr (1958/2000: 227) put it, being a 'microcosmic society', Ryukyu was:

> so delicately balanced in population versus meager resources and limited opportunity, and so precariously placed on political frontiers. The balance of moral obligation felt toward China versus political and economic obligation to Satsuma had been neatly maintained through two centuries, but it could be preserved only under conditions of extreme isolation.

That isolation came to an end at the turn of the early nineteenth century, following the increasing presence of Western vessels sometimes backed by warships, notably from Britain, the USA and also France under Napoleon. Driven by lucrative trading interests with countries in East and Southeast Asia, these Western maritime powers were all eager to gain a foothold around the coastal waters of the Ryukyu Kingdom (see Part Three, 'Between two worlds', 1797–1878, Kerr 1958/2000: 237–378).

Cungtaplok, early seventeenth century

Yugu sasin chŭngdamnok 琉球使臣贈答錄 (literally 'A record of exchange of poetic verses with the Ryukyu ambassadors', hereafter *Cungtaplok*) is a record of

158 Wong Tak-sum

brush-talk interaction between envoys from Chosŏn and Ryukyu to Ming China in Peking. In 1611, emissaries from various tributary states travelled to Peking to pay tribute to the Ming emperor Shenzong 神宗 (1563–1620, better known as the Wanli Emperor 萬曆帝, r. 1572–1620). During this trip, the Chosŏn envoy, Yi Su-Kwang 李睟光 (1563–1629) met two emissaries from Ryukyu, Sai Ken 蔡堅 (1587–1647) and Ba Seiki 馬成驥.[8] Not only did they improvise and exchange poetic verses, Yi also took this opportunity to ask about the geographical location, political and socioeconomic conditions of the Ryukyu Kingdom in the form of questions and answers through brush-talking. These brush-talk records were later compiled and included in the *Cungtaplok*, which now forms an integral part of the (Korean) 'Travelogue to Peking' 燕行錄 (Kor: *Yenhaynglok*; Mand: *Yanxinglu*, see Lim 2006 for details). In this collection, in addition to the brush conversations, 17 poems were also included, of which 15 were composed by Yi, and one each by Sai and Ba. This work was later published in scroll 10 of 'Classified notes by Master Cipong' (*Chi-Pong Sŏnsaeng Chip* 芝峯先生集) in Korea in 1633. Digitalized images of this work are freely available at the 'Kotenseki Sōgō Database of Japanese and Chinese Classics' 古典籍総合データベース of Waseda University Library (2021).[9] Figure 6.1 shows a scanned copy of the first page of the edited brush-talk records in *Cungtaplok* (compare photocopied version published in Korea, S.-K. Yi 1633/1991).

At the turn of the millennium, *Cungtaplok* was photocopied and reprinted as part of 'Complete works of *Yŏnhaengnok*' 燕行錄全集 (vol. 10, S.-K. Yi 1633/2001) in Korea; it also formed part of 'Complete edited works of Travelogue to Peking' 燕行錄全編 (vol. 5, S.-K. Yi 1633/2010) published in China. Recently, the Institute for the Translation of Korean Classics also published a text-searchable version of the entire 'Classified notes by Master Chi-Pong' 芝峯先生集 online in the 'Comprehensive Database of Korean Classics 韓國古典綜合DB.[10] Users can read the source text in its entirety along with its translation in modern Korean, see selected images of the original work, as well as perform keyword searches. Figure 6.2 shows a screenshot of this database displaying a typeset version of the

---

8 Immediately before the brush conversations, it was stated that

> The Ryukyu Kingdom is located at Eastern South Sea. The ambassadors, Sai Ken, Ba Seiki, and the seventeen attendants, all wearing clothes from the Celestial Empire [*i.e.* Chinese-style clothes], said that they departed from [their] home country in the ninth [lunar] month of the year 1610 and travelled to Fujian by sea in five days. Then they travelled 7,000 *li* by land from Fujian and arrived at Peking in the eighth [lunar] month of the year 1611. They do not sleep on heatable brick beds; they even bathe during severe winter. In terms of appearance and language, they look like Japanese to some extent.

(琉球國在東南海中．使臣蔡堅．馬成驥．從人并十七人．皆襲天朝冠服．自言庚戌九月離本國．水行五日抵福建．由福建陸行七千里．辛亥八月達北京．寢處不抃炕突．雖盛冬必沐浴．狀貌言語．略與倭同． Source: S.-K. Yi 1633/2001: 168).

9 Accessible at www.wul.waseda.ac.jp/kotenseki/html/he16/he16_02433/index.html.
10 Accessible at https://db.itkc.or.kr/

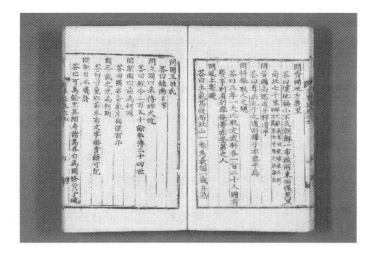

Figure 6.1 Sample digitalized image of the brush-talk record in 'A record of exchange of poetic verses with Ryukyu ambassadors' (*Yugu sasin chŭngdamnok* 琉球使臣贈答錄. S.-K. Yi 1633/2001. 1633/2010).

Source: Adapted from the 'Kotenseki Sōgō database of Japanese and Chinese classics' at Waseda University Library

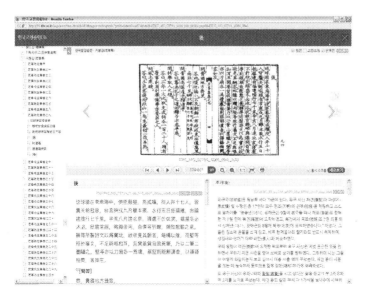

Figure 6.2 Screenshot showing an edited version of the original text, its translation in modern Korean, and a photocopy of the typeset brush-talk record in 'A record of exchange of poetic verses with Ryukyu ambassadors' (*Yugu sasin chŭngdamnok* 琉球使臣贈答錄. S.-K. Yi 1633/2001) from 'Comprehensive Database of Korean Classics' 韓國古典綜合DB.

original Sinitic text, its modern Korean translation, and the digitalized image of the first page of the original *Cungtaplok*.

Studies focusing on this brush-talk are few and far between. Fu and Huang (2018) discuss the literary exchange in this brush-talk as well as another Chosŏn-Annam brush-talk which took place in 1597, while Yi (2016) focuses on the diplomatic exchange between Yi and Sai. To my knowledge, no attempt has been made to conduct a linguistic analysis of this document, which is the focus of this chapter.

Ryukan hitsudan 琉館筆譚, early nineteenth century

After the Ryukyu Kingdom became a vassal state of the Satsuma daimyō, Japan set up an institution in Kagoshima 鹿兒島 called Ryukyu-kan 琉球館, providing a place for the missions, dignitaries, students, etc. from Ryukyu to stay and work, in effect functioning as a liaison office cum residence for traveling Ryukyuans (Kerr 1958/2000: 168; Sakai 1968: 134). The building was destroyed during the bombardment of Kagoshima in 1863, unfortunately. *Ryukan hitsudan* records the brush-assisted conversation between a Ryukyu official and a Satsuma official in 1803 which took place at the Ryukyu-kan.

Kamida Peichin 嘉味田親雲上 (1747–1805, also called Yō Bunpō 楊文鳳), was a Ryukyu scholar-official. In summer, 1803, during his stay at Ryukyu-kan in Satsuma, he was engaged in poetic exchange as well as brush conversation with Ishizuka Saikō 石冢崔高 (1803, 1803/1808), a Satsuma official. Ishizuka was a Chinese interpreter (Jap: *Tōtsūji* 唐通事) of the Satsuma domain. Kamida could speak neither Japanese nor Mandarin but he could read and write Literary Chinese. With no shared vernacular, brush-talking turned out to be the most convenient mode of communication for literati of Sinitic like Kamida and Ishizuka, as elsewhere in premodern and early modern East Asia (cf. the Sinographic cosmopolis, Koh & King 2014):

> 見一二才子 文鳳不識官話 言語不通 書字通言 聞其大略耳
>
> 'I met a couple of gifted scholars (in Fujian). Being not able to speak in Mandarin, Kamida (I) had language barrier (with them). Through brush-talking, I managed to have a brief discussion with them' (*Ryukan hitsudan*.)

Their surviving brush-talk records consist of eight themes as follows (Iwamoto 2013):

1 a brief introduction of the brush-talk
2 self-introduction by Ishizuka
3 Kamida's experience of brush-talk exchange in Ryukyu with envoys from China
4 Kamida's drifting experience to Taiwan
5 Kamida's experience at the Ryukyu outpost in Fuzhou
6 mechanism for selecting the principal officials in the Ryukyu kingdom

7   Ryukyu's education system
8   Kamida's exchange with the vassal of the Satsuma daimyō, Yamamoto 山本

The brush-talk records were later collected by Ishizuka and published as the *Ryukan hitsudan*. The poetic exchanges were also collected (but were lost, according to Y. Wang 2015):

石崔高訪其旅館，一見如舊，於是以其相贈答詩什及其筆談語錄為一卷，題為琉舘筆談，以誌奇遇於後日也，其詩又別為一冊。[11]

Ishizuka Saikō visited his hostel [and had brush conversation with Kamida]. Even though this was the first time they met, their interchange was like an encounter between old friends who also engaged in poetic exchange. Their brush-talk records were collected and compiled as the *Ryukan hitsudan*, an adventurous encounter preserved for posterity. Records of their poetic exchange were also printed in a separate booklet.

(*Ryukan brush-talk* 1803)

At present, two versions of *Ryukan hitsudan* have survived, namely, the Hawley version (n.d.) and the Tsukuba version (1808).[12] A copy of *Ryukan hitsudan* may be found in the Sakamaki/Hawley collection of the University of Hawai'i at Manoa Library. The digitalized images of this version are accessible from the website of the Ryukyu/Okinawa Special Collection Digital Archives (琉球・沖縄関係貴重資料デジタルアーカイブ) at the University of the Ryukyus Library (2021).[13] The version was also reprinted and included in the second series of 'A compilation of the inherited Sinitic documents from Ryukyu' 傳世漢文琉球文獻輯稿(第二輯) (Zhai 2015: 155–172).

The Tsukuba version, an anonymous handwritten copy of Ishizuka's original manuscript dated the eleventh lunar month of 1808,[14] is also accessible from the library website of the University of Tsukuba.[15] Notice that its *kanji* title is 琉舘筆談, where the second sinogram is written as 舘, an allograph of 館 (Figure 6.4).

---

11 In the original text, Ishijuka identified himself as 石崔高, rather than his full name 石冢崔高. It was a custom for Ryūkyū and its neighbouring region to adopt a Chinese-style name (Iwamoto 2013).
12 The last sinogram of its title in *kanji* is 譚 (viz. 琉舘筆譚, Figure 6.3), where the two orthographic variants, 筆談 and 筆譚, were held to be interchangeable and semantically equivalent.
13 Retrieved January 24, 2021, at https://shimuchi.lib.u-ryukyu.ac.jp/collection/sakamaki/hw544/2; also: http://manwe.lib.u-ryukyu.ac.jp/d-archive/viewer?&cd=00061140.
14 '文化戊辰十一月借抄石冢崔高稿本了', written at the end of the last page of the Tsukuba version.
15 Retrieved January 24, 2021, at www.tulips.tsukuba.ac.jp/limedio/dlam/B95/B952222/1/vol09/tsb/2162.htm; see also www.tulips.tsukuba.ac.jp/opac/volume/1543513.

Figure 6.3 Sample digitalized image of the first page of *Ryukan hitsudan* 琉館筆談, the Hawley version.

Source: Adapted from the Ryukyu/Okinawa Special Collection Digital Archives

Ryukan hitsudan has received the attention of only a handful of scholars. Both Iwamoto (2013) and Y. Wang (2015) have briefly introduced this brush-talk record and compared its content in the Hawley and Tsukuba versions. In addition to a brief linguistic analysis, Iwamoto (2013) also provides annotations and a translation of this document in Japanese. Zhou (2015) discusses the social customs of Fujian and Taiwan during the early nineteenth century as reflected in the interactions between the brush-talkers in this record. On the basis of such writing-mediated interactions, Zhou (2019) further points to the prosperity of Amoy, a port city opened to merchants of several European countries since 1684 and analyzes the Sino-Ryukyuan relations during that historical period. To my knowledge, no attempt has been made to examine this brush-talk record from a linguistic or discourse-pragmatic perspective.

According to Y. Wang (2015), the Tsukuba version adheres more faithfully to the original manuscript written by Ishizuka. For this reason, the analysis of *Ryukan hitsudan* in the present chapter will be based on the Tsukuba version.

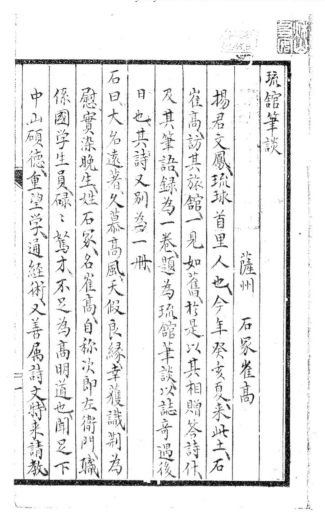

Figure 6.4 Digitalized image of the first page of *Ryukan hitsudan* 琉館筆談, the Tsukuba version.

Source: Adapted from the website of the University of Tsukuba Library

Linguistic features in two surviving Ryukyuan brush-talk records: a comparison

Classical Chinese is modeled on Old Chinese, which is the Chinese language spoken during the first millennium BCE (Norman 1988: 20). During the period of imperial China, although most Chinese literati consciously attempted to imitate the classical lexico-grammatical style of model essays written before the Han dynasty (206 BCE–220 CE), their writings were colored to some degree by their respective vernaculars (Norman 1988: 105). For a similar reason, in these two brush-talk records, although both are written principally in Classical Chinese, linguistic features more commonly attested in Middle Chinese and Early Mandarin are also observed. In what follows, we will focus on and exemplify these features. The lexical-grammatical items appearing in these texts will be cross-checked and validated with those in the following corpora:

(i)   Academic Sinica Tagged Corpus of Old Chinese (first millennium, BCE)[16]
(ii) Academic Sinica Tagged Corpus of Middle Chinese (ca. 1–750 CE)[17]
(iii) Academic Sinica Tagged Corpus of Early Mandarin Chinese (ca. 750–1800 CE)[18]

As is well known, Old Chinese (also commonly referred to as Archaic Chinese) is characterized by four salient function words, namely *zhi* (之, commonly functioning as adnominalizer or general purpose pronoun, Pulleyblank 1995: 64), *hu* (乎, typically functioning as question particle, Pulleyblank 1995: 139), *zhe* (者, subject marker or nominalizer, Pulleyblank 1995: 66), and *ye* (也, affirmative sentence final particle, Pulleyblank 1995: 20, 118). These particles can be found in both *Cungtaplok* and *Ryukan hitsudan*. For example:

(1) 問：貴國尚儒道乎？釋道乎？ (*Cungtaplok*, 1611)
    苔曰：尊尚孔子之道。
    Q: 'Your esteemed nation reveres Confucianism? Buddhism?'
    A: '(We) revere the philosophy **of** Confucius (i.e. Confucianism).'
(2) 楊曰：. . . 亦聞足下名，欲見之。 (*Ryukan hitsudan*, 1803)
    Yō: . . . 'I have also heard of your name, and want to see **you**.'
(3) 石曰：. . . 碌碌駑才，不足為高明道也。(*Ryukan hitsudan*, 1803)
    Ishizuka: . . . 'Being so mediocre and deficient in talent, I am not (good) enough to be mentioned by any brilliant person (i.e. I am inferior to you).'

In example (1), Yi asked Sai whether they revered Confucianism or Buddhism. He made use of the question particle 乎 (*hu*) to mark the end of the two parallel questions. Sai replied that they revered the philosophy of Confucius, whereupon he used 之 (*zhi*) to mark the genitive case of *Confucius* (孔子之道, 'the philosophy **of** Confucius'). In example (2), Yō said that he also heard of Ishizuka and wanted to see him. In Classical Chinese, 之 serves different lexico-grammatical functions depending on how it is used. In this context, it is used as a pronoun referring to the person being addressed, namely Ishizuka. In example (3), Ishizuka's expression of humility that his talent was deficient compared with Yō was

---

16 Institute of Linguistics, Academic Sinica (2021a): http://lingcorpus.iis.sinica.edu.tw/ancient/.
17 Institute of Linguistics, Academic Sinica (2021b): http://lingcorpus.iis.sinica.edu.tw/middle/.
18 Institute of Linguistics, Academic Sinica (2021c): http://lingcorpus.iis.sinica.edu.tw/early/.

marked by 也 (*ye*) at the end of this affirmative sentence. All this shows that lexico-grammatical elements of Old Chinese are frequently observed in these two brush-talk records.

In terms of linguistic resources, while the bulk of the brush-talk record was written unmistakably in Old Chinese, features of Middle Chinese are also observed occasionally, for instance:

(4) 問：距日本幾許？ (*Cungtaplok*, 1611)
Q: '**How many** (units of distance, i.e., how far) is Ryukyu away from Japan?'

In example (4), Yi raised a question regarding the geographical distance between Ryukyu and Japan. He used a bisyllabic interrogative marker 幾許 (*jixu*, 'how many'). While this bisyllabic word cannot be found in the *Academic Tagged Corpus of Old Chinese*, it was first attested in the Eastern Han period (25–220 CE). For example:

(5) 河漢清且淺，相去復幾許？ [19]
'The River of Heaven is clear and shallow; What a little way lies between them!'
Lit. 'The Yellow River and Han River is clear and shallow; **How many** (units of distance) are we/they apart?'
To inquire about distance in Old Chinese, 幾何 (*jihe*) would be used instead, for example:

(6) 唯與訶，其相去幾何？ [20]
'The (ready) 'yes,' and (flattering) 'yea;' – Small is the difference they display.'
Lit. 'For the "yes" and "yea", **how far** are they apart (from each other)?'
Example (7) shows a feature of Middle Chinese observed in *Ryukan hitsudan*:

(7) 楊：．．．遇土人出來救命。 (*Ryukan hitsudan*, 1803)
Yō: . . . '(We) met some natives, who **came out** and rescued (our) lives.'

Yō mentioned that during one of his diplomatic missions, the junk drifted ashore in Taiwan. Fortunately, they were rescued by the local people in Taiwan. In this sentence, the compound verb 出來 (*chulai*) 'to come out' is formed by two-directional verbs, namely, 出 (*chu*) 'to exit' and 來 (*lai*) 'to come'. This verb phrase, first attested in the North and South Dynasties (420–589), is not found

---

19 Source: Poem no. ten. 古詩十九首 ('Nineteen Ancient Poems'. second century CE. translated by Ho 1977: 75). Originally with no title. this poem was subsequently known by its first verse. 迢迢牽牛星. 'The distant herdboy star'.
20 Source: 道德經 (Tâo Teh King). ca. third century BCE. translated by James Legge. Lao Tsŭ (1891: 62).

in the *Academia Sinica Tagged Corpus of Old Chinese*. Example (8) is dated the fifth century CE:

(8) 汝速出來，與汝好鼻。²¹
'**Come out** quickly; I am giving you a beautiful nose.'
To convey the same meaning in Old Chinese, what was used was not a compound verb, but a monomorphemic verb 出 (*chu*, cf. W. Li 2018). For example:
(9) 樂正子春下堂而傷其足，數月不出。²²
'The disciple Yo-kăng Khun injured his foot while descending from the hall, and for some months was not able to **go out**.'

Attested in these two brush-talk records are not only features of Middle Chinese, but those of Early Mandarin as well. Example (10) illustrates the use of an Early Mandarin word, 俺䓁 (*andeng*) as a first-person plural pronoun when Sai told Yi that he had also passed the civil service examination. This word is more commonly written as 俺等, where 䓁 is an allograph of 等. It is formed by adding the plural suffix 䓁 (*-deng*) after the first-person singular pronoun 俺 (*an*).

(10) 荅曰：俺䓁亦登弟之人。(*Cungtaplok*, 1611)
A: '**We** also passed the civil service examination.'

In Old Chinese, 吾 (*wu*) was frequently used as the first-person singular pronoun in subject case while in Middle Chinese and modern Mandarin 我 (*wo*) is syntactically independent, in that it may occur in the subject or object position. The pronoun 俺 (*an*) is found in neither the *Academic Tagged Corpus of Old Chinese* nor the *Academic Tagged Corpus of Middle Chinese*. It was first attested in the Southern Song period (1127–1279). For example:

(11) 俺略起，去洗耳。²³
'**I** stand up slowly and go wash my ear.'

Another Early Mandarin feature found in *Ryukan hitsudan* is 係 (*xi*), as shown in example (12), where Ishizuka told Kamida that he was currently studying at the Imperial College of Ryukyu:

---

21 Source: Gunavaddhi's Chinese translation of the *Sutra of One Hundred Parables* 百喻經, Saṅghasena 1990/490, trans. Fung 2019: 70).
22 Source: 禮記．祭義 ('The meaning of sacrifices, *The Book of Rites*'), translated by James Legge (1885: 228).
23 Source: 夜游宮·苦俗客 (Kusuke, Yeyougong, by 辛棄疾 Xin Qiji), cited in Wu (1947: 21).

(12) 石曰：職係國學生員 (*Ryukan hitsudan*, 1803)
 Ishizuka: 'I **am** studying in a school for samurais in Satsuma domain.'
 Lit. '(My) occupation **is** Imperial College student.'

In example (12), the copulative verb 係 (*xi*) is used to link up two typically interchangeable noun phrases, here syntactically the subject 職 (*zhi*) 'occupation' and the nominal predicate 國學生員 (*guoxue shengyuan*, 'student of Imperial College'). The copulative usage of *xi* was only attested in the *Tagged Corpus of Early Mandarin* but not the other two corpora. The grammaticalization of *xi* as a copulative verb was a relatively late development, which took place during the Southern Song period. For instance:

(13) 以下係人倫。[24]
 'The following (text) **is** (about) human relationships.'

In example (13), similarly, the copulative verb *xi* serves to link up the subject 以下 (*yixia*, 'the following') and the nominal predicative 人倫 (*renlun*, 'human relationships'), in addition to expressing co-referential identity between 'the following text' and 'human relationships'.

Although most parts of these two texts were written in Classical Chinese, from these examples, it can be observed that not only are features of Old Chinese commonly used, but also those of Middle Chinese and Early Mandarin. As mentioned, coloring Classical Chinese texts with elements of the contemporary vernacular is for centuries a common characteristic of works written by Chinese literati in imperial China. However, in these two brush-talk records, all the authors were literati from East Asian nations beyond China. What implication is there for features of Middle Chinese and Early Mandarin to appear in Ryukyuan-Japanese brush-talk interactions?

Ever since the spread of sinograms from Ancient China to other parts of the Sinosphere, it is well acknowledged that the literati in these nations were keen on studying Confucian classics, which were mostly published during the Spring and Autumn period (770–476 BCE) and which were written in Old Chinese (Handel 2019: 67; Lurie 2011: 1). Nevertheless, features of Middle Chinese and Early Mandarin are also commonly found in the brush-talk records written by literati from Japan, Ryukyu and Chosŏn. This suggests that the literati of Sinitic were keen on learning not only the Confucian classics, but they were also attracted by other works of what may be called 'vernacular literature' in China, possibly as a gateway for learning spoken Chinese when access to native speaker input – colloquial Mandarin Chinese, or some other topolect – could be found. In fact, textbooks of Early Mandarin published in these nations can be traced back to the

---

24 Source: 朱子語類 ('Thematic discourses of Master Zhu'). J.-D. Li (1270/1986: 230).

168 *Wong Tak-sum*

fourteenth century (Lin 2015). For instance, *Hakusei Kanwa* 白姓官話 (Setoguchi 1994) is a Mandarin primer for Ryukyuan speakers published in 1750 (Setoguchi & W. Li 2004), where dialogues pertaining to Ryukyu's political institutions, customs, festivals, *etc.* were used to teach colloquial Mandarin (Figure 6.5). For a brief introduction of this work in Chinese, please refer to Setoguchi (1993).[25]

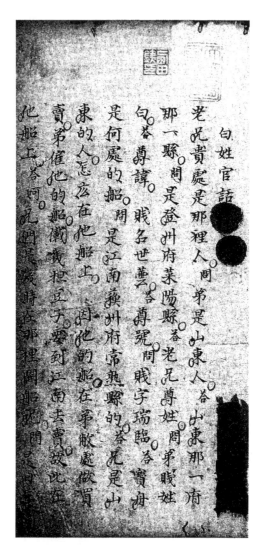

Figure 6.5 An excerpt of *Hakusei Kanwa* 白姓官話 ('Haku's Mandarin').

Source: Adapted from Setoguchi (1994: 228)

25 Modern reprint of other Early Mandarin textbooks from Ryukyu can also be found in Z. Chen (2021) and Takatsu and J. Chen (2013).

Discourse-pragmatic features in the two surviving brush-talk records

While the linguistic features observed in these two surviving brush-talk records were analyzed in the previous section, the discourse-pragmatic features therein are also worth discussing. Table 6.1 presents some basic statistics of the two brush-talk records.

The number of turns in these two brush-talk records is quite similar: there are 14 adjacency pairs in *Cungtaplok* and 16 in the *Ryukan hitsudan*. However, the difference between their average lengths is 70 sinograms (17.8 vs. 87.5), which is quite large. This may be explained by the nature of these two brush-talks.

Cungtaplok is a record of a rather formal diplomatic event between the envoys of two East Asian nations. The primary aim of their mission to Peking was to pay tribute to the emperor of China while Yi Su-Kwang's intention of brush-talking was to solicit information concerning the Ryukyu Kingdom. Accordingly, the purpose of the brush-talk is more transactional than interactional (Brown & Yule 1983) – transaction of factual information – hence the shorter average length, which is more or less expected. The shortest turn is shown in example (14), where Yi asked about the family name of the Ryukyu king, with Sai giving a brief affirmative response consisting of only two sinograms:

(14) 問: 國王姓氏？ (*Cungtaplok*, 1611)
    荅曰: 姓尚。
    Q: '(The) King's family name?'
    A: '(His) surname (is) Shoo.'

On the other hand, the *Ryukan hitsudan* is a travelogue brush-talk, which was produced when Ishizuka visited the place where Kamida was staying while he was traveling in Japan. The two brush-talkers appeared to be well acquainted with each other despite the fact that it was their first encounter. This

Table 6.1 A comparison of the basic statistics in *Cungtaplok* and the *Ryukan hitsudan*

	Yugu sasin chŭngdamnok (琉球使臣贈答錄)	*Ryukan hitsudan* (琉館筆談)
Year of conversation	1611	1803
text length	*ca.* 500	*ca.* 2,800
#turns	14 adjacency pairs	16 adjacency pairs
minimum length	2 sinograms	13 sinograms
maximum length	40 sinograms	639 sinograms
average length	17.8	87.5

170 Wong Tak-sum

brush-talk record covers miscellaneous topics without a dominant theme, from the mechanism for selecting Ryukyu officials to Kamida's experience of staying in Fuzhou in Qing China. This is quite typical of an interactionally oriented brush-talk, where the turns are expected to be longer or even lengthy. In the case of *Ryukan hitsudan*, the longest turn consists of 639 sinograms, where Kamida recounted his experience of boat drifting in Taiwan (for details of this turn, see Appendix).

In a typical daily conversation, pronouns like *you* and *I* are frequently used. In these two brush-talk records, however, personal pronouns are rarely observed. Instead, self-address and other-referencing are more commonly marked by honorific terms.

In *Cungtaplok*, every question raised by Yi was about Ryukyu's national condition. For example:

(15) 問：貴國有三國分立，皆號琉球云，信否？(*Cungtaplok*, 1611)
    荅曰：否。本國方都中山，而設都三處...
    Q: '**Your esteemed nation** is formed by three kingdoms. It is said that all of them are called Ryukyu. Is it true?'
    A: 'No. **Our nation**'s major capital is in Chūzan. There are three capitals in our nation...'

In example (15), Yi asked for confirmation whether Ryukyu was made up of three kingdoms as it was widely believed. However, in this sentence, neither the second-person pronoun nor the name of Sai's country, Ryukyu, appears. Instead, Yi used the term 貴國 (*gui guo*) to refer to Ryukyu, where 貴 (*gui*) means 'valuable'. However, used in collocation with 國 (guo, 'country'), *gui* functions as an honorific term denoting the superiority of the country of the listener or addressee, viz. 'your esteemed home country'. In *Cungtaplok*, *gui guo* appears eight times, of which six tokens were used by Yi. In fact, Yi also used another term 貴地 (*gui di*, 'your esteemed soil') in reference to Sai's esteemed home country. As for Sai, one token of the first-person plural pronoun 俺等 (*an deng*), was used, as cited in example (10). He also used *gui guo* once when referring to Yi's esteemed home country, Chosŏn. On the other hand, when Sai mentioned his own country Ryukyu, as in example (15), 本國 (*ben guo*, 'my own nation') was used, where 本 (*ben*) is a non-honorific, neutral determiner meaning 'one's own'.

In the *Ryukan hitsudan*, similarly, canonical personal pronouns are rarely used. In the whole passage, only five tokens of the first-person singular pronoun 我 (*wo*) and one token of the second-person singular pronoun 汝 (*ru*) are found. In most cases, Kamida referred to himself by using his given name in full, that is, 文鳳 (*Bunpō*), or just the last syllable 鳳 (*Pō*). For example:

(16) 楊曰：...鳳既海外小儒，無經術...(*Ryukan hitsudan*, 1803)
    Yō: '...**Pō** is an inferior literatus from overseas, who knows very little about the Confucian classics...'

On the other hand, Ishizuka invoked six tokens of 足下 (zu xia)[26] to address Kamida. For instance:

(17) 石曰：．．．幸獲識荊為慰，實染晚生．．．聞足下中山碩德．．．(*Ryukan hitsudan*, 1803)
Ishizuka: '... I am so lucky and glad to have a chance to meet you [the first time], which will affect me a lot. ... I heard that **you** are a great scholar in Chūzan ...'

In example (17), Ishizuka mentioned that before their first encounter, he had heard that Kamida was famous for his great virtue in Chūzan. For this indexical meaning, rather than using a canonical second-person pronoun like 汝 (*ru*), Ishizuka used the honorifically loaded expression 足下 (*zu xia*) in reference to Kamida. After that, when Ishizuka went on to introduce himself, he used a humble term 晚生 (*wan sheng*, lit. 'born later') rather than 我 (*wo*, 'me') for self-address. Similar to the *Cungtaplok*, both Kamida and Ishizuka used terms like 貴國 (*gui guo*), 貴地 (*gui di*) and 本國 (*ben guo*) in reference to the interlocutor's country and their own, respectively.

Conclusion

In this chapter, we have introduced two Ryukyuan brush-talk records. The first one is 'A record of exchange of poetic verses with Ryukyu ambassadors' (*Yugu sasin chŭngdamnok* 琉球使臣贈荅錄), a brush-assisted conversation between literati of Sinitic from Ryukyu and Chosŏn in the early seventeenth century. It is more characteristic of transactional as opposed to interactional communication (Brown & Yule 1983) in that the brush-talkers, being strangers or new acquaintances, are mainly engaged in relatively short questions and answers. The second, 'A brush-talk record at the Ryukyu residence' (*Ryukan hitsudan* 琉館筆談), involves writing-mediated brush-assisted conversation in the early nineteenth century between a Ryukyuan and a Japanese who were already quite acquainted with and admired each other. Unlike the former, therefore, the latter is more typical of interactional than transactional communication, with the conversational goal being the solicitation and exchange of opinions, sometimes requiring an extended narrative (see Appendix for an instructive illustration).

The lexical-grammatical markers found in these two brush-talk records were compared with those in three historical corpora developed by Academia Sinica. It was found that lexico-grammatical markers of Old Chinese, Middle Chinese, and Early Mandarin are all attested in both records, including the first-person and second-person pronouns, *wo* 我 ('I'), *andeng* 俺等 ('we'), *ru* 汝 ('you'). This suggests that, despite being separated by almost 200 years, all the brush-talkers

---

26 Literally 'beneath one's feet', with an implication that the addresser only dare look at the ground under the addressee's feet and, in so doing, lower one's head to show respect.

in these two records all had a relatively good command of Classical Chinese literature, in addition to being rather familiar with vernacular literature written by Chinese literati.

As for discourse-pragmatic features, both brush-talk records exhibit a contrast between a typical interactional brush-talk and a typical transactional brush-talk, as evidenced, for example, in their average length of a turn (Table 6.1). We have also observed that, in accordance with Classical Chinese usage, canonical personal pronouns were used infrequently while a variety of honorific terms was used: 貴國 (*gui guo*, 'your esteemed country'), 本國 (*ben guo*, 'my own country'), 足下 (*zu xia*, lit. 'beneath your feet', metaphorically 'your esteemed self'), and 晚生 († *Wan sheng*, lit. 'later born', metaphorically 'my humble self'). Such a discourse-pragmatic practice was not unlike stylistic patterns of formal written communication so typical of personal letters in premodern and early modern East Asia.

References

Akamine, M. [赤嶺守] (2004). 琉球王国: 東アジアのコーナーストーン ('The Ryukyu kingdom: Cornerstone of East Asia'). Tokyo: Kodansha Limited.

Akamine, M. [赤嶺守] (2017). *The Ryukyu kingdom: Cornerstone of East Asia* (L. J. Terrell, Trans.). Honolulu: University of Hawai'i Press.

Brown, G., & Yule, G. (1983). *Discourse analysis*. Cambridge: Cambridge University Press.

Cen, L. [岑玲] (2014a). 清朝中國に漂著した琉球船乗員の言語接觸 ('Language contact with the crew of Ryukyu's drifting ships during the Qing Dynasty'). *Journal of East Asian Cultural Interaction Studies* 東アジア文化交渉研究 7: 449–461. Retrieved February 16, 2021, from https://kuir.jm.kansai-u.ac.jp/dspace/handle/10112/8264.

Cen, L. [岑玲] (2014b). 清朝官員與漂流到中國的琉球船乗員的言語接觸 ('Language contact between Qīng government officials and the crew of Ryukyu drifting ships'). *National Maritime Research* 國家航海 7: 1–13.

Chen, T.-T. (1968). Investiture of Liu-Chiu kings in the Qing period. In J. K. Fairbank (Ed.), *The Chinese world order: Traditional China's foreign relations* (pp. 135–164). Cambridge, MA: Harvard University Press.

Chen, Z. [陳澤平] (Ed.). (2021). 琉球官話課本三種——校註與研究 ('Three Mandarin textbooks from Ryukyu: Proofreading, annotation and study'). Fuzhou: Fujian People's Publishing House.

Fu, Y., & Huang, L. [付優、黃霖] (2018). 混響的聲音: 朝鮮朝燕行使與安南、琉球使者的文學交流——以李睟光《安南使臣唱和問答錄》和《琉球使臣贈答錄》為中心 ('Voice reverberation: Literary exchange between Chosŏn envoys travelling to Peking and envoys from Vietnam and Ryukyu: Focusing on the "Records of poetic improvisation and chanting plus verbal exchange with Vietnam ambassadors" and "A Record of [poetic] exchange with the Ryukyu ambassadors" by Yi Su-Kwang'). *Dongjiang Journal* 東疆學刊 35(1): 40–45.

Han, S. [潘相] (1768). 琉球入学見聞録 ('An eye-witnessed account of Ryukyuans entering school'). Ryukyu: Ranbun Sho'oku. Retrieved March 2, 2021, from https://shimuchi.lib.u-ryukyu.ac.jp/collection/sakamaki/hw79001.

Handel, Z. (2019). *Sinography: The borrowing and adaptation of the Chinese script*. Leiden & Boston: Brill.

Heinrich, P., Miyara, S. [宮良信詳] & Shimoji, M. [下地理則] (Eds.). (2015). *Handbook of the Ryukyuan languages: History, structure, and use*. Berlin: De Gruyter Mouton.

Higa, S. [比嘉春潮] (1962). 琉球文献目録 ('A bibliography of the Ryukyus'). Naha: University of the Ryukyus.

Higaonna, K. [東恩納寬惇] (1950). *Outline of Okinawan history*. Naha: Relief Association for Okinawa & Ogasawara Islands.

Ho, K. P.-H. [何沛雄] (Ed. & Trans.). (1977). *The nineteen ancient poems* 古詩十九首. (Original work written 1st & 2nd century). Hong Kong: Kelly & Walsh.

Institute for the Translation of Korean Classics [韓國古典翻譯院]. (2021). 芝峯先生集 ('Classified notes by Chi-Pong'). 韓國古典綜合DB (Comprehensive database of Korean classics). Retrieved January 24, 2021, from https://db.itkc.or.kr/dir/item?grpId=hj#/dir/node?grpId=hj&dataId=ITKC_MI_0273A.

Institute of Linguistics, Academic Sinica [中央研究院語言學研究所] (2021a). 中央研究院上古漢語標記語料庫 ('Academic Sinica tagged corpus of old Chinese'). 中央研究院古漢語語料庫 (Academia Sinica Ancient Chinese Corpus). Retrieved January 24, 2021, from http://lingcorpus.iis.sinica.edu.tw/ancient/.

Institute of Linguistics, Academic Sinica [中央研究院語言學研究所] (2021b). 中央研究院中古漢語標記語料庫 ('Academic Sinica tagged corpus of middle Chinese'). 中央研究院古漢語語料庫 (Academia Sinica Ancient Chinese Corpus). Retrieved January 24, 2021, from http://lingcorpus.iis.sinica.edu.tw/middle/.

Institute of Linguistics, Academic Sinica [中央研究院語言學研究所]. (2021c). 中央研究院近代漢語標記語料庫 ('Academic Sinica tagged corpus of early mandarin Chinese'). 中央研究院古漢語語料庫 (Academia Sinica Ancient Chinese Corpus). Retrieved January 24, 2021, from http://lingcorpus.iis.sinica.edu.tw/early/.

Ishizuka, S. [石冢崔高] (1803). 琉館筆譚 ('Brush-talk records at the Ryukyu residence'). Retrieved January 24, 2021, from https://shimuchi.lib.u-ryukyu.ac.jp/collection/sakamaki/hw544.

Ishizuka, S. [石冢崔高] (1803/1808). 琉館筆談 ('Brush-talk records at the Ryukyu residence'). Retrieved January 24, 2021, from www.tulips.tsukuba.ac.jp/limedio/dlam/B95/B952222/1/vol09/tsb/2162.htm.

Iwamoto, M. [岩本真理] (2013). 『琉館筆譚』翻字、注釈 ('Translation and annotation of "Ryukan hitsutan"'). *Studies in the Humanities* 人文研究：大阪市立大学大学院文学研究科紀要 64: 179–196. Retrieved January 24, 2021, from https://dlisv03.media.osaka-cu.ac.jp/il/meta_pub/G0000438repository_KJ00008390119.

Kerr, G. (1958/2000). *Okinawa: The history of an island people*. North Clarendon, VT: Tuttle Publishing.

Koh, J., & King, R. (2014). *Infected Korean language, purity versus hybridity: From the Sinographic cosmopolis to Japanese colonialism to Global English*. Amherst, NY: Cambria Press.

Lao Tsŭ [老子] (1891). 道德經 (*The tâo teh king*. J. Legge, Trans.). In *The scared books of China: The texts of Tâoism* (pp. 1–124). (Original work written 5th century BC). Oxford: Oxford University Press. Retrieved January 27, 2021, from https://oll.libertyfund.org/title/tzu-the-texts-of-taoism-part-i.

Legge, J. [理雅各] (Ed. & Trans.). (1885). *The Lî Kî, XI-XLVI* ('The Book of Rites', in *The scared books of China: The texts of Confucianism*). (Original work published 5th century BCE). Oxford: Clarendon Press. Retrieved February 7, 2021, from https://oll.libertyfund.org/title/legge-the-sacred-books-of-china-the-texts-of-confucianism-part-iv-the-li-ki-xi-xlvi.

Li, J.-D. [黎靖德] (Ed.). (1270/1986). 朱子語類 ('Thematic discourses of Master Zhu'). Peking: Zhonghua Book Company.

Li, W. (2018). Multi-verb constructions in Old Chinese and Middle Chinese: From verb serialising to verb compounding. *Asia-Pacific Language Variation* 4(1):103–133.

Lim, K.-C. [林基中] (2006). 燕行錄研究 ('Studies in travelogues to Peking'). Seoul: Iljisa.

Lin, C.-H. [林慶勳] (2015). 域外漢語探索——論長崎唐話的表現特色 ('An exploration of overseas Chinese language: Characteristics of Nagasaki Tanghua'). *Journal of the Chinese Department, National Chung Hsing University* 興大中文學報 37: 1–36. Retrieved January 24, 2021, from http://chinese.nchu.edu.tw/files/users/189/37-10.pdf.

Lurie, D. B. (2011). *Realms of literacy: Early Japan and the history of writing*. Cambridge, MA: Harvard University Asia Center.

Mansfield, S. (2017, April 8). Disputatious legacies: Examining the historic ties that bind Okinawa and China. *Japan Times*. Retrieved March 2, 2021, from www.japantimes.co.jp/life/2017/04/08/lifestyle/disputatious-legacies-examining-historic-ties-bind-okinawa-china/.

Norman, J. (1988). *Chinese*. Cambridge & New York: Cambridge University Press.

Okinawa Prefectural Library [沖縄県立図書館] (1924). 琉球史料目錄 ('A catalogue of the historical documents of Ryukyu'). Naha, Okinawa: Author.

Pulleyblank, E. G. [蒲立本] (1995). *Outline of Classical Chinese grammar*. Vancouver: University of British Columbia Press.

Sakai, R. K. (1968). The Ryukyu (Liu-Chiu) islands as a fief of Satsuma. In J. K. Fairbank (Ed.), *The Chinese world order: Traditional China's foreign relations* (pp. 112–134). Cambridge, MA: Harvard University Press.

Sakamaki, S. (1963). *Ryukyu: A bibliographical guide to Okinawan studies*. Honolulu: University of Hawaiʻi Press.

Sakamaki, S. (1964). *Ryukyuan names: Monographs and lists of personal and place names in the Ryukyus*. Honolulu: East-West Center Press.

Saṅghasena [僧伽斯那] (1990). Po Yü Ching 百喻經 ('The sūtra of one hundred parables'). (Gunavaddhi 求那毗地, Trans.). In J. Takakusu & K. Watanabe [高楠順次郎、渡辺海旭] (Eds.), 大正新脩大藏經 第四冊 ('Taishō revised tripiṭaka') (vol. 4, pp. 543–558). Taipei: Shyh Hyah International Co., Limited (Original work written 490). Retrieved February 7, 2021, from https://cbetaonline.dila.edu.tw/zh/T0209_002.

Saṅghasena [僧伽斯那] (2019). *The sutra of one hundred parables* 百喻經 (M. M. Y. Fung 馮張曼儀, Trans.). Hong Kong: The Centre for the Study of Humanistic Buddhism, The Chinese University of Hong Kong (Original work written in 490).

Setoguchi, R. [瀨戶口律子] (1993). 琉球官話課本簡介 ('A brief introduction to the Mandarin textbooks from Ryukyu'). *Current Research in Chinese Linguistics* 中國語文通訊 25: 35–36.

Setoguchi, R. [瀨戶口律子] (1994). 白姓官話全訳 ('A complete translation of "Hakusei Kanwa" Mandarin'). Tokyo: Meiji Shoin.

Setoguchi, R., & Li, W. [瀨戶口律子、李煒] (2004). 琉球官話課本編寫年代考證 ('A textual research of the compiling years of Ryukyu's four Mandarin Chinese textbooks'). *Studies of the Chinese Language* 中國語文 2004(1): 77–84.

Takahashi, T. [高橋俊三] (2002). 「三字經俗解」の翻字および訳注 ('Transliteration and annotated translation of the *Sanjikyou Zokkai*'). *Journal of Japanese Language and Japanese Literature, Okinawa International University* 沖縄国際大学日本語日本文学研究 2002: 44–167.

Takatsu, T., & Chen, J. [高津孝、陳捷] (Eds.). (2013). 琉球王國漢文文獻集成 ('A collection of Sinitic documents from the Ryukyu Kingdom'). Shanghai: Fudan University Press.

The First Historical Archives of China [中國第一歷史檔案館] (1993). 清代中琉關係檔案選編 ('Selected records from Sino-Ryukyu relation archive of Qing dynasty'). Peking: Zhonghua Book Company.

University of the Ryukyus Library [琉球大学] (2021). 琉球・沖縄関係貴重資料デジタルアーカイブ (Ryukyu/Okinawa Special Collection Digital Archives). University of the Ryukyus Library 琉球大学附属図書館. Retrieved January 24, 2021, from https://shimuchi.lib.u-ryukyu.ac.jp/.

Wang, Y. [王勇] (2015). 《琉館筆談》解題並影印 ('Synopsis and photocopy of *Ryukan hitsudan*'). 東亞筆談 (Brush-talking in East Asia) 6: 10–16. Retrieved January 24, 2021, from http://d2.datahistory.cn/files/1075245b84bdae/news/5776785d245558/4707695d245577.pdf.

Wang, Y.-F. [汪毅夫] (Ed.). (2012). 傳世漢文琉球文獻輯稿 第一輯 ('A compilation of the inherited Sinitic documents from Ryukyu (Series 1)'). Amoy: Lujiang Publishing House.

Waseda University Library. (2021). Kotenseki Sougou database of Japanese and Chinese classics 古典籍総合データベース. Waseda University Library. Retrieved January 24, 2021, from www.wul.waseda.ac.jp/kotenseki/.

Wu, Y.-Y. [胡雲翼] (Ed.). (1947). 辛棄疾詞 ('Poetic works by Xin Qiji'). Shanghai: Shanghai Jiaoyu Shudian.

Yi, S.-H. [李聖惠] (2016). 北京에서 만난 朝鮮과 琉球 使臣의 民間외교 – 李睟光의「琉球使臣贈答錄」을 中心으로 ('Nongovernmental diplomacy between the envoys of Joseon and Yugu in Beijing – Focusing on Yi Su-gwang's "Yugu Sasin Jeungdaprok"'). 圃隱學研究 (Journal of the Association of Poeun Studies) 18: 239–261. Retrieved January 24, 2021, from www.kci.go.kr/kciportal/landing/article.kci?arti_id=ART002187448.

Yi, S.-K. [李睟光] (1633/1991). 芝峯先生集 ('Classified notes by Chi-Pong'). Seoul: Institute for the Translation of Korean Classics. Retrieved January 24, 2021, from www.wul.waseda.ac.jp/kotenseki/html/he16/he16_02433/.

Yi, S.-K. [李睟光] (1633/2001). 琉球使臣贈答錄 ('A record of exchange of poetic verses with Ryukyu ambassadors'). In K.-Z. Lim 林基中 (Ed.), 燕行錄全集 卷十 ('Complete works of Yenhaynglok') (vol. 10, pp. 161–181). Seoul: Dongguk University.

Yi, S.-K. [李睟光] (1633/2010). 琉球使臣贈答錄 ('A record of exchange of poetic verses with Ryukyu ambassadors'). In H. Hong [弘華文] (Ed.), 燕行錄全編 第一輯第五冊 ('Complete edited works of Yanxinglu, series 1') (vol. 5, pp. 357–363). Guilin: Guangxi Normal University Press Group.

Zhai, J.-M. [翟金明] (Ed.). (2015). 傳世漢文琉球文獻輯稿(第二輯) ('A compilation of the inherited Sinitic documents from Ryukyu (Series 2)'). Amoy: Lujiang Publishing House.

Zhou, C.-H. [周朝暉] (2015). 琉球使節眼中嘉慶初年的閩臺世態風情——以《琉館筆談》為例 ('Social customs of Fujian and Taiwan during the early 19th century as seen through the eyes of the envoy from the Ryukyu Kingdom: A study based on *Ryukan hitsudan*'). *Fujian-Taiwan Cultural Research* 閩臺文化研究 2: 29–34.

Zhou, C.-H. [周朝暉] (2019). 嘉慶初年琉球使節眼中的廈門 –《琉球筆談》漫讀劄記 ('Amoy in the eyes of the Ryukyu envoy during the early Jiaqing era: Notes after deep reading of *Ryukyu hitsudan*'). *Journal of Gulangyu Studies* 鼓浪嶼研究 9: 173–178.

Appendix: The longest turn in *Ryukan hitsudan* (1803)

石曰、聞旧年貴舟、欲徃福州、因風不順、漂到台湾、有之乎、願聞其詳

楊曰、正是如命、夲國二隻貢船、在那霸、一同開駕、在洋遇風、一隻船於今未知存亡下落、鳳莟船漂至台湾地方、船即破矣、所載公私貨物、悉為烏有、通船八十名、遇土人出來救命、方得上岸、寫字通意、始知其為台湾也、艱難萬狀、不可形容也、其地官員分付土人、借屋居住、得免飢渴、文鳳賦詩謝恩、先是地方官、待鳳莟、甚是輕賤、鳳莟叩頭礼拜、而不肯為答礼、及見其地方官、或秀才莟、以詩与鳳相為贈答、皆下坐答拜、前倨者、後皆恭也、鳳竊謂同舟者、誰道文章不值錢、今日方見文字值錢的、衆人皆笑、台湾贈荅詩、載在別冊、

Ishizuka: I heard that on the way to Fuzhou last year, your esteemed junk drifted to Taiwan due to typhoon. Is that true? I would like to hear more about it.

Yō: That's true! I will follow your command. Two tribute ships from my nation that departed from Naha at the same time encountered a typhoon. The other junk is still missing to this day. My junk wrecked when it drifted to Taiwan. The tributes and personal belongings on board were all gone. There were eighty of us. We met some natives who came to our rescue and helped us to go ashore. I only knew that we landed in Taiwan after communicating with the people in writing. The ordeal that we had to go through is beyond what words can describe. The officials there ordered the native people to let us live in their houses. In this way, we were free from hunger and thirst. Bunpō composed poems to express our profound gratitude to them. At first, the local officials looked down on Pō and my shipmates. We kowtowed to show our humility, but they gave not the slightest gesture to acknowledge our respect. I met other local officials and government school students there as well as other people. We were all engaged in poetic exchange and they treated me politely. (Suddenly,) all those who had been irreverent to me previously paid me respect after that. I told my shipmates in confidence, "Who said that written words are not worth a penny? Today we eventually see how valuable written words can be." Everybody laughed. The poetic exchanges we produced in Taiwan were collected in a separate volume.

一日在台湾新莊分府、旅思淒愴、口占一詩、貼于座隅、地方諸官群來見之、自是敬禮甚篤、一日出外間、遊縣中、上人爭先來迎、或有詩稿求和、或攜花箋求書字、鳳毫不推辭、各應其求即苔、所過館驛十人、求書甚多、後來不能悉應、或書字到夜深、或送酒肴、或携管絃來慰、凡経過地、往〻如此、有僧佛祖、年十六秀才、謝鴻恩、年十八、皆好文字、日夜出入旅舘、起居安慰、情意甚歡、留十餘日、從至竹塹分府、相去十餘里、其両人跟隨來如前、欵待、其地宰官、奉政大夫吉壽者、北京人、清朝今上皇帝親眷也、即日來舘慰劳、談話之間、即席賦詩一章、以獻、府官見而賞之、袖而帰、次日遣其子、寄贈次韻詩、并見惠美酒一罈、又次日遣其孫、贈以好茶、在此間、官府一家、三人毎來慰問、其孫年方十四、容貌秀雅、常從十多個人、乗一座大轎來、叫我寫字、不幾日寫字、不幾日、自此起程、東行西轉、至台湾城、一日城中衆官、集于大守正堂、有謁見之礼、大守姓曰慶、名曰保、其日坐堂上、問鳳等道琉球海外小邦、而今被中華風教、至於文字、亦頗有通之者、顧左右取筆硯米面試鳳、出班、対曰、開外遠人不識礼數、敢不獻醜、以谢髙恩、即書七言律詩以呈、慶保見之、賞文鳳以詩一函、親筆對聯及衣服等物、此飄流之一二也、事不能盡述也

One day, in the office of the vice governor at Hsinchuang, feeling melancholic due to travel sickness, I composed a poem, recited it out loud and pasted it near my seat. It attracted throngs of local officials to come and read it. Thereupon they became extremely polite with me. Another day, when I was travelling in the county, the virtuous admirers elbowed their way just to greet me. Some passed me a poem seeking a poetic response; others brought beautiful letter papers requesting me to improvise anything in writing. To such entreaty, Pō never declined but complied at once. When I stopped at the roadside inns, many native people made similar requests for my calligraphy. I did not manage to meet all their requests eventually. Sometimes I wrote until the dead of night. Some would deliver food and alcoholic beverages; others would bring a string instrument and improvise it to express appreciation. It was by and large like that every time I visited a new place. Then I met a priest, who was sixteen, and a government school student called Xie Hongen, who was eighteen. They both enjoyed writing very much and took good care of me day and night. We enjoyed our intellectual exchange very much. Having stayed there for more than ten days, I decided to move to the office of the vice governor at Poocaal's (now Hsinchu). It was more than ten *li* away but they went with me and entertained me as much as they had done previously. On that day, the prefectural magistrate (of the Taiwan Prefecture) Ji Shou, who was a relative of the Qing emperor, came to the Ryukyu residence and expressed his consolation and sympathy. During our discussion, I improvised a poem and presented it to him. Having read it, he gave me praise, put it in his sleeve and returned (to his office/home). The next day, he sent his son to present me a poem using the same rhyme as the one in mine, plus a jar of nice alcoholic beverage. On the next day, he sent his grandson and presented me some nice tea. While I was there, the magistrate family, three of them, would often come to console me. His grandson, 14, was a good-looking young man. Seated invariably in a big sedan chair accompanied by more than 10 servants every time he arrived, he would ask me to write something every couple of days. Then I left for the capital of Taiwan (Prefecture), arriving after many twists and turns. One day, the officials in the city gathered at the main hall of the governor's office for a formal reception. The governor was surnamed Qing, with Bao as his given name. On that day, he asked Pō and my shipmates at the hall (of his office). "(Even though) Ryukyu is a small country overseas, now it has adapted the customs and teachings from China, some of you are also proficient in our written language." Thereupon he asked his servants to get the stationery to test my ability on the spot. I stepped out and replied, "I am from a remote place and ignorant of the etiquette. I dare not hide my incompetence. (Allow me to write something to) express my deep gratitude for your great favors." Immediately after that, I improvised a heptasyllabic octave and presented it to him. Having read it, Qing Bao rewarded me with a poem in a letter, an antithetical couplet, some clothes and a few other things. These are some of the things (I recall) during my drifting story. It is impossible to tell the full story.

Part 2
Brush-talk involving diplomatic envoys in East Asia

7 Sinitic brush-talk between Vietnam and China in the eighteenth century

A study of Vice-Envoy Lê Quý Đôn's mission to Qing China[1]

Nguyễn Tuấn-Cường and Nguyễn Thị-Tuyết

Lê Quý Đôn and *A complete record of an embassy to the North* 北使通錄

Lê Quý Đôn 黎貴惇 (1726–1784), a senior scholar-official during the Restored Lê period (1533–1789), served in court for several generations after achieving the top-ranked position in the civil service examination in 1752. His exemplary literary career made him a widely acclaimed eighteenth-century scholar who commanded encyclopedic knowledge of the Great Việt 大越.[2] In 1758, he was appointed as Vice-Envoy (1758–1762) on a diplomatic mission to Qing China, the second most important figure in a delegation of 25 people headed by the Chief Envoy Trần Huy Mật 陳輝謐 (1710–?). The delegation departed from the capital Thăng Long 昇龍 (now Hanoi) in the first lunar month[3] of 1760 and returned to their home country in spring, 1762. The more than four-year mission including a two-year journey to Peking and back was intended to fulfill Annam's[4] obligation to make up for two tribute visits to the celestial capital scheduled in 1756 and 1759. The envoys' main duty was to report on two important events: the funeral of King Lê Ý Tông 黎懿宗 (1719–1759; r. 1735–1740) and the coronation of King Lê Hiển Tông 黎顯宗 (1717–1786; r. 1740–1786). The journey took place at a time when Vietnamese-Chinese relations were politically rather stable.

'A complete record of an embassy to the North' 北使通錄 (hereafter, *A complete record*, Lê 1763) was based on Lê Quý Đôn's travel diary where important events and personal reflections were recorded. Today, only a single copy is

---

1 The authors would like to thank the three editors of this volume for their insightful and helpful comments on earlier drafts of our manuscript.
2 For details about Lê Quý Đôn's life and career, see Zhong Caijun (2012); Nguyễn Tài Đông (2008).
3 The dates are all recorded according to the lunar calendar. For convenience's sake, all lunar months and days will be presented in digits, with the month preceding the day separated by a colon. Thus, '03:05' would mean 'the 5th day of the 3rd lunar month'.
4 An Nam (安南, also spelled as Annam), literally 'the Pacified South', was an alternative name of the Great Việt 大越; both referred to Vietnam during the monarchical period (938–1945).

DOI: 10.4324/9781003048176-9

archived at the Institute of Sino-Nom Studies in Hanoi (call number A.179). This work consists of four volumes, of which volumes 2 and 3 are missing (i.e., only volumes 1 and 4 remain). Volume 1 documents preparatory activities before the mission started; volume 4 records events during the homeward journey covering a period of about half a year, from 06:28, 1761, in Hezhou 和州, Anhui Province to 01:07, 1762, upon arriving at the border gate in Taiping Prefecture 太平府, Guangxi Province. Although incomplete, this surviving travel diary contains interesting details with lingua-cultural import as well as historical value in such aspects as contemporary history, culture, intellectual exchange on issues of shared academic interest, and of course diplomatic relations between Annam and China vis-à-vis other East Asian neighbors.[5]

In official Vietnamese-Qing diplomatic encounters, bilateral verbal exchange mediated by an interpreter was the default mode of official communication and face-to-face interaction. The 1760–1762 delegation included three interpreters (listed as 通事 or 通士): Nguyễn Đình Ngạn 阮廷彥, Nguyễn Đình Thiệm 阮廷贍, and Trương Đình Tài 張廷財. They were in charge of interpreting during official meetings between the envoys and Qing authorities, central or provincial. By contrast, in their private capacity, the envoys tended to rely on Sinitic brush-talk 漢文筆談 when meeting with Chinese people or interacting with envoys from other polities. In this study, we will analyze the Sinitic-based brush conversations between Lê Quý Đôn and the Chinese people as documented in volume 4 of *A complete record* (on Sinitic brush-talk in Vietnam and in East Asia in general, see, e.g., Yu & Liang 2013; Clements 2019; Nguyễn & Nguyễn 2019, 2020; Wang & Xie 2015; Li et al. 2020).

Brush-talk activities of Lê Quý Đôn in *A complete record*

According to *A complete record* (volume 4), during the delegation's return journey from the Chinese capital, there is clear evidence of ten writing-mediated conversations between the envoys of the Great Việt and their Chinese interlocutors, as evidenced in such expressions as 'used/grabbed an ink brush to write' (以筆寫, folio 13a; 取筆寫, 76b), 'used an ink brush to question and answer' (以筆問答, 28b), 'used an ink brush to question and answer each other' (以筆硯相問答, 61b), 'used an ink brush to discuss poetry' (以筆談詩談文, 6b), or 'sat and wrote' (坐書, 81b). There were ten other writing-mediated exchanges that either specified conversations with interpreters 通事 (n=4, see <1>, <3>, <5>, and <14>, Table 7.1) or were clearly laid out in question-and-answer mode (n=8), although no mention was made of the use of ink brushes and paper. The following analysis is based on these twenty writing-mediated brush conversations between envoys of the mission and the Qing people they met during their return journey (see Table 7.1).

---

5 北使通錄 is also available in Vietnamese translation by Nguyễn Thị Tuyết 阮氏雪 (see Lê 1763/2018, *Bắc sứ thông lục*). For the original Sinitic texts, see call number A.179 archived at the Institute of Sino-Nom Studies in Hanoi.

Brush-talk between Vietnam and China 183

Table 7.1 Basic information about 20 (brush) conversations in question-and-answer mode as documented in 'A complete record of an embassy to the North' 北使通錄 (vol. 4)[6]

No.	Date & Time	Place	Participants	Form	Topic	Folio
1st lunar month, 1761						
1	Noon, 01:10	Temple of Confucius 孔廟 and Imperial Academy 國子監, Peking	Annam envoys and Shi Zhouhan 史周翰, Zhang Yuanguan 張元觀	Oral interpreting	Envoy asked to observe ritual tools in the Temple of Confucius.	59b
2	Afternoon, 01:10	Temple of Confucius and Imperial Academy, Peking	Annam envoys, Zhang Yuanguan XE, "Trương Nguyễn Quản", and Zhang Fengshu 張鳳書	Brush-talk	Motivation, learning attitude and respect; reverent worship of Temple of Confucius and Imperial Academy; Envoy asked to observe books on ritual tools and ceremony at the Temple of Confucius.	61b – 62a
8th lunar month, 1761						
3	Mid-noon, 08:05	Dehua 德化, Jiujiang 九江, Jiangxi Province 江西省	Lê Quý Đôn and Qin Chaoyu 秦制釪	Oral interpreting, Brush-talk	Discussed court rituals, the social situation, customs, and local specialities of Annam	6b – 7b
4	From Tỵ 巳 hour (9–11 am) until evening, 08:14	Wuxue 武穴, Guangji 廣濟, Huangzhou 黃州, Hubei Province	Lê Quý Đôn and Qin Chaoyu	Brush-talk	'A review and criticism of books' 群書考辨, 'Reflective reading notes' 讀書記, and 'Book of poetry' 討經	8b – 10b
5	From Thân 申 hour (3–5 pm) until late at night, 08:16	Pantang 潘塘, Tongcheng 桐城, Huangzhou	Lê Quý Đôn and Qin Chaoyu	Oral interpreting, Brush-talk	*A review and criticism of books*, the civil service examination system, and the system for selecting assistants to envoys	10b – 11b
6	From evening to midnight, 08:27	On the Imperial Commissioner's boat docked at Huangzhou	Lê Quý Đôn and Qin Chaoyu	Brush-talk	'Records of model sages and nobles' 聖賢範錄; mutual friends	13a – 14a

(*Continued*)

6 With few exceptions, the English translations of traditional Chinese institutions and titles of scholar-officials below are essentially based on Hucker (1985).

Table 7.1 (Continued)

No.	Date & Time	Place	Participants	Form	Topic	Folio
9th lunar month, 1761						
7	09:09	Wuchang 武昌, Hubei Province	Lê Quý Đôn and Zuo Peng 作朋	(unclear)	Ceremonies to welcome envoys; envoys' command of Mandarin; books and published works; the capital; clothing system; the custom of disheveled hair 披髮, etc.	16a – 16b
10th lunar month, 1761						
8	10:01	Changsha 長沙, Hunan Province	Lê Quý Đôn and Guo Can 郭參	(unclear)	Envoys' costumes, challenged with antithetical couplets	24a – 25a
9			Lê Quý Đôn and Yong 永氏, the Provincial Chief	(unclear)	The well-being of the mission, bureaucracy system, and the court of Annam	25a – 25b
10	From Tỵ 巳 hour (9–11 am) until evening, 10:21	Yongzhou 永州, Hunan Province	Lê Quý Đôn and Qin Chaoyu	Brush-talk	Homesickness; civil service examination, court officials and local officials; *A review and criticism of books*, and *The Book of poetry*	28b – 29b
11	Evening, 10:22	Yongzhou, Hunan Province	Chief Envoy Trần Huy Mật and Qin Chaoyu	(unclear)	Duties of the Chief Envoy; the system for selecting assistants accompanying the envoys, etc.	29b
11th lunar month, 1761						
12	From Thân 申 hour (3–5 pm) until late at night, 11:05	Darongjiang 大榕江, Xing'an 興安, Guangxi Province	Lê Quý Đôn, Trần Huy Mật and Qin Chaoyu	Brush-talk	Border areas between the two countries, climate, customs of the states in the South, envoys' families, etc.	31b – 34a
13	11:08	Guilin 桂林, Guangxi Province	Trần Huy Mật, Lê Quý Đôn and Xiong Xuepeng 熊學鵬	(unclear)	Request to local officials for delegation's travel route and itinerary from Wuzhou 梧州 to Nanning 南寧	34b

Brush-talk between Vietnam and China   185

14	Evening. 11:10	Guilin, Guangxi Province	Interpreters and Ye Cunren 葉存仁. Qing Accompanying Official 伴送官 named Luo Xiu 羅繡	Oral interpreting	Request for dropping the character 'Barbarian' 夷, and changing the title to 'Envoys of Annam' 安南國使	46a – 46b
12th lunar month, 1761						
15	12:26 past 11 pm	Taiping Prefecture 太平府. Guangxi Province	Envoys and De Bao 德保. Gu Ruxiu 顧汝修	(unclear)	Two capitals of Annam: the Emperor and Lord Trịnh Sâm 鄭森 (1739–1782); Annam as a peaceful country with a respectful and obedient (恭順) court; composing poems (couplets)	66b – 67b
16		Taiping Prefecture. Guangxi Province	Lê Quý Đôn and Cha Li	(unclear)	Literature and poetry past 11 pm	67b
17	12:27	Taiping Prefecture. Guangxi Province	Lê Quý Đôn and Ouyang Min 歐陽敏	(unclear)	Discussed poems	67b
18		Taiping Prefecture. Guangxi Province	Lê Quý Đôn and Zhu Peilian	Brush-talk	Historical changes in geographical boundaries of Annam	67b – 71a
19	Past noon. 12:29	Taiping Prefecture. Guangxi Province	Lê Quý Đôn and Zhu Peilian	Brush-talk	*Records of model sages and nobles* and *A review and criticism of books*	76b
1st lunar month, 1762						
20	01:03	Taiping Prefecture. Guangxi Province	Lê Quý Đôn and Zhu Peilian	Brush-talk	Border area and geography: Vietnamese people's worship of Master Xie 解縉; building of ramparts and fortresses; and Việt Thường 越裳 people's offer of pheasants as tribute items	78a – 81b

The people regularly engaged in brush-talk with Lê Quý Đôn may be subdivided into three groups. The first group consisted of local officials receiving the envoys in their return journey, including Surveillance Commissioner 按察使 Zuo Peng 作朋, a Metropolitan Graduate 進士 (from Hubei Province); Guo Can 郭參, a subordinate of Provincial Governor 巡撫 Feng Qian 馮鈐 (Hunan Province); Provincial Governor Xiong Xuepeng 熊學鵬 (Guangxi Province), a Metropolitan Graduate in 1730; Provincial Administration Commissioner 布政使 Ye Cunren 葉存仁 (from Jiangxia 江夏); two Imperial Commissioners 欽差冊使官 De Bao 德保 and Gu Ruxiu 顧汝修; Defense Command Lieutenant Governor 協鎮 Ouyang Min 歐陽敏; Provincial Education Commissioner 提督學政 Zhu Peilian 朱佩蓮; and Acting Circuit Intendant 暑道臺官 Zha Li 查禮. The second group comprised Qing court officials in Peking, including Shi Zhouhan 史周翰, Zhang Yuanguan 張元觀, Zhang Fengshu 張鳳書, and Qin Chaoyu 秦朝釪. The third group was made up of envoys encountered in Peking, including three from Chosŏn: Chief Envoy Hong Kye-hŭi 洪啟禧, two Vice-Envoys Cho Yŏng-chin 趙榮進 and Yi Hwi-chung 李徽中, and two from the Ryukyu 琉球 Kingdom: Tei Kōtoku 鄭孝德 and Sai Seshō 蔡世昌. The conversational exchanges with the envoys of Chosŏn and Ryukyu were all mediated by Sinitic brush-talk. Unfortunately, these multi-national brush-talk records were lost.

The writing-mediated face-to-face interactions with regional officials at provincial level sometimes took place spontaneously, swiftly, and briefly, other times over an extended period if pre-arranged at appointed times upon invitation. Most of the conversational exchanges with local officials were usually routine and short; these would typically go through an interpreter. For topics involving lengthy deliberation, however, brush-talk tended to be preferred. Compared with speech-based interaction mediated by an interpreter, writing-mediated brush conversation would take longer, but it had the advantage of allowing for meaningful, in-depth exchange of personal or private views, which would complement the viewpoints presented officially out of national interest. Most of the brush-talks took place on the boat of Imperial Commissioner Qin Chaoyu or in the offices of the regional officials where Lê Quý Đôn was invited to meet with enthusiastic local scholars and literary figures. As shown in Table 7.1, many brush conversations lasted from noon till late evening, a few until late at night.

In *A complete record*, there are six brush conversations between Lê Quý Đôn and Qin Chaoyu, who was sent to escort the envoys of Annam back to their country from 03:01 to 11:12, 1761, departing from Peking to Guilin before returning to the celestial capital. Qin was the one who held the most brush-talks with the envoys of Annam, frequently and prolonged, and the topics of their brush conversations were often revisited as he spent nearly a year traveling by boat with the delegation during their return journey. Lê also conducted brush-talks with Zhu Peilian for three consecutive times, each time lasting from early afternoon to the evening as it was right before the New Year's Eve of 1762 when the delegation had to stay and wait at the border gate until it reopened in the new year. In addition, Lê improvised short poems in writing with Zha Li, who welcomed the delegation at the entry point in China and saw the delegation off two years later in their return journey at the border. The brush-talks of Lê Quý Đôn with Qin Chaoyu, Zhu Peilian, Zha Li usually lasted a few hours because their conversational topics were often intellectually rich, exchanging views on books of shared academic or historical interest but also studies of Chinese classical canons, culture, and poetry.

Of the twenty writing-mediated brush-talks in the form of questions and answers in Table 7.1, ten took place during the delegation's return journey, including two brush-talks involving interpreters and eight where no interpreters were present. In those brush-talks attended by interpreters, the mode of communication was usually a mixture of writing-mediated interaction and speech-based conversation, with brush-talk being the dominant mode of intellectual exchange. By contrast, the speech-based mode was only secondary, being restricted to greetings and other conversational routines before the brush-talk started, such as inquiries about the availability of interpreters. In what follows, we will cite three excerpts to illustrate brush-assisted interactions involving interpreters, who sometimes talked to the Chinese interlocutors directly in Chinese.

On 09:09, the Vietnamese envoys were received by Hubei Surveillance Commissioner Zuo Peng in the presence of some enthusiastic scholars and literary figures:

問: 貢使能官話否?	Surveillance Commissioner [Zuo] asked: 'Do the envoys speak Mandarin?'
曰: 不能。	Interpreter: 'They don't'.
問通上曰: 貴國多書籍否?	[Zuo] asked the interpreter: 'Are there many books in your country?'
使答曰: 經、史、子、集, 亦略備觀覽, 安敢比中國之富。...	Envoy [Lê] answered: 'Confucian classics, historical records, philosophical writings and miscellaneous works are available and enough to read. But they are no match for the collections in China'. (Folio 16b)

On 08:16, after Lê Quý Đôn and Qin Chaoyu had a brush-talk about the book *Sử biện* (史辨, 'Critical historical review'), Qin Chaoyu served rice and wine, and asked the interpreters casually:

曰: 三位貢使. 想係貴國選擇而來?	[Qin]: 'The three envoys were selected by your esteemed country for this mission, I suppose?'
仍[乃]教他代對曰: 奉使天朝, 豈敢不重其選? 但三貢使. 亦以位次當行, 非極選也。	Vice-Envoy [Lê] told the interpreter to answer on his behalf [orally]: 'We are entrusted to pay a tribute visit to the Celestial Empire, how can we not select carefully? But the three envoys were selected based on ranking rather than on merits.'
伊又曰: 國中想如三位者甚少?	He [Qin] asked again: 'Few in [your] country can compare with the three envoys, I suppose?'

(*Continued*)

伊曰: 然。	The interpreter said: 'Yes.'
甲副官語他改對曰: 國中才學名臣極多, 如大貢使上尚書侍郎十數人, 二貢使三貢使之列在翰林東閣有名望者亦眾。	Vice-Envoy [Lê] told the interpreter to correct himself: 'There are many talented scholar-officials in the country; there are over a dozen knowledgeable scholar-officials like the Chief Envoy [Trần Huy Mật] at the Vice-Minister rank. Reputed scholars comparable to second- and third-ranked envoys who merit a position in the Eastern Imperial Academy are also not rare.'
伊笑曰: 雖然亦為罕得之才。 . . .	He [Qin] laughed and said: 'However, gifted scholars [like the three envoys] are rare.' (Folio 11a – 11b)

On 10:01, 1761, Lê Quý Đôn met with local scholars and literary figures before Yong, the Administration Commissioner of Hunan Province. They were accompanied by interpreter Nguyễn Đình Ngạn:

曰: 貢使不通官話, 何能對得?	[Yong] said: 'The Envoys [=you] do not speak Mandarin; how could you communicate [with our Emperor]?'
曰: 那時跪, 使通事代對。. . .	[Lê]: At that time [when meeting with your Emperor,] we bent on our knees, and requested the interpreter to respond on our behalf. . . .
退辭, 出送至門外,復回[, 問]: 官何處人能說話?	[When the envoy] excused himself, [Yong] went to the gate to see him off. [Yong] asked [the interpreter] again: 'Where are you from; how come [you] can speak [Mandarin]?'
曰: 本國海陽人。	[Nguyễn]: '[I am from] Hải Dương Province of my country.'
問: 有官職否?	[Yong]: '[Do you] have an official title?'
曰: 小職色。. . .	[Nguyễn]: 'Just a low-ranking officer.' (Folio 25a – 25b)

Clearly, the aforementioned conversational records were only partly writing-mediated. The questions and responses were largely speech-based thanks to the presence of one or more interpreters. While the envoys, including Lê Quý Đôn, were non-conversant in Mandarin, there is some indication that they could follow the verbal interaction between Qing Chinese officials and their interpreters to some extent.

Brush-talk contents

When official business was over, most of the communication activities recorded during the delegation's return journey were rather routine. These included welcoming and bidding farewell, contacting the local offices about supervisory arrangements from making boat schedule arrangements to escorting the delegation to the national border. Based on the content of these brush-talks, four topical focuses are discernible: (i) academic exchange about history, geography, and Confucian classics; (ii) culture and customs of Annam; (iii) paintings and poetry; and (iv) socializing. In the following, we will illustrate them with one or two examples each.

Brush-talking about history, geography, and Confucian classics: intellectual exchange

In *A complete record*, Lê stated the purpose of his academic exchange via brush-talk clearly as follows (Lê Quý Đôn 1763: vol. 1, folio 32a):

> 僕忝自遠方來朝上國，深欲與賢士大夫接識，講論典籍，考究禮樂，得求教益。
>
> I came to the Superior Country from afar, look forward to meeting the great sages and nobles, discussing classical and literary works, studying rites and music in the hope of benefiting from [your] fine teaching and sharing.

Besides his diplomatic mission, Lê was most interested in the political figures of the North and academic studies of Confucianism. In view of the intellectual currents and debates on classical Chinese canons and research in historical studies by Qing scholars, Lê consciously brought along his two own books in anticipation of informed discussion and in-depth exchange of views with Chinese scholars. The two books were 'A review and criticism of books' 群書考辨 (Lê 1757) and the 'Records of model sages and nobles' 聖模賢範錄 (Lê 1750).[7] According to *A complete record*, the literati from the North and Lê had fruitful discussions on many aspects of historical studies, classical Chinese canons, and literary works, as well as geography.

For instance, on 08:14, Qin Chaoyu and Lê Quý Đôn discussed various historical events. The two began by exchanging views toward *A review and criticism of books* before extending their discussion to other historical issues. This book consisted of four volumes, covering the history of China from the Xia 夏 (ca. 2100–1600 BCE), Shang 商 (ca. 1600–1050 BCE), and all the dynasties up to the Song 宋 (960–1279 CE). Qin was particularly interested in the Yellow Turban (*Huangjin* 黃巾) uprising during the Eastern Han 東漢 (25–220 CE) and the White Lotus Sect (*Bailian jiao* 白蓮教) of the Song dynasty. After their brush-talk exchange, Qin praised Lê that 'the Envoy does have an eye for history' (可見讀史有眼, folio 9b), and that Lê was 'good at reading history and understanding its essence' (可謂善讀史而得其要領者也, folio 20b).

When Qin presented the 'Reflective reading notes' 讀書記 for Lê to read, they immediately had a good discussion about studies of Confucian classics, focusing on the 'Book of poetry' 詩經. When commentaries of Zhu Xi 朱熹 were brought

---

7 There is one copy archived at the Institute of Sino-Nom Studies, call number VHv.275/1–4.

up, Lê quoted 'The Analects' 論語. To challenge Zhu Xi's views, Lê supported his argument by citing opposing opinions by Lü Donglai 呂東萊 (1137–1181) and the 'Comprehensive Examination of Literature' 文獻通考 by Ma Duanlin 馬端臨 (1254–1323). Lê showed an unmistakable predilection for classical learning 古學 and had high praise for Confucian scholarship conducted during the Han dynasty, in keeping with the prominent intellectual currents of textual criticism and evidential research 考據學 so prevalent during the Qing dynasty. Qin did not agree with Zhu Xi's viewpoints entirely even though he remained respectful of Zhu. His attitude may be seen as 'the middle way' 中道, which is characterized by eclecticism 折衷學派 between the Confucian scholarship of the Han and Song dynasties.

In the eighth lunar month of 1761, Lê Quý Đôn had four extended brush conversations with Qin Chaoyu (08:16, 08:27, 10:21, and 11:05), continuing their writing-mediated sharing and exchange earlier (08:05 and 08:14). As before, in-depth discussions were held focusing on the content in three books: *A review and criticism of books*, *Records of model sages and nobles*, and the *Book of poetry*. The main topics in these four brush conversations were mainly related to historical studies and Confucian classics as found in various published works on studies of history, critical commentaries, investigative research, as well as selected excerpts from the Confucian classics, in keeping with mainstream academic interests and concerns of Qing scholars.

Geography along the border regions between Annam and Qing China was the main topic of the brush-talk and letter correspondence between Lê Quý Đôn and Zhu Peilian.[8] On 12:27, before the Lunar New Year's Eve to 1762, Lê visited the Chief Provincial Education Commissioner of Guangxi Province, Zhu Peilian. Through brush-talks, Zhu asked about some locations in Giao Châu 交州 and how they were called historically. Zhu appreciated Lê's elaborate response and commented that 'Everything [the Envoy] raised is precious advice' (承示一條, 誠如尊諭, folio 70a). At the end of the brush-talk, Zhu handed over a complete set of papers listing all districts and provinces prior to the Ming dynasty and requested Lê to indicate historical changes in geographical boundaries and names of those regions. On that occasion, Lê also took out both the *Records of model sages and nobles* and *A review and criticism of books*, and requested Zhu for comments and to write a preface for each of them. On 01:03,

---

8 Liam C. Kelley (2005: 215) also mentioned the brush conversation and letter correspondence between Lê Quý Đôn and Zhu Peilian in footnote 49:

> How Southern envoys communicated with Northern officials varied depending on the occasion and also perhaps on the status of the Northern official. Le Quy Don and Zhu Peilian communicated at times by exchanging letters and at times by engaging in 'brush talks' (*but dam/bitan*), where both men sat at a table and wrote questions and answers to each other. For an example of a brush talk between Le Quy Don and Zhu Peilian, see Le Quy Don, *Bac su thong luc* [A complete record of an embassy to the North], (1760), A. 179, 68a – 71a.

1762, Lê returned and gave Zhu the answers he was looking for. Thereupon they had a fascinating brush-talk on various historical changes in geographical boundaries of specific regions in Annam, Lê's own literary works, as well as a great variety of cultural and historical issues in Annam. Guided by serious inquiry and academic rigor, they thoroughly researched changes in geographical boundaries through time by looking up relevant references and credible published sources, in keeping with the critical stance of Qing scholars who subscribed to the mainstream school of evidential research or textual criticism 考證學派/考據學.

The brush-talks on studies of classical Chinese canons and history, like those on changes in geographical boundaries, were among the most stimulating and academically demanding exchanges between the Annam delegation and their Chinese brush conversation partners. Being the most knowledgeable scholar-official from Annam, Lê Quý Đôn took advantage of his position as the Vice-Envoy to seek the views of Qing scholar-officials by conversing with them in writing. In particular, to satisfy his intellectual curiosity and interests in various political and academic issues, he would try to apply the method of textual criticism which was so trendy and popular at that time. In this regard, Lê's brush-talk records collected in his 1763 *A complete record* are truly a highlight of Vietnamese-Chinese academic exchange – unparalleled in the past and probably unsurpassed in the rest of the monarchical period of Vietnam.[9]

Brush-talking about the culture and customs of Annam

Annam culture and customs were among the topics that many Chinese officials were interested in and curious about. In particular, Zhu Peilian raised many questions when brush-talking with Lê Quý Đôn. Following is one such question concerning the rumored offering of white-eared pheasants by Việt Thường people 越裳氏 to ancient China during the Zhou dynasty (1045–221 BCE):

曰：有一說欲奉呈。史載越裳氏朝周獻白雉事，容或有之？	[Zhu]: 'There is one hearsay that [I] would like to consult [you]. Some history books stated that the people of Việt Thường offered white-eared pheasants as tributes to the Emperor of Zhou dynasty. May [I] ask is that true?'

(*Continued*)

---

9 The content of Lê Quý Đôn's academically focused brush-talk records in *A complete record* is very rich; it will be reported in a separate study. On more details of academic exchange between Lê Quý Đôn and Qing scholars and their relationships, see Nguyễn Kim Sơn (1995).

[曰]: 其謂由扶南、林邑海際朞年而至其國，無不謬安。越裳在交趾南，舊驩州，今本國乂安處也。林邑舊占城國，今本國廣南處也，在乂安外。扶南又在林邑之外，乃占城、臘地，又外此則近於西海諸國，莫知所極矣。今云由扶南達越裳，非惟後世未嘗開，　　周時亦無此路也。....凡此皆王子年《拾遺記》怪誕之說。史遷本無是言，後儒收入外史，不可勝辨。

伊覽之，欣然曰：真快論也，令人欽嘆！

[Lê]: 'It took a whole year to get to Zhou China by sea from Phù Nam 扶南 and Lâm Ấp 林邑. Việt Thường 越裳 was located in the south of Giao Chỉ 交趾, formerly known as Hoan Châu 驩州, now the Nghệ An 乂安 of our country. Lâm Ấp was formerly the country Chiêm Thành 占城國; it is now the Quảng Nam 廣南 region of our country outside of Nghệ An. Phù Nam is located outside of Lâm Ấp; it belongs to the land of Chiêm Thành and Chân Lạp 真臘. And the exterior of Phù Nam is close to the countries in Tây Hải 西海, and we do not know their boundaries. Now it is said that the road from Phù Nam to Việt Thường not only has not been cleared by the next generations, but the Zhou dynasty also had no such path. . . . Those myths that have been passed down [i.e., the theory that Việt Thường offered pheasants as tribute goods to the Zhou dynasty] are all absurd claims in the 'Records of neglected matters' 拾遺記 of Wang Zinian 王子年. Those records were not found in the work of Sima Qian 司馬遷. Later, the Confucian scholars included that unsubstantiated hearsay in their works, making the posterity confused.'

[Zhu] read and said delightfully: 'This commentary is really interesting, truly admirable.' (Folia 82b-83a)

This brush-talk record provides evidence that as early as the eighteenth century, Lê Quý Đôn had demystified the theory of Việt Thường people offering white-eared pheasant to the Zhou dynasty. Such an absurd hearsay was misrepresented in the 'Records of neglected matters' 拾遺記. Elsewhere, Lê also cited many sources to refute the claim that Xie Jin 解縉 (1369–1415) was worshipped by people in Annam. Lê also discussed, through brush-talk, the existence of soil ramparts 土壘 in Annam after the wars with Yuan and Ming dynasties. His explications were so insightful and convincing that Zhu praised Lê for correcting various historical and cultural misrepresentations.

Also, Lê Quý Đôn conducted brush-talks with other Chinese officials on a wide range of topics, including the status of the successor to the throne in Annam, work conditions in the six national departments and the Hanlin Academy, the administrative hierarchy in court, the number of officials and the costumes required by court rituals, the relationships between court officials and regional officials, the civil service examination system 科舉 and the age limit of candidates for the examination, the importance of the Metropolitan Graduate 進士 rank, but also geographical topics like historical landmarks, regional customs and products, local climate and boat traffic conditions.

One such example may be found in the brush-talk between Lê Quý Đôn and the Administration Commissioner named Yong 永氏 on 10:01, 1761 in Changsha, Hunan Province concerning the king of Annam and the civil service examination system:

曰: 貴國老王何年駕薨?	[Yong]: 'In which year did the former king of your esteemed country pass away?'
曰: 己卯年六月月。	[Lê]: 'The sixth month of 1759.'
曰: 今王何親?	[Yong]: 'How are they related, the former king and the present one?'
曰: 先王之姪。	[Lê]: '[The present king is] the nephew of the former king.'
曰: 先王有幾子?	[Yong]: 'How many children did the former king have?'
曰: 最多。	[Lê]: 'The most.'
曰: 何不立子而立姪?	[Yong]: 'Why not enthrone his own son instead of the nephew?'
曰: 先王原係以弟繼兄，遺命復傳國於兄之子。今王乃先尊諡純王嫡統。	[Lê]: 'The former king inherited the throne from his brother; before he passed away, he left a will stating that the throne be passed on to his brother's son. The present king is the eldest son of the king before the former king, whose posthumous title was Thuần Vương 純王.' (Folio 25a – 25b)

At brush-talk <5>, after discussing the Confucian classics, Qin Chaoyu asked Lê about the civil service examination in Annam:

又問：士子幾歲應試?	[Qin] asked again: 'What is the eligible age for candidates to take the examination?'
副使曰：不泥年齒，任人就考，本國常有十三、十四歲已中舉人者。	[Lê]: 'We are not concerned about age. In our country, there are people who passed the local examination and acquired the Metropolitan Graduate qualification at age 13 or 14.' (Folio 11b)

As evidenced in these writing-mediated exchanges, Sinitic brush-talk between the envoys and local Chinese officials was a productive mode of intercultural communication for both sides not only to promote cultural exchange and enhance mutual understanding by correcting any inaccurate historical representations but also to cultivate good relations between Vietnam and China at both the national and interpersonal levels.

Brush-talking about paintings and poems

One of the key characteristics of writing-mediated brush conversation in Sinitic is its semiotic potential and pragma-linguistic affordance for brush-talkers to showcase their flair in literary and calligraphic talents by improvising poetic exchange interactively, which is possibly a *sui generis* lingua-cultural phenomenon in Sinographic East Asia until the 1900s (see Chapter 1). This is especially evident when the brush-talkers were engaged in composing couplets or poems that require strict adherence to a specific rhyming scheme, suggesting among other things their passion and delight in poetic improvisation. It is not surprising, therefore, to find no less than 260 poems recorded in a separate book authored by Lê Quý Đôn, entitled 'Quế Đường collection of poems' 桂堂詩集 (Lê n.d.).[10] Most of the poems were composed by Lê, the Chinese scholar-officials or the Chosŏn envoys that were collected during the four-year mission. In terms of topics, a large percentage of the poems and couplets involved making compliments on paintings, suggesting that poetic exchange inspired by appreciation of paintings was a rather commonplace activity throughout the Annam delegation's travel in Qing China. However, apart from compilations of improvised calligraphy exchanged between the Annam envoys and Qing Chinese scholar-officials, in *A complete record* there was hardly any mention of events involving Sinogram-based poetic improvisation and chanting of Sinitic poems (*Hán thi thù xướng* 漢詩酬唱).[11] One such rare example was found on 10:01, 1761 in Changsha, when Lê met with Hunan Provincial Governor Feng Qian and local scholars including Guo Can 郭參. After brush-talking for a while, Guo asked:

聞貢使兩榜文官，有一對請教。隨即寫曰：安南貢使，安南使乎，使乎？	[Guo] I heard that the Envoy passed at second place in the civil service examination, I have a couplet and would like to consult with you. And then he wrote: 'Envoy of Annam, Envoy of Annam, what a worthy Envoy!'
應曰：天朝聖皇，天朝皇哉，皇哉! 此下句出《文選》。伊曰：好，說得太好了!	[Lê] rejoined: 'Emperor of Celestial Empire, Emperor of Celestial Empire, what a worthy Emperor!' The latter couplet from *Wenxuan* ('Selections of Refined Literature'). Guo praised: 'Excellent! Excellent counterpoint!' (Folio 24b)

The relatively infrequent poetic improvisation through brush-talk documented in *A complete record* probably reflects Lê Quý Đôn's preference of presenting the envoys' poetic exchange with others in a separate volume. Content-wise, therefore, *A complete record* focuses on miscellaneous conversational topics arising from the delegation's brush-talk interaction with people they met during their two-year return journey to the celestial capital, including history, Confucianism, literature, culture, geography, and the like.

10 There are three copies of *Quế Đường collection of poems* archived at the Institute of Sino-Nom Studies (Hanoi, call number A.576 and VHv.2341; Vietnam Institute of Literature, call number HN.32).
11 Compare 唱和: Mand. *chànghè*, Jap. *shōwa*, Kor. *changhwa*, Vi. *xướng hoạ* ('chanting').

Socializing brush conversations

There are also several socializing brush conversations that clearly involved participant roles of a non-official, private capacity, showing a level of intimacy that may be characterized as 'heart-to-heart talk', the purpose being to express personal concerns about the brush conversation partner(s)' well-being. This happened when the Qing Chinese brush-talker asked about the Annam delegation's feelings when traveling in China, whether they felt any homesickness or experienced any difficulties arising from climatic differences between the North and the South, living conditions of their family members, and so forth. Such relationship-focused questions were most probably geared towards rapport-building, cementing personal friendship, and tightening up both sides' emotional bond. For instance, in brush-talk <9>, the Administration Commissioner Yong asked about the delegation's travel arrangements:

問: 何日出京?	[Yong]: 'What day did the Envoy leave the Capital [for the South]?'
曰: 三月初一日。	[Lê]: 'The first day of the third lunar month.'
曰: 何故至茲方到此?	[Yong]: 'Why did it take so long for the delegation to arrive?'
曰: 上水逆風不順。	[Lê]: 'The wind was blowing in the opposite direction, not favorable.'
曰: 風水不順，亦不至此遲滯，必有緣故。	[Yong]: 'Even the wind was unfavorable, it could not have delayed the boat for that long. There must be some other reason.'
曰: 不敢說，由江南船戶到處販賣，以是酖閣[耽擱]。	[Lê]: '[I] dare not say, [but actually] because the boat owner of Jiangnan went everywhere for trading business, that's why the boat arrived late.'
伊曰: 原來如此，當為相催，使貢使早早還國也。	He said [Yong]: 'Is that so? [I] will urge them so that the Envoys can go home soon.' (Folio 25b)

Likewise, in brush-talk <12>, the Imperial Commissioner Qin Chaoyu asked about the envoys' families, including questions about the age of Chief Envoy, and the age and occupation of Vice-Envoy's father.

問: 大貢使幾歲?	[Qin]: 'How old is the Chief Envoy?'
其答之。	Chief Envoy [Trần Huy Mật] answered.
問: 二貢使太翁尊年?	[Qin]: 'How many golden years has the esteemed father of the Vice-Envoy passed?'
曰: 家親今七十歲。	[Lê]: 'My father is 70 years old.'
曰: 尊居何職?	[Qin]: 'What is [his] esteemed official title?'
曰: 現奉致仕，迴復內閣辦事。	[Lê]: '[He] has retired but is still working in the cabinet.'
曰: 老亦多事否?	[Qin]: '[Your] aged [father] must have many duties. Right?'

(Continued)

曰: 從容隨朝，亦無甚事。	[Lê]: 'Depending on the court affairs, [he does] not have that many duties.'
伊曰: 二位貢使，役行日久，家中想念，當為言於撫臺大人使得早早進行回國也。	He said [Qin]: 'Both envoys have been duty-bound [away from home] for so long; [your] family must miss you a lot. [I] will talk to the Provincial Governor to let the delegation go home soon.'
曰: 多謝盛情。	[Lê]: '[We are] very much obliged to your kindness.' (Folio 33b)

In terms of length, brush conversations on traditional culture, conversational routines, or poetic improvisation tended to be shorter, usually no more than a few hundred sinograms. By contrast, brush conversations involving academically focused exchange of views were often longer and more elaborate, reaching a thousand or even a few thousand sinograms. This is because, apart from the fact that writing was in general more time-consuming than speaking, to make a point or one's argument convincing, cross-referencing to and quotation of original texts in ancient classics was often deemed necessary, not to mention the brush-talkers' own elaboration of viewpoints and sharing of personal insights.

Conclusion

Historically, brush-talk was a unique writing-mediated mode of communication that helped supplement or even replace the conventional form of verbal communication when it was deemed more effective than speech-based interaction. In the absence of a shared spoken language, Sinitic brush-talk was an age-old lingua-cultural practice that helped literati of Sinitic overcome the language barrier. This was commonplace between diplomats and scholar-officials gifted with deep-rooted knowledge of shared Sinitic-based literary heritage from different parts of Sinographic East Asia when they were engaged in cross-border communication. At the same time, brush-talk was also a mode of communication that made it easier for the parties to connect, deliberate issues of academic import at an intellectually deep and sophisticated level, resolve any problems arising and, in the case of envoys from different countries, build closer rapport as well as cement friendship between their countries – or managing 'public relations' in modern terminology. Lê Quý Đôn's friendship with Qin Chaoyu and Zha Li are typical of personal relationships that were built and nurtured through brush-talk. Likewise, thanks to Sinitic brush-talk, Zhu Peilian and many other Qing scholars acquired a more accurate understanding of Annam's cultural history. Chosŏn Vice-Envoy Yi Hwi-chung 李徽中 once wrote:

差幸同文論古字，共存舊製撫身章。

Luckily the two countries [Chosŏn and Annam] are from the same cultural sphere, [which enables us to] discuss the ancient characters, keep our shared literature and dress elegantly.[12]

Writing-mediated Sinitic brush-talk being such an effective communication tool, it would be nice if it could be revitalized today in diplomatic circles to enhance international relations, among other objectives. Lê Quý Đôn wrote in the preface of *A complete record*:

乃知人心不異以誠正相待，以文字相知，即四海皆兄弟也。(vol. 1, folio 3b)

We now know that people's hearts are the same, if we treat each other with sincerity, and to get to know each other through Sinitic-based writing, then we are all brothers in this world.

The brush-talk interactions embedded in *A complete record*, be they long or short, reflect the shared concerns of Lê and the Qing scholar-officials regarding the political situation, civil service examination system, rituals and ceremonies, historical shifts in national boundaries, Annam's culture, customs as well as developments in contemporary Confucian ideologies. Their academically focused exchange on Confucianism, review of classical works, historical events, and research on historical shifts in national boundaries in the border regions are intellectually rich and complex topics. No wonder their brush conversations could last for several hours and, being written, provide a window that affords us a glimpse into the little-known academic exchange at an interpersonal level in the history of diplomatic relations between the Great Việt and China. It is in this sense that the Sinitic brush-talks bequeathed by scholar-officials like Lê Quý Đôn are so valuable for research in intellectual exchange between Vietnamese and Chinese scholars in cross-border communication contexts. It is also noteworthy that some of those brush conversation events would result in solid emotional bonds and convivial relations between the brush-talkers over an extended period.

Last but not least, the selected brush conversations excerpted from *A complete record* conjure up a portrait of Lê Quý Đôn as a fine Confucian scholar-official with erudite knowledge – a diplomat with great respect for high standards, plus a strong sense of national pride and dignity, but also a politician who was mindful of the importance of cultivating good neighborly relations with Qing China. Such brush-talk materials have greatly enhanced our understanding of the authentic characters of individual diplomats like Lê Quý Đôn, but also the important roles they played as prominent historical figures of early modern Vietnam, China, and to some extent, elsewhere in Sinographic East Asia.

---

12 Lê Quý Đôn. *Quế Đường thi tập* ('Quế Đường collection of poems' 桂堂詩集). VHv.2431. folio 32a.

References

Clements, R. (2019). Brush talk as the 'lingua franca' of East Asian diplomacy in Japanese-Korean encounters, c. 1600–1868. *The Historical Journal* 62(2): 289–309.

Hucker, C. (1985). *A dictionary of officials titles in late imperial China*. Stanford: Stanford University Press.

Kelley, L. C. (2005). *Beyond the bronze pillars: Envoy poetry and the Sino-Vietnamese relationship*. Honolulu: University of Hawai'i Press.

Lê, Q.-Đ. [黎貴惇] (n.d.). *Quế Đường thi tập* 桂堂詩集 ('Quế Đường collection of poems'), archived at the Institute of Sino-Nom Studies, call number A.576 and VHv.2341; and Vietnam Institute of Literature, call number HN32.

Lê, Q.-Đ. [黎貴惇] (1750). *Thánh mô hiền phạm lục* 聖模賢範錄 ('Records of model sages and nobles'), archived at the Institute of Sino-Nom Studies, call number VHv.275/1–4.

Lê, Q.-Đ. [黎貴惇] (1757). *Quần thư khảo biện* 群書考辨 ('A review and criticism of books'), archived at the Institute of Sino-Nom Studies, call number A.252.

Lê, Q.-Đ. [黎貴惇] (1763). *Bắc sứ thông lục* 北使通錄 ('A complete record of an embassy to the North'), archived at the Institute of Sino-Nom Studies, call number A.179.

Lê, Q.-Đ. [黎貴惇] (1763/2018). *Bắc sứ thông lục* ('A complete record of an embassy to the North', Nguyễn Thị Tuyết [阮氏雪], Trans.). Hanoi: University of Education Press.

Li, D. C. S., Aoyama, R., & Wong, T.-S. (2020). Silent conversation through brushtalk (筆談): The use of Sinitic as a scripta franca in early modern East Asia. *Global Chinese* 6(1): 1–24.

Nguyễn, H.-T., & Nguyễn, T.-C. [阮黃申、阮俊強] (2019). 越南與諸國筆談概論 ('An outline of brush-talk between Vietnam and other countries'). In H. He & T.-C. Nguyễn [何華珍、阮俊强] (Eds.), 越南漢喃文獻與東亞漢字整理研究 ('Research on Vietnamese classical texts and East Asian sinograms') (pp. 101–117). Peking: China Social Sciences Press.

Nguyễn, H.-T., & Nguyễn, T.-C. [阮黃申、阮俊强] (2020). Sinitic brushtalk in Vietnam's anti-colonial struggle against France: Phan Bội Châu's silent conversations with influential Chinese and Japanese leaders in the 1900s. *China and Asia* 2(2): 270–293.

Nguyễn, K.-S. [阮金山] (1995). Về sự tiếp xúc của Lê Quý Đôn với học thuật đời Thanh Trung Quốc thế kỷ XVII – đầu thế kỷ XVIII ('On Lê Quý Đôn's contact with Qing scholarship in the seventeenth and early eighteenth centuries'). *Tạp chí Nghiên cứu Trung Quốc* (Journal of Chinese Studies) 3: 59–65.

Nguyễn, T.-Đ. [阮才東] (2008). 黎貴惇的儒學研究 ('A study of Lê Quý-Đôn's Confucian learning'). Unpublished PhD dissertation. Taipei: Fu Jen Catholic University.

Wang, Y., & Xie, Y. [王勇、謝詠] (Eds.). (2015). 東亞的筆談研究 ('Studies on brush-talk in East Asia'). Hangzhou: Zhejiang Gongshang University Press.

Yu, X.-D., & Liang, M.-H. [于向東、梁茂華] (2013). 歷史上中越兩國人士的交流方式：筆談 ('Historical mode of communication between Chinese and Vietnamese people: Brush-talk'). 中國邊疆史地研究 (*Journal of China's Borderland History and Geography Studies*) 4(23): 108–116.

Zhong, C.-J. [鍾彩鈞] (Ed.). (2012). 黎貴惇的學術與思想 ('Lê Quý Đôn's scholarship and thoughts'). Taipei: Institute of Chinese Literature and Philosophy, Academia Sinica.

8 Lingua-cultural characteristics of brush-talk

Insights from *Ōkōchi Documents* 大河内文書

Wang Baoping

Introduction

Sinitic brush-talk (*bǐtán* 筆談, also known as *bǐyǔ* 筆語 or *bǐhuà* 筆話) is a sinogram-based modality of written communication between literati within Sino-graphic East Asia, interactively and face-to-face. One early, famous example may be traced back to the Northern Song dynasty (960–1127 CE). During his visit to China, the Japanese monk Chōnen (奝然, Mand: Diaoran, 938–1016) was received in audience by Emperor Taizong 宋太宗, and responded to his questions in writing because his knowledge of spoken Chinese was inadequate to make himself understood. His written response was described and documented in *the History of Song* 宋史 as follows:

> Chōnen's clerical script (*lishu* 隸書) handwriting was elegant, but he did not speak any Chinese. When asked about the people and customs in his country, he brushed his response thus: 'We have "Five classics" plus Buddhist texts, and a seventy-volume "Bai Juyi Collection", all procured from China'.[1]

Through Sinitic brush-talk, Chōnen was able to enlighten his hosts with a range of novelties about Japan, from agricultural and commercial activities to stockbreeding and local products, but also their emperor. All this provided useful information for the section concerning the history of the island state and its people in China's official history record. Over 500 years later, in the mid-sixteenth century, another transcultural encounter triggering the use of writing-mediated communication in Sinitic again made history. In 1543, a Portuguese ship drifted to Tanegashima Island 種子島 in Japan. According to one historical record (鉄砲記, Mand: *Tiěpàojì*; Jap: *Teppōki*, 'The matchlock gun incident'), 'on board were a hundred odd passengers; their appearance was queer, speaking an alien tongue.

---

1 "奝然善隸書，而不通華言，問其風土，但書以對云：國中有《五經》書及佛經、《白居易集》七十卷，并得自中國" (from *History of Song*, volume 491, Biographies 250: Foreign States 7 – Ryukyu Islands, Dingan, Bohai, Japan, Tangut; 《宋史》卷四百九十一 列傳第二百五十，外國七：流求國、定安國、渤海國、日本國、党項, Toytaya 1977: 14131).

DOI: 10.4324/9781003048176-10

To local beholders, they all looked strange indeed'.[2] It so happened that among those washed ashore was a Confucian scholar from Ming China called Wufeng 五峰, who 'used a stick to write on the sand',[3] which managed to get his meanings across and facilitated communication timely before the volatile confrontation evolved into deadly skirmishes. What is more, after this incident, Japanese militants became aware of Western firearms and cannon balls, triggering thereby a game-changing military reform toward the manufacturing of artillery firearms and modern warfare, with the one-on-one calvary-driven combat tactics giving way to infantry-centered battle techniques. Marveling at the outcome of this fateful historical incident, the author remarked that 'Written words took the place of speech to convey Wufeng's meanings effectively, making him feel as if he had crossed paths with well-acquainted friends in alien land, thanks to the sharing of similar-sounding words, which made our give-and-take possible in the first place' (Nanpo 1971).[4]

Sinitic brush-talk data sources, being rather unique to Sinographic East Asia, have attracted increasing attention of scholars working on related research areas within humanities areas recently.[5] This chapter gives a brief overview of this modality of face-to-face communication by drawing on interaction between Chinese, Japanese, and Korean brush-talkers during the early Meiji period (1868–1912), as exemplified in the *Ōkōchi Documents* 大河内文書 (Wang 2016).

Why engaged in Sinitic brush-talk

In the extant literature of traditional works on philology, there is hardly any mention of Sinitic brush-talk 漢文筆談, which is aptly and succinctly defined in the *Comprehensive Dictionary of the Chinese Language* 漢語大詞典 as 'written conversation' 書面談話. Little is known about the circumstances under which written conversation is conducted in place of speech. Based on my own research, Sinitic brush-talk typically took place in three types of situations, which may be characterized as: involuntary brush-talk 被動筆談, cultural brush-talk 文化筆談, and espionage brush-talk 情報筆談.

---

2 "船客百餘人，其形不類，其語不通。見者以為奇怪矣" (Nanpo Bunshi 南浦文之1971).
3 "以杖書于沙上". According to Nanpo (1971), Wufeng's real name was Wang Zhi 王直, a Ming Chinese firearms smuggler.
4 "偶遇五峰，以文字通言語，五峰亦以為知己之在異邦也。所謂同聲相應，同氣相求者也。"
5 Leading researchers who have been engaged in the compilation of Sinitic brush-talk manuscripts include: Sanetō Keishū 実藤恵秀, Matsuura Akira 松浦章, Chen Jie 陈捷, Liu Yuzhen 劉雨珍, Wang Baoping 王寶平. Other researchers who have conducted systematic analysis of Sinitic brush-talk from different vantage points are Zhang Weixiong 张偉雄, Uozumi Kazuaki 魚住和晃, Nakamura Shirō 中村史郎, Ihara Takushū 伊原澤周, Dai Dongyang 戴東陽, and Wang Yong 王勇.

Involuntary brush-talk 被動筆談

Involuntary brush-talk refers to the reliance on communication through writing because speech was not a feasible option. The 'brush' in *brush conversation* refers to a historically widely attested mode of communication in Sinographic East Asia until the late nineteenth and early twentieth century. Since then, however, in keeping with technological changes in handwriting activities, the brush has yielded to other modern writing instruments such as fountain pen, pencil, and ball pen. For our purpose, we will use the term 'involuntary brush-talk' to refer to historical situations where the brush, along with ink and paper, was considered the unmarked or default writing instrument and stationery to conduct written conversation interactionally, which was often but not always a negative choice. When modern instruments and stationery are involved, the term 'pen-talk' will be used.

Pen-talk can take place between interlocutors with a shared spoken language, for example, when an interlocutor is physiologically prevented from speaking due to serious sickness or after undergoing surgery affecting any of the articulatory organs (see also Chapter 1). Such situations may be found in the past or present, in multilingual as well as monolingual communities. For instance, there is a relatively recent, widely reported case in Japan where a 'first hostess' (Saitō Rie 斉藤里恵) working in the red-light district Ginza of Tokyo made a name by engaging her clients in pen-talk because she had lost the ability to speak. Selected documented content of her pen-talk with her clients attracted a lot of media attention, electronic and print. Her 2009 autobiography 《筆談ホステス》 ('Pen-talk hostess') was a great success. Apart from interesting and vivid details featuring lively interaction with her clients in writing, many readers were also impressed by her personality, sincerity, knowledgeability, and writing skills. Such involuntary pen-talk clearly would not have been necessary if she had been able to speak and interact with others in speech. Be it brush-talk (premodern and early modern) or pen-talk (modern), situationally it is/was an involuntary social practice as speech would be/have been preferred. There is thus continuity in what is termed here as 'involuntary brush-talk' in reference to the same contingent social practice – contingent because the interlocutors have at least one shared spoken language at their disposal but are inconvenienced to speak for one reason or another.

Cultural brush-talk 文化筆談

Involuntary brush-talk is a negative choice. By contrast, cultural brush-talk is a preferred option despite the availability of interpreting service. This is clearly evidenced by a large amount of Sinitic brush-talk data generated by late Qing government officials in Japan in their face-to-face brush conversations with their Japanese hosts. For decades since the arrival of the first Qing Chinese legation led by the Consul He Ruzhang 何如璋 (1838–1891) at Tokyo in 1877, 'silent conversation' between individual Chinese embassy staff and Japanese visitors through Sinitic brush-talk – in different numbers and combinations – has yielded plenty of writing artifacts, of which a sizable amount has survived thanks to the unfailing enthusiasm and meticulous care of some of the brush-talkers to collect and preserve the loose sheets of brush-talk proceedings, subsequently often annotated and bound into book form. As the topics in Chinese-Japanese Sinitic brush-talk tended to touch upon broadly defined cultural issues, their writing-mediated communication, interactively and face-to-face, may be characterized as cultural brush-talk.

One such brush-talk enthusiast was Ōkōchi Teruna 大河内輝声 (1848–1882), the last feudal lord of Takasaki domain 高崎藩 (south of Gunma Prefecture 群馬県 today) and a frequent visitor at the Chinese embassy. The intensity of his zeal in Sinitic brush-talk may be gauged by his own words: 'day-in-day-out working indefatigably on piles of loose sheets stacked up like a hill, indulging in creating orderly discourse out of disorderly improvisations'.[6] There is also clear evidence of brush conversation being preferred to speech-based interpreting:

> From now on, in my exchange with the two Consuls at the embassy, my wish is to dispense with Wei [the interpreting officer Wei Limen 通辯官魏梨門], an impediment to our smooth brush conversation. Please take note: How ingenious if [each of us could] stick to our own brush (頭毛錐)![7]

Essentially the same point was reiterated elsewhere in a poem – a heptasyllabic quatrain – by Minamoto no Keikaku 源桂閣, Ōkōchi's appellation (*Ōkōchi Documents*, 戊寅筆話, 28 Feb 1878, Wang 2016: 1362):

不假辯官三寸舌	Let's not rely on the interpreter's three-inch tongue,
只揮名士一枝毫	Behold the esteemed scholar's brush in action.
莫言東海幾蠻語	Speak no barbarian language of the Eastern Sea,
叙談通情何可勞	What better way to exchange words and emotions.

These words offer strong evidence of Ōkōchi's predilection for brush-talking with his soulmates from across the sea, which he found superior to attending to an official interpreter's regurgitation of whatever verbiage uttered in speech (*Ōkōchi Documents*, see preface, Wang 2016). While more evidence is needed to impute to him a despicable attitude towards interpreting in general, we can be sure that for Ōkōchi, engaging a go-between for speech-based interpretation was no match for the direct heart-to-heart communion mediated by a 'talking' brush 叙談通情 (cf. Clements 2019). While this is incontestable, one must not lose sight of the fact that for Sinitic brush-talking to serve as an alternative mode of communication, profound knowledge of the Sinitic literature was required. This was exactly the case of Ōkōchi, a scholar and admirer of Chinese culture whose solid training was

---

6 "終日不知倦，紙疊作丘，奇論成篇" (Wang 2004: 61).
7 "自今以後，每訪兩公使,不宜待魏少年之陪侍，卻為筆話之妨害，請君銜之。單貨一枝頭毛錐，尤為妙" (*Ōkōchi Documents*, 戊寅筆話, 25 Feb 1878, Wang 2016: 1355).

grounded in the voracious reading of Chinese classics, canons, and literary works. In his own words:

慶應年間，余結交於西洋人，講習其藝術，窺其所爲，無事不窮其精妙者，大喜其學之窮物理，以能開人智。明治初，余解組掛冠，卜棲墨江。自是後，以無用于世，乃改轍結交清人。相識日深，情誼月[越]厚，而其交遊之妙，勝於西洋人遠矣。蓋西洋人神氣穎敏，行事活潑，孜孜汲汲，覃思於百工器用製造也。至清國人，則不然，百官有司，廟謨之暇，皆以詩賦文章，行樂雅會，善養精神，故性不甚急也。	I came across some westerners during the Keiō era, learned about their art and observed their deeds through mutual exchange, and couldn't help marveling at the ingeniousness of what they are able to accomplish. I am elated by their studious inquisitiveness, which bears great potential to enlighten the human mind. In the early Meiji years, I stepped down from my government post, and have since been staying in Sumie. Befriending westerners having yielded so little contribution to society, I decided to switch and make friends with people from Qing China instead. Our acquaintance and intimacy grew steadily with time: in terms of the quality of our give-and-take, previous interactions with westerners are simply beyond comparison. Westerners are quick-witted if pretentious, diligent and swift in fabricating all kinds of tools and their applications. This is not true of people from Qing China, whose officials of different ranks can readily engage in poetry writing and literary composition over and above their official duties. They know how to entertain themselves and their guests at meetings, cultivate interests and conserve energy, hence they seldom do things in a rush.

After appreciating contrastive differences between Chinese and Western cultures, Ōkōchi came to the conclusion that

> for merchants in the capital, business-minded people and profit seekers the world over, befriending westerners is their best choice; for those who fancy leading a relaxing life in a remote area and enjoy amusing themselves with poetry and wine, making friends with people from Qing China would be more suitable for them.[8]

Clearly, Ōkōchi felt that compared with westerners' obsession with excelling in tool making, Chinese people knew how to conserve energy and lead a pleasurable life through poetry writing and literary composition, as well as entertaining themselves and guests at scholarly encounters.

---

8 "京畿之商賈、天下之人士，其求名趨利輩，宜交西洋人；高臥幽棲，詩酒自娛之人，宜交清國人也" (Wang 2004: 62).

Regarding the popularity of cultural brush-talk as a transcultural social practice, one important motivation was a conscious act, on the part of many brush-talkers, to keep a historical record for future reference (cf. Clements 2019). Sinitic brush-talk interaction yielded plenty of artifacts on paper; if preserved with care, such artifacts have the potential to last a long time. As noted by Confucianist merchant 儒商 Wang Tizhai 王惕齋, 'verbal duel fades instantly, while brush conversation is long-lasting'.[9] Likewise, after tidying up his brush-talk records with Li Shuchang 黎庶昌, the second Qing China ambassador to Japan, Miyajima Seiichirō 宮島誠一郎 (1838–1911) wrote affectionately, 'the brush-talk with Li Shuchang at farewell, which is on the right, will be stored in the painting gallery for appreciation by my offspring'.[10] Nor was he contented with these words alone; the original manuscripts were carefully bound together as a work of art and shown to the third ambassador to Japan Li Jingfang 李經方 and other embassy staff for appreciation. What is more, Li Jingfang was invited to write an epilogue for it (Wang 2014). A further instructive illustration may be found in the brush conversation between ambassador He Ruzhang and Meiji Sinologists Kametani Shōken 亀谷省軒 (1838–1913) and Washizu Kidō 鷲津毅堂 (1825–1882), as follows:

RZ	人生不百年，常懷千歲憂。[11] 若果活百年，厥憂當萬秋。此語可作注腳。	One lives rarely a hundred years but grieves for a thousand. If one should become a centenarian, would worries not multiply to ten thousand. This may serve as a footnote.
SX	後來歷史當大書：光緒何年何某出使日本。敝土儒林傳亦當特書：鷲津某與何公使筆話，何公使評其文。然則此筵上人皆係千古。自今百年後有人詫賞：此係何公使與鷲津毅堂筆話之書。亦猶今之想像高野山。	Subsequent history should elaborate: appointed as ambassador to Japan in a particular year under Emperor Guangxu. Our biographies of famous scholars should also give special mention of Washizu brush-talking with Ambassador He, who read and commented on his writing. But then all of us around the table will have perished. Perhaps someone will find this amazing a hundred years later: this is a brush-talk record between Ambassador He and Washizu, which was as important/great as what happened in Mount Kōya.
KK	我願傳此事於兒孫。待百年之後，漸漸賣之而立一家產。	I am willing to pass this to my offspring. A hundred years later, this will sell and allow them to make a fortune.

---

9 "舌戰一時消滅，至筆話永世不朽" (*Ōkōchi Documents*, 戊寅筆話, 25 Feb 1878, Wang 2016: 1354).
10 "右一綴與黎庶昌蒓齋臨別之筆談，藏之畫齋，以貽子孫" (《栗香齋筆話二》, 27 Feb 1885, end-of-volume remark, Wang 2014: 188).
11 The first half of this pentasyllabic octave was a slightly modified version of a widely acclaimed poem: 人生不滿百，常懷千歲憂 (*rénshēng bù mǎn bǎi, cháng huái qiānsuì yōu* 'One lives rarely a hundred years, but grieves for a thousand.').

RZ	東坡云:人生四十,始曉作家。觀君此言,真是曉作家之人。	Su Dongbo once said: one only gets to know how to manage family affairs by forty years of age. Seeing your words makes me convinced that you really know how to manage your family.
YT	自信後五百年,必為五百金。	I am confident that five hundred years later, this will be worth five hundred taels of gold.
RZ	須令其加倍。	Should be at least doubled.
KK	五百年而五百金?!今日我獨雖有五百金,可買之人,決不賣!	Five hundred taels only in five hundred years?! Even if my entire assets amount to only five hundred taels of gold today, should there be a buyer, I won't sell it for sure!
RZ	即賣亦可,第不收今日紙幣	Selling now is fine, but for the moment my humble self will not accept today's paper currency.

KK: Keikaku 桂閣 RZ: Ruzhang 如璋 SX: Shengxuan 省軒 YT: Yitang 毅堂
Source: *Ōkōchi Documents*, 庚辰筆話, 9 Jan 1880, Wang (2016: 2461–2462)

Apart from the humor and hyperbole intended for a good laugh, the blissful cacophony of preserving for five hundred years their brush-talk manuscript suggestively worth five hundred taels of gold, expecting future historians to give it a full elaboration, was uttered not entirely on impulse but probably reflected a collective wish. Such a yearning for visibility transcending time and space was arguably the driving force behind their conscious decision to preserve brush-talk manuscripts where possible.

Espionage brush-talk 情報筆談

Subject to the whims of the brush-talker and the sensitivity of information exchanged through brush conversation, politically valuable intelligence thus gathered could unsurprisingly end up serving ulterior motives and purposes like espionage. This was especially common when the participant role on the Chinese side – plausibly oscillating between government official and private acquaintance – was blurred after friendship gradually became cemented through deep brush-talk repeatedly. One instructive case involved Miyajima Seiichirō (宮島誠一郎, 1838–1911), a former retainer of Yonezawa domain 米沢藩 (today's Yamagata Prefecture 山形県) and an official historian at the Bureau of Historical Compilation. A writer of poetry in Chinese or Sinitic (漢詩 *kanshi*), he held China and its culture in high esteem, which led him to seek enlightenment from Chinese scholar-officials like Huang Zunxian 黃遵憲. Of all the envoys attached to the Chinese embassy in Japan, Li Shuchang, one of four disciples of Zeng Guofan 曾國藩 (1811–1872), was the one he admired the most, from whom he would solicit expert opinion and commentary on his draft *kanshi*, and and seek advice on the study plan of his beloved son Daihachi 宮島大八 (1867–1943) in China. Being like-minded in many ways, Miyajima and Li became very good friends, exchanging letters when meeting in person could not be arranged. In Miyajima's own words, 'seven years of collegiality with Li Shuchang have turned us into intimate friends, and the power of our trust for each other is strong enough to break a gold bar'.[12]

On the other hand, Miyajima exploited Li's unsuspecting trust and collected politically sensitive intelligence for his own government. For instance, on 6 January 1885, just before Li was about to return to China, during a brush conversation with Miyajima he hinted that the Qing government was seriously considering abandoning Ryukyu in exchange for Japan's non-intervention in Korea. Repeatedly Li stressed that 'what we discussed is private conversation between us; it should not be disclosed to any third party'.[13] That reminder did not seem to put Li's apprehension to rest. The next day Li wrote Miyajima a letter, reiterating that 'our brush conversation yesterday was merely our collegial exchange of views in private; by all means please keep it to yourself and refrain from disclosing it to others'.[14] To those words of caution, Miyajima promptly responded reassuringly that 'private words will certainly not be mixed up with official matters; our brush-talk manuscript is buried at the bottom of the cabinet. Your Esteemed Self, please be assured and have no worries'.[15] That reassurance turned out to be no more than a smokescreen, however. Historical records indicate that Miyajima reported what he had learned from the Chinese ambassador to Prime Minister Itō Hirobumi 伊藤博文 (1841–1909) with minimum delay (for more details, see Liu, this volume). That was by no means an isolated example. Shortly after Li Shuchang was re-appointed as ambassador to Japan, he and Miyajima were engaged in a heart-to-heart brush conversation on the current political situation. Li opined that the future of Ryukyu and Korea had better be strategically bundled and disentangled together, and that the primary concern that called for urgent action was to preempt Russia's invasion of Korea. To this end, Li proposed that China and Japan form an alliance and sign an agreement discreetly pledging mutual support with a view to restoring Asia's vitality. Two days after Li confided his personal opinion to Miyajima in their brush conversation, the latter passed a copy of that manuscript to Associate Counselor Yamagata Aritomo 山縣有朋 (1838–1922), who then submitted it to the Meiji emperor on the same day.

Brush conversation: interactional features characteristic of speech

Sinitic brush-talk being written conversation, linguistically its interactional patterns are characteristic of both speech and writing, which will be discussed and illustrated later. First, like in any conversation, it takes at least two persons to conduct brush-talk. Dyadic or involving more than two brush-talkers, interaction tends to be dominated by question and response, with or without a clear topical

---

12 '黎君蒓齋與余交七年，情最親密，誠爲斷金' (Wang 2014: 190).
13 '此不過兩人私談，幸勿與外人見則可' (Wang 2014: 191).
14 '昨日筆譚，此不過我兩人至好之私言，千萬藏之于心，不必示人爲幸' (Wang 2014: 191).
15 '私言固不與公事關涉，筆譚深藏之于匣底，幸勿勞尊慮' (Wang 2014: 191).

focus, long-winded or short-lived. Digression is not uncommon. In terms of content, as in casual conversation through speech, any topic may surface in brush-talk, from serious to trivial, scholarly to mundane. Intimate details of private affairs are well within the scope of brush-talking; personal relationship with the opposite sex, if invoked, is hardly surprising. Compared with written discourse, Sinitic brush-talk can be topically diverse, sometimes drifting to the point of lacking coherence or losing focus, unavoidably depending on the context.

In 1968, with the much-anticipated publication of 'Posthumous manuscript of brush conversation between Huang Zunxian and his Japanese friends' 黃遵憲與日本友人筆談遺稿,[16] the indefatigable efforts of Cheng Tsu-yu 鄭子瑜 and Sanetō Keishū 実藤惠秀 finally bore fruit. What followed was an anticlimax, however. Rather than traces of 'attitudinal change or intellectual growth' as expected, it turned out that the conversational exchange in their documented brush-talk interaction rarely goes beyond 'mundane matters' and 'quotidian trivialities', hence a big letdown to the reader.

According to Wang Xiangrong (1987), who expressed utter disappointment with the publication of the *Posthumous manuscript*, he had high expectation of finding some clues to Huang Zunxian's role in the coup d'état of Empress Dowager Cixi 慈禧太后 (1835–1908) that put an end to the 1898 Hundred Days' Reform 戊戌變法/百日維新. Wang recalled making that point to Sanetō several decades earlier in 1944. Since Huang had served as a counselor to Qing government's Consul He Ruzhang in Japan, a diplomatic appointment that predated his active involvement in that 1898 coup, Wang Xiangrong very much looked forward to finding traces of his inner thoughts in his brush-talk interaction with the Japanese hosts, in particular his personal reflections and viewpoints which took shape while in Japan and which subsequently exerted tremendous influence on his political stance after returning to China. The first-hand brush-talk data source in the *Posthumous manuscript* thus appeared to be promising in offering some enlightenment to that important missing link. As Wang Xiangrong further explained, while browsing the archives he had come across similar brush-talk data sources produced by Liu Shoukeng 劉壽鏗 and Governor of Hyōgo Prefecture 兵庫県知事, Sufu Kōhei 周布公平, Ma Xiangbo 馬相伯, and Zheng Xiaoxu 鄭孝胥, but he recalled finding nothing of import after thumping through over a dozen bound brush-talk manuscripts. Sanetō, too, found that difficult to believe. Wang Xiangrong suspected that the search proved futile because the dataset was too small, and so he kept banking his hope on other data sources. But then after going through the *Ōkōchi Documents* and the *Posthumous manuscript*, where pages after pages were filled with an exchange of trivial remarks on mundane topics bordering on bad taste, he could not help raising a query to Sanetō. In his response, Sanetō confirmed that when browsing the archives of brush-talk manuscripts produced by Qing China's representatives 理事 and their Japanese friends at the Representative Office of China in Kōbe 神戶理事府, he had come across

---

16 Published by Association for East Asian Literature, Waseda University.

deliberation of more business-like topics. He recalled that the size of the original paper might vary, but content-wise conversational exchanges on mundane topics were few and far between, let alone the sharing of intimate details of one's private life involving the opposite sex. All this begs the question: why did quotidian trivialities figure so prominently in Ōkōchi's voluminous brush-talk manuscripts (Wang 1987; Zong 1992: 6–7)?

To this question, Wang Xiangrong offered an explanation by way of an afterthought. He now found that 'content bias' perfectly reasonable and unsurprising. In their diplomatic capacities as official representatives of Qing China, naturally, they should refrain from discussing sensitive issues or divulging personal views towards political issues on paper. Although Ōkōchi was a nobleman, he did not have any official or formal capacity to represent the Japanese government. On the contrary, his social interaction with Qing embassy staff was premised on friendship at a personal level and therefore entirely private. In their brush conversation with Ōkōchi, therefore, bringing up political issues or formal business related to national interests would be topically out of place and situationally inappropriate. That said, was Huang Zunxian ever engaged in more serious discourse with his Japanese brush-talkers? The answer is definitely: 'Yes', except that when that happened, the brush-talk artifacts would hardly be kept in his personal files. Such manuscripts, if they existed, would more likely find their way to the Qing embassy archives in Tokyo 東京使署檔案館, and it is doubtful any surviving records could be found today. As a closing remark, Wang Xiangrong noted that intellectual exchange on some serious topics did crop up in brush conversation between Ōkōchi and Huang Zunxian, but only once in a very long while, no wonder such data source is tiny quantity-wise.

Wang Xiangrong's explanation sounds reasonable: no formal business when meeting informally. In my view, however, a more determining factor is grounded in the nature of unscripted conversation itself: the more participants (here: brush-talkers), the more topically diverse as one distraction may easily drift to another. This is exactly one salient characteristic of writing-mediated casual conversation which sets it apart from carefully edited writing in print. So long as brush-talk is recognized situationally as a site of interaction-embedded casual conversation, albeit writing-mediated, the kind of person as evidenced in Huang Zunxian's brush-talk interaction in the *Posthumous manuscript* comes closer to historical reality. For one thing, a desire for food and sex are integral to human nature. Sex is no taboo in conversation between young people, male or female. If it is treated like one and banned where traditional Chinese values prevail, it would be like burying one's head in the sand. Huang Zunxian and his colleagues were well into their thirties; being away from home over an extended period, it is perfectly understandable if sex as a topic should figure in their private brush conversation with close friends. Suppressing such brush-talk data would in no way deny that sex-related remarks did come up in their writing-mediated conversational exchange. That Sanetō Keishū and Cheng Tsu-yu, editors of the two respective *Posthumous manuscript* volumes, were daring enough to preserve such brush-talk artifacts was no simple feat. In particular, that the Chinese editor Cheng Tsu-yu defied all odds to publish the original brush conversation manuscript verbatim, was truly remarkable (Wang 2014).

Other linguistic features characteristic of speech include a small vocabulary range, the use of short clauses or phrases, and relatively simple and sometimes truncated sentence structures such as syntactic dislocation, supplementation, insertion and, above all, ellipsis (cf. Lü Shuxiang 1998: 7). What about nonverbal communication such as facial expressions, gestures, and body language which have been shown to accompany speech-based social interaction? Sinitic brush-talk is sometimes characterized as silent conversation. Although historical brush-talk data is devoid of visual details, evidence may sometimes be adduced from what transpired during the brush-talkers' interaction in writing, which is occasionally reinforced or triangulated by other textual features such as ellipsis, repetition, and pause. One such example may be found in the brush-talk record compiled by Miyajima Seiichirō. In his brush conversation with Li Shuchang on 22 July 1883, he wrote:

> Li's words were imbued with sincerity; when he wrote 'rare are my compatriots who have a deep understanding of foreign countries and affairs' and 'our Emperor is feeble, regal power being inaccessible to him', he looked worried and kept sighing. I was deeply moved when he brushed these words, which were loaded with emotions straight from the bottom of his heart.[17]

The actual interactional context may be beyond us, but it does little to stop the reader from visualizing and imagining a worrying Li Shuchang, thanks to the consciously collected and carefully preserved brush-talk manuscript by Miyajima. Another instructive example took place in the spring of 1884. Hayashi Gakusai 林學齋 (1833–1906), the twelfth-generation descendant of Confucian scholar Hayashi Razan 林羅山 (1583–1657) working under the Tokugawa shogunate, gave a banquet in honor of Qing China diplomat Huang Yinmei 黃吟梅 at his residence in the company of a Japanese monk called Kōgan 高岡. The banquet took place in a chamber. Since not a sound was heard from the chamber for a long while, the servants became concerned but were startled by what they beheld as they came close to the chamber: without uttering a sound, the trio were busy finger-drawing and writing on paper, punctuated by an appreciative smile when exchanging mutual gaze.[18] These lively descriptions of the three brush-talkers in action suggest that while they might be speechless, there was no shortage of emotionally-laden body language during their conversational interaction. While

---

17 '黎氏發言實爲至誠，書寫·敞邦明悉外邦情事之人不多·、·主上幼弱，大權不能自持·時，愁嘆溢于色，句句流滿肺腑，感動我心' (Miyajima Seiichirō, 22 July 1883, original in Japanese, Chinese translation by author and emphasis added).
18 '三人宛如啞人，時而以手摹畫，時而相視而笑，不停地在紙上塗寫'(Sanetō Keishū 1964: 11, original in Japanese, Chinese translation by author).

this point received explicit mention and portrayed vividly here, such fine details of nonverbal meaning-making would typically be ignored in other surviving brush-talk records.

Brush conversation: interactional features characteristic of writing

First and foremost, unlike other written outputs that were planned and edited before publication, brush conversation captured brush-talkers' spontaneous improvisation and left a verbatim record of their interaction when completed. Brush-talking usually took place in a private and restricted setting. In informal settings, with no prior knowledge nor time to consider whether their improvisation would eventually be made public, brush-talkers would usually 'speak their mind' by following their heart, showing little or no concern of the brushed content. In general, therefore, brush-talk manuscripts are faithful, unedited records of what actually transpired in writing-mediated conversation, be it morphographic sinograms or sketches intended for some aesthetic or practical purpose. It is in this sense that Sinitic brush-talk records were functionally akin to twentieth-century electronic recordings of speech, reproducing the original flavor of both the content and style of brush conversation, complete with other ecological marks that made Sinitic brush-talk possible in the first place, including paper, calligraphy, the hue of the ink, shift in fonts, highlighting and deletion, (attempted) correction and even unintended smearing. This is why the originality of both form and content is probably the defining characteristic of brush-talk literature in general.

Another correlate of free improvisation is that there is no limit to the semiotic resources that were at the disposal of individual brush-talkers. Block-shaped sinograms might be written horizontally or vertically, from left-to-right or right-to-left; sinograms might also be annotated with kana if so desired, supplemented with drawing if need be. Figure 8.1 shows an artifact produced during the brushed encounter between Ōkōchi and Guangdong painter Luo Xuegu 羅雪谷 (Wang 2016: vol. 4, p. 37). To facilitate pronunciation, Ōkōchi inserted phonographic Japanese kana アン on the right-hand side of the sinogram for 'nightingale' 鶯, and provided both the *on* and *kun* readings of the bisyllabic Chinese word 杜鵑 'cuckoo' in Japanese (*on*: トケン on the right; *kun*: ホトトキス on the left). This is one good illustration of the affordance and flexibility of brush-talking as a conventionalized practice of and productive site for transcultural meaning-making, be it intellectually or aesthetically oriented. Figure 8.2 is even more interesting, if somewhat provocative. Here the same brush-talking duo were manifestly engaged in a lively comparison of what may be termed 'toilet culture' 厠坑文化 in China versus in Japan. Without going into lengthy details, it does not take much imagination to conclude that Ōkōchi must be enormously proud when explaining how the four different toilet pit designs catered for specific needs of individual toilet-users. Apart from the rough sketch for differentiating the four different defecation needs – one each for urine, urgent, soft,

Lingua-cultural characteristics 211

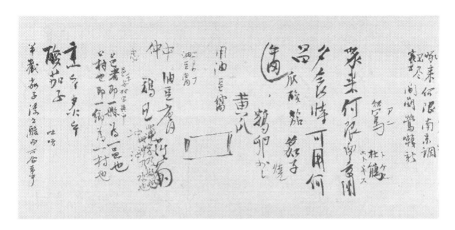

Figure 8.1 Ōkōchi Documents. Luó yuán tiě 羅源帖. vol. 4. p. 37.

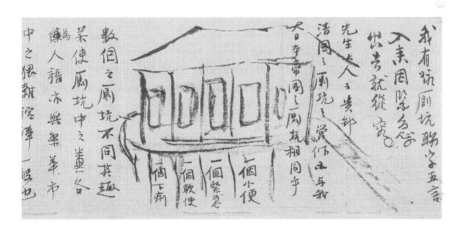

Figure 8.2 Ōkōchi Documents. Luó yuán tiě 羅源帖. vol. 8. p. 406.

and diarrhea,[19] Ōkōchi made reference to his own country as 'our Great Imperial Japan' 我大日本帝國.[20]

A further characteristic of writing-mediated Sinitic brush-talk is an exchange of poetic verses (cf. poetic brush-talk, 詩文筆談; compare: Li & Aoyama; Liu;

---

19 "一個小便，一個緊急，一個軟便，一個下痢".
20 Notice that in that same sentence and turn. out of politeness and etiquette. Ōkōchi referred to Luo's country as 'your esteemed Qing state' 貴邦清國. Another source of pride might be modern toilet management (separating diarrhea defecation for better sanitation and control of transmission of disease). This fine detail in Chinese-Japanese intercultural communication during the late Qing and Meiji era would have been lost without this brush-talk anecdote and illustrated artifact in Figure 8.2.

Nguyễn & Nguyễn; Wong, this volume). In Sinographic East Asia, whether their purpose of the meeting was official or unofficial, literati of Sinitic were often tempted to compose poetic verses using brush, ink, and paper to lend expression to their feelings (Clements, this volume). As this was usually reciprocated, typically following the same rhyme pattern if what was improvised was a poem. Such a ritual-like activity came to be called 筆談唱和 (Kor: *p'iltamch'anghwa*, 'brush-talk cum socializing chanting of poetic verses'; cf. 唱和: Mand: *chànghè*, Jap. *shōwa*, Kor. *ch'anghwa*; 'chanting'). In transcultural encounters, even though the brush-talkers had no shared vernacular, they could normally rely on the meanings of individual sinograms to make out what the poetic improvisation was about. What is interesting is that, at the receiving end, rather than the poetic work being recited in the composer's language (in which case intelligibility would be blocked), both phonetically and semantically the aesthetic content would usually be appreciated via the reader's own vernacular. This communication dynamic underlying writing-mediated, Sinitic-based brush conversation is characterized by Li (2020) as 'intersubjective' reading (see also Li & Aoyama, this volume). That comprehension and appreciation were possible via the visual-reading mode rather than auditory-acoustic mode may be explained by the morphographic nature of the Sinitic script: with very few exceptions most sinograms were morphemic units whose meanings were semantically rather stable in their respective incarnations in other East Asian languages during the premodern and early modern period.

Poetic brush-talk, of which exchange of poems was a sub-genre, was a common ritual-like activity at meetings between literati of Sinitic from different parts of East Asia. It might be embedded as part of a formal business-like brushed encounter (e.g., envoys' meeting with their hosts), or it might be the purpose of the brush-talk event unto itself (say, between friends). So common was the exchange of poems among literati of Sinitic that a special term *ch'anghwa* 唱和 was coined by Korean literati in reference to a body of literature (Zhang 2012: 335), as found in a few Korean monographs devoted to this poetic genre of brush-talk outputs. For example, a Sinitic brush-talk dataset collected during the official visits of Korean envoys (*t'ongsinsa* 通信使) to Japan entitled 筆談唱和 (*P'iltamch'anghwa*, in photocopies) was published by Yonsei University (Kim 2011; Hur 2011a, 2011b; Koo 2011; see also Jang; Koo & Joo, this volume).[21] The prominence of improvisation and exchange of poetry in early modern East Asia is also copiously attested in *Ōkōchi Documents*.

Spoken and written language are two modes of communication between humans. Provided it is shared by the interlocutors, spoken language is no doubt quicker and more convenient. Whereas words are lost as soon as they are uttered in speech, written language on a durable surface has the potential to transcend time and space. Based on the affordance of Sinitic brush-talk briefly discussed earlier, brush-talking is arguably far more than a simplistic substitute or surrogate

---

21 The term 筆談唱和 seemed to have been coined much later. See *Sōkanhitugo Shōwashū* 《桑韓筆語唱和集》 published in 1682 in Japan (accessible from Tokyo Metropolitan Library, 東京都立圖書館藏).

for speech; rather, what is conveyed through brush-talking not only complements but also extends the semiotic potential of the vernaculars of all the brush-talkers present. Holistically, therefore, the communicative effect of brush-talking is richer than that of speech or writing alone. Put differently, the affordance or semiotic potential of Sinitic brush-talk may be characterized as '1 + 1 ≥ 2'.

As for the genre and linguistic resources used by literati of Sinitic when engaged in brush conversation, Classical Chinese or Literary Sinitic (*wényán* 文言) was the most often used, which is lexico-grammatically different from vernacular-style writing (*báihuà* 白話). In China, vernacular writing used to be restricted to colloquial works such as novels and essays that were intended for popular consumption by a mass readership. After the Song (960–1279) and Yuan (1271–1368) dynasties, however, elements of vernacular writing began to find their way into some academically oriented works and even government documents. It was not until after the 1919 May Fourth New Culture Movement that vernacular writing became more and more widely accepted in Chinese society at the expense of Classical Chinese. Before the May Fourth Movement, as Japanese readers had limited access to the body of vernacular-based Chinese literature, naturally Literary Sinitic was their preferred choice when brush-talking,[22] albeit unavoidably showing the influence of their native Japanese sometimes, a style that was self-mockingly referred to as 和臭文言 or 'Japanese-flavored Sinitic' (literally 臭: 'stinking'). Following is one instructive extract of Sinitic brush-talk collected by Ōkōchi, who adopted the appellation Keikaku 桂閣 (Liu 2010: 190; Wang 2016: 2105–2106). The context was a banquet called 'Longevity banquet' (*Wanshouyan* 萬壽筵), which was also attended by Chinese scholars including Wang Zhiben 王治本 (appellation Qiyuan 黍園) and Wang Yinmei 王吟梅 (appellation 琴仙 Qinxian).

KK	擇其可適口者徐徐下箸，決勿促之。	Better choose what we like, and pick the food slowly with chopsticks, no rush.
QY	先下箸方知其適口。	We must pick and try the food first before we know whether we like it.
KK	此羹叫何？其中以何物制之？	This soup, <u>what is it called</u>? What is it made of?
QY	魚翅。	Shark fin.
KK	此酒叫何？以何物釀之？	<u>What is</u> this wine <u>called</u>? What material is used for brewing?
MS	紹興酒。	Shaoxing wine.
KK	此物<u>何的</u>?	This thing, <u>what is it</u>?
QX	鷄肫、杏仁、糯米。又クヘ、クヘト言フ[23]	Chicken gizzard, almond, sticky rice. (They all said to me: 'Eat! Eat!')
KK	弟以徐徐下箸爲好，意先試問其名與其製，而爲後<u>學</u>亦頗可。	My humble self had better pick food slowly, first to find out what the food is called and how it is prepared, and then <u>to learn</u> how to prepare it <u>later</u>.

(*Continued*)

22 Occasional use of vernacular elements from Chinese colloquial works cannot be ruled out.
23 In Chinese: 他們又對我說:"吃! 吃!"

214 *Wang Baoping*

QY	炒鶏。	Fried chicken.
KK	此物爲何？	This thing, <u>what is it</u>?
QX	海蜇，海中物。	Jelly fish, seafood.
	皆々にてサークへ、サーク へト言フ[24]	(They were all saying: 'Eat! Eat!')
KK	弟非饕餮之輩，徐徐下 箸，<u>決勿勞意</u>。	My humble self is no glutton, I will pick my food with chopsticks slowly, so please <u>do not be concerned</u>.

KK: Keikaku 桂閣 MS: Meishi 梅史 QX: Qinxian 琴仙 QY: Qiyuan 黍園
Source: *Ōkōchi Documents*, 10 Aug 1878, Wang (2016: 2105–2106); see also Liu (2010: 190)

Japanese-flavored Sinitic is discernible in a number of expressions (Table 8.1). A few collocations had no currency in Chinese (i–iii) and so they were probably incomprehensible to Chinese readers out of context. With concrete pragmatic details like speaker identities and purpose of interaction, however, any linguistic ambiguity arising would become clear in context. In the transcultural encounter featuring a banquet at the Chinese embassy in Meiji Japan exemplified earlier, the Chinese hosts had no problem understanding Ōkōchi's inquiries about Chinese food and wine (cf. 叫何, 何的, and 爲何 in Keikaku's questions), as reflected in their response. The same may be said of Ōkōchi's expression 決勿勞意 which, though a collocational oddity to Chinese eyes, was nevertheless interpretable by virtue of the literal meanings of each of the four morphographic, polysemous sinograms, which may be roughly glossed as 'definite-not-bother-intent' (i.e., 'do not be concerned').[25] Likewise, while the collocation 後學 normally means 'a junior scholar (late-comer in academia)' in Chinese, Ōkōchi used it for its literal meaning 'to learn later' and 'for future reference', which did not seem to occasion any misunderstanding to his hosts. There is yet another interesting interactional feature in this extract. Twice after responding to Ōkōchi's question, the Chinese

Table 8.1 Japanese-flavored Sinitic expressions and their corresponding meanings in Chinese

Japanese-flavored Sinitic expression	*Intended meaning in Japanese*	*Meaning in Chinese (if interpretable)*
i 叫何	what is it called?	call what?
ii 何的	what is it?	of what?
iii 決勿勞意	please do not be concerned	must not border you
iv 爲何	what is it?	why?/is what?
v 後學	to learn later	後進學者 'a junior scholar (late-comer in academia)'

24 In Chinese: 他們都異口同聲地說："吃! 吃!"
25 For this idiomatic meaning in Mandarin Chinese, one might say: 一定不要勞您費神 (*Yīdìng bù yào láo nín fèishén*).

hosts appeared to encourage him to try the unfamiliar food items: chicken gizzard, almond, sticky rice, and jellyfish. This point was noted twice within brackets (e.g., 皆々にてサークへ、サークへト言フ, 'They were all saying: "Eat! Eat!"'). As reference was made to 'everybody' (皆々), the bracketed words must have been inserted by the brush-talk manuscript collector after the event.

What about the genre and linguistic resources used by the Chinese brush-talkers? There is no doubt that both Classical Chinese and vernacular Chinese elements were at their disposal. The latter would rarely show up, however, given potential intelligibility problems to their Japanese counterparts, plus the fact that vernacular writing was no match in prestige to lexico-grammatical elements proper to the Classical canons and registers. This said, to minimize undue communication problems, while expressing themselves in Classical Chinese, Chinese brush-talkers would usually refrain from using obscure lexis or esoteric rhetorical elements like quadrisyllabic expressions 四字詞 embedded with allusions specific to Chinese history.

Coda

Sinitic brush-talk may be regarded as a cultural artifact of the Sinographic cosmopolis in early modern East Asia. Brush-talk 筆談, along with invitational preface or postscript (xùbá 序跋) for a monograph, exchange of poetic verses or socializing chanting 唱和, and epistolary correspondence 書信 together made up the most salient types of records arising from Chinese-Japanese transcultural interaction (Wang 2010). After the First Sino-Japanese War (1894–1895), following the gradual decline of Sinitic in a once vibrant Sinographic East Asia, such a confluence of sinogram-based, writing-mediated transcultural interaction in cross-border communication contexts has accomplished its historical mission. Like the exchange of poetic verses, brush-talk as a quintessential mode of communication between literati of Sinitic from different walks of life without a shared vernacular is now very much a thing of the past. Even though pen-talk is still practiced in the twenty-first century between literate users of Sinitic – Chinese and Japanese so to speak, it is much less common and contingent on both sides being eager to make meaning (see Chapter 1). In that huge repository of organically related *kanbun* data sources 漢文資料 bequeathed by Sinitic brush-talkers – a philological jewel in premodern and early modern East Asia, much remains to be discovered and investigated through careful research and fine-grained analysis, both in terms of the unique writing-mediated interactional patterns inherent to Sinitic-based brush conversation and the historically promising interdisciplinary substance they carry.

References

Clements, R. (2019). Brush talk as the 'lingua franca' of East Asian diplomacy in Japanese-Korean encounters, c. 1600–1868. *The Historical Journal* 62(2): 289–309.

Hur, K.-J. [許敬震] (Ed.). (2011a). 통신사 필담창화집 문학연구 (通信使筆談唱和集文學研究, 'A study in the literature of Chosŏn envoy's brush-talk and poetic exchange collections'). Seoul: Bogosa.

Hur, K.-J. [許敬震] (Ed.). (2011b). 통신사 필담창화집 문화연구 (通信使筆談唱和集文化研究, 'A study in the culture of Chosŏn envoy's brush-talk and poetic exchange collections'). Seoul: Bogosa.

Kim, H.-T. [金亨泰] (2011). 통신사 의학 관련 필담창화집 연구 (通信使醫學關聯筆談唱和集研究, 'A study in Chosŏn envoys' brush-talk and poetic exchange collections pertaining to medicine'). Seoul: Bogosa.

Koo, J.-H. [具智賢] (2011). 通信使筆談唱和集の世界 ('The world of Chosŏn envoys' brush-talk and poetic exchange collections'). Seoul: Bogosa.

Li, D. C. S. (2020). Writing-mediated interaction face-to-face: Sinitic brush-talk (漢文筆談) as an age-old lingua-cultural practice in premodern East Asian cross-border communication. *China and Asia* 2(2): 193–233.

Liu, Y. [劉雨珍] (Ed.). (2010). 清代首屆駐日公使館員筆談資料彙編 ('A collection of brush conversations by the staff of the first Qing Embassy to Japan'). Tianjin: Tianjin Renmin Press.

Lü, S. [呂叔湘] (1998). 語文常談 ('General Issues on language'). Peking: SDX Joint Publishing Co.

Miyajima, S. [宮島誠一郎] (1883). 養浩堂私記 ('Intimate notes of Yōkōdō') (vol. 5). Retrieved 23 April 2021 from https://dl.ndl.go.jp/info:ndljp/pid/11536065?tocOpened=1.

Nanpo, B. [南浦文之] (1971). 南浦文集 ('Nanpo collection of essays'). In 新薩藩叢書 (四), 鉄砲記 (Teppōki, 'The matchlock gun incident', vol. IV, Shin Satsuhan Series). Tokyo: Reikishi Toshosha.

Sanetō, K. [実藤恵秀] (Ed.). (1964). 大河内文書:明治日中文化人の交遊 ('Ōkōchi documents: Friendship between Japanese and Chinese intellectuals during the Meiji period'). Tokyo: Heibon Sha.

Toγtaγa (Ed.). (1977). 宋史 ('History of song'). Peking: Zhonghua Book Company.

Wang, B. [王寶平] (2004). 晚清東遊日記彙編・中日詩文交流集: 源輝聲《芝山一笑後序》('Compilation of Japan travelogues during late Qing: Collection of Sino-Japanese Interaction on Poetry and Essay: *Epilogue of Shizan Isshō* by Ōkōchi Teruna'). Shanghai: Shanghai Lexicographical Publishing House.

Wang, B. [王寶平] (2010). 日本典籍清人序跋集 ('A collection of forewords in Japanese scholarly works written by Qing Chinese literati'). Shanghai: Shanghai Lexicographical Publishing House.

Wang, B. [王寶平] (2014). 日藏黎庶昌與宮島誠一郎筆談記錄 ('Records of brush-talk between Li Shuchang and Miyajima Seiichirō'). *Wenxian* 文獻 6: 184–191.

Wang, B. [王寶平] (Ed.). (2016). 日本藏晚清中日朝筆談資料——大河內文書 ('Late Qīng brush-talk materials in Japan: Collection of brush conversations between Chinese, Japanese and Koreans in Ōkōchi documents'). Hangzhou: Zhejiang Ancient Books Publishing House.

Wang, X. [汪向榮] (1987). 一部中日文化交流史的寶貴資料——《黃遵憲與日本友人筆談遺稿》('Lecture on a valuable monograph on the Sino-Japanese history of cultural interaction: *Posthumous manuscript of brush-talk between Huang Zunxian and Japanese friends*'). January 15. Peking.

Zhang, B. [張伯偉] (2012). 域外漢籍研究入門 ('Introduction to research on foreign Sinitic literature'). Shanghai: Fudan University Press.

Zong, T. [宗廷虎] (Ed.). (1992). 鄭子瑜的學術研究和學術工作 ('Cheng Tsu-yu's academic research and academic endeavors'). Shanghai: Fudan University Press.

9 The charm and pitfalls of Sinitic brush-talk

A study of brush conversation records involving the first legation staff of Late Qing China in Japan (1870s–1880s)[1]

Liu Yuzhen

Introduction

Sinitic brush-talk (Mand: *bǐtán* 筆談, also called *bǐhuà* 筆話, *bǐyǔ* 筆語) refers to written communication using brush, ink, and paper in place of spoken language. It was one of the most commonly adopted modes of interpersonal communication between people from diverse language backgrounds within Sinographic East Asia since antiquity, synchronously and face-to-face. It was widely attested in different East Asian regions involving traveling literati of Sinitic, bringing them into contact with other East Asian brush-talkers, including government envoys, scholars, monks, literati well-versed in Sinitic, merchants, boat drifters, missionaries, etc. In spatial terms, core to the polities within Sinographic East Asia were territories covered by today's China, Japan (including Okinawa, formerly the Ryukyu kingdom), North Korea and South Korea (Chosŏn), and Vietnam (Annam). Without a doubt, Sinitic brush-talk was one of the most widely practiced modes of cross-border communication in premodern and early modern East Asia. In recent years, Ge Zhaoguang 葛兆光 2018 advocates 'seeing China from the peripheries' 從周邊看中國. Brush-talk materials represent a veritable treasure house providing a rich data source in support of burgeoning research in this regard (see, e.g., Ihara 2003).

In the two volumes of 清代首屆公使館員筆談資料彙編 ('A collection of brush-talks by the staff of the first Qīng Embassy to Japan') compiled by the author (Liu 2010), six brush-talk data sources are covered.[2] The brush-talkers

---

[1] The research carried out in this chapter was entirely supported by China's 'Major Projects of the National Social Science Fund' 國家社科基金重大項目 (project title: 'Sinitic brush-talk in Sinographic East Asia: Historiography and research' 東亞筆談文獻整理與研究, project no. 14ZDB070).

[2] (i) Brush-talk with 大河內輝聲 Ōkōchi Teruna and others; (ii) with 宮島誠一郎 Miyajima Seiichirō and others; (iii) with 芝山一笑 Shizan Isshō; (iv) with 岡千仞 Oka Senjin and others; (v) with 增田貢 Masuda Mitsugu; and (vi) with Chosŏn (Korean) envoys to Japan.

DOI: 10.4324/9781003048176-11

involved were envoys, scholar-officials, and literati well-versed in Sinitic from China, Japan, and Chosŏn who had received a solid foundation in Sinitic-based education since their childhood. Thus, they were familiar with literary classics from China and were able to express themselves freely using Sinitic, the scripta franca (Denecke 2014) within the Sinographic cosmopolis (Koh & King 2014) to compensate for the lack of a shared spoken language. After getting acquainted through brush-talking, the brush-talkers would often engage in literary improvisation and poetic exchange in part to deepen their emotional bond, a writing-mediated pattern of social interaction with *sui generis* charm so specific to Sinitic brush-talk 漢文筆談. On the other hand, compared with speech-based interaction, the written artifacts generated in the process of brush-talking would make excellent materials for those whose ulterior motive was to probe or gather secret intelligence for the purpose of espionage. This is how, as a conventional cross-border communication practice, brush conversation in Sinitic was sometimes exploited and became a diplomatic pitfall for those who were caught off guard and less vigilant. This chapter discusses and exemplifies the charm and pitfall associated with Sinitic brush-talk with the help of surviving records of brush-talk involving the first embassy staff of Qing China in Japan during the 1870s and 1880s.

The first Qing legation to Japan: historical background

Being neighbors separated by the Sea of Japan and East China Sea, China and Japan have had a history of intercultural exchange for well over one thousand and five hundred years. The onset of their formal diplomatic relations in the early modern period can be traced to the signing of the 'Sino-Japanese Friendship and Trade Treaty' 中日修好條規 in 1871. There were altogether 18 articles, of which two of the most important are Articles One and Six (Wang 1957: 317–319):

第一條: 嗣後大清國、大日本國倍敦和誼，與天壤無窮。即兩國所屬邦土，亦各以禮相待，不可稍有侵越，俾獲永久安全。

Article One: Hereinafter, the harmony and amity between the Great Qing and the Great Japan will be doubly enhanced, eternally and boundlessly. Within the territories of both nations, they should treat each other with due respect and should not undertake the slightest act of territorial infringement in order that safety be secured in permanence.

第六條: 嗣後兩國往來公文，中國用漢文，日本國用日本文，須副以譯漢文，或只用漢文，亦從其便。(《同治條約》卷二十)

Article Six: Hereinafter, for official diplomatic documents exchanged between the two nations, China will use Classical Chinese while Japan will use Japanese, the latter to be accompanied by a translation in Classical

Chinese. Japanese documents may also be written in Classical Chinese only, if deemed more convenient.

(Scroll 20, Tongzhi Treaty; see National Archives of Japan 2021 for the Japanese version)[3]

Article One stipulates mutual non-aggression of sovereign and dependent territories. This article was highly relevant in subsequent Sino-Japanese negotiations on Ryukyu's political status as a tributary state, which was frequently cited by first Ambassador He Ruzhang 何如璋, Vice-Envoy Huang Zunxian 黃遵憲 and other Qing embassy staff. Article Six defines the use of Classical Chinese or Sinitic (漢文, Mand.: *hanwen*; Jap.: *kanbun*) in bilateral diplomatic communication, which has profound historical influence and significant political and cultural implications for Sino-Japanese diplomatic relations.

On 30 November 1877, the first Qing legation to Japan led by Ambassador He Ruzhang 何如璋 (1838–1891), Vice-Envoy Zhang Sigui 張斯桂 (1817–1888), and Counsellor Huang Zunxian 黃遵憲 (1848–1905) arrived at Nagasaki. They reached Yokohama on December 16 and stayed at a residence arranged by the Japanese Ministry of Foreign Affairs. Then on December 28, through the Foreign Minister and officials of the Ministry of the Imperial Household, the trio presented the Qing government's letter of credence to the Meiji Emperor. This was followed by a formal meeting with senior officials and consultants of the Meiji Great Council of State, including Sanjō Sanetomi 三條實美 (1837–1891), Iwakura Tomomi 岩倉具視 (1825–1883), and Ōkubo Toshimichi 大久保利通 (1830–1878) before returning to Yokohama that evening (He 2010: 76).

On 15 January 1878, Huang Zunxian rented Gekkaiin 月界院 at Zōjō-ji 増上寺 of Shibayama 芝山 in Tokyo as the location of the Chinese embassy. Despite the serenity and beautiful surroundings, a lack of space eventually made it necessary for the embassy to move to the former site of Peers' Club (Kazoku Kaikan 華族會館) at Nagatachō 永田町 ten months later. Most of the brush-talk events involving the legation staff and their Japanese friends took place at these two sites.

Although Ambassador He had appointed a Japanese translator, Ōga Kakutai 鉅鹿赫泰 (1860–1933, Chinese name Wei Limen, variously written as 魏梨門 or 魏鯉門), as a member of the Qing legation before departing for Japan from Tianjin, the first Chinese legation faced a perennial handicap, namely the translation workforce was seriously understaffed and inadequate relative to the huge demand for translation and interpretation tasks (Wang 2007; Yan 2009: 187–241). This helps explain why, in routine encounters between the legation

---

3 JACAR (Japan Center for Asian Historical Records). '大日本国大清国修好条規、通商章程、及両国海関税則 (C1)'. 外務省外交史料館 (Diplomatic Archives of the Ministry of Foreign Affairs of Japan). Ref. B13090891200. Retrieved March 30, 2021. from www.jacar.archives.go.jp/aj/meta/image_B13090891200.

staff and Japanese visitors, speech-based interaction was often not an option and that writing-mediated brush-talk was looked upon as the unmarked mode of face-to-face communication.

The arrival of the first Chinese embassy during the early Meiji period created excitement among Japanese Sinologists as well as elites who were well versed in Chinese literary classics. They were enthusiastically embraced, as shown in the epilogue of Huang Zunxian's 'Poems on miscellaneous subjects from Japan' 日本雜事詩, where the Sinologist scholar Ishikawa Kōsai 石川鴻齋 (1833–1918) was quoted as saying:

> 入境以來，執經者、問字者、乞詩者，戶外履滿，肩趾相接，果人人得其意而去。
>
> Ever since the Chinese embassy arrived, [Japanese] people kept queuing up outside. Some sought advice or clarification on Chinese classics/canons; still others entreated improvisation of poetic verses as a gift. There were so many people waiting outside [the embassy] that hardly any space was left between their toes and shoulders. Eventually everyone would leave with deep satisfaction.
>
> (Chen 2005: 793)

There was indeed no shortage of eager visitors at the Chinese embassy. Embassy staff like He Ruzhang, Zhang Sigui, and Huang Zunxian had to spare time beyond their routine duties meeting their Japanese acquaintances frequently and interacting with them through brush-talk. In terms of topics, there seemed no bounds to what could be invoked during their brush conversation, from the far-flung universe to our mundane world, from metrical patterns of poetry composition to ancient laws and regulations, not to mention languages and how they are written as well as customs and rites unique to specific ethnic groups. Taken together, the surviving brush-talk records involving Chinese embassy staff suggest that it was a most pleasant experience for the hosts and guests alike. In metaphorical terms, such records may be likened to a magnificent, awe-inspiring scroll painting where the prologue of formal Sino-Japanese diplomatic relations and intercultural exchange during the early modern period was unveiled.

Since the diplomats dispatched by the Qing government to Japan were mostly scholar-officials who were well versed in literary and poetic composition, the poetic improvisation and socializing chanting 漢詩酬唱 produced during their brush-talk interaction with Japanese elites was often an indispensable part of their light-hearted encounters and merry-making exchange. In the following, I will first focus on three separate brush-talk events to illustrate the charm that emanates from writing-mediated poetic improvisation by literati well-versed in Literary Sinitic from Qing China, Japan but also Chosŏn, before discussing and exemplifying how brush conversation was abused for collecting secret intelligence at the state level.

Enjoying magnificent scenes of blossoming flowers overseas for the first time (16 April 1878)

The Japanese Sinologist Ōkōchi Teruna 大河內輝聲 (1848–1882) visited the embassy for the first time on 25 February 1878 and had wonderful brush conversations with Ambassador He and Vice-Envoy Zhang. Since that day, Ōkōchi frequented the embassy almost every day. Notwithstanding piercing winds, heavy downpours, or other adverse weather conditions, the single-minded Ōkōchi would remain undeterred because he enjoyed the company of his Chinese friends so much. By April the same year, Ōkōchi started planning to organize for them a spring outing to enjoy the magnificent scenes of cherry blossoms.

Ōkōchi Teruna, a daimyo of the Takasaki domain 高崎藩 (south of Gunma Prefecture 群馬県 today) during the late Tokugawa shogunate, was re-appointed as a domain governor 藩知事 in 1869 at the beginning of the Meiji era. After the abolition of the daimyo system in 1871, he retained his exalted lineage 華族 identity. When interacting with Chinese people who were well-versed in literary writing, Ōkōchi would indicate that writing-mediated brush conversation was what he would prefer, even though his Chinese interlocutor(s) might speak some Japanese or be accompanied by an interpreter. His primary purpose was to collect 'inked treasure' 墨寶 from them, so that he could compile them neatly into bounded volumes for safe keeping on one hand, and for perpetual remembrance by the Ōkōchi family's posterity on the other (Sanetō 1961).

The invitational outing organized by Ōkōchi took place on 16 April 1878. It was well attended by Chinese embassy staff including He, Zhang and Huang, but also two Chinese literary writers living in Japan, the Wang brothers: Wang Zhiben 王治本 (1835–1908) and Wang Fanqing 王藩清 (1847–1898). They were joined by their Japanese friends Katō Ōrō 加藤櫻老 (1811–1884), Uchimura Suisho 内村綏所 (1833–1907), among others. Their destination was Mukōjima Island 向島 along the Sumidagawa River 隅田川, a highly popular spot in Tokyo for enjoying magnificent views of cherry blossoms and commonly referred to poetically by the Chinese guests as Mochuan 墨川. Amidst their feasting, drinking and appreciation of breathtaking scenes of blossoming flowers, the brush-talkers enlivened the conviviality by improvisation and exchange of Sinitic poetry (漢詩, Mand. *hanshi*, Jap. *kanshi*), including the three senior Chinese embassy staff, and of course Ōkōchi himself.

The planned outing had been inconvenienced by the rain in the preceding days. On April 16, however, bright sunny weather and fresh air finally took over, projecting the cherry blossoms of the season in full bloom. Thanks to Ōkōchi, it was such a wonderful time of the year to visit Mukōjima Island, which was crowded with visitors. Katō Ōrō played several tunes of Japanese court music 雅樂 for the Chinese guests with the instruments he brought with him, including *sheng*[4] and flageolet.[5] This triggered commendation by Huang Zunxian (Liu 2010: 71):

殊使人飄飄有淩雲氣

the music charmed all [of us], making [us] mellow as if [we were] hovering in the sky

Thereupon Ōkōchi invited Ambassador He and Vice-Envoy Zhang to grace the joyous occasion with poetic verses. He Ruzhang showed his flair and brushed a poem:

十里春風爛漫開	Cherry blooms in full bloom dot the long dike in spring breeze,
墨川東岸雪成堆	Petals tower the eastern bank of Mochuan like snow hills.
當筵莫惜詩兼酒	Spare no effort composing poems while feasting and relishing *sake*,
如此花時我正來	Amidst such splendid flowers I come by happenstance.

The first two verses depict Mochuan 墨川 (i.e., Sumidagawa River 隅田川), the long dike on the eastern bank, boundless clusters of cherry blossoms in full bloom, and powder-like cherry petals piling up like snowdrifts. The third and fourth verses express the delight of improvising poetry and sipping *sake* while enjoying the wonderful scenes of cherry blossoms in good company. In response, Ōkōchi composed a poem following the same rhyme (Liu 2010: 74):

絕勝西園雅會開	The *Elegant Gathering at Western Garden* was no match for our outing,
春花爛漫似雪堆	Falling spring flower petals pile up like snowdrifts.
櫻桃休作桃源想	Make no mistake, cherry blossoms are no *Peach Blossom Spring*,
為賦淵明歸去來	Reminiscent of *Come Away Home* by Tao Yuanming.

The first verse alludes to the *Elegant Gathering in the Western Garden* involving the Chinese literary figures Su Dongpo 蘇東坡 (1037–1101), Huang Tingjian 黃庭堅 (1045–1105), and Qin Guan 秦觀 (1049–1100) of the Northern Song dynasty, and asserts that it was absolutely no match for the breathtaking scenes of cherry blossoms and the ambience of the outing on that day. The second verse echoes the first two verses by Ambassador He by comparing massive falling cherry petals to powdery snowflakes. The last two verses are clear allusions to *The Peach Blossom Spring* 桃花源記 and *Come Away Home* 歸去來辭 by the celebrated Jin

---

4 笙, a free reed mouth organ, with wooden pipes stuck into a gourd; a small gourd-shaped musical instrument with 13 reeds, Jap: *shō*.
5 篳篥, a cylindrical double reed wind instrument used to perform ritual music in the court of imperial China since ancient times, Jap: *hichiriki*, Mand: *bìlì*.

dynasty poet Tao Yuanming 陶淵明 (365–427). These allusions attest to Ōkōchi's solid foundation in Classical Chinese literature as well as his erudite knowledge of China's deep-rooted cultural heritage.

Then, on the jovial remark written by Vice-Envoy Zhang 酒地花天，興高釆烈 ('a great time indulging in fine booze, truly ecstatic and overjoyed'), Ambassador He drew a small circle next to the character 高 (*gao*), hinting to the others that the 'ao' rhyme should be followed in subsequent poems. Thereupon Chinese and Japanese poets embarked on a new round of *hanshi* improvisation and exchange.

Vice-Envoy Zhang took the lead and brushed the following poem:

春風花事醉櫻桃	Feeling mellow viewing cherry blossoms in spring breeze.
人影衣香快此遭	Viewers' attire adds fragrance to my ecstasy.
歸去欲攜花作伴	Tempted to bring some flowers with me home.
折枝不怕樹頭高	No fears breaking branches while mounting those trees.

This poem depicts a tipsy feeling while reveling and enjoying the scenes of massive cherry blossoms in full bloom amidst spring breeze, with the third verse 歸去欲攜花作伴 ingeniously echoing Ōkōchi's clever use of 歸去來, an unmistakable allusion to Tao Yuanming's *Come Away Home*. Ambassador He then carried on and improvised another heptasyllabic quatrain as follows:

飛觴不惜醉蒲桃	Toasting *sake* under cherry blossoms till drunk.
海外看花第一遭	Beholding flowers the first time ever away from motherland.
有客正吹花下笛	There goes a piper playing his flute under the tree.
陽春一曲調尤高	Simple enchanting tunes echo our high spirits.

The second verse marks the poet's delightful feeling viewing spring flowers for the first time in Japan, a beautiful and memorable anecdote in the history of Sino-Japanese cultural exchange indeed. The last two verses are a tribute to the ritual music performed by Katō Ōrō. Huang Zunxian followed suit:

長堤十里看櫻桃	Viewing cherry blossoms on a long dike.
裙屐風流此一遭	Elegantly unbridled like the rich for once.
莫說少年行樂事	Don't say indulgence is the privilege of the young.
登樓老子興尤高	What a delight for old folks to trot up here high.

The first two verses echo those by He and Zhang, highlighting the joy of beholding flowers on a long dike for the first time, which is reminiscent of similar events involving literary talents of the Wei-Jin period (220–420). The last two make reference to the jubilance of He and Zhang and other Chinese guests, who did not mind trotting upstairs despite their age just to gain a better view of the breathtaking flower scenes. It was Ōkōchi who volunteered the finale in this round, keeping to the same rhyming scheme (Liu 2010: 74):

墨堤十里放鶯桃	The long Mochuan is dotted with cherry blossoms,
詩酒來遊快此遭	Such a charming outing composing poems while relishing *sake*.
博得華筵才子賦	Admiring literary talents' poetry amidst a lavish meal,
洛陽紙價一時高	Drives the Luoyang paper price up high.

In the bound volume compiled by Ōkōchi, he added a personal note after the first verse '月令注以鶯鳥所含，故名' (In *Explanatory notes* 釋文 of 'Proceedings of Government in the Different Months, The Classic of Rites' 禮記·月令, Lu Deming 陸德明 (550–630) explained the inspiration for the allusion to 鶯桃 as follows: in Chinese, *yingtao* 櫻桃 'cherry blossom' is also called *yingtao* 鶯桃 'oriole-cherry', because orioles are fond of holding cherries by the mouth).[6]

The last two verses make reference to paper price being pushed up in Luoyang (洛陽紙貴), an allusion to the immense popularity of 'Poetic essays on the two capitals' 二京賦 by Zhang Heng 張衡 (78–139), suggesting the high quality of the poetic works produced by the Chinese guests. The rhyme of the first, second and fourth verses in subsequent poems must adhere to the same rhyming scheme initiated by Vice-Envoy Zhang Sigui, namely *táo* 桃, *zāo* 遭 and *gāo* 高, plus Ōkōchi's ingenuity in selecting characters bearing the same rhyme that are embedded in traditional Chinese allusions. All this demonstrates the profundity of Ōkōchi's impressive self-cultivated knowledge in Sinology.

The poems arising from such a flower-viewing outing and experience were later recorded respectively in Huang Zunxian's *Poems on Miscellaneous Subjects from Japan* 日本雜事詩 (poem numbers 122 and 123) and 'Ode to Cherry Blossoms' 櫻花歌. That event also received a mention in a letter written by Huang to Miyajima Seiichirō dated 10 January 1891 during his subsequent tenure as Counsellor at the Chinese embassy in Britain. In that letter, Huang gave a sentimental outpouring of his reminiscence, how much he thoroughly enjoyed visiting places of historical significance in Japan, in particular that memorable day when he, accompanied by like-minded literary talents, was able to contemplate cherry blossoms along the Mojiang up close, sipping fine *sake* in the midst of collective poetic exchange and chanting of *hanshi*. All this attests to the deep impression that such a flower-viewing outing had left the participating embassy staff.

---

6 《禮記·月令》:「是月也，天子乃以雛嘗黍，羞以含桃，先薦寢廟」 'in this month the son of Heaven partakes of it along with pullets, and with cherries set forth beside them, first offering a portion in the apartment behind the ancestral temple' (trans. James Legge 1885: 274). According to the *Explanatory notes* 釋文 by Lu Deming:「含，亦作函。一說鶯鳥所含，故亦名鶯桃。」 (Zhang & Chen 1716/2005: 178, see also https://kangxizidian.com/v1/index.php?page=178).

Enjoying poetic exchange with kindred spirits under the same roof (14 June 1878)

Miyajima Seiichirō 宮島誠一郎 (1838–1911), appellation 養浩堂 Yōkōdō, was a samurai of the Yonezawa domain 米澤藩 (south of the Yamagata Prefecture 山形県 today) during the late Tokugawa shogunate. Educated and trained in Sinology from a very young age, he was precocious and his gifted learning abilities were widely recognized. After serving as a teaching assistant at the Kōjōukan 興讓館, a training school for samurais, he was dispatched by the Yonezawa domain as an agent to collect intelligence in Edo and Kyōto. During the Boshin War (戊辰戰爭, 1868–1869), he sought to unite the northeastern domains indefatigably to form an alliance.

During the Meiji period, he had served in the legislature 左院, Office of Historical Documentation 修史館, Imperial Household Agency 宮内省, Office of the Exalted Lineage 華族局, and Office of Peerage 爵位局. In 1896, he was appointed by the Imperial Court as a member of the House of Lords 貴族院議員. Among the works he authored were 'Prelude to the Compilation of the National Constitution' 國憲編纂起原 and 'Yōkōdō Collection of Poems' 養浩堂詩集. Based on available brush-talk records, Miyajima visited the Chinese embassy located at Gekkaiin 月界院 at Shibayama 芝山 for the first time on 15 February 1878 and was engaged in lengthy brush conversation with Ambassador He and Vice-Envoy Zhang. His first encounter with Huang Zunxian took place on April 19. They were instantly attracted by each other's intellectual charm and regretted not having met earlier. Such sentiments intensified after the relocation of the Chinese embassy to Peers' Club in November of that year. Miyajima's home being just a street away, brush conversations between them were held more frequently.

On 14 June 1878, Miyajima invited several Chinese embassy staff including He, Zhang and Huang to a banquet at his residence. Also invited were Japanese acquaintances, all Sinologists, including Shigeno Seisai 重野成齋 (1827–1910) and Aoyama Nobutoshi 青山延壽 (1820–1906). While feasting, Shigeno, Aoyama, and other Japanese guests exchanged views with Huang on various daily necessities from tobacco and oyster sauce to seaweed (kelp) and shark's fin. This led Shigeno to write:

> 魚翅得他物成味，可知人亦藉交遊成德，所謂以友人輔德。異邦殊域，握手交歡，見其所未見，聞其所未聞，洵人生之幸福也。

> It takes other ingredients for shark's fin to become tasty. Likewise, the shaping of virtue and moral character hinges on our interaction with friends. This is what we mean by developing virtue and morality through acquaintances. In a foreign country and alien territory, [we] shake hands to signal friendship, see things never encountered or unheard of, what a blessing and enchanting thing in life.

In this brush-talk excerpt, a strong sense of camaraderie and communion is in evidence, while their intellectual exchange exudes wisdom characteristic of Daoism.

This prompted Huang Zunxian to comment that:

由小物悟入交遊，足仰大德，其所云之，僕亦同之。敢謝厚意，並志私喜。

From the minutiae, [you] derive insights on the cultivation of friendship, [your] great virtue is truly admirable. That which [you are] alluding to, I abide by, too. [May I] thank you for your deep affection, and express [my] personal delight.

(Liu 2010: 452)

Thereupon Miyajima composed a heptasyllabic quatrain in response:

縱有靈犀一點通	Though our hearts are linked up as one,
舌難傳語意何窮	Our tongues can't convey our thoughts, are our meanings ever lost?
交情猶幸淡如水	Luckily our relations are tasteless like water,
滿室德熏君子風	This space is filled with virtuous scent and gentlemanly allure.

The aforementioned poems figured in the original brush-talk record. The first two verses allude to 心有靈犀一點通[7] in a poem 'No Title' 無題 by Tang poet Li Shangyin 李商隱 (813–858). Notwithstanding intellectual communion in Chinese-Japanese interaction that was made possible by brush-talking in Sinitic, one can sense a concern for a lack of a shared spoken language, which somehow made it difficult for both sides to speak their mind incisively and comprehensively.

The third and fourth verses contain a reference to 君子之交淡若水 ('the intercourse of superior men is tasteless like water'; source: 'The Tree on the Mountain', Zhuangzi 莊子·山木, *trans.* James Legge 1891: 35), commending that the brush-talkers present were all morally erect and manifestly modest, self-disciplined gentlemen.[8]

In response, Huang Zunxian reciprocated with yet another poem following the same rhyming scheme:

---

7 The relevant verses of the Tang poem by Li Shangyin reads as follows: 身無彩鳳雙飛翼 心有靈犀一點通, 'A phoenix's wings we lacked to fly as a pair, but linked were our hearts by the rhino horn's magical might'. Gloss: 'Legend has it that the horn of a rhinoceros has telepathic powers, being so sensitive that its tip is capable of transmitting information to one's brain instantly.' (Adapted from: https://en.wiktionary.org/wiki/心有靈犀一點通, retrieved February 28, 2021).
8 When subsequently copying and editing the manuscripts for publication, Miyajima replaced 縱有 ('although') in the first verse with 自有 ('given'), and similarly replaced 淡如水 ('tasteless like water') in the third verse with 深如海 ('ocean-deep'). This generated quite a lot of problems for researchers in the process of compiling and proofreading brush-talk materials (Liu 2010: 452–453).

舌難傳語筆新通	Our tongue can hardly convey our thoughts, but an innovative brush can take its place.
筆舌瀾翻意未窮	Brush-talking non-stop in no way exhausts our meanings.
不作佉盧蟹行字	Forget about crab-walk Kharoṣṭhī words written horizontally.
一堂酬唱喜同風	Enjoy poetic exchange with kindred spirits under the same roof.

The first two verses are clearly conceived as a response to Miyajima's observation, but with a twist: while oral communication through speech is not an option in social interaction between Chinese and Japanese literati of Sinitic, neither intellectual exchange nor the development of friendship is hindered thanks to their shared convention of and ability to conduct brush conversation. The third verse invokes an old written language in ancient India called Kharoṣṭhī (qūlú 佉盧), which is written horizontally from right to left. Here, 佉盧蟹行字 ('crab-walk Kharoṣṭhī words') refers metaphorically to languages that are similarly written horizontally in Europe and America. Their written forms are in stark contrast with Sinitic, which is written with sinogram-based characters that were widely used within Sinographic East Asia, whereby literati could 'speak their mind' through brush-talk, including the possibility of engaging in poetic improvisation and exchange blithely with fellow kindred spirits under the same roof.

Finally, Ambassador He Ruzhang ended the poetic exchange with the following heptasyllabic quatrain (Liu 2010: 453):

何須機電翻神通	Why rely on electrical devices to do magic?
寸管同摻用不窮	Brush barrels are short and thin, but what is written is easy to keep.
卷則退藏彌六合	When rolled up, paper and brush lie hidden and inconspicuous; unrolled, they fill the universe;
好揚聖教被殊風	Let the teachings of the sages be spread and vindicated.

Along with this poem is a note that says:

近西人有電器，名德律風，足以傳語，故以此為戲

recently westerners came up with an electrical device called telephone, enabling (people to) talk remotely, hence the playful allusion to that device.

The first two verses applaud the function of brush-talk as a means of conversational exchange, which is far better than the telephone, in that the brushed content can be kept conveniently, making it rather easy to spread the teachings of the sages. While invoking a recently invented modern device like the telephone in poetic improvisation helps extend the stock of traditional imageries, the last verse sounds somewhat pedantic, which is why judging from the points of view of aesthetic and artistic values in poetry writing, Ambassador He's poetic improvisation seems no match for that of Counsellor Huang Zunxian.

Conducting brush conversation and conveying personal feelings through poetic exchange in Sinitic appears to be a unique mode of communication between literati who were well-versed in literary classics and sinogram-based literature, which seems unparalleled in other cultures beyond Sinographic East Asia. As Huang puts it so well, the quintessential function and exquisite value of Sinitic brush-talk lies in 'enjoying poetic exchange with kindred spirits under the same roof' (一堂酬唱喜同風).

Brush-talking on paper is like flying over clouds; music produced from *sheng* makes the rain boiled (29 August 1880)

On 29 August 1880, the Japanese Ambassador to Chosŏn, Hanabusa Yoshimoto 花房義質 (1842–1917) invited not only three visiting Chosŏn envoys to Tokyo, Kim Koeng-chip 金宏集 (1842–1896),[9] Yi Cho-yŏn 李祖淵 (1843–1884), and Kang Wi 姜瑋 (1820–1884), but also He Ruzhang and Huang Zunxian to meet at the Ai'i Villa 曖依村莊 of Shibusawa Eiichi 渋沢栄一 (1840–1931) at Asukayama Mountain 飛鳥山 in Tokyo. At the end of the 1880 mission, Kim took with him a copy of 'Chosŏn Strategy' 朝鮮策略 by Huang Zunxian back home, and emerged as one of the active advocates of the enlightenment movement in Chosŏn 朝鮮開化運動. He was later appointed as Second State Councillor 左議政 and served as Prime minister three times. Among the political initiatives that he tried to push forward were reform of the bureaucratic system 官制改革, abolition of the civil service examination 科舉, and the cutting of the male's braid 斷髮令. In 1896 he died during a coup and was granted the posthumous title of Ch'ung-hŏn 忠獻.

In August 1880, Kim was appointed by the Counsel 禮曹 of the Chosŏn Ministry of Rites as one of the 58 envoys to Japan, many of which made significant contributions to the subsequent enlightenment movement in Chosŏn. The delegation arrived in Tokyo on August 11 where they stayed for about a month before heading back to Chosŏn on September 8, reaching Pusan on September 15. While in Japan, Kim had six rounds of brush conversations with He Ruzhang and Huang Zunxian. To make up for what could not be adequately conveyed through brush-talk, Ambassador He instructed Huang Zunxian to write up a policy document, *Chosŏn Strategy*, as a departure gift for Kim.

According to the brush-talk records as stated in the 'Miyajima Documents' 宮島文書, on August 29, 'the literary talents well-versed in Sinitic from the three nations drank jubilantly and wielded their writing brush generously, meeting up at noon and breaking up late at night' (三國文士，歡飲揮毫，正午來會，到晚始散), suggesting what a lively, intellectually fruitful and pleasurable event it must have been. Miyajima told Kim about his expectation that the unusual meeting

---

9 Kim Koeng-chip, originally named Kim Hong-chip 金弘集, changed his name out of taboo because the first syllable of his bisyllabic given name 弘 coincided with the counterpart of the Qing Emperor Gaozong Hongli 清高宗弘曆 (1711–1799), who reigned from 1735 to 1796.

involving the literary talents of the three Sinographic nations would mark the beginning of a prosperous Asia:

> 今日之會，係三國集一堂，曠古所稀，是為興亞之始。

> Our meeting today, with virtuous and able men from three nations converging at one spot, is rare and unprecedented. This augurs the onset of a prosperous Asia.

In February 1880, Miyajima and Sone Toshitora 曾根俊虎 (1847–1910) championed the formation of the Association of Asian Revival (Kōa-kai 興亞會); their names, along with that of the Qing Ambassador He Ruzhang, were included in the list of supporters. During the brush-talk with Kim, Miyajima recalled accompanying Kim on their visit to the Asakusa Library (Asakusa Bunko 淺草文庫) during their first encounter, and reiterated his expectation and wish that amicable relations between the three Sinographic nations would be sustainable and long-lasting:

> 一昨日始拜道范，不堪欣喜。又得陪觀淺草文庫，庫中書籍紛雜，不便縱觀，想應心悶。今日天晴，遠路幸蒙枉顧。是為交歡之始。自今以後永好，謀三國之益，不堪渴望。

> I am very pleased to have visited you for the first time the day before. You also accompanied me to visit the Asakusa Library. The books there are messy; reading there is not so convenient. You might have found it irksome. Today is sunny. You have come a long way to visit me, a good start of our friendship. Hitherto let us keep up our friendship forever. To further the interests of our three countries is my deepest wish.

At this point, Ambassador He wrote:

> 栗香先生深重同洲之誼，所慮深且遠。今日之會，素非偶然。

> Mr Kurika [Miyajima] cares so much about friendship between confreres from the same continent [Asia]. Your concerns are deep and far-reaching. Our meeting today is by no means unplanned.

There is thus evidence that the meeting was thoughtfully arranged by Miyajima out of his wish for fostering friendly relations between China, Japan and Chosŏn. To this remark by Ambassador He, Miyajima responded thus:

> 僕自何公使之東來，相交尤厚且久矣。其意專在聯絡三大國，而興起亞洲。今先生之來，若同此志，則可謂快極。

> Since Ambassador He made your east-bound journey to Japan, [you and] I have established deep and long-lasting amicable relations. The goal is to connect the three nations in order to make Asia prosper. Now that Ambassador He is here, [I] would be hugely gratified if [we are all] like-minded in pursuit of this goal.

From this thread of brush-talk interaction, Miyajima's sincerity and eagerness is clearly evidenced by his reiteration of the importance of connecting the three East Asian nations as a stepping-stone towards propelling Asia to prosperity. At this memorable juncture amidst the joyous encounter and unfettered intellectual exchange between the literary talents from China, Japan, and Chosŏn, Huang Zunxian, getting mellow after several rounds of *sake*, improvised the following poem:

滿堂賓客 三國之產	This place is filled with guests from three countries.
更無一人 紅髯碧眼	None has red hair and green eyes.
紙筆雲飛 笙歌雨沸	Brush-wielding on paper is like flying in the clouds, *sheng* music makes the rain boiled.
皆我亞洲 自為風氣	Such a practice is unparalleled, unique to us Asia.
人生難得 對酒當歌	Chanting and savoring spirits, such moments are rare in life.
今我不樂 復當如何	If not rejoicing at this moment, what else are we to do?
縱橫戰國 此樂難得	Warring states are everywhere, rare is such pleasure.
奚怪有人 閉關謝客	Who can blame us when doors are closed and guests turned away?

In this poem, reference is made to a famous verse from *A Short Song* 短歌行 by Cao Cao 曹操 (155–220): 'I lift my drink and sing a song, for who knows if life is short or long?' 對酒當歌 人生幾何, reflecting the poet's intense exhilaration occasioned by the convivial sharing between the literary talents from the three countries. At the same time, through 'red hair and green eyes' 紅髯碧眼, the poet expresses utter discontent with humiliating suffering of East Asians in the face of Western powers' hegemony. The poem ends with a yearning for an open, modern, and enlightened Chosŏn.

In the middle of the banquet, Miyajima and the Korean envoy Kang Wi jointly composed a pentasyllabic quatrain as follows (Liu 2010: 551–552):

素心蘭馥鬱	Chypre is so fragrant,
可以訂交情 (宮島)	Can be used to seal our friendship. (Miyajima)
一去滄溟滴	Departing is like a water droplet falling into the sea,
何由急遠程 (姜瑋)	Why rush to embark on a long journey? (Kang)

Miyajima compared his amiable relationship with Kang to strongly flavored Chypre, while Kang's verses made it clear that he was reluctant to leave and could not bear to part with Miyajima. The next day, Miyajima visited Kim at his Honganji 本願寺 residence in Asakusa 淺草. In their brush conversation, he invited Kim to write a postscript for his *Yōkōdō Collection of Poems* 養浩堂詩集. Thereupon Kim improvised a couplet as a gift:

真緣已採三山藥 別意將回八月槎

It was true destiny that allowed me to gather herbal medicine from Three Immortal Mountains 三神山. For my return journey, I will take the scheduled ship back in the eighth lunar month.

As for the postscript, Kim wrote (Liu 2010: 553–555):

余得晤栗香先生數次，襟度淵雅，英華襲人。今讀其《養浩堂集》，可謂詩若其人，不覺心折。臨行書此，以志景仰。「何時一尊酒，重共細論文」為君一誦，黯然而已。歸林歸客金宏集拜識。

> I had the honour to meet with Mr Kurika [Miyajima] several times. [Your] broad-mindedness and congenial attitudes are profound and elegant. [Your] high esteem commands respect. Reading [your] *Yōkōdō Collection of Poems* now, I get the same feeling when talking to [you]. I am deeply humbled. This [postscript] is written to record my admiration and respect before my departure. "When will we share a cask of wine, and be engaged in literary exchange again?" Chanting (this couplet) once for such a genteel friend can hardly put the melancholy in me to rest – Respectful notes by Kim Koeng-chip, a homeward bound returnee.

In the postscript, Kim lauded Miyajima as a person but also the gracefulness and elegance of his poetry. He cited the last two verses in the poem *On a Spring Day Thinking of Li Bai* 春日憶李白 by the famous Tang poet Du Fu 杜甫:

何時一尊酒 重共細論文

When will we share a cask of wine, and be engaged in literary exchange again?

to express his strong craving to meet Miyajima merrily again over fine spirits and literary exchange. All this demonstrates how, for the literary talents of China, Japan, and Chosŏn, improvisation and chanting of sinogram-based poetry 漢詩酬唱 had already become an unmarked mode of cross-border interaction that allowed for intellectual exchange, albeit writing-mediated, in addition to being a catalyst toward deepening convivial relations interpersonally.

Espionage and collection of secret intelligence: a pitfall of brush conversation

Of the brush-talk materials compiled by Liu (2010), those from the *Ōkōchi Documents* 大河內文書 involve mainly topics on everyday life, be they elegant or mundane, mostly unrelated to national diplomacy or political issues (see Wang, this volume). By contrast, the brush-talk records in *Miyajima Documents* show a penchant for a particular purpose, namely to collect secret intelligence. This characteristic is especially apparent when relevant parts of the brush-talk events concerning Ryukyu are compared with those in Miyajima's (1872) personal diary 養浩堂私記二 ('Intimate Notes of Yōkōdō', vol. 2). The extent to which brush-talk could be exploited for espionage purposes is clearly evidenced in Miyajima's *Intimate Notes*, which contains elaborate details regarding the secrets behind Sino-Japanese negotiations and their respective concerns over the tributary status of Ryukyu.

On one hand, through poetic improvisation and socializing, Miyajima was able to develop friendship and gradually deepen his convivial relations with embassy staff like He Ruzhang 何如璋, Huang Zunxian 黃遵憲, and Shen Wenying 沈文熒. On the other hand, the strategic positioning of Miyajima as a friend and the personal relations that he informally enjoyed were clearly exploited by Miyajima as a hidden conduit for collecting much coveted secret intelligence regarding the Qing government's stance toward Ryukyu in Sino-Japanese negotiations. Such valuable diplomatic information was swiftly conveyed to senior Meiji officials like Ōkubo Toshimichi and Iwakura Tomomi, in effect making Miyajima's information about the Qing court's attitudes and actions a crucial reliable source of secret intelligence for the Meiji government.

As stated in scroll 2 of Miyajima's (1872) *Intimate notes*, on account of Miyajima's profound and solid foundation in Sinology, the Ministry of Foreign Affairs had considered appointing him as the Japanese official in charge of liaison with Qing officials. Such a formal functional role would have facilitated communication through brush conversation with Chinese embassy staff like Ambassador He and Vice-Envoy Huang, frequently and conveniently:

> 頃者，外務省有內諭，願採用余為清國應接之差

> Just now, the Ministry of Foreign Affairs issued an internal communication, entreating me to serve as the official in charge of liaison with Qing officials.

After careful consideration, however, Miyajima declined the proposed appointment and offered the following reason (Liu 2001: 9):

> 予亦左院廃院以来ハ、深ク時勢ヲ考ル処アリ。軽々挙動，一時ノ栄利ヲ貪ル，素ヨリ好マサル所，況ヤ清国公使今日ノ談話ハ，両国交歓ノ始メニシテ，僅ニ皮膚ノ談而已。其心術如何ハ，却テ閑接ノ交際ニ在リ。今若シ公然外務省ニ奉職セハ，他日有事ノ日，却テ嫌忌ヲ免カレス。

> Ever since the abolition of the Legislature, I have been following the current political situation very carefully. Acting in a rush for the sake of instant fame or profit without considering possible consequences is never what I would like to do. Moreover, engaging in brush conversation with the envoys from Qing China today is the beginning of formalized relations between the two countries. What we exchanged was only skin-deep. To unveil more nuanced thinking or innermost thoughts on their part, we can only find out through casual conversation and verbal exchange. If I am officially appointed as a diplomat of the Ministry of Foreign Affairs, I would be incriminated and could hardly escape undue allegations should anything go wrong in future.

The said appointment was thus declined after exchanging views with Ōkubo, who told Miyajima that casual conversation and informal socializing with Chinese embassy staff could better serve the Japanese government's interests, and further cautioned him to attend to the convivial collaboration and strive to maintain peaceful relations between the two nations (Liu 2001: 9). That was the background of how Miyajima subsequently positioned himself as a private, well-acquainted friend of the embassy staff, and how he was able to use that special identity as camouflage to collect diplomatically sensitive intelligence emanating from the Qing court vis-à-vis the Meiji government, a veritable secret agent so to speak.

Of all the complex issues confronted by the first ambassador to Japan He Ruzhang, Sino-Japanese negotiations on the tributary status of Ryukyu topped the list. The Ryukyu islands 琉球群島 are located between Japan and Taiwan. It had been an independent kingdom for over 500 years. In 1372, the Ming Emperor Taizu 明太祖 dispatched Yang Zai 楊載 to the three Ryukyu principalities of Chūzan 中山, Hokuzan 北山, and Nanzan 南山 to negotiate their acceptance of Ming dynasty as the sovereign state and their tributary status, which was successful. The three kingdoms thus became a tributary and started sending envoys to Ming China periodically.

In the next 500 years until the late Qing period, China formally dispatched Imperial Chinese missions 冊封使 to Ryukyu twenty-four times (sixteen times during the Ming dynasty, eight during the Qing). The relationship between Ryukyu as a tributary and China the sovereign state was thus unquestionable throughout this period. In 1609, Shimazu Iehisa 島津家久 (1576–1638), the daimyo of Satsuma domain 薩摩藩主 in Japan invaded Ryukyu and kidnapped King Shō Nī 尚寧 (1564–1620). On one hand, control of Ryukyu became more stringent; on the other hand, Ryukyu was allowed to continue pledging political allegiance to Qing China by sending envoys to Peking periodically – a policy that was not disclosed to China, however. Thus began a long period, for well over a century, when the Ryukyu kingdom practiced dual allegiance or subordination in that it accepted to be a tributary of both China and Japan. At the onset of the Meiji Restoration (1868–1912), the Japanese government abolished the Ryukyu Kingdom in 1872 and installed the Ryukyu domain 琉球藩 instead, thereby triggering the demand that Ryukyu should hitherto stop sending envoys to China. To counter this move, the king of Ryukyu sent a special envoy to the Qing court to solicit assistance, thus unveiling a long negotiation on the dependency status of Ryukyu in the early modern history of Sino-Japanese diplomacy (see also Wong, this volume).

According to Miyajima's (1872) *Intimate notes*, the first mention of the embassy staff's attitudes towards the Ryukyu issue was dated 1 December 1878:

十二月一日，訪清公使何如璋筆談，頗有關係於東洋，不啻琉球一事，以記之。

On the 1st of December, I visited the Qing ambassador, He Ruzhang, and had brush conversation with him. Much of that exchange was related to Japan, not only concerning Ryukyu, hence these notes.

In their brush conversation, Ambassador He was mainly concerned about the possible perils of Russia's southward move, advocating that China, Japan, and

Chosŏn should form an alliance to counteract the Russian threat. Toward the end, Ambassador He wrote (Liu 2010: 469):

> 頃者照貴外務，告琉球之事，外務未有答。中東本宜唇齒相依，此球在中東之間頗好，若有謬落外人之手，則忽為東洋禍根，今之時不可不有兩便之法，如何？

> I just informed your esteemed country's Ministry of Foreign Affairs about the Ryukyu issue, but they have not replied yet. The well-being of China and Japan is closely connected and mutually dependent. It is not a bad idea for Ryukyu to continue having tributary relations with both of our countries. Should Ryukyu fall into the hands of an outsider, it would instantly become the bane of Japan. Now, there has got to be a mutually beneficial way out. What do you think?

On this note, Miyajima gave the following comment:

> 此般何公使始言琉球之事，蓋球人訴何公使乎？

> The way Ambassador He raised the Ryukyu issue just now, did any Ryukyuan complain to Ambassador He?

According to the *Ōkōchi Documents*, ten days before, on November 21, two envoys from Ryukyu embassy 琉球使館, surnamed Shō 尚 and Mō 毛, respectively, had visited the Qing embassy. In fact, while the entire Chinese legation stopped by Kōbe on their way to Tokyo, already a Ryukyu envoy Ma Kenshee 馬兼才 requested to see them. He presented the secret imperial order 密敕 of Shō Tee 尚泰 (1843–1901, a.k.a. Shō Tai), the king of Ryukyu, collapsed and broke out crying, entreating the Qing ambassador to come to Ryukyu's rescue (Chen 2005: 130). On 7 October 1878, Ambassador He had sent a strongly-worded diplomatic note addressed to the Japanese Foreign Minister Terashima Munenori 寺島宗則 (1832–1893), protesting against the Meiji government's edict that Ryukyu's centuries-old practice of sending tributary envoys to Ming and Qing China would be stopped forthwith:

> 今忽聞貴國禁止琉球進貢我國，我政府聞之，以為日本堂堂大國，諒不肯背鄰交欺弱國，為此不信不義、無情無理之事。[10]

> Just learned that your esteemed nation had forbidden Ryukyu to send tributary envoys to our country. After being informed of this, our Government

---

[10] In the original brush-talk record, the character "背" is not found. It is however most probably a misprint, as evidenced in corresponding Japanese sources. For example, according to the *Documents on Japanese Foreign Relations* 1936, vol. 11, no. 126, p. 272, 十一月二十一日　寺島外務卿ヨリ清国公使宛, in the reply letter written by Terashima Munenori 寺島宗則, he mentioned "...諒ルニ肯テ隣交ニ背キ弱國ヲ欺キ...".

was of the view that a great, respectable nation like Japan would presumably not betray her congenial neighbor and intimidating a weak country, and in so doing defying justice and violating trust by committing such an insolent and unreasonable act.

(see Ministry of Foreign Affairs of Japan, *Documents on Japanese Foreign Relations*, 1936, vol. 11, no. 125, p. 271, 十月七日　清国公使ヨリ寺島外務卿宛, 'Oct. 7, From Qing envoy to Foreign Minister Terashima')

In response, the Japanese government decidedly dodged its political will to prevent Ryukyu from continuing to make tributary trips to China with a view to ultimately annexing it. Instead, the Japanese government accused Ambassador He for making baseless allegations using 'illusory verbal abuse' 假想之暴言,[11] and for demanding an apology from the Japanese side, thus turning the Sino-Japanese negotiations into a stalemate (Kerr 1958/2000; Mi 1998: 177–202).

On 26 February 1879, Ambassador He sent another diplomatic note to the Foreign Ministry of Japan, demanding the re-opening of negotiations, but did not get any response. Instead, the Japanese government speeded up the pace of annexing Ryukyu. In the face of the Meiji government's uncompromisingly stern measures, on one hand, Ambassador He had to report to the Qing Foreign Office 總理衙門 and keep Li Hongzhang 李鴻章 (1823–1901) informed of the latest development timely. On the other hand, Ambassador He consciously used Miyajima's connection as a window for keeping the line of negotiation and communication with the Japanese government open. For this purpose, Ambassador He sent Huang Zunxian and Shen Wenying to visit an ailing Miyajima who was recovering from illness. Tension was high during and beyond their brush conversation, as stated in scroll 2 of Miyajima's (1872) *Intimate notes* (cf. Liu 2001: 10):

三月一日[12]，清使館ヨリ黃參贊遵憲，沈知州文熒来訪，筆談頗ル劇談球事，余答辨太タ苦ム。

On the 1st of March, the Qing Counsellor, Huang Zunxian, and the prefect designate (of a county in Shaanxi) Shen Wenying paid me a visit. Most of our brush conversation focused on Ryukyu issues. I had a hard time answering tough questions raised by them.

Their brush conversation touched upon the Chinese legation staff's preparation for returning to China given Japan's resolute decision to annex Ryukyu and turn

---

11 Source: Ministry of Foreign Affairs of Japan, *Documents on Japanese Foreign Relations*, 1936, vol. 11, no. 126, p. 272, 十一月二十一日　寺島外務卿ヨリ清国公使宛, 'Nov. 21, From Foreign Minister Terashima to Qing ambassador'.
12 According to the original brush-talk materials, *Miyajima Documents*, notes in section C9, and 'Questions and Answers', it was dated March 2 (Waseda University Library Collection).

it into a Japanese prefecture 廃琉置県, as explained by Huang Zunxian (Liu 2010: 474):

> 貴政府若有事於球，非蔑球也，是輕我也。我兩國修好條規第一條即言：「兩國所屬邦土，務各以禮相待，不可互有侵越。」 條規可廢，何必修好？故必絕聘問，罷互市。吾輩不得不歸也。

> If your esteemed government takes action on Ryukyu, you despise not Ryukyu, but our country! According to Article One of the 'Sino-Japanese Friendship and Trade Treaty', 'Within the territories of both nations, they should treat each other with due respect and should not undertake the slightest invasive act.' If this Article is not followed, why bother cultivating friendship? So we will stop visiting and sending envoys (to your country), and stop all the trading activities between our two nations. Returning to China will be the only option left for us.

Huang cited Article One of the 'Sino-Japanese Friendship and Trade Treaty' to refute Japan's annexation plan, which would amount to an infringement of China's sovereign territory. Shen further warned that military action from the Chinese side could not be ruled out:

> 今貴邦政府貪其地而不顧理之是非，將來用兵而致禍患，僕甚不解其惑也。

> Now the government of your esteemed country is trying to annex Ryukyu out of greed, in blatant disregard of what is right and wrong. In future this may lead to warfare and disaster. I don't understand [why you seem to have lost your senses].

According to his (1872) *Intimate Notes*, on March 10, Miyajima submitted the brush conversation record with Huang and Shen to Minister Iwakura, who remained undaunted and advised Miyajima as follows:

> 廟堂ノ議今日既ニ已ニ決定イタシ，今此蜘躇セハ，先年大久保ノ施行モ前後順序ヲ成サス，此上ハ断然廃藩シテ内地一般ノ施政ヲ為ヨリ外ナシ。此筆談ハ尋常文事ノ談ニ非ス，國事上頗ル大關係ヲ保有スレハ，掛リノ參議一人丈ケニ，内密ニ示スヘキニ付，一本寫取。

> The court has made the decision today. If we remain indecisive on this issue, then the implementation and logical sequence of Ōkubo's action planned a few years ago will be disrupted. Thus, apart from abolishing the Ryukyu domain resolutely, which is in line with national governance for the rest of Japan, there is no other option. What is covered in this brush-talk is no ordinary matter; it is immensely critical for our nation. As an internal top secret, it can only be shown to the Chief Counsel. Please write up a copy of the brush-talk.

Before leaving, Miyajima (1872) pleaded absolute confidentiality with Iwakura:

小子モ外露候テハ清人交際ノ道ヲ失候ニ付，何クマデモ内密ニ被成下度申述候事。

If this information is leaked, it would damage my relationship with Qing people, and so please make sure to keep it secret.

On March 11, the Japanese government dispatched Matsuda Michiyuki 松田道之 (1839–1892) as head of a contingent of army and police force to Ryukyu swiftly. Shortly after arriving at Ryukyu on March 27, Matsuda proclaimed the abolition of Ryukyu domain, installed Okinawa Prefecture 沖縄県 in its place, and further demanded that the Ryukyu palace at Suigusiku 首里城 be handed over by March 31. On April 4, the Meiji government decreed nationwide that the Ryukyu domain had been abolished and given way to Okinawa Prefecture. The following day Nabeshima Naomasa 鍋島直彬 (1843–1915) was appointed as the first county magistrate of Okinawa. On May 27, the monarch of Ryukyu, King Shō Tee, was relocated to Tokyo, thus putting an end to Ryukyu's political status as an independent kingdom.

Amidst the stalemate of Sino-Japanese negotiations over the future of Ryukyu, in June 1879, Ulysses Simpson Grant (1822–1885), former President of the USA, was traveling around the world on his way to Japan via China. Li Hongzhang took that opportunity to entreat Grant to serve as a mediator for China. Departing from Peking on June 2, Grant arrived at Nagasaki on June 21 and reached Yokohama on July 3. On the Japanese side, it was Miyajima who, through intensive brush conversation with Shen, picked up the intelligence that Grant had been entrusted with the task of mediation by and for the Chinese. While visiting the Chinese embassy on June 20, Miyajima felt strongly that Ambassador He did not have peace of mind regarding Japan's annexation of Ryukyu and turning an independent nation into a Japanese prefecture. On July 18,[13] Miyajima called at the Chinese embassy again. According to his *Intimate notes*, it was then when Shen Wenying was caught off guard in their brush conversation and leaked the purpose of Grant's visit to Japan inadvertently:

彼駐北京一月，我政府托球事於彼，彼來貴邦，為我作排解，僕輩望之。

He [Grant] is staying in Peking for a month. Our government entrusted him with mediation of the Ryukyu issue. He came to your esteemed nation to resolve the problem on our behalf. We hope that he can help us.

---

13 There is again some discrepancy regarding the date. According to the 'Questions and Answers' 問答錄, this took place on August 4.

Miyajima was elated for obtaining such a crucial piece of intelligence, as he wrote in his (1872) *Intimate notes* (cf. Liu 2001: 12–13):

> 以上筆談事件、頗ル緊要、就中米国克蘭徳清国ノ托ヲ受テ、球事ヲ周旋スルニ至テハ、實ニ是レ緊要中ノ緊要ニ、沈氏ノ雅量ニ非レハ、決シテ之ヲ外洩セス。乃チ黄遵憲ハ彼ノ枢機ニ参スレハ、未タ寸言モ克蘭徳ニ関係スル⏋ヲ聞カス。

> The brush-talk mentioned above is rather important. Grant, an American, was entrusted by Qing China to serve as a mediator on the Ryukyu issue. This is the most important point of all. Without Shen's genteelness, this secret would not have been divulged. Should Huang Zunxian be the key person or nexus, he would not have said a single word about Grant's mediation.

Immediately after obtaining this secret information, Miyajima reported it to Minister Iwakura (Miyajima 1872; cf. Liu 2001: 13):

> 岩倉右府大ニ喜ンテ、曰ク、今ヤ克蘭徳氏 琉球ノ事ヲ聖上ニ奏陳シ、又政府ニモ忠告セリ、然レ圧甞テ清廷ノ請願ヲ受テ周旋スル⏉ヲ不知。今此言ヲ得テ實ニ一層ノ考慮ヲ増ス。然ラハ則我ヨリ先ツ着手スヘシト。

> Minister Iwakura said with great delight, 'now that Grant had presented the Ryukyu issue to the Tennō and advised our government, but we did not know he had been entrusted by the Qing government to serve as a mediator. Now that we know, we should mull over it carefully before deciding what to do next'.

On July 12, the Meiji government appointed Itō Hakubun 伊藤博文 (1841–1909), Saigō Jūdō 西郷従道 (1843–1902), and Yoshida Kiyonari 吉田清成 (1845–1891) to receive Grant officially, accompanying him on a tour to famous touristic attractions like Nikkō 日光 and Hakone 箱根. In the process, they persuaded Grant to relinquish his pro-China stance. After returning to Tokyo on August 19, several ministers including Ōkuma Shigenobu 大隈重信 (1838–1922), Iwakura Tomomi 岩倉具視, and Yoshida Kiyonari 吉田清成 called at the Enryōkan 延遼館 residence where Grant was staying to reiterate the Japanese viewpoint toward the Ryukyu issue.

On August 16, Miyajima visited the Chinese embassy again trying to engage Shen in brush-talk, the primary purpose being manifestly to probe what Grant might have said to Ambassador He upon his return from Nikkō (Miyajima 1872; cf. Liu 2001: 13):

> 此時克蘭徳日光ヨリ帰ル。想フニ必ス清公使ニ告ルモノアルヘシ。其情状ヲ探偵セントス。

> By this time Grant must have returned from Nikkō. Guess he might have said something to the Qing Ambassador. Find out what he said.

But Shen told him that (Liu 2010: 494):

既彼居間，且俟其復音。刻下亦無事，俟彼回來再看。

Since he is mediating, let us wait for his reply. There is nothing [that we can do] for the time being. Let us see what to do after he has come back.

On August 20, Miyajima (1872) wrote (cf. Liu 2001: 13):

岩倉右府ニ面シ，沈文熒ニ内話ヲ委細ニ談シ，且機密ニ攻略ヲ聞ク。

[I] met Iwakura face-to-face and discussed what Shen Wenying confided in me in detail, and also listened to Iwakura's secret political strategies.

While it is impossible to tell what exactly was meant by 'secret political strategies', it may be inferred that Iwakura must have demanded further specific information from the Chinese embassy and instructed Miyajima to step up his efforts to obtain more secret intelligence. At the diplomatic level, fierce, contentious negotiations of various scenarios over the future of Ryukyu continued meanwhile.

It was only after the site of such negotiations was shifted to Peking that cordial relations in brush-talk interactions between Miyajima, Ambassador He and Huang Zunxian were restored. Such cordial relations lasted until the end of Ambassador He's tenure in Japan largely thanks to Miyajima's efforts. On 16 February 1882, shortly before Ambassador He was about to begin his homeward-bound journey, Miyajima raised an issue of serious concern to the Meiji government (Liu 2010: 594–595):

宮島: 臨別一言，如公與我則可謂千載之知己也。頃僕與一親友深慮兩國利害，說某大臣。大臣深嘉納之，曰以琉球一事，決不至開禍端。於貴國也，此事不在世人所知，敢告之閣下。	Miyajima: [My] words before [your] departure: our intimate friendship can last for a thousand years. Just now, with a close friend who is deeply concerned about possible consequences that could happen to our nations, we lobbied a particular minister together. That minister deeply applauded and accepted our view, saying that the Ryukyu issue would in no way trigger any disaster. Not many people in your esteemed nation are aware of this. I take the liberty to inform your honorable self.
子峨: 兩國絕不因此小事開大爭端，我政府亦是此意。	Zie [Ambassador He]: Our nations should under no circumstances start a serious dispute over such a trivial matter. This is also our government's stance.

According to Miyajima's (1872) *Intimate notes*, the 'close friend' and 'a particular minister' alluded to here referred to Yoshii Tomozane 吉井友実 (1827–1891) and Iwakura Tomomi, respectively. By raising such a sensitive question just before Ambassador He was about to leave Japan, Miyajima clearly wanted to probe into the Chinese stance toward Japan's annexation of Ryukyu, in particular the extent to which Qing China was ready to undertake military action against Japan. In response, Ambassador He confided to Miyajima unequivocally that the Qing court would never consider going to war with Japan over Ryukyu. This point was elaborated toward the end of his (1872) *Intimate notes* as follows (cf. Liu 2001: 14):

> 右臨別ノ一言，両国ノ関係スル処，誠ニ重大ノ事件ナリ。苟モ何公使ヲシテ帰廷，此処ニ注意アラシメハ，両国ノ蒼生，此幸福ヲ得ル，豈鮮少ナランヤ。余五年ノ際，区区ノ微衷，私交ヲ結ヒ，憂慮スル所ノ者，此一点ニ在リ。此事外交機密ニ関係スルヲ以，特ニ漏洩ヲ戒ムノミ。

As stated in the previous words before departure, at stake was one crucial, pivotal issue of concern to both nations. If Qing Ambassador He Ruzhang could remain vigilant of this point after returning to his home country, that would be no small contribution to the well-being of the masses in both nations! This has been on my mind in the past five years. My wish to seal a heart-to-heart friendship [with Chinese envoys] is exactly driven by such a concern. This being a diplomatic secret, extra caution against leakage is in order.

Miyajima clearly had no wish to see any military confrontation erupting between China and Japan. This notwithstanding, there can be no doubt that in the long process of Sino-Japanese negotiations over the Ryukyu kingdom's tributary status, he went out of his way to exploit the convenience of frequent brush conversations with Chinese embassy staff and turn them into opportunities for collecting diplomatic intelligence and national secrets through Sinitic brush-talk and report them to the Meiji government swiftly. Such acts of espionage continued after the second ambassador, Li Shuchang 黎庶昌 (1837–1898), assumed duty. In their poetic improvisation and brush-talk interaction, Miyajima kept up his efforts to gather sensitive and invaluable intelligence over Ryukyu issues for the Meiji government, thereby inflicting huge damage and untold losses in Qing Chinese diplomacy.

Coda

Based on the aforementioned illustrations, there is ample evidence that literary improvisation and poetic exchange through Sinitic brush-talk formed a crucial, conventional mode of cross-border communication between well-educated elites from China, Japan, and Chosŏn within Sinographic East Asia. This point is clearly reflected in surviving brush-talk records involving members of the first legation dispatched by Qing China to Japan during the early Meiji period. With few exceptions, the Chinese embassy staff were scholar-officials who were well-versed in Classical Chinese canons, literary works, and traditional Chinese culture. Much the same, *mutatis mutandis*, may be said of their Japanese counterparts, be they powerful politicians, aristocrats, or influential leaders. Their shared literary heritage and, above all, shared knowledge of a body of sinogram-based Classical literature enabled some Chinese embassy staff like Huang Zunxian to develop deep personal bonds and convivial relations with their Japanese acquaintances through brush conversation, including improvisation and exchange of poetry as exemplified earlier. Through this process, many would have no hesitation recognizing each other as genuine soulmates. Here lies the most charming aspect of Sinitic brush-talk no doubt.

That notwithstanding, it must be pointed out that the Chinese embassy staff's outpouring of personal feelings that they confided in the heat of brush conversation was exploited by their Japanese brush conversation partners to probe secret intelligence out of national political interests. This is how Sinitic brush-talk could become a pitfall to the disadvantage of the government when national secrets – be it stance, policy, action, or plan – were compromised. In addition to delicate questions concerning their East Asian neighbor Chosŏn, the political status of Ryukyu was another thorny diplomatic issue because, for decades, the political allegiance of Ryukyu to late Qing China and Meiji Japan as a tributary state had been a delicate diplomatic issue between the two sovereign nations.

Ample records of brush conversation between Miyajima Seiichirō and the Chinese embassy staff, notably Ambassador He Ruzhang, Vice-Envoy Zhang Sigui, Counsellor Huang Zunxian, and supporting staff Shen Wenying, have shown that while cultivating convivial relations by conducting literary and intellectual exchange using brush, ink, and paper, Miyajima consciously abused such personal relations by collecting politically sensitive information and probing national secret intelligence concerning Ryukyu and Chosŏn for the Meiji regime at the expense of Qing China's national interests.

For want of space, this chapter has discussed and exemplified two aspects of Sinitic brush-talk: the literary charm it manifestly possesses, but also the pitfall it may occasion in the hands of malicious brush-talkers. Both the *Ōkōchi Documents* and the *Miyajima Documents* contain a huge number of brush-talk records which are immensely rich in content. There are no doubt many other obscure or hidden aspects that have yet to be uncovered, awaiting careful research and fine-grained analysis.

References

Chen. Z. [陳錚] (Ed.). (2005). 黃遵憲全集 ('A complete collection of Huang Zunxian'). Peking: Zhonghua Book Company.
Denecke. W. (2014). Worlds without translation: Premodern East Asia and the power of character scripts. In S. Bermann & C. Porter (Eds.). *A companion to translation studies* (pp. 204–216). Chichester: Wiley-Blackwell.
Ge. Z. [葛兆光] (2018). *What is China? Territory, ethnicity, culture, and history* (M. G. Hill. Trans.). Harvard: Harvard University Press.
He. R. [何如璋] (2010). 使東述略 ('A précis of my diplomatic mission in Japan'). In Z.-Q. Wu & Y.-X. Wu [吳振清、吳裕賢] (Eds.). 何如璋集 ('A collection of He Ruzhang's work') (pp. 65–82). Tianjin: Tianjin Renmin Press.

Ihara, T. [伊原澤周] (2003). 從"筆談外交"到"以史為鑒"—中日近代關係史研究 ('From "brush-talk diplomacy" to "drawing lessons from history": A study in the history of Sino-Japanese relation at modern times'). Peking: Zhonghua Book Company.

Kerr, G. H. (1958/2000). *Okinawa: The history of an island people* (revised edition). Boston: Tuttle Publishing.

Koh, J., & King, R. (2014). *Infected Korean language: Purity versus hybridity*. Amherst, New York: Cambria Press.

Legge, J. [理雅各] (Ed. & Trans.). (1885). *The scared books of China: The texts of Confucianism (Part III: The Lî Kî, I-X*, 禮記 *The book of rites)*. Oxford: Clarendon Press (Original work published 5th century BC). Retrieved March 15, 2021, from https://archive.org/details/sacredbooksofchi3conf.

Legge, J. [理雅各] (Ed. & Trans.). (1891). *The writings of Kwang-Tze(Zhuangzi): Books XVIII-XXXIII* 莊子. In *The scared books of China: The texts of Tâoism (Part II)* (pp. 1−234). Oxford: Clarendon Press (Original work published 3rd century BC). Retrieved March 15, 2021, from https://archive.org/details/sacredbooksofchi028287mbp.

Liu, Y. [劉雨珍] (2001). 黄遵憲と宮島誠一郎の交友に関する総合的考察 —『宮島誠一郎文書』を手がかりに ('A comprehensive study in the camaraderie between Huang Zunxian and Miyajima Seiichirō: Using *Miyajima Seiichirō's Documents* as illustration'). *The Journal of Social Science* 社会科学研究 26: 1−35.

Liu, Y. [劉雨珍] (Ed.). (2010). 清代首屆駐日公使館員筆談資料彙編 ('A collection of brush-talks by the staff of the first Qing Embassy to Japan'). Tianjin: Tianjin Renmin Press.

Mi, Q. [米慶餘] (1998). 琉球歷史研究 ('A study of the history of Ryukyu'). Tianjin: Tianjin Renmin Press.

Ministry of Foreign Affairs of Japan [外務省] (1936). 日本外交文書 ('Documents on Japanese Foreign Relations'). Tokyo: Author.

Miyajima, S. [宮島誠一郎] (1872). 養浩堂私記二 ('Intimate notes of Yōkōdō') (vol. 2). Retrieved January 24, 2021, from https://dl.ndl.go.jp/info:ndljp/pid/11536065?toc Opened=1.

National Archives of Japan (2021). Sino-Japanese friendship and trade treaty, Japan Centre of Asian Historical Records. Retrieved March 15, 2021, from www.jacar.archives.go.jp/aj/meta/image_B13090891200.

Sanetō, K. [実藤恵秀] (1961). 清代中日文人筆話手稿的發現和整理 ('The discovery and compilation of manuscripts of brush conversation between Qing Chinese and Japanese literati of Sinitic'). 南洋學報 *Journal of the South Seas Society* 17(1): 1−3.

Wang, B. [王寶平] (2007). 甲午戰前中國駐日翻譯官考 ('A study in the China's interpreting officials in Japan before the First Sino-Japanese War'). 日語學習與研究 *Journal of Japanese Language Study and Research* 2007(5): 57−64.

Wang, T. [王鐵崖] (Ed.). (1957). 中外舊約章彙編 ('Collection of China's historical treaties with foreign countries') (vol. 1). Peking: SDX Joint Publishing Company.

Yan, L. [閻立] (2009). 清末中國的對日政策與日語認識 ('China's Japan policy and knowledge of Japanese during late Qing'). Tokyo: Tōhō Shoten.

Zhang, Y., & Chen, T. [張玉書、陳廷敬] (Eds.). (1716/2005). 康熙字典 ('Kangxi dictionary'). Peking: Zhonghua Book Company. Retrieved from https://kangxizidian.com/.

10 Japanese-Korean brush-talk during the early Edo period, 1603–1711

Koo Jea-hyoun and Joo Ian

Introduction

In 1637, the Korean envoys dispatched to Japan returned to Korea. When King Injo 仁祖 (1595–1649; r. 1623–1649) asked them about the Japanese literati, the Chief Envoy Im Kwang 任絖 (1579–1644) replied:

不成文理，詩則尤不好。

Lacking in literary flair, the quality of poetry is particularly poor.

Kim Se-ryŏm (金世濂 1593–1646) (1637), the Vice-Envoy likewise answered:

沿路及江戶多有來問者。皆以理氣性情等語爲問。不可以蠻人而忽之。

Many people on the way to and from Edo came to ask questions about the *Principle, Force, Nature, and Emotion* [Neo-Confucianist philosophy] and the like. We should not neglect them and treat them as barbarians.

These two replies reflect the Japanese scholars' wish to visit the Koreans and exchange views with them on Neo-Confucianism; they also reveal the Korean envoys' rather condescending attitude toward the Japanese literati. Under what circumstances did the Korean envoys engage in intellectual and poetic exchange with their Japanese hosts? Why were the Japanese interested in Korean Neo-Confucianism?

Before the twentieth century, Literary Sinitic[1] (Kornicki 2018, hereafter Sinitic) was the written lingua franca in China, Japan, Korea, Vietnam, and Ryukyu (cf. 'scripta franca',[2] Denecke 2014: 209; Clements 2019: 308). Sinitic is different from spoken Chinese vernaculars such as Mandarin or Cantonese, because it is a fossilized written language that was spoken approximately 2,000 years ago but

---

1 When reference is made to the use of Classical Chinese (*wényán* 文言) within the Sinosphere, the term 'Literary Sinitic' or 'Sinitic' is preferred.
2 Some scholars contend that it is more appropriate to say 'scriptum francum', given that 'scriptum' in Latin is neutral by gender (Genus) (see Man 2002: 112).

DOI: 10.4324/9781003048176-12

had been used as a written language for over two millennia within the Sinographic cosmopolis in East Asia (Norman 1988: 109; Koh & King 2014). It is further distinct from other classical languages, such as Latin or Sanskrit, because it is written in Chinese characters, which is a morphographic, non-phonographic writing system. Thus, it allowed two speakers of different first-language backgrounds to communicate with each other through brush-assisted handwriting, even though they may pronounce each sinogram very differently. Such a mode of communication is comparable to two mathematicians with no shared spoken language exchanging mathematical ideas solely via mathematical formulae.

Sinitic was most commonly used in China, Japan, Korea, Vietnam, and Ryukyu, societies that until the end of the nineteenth century were known collectively as the Sinosphere 漢字文化圈. Typologically distinct languages were spoken in these fives polities, such as Mandarin (Sino-Tibetan), Japanese (Japonic), Vietnamese (Austroasiatic), and Korean (Koreanic), to name a few. Sinitic thus served as the scripta franca for international communication, similar to the role of English today.

Sinitic was commonly used as a written language in Chosŏn Korea 朝鮮 (1392–1910) within its borders. Even after the invention of the Korean alphabet, *hangŭl* in 1443, Sinitic remained the written language for formal purposes until the end of the nineteenth century. The Chinese-based Korean writing technique 'clerical writing' (*Idu* 吏讀) was also used, but its usage was functionally complementary to the formal use of Sinitic (Kornicki 2018: 57; cf. Handel 2019).

In Japan, Classical Chinese was not used as extensively throughout the Edo period (1603–1867). Literary written Japanese, *Sorobun* 候文, was used instead. Sinitic was mainly used by Buddhist monks to access the Buddhist scriptures translated from Sanskrit into Chinese, which typically consisted of a mixture of (written) Classical as well as (spoken) Chinese vernacular elements depending on the translator (Mair 1994).

Prior to the Edo Period, there was little exchange between Japan and other countries that used Classical Chinese as the main written language. Japan had no formal diplomatic relations with China. Envoys from Chosŏn were also very irregular. In addition, diplomatic relations with Chosŏn were conducted via Tsushima 対馬, the Japanese island closest to the Korean peninsula. Tsushima was a barren island, and it maintained its economy through trade with Chosŏn. By accepting nominal government posts from the Chosŏn court, Tsushima received its right to conduct trading activities with Chosŏn; in other words, Tsushima was semi-subordinate to Chosŏn, if only in name (Chong 2010). Because many Tsushima islanders were fluent in Korean, they were in charge of interpreting for the Korean envoys.

However, with the establishment of the Tokugawa shogunate and the beginning of the Edo Period in 1603, the use of Sinitic in Japan began to change. Neo-Confucianism, a new school of Confucianist ideology founded by the Song philosopher Zhu Xi 朱熹, rapidly gained support under Tokugawa Ieyasu 徳川家康 (1542–1616) (Nosco 1984). The emerging new social class of Confucianists 儒者 consisted of intellectuals literate in Sinitic. Mainly employed by the feudal lords (*daimyōs* 大名), they played a role in acquiring knowledge in Sinitic literature and imparting such knowledge to their lords. A cultural need arose after the end of the long *Warring States* period 戦国時代 (1467–1615) and the Confucianists were well placed to fulfill that need.

The emergence of a class of Confucianists facilitated the use of Classical Chinese as a scripta franca to communicate with the Koreans. Each time a new Shōgun came to the throne, Chosŏn would dispatch envoys to the Tokugawa bakufu 幕府, totaling twelve times from 1607 to 1811 (see also WANG Yong, this volume). The envoys were dispatched on a fairly regular basis. A Chosŏn mission consisted of nearly five hundred Koreans; they were guided by Tsushima islanders and traveled all the way to Edo (江戸, today's Tokyo). They would deliver the letter of credence 国書 from the Chosŏn King to the bakufu, receive the reply letter, and return to Korea via the same route. The local daimyōs would provide room and board and order the Confucianists to serve the Koreans. Japanese Confucianists would routinely ask for the writings, drawings, or poems from the Koreans in part to satisfy the exotic tastes of their feudal lords.

Gradually the Confucianists came to realize that it would be much more practical to directly communicate with the Koreans via brush-talk rather than relying on the Tsushima islanders' interpretation. As mentioned, the status of written Chinese as a scripta franca and its morphographic nature made it possible for writing-mediated brush conversation to take place between the Japanese and Koreans who did not have a shared spoken language. Being more conversant than their Japanese counterparts in general, the Korean literati tended to feel that they were gifted with excellent skills in Sinitic. Moreover, since the Koreans considered themselves superior to the Japanese based on their skills in poetry writing and meaning-making through brush-talk, the Japanese found brush-talking with Korean visitors a good opportunity to prove their Sinitic skills. The number of Japanese Confucianists wishing to meet with the Koreans grew exponentially each time the Chosŏn mission was received. Some well-versed Japanese literati were able to engage in extended poetic improvisation and long brush-talks with Koreans.

The Korean envoys and the Japanese literati also engaged in poetic exchange and socializing chanting (唱和, Jap: *shōwa*; Kor: *ch'anghwa*) consisting of improvising poems in Sinitic (Kwŏn 2010). While the brush-talk, poetic exchange, and exchange of personal letters were routinely collected, edited, and published by the Japanese hosts, the Korean delegates would record their own experiences in Japan in the form of diaries or travelogues.

The beginning of *t'ongsinsa* missions

The Korean envoys dispatched to Edo Japan in 1636 started brush-talking on diplomatic matters as ambassadors of cultural exchange between the two countries. The envoys were officially designated as *t'ongsinsa* 通信使, literally 'transmit-trust envoy'. Prior to this, the official Korean title of the first three missions to Edo Japan (1607, 1617, 1624) was called 'Respond cum Return Envoy' (*Hoetap kyŏm Swaehwansa* 回答兼刷還使), because the envoys were dispatched to deliver the Korean reply to the Japanese demand and to bring the Korean captives in Japan back home. In 1617 and 1624, the main duty of the Chosŏn envoys was to find those Koreans stranded in Japan and to bring them home.

But the Edo bakufu kept demanding Chosŏn to dispatch *t'ongsinsa* missions to Japan. Tsushima, as the diplomatic mediator, received pressure from the bakufu but was aware that Korea would not accept such a request. What Tsushima ended up doing was to alter the contents of the credentials presented by both countries. In effect, whereas Korea sent their 'Respond cum Return Envoys', the Japanese side was under the impression that they were sent in the name of *t'ongsinsa*. Thus, both sides operated with this misunderstanding during the three Chosŏn missions to Edo Japan in 1607, 1617, and 1624.

In 1631, Yanagawa Shigeoki 柳川調興 (1603–1684), a Tsushima Elder 家老, exposed to the bakufu that Korea in fact had not sent any *t'ongsinsa*. Yanagawa performed well in Japanese-Korean diplomacy, as well as maintaining good relations with the bakufu. Being ambitious, Yanagawa aimed to exploit and control the Japanese-Korean relations and eventually rise from a retainer of Tsushima domain to a liege lord or vassal of the Tokugawa Shogunate, the center of state power. Thus, he exposed to the bakufu the manipulation of the credentials by Sō Yoshinari 宗義成, the daimyō of Tsushima. But the bakufu would not tolerate treason and ended up siding with Sō and sending Yanagawa into exile instead.

Sō, however, had to prove to the bakufu that he could serve as a mediator in Japanese-Korean diplomatic relations in the absence of Yanagawa. To do so, he had to persuade Korea to send a real *t'ongsinsa* mission. At that time, the Later Jin 後金 (Manchurian: *Aisin Gurun*, 'golden state', 1616–1636) khanate was expanding its power in the north of Chosŏn Korea. To alleviate the threat from the north and step up with defense, Korea desperately wanted peace with its southern neighbor. To do so, Korea judged that it was in their best interest not to jeopardize their amicable relations with the Sō clan. Thus, they decided to dispatch *t'ongsinsa* envoys at Sō's request. On the other hand, many of the Korean captives were already brought back home, while others were reluctant to return to Korea because they had already been accustomed to life in Japan.

The dispatch of *t'ongsinsa* missions was not only important diplomatically but also in terms of cultural exchange between Japan and Korea. In 1636, a small group of 'talents on horse' 馬上才 were dispatched together with the envoys, gaining much popularity in Japan. This shows how the *t'ongsinsa* mission started morphing into a kind of cultural event. The earliest Korean envoys were preoccupied with negotiating for the repatriation of Korean prisoners of war and tried to dodge writing poems during their mission. At that time, Korean *t'ongsinsa* envoys regarded writing poems as merely an idle activity to kill time. The early envoys were trying to avoid being criticized for wasting time on poetry-writing rather than focusing on their primary duty of negotiating for the repatriation of Korean war captives. But as the mission was formally retitled as *t'ongsinsa*, the poetic exchange came to be seen as an important means to ascertain and sustain amicable diplomatic relations between the two countries.

The first Japanese-Chosŏn brush-talks

Fujiwara Seika

The oldest Japanese-Chosŏn brush-talk record could be traced to Fujiwara Seika 藤原惺窩 (1561–1619). Fujiwara was the founder of the Japanese school of Classical Chinese literature. One of his works contained brush-talk with Kang Hang 姜沆 (1567–1618) and other war captives from Chosŏn. Being a Confucianist, Kang had exerted tremendous influence on Fujiwara. During the second Japanese invasion of the six-year Imjin war 丁酉再亂 (1597–1598), Kang fought back against the Japanese army by transporting military provisions and raising an army. He was subsequently captured and transported to Japan. After he was sent to the Fushimi castle 伏見城, he met with Fujiwara, who was patronized by Akamatsu Hiromichi 赤松広通 (1562–1600), the castellan of Tatsuno 竜野, Harima 播磨. The encounter with Fujiwara led Kang to participate in the Japanese translation of the 'Four Books and Five Classics' 四書五經 and the publication of other Confucian works. Since the Japanese translations of the 'Four Books and Five Classics' were used as textbooks for early Confucianist education in Japan, Kang exerted tremendous influence on the formation of Japanese Confucianism.

Fujiwara had already encountered Koreans when he was a monk, although no brush-talk records by him survived. In 1590, when a Korean mission was dispatched to meet with Toyotomi Hideyoshi 豊臣秀吉 (1537–1598) in Edo Japan, Fujiwara visited the envoys at their residence and exchanged brush-talk and poems with them. Hŏ Sŏng 許筬 (1548–1612), the Third-Envoy (*sŏchanggwan* 書狀官), wrote 'About the name Sairitsushi' 柴立子說. *Sairitsushi*, literally 'standing old tree', was Fujiwara's pen name. That meeting with Kang Hang left a deep impression on Fujiwara, who eventually abandoned monkhood to become a Confucianist (Kwak 2010).

Hayashi Razan

Fujiwara, having grown into the first Japanese Confucianist, turned down the invitation of the bakufu to serve as an official and recommended his disciple Hayashi Razan 林羅山 (1583–1657) instead. Hayashi then became the first 'Confucian official' 儒官 of Edo Japan. In 1607, he taught the classics to the second Shōgun Tokugawa Hidetata 徳川秀忠. He also took charge of finding foreign books or doing research for the bakufu and the first Shōgun Tokugawa Ieyasu, who retreated to Sunpu 駿府 (today's Shizuoka 静岡県).

Hayashi's list of works included the brush-talk he had with the Koreans, allowing us to discern the types of people he encountered. His first brush-talk record was a brush conversation with Sa'myŏngdang 四溟堂 (1544–1610). Hayashi, aged 23, visited Sa'myŏngdang in the second lunar month of 1605 when the latter was staying at Fushimi. Sa'myŏngdang was not only a monk well versed in Sinitic but also a leader of warrior monks who gained many victories against the Japanese army during the Imjin war. He was dispatched to Japan under the title 'envoy to probe the enemy' (*t'amjŏksa* 探敵使) in 1604, in response to the Tokugawa bakufu's proposed restoration of diplomatic relations, a peace initiative mediated by Tsushima. The Chosŏn court purposely included a monk among the envoys based on the fact that Japan was a Buddhist country. His brush-talk with Hayashi was very brief, with Sa'myŏngdang asking Hayashi about his knowledge of Confucianism and Hayashi's short responses. At the end of the brush-talk, Sa'myŏngdang complimented Hayashi on his talent. The fact that Hayashi met with Sa'myŏngdang to inquire about Confucianism even though he was a monk suggests that Hayashi viewed Chosŏn as a country where Confucianism was more developed.

After he was employed by the bakufu, Hayashi met Chosŏn envoys more actively, but it was only in 1636 that he began engaging in brush-talk with them in earnest. The bakufu, in order to prevent the recurrence of the manipulation of credence letters, adopted the policy of *Iteian* Rotation 以酊庵輪番制. *Iteian* was the name of a temple in Tsushima where diplomatic documents between Japan and Chosŏn were handled. Under the policy of Iteian Rotation, the bakufu would send monks from Kyoto to Iteian on a rotating basis, the purpose being to inspect the diplomatic documents so that the bakufu could have better control over Japanese-Chosŏn diplomacy (Hong 2013). At the same time, the bakufu started to write the Japanese credentials on their own in place of seeking Tsushima's assistance. As the first Confucianist official of the bakufu, Hayashi had to attend to one of the important tasks: the writing of the credentials. But the bakufu was familiar with neither the style of diplomatic documents nor the official terminologies, unlike Tsushima interpreters who were familiar with the conventions in Korea. This led to frequent complaints from the Chosŏn envoys. In order to prevent further blunders, it became customary for the person in charge of the Japanese credentials to consult the Korean envoys beforehand. This gave Hayashi plenty of opportunities to visit the Korean envoys and to engage in brush conversation with them.

What kinds of topics did Hayashi 'talk' about with the Korean envoys in 1636? What they discussed may be discerned by reading *Record of sea travel* 海槎錄, a journal written by Kim Se-ryŏm, the Vice-Envoy on that mission. According to Kim's journal records, on 12:13, 1636, Hayashi came and asked him about certain Chinese characters used in Confucian classics. Kim was impressed by Hayashi's knowledge of Sinitic and answered his questions thoroughly. From this example, we can infer that Hayashi and Kim not only met for official purposes, but also exchanged information on matters of personal interest.

While discussing Confucianism and Confucianists in Chosŏn, Hayashi inquired about Chosŏn's landscape, customs, and products. He also asked about 'the method of raising hawks' (*yang'ŭngbang* 養鷹方). Thereupon Kim reprimanded Hayashi for asking trivial questions like raising hawks and dogs when he was expecting more serious questions. To Kim's rebuke, Hayashi apologized. Kim then let Kwŏn Ch'ik 權伋 (1599–1667), a 'teacher of formal diplomatic writing' 吏文學官, answer Hayashi's questions. Hayashi's writings do not contain brush-talk with Kim, but there are some records of brush-talk with Kwŏn and the secretary Mun Hongjŏk 文弘績. Content-wise, most of the brush-talks are concerned with the national administration, culture, and products of Chosŏn.

Kim's attitude to Hayashi's question provides a striking contrast between what it meant to be a Confucianist in Chosŏn and in Japan. Kim had won first place in the national civil service examination. He was an elite bureaucrat who served important roles, such as lecturing on Chinese classics to the prince. For elite bureaucrats like him, studying the classics was first and foremost to study political philosophy regarding how to participate in state administration. They were not interested in books providing technical or practical knowledge such as medicine, interpretation, the raising of hawks, and the like.

But being a Confucian official, Hayashi was not in a position to provide political advice or wield political authority. While he served as tutor of the Shōgun on Chinese classics, it was for the Shōgun's personal education and interests and not for promoting his own personal views of a particular school of political philosophy. It was thus more important for Hayashi to gain practical information from books written in Sinitic, such as cracking the complexity of certain Chinese characters but also the art of raising hawks effectively. Hawk hunting was the most luxurious hobby for a daimyō (as for Korean aristocrats as well), and hawks were among the gifts that the Korean king presented to the Shōgun.

Hayashi had the exceptional opportunity to engage in brush conversation with Vice-Envoy Kim upon the latter's invitation. Kim had a high regard for Hayashi's knowledge of Confucian classics. Even though there were Tsushima people fluent in Korean taking charge of interpretation, brush-talk was preferred probably because it was an opportunity for both sides to showcase their erudition as well as membership within the Sinosphere. In 1643, Hayashi entertained the Korean envoys for the second time, along with his own sons. The *t'ongsinsa* mission in 1655 was received by his son Hayashi Gahō 林鵞峰 (1618–1680), and the one in 1682 was received by his grandson Hayashi Hōkō 林鳳岡 (1644–1732). Up until 1811, the year of the last *t'ongsinsa* mission, all the descendants of the Hayashi clan entertained the Chosŏn envoys in their capacity as the Confucianist official of the bakufu. After each mission, the brush-talks and the poetic exchange with the Korean envoys were edited and compiled for publication. These compilations, however, did not include Hayashi's questions for Kim Se-ryŏm. It only included Hayashi's polite reception and the poems he improvised as the official host representing the bakufu.

The publication of brush-talk collections

'Collection of Chosŏn brush-talk' 朝鮮筆談集

For generations, the Hayashi clan met with the Chosŏn envoys, exchanged poems and engaged in brush conversation with them. But it is only in 1748 that the records of these encounters were published. The records had been kept in the form of bound volumes, perhaps because the Hayashi's, as a family of Confucian officials under the bakufu, needed them for internal purposes. The Hayashi's kept a diverse array of brush-talk interactions and exchanged collections of poetry published by others. The 'Annotation of the Asakusa library catalog' 淺草文庫書目解題, compiled by Murayama Tokujun 村山德淳 (1832–1893) in the Meiji era, allows us to estimate how many books the Hayashi clan actually possessed. The primary source of the Asakusa library was the collection of 'Shōheizaka School' 昌平坂學問所, which was previously the school of the Hayashi family during the late Edo period before it became a national school. Thus, the Asakusa library has its roots in the private collection of the Hayashi's literary treasures. Included in Murayama's list is a cluster of 42 documents classified as the 'Cluster of brush-talks with Korean visitors' 韓客筆談類. They were all commercially printed books, suggesting that they were probably among the most popular books of their time.

The first one of this cluster of 42 documents is the 'Collection of Chosŏn brush-talk' 朝鮮筆談集 compiled by Ishikawa Jōzan 石川丈山 (1583–1672). Ishikawa was the first true Sinitic poet of the Edo Period. He formerly served Tokugawa Ieyasu as a samurai and fought for the Siege of Osaka. He lost his status of samurai after breaching a military command and became a monk. Having learned Confucianism from Fujiwara Seika, he built 'the Hall of Poet-Muses' (*Shisendō* 詩仙堂) in his later years and spent his time there writing poems in Sinitic. Shisendō also served as a forum for poetic exchange.

The Korean appearing in Ishikawa's collection is Kwŏn Ch'ik who, as mentioned earlier, was a teacher of formal diplomatic writing 吏文學官 and had a brush conversation with Hayashi Razan at the order of Kim Se-ryŏm. *Imun* 吏文 refers to various official documents to be sent abroad, which the *hakkwan* 學官 was responsible for. Kwŏn was well known for his writing skills and was recommended by Im Kwang to participate in the mission as the Chief-Envoy's attendant. He was also famous for being the author of *Kangnojŏn* 姜虜傳, a novel based on the Battle of Sarhū 薩爾滸之戰 (1619) between Later Jin and Ming-Chosŏn allied forces, which he claimed to have participated in.[3]

In the first lunar month of 1637, the Korean envoys stayed in Honkoku Temple 本圀寺 in Kyoto after their visit to Edo. Because he was curious about how well the Koreans wrote Sinitic poems, Ishikwawa visited that temple, where he met Kwŏn. Having met for the first time, Kwŏn and Ishikawa learned about each other through brush-talk. The two had one thing in common: they were both talented in poetry writing. Ishikawa was also interested in Kwŏn's several visits to China, where he wanted to visit as well. As soon as he met Kwŏn, Ishikawa gave him his book of poetry as a gift. During their brush conversation, he requested Kwŏn to take a look at his book, give comments, and make suggestions for revision.

Ishikawa wrote to Kwŏn very politely, referring to him as a *Professor of poetry* 詩學教授 and consistently addressing him as *scholar* 學士. Even though he was 15 years older, Ishikawa was willing to learn from Kwŏn. At first, Kwŏn politely declined Ishikawa's request, saying that he was unable to concentrate because he was so tired after a long trip. But the interactional pattern of the brush-talk

---

3 According to Kwŏn (2019: 57–58), Kwŏn Ch'ik might not have participated in the Battle of Sarhū.

changed after Kwŏn asked Ishikawa specifically about literary figures and activities in Japan. This is in stark contrast with Kwŏn's brush-talks with other Japanese, probably because he was impressed by Ishikawa's academic talents after seeing his poems and their brush-talk interaction.

Kwŏn claimed that no Japanese writer could match Ishikawa's poetry. He described Ishikawa as the 'Li Bai and the Du Fu of Japan' 日東之李杜. Li Bai and Du Fu are historically the best-known poets of the 'Prosperous Tang' 盛唐 period, which was widely regarded as the pinnacle of creativity in Chinese poetry composition. Thus, Kwŏn was praising Ishikawa as the best poet in Japan. Kwŏn also wrote a foreword for Ishikawa's book of poetry, which says 'the metrics [of Ishikawa's poems] are close to the Prosperous Tang and the rhythm is a sequel to the "Major Court Hymns"' 律逼盛唐 韻賡大雅. Kwŏn's praise left a great impact on the Japanese world of poets of that epoch. According to Ishikawa's friend Noma Seiken 野間靜軒 (1608–1676), this event boosted Ishikawa's fame considerably as more and more people came to learn poetry from him. Noma also met Kwŏn, but only Ishikawa was praised as such. On 05:15, 1638, one and a half years after meeting Kwŏn, Ishikawa compiled his brush-talk with Kwŏn to show it to his friends visiting Shisendō. The printed copies accessible today were commercially published in 1682 and 1711, as public interest on *t'ongsinsa* envoys grew in each of the subsequent Chosŏn missions to Edo Japan.

The *Collection of Chosŏn brush-talk* illustrated Ishikawa's meeting with a Korean alone, with neither card nor letter showing his social status or ability. Kwŏn's praise of him as the best poet in Japan toward the end of their brush conversation may serve as a remarkable episode of a Japanese-Chosŏn encounter for the newly emerged class of Japanese Confucianists. The *Collection* must have been a popular commercial publication among the Confucianists, especially in the seventeenth century when the Japanese publication industry began to prosper (Clements 2015).

In 1695, Kwŏn's collection of 50 Chinese poems, the 'Must-reads for poets' 詩人要考集, was published in Kyoto by *Shōrindō* 書林堂. It consists of 50 poems, each with a portrait of its poet, and an appendix explaining the nuts and bolts of poetry writing in Sinitic. Its introduction states that Kwŏn selected the 50 poems from the 'Beads of poetic styles' 聯珠詩格 that he edited and took the manuscript with him to Japan. Someone in Japan got it from Kwŏn and kept it until the publisher Shōrindō obtained and published it. Although Kwŏn selected the poems, the poems themselves were all written by Chinese poets, with an appendix added by the Japanese publisher. Thus, the book has little to do with Chosŏn. Nevertheless, on its cover was written 'Selected by the Chosŏn scholar Kukhŏn' 朝鮮學士菊軒撰 (Kukhŏn being Kwŏn's pen name), suggesting how highly Chosŏn scholarship was respected and trusted by the Japanese literati during the early eighteenth century.

'Collection of Kyerim poetic exchange' 鷄林唱和集

The publication of the *Collection of Chosŏn brush-talk* in 1636 in Japan was rather an exceptional case, as no other similar collections were published following the Chosŏn missions of 1643 and 1655. The publication was made possible by Hayashi and Ishikawa, who were prominent intellectuals of their time. It was only in 1682 that collections of brush-talk and poetic exchange began to be published in large quantities in Japan. The publication process was so fast that the brush-talks held when the Korean envoys were heading to Edo were already published by the time they were returning home. This was clearly related to the rapid development of the Japanese publication industry and the growth of the Japanese readership of literature in Sinitic (Clements 2015).

The 'Collection of Kyerim poetic exchange' 鷄林唱和集 (Jap: *Keirin shōwashū*; Kor: *Kyerim changhwajip*, Seo 1711), is perhaps the largest collection of Japanese-Korean brush-talk and poetic exchange to date, consisting of works from 115 literati. Together with its sequel 'Collection of the poetic exchange of seven poets' 七家唱和集 (Jap: *Shichika shōwashū*; Kor: *Chilga changhwajip*), the *Kyerim* collection comprises most of the brush-talk and poetic exchange produced and collected in 1711.

The brush conversations in the *Kyerim* collection afford us a glimpse into the Literary Sinitic world in Japan during the early eighteenth century. The Japanese monks, who were experts in Classical Chinese literature, only had brief conversations with the Korean envoys because the two groups could not find common topics to talk about. But the newly emerged class of Japanese Confucianists made an effort to engage in extended brush conversations with the Korean literati. The Japanese Confucianists, skilled in Sinitic, could freely converse with the Korean scholars and had the privilege to meet with them on different occasions. They were at the forefront of the Sinitic-based literature in Japan.

The difference in sociocultural status between Japanese and Korean scholars

When the Confucianists, employees of the daimyōs, met the Korean literati, they called themselves 'serving tutors' 侍講 or 'historian ministers' 史臣. This is because their main job was to tutor their lords on Chinese classics or write documents for them. After the *han* schools 藩校 were established, they used their titles such as 'chief teacher' 學頭, 'writer' 文學, or 'secretary' 書記. Although they rarely gave political advice, they were principally experts in Sinitic-based literature in charge of Chinese books or written documents. Their Sinitic literacy was crucial in deciphering the Chinese books delivered by Chinese merchants, which contained the most advanced knowledge of their time. Thus, the questions posed by the Confucianists in 1711 were similar to those posed by Hayashi Razan in 1636: They were mainly about Korea, the Confucian classics, and other books in Chinese. The Confucianists wanted to verify and expand their knowledge of Korea through their exchange with the envoys, as well as proving their ability by winning recognition from the Koreans. On the other hand, the Korean literati were bureaucrats(-to-be), selected through national civil service examinations. Because all the envoys were bureaucrats, they behaved like bureaucrats with diplomatic missions even when engaged in brush-talking privately, which helps explain why they would never express anything that might be critical or tarnish the reputation of their own country.

The Korean envoys were interested in the politics of Japan and other countries. Okajima Kanzan 岡島冠山 (1674–1728), who wrote Mandarin textbooks and translated Mandarin into Japanese, met Chŏng Ch'ang-ju 鄭昌周 (1652–?), a Korean-Chinese interpreter among the Korean envoys on the 1711 mission. Chosŏn included Japanese interpreters in their missions to China and Chinese interpreters in their missions to Japan, in the hope of establishing contact with foreigners in China or Japan so as to obtain valuable information from third parties. Even though Okajima and Chŏng could have talked about their shared interest in learning Mandarin, Chŏng rather showed interest in Okajima's hometown Nagasaki, questioning the number of Chinese merchant ships entering Nagasaki and their relationship with Japan. This is one example showing that the envoys, including the interpreters, were devoted to their duty of collecting information or intelligence about the political situation of other countries.

In sum, there was a gap between the interests and the attitudes of Korean envoys and diplomatic bureaucrats on one hand and Japanese literati and intellectuals on the other. This led to a divergence of the 1711 Japanese-Korean brush-talks into two types: One being poetic exchange between the Korean poets and the Japanese literati, the other being medical exchange between Japanese and Korean medical doctors.

As mentioned earlier, despite being positioned as 'Confucian officials' 儒官, the Japanese literati were closer to a class of scholars than that of bureaucrats in accordance with a hierarchy of national ranks and files, unlike their Chosŏn counterparts. Apart from becoming experts of Confucian classics and other literary works from China, they were also expected to familiarize themselves with specialized technical knowledge of foreign origin, especially from China as printed in Chinese books. This is clearly illustrated by the Japanese term 'Confucian doctor' 儒医, which literally combines two areas of expertise in one and the same person, namely medical doctor with a good command of medical knowledge, but also a scholar of Confucian classics. What these two areas of knowledge have in common is that both required a high level of reading skills in written Chinese. Such a status or practice being unknown in Chosŏn Korea, of particular interest are a number of 'knowledge gaps' that are discernible in several brush-talk records in the *Collection of Kyerim poetic exchange*.

One instructive example may be found in the brush-talk record produced by Inō Jakusui 稲生若水 (1655–1715). When he met the Chosŏn *chesulgwan* (製述官, 'official in charge of writing') and other secretaries 書記, Inō indicated that he was compiling a 'list of plants and animals' 庶物類纂 under the auspices of Maeda Tsunanori 前田綱紀 (1643–1724), lord of the Kaga Han 加賀藩. Functionally it was meant to be an encyclopedic introduction to about 3,590 species of animals and plants, a monumental undertaking that was only brought to completion in 1738 by his disciple Niwa Shōhaku 丹羽正伯 (1691–1756). In this brush conversation, therefore, Inō's interest focused exclusively on animals and plants. For instance, Inō took the trouble of showing real fish and, after explaining their habits in great detail, asked whether they existed in Chosŏn and what they were called.

Compared with the very detailed question raised by Inō, Chosŏn literati's answers were simplistic and uninformative to say the least, as none of them possessed the expert knowledge needed to provide an enlightening response. Inō also had a brush conversation with the 'good doctor' (*yangŭi* 良醫) Ki Tu-mun 奇斗文. He brought along plant specimens and asked Ki rather specific questions one after another. Ki was able to give sensible responses based on his knowledge of herbal medicine. In terms of intellectual competence, Inō seemed to come closer to being a good doctor than a *chesulgwan*. This trend can also be seen in the brush-talk of Takeda Shun'an 竹田春庵 (1661–1745), who was also a Confucian scholar and medical doctor from Fukuoka. He sent a long list of questions to *chesulguan* Yi Hyŏn 李礥 and *yangŭi* Ki Tu-mun, respectively. Takeda's questions in both lists showed remarkable similarity between his attitudes toward Confucian classics and books on medicine. There was hardly any difference between the way he treated scholarly questions concerning Confucian classics and those concerning Chinese drugs. What they had in common was his determination to fill unknown knowledge gaps, be they questions related to Confucian canons or Chinese medicine.

Korean and Japanese literati had rather different views toward Neo-Confucianism. For the Koreans, it was the foundation of Chosŏn society, whereas, for the Japanese, it was simply a part or branch of technical knowledge in Sinitic literature. To interpret Confucian classics was a question of ideology for the Koreans, but for the Japanese, it was simply a matter of deciphering technical know-how in Chinese. This is probably why exchange between the Korean envoys and Japanese Confucianists gradually changed topically from scholarly discussions to poetic exchange out of concern for courtesy and amity.

The medical doctors on both sides, on the other hand, did not have any ideological taboos between them. They were thus able to engage in discussion and exchange of medical knowledge freely. Starting from 1711 and throughout the eighteenth century, various records of Japan-Chosŏn brush-talk related to medicine were published in Japan (Hur 2010). This was because, as mentioned earlier, cultural exchange had become an important part of the *t'ongsinsa* mission, including exchange of medical knowledge, not least because by the eighteenth century, Chosŏn Korea's stature in the study of medicine was highly respected and well acknowledged by Japan as well as China (Ham et al. 2007).

Conclusion

In this chapter, we have illustrated how the newly emerged class of Japanese Confucianists were engaged in brush conversation and exchanged poetry with the Korean envoys during the early Edo period. The Korean envoys were the only national envoys dispatched to Japan, unlike the Dutch envoys dispatched by the Dutch East India Company or the Ryukyuan envoys who followed the Satsuma domain's instruction. Because Chosŏn was a country bordering on and exchanging envoys periodically with China, she was able to trade with and observe China directly, unlike Japan, where Chinese books and goods could only be brought in through imports via merchant ships. The Japanese Confucianists, admiring China, were eager to meet and talk with Korean envoys, whose evaluation of their literary performance had great authority and impact among the Japanese literati. As the Japanese Confucianists grew in numbers, the types of Japanese literati the Korean envoys met diversified, which is reflected in the *Collections of Kyerim poetic exchange*.

However, whereas the Confucianists in Korea were bureaucrats selected via national civil service examinations, the Confucianists in Japan had inherently different social statuses given that political power rested with hereditary warrior lords. Thus, both sides entered into transcultural brush conversations with rather different objectives and expectations: The Korean diplomats were bureaucrats who wanted to maintain good diplomatic relations with the Japanese literati through writing while not forgetting to fulfill their duty of gathering information and intelligence. On the other hand, the Japanese literati were experts on technical knowledge, expecting intellectually rich discussions with and enlightening teachings by the Korean literati. The Japanese-Korean brush-talks during the early Edo period allow us to observe how the two groups of Confucianists, despite their linguistic and sociocultural differences, exchanged lingua-cultural and technical knowledge through the scripta franca that they shared, namely Classical Chinese or Literary Sinitic (Kornicki 2018).

References

Chong, D.-H. (2010). Making Chosŏn's own tributaries: Dynamics between the Ming-centered world order and a Chosŏn-centered regional order in the East Asian periphery. *International Journal of Korean History* 15: 29–63.

Clements, R. (2015). *A cultural history of translation in early modern Japan*. Cambridge: Cambridge University Press.

Clements, R. (2019). Brush talk as the 'lingua franca' of East Asian diplomacy in Japanese-Korean encounters, c. 1600–1868. *The Historical Journal* 62(2): 289–309.

Denecke, W. (2014). Worlds without translation: Premodern East Asia and the power of character scripts. In S. Bermann & C. Porter (Eds.), *A companion to translation studies* (pp. 204–216). Chichester, UK: Wiley-Blackwell.

Ham, J.-S. [咸晸楨] et al. (2007). 18 世紀 朝鮮通信使 醫官과 儒醫의 役割 – 醫學問答을 中心으로 – (The role of medical officers and Confucian doctors in the 18th century in Joseon). 韓國漢醫學研究院論文集 *Korea Journal of Oriental Medicine* 13(1): 19–27.

Handel, Z. (2019). *Sinography: The borrowing and adaptation of the Chinese script*. Leiden: Brill.

Hong, S.-T. [洪性德] (2013). 朝鮮後期 韓日外交體制와 對馬島의 役割 ('The role of Tsushima domain in Chosŏn-Japan relations in the late Chosŏn period'). 東北亞歷史論叢 *Journal of Northeast Asian History* 41: 137–180.

Hur, K.-J. [許敬震] (2010). 朝鮮 醫員의 日本 使行과 醫學筆談集의 出版 樣相 (Japanese travels of Joseon medicine and the aspects of publication of collections of medical written conversations). 醫史學 *Korean Journal of Medical History* 19(1): 137–156.

Ishikawa. J. [石川丈山] (1711). 朝鮮筆談集 ('Collection of Chosŏn brush-talk'). 日本國立公文書館 (National Archives of Japan). Retrieved June 26, 2021, from www.digital.archives.go.jp/img/1232493.

Kim, S.-R. [金世濂] (c. 1637). 海槎錄 ('Record of sea travel'). Unpublished manuscript. 韓國 國立中央圖書館 (National Library of Korea). Retrieved July 24, 2021, from https://db.itkc.or.kr/dir/item?itemId=GO#dir/node?grpId=&itemId=GO&gubun=book&depth=3&cate1=Z&cate2=&dataGubun=%EC%84%9C%EC%A7%80&dataId=ITKC_GO_1387A&upSeoji=ITKC_GO_1373A.

Koh, C.-S., & King, R. (2014). *Infected Korean language, purity versus hybridity: From the Sinographic cosmopolis to Japanese colonialism to global English*. New York: Cambria Press.

Kornicki, P. F. (2018). *Languages, scripts, and Chinese texts in East Asia*. Oxford: Oxford University Press.

Kwak, C.-R. [郭貞禮] (2010). 岳麓許筬과 에도(江戶) 儒學의 勃興 – 후지와라 세이카 (藤原惺窩)와의 酬唱詩와 「柴立子說」을 中心으로 – (Ak-Rok Huh Seong and sudden rise of Edo Confucianism: Focusing on poetic exchange with Fujiwara Seika and 'About the name Sairitsushi'). 語文研究 *The Society for Korean Language & Literary Research* 38(3): 411–437.

Kwŏn, C.-W. [權政媛] (2010). 筆談과 唱和의 同異性 考察 – 日本使行記를 中心으로 – (An inquiry into similarities and differences between Pildam and Changhwa – focusing on Japanese envoys' remarks). 漢字漢文教育 (Han-Character and Classical written language Education) 25: 413–439.

Kwŏn, H.-R. [權赫來] (2019). 深河戰鬪 戰爭捕虜 姜弘立의 두 形象 – 『柵中日錄』과 <姜虜傳>의 對比를 中心으로 – (Two shapes of a captive General Kang Hong-lip in Simha War: Focusing on the contrast between Ch'aekchung-illok and Kanglo-chŏn). 洌上古典研究 *Yeol-sang Journal of Classical Studies* 68: 41–75.

Mair, V. H. (1994). Buddhism and the rise of the written vernacular in East Asia: The making of national languages. *The Journal of Asian Studies* 53(3): 707–751. doi: 10.2307/2059728.

Man, J. (2002). *Gutenberg: How one man remade the world with words*. New York: Wiley.

Norman, J. (1988). *Chinese*. Cambridge: Cambridge University Press.

Nosco, P. (1984). Introduction: Neo-Confucianism and Tokugawa discourse. In P. Nosco (Ed.), *Confucianism and Tokugawa culture* (pp. 3–26). Princeton, NJ: Princeton University Press.

Seo, Y. [瀨尾用拙齋] (Ed.). (1711). 鷄林唱和集 ('Collection of Kyerim poetic exchange'). Kyoto: Keibunkan [奎文館]. 日本國立公文書館 (National Archives of Japan).

11 Brush-talk between Chosŏn envoys and Tokugawa literati

Contesting cultural superiority and 'central efflorescence' 中華, 1711–1811

Jang Jin-youp

Introduction

The term *t'ongsinsa* 通信使 refers specifically to envoys dispatched by Chosŏn to Tokugawa Japan after the Japanese Invasion (1592–1598, Imjin War 壬辰倭亂), which involved altogether twelve missions from 1607 to 1811, of which four took place during the eighteenth century (1711, 1719, 1748, 1763–64).[1] Whereas negotiating post-war diplomatic relations and repatriation of prisoners were the main goals of early missions, from the late seventeenth century onwards, when the Chinese World Order in East Asia began to stabilize (Fairbank 1968), cultural exchange through *t'ongsinsa* visits played a crucial role in cultivating friendly interstate relations. During their visits, partly due to a lack of a shared spoken language, Chosŏn envoys were routinely engaged in poetic improvisation and exchange as part of their writing-mediated brush conversations (brush-talks) with Japanese scholars, poets, doctors, and monks. Notwithstanding the presence of Korean-Japanese interpreters, the literati on both sides clearly preferred to engage in brush conversation directly. This was probably motivated by a strong sense of communion emanating from shared membership within the same Confucian civilization by virtue of the fact that their intellectual exchange was grounded in a shared body of Classical canons and literary works in Chinese, 'a shared storehouse of civilized learning' for literati in Sinographic East Asia (Clements 2019: 308). Compared with speech-based communication through interpreters, brush-talk was perceived to be superior not only because it allowed for more in-depth exchange of views, but it also enabled the brush-talkers to perform other aesthetic feats from calligraphy and various visual art forms to poetic improvisation (Clements 2019). As a result of such exchanges from 1636 (the fourth mission) to 1811 (the twelfth), no less than 170 books of brush-talk records 筆談唱和集 were produced in Korea and Japan, the majority being compiled and edited by Japanese

---

[1] The eleventh mission departed Chosŏn and arrived at Tsushima in 1763. By the time it reached Edo and other big cities like Osaka, Kyoto, and Nagoya, it was 1764. Thus, whereas the Koreans regarded it as the 1763 mission, the Japanese called it 1764 mission, hence the notation 1763–64.

literati and circulated as handwritten copies or printed volumes (see Takahashi 2007, 2009; see also Jang 2017).

Based on a systematic review of brush-talk records from the seventeenth to the nineteenth centuries, this chapter presents evidence of Japanese-Korean writing-mediated dueling since 1711, contesting for the status of 'central efflorescence' 中華 or 'standard of civilization'. Chosŏn *t'ongsinsa* visits to Japan were clearly exploited by both sides as a gateway to compete for cultural superiority. I will briefly examine the historical background before exemplifying such dueling and contestation using brush-talk excerpts from 1711 to 1811 in Japanese-Korean poetic exchange 詩文唱和 and brush-talk records.

Brief review of the relevant literature

The study of brush-talk records produced during Chosŏn's missions to Japan began in earnest with Yi Wŏn-sik's (1991) book and the publication of 'A compilation of the records of Chosŏn missions to Japan' (*Taikei Chōsen Tsūshinshi* 大系朝鮮通信使) by Sin and Nakao (1993–94). Takahashi (2007, 2009) provides a more accurate and up-to-date list of such records. Yi Hye-sun (1995) is an early example of the use of *t'ongsinsa* brush-talk data to analyze cultural exchange between Korea and Japan. In Korea, since the 2000s, research on brush-talk interactions produced during Chosŏn missions has been active, and over 100 articles have been published so far. Among them, two published doctoral dissertations are particularly worthy of mention. Koo (2006) analyzes brush-talk records of 1763–64, while Shin (2011) is a study of the brush-talk records of 1811. Hur (2010) gives an overview of the main characteristics of brush-talk exchange between Korea and Japan. Regarding scholarly works in English, Clements's (2019) study of Chosŏn *t'ongsinsa* missions to Japan provides empirical evidence by drawing on successive envoys' travel journals, their brush-talk records, as well as artistic illustrations such as paintings to show that even though Sinitic brush-talk was not included as part of the protocol in diplomatic exchange, there is extant evidence of its prominent role at various points – ceremonial or otherwise – during Chosŏn's *t'ongsinsa* missions to Japan. Clements also discusses the functional role of Chinese characters or Literary Sinitic in Sinographic East Asia which, following Denecke (2014), is more appropriately characterized as a 'scripta franca' than a 'lingua franca', given that Sinitic brush-talk is essentially writing-mediated rather than speech-based.

Several studies are particularly relevant to the theme of this chapter. Fuma (2008, 2015) provides an informative overview of the confrontation between Korean Zhuzi 朱子 Studies and Japanese Sorai 徂徠 studies during Chosŏn missions to Japan from 1748 to 1811. Despite being criticized by Korean researchers for biased interpretation of brush-talk data, Fuma's (2008, 2015) book is a pioneering scholarly work in that the full spectrum of academically oriented dialogue between Chosŏn Korea and Tokugawa Japan is empirically supported by evidence of brush-talk interactions recorded during the *t'ongsinsa* missions. Huh (2012) discusses the dispute between Arai Hakuseki 新井白石 (1657–1725) and the

1711 Chosŏn mission over Chosŏn's dress and clothing styles, while Yi Hyo-wŏn (2017) draws attention to the confrontation between a Sorai School scholar and the Chosŏn mission in 1748 surrounding Japan's clothes and Confucian rites and rituals. This chapter is an extension of the author's doctoral thesis published in 2017, which analyzes the brush-talk records of the 1763–64 mission and Korean-Japanese competition over the legitimacy of their respective claims for central efflorescence status.[2]

Background to contestation between Chosŏn envoys and Japanese literati

As the Ming dynasty (1368–1644) gave way to the Qing (1644–1911), the 'barbarian' Manchus' ascent to the Chinese throne sent shock waves to Chosŏn, the 'model tributary' of the Sinocentric 'center' (Chun 1968: 90). Elsewhere in Sinographic East Asia, there was widespread skepticism whether China could legitimately lay claim to the hitherto Han-specific central efflorescence (Mand: *zhōnghuá*, Jap: *chūka*, Kor: *chunghwa*, Viet: *trung hoa*) status. Now that the bearer's position was deemed vacant following the demise of the Ming, which polity best merited that status thus became an open question. While the two eastern neighbors, Korea and Japan, had both been influenced by Chinese culture, the extent of such influence was far greater in Korea due primarily to geographical proximity. Korean literati, who had long been proud of themselves as 'Little China' 小中華, firmly believed that their civilization had always adhered to Confucianist culture and values closely. By contrast, Confucianism was embraced in Japan rather late. Historically, until the Tokugawa period, Japan had little interest in emulating institutions inspired by Confucian philosophy and values, but that changed after Confucianism was systematically introduced since the late seventeenth century in Japan, probably as a result of the teaching and influence of late Ming Confucian scholar Zhu Shunshui 朱舜水 (1600–1682), who spent the last two decades of his twilight years serving as a guest teacher of the *daimyō* of the Mito 水戸 domain and advisor of Tokugawa Mitsukuni 德川光圀 (1628–1701) (see Li 2020: 209–216).

The advent of the Qing era made the Korean literati convinced that Chosŏn was the natural custodian and only legitimate bearer of central efflorescence status in the world. This thought, called 'Chosŏn central efflorescence' 朝鮮中華主義, became mainstream among the ruling class of Chosŏn who mourned the demise of the Ming dynasty, whose assistance during the Imjin War was greatly appreciated. They pledged that Chosŏn would continue to adhere to the fine teaching of ancient Chinese sages until the Han Chinese revival. Meanwhile, disgruntled with the Chinese World Order (Fairbank 1968) after diplomatic relations with the Ming dynasty was severed at the beginning of the Bakufu period, Japan under the Tokugawa shogunate

---

2 Owing to space limitation, I regret that many other relevant publications written in Korean or Japanese could not be cited.

gradually evolved its own 'center-periphery' concept or awareness of central efflorescence 日本型華夷観念意識, whereby Japan was positioned as the new center of 'all-under-heaven' 天下. Such a mindset of Japan being the new central efflorescence gradually took hold after China came under the Manchus' 'barbarian' rule from the mid-seventeenth century onward (Toby 1991/2013: 126–127).[3]

It took several Chosŏn missions before the Japanese aspiration and claim became apparent to the Korean envoys. In short, the century-long intensification of Japanese-Korean identity negotiation vying for the culturally superior central efflorescence status was rooted in a widely shared perception among Japanese and Korean literati that from the mid-seventeenth century onwards, the traditional 'efflorescence-barbarian' distinction was in tatters, and that the Manchus, being a 'barbarian' tribe, could no longer lay claim to such a prestigious role and status.

Among the Japanese who received Chosŏn envoys and participated in brush-talk interaction with them were mostly scholars, poets, monks, and doctors who were familiar with Confucian classics and values. At the peak of Japanese-Korean cultural exchange through *t'ongsinsa* visits to Japan in 1763–64, approximately five hundred Japanese brush-talkers were involved. Various schools of thought were represented, including Sorai studies 徂徠學, anti-Sorai studies 反徂徠學, Zhuzi studies of Neo-Confucianism 朱子學, eclecticism 折衷學 and evidential research 考證學. What they had in common was knowledge of Confucianism, the shared heritage of Confucian teachings and values that were constitutive of central efflorescence in Chinese civilization 中華文明, which made communication between the Japanese and Korean literati possible in the first place.

The contestation concerned the legitimacy and bearer status of central efflorescence. The challenge consisted of Japan's assertive claim for a new world order in which Japan would advance from the periphery to the center vis-à-vis once efflorescent China and 'Little China' Chosŏn. The Japanese tried to prove their cultural superiority by demonstrating advances not only in aggregate quality outputs of Confucian scholarship that they were so proud of but also the preservation of ancient Chinese rites, rituals, music, and other forms of cultural heritage 禮樂文物. Such contestation became more and more evident as *t'ongsinsa* exchanges intensified, culminating in the eleventh mission in 1763–64. In the following, I will briefly explain when and how the idea of competition emerged among Japanese Confucians.

Hayashi Razan 林羅山 (1583–1657) was an influential Japanese scholar who took part in early brush-talk exchanges between Chosŏn envoys and their Japanese hosts during the seventeenth century. From the fourth (1636) to the sixth (1655) *t'ongsinsa* exchanges, he engaged in brush-talk with Chosŏn envoys together with his family members, colleagues, and disciples. These Confucian scholars did not confront the Korean literati ideologically in their poetic exchange or brush conversations. While Razan was sometimes critical of Korean history studies and literary works, he was nevertheless convinced that Japanese scholars

---

3 Page references based on the Korean version of Toby's (1991) book (2013 ed., trans. by Y.-J. Huh. [許恩珠]).

were no match for their Korean counterparts in Chinese poetry composition and knowledge of Confucian classics. By 1682, during the seventh *t'ongsinsa* mission, as the Confucian scholars in Japan grew in number, both sides began to take brush-talk performance more and more seriously. In addition to Hayashi and his family, many other scholars participated in brush conversation with Chosŏn envoys (H.-S. Yi 1995: 94). Up until this point, no evidence of writing-mediated dueling was discernible in Japanese-Korean brush-talk interactions. At the early stage of *t'ongsinsa* exchange, asymmetry in lingua-cultural abilities to engage in brush-talk interaction made the Korean envoys feel strongly that their Japanese hosts were not up to par. Given that the capacity to engage in brush-talk and Sinogram-based poetic improvisation of *hanshi* 漢詩酬唱 (cf. 唱和, Mand: *chànghè*, Jap: *shōwa*, Kor: *changhwa*, Viet: *xướng họa*, 'chanting in harmony', Clements 2019: 295), was a prerequisite for meaningful cross-cultural exchange, Japanese literati who were latecomers in the systematic study of Chinese literature and Confucian classics had no choice but to learn from their counterparts in Chosŏn. That explains the condescending attitude of early *t'ongsinsa's*, as shown in their open criticisms of their Japanese hosts' writing-mediated improvisation enacted through brush conversation.

From the eighteenth century onward, however, there emerged among Japanese literati of Sinitic a popular belief that capacity-building in the studies of Confucianism had matured, rivaling Chosŏn or even Qing China. The idea that Japan outperformed Chosŏn not only militarily 武, but also in writing 文 gradually took shape. Such a perception was grounded in rapid advances in academic studies since the Genroku 元禄 (1688–1704) period, in particular Zhuzi studies of Neo-Confucianism 朱子學, Jinsai studies 仁斎學 and Sorai studies 徂徠學. These intellectual currents thrived following the steady expansion in the number of scholars and literati of Sinitic resulting from the dissemination of Confucian thoughts and knowledge initiated by some *daimyō's* 大名 and the shogunate. Japanese life and culture were basically dominated by Buddhism and Shintoism, and the ruling samurais were principally guided by the samurai spirit (*bushido* 武士道, Watanabe 1985/2007: 23–41).[4] Even though the influence of Confucianism in society was moderate, the development of Japanese *kangaku* 漢學 in the early seventeenth and eighteenth centuries was still remarkable as gauged by the quality of Sinitic-based scholarship and number of literary works. Following the emergence of a class of experts with strengths in Confucian studies and Sinitic writing, growing numbers of Confucian scholars increasingly took pride in their academic excellence and began to take brush-talk exchange seriously. In their view, being the upholder of ancient Chinese civilization, Japan fully deserved the claim to the status of central efflorescence. Unsurprisingly, such a claim was bitterly contested by Korean envoys who held fast to their superior cultural identity as well as the legitimacy of 'Little China' status until the very end of their *t'ongsinsa* exchange

---

4 Page references based on the Korean version of Watanabe's (1985) book (2007 ed., trans. by H.-K. Pak [朴鴻圭]).

with Japan in 1811. In the following, we will examine the early forms of positioning and contestation that began in 1711, and how it evolved in subsequent *t'ongsinsa* visits.

Arenas of Korean-Japanese competition, 1711–1811

'Brush battle' 筆戰 *as the site of competition*

In 1711, Yamagata Shūnan 山縣周南 (1687–1752) and Ando Tōya 安藤東野 (1683–1719), among others, compiled a collection of brush-talks that made a mockery of Chosŏn envoys, including in its title: 問槎畸賞 ('Unique sights of Chosŏn envoys', Akimoto 1712). Their teacher, Ogyū Sorai 荻生徂徠 (1666–1728), wrote a preface where he commented that the poetry of Chosŏn envoys resembled crude poetic imitations of the Song period 宋詩, which was no match for the Sorai School writers' passionate and elegant poems inspired by the works of Qin-Han times and Tang dynasty at its best. Following is a selection of Sorai's comments on the poems by Yi Hyŏn 李礥, Chosŏn's 'official in charge of writing' (*chesulgwan* 製述官), who was better known by his penname Tonggwak 東郭:

• 東郭詩 是爲第一 只是村氣滿目	This poem is the best of Tonggwak's poems, but it is replete with rustic airs.
• 這甚俚語	This sounds very colloquial.
• 似工却醜 宛然宋人 面目可憎	Seemingly exquisite but dreadfully so, reminiscent of Song people, abominable.
• 如讀俗牘	As if reading a vulgar letter.
• 何不將艸字押	Why didn't he follow the rhyme of [the sinogram] 艸?

On the other hand, the Korean envoy's comments on the poems of Yamagata, penname Jikō 次公 are far more positive:

• 淵淳可法	Profound and lucid, truly a model.
• 典麗宏雅 冠冕當世 自是大家	Graceful, elegant and splendid, stately work of our time, no doubt a master
• 大氏次公七律 色澤似仲默 神理肖于鱗 而骨格原諸右丞 所以爲妙	Jikō's heptasyllabic octave has Zhongmo's flavor, reminiscent of Yulun's style, while structurally it gives the feel of a senior minister's masterpiece, so ingenious!

Whereas Yi Hyŏn was rated as a celebrated writer by the Japanese literati until the end of *t'ongsinsa* exchanges, his poems were criticized by Sorai as unworthy as they did not even rhyme properly. By contrast, his own disciple Yamagata's poetry was hailed as a virtuoso exuding rigor 法度 and ingenuity 妙處. Sorai's promotion of his own school's poetic excellence, in sharp contrast with his denigration of Chosŏn's literary improvisation was indicative of an attempt to uplift the status of Sorai School which hitherto had not been acknowledged in Japan. Such a prejudice took its toll as it perpetuated a negative perception among subsequent generations of Japanese literati that Chosŏn poets were mediocre and ignorant of proper rhyming scheme, and their works unsophisticated and produced hastily with no literary interest. By 1763–64, such a perception became virtually received wisdom among Japanese literati. Unlike the early days of *t'ongsinsa* exchange, Japanese literati of the eighteenth century who were far more confident in composing Classical Chinese poetry (*hanshi* 漢詩) regarded poetic exchange with Chosŏn envoys as a site of interstate rivalry that came to be called 'battle of writing' 文戰 or 'brush battle' 筆戰. Such a stance, which might have helped offset the self-doubt and anxiety of Japanese literati and boost their confidence when engaged in poetic improvisation vis-à-vis Chosŏn envoys, clearly became more and more apparent with time, as evidenced in the prefaces of various brush-talk volumes like those exemplified here:

讀之則非唐非明, 有一種之體裁焉. 若逢場帆前之數語, 橘花蟬聲之重出, 則瑣俚可厭矣. 要之則彼邦汲汲乎場屋擧業, 爲祿利之捷徑, 無千秋不朽之志矣則可. (Miyase 宮瀨龍門 1748)

The writing of this work is neither Tang- nor Ming-style but has a style of its own. The monotonous words we use when we meet and break up, repeated allusion to orange blossoms and the buzzing and clicking of cicadas sound abominable. In that country, people are eager to learn the classics for the sake of participating in the civil service examination (Mand: *kēejǔ* 科擧, Kor: *kwagŏ* 科擧), a well-known shortcut for making money or hoarding wealth by taking up official positions, especially for those with no ambition to strive toward making a name for posterity.

然而皆操其土風, 蘇, 黃末派之雄耳. 如夫筆語者, 應酬敏捷, 頗似得縱橫自由者也, 是其生平之所業, 習慣如天性, 而唯是應務而已, 何有文章之可觀? 蓋韓土取士之法, 一因明制, 廷試專用濂閩之經義, 主張性理, 以遺禮樂, 故文唯主達意, 而修辭之道廢矣, 宜乎弗能知古文辭之妙.[5]

However, their works exhibit an indigenous [Korean] style, reminiscent of the waning influence of [Song Chinese poets] Su Shi 蘇軾 and Huang Tingjian 黃庭堅. They were dexterous at brush-talking, very much at ease and seemingly unhindered. That natural instinct was no doubt a result of handling habitual routine tasks on the job. By contrast, the quality of their brush-talk is never matched by their literary composition. This is because the selection of officials in Chosŏn follows the system modeled on Ming China. The Chosŏn

---

5 Preface of Yamane Kayō 山根華陽 (1697–1772) in 長門癸甲問槎 ('Chosŏn envoy who visited Nagato in 1763–1764') by Taki (1765).

court only accepts the Lian 濂 doctrine of Zhou Dunyi 周敦頤 and Min 閩 doctrine of Zhu Xi 朱熹, whereby human nature 人性 and laws of nature 天理 were foregrounded to the neglect of proper rites, rituals and music 禮樂. Consequently, whereas their literary compositions can get across their ideas, rhetorical principles and poetic elements are ignored. It would be fair to say that what makes ancient literary compositions ingenious eludes them entirely.

It should be noted that the Chosŏn envoys' poems in question were mostly impromptu improvisations during *t'ongsinsa* exchange with their Japanese hosts; they are in no way representative of the quality of Chosŏn poetry in general. The Chosŏn literati had to improvise poetry composition on demand all day long, amounting to thousands of poems per Chosŏn mission in Japan collectively. For instance, Clements (2019: 298) notes that 'Sin Yu-han [申維翰] (1681–1752), secretary of mission to the 1719 Korean embassy, recorded in his diary that he was bombarded with requests for brush conversation and poetry exchanges'. It would be understandable if a lack of topical variety and literary style in Chosŏn poetry is in evidence. Where the content appeared to be bland, like 'the monotonous words we use when we meet and break up' 逢場帆前之數語, this hardly warrants the conclusion that Chosŏn poetry was a poor imitation of Song-style colloquialism or a cliched product of the civil service examination. By dismissing Chosŏn's poetry as low-quality imitations and positioning it at the opposite end of fine, superior poetic style which was characteristic of prosperous Tang 盛唐 and the archaic style of the Former and Later Seven Masters 前後七子 during the Ming dynasty, Sorai School literati uplifted the prestige of their writing while projecting a distorted view of Chosŏn's poetry. Such an undue comparison and contrast also did much to fuel an awareness that Chosŏn and Japan were at war, albeit mediated by poetic exchange in writing, with Japan standing out clearly as the winner being the inescapable conclusion. Following is one instructive example:

昔者神皇后一張桑弓, 制服三韓, 武德永威, 待之以狗. 近世豊臣王提三尺劍, 自將伐韓, 八道風靡, 餘勇獵虎. 吾日本之於朝鮮, 蓋以此二役, 盛爲國譽矣. 今俊卿之詩, 神后之弓也. 修之以文、施之以道, 漢魏振其旅、李杜拜其將, 風雅爲絃、比興爲矢, 圓朗以引滿、秀華以射發, 而無不中也, 其盛矣乎! 俊卿之書, 豊王之劍也. 金英爲筆, 鐵精爲墨.[6]

In the past, the Three Han [on the Korean Peninsula: Pyŏnhan 弁韓, Chinhan 辰韓, and Mahan 馬韓] were subdued once the Empress Jingū 神功皇后 opened her formidable bow. Her military prowess was awe-inspiring, treating the Koreans like dogs. More recently, King Toyotomi no Hideyoshi 豊臣秀吉 wielded his one-meter sword and led his troops to conquer Chosŏn and brought all Korean subjects under control, with spare potent force to subdue a tiger. These two battles against Chosŏn are laudable of our great nation.

---

6 Preface in 賓館唱和集 ('Record of poetic improvisation at a lodge') by Taira (1764).

Now, the poetry of Taira no Shunkei 平俊卿 is just as mighty as Empress Jingū's bow. His brush and writing skills were guided by the Way 道. His literary 'army' is reminiscent of Han and Wei 漢魏, led by 'Generals' worthy of celebrated Tang poets Li Bai and Du Fu 李杜. Like in the *Book of Odes* 詩經, Shunkei employed major literary devices 'implied comparisons' (*feng* and *ya* 風雅) as his bowstrings, 'explicit comparisons' (*bi* and *xing* 比興) as his arrows. When arrows of grandeur are unleashed from his bowstring of glamor, no targets will be missed. What a mighty poet he is! Shunkei's poetry is like King Hideyoshi's sword; in his hands, brush and ink are just as formidable as fine metal and iron of the blade.

It can be seen that the rivalry that manifested in brush-talks was metaphorically compared to 'battle of writing' 文戰 and 'brush battle' 筆戰, which was not uncommon elsewhere within Sinographic East Asia 漢字文化圈 (cf. 'battle without weapons' 白戰). However, what these metaphors meant for the Japanese Confucians differed from their usual meanings elsewhere, in that military prowess 武威 so dear to the samurai class in the battlefield was extended to the arena of Chosŏn's writing-mediated *t'ongsinsa* exchange (i.e., 文戰, Koo 2011). Notwithstanding the denigration and criticism of Chosŏn envoys' poetic improvisation in Japanese brush-talk volumes as shown in the preface section, however, the ambience of brush interaction was mostly convivial or diplomatic according to the actual brush-talk records, with no shortage of praise or admiration from one side followed by polite, humble rejoinders 和答詩 by the other.

The books containing brush-talk records of *t'ongsinsa* exchange were edited by Japanese literati and distributed in Japan. In the preface section, which was intended primarily for domestic readers in Japan, some of the editors appeared to elevate their status by denigrating the Korean envoys with remarks bothering on abusive language (Hur 2010: 85–94), even though the criticisms there were inconsistent with what had actually transpired during the brush-talk interactions. Why were the compilers and editors so critical of Chosŏn envoys' poetry? One possible explanation is that they were reacting to their peers' excessively polite, overly humble or even submissive stance several decades earlier, whereby Chosŏn poetry was rated highly, to the point of self-deprecation by requesting 'correction' of their own poetic improvisation. Whether or not such requests were genuinely motivated by a lack of poetic flair, it did not matter; what really mattered to the Sorai school of scholars was that such a stance generated ill feelings and a sense of shame that hurt their self-esteem badly.

Secondly, the *t'ongsinsa* envoys' lack of a corresponding competition mindset might have reinforced competitive sentiments among the Japanese literati. Poetry writing being such a common everyday activity for Korean literati, there was no shortage of literary talents in Chosŏn. Those selected to serve as officials in charge of writing 製述官 and secretaries 書記 were particularly acclaimed for this. In *t'ongsinsa* exchanges of earlier missions, the envoys' journals often contained remarks how they felt obliged to help improve the poetic improvisation of Japanese literati and monks, which were often crude and sometimes incomprehensible. Such a readiness to serve was often coupled with a feeling of being duty-bound to accede to Japanese literati's requests for poetry day and night, in the hope that their aggressiveness could be tamed by practicing literary writing 文.

Being convinced of Chosŏn's superiority in Sinitic-based literary writing and given the marked difference in their levels of performance, it is not surprising that in early *t'ongsinsa* visits, few if any Chosŏn literati would consider their Japanese counterparts as competitors when engaged in poetic improvisation and exchange with them. But even by the mid-eighteenth century, when Japan's capacity to conduct critical studies in (Neo-)Confucianism began to win Korean recognition through the discovery of outstanding scholars like Arai Hakuseki 新井白石 in 1682 and Gion Nankai 祇園南海 (1676–1751) in 1711, few if any Korean literati would harbor any disdain when engaging their Japanese hosts in poetic exchange. This is especially evident during the 1763–64 mission, where the Japanese performance in poetic improvisation left the Korean envoys a deep impression, including the *chesulgwan* Nam Ok 南玉 (1722–1770), and the secretaries Sŏng Tae-chung 成大中 (1732–1809) and Wŏn Chung-kŏ 元重擧 (1719–1790). Quite the contrary, there was little doubt that Japan already ranked among the 'civilized' states on par with dynastic China and Chosŏn, including making inquiries about exemplary poetic and other scholarly works in Japan, with a view to taking them home for sharing with a wider Korean readership. In this regard, the brush-talk records contain a wealth of such earnest exchange of views. Although disagreements did arise, they were dwarfed by ample evidence of collegiality, camaraderie and mutual respect in Japanese-Korean brush conversations.

It would seem that at stake was largely a psychological barrier, namely the Japanese literati circles' difficulty to accept the widely perceived asymmetrical levels of competence and literary talents vis-à-vis their Korean counterparts. This is clearly epitomized by the epilogue of the book of brush-talk records of the 1811 mission, the last *t'ongsinsa* exchange. In that volume entitled 接鮮瘖語 ('Silent conversation with Chosŏn people') edited by Matsuzaki Kōdō (松崎慊堂 1771–1844) (1811/2018), one finds evidence of a concerted attempt by several Japanese scholars to redress that perceived imbalance, including Hayashi Jussai 林述斎 (1768–1841), better known by his title as the *Daigaku-no-kami* 大學頭 ('head of the national school'), and his disciple Kōdō. Whereas the brush-talk records were published intact, the book ends with an epilogue, 接鮮紀事 ('Record of meeting Chosŏn people') where the plan to meet with Chosŏn envoys from the preparatory stage to the actual proceedings were laid out succinctly in a summary.

According to traditional practice, the three Chosŏn envoys 三使, the *chesulgwan* and the secretaries were expected to meet with the *Daigaku-no-kami* of the Hayashi family and his disciples to engage in poetic exchange and brush conversation. In 1811, however, Jussai put up some conditions before the meeting with the envoys could be arranged. First, the envoys should make a formal request for an audience. Second, the attire of the Japanese side would be less formal so as to create an impression of parity in social status. Third, instead of writing himself, Jussai would have a secretary dictate his words. Finally, the Japanese side would not initiate the first poem. While there is no independent evidence to assess how the Korean side reacted to these conditions, according to Kōdō's record, the attitude of the *chesulgwan* and others were very polite, unlike in previous *t'ongsinsa* exchanges. Further, he said the Chosŏn *chesulgwan* and secretaries looked ridiculous for they insisted on being proud of their inferior literary skills, and that what they wrote in their brush-talk interaction was so rough that he could hardly make sense of the content without extensive rewriting. On the basis of such evidence, Kōdō along with Jussai proclaimed having 'won' and finally triumphed over their archrival after 200 years of literary competition, and finally restored the national pride by achieving parity with Chosŏn.

But the 'story' in the epilogue did not quite match what actually transpired in their brush-talk records. Jussai began by requesting Chosŏn literati to write a preface for a collection of poems composed by a Japanese poet, a polite expression of goodwill and ice-breaker not unlike previous *t'ongsinsa* exchanges. Rather than sticking to the condition of not composing the first poem, however, Jussai ended up taking the lead to compose one himself after it became clear that no Chosŏn envoy was willing to take that symbolic first step. Apart from putting an end to that stalemate, Jussai was probably eager to solicit poetic response from Chosŏn literati, whose potential literary value was too enticing to resist. There are other details suggesting that the brush-talk atmosphere was friendly, not unlike previous *t'ongsinsa* exchanges. For one thing, at the 1811 mission, the envoys presented to their Japanese hosts the calligraphy and paintings of leading literary figures in Seoul, which had been difficult to obtain in Japan. It might be a small gesture, but it was enough to convey the Korean envoys' goodwill, despite the portrayal of Chosŏn people being arrogant and rude.

What is intriguing is that the original intent – the planned 'imagined competition' scenario – was left intact in Kōdō's book rather than being edited out. Given the target Japanese readership, one cannot help concluding that such a 'proud' experience of the Japanese literati was deliberately intended and framed as a 'success story' for nationwide circulation. Of interest to us here is that the epilogue in Kōdō's book provides clear evidence of the Japanese plan to engage Korean *t'ongsinsa* in poetic competition by stipulating guidelines for brush-talk interaction before they even met, except that those 'imagined competition' guidelines fell short of being implemented, possibly due to the complexity and constraint of writing-mediated brush-talk interaction. Such a 'competition' mindset was not new; in fact, it could be traced back a century earlier to the 1711 mission, when the Japanese literati first proposed replacing exchange of poetry with poetic competition, which proved to have lasting influence for subsequent generations of Japanese literati.

Thus the literary elites from both sides were guided by rather different perceptions of their rivals' mindset. Be it exchange or competition, there is no doubt that the Japanese literati were eager to impress their Korean visitors with their poetic flair and literary talents through brush-talk interaction, which was perceived as a site of confrontation or a game of competition for ascertaining Japanese superiority, even though this was not apparent judging from the brush-talk records. On the other hand, the same records suggest that the Korean literati appeared to be completely unaware of their Japanese hosts' competition-prone mindset. This is especially striking because since at least the 1763–64 mission, the quality of Japanese literature had already been acknowledged.

Maintaining rites and rituals versus preservation of ancient Confucian heritage

Further compelling evidence of contestation may be found in brush-talk exchange on various aspects of Confucian heritage, including rites and rituals but also music. Confucian heritage comprised dress style, clothing and ornaments 衣冠服飾, the civil service examination system, and music for the national rituals and the four ceremonial occasions: ceremony of coming-of-age, marriage, funeral, and ancestor worship 冠婚喪祭. Of these, dress style was one of the popular topics since the early days of *t'ongsinsa* exchange, probably because attire and clothing were among the most visible aspects of civilization. Based on limited brush-talk records before the 1682 mission, Chosŏn was overtly recognized for her Confucian attire and headdress tradition 衣冠傳統 which could be traced back to the rites and rituals of the Zhou period 周禮. Among the most frequently mentioned laudatory comments by Japanese literati was Chosŏn's preservation of fine customs dated from the Yin 殷 (also known as Shang 商, ca. 1600–1044 BCE) and Zhou 周 (ca. 1100–256 BCE) dynasties thanks largely to the foundation laid by Kija 箕子. By 1711, the first mission in the eighteenth century, the scale of brush-talk interaction was expanded considerably, much of which focused on the give-and-take concerning Chosŏn's ancient Chinese rites, rituals, music and other forms of cultural heritage 禮樂文物. In the early days of *t'ongsinsa* exchange, therefore, there is clear evidence of Chosŏn being recognized by Japanese literati as the guardian of Confucian culture and upholder of Chinese civilization 中華文明, an unmistakable trend in seventeenth-century brush-talks indeed. One possible explanation is that unlike in Chosŏn, access to government positions and officialdom by excelling in Confucianist scholarship at the civil service examination was beyond the reach of the newly emerging class of Japanese Confucians, simply because such an important life-changing Confucianist institution did not exist in Japan where *bushido* and the samurai class prevailed culturally if not sociopolitically.

Back in 1711, Arai Hakuseki challenged Chosŏn's status as the custodian of central efflorescence (cf. 'Little China'), a mutual perception that had been shared in previous Chosŏn missions. That challenge was spelled out in the brush-talk records 'Brush-talk at the feast' 坐間筆語.[7] Hakuseki asked why Chosŏn would insist on retaining the Ming Chinese dress and clothing style while the other neighboring periphery states which looked to the Qing dynasty as the center would model their dress and clothing style on that of the Manchus. To this query, the Chief-Envoy 正使 Cho T'ae-ŏk 趙泰億 replied that the Chosŏn Dynasty, being the guardian of central efflorescence, was the only state under the Heaven 天下 to preserve the traditional dress and clothing style of China. Further, Cho added that the Qing regime had no interest in imposing their style on Chosŏn knowing fully well that

---

7 This brush-talk book consists of two parts: 坐間筆語 ('Brush-talk at the feast') and 江關筆談 ('Brush-talk at Edo edited at Akamagaseki 赤間關'), the latter was also included in 東槎日記 ('Journal of travel to Japan') authored by Chosŏn Vice-Envoy 副使 Im Su-kan 任守幹 during the 1711 mission.

Confucian rites and rituals were followed there 禮儀之國 (see Chun 1968). Then Hakuseki expressed disappointment upon seeing Chosŏn envoys being clothed in Ming attire because he had expected to see, as symbolic evidence of central efflorescence, a clothing style befitting the golden era of the Yin (Shang) dynasty in the distant past rather than the Ming, Chosŏn's powerful neighbor barely a century earlier. This suggests that, for Hakuseki, instead of being a visually salient manifestation of culture and civilization, people's dress and clothing style reflected their nation's political dependency along a power hierarchy (Huh 2012).

However, there is no evidence of Hakuseki's critical views being conveyed to the Korean envoys interactively. There are two versions of 'Brush-talk at Edo edited at Akamagaseki' 江關筆談 brush-talk records. The one in 'Journal of travel to Japan' 東槎日記 was edited by Chosŏn envoy Im Su-kan 任守幹; the other one appended to 'Brush-talk at the feast' 坐間筆語, compiled by Hakuseki (Arai & Cho 1789), was based on the Korean version sent to him by Im Su-kan. Interestingly, Hakuseki's deprecating remarks are found in *Brush-talk at the feast* 坐間筆語 he authored, but not in the Korean version, suggesting that such remarks were subsequently inserted while the Japanese edition was edited. As in the subtle competition in poetry exchange, sometimes words representing the real thoughts of leading Japanese literary figures that were unsaid during the actual brush conversations appeared to be added to the edited version, apparently 'for the record' after the Chosŏn mission was over. Incidentally, it was through those post-*t'ongsinsa* exchange remarks that we learned about the critical stance of Japanese intellectuals for the first time in 1711.

On the other hand, in the latter part of *Brush-talk at Edo edited at Akamagaseki* 江關筆談 (both versions), their brush conversation also touched upon conventional headdresses 冠帽 originated in imperial China as follows:

平泉曰: 欲著幅巾. 先著緇冠. 制在《家禮》圖式. 可考.	P'yŏng-ch'ŏn [Chief-Envoy Cho T'ae-ŏk] said: Before wearing a headcover, one must first wear a headdress made of black silk. This dress pattern is recorded in 'Family rites of Zhuxi' (*Zhuzijiali* 朱子家禮) where it can be verified.
白石曰: 副使從事所戴. 似本邦所謂錦繡冠. 又曰: 下官前歲觀光於上國. 幸及見天朝冕弁之制. 蓋是上世之物. 且本邦文物出於三代之制者不少. 如僕所戴者. 卽是周弁之製. 亦如深衣之製. 校之《禮經》. 則知漢唐諸儒漫費其說也.	Hakuseki said: What Vice-Envoy and the Third Envoy wear resembles *kinsukan* in our nation. He added: I visited Kyoto two years ago. Luckily I was able to see (the definite object of) ancient China's conventional design of headdresses. Further, quite a number of the (cultural) products used by literati in our nation are made according to the designs from Xia, Shang, and Zhou dynasties. For instance, the hat that I am wearing was made according to the hat used in Zhou dynasty. In addition, for the making of *shenyi* ('a gown worn by Confucians'), if you study the 'Book of Rites' 禮經 closely, you would know what the Han and Tang literati said were all nonsense.

(*Continued*)

南岡曰: 深衣之制, 司馬公以後自有定論. 貴邦豈有他本耶?	Nam-gang [Third-Envoy, Yi Pang-ŏn 李邦彥]: The final version of the conventional design of *shenyi* was firmly established by Master Sima Guang. How could your esteemed nation reconstruct the conventional design, or was it based on some other source?
白石曰: 考之《禮經》而可也. 漢唐以來諸儒紛紛之說, 何足以徵之也? 本邦之俗所稱吳服者, 蓋與深衣之制大同小異耳.	Hakuseki: We can reconstruct the conventional design according to the *Book of Rites*. The opinions given by the literati from Han dynasty on were diverse. How can we adopt their views? The so-called (style of) *Gofuku* (Wu-style clothes) in our nation is rather similar to the conventional design of *shenyi*.

Here, Hakuseki took pride in Japan's preservation of ancient Chinese dress and clothing style, as shown in the Tennō's costume and other formal attire when performing state duties in Kyoto, which could be traced back to the ancient Chinese era of 三代 ('three dynasties' Xia, Yin, and Zhou). For illustration, he pointed to the hat he was wearing, which resembled the headdress dated during the Zhou dynasty. Further evidence of Japanese preservation of fine cultural practices of ancient Chinese origin included *Gofuku* 吳服 'Wu-style clothes', which was replicated after the design of *shenyi* 深衣 (a gown worn by Confucians) as stated in the 'Book of Rites' 禮經 (cf. 禮記); even the standard outfit for samurais was said to be modeled on the robes of ancient kings in China (Huh 2012: 134–135). To reinforce this argument, during the banquet hosted in honor of the three Chosŏn envoys, Hakuseki arranged for musical performance featuring the ancient music (*kogaku* 古樂) of Kyoto – another subtle allusion to Japan's consistent adherence to ancient Chinese culture.

Since the brush-talk records edited by Hakuseki were not published in printed form until 1789, their impact on subsequent *t'ongsinsa* exchanges appeared to be limited. This notwithstanding, according to brush-talk records of the 1748 mission, a similar stance of Japan being the custodian of central efflorescence was in evidence. There, the Sorai School Confucians likewise asserted Japanese superiority in retaining ancient Chinese rites, rituals, music, and other forms of cultural heritage 禮樂文物. They regarded the ancient system and rituals (including music) as representing the essence or *dao* 道 of Confucian teachings: the older the practice, the more valuable it would be, hence the emphasis that Japan had preserved Confucian rites and rituals dating back to the three dynasties 三代 (viz. Xia 夏, Shang 商, and Zhou 周) in ancient China. Such a static, absolutist Confucianist criterion of central efflorescence, which was largely an outgrowth of the viewpoint championed by the Neo-Confucian scholar Hakuseki, differed diametrically from that of Chosŏn, which was dynamic and constantly evolving, in keeping with changes in social practices through time. In short, the question, which side embodied the essence of central efflorescence, was hotly debated. Such contestation or dueling was often embedded in ideological debates concerning one's preferred Confucianist orientation. For instance, Chosŏn literati's predilection for

Zhuzi studies, in the form of critique and defense, was a major theme in the 1748 brush-talk records; it also figured prominently in the *t'ongsinsa* exchange during the 1763–64 Chosŏn mission.

Japan's aspiration to be seen as the custodian of central efflorescence began to appear in the brush-talk records of *t'ongsinsa* exchange in 1748. Of the writing-mediated debates there, the one between Matsuzaki Kankai 松崎観海 (1725–1776) and Yi Pong-hwan 李鳳煥 (1710–1770) detailed in 'Records of meetings with Chosŏn envoys' 來庭集 (Matsuzaki 1748)[8] was particularly noteworthy (H.-W. Yi 2017). After discussing specific issues related to Zhuzi studies, the two statesmen then exchanged views about court music, and rites and rituals 禮樂制度.

Riding on a defensive note in response to Kankai's criticism of Zhuzi Studies, Yi queried why proper rites and rituals for various ceremonies did not seem to exist in Japan and asked whether the scholar-officials in Kyoto knew how to address that problem. To this provocative question, Kankai responded that historically under the influence of Shintoism, court rituals along with rites and customs in Japanese society were generally rustic and simple 忠厚質朴. It was only after Japan had become acquainted with ancient Chinese customs and cultural practices during the Han dynasty (206 BCE–220 CE) that many similar institutions were set up. Consequently, during the reigns of Enki 延喜 (901–940) and Tenreki 天曆 (947–957), a well-established system of court music and rites and rituals comparable to that of the Zhou dynasty was introduced. Unfortunately, such a system was largely obliterated during the Sengoku period 戰國 (1467–1590), except in Kyoto where it was retained. Kankai then said reassuringly that following the unification of Japan under Tokugawa Ieyatsu 德川家康 (1543–1616), the nation had been well governed, and that he had no doubt that the fine old institutions inspired by Confucian culture would be restored once a decree from the emperor was issued.

It turned out that Kankai's clarification begged further questions from Yi, who doubted the claim that manners or clothing style could be altered overnight by decree; nor was it apparent to him how Kyoto where he passed by differed from other places in Japan. Above all, from what he could observe, the attire expected of four ceremonial occasions – the coming-of-age, marriage, funeral, and ancestor worship 冠婚喪祭 – was most disappointing, a far cry from Confucian rites and rituals indeed. Yi Pong-hwan added mockingly that in Japan, the clothing of the commoners in the street could hardly cover their whole bodies.

Even though he knew full well that real power in Japan resided not with the emperor but the shogun, Kankai adamantly tried to buttress Japan's right to the claim of being the custodian of central efflorescence, apparently on the assumption that the Japanese emperor would issue any decree even without the shogun's

---

8 Given that *laitei* 來庭 in Japanese referred specifically to 'envoys of a tributary 諸侯國 on a mission to the suzerain state 天子國', the Japanese positioning as the suzerain state vis-à-vis Chosŏn was unmistakable.

consent. In fact, prior to this debate, he had come across as highly confident in his brief introduction of the Sorai School's literary theory and critique of Zhuzi Studies in Chosŏn. Yi's provocative question was arguably directed at undermining his confidence, suggesting shrewdly how pointless it would be for Japanese Confucians to criticize the leading scholars of Zhuzi studies (viz. 程朱: 程子 and 朱子) and to engage in abstract deliberation of their doctrines while the spirit of Confucian rites and rituals was completely ignored in Japanese society. Conceivably Kankai must have been somewhat embarrassed in the face of Yi Pong-hwan's sharp-witted argument, which was clearly provocative but not unreasonable.

In this 1748 brush-talk, Kankai was on the defensive vis-à-vis the Chosŏn envoys' criticism. In the *t'ongsinsa* exchange of 1763–64, the Sorai school scholars appeared to take extra care to shun direct confrontation with the envoys, even though there was no shortage of assertion of Japan's superior civilization, resulting in dueling and contestation. When the Chosŏn literati argued for laudable, exemplary Confucian rites and rituals and other institutions in Chosŏn, the Japanese hosts would counter-argue how immensely proud they were with the retention of some of the oldest Chinese institutions in Japan. Their dueling and contestation, enacted through brush conversation, focused on the question, which side better deserved the attribute of central efflorescence, which had become void as the Han Chinese Ming dynasty had given way to the 'barbarian' Qing. Interestingly, what the Japanese Confucians refrained from 'verbalizing' through writing-mediated brush-talk, they would insert them at will in the post-mission editing of brush-talk records of *t'ongsinsa* exchange. In this sense, what was subsequently published in print was not really a faithful record of the actual brush conversations.

Compared with the Korean envoys' stance during the earlier mission in 1748, in 1764 the three Chosŏn literati – Nam Ok, Sŏng Tae-chung and Wŏn Chung-kŏ – were much more assertive in their refutation of what in their view were heretic offshoots of Confucianism in Japan. Accordingly, in the process of answering questions about Confucian rites and rituals, customs and cultural practices in Chosŏn, the three envoys made a concerted effort to portray how the spirit and value of central efflorescence were materialized by successive generations of Koreans through social practice in their daily lives, which was why and how Chosŏn would better merit the attribute of central efflorescence. For example, when asked what their headdress was called, the envoys provided not only the name of their headdress but also grounded its use by historical figures in well-known literary works as follows:

稟: 學士所著冠, 其名云何?
答: 司馬溫公獨樂園中所著冠也. 名溫公冠. 儒者著之.
(寶曆甲申朝鮮人贈答錄)

Question (Toriyama Sugaku 鳥山崧岳): The hat you are wearing, what is it called?
Answer (Nam Ok 南玉): This is what Master Sima Wen wore in *Duleyuan*, so it is called *On'gonggwan* (Mand: *wengongguan*). Confucians wear this hat.
('A record of poetry exchange in 1764', Toriyama 1764)

龍山問: 公衣冠名何? 退石答: 冠幅巾衣道袍. 乃古聖賢所 着. (問槎餘響)	Ryūzan asked: The hat and dress (that you are wearing), what are they called? T'oe-sŏk answered: The hat is *pokkŏn* (Mand: *fujin*), and the dress is *to'p'o* (Mand: *daopao*). These are what the ancient sages wore. ('Echoes that remained after meeting Chosŏn envoys'. Ito 1764)

Not only formal attire and dress style, but similar give-and-take was also found with regard to other topics like specific rituals and the civil service examination. The three envoys provided concrete details, including their societal merits and cultural values. The ultimate purpose of explicating Chosŏn customs and institutions such as Confucian attire and dress style, music, rites and rituals, and the civil service examination was to instill their inherent value and virtue, which had been working so well in Korean society through practice. By engaging their Japanese hosts in deliberations of Confucian court music, and rites and rituals through brush conversation, the Chosŏn literati were eager to teach the Japanese about rites and rituals 禮. In short, the strategy adopted by Chosŏn envoys of the 1763–64 *t'ongsinsa* mission was 'converting barbarians to civilized people by adapting advanced Chinese culture' (用夏變夷, Mand: *yongxiabianyi*; Kor: *yong habyŏn-i*). For this strategy to yield its intended effect, the Japanese Confucians must be convinced of the merits of translating Confucian rites and rituals into practice in society. Should this happen, the goal of making the Japanese Confucians appreciate the spirit and essence of Confucian civilization – by implementing proper rites and rituals in society as successive generations of Koreans had demonstrated since antiquity – would have been achieved. Although in Wŏn Chung-kŏ's estimate, that goal had been achieved to some extent (see his journal 乘槎錄, 'Journal of travel by sea', Wŏn 1764), his optimism was completely futile according to the actual brush-talk records of *t'ongsinsa* exchange compiled by the Japanese Confucians. There is no evidence of Japanese Confucians being willing to emulate and learn from the Koreans in this regard.

During the 1763–64 Chosŏn mission, through *t'ongsinsa* exchange, the Japanese literati tried to prove that the intrinsic value of central efflorescence was fully embraced in their culture. What they valued the most and upheld as the ultimate criterion was 'antiquity' 古. This philosophy of Tokugawa Confucians was based on the belief that historically, Confucianism at its ideal state in terms of impeccable governance 至治 was found purportedly during the three dynasties Xia, Shang, and Zhou. From this belief, a principle was derived, which may be glossed as 'the older an institution or practice, the closer it is to the original *dao* 道'. Then, following this golden principle, Japanese Confucians became convinced of their central efflorescence position after 'discovering' three antiquities 古代文物 exhibiting ancient Chinese influence that were found only in contemporary Japan: (i) the formal attire and dress style of the court in Kyoto from emperor to officials, (ii) the ancient music that pre-dated the Sui (581–618) and Tang (618–907) dynasties, and (iii) the ancient classics produced before Qin (221–206 BCE). These were regarded by Japanese

Tokugawa Confucians as strengths that were unparalleled by Ming or Qing China, not to mention Chosŏn. From the visiting Chosŏn envoys, they realized that Korean rites and rituals, music and dress style were modeled on the Song (960–1279) and the Ming (1368–1644), which was nowhere near the Zhou Dynasty on the Japanese scale of antiquity (c. 1100–256 BCE). This led the Japanese Confucians to conclude that Chosŏn did not measure up as a contender for the central efflorescence position. Such a similarly disdainful stance had already been in evidence half a century earlier in Arai Hakuseki's *t'ongsinsa* exchange with earlier Chosŏn envoys in 1711.

The arguments adopted by the Japanese intellectuals may be summarized as follows. Since the Song Dynasty, ancient music in China had been lost, while proper attire and clothing styles had also undergone tremendous changes with time, resulting in contemporary Chinese being required to wear a queue 辮髮 and put on dresses that used to be regarded as foreign and barbarian 胡服. Ancient classics had disappeared in China, but many of the ancient books from dynastic China had survived in Japan; some were transported back to China. As for Chosŏn, her dresses and clothing style were adapted from the Ming era, and the origin of her music was unclear, being ignorant of how ancient Chinese musical instruments were made. Likewise, ancient Chinese classics were also rare. Academic studies of Confucianism were heavily influenced by Zhuzi 朱子 whose views were held to be the standard, which were used as the criteria for rating students' performance at civil service examinations. By comparison, Japan occupied an unrivaled position in East Asia in terms of preserving the spirit and value of central efflorescence.

The approach to the notion of central efflorescence among Japanese and Korean literary circles were thus drastically different. Despite Japanese appreciation of Chosŏn's claim of being *the* model, they showed little understanding of how it was implemented in Korean society, let alone the reason for the pride so derived. Primordial for Korean intellectuals was not 'old' 古 *per se*, but 'practice' 行 in keeping with the times. What mattered most was the implementation of Confucian rites and rituals and their societal observance in everyday lives following social changes through time. Such an approach constituted proof of Koreans' deep, collective internalization of Confucian values as manifested in their social systems from education and civil service examination to the rites and rituals required for specific ceremonial occasions. By contrast, Japanese Confucians embraced Confucianism as an academic discipline within a 'foreign studies' tradition and, as such, their endeavors were confined to scholarly debates between literary figures, which stopped short of 'applying' the insights thus obtained to the political arena. Accordingly, the aim of 'learning' the systems of court music, rites, and rituals was not for practice, but for the sake of accumulating knowledge through historical evidential research 考證學. From the Korean point of view, Japanese studies of Confucianism were divorced from Confucian rites and rituals and corresponding sociocultural practices, and so they found it difficult to see how the Japanese approach could advance toward central efflorescence. By contrast, the Chosŏn dynasty had never stopped putting the spirit and values of Confucian rites and rituals into practice, which is why they believed that Korea fully merited the appellation 'Little China' 小中華 since antiquity.

It is difficult to say which side prevailed in this competition, largely because very different criteria and standards of central efflorescence were followed. What is clear is that Korean-Japanese dueling and contestation peaked during Chosŏn mission in 1763–64, both in terms of the quality and quantity of *t'ongsinsa* exchange enacted through brush-talk interactions with their Japanese hosts. There is no doubt that in the process, both sides got to know each other a lot more deeply.

Significance of dueling in brush-talk records of Chosŏn *t'ongsinsa* visits: positioning and negotiating status in universal Confucian civilization

The eighteenth century marked the beginning of Japanese assertion for cultural superiority within the realm of universal Confucian civilization. This assertive stance was played out subtly when the Chosŏn envoys were engaged in brush conversation with their hosts during their missions to Japan. From the mid-eighteenth century onwards, Chosŏn's previously self-evident position as the guardian of the culturally prestigious central efflorescence position was challenged. In 1711, Ogyū Sorai first made known his view that Chosŏn envoys' poetry was inferior by circulating brush-talk records with his commentaries. Also in 1711, Arai Hakuseki disputed Chosŏn's self-complacent claim of being the successor and upholder of central efflorescence and argued that Japan was the true custodian of ancient Chinese rites and rituals and other forms of cultural heritage 禮樂文物.

Poetry exchange during subsequent Chosŏn missions was pervaded by a sense of imagined rivalry and subtle contention. This trend was especially apparent during the 1763–64 mission, culminating half a decade later in Japanese literati's unilateral proclamation of victory in 1811, as evidenced in the epilogue of a book of brush-talk records by Kōdō. On the other hand, Hakuseki's arguments were reiterated by various Japanese literati, especially among Sorai School scholars from 1748 to 1763. The Chosŏn literati countered that the spirit of Confucius's teachings was internalized by Koreans through painstaking study and scholarly investigation, while Confucian rites and values were fully reflected in as well as actualized through collective behaviors and cultural traditions in society.

The increasing assertiveness and confidence of Japanese literati may be explained by several factors. The emergence of academic leaders such as Ogyū Sorai was certainly an impetus as they helped attract followers to embark on scholarly studies of Confucianism. Sinitic-based literature also thrived during the Tokugawa period, reinforcing the pride of Japanese Confucians as they saw a steady and healthy cycle of scholarly inquiries and literary creativity, to the point that adherents of Sorai studies took pride in outshining Zhuzi studies, an intellectual current of Chinese origin popularized in Chosŏn.[9] During the eighteenth

---

9 Academic exchange between Korea and Japan was very much a site of intense competition along multiple fault lines. The divide between Zhuzi studies and Sorai studies may be regarded as the primary site of confrontation. The emergence of scholarly orientations like eclecticism 折衷學 and

century, among Japanese literati, competition for scholarly merits in the name of poetry exchange with Chosŏn envoys gradually gravitated toward a 'brush battle' 筆戰, an allusion to a symbolic association whereby Koreans were subdued not only militarily, but also in the realm of writing by the brush. Where a lack of Confucian-style social systems like those in Chosŏn appeared to put the Japanese side on the defensive, such an apparent disadvantage was cleverly offset by the argument that ancient Chinese civilization with its fine traditions and cultural practices were far better preserved in Japan. This argument was further reinforced by her upkeep of old Confucian classics that had been lost in dynastic China, but also fine creative works from literary criticism to belles lettres. All this lent support to Japan's claim to academic excellence in the study of Confucianism.

Underpinning the subtle contention for central efflorescence status was a collective desire and self-consciousness of Japanese Confucians to win the Chosŏn literati's recognition and consent of Japan's excellence in scholarly pursuits and literary creativity. But why? This may be explained by the 'coming of age' of Japan's place in the scholarly studies of Confucianism. Unlike Chosŏn, Japan was a late starter in this regard. It had been barely two hundred years since a critical mass of young scholars started learning Confucianism in earnest, with the objective of adapting its merits to Japanese society. As a school of philosophical and academic inquiry, Confucianism in eighteenth-century Japan was relatively young – no more than a hundred years following the rise of two celebrated scholars, Ogyū Sorai and Itō Jinsai 伊藤仁斎 (1627–1705). It was against this background that the arrival of *t'ongsinsa* envoys gave rise to occasions when Japanese interpretations of Confucianist teachings entered into competition with alternative philosophical orientations elsewhere within the Sinographic cosmopolis – Chosŏn in this case. Whereas poetic exchange and the spirit and values of Confucian principles and practices constituted the substance of literary contention and philosophical debate, writing-mediated communication enacted through brush-talk enabled the Japanese Confucians to appreciate alternative intellectual orientations and developments like those embraced by Korean Confucians. In short, having evolved an indigenous school of Confucianism, Japanese Confucians were obliged to address the question, what is the position of the Japanese orientation vis-à-vis the universal Confucian civilization practiced elsewhere in Sinographic East Asia, as defined by their extent of adherence to the essentialist notion of central efflorescence 中華? In other words, through encounters with a significant 'other' made possible by periodical *t'ongsinsa* visits, subtle rivalry or contention as evidenced in the Japanese literati's stance and reaction clearly amounted to a

---

evidential research 考證學 – evidently a result of influence of Qing scholarship – made such scholarly debates even more complex. All told, those academically oriented debates may be interpreted as a natural correlate of diverged intellectual currents as both sides pursued competing approaches to the essence of *dao* 道 in Confucianism. What seems clear is that by 1763–1764, the Sorai scholars were joined by their ideological comrades of other persuasions in their collective claim that hitherto, East Asian scholarship surrounding the study of Confucianism should look to Japan for philosophical orientation and intellectual leadership.

quest for Japan's Confucianist identity within the universe of Confucian civilization at large.

How did Chosŏn's scholarly circles react to the increasingly apparent Japanese assertion of cultural superiority? There is some evidence of 'barbarian' Japan being gradually recognized and accepted as a member of the 'civilized world'. This may be gauged by the travel journals of the three literati, Nam Ok, Sŏng Tae-chung, and Wŏn Chung-kŏ written during their 1763–64 mission to Japan. According to their personal evaluation and commentaries, whereas certain interpretations of Confucianism in Japan might be objectionable or even be seen as heretic, by and large, all three Korean scholars reckoned that Confucian studies and literary creativity in Japan merited a place in the universal Confucian order. Based on the outstanding Japanese literary figures they had encountered, the rapid development of and rigor in producing Confucian scholarship, admiration of Confucian values, and passion with which literary works were created, coupled with love of Confucian classics and their abundance in literary circles, Tokugawa Japan was clearly making big strides toward meeting the Confucianist ideal of central efflorescence. That was new to keen Korean observers of the Japanese: the samurais' valor 武 intrinsic to the spirit of *bushido* that the Japanese were immensely proud of was for the first time matched by an equally strong craving for cultural superiority, leadership in Confucianist philosophy, and literary creativity through writing 文.

One important reason why it took a long time for Korean awareness of Japanese assertiveness for cultural superiority to take shape was largely because such intentions were hardly discernible in their actual brush-talk interactions. Instead, the give-and-take appeared to be focused on intellectual exchange regarding Confucian philosophy and literary standards. Through such writing-mediated exchanges, just as Chosŏn scholars gradually realized that the Japanese counterpart's aspiration for membership and a position in the 'center of universal civilization' 普遍文明 was beyond dispute, so too did the Japanese Confucians muster up confidence in rising up to Chosŏn as an equal through their own Confucianist vision and literary fervor. It is in this sense that reconfiguration of Confucianist civilization at the interstate level has taken place as a direct result of *t'ongsinsa* missions to Japan.

Finally, while the Confucian order was widely held to be universal in eighteenth-century East Asia, it goes without saying that what that meant in Korea and Japan – both being at the peripheries relative to the proverbial center, China – differed vastly given their respective cultural preferences and value judgments. No wonder the ideal attributes and standards of central efflorescence, despite their indisputable and fully acknowledged Han Chinese origin, were interpreted rather differently, and that neither side felt convinced by the other's arguments and evidence presented during their writing-mediated 'brush battles'. What is interesting is that such contention and dueling would not have been so vividly preserved had it not been for the fact that Japanese and Korean intellectuals found common ground in using Sinitic-based sinograms as the shared linguistic resources for their writing-mediated brush conversations.

References

Akimoto, T. [秋本澹園] (Ed.). (c. 1712). 問槎畸賞 ('Unique sights of Chosŏn envoys'). Publisher unknown. Retrieved May 30, 2021, from www.wul.waseda.ac.jp/kotenseki/html/he16/he16_01392/index.html

Arai, H., & Cho, T.-Ŏ. [新井白石、趙泰億] (1789). 坐間筆語(附江關筆談) ('Brush-talk at the feast/Brush-talk at Edo edited at Akamagaseki 赤間關'). Kyōto: Hachimonjiya Shōbē. Retrieved May 30, 2021, from http://base1.nijl.ac.jp/iview/Frame.jsp?DB_ID=G0003917KTM&C_CODE=OCHA-00772.

Chun, H.-J. (1968). Sino-Korean tributary relations in the Qing period. In J. K. Fairbank (Ed.), *The Chinese world order: Traditional China's foreign relations* (pp. 90–111). Cambridge, MA: Harvard University Press.

Clements, R. (2019). Brush talk as the 'lingua franca' of East Asian diplomacy in Japanese-Korean encounters, c. 1600–1868. *The Historical Journal* 62(2): 289–309.

Denecke, W. (2014). Worlds without translation: Premodern East Asia and the power of character scripts. In S. Berman & C. Porter (Eds.), *A companion to translation studies* (pp. 204–216). Malden, MA: Wiley-Blackwell.

Fairbank, J. K. (Ed.). (1968). *The Chinese world order: Traditional China's foreign relations*. Cambridge, MA: Harvard University Press.

Fuma, S. [夫馬進] (2008). 燕行使와 通信使 ('Chosŏn envoys to Peking and Chosŏn envoys to Japan'). Seoul: Sinsŏwŏn.

Fuma, S. [夫馬進] (2015). 朝鮮燕行使と朝鮮通信使 ('Chosŏn envoys to Peking and Chosŏn envoys to Japan'), revised and enlarged edition of Fuma (2008). Nagoya: Nagoya University Press.

Huh, Y.-J. [許恩珠] (2012). 東아시아 官服 制度와 近世 朝日의 自意識·相互認識 —朝鮮의 文明教化論과 日本의 文明自立論 ('The official uniform system of East Asia and Korea's and Japan's self-awareness and mutual perception in premodern times: Chosŏn's civilization and enlightenment theory and Japan's civilization self-reliance theory'). 日本學研究 *The Journal of Japanese Studies* 35: 121–143.

Hur, K.-J. [許敬震] (2010). 筆談과 漂流記의 現場에서 編輯 및 出版까지의 距離 ('The distance from the site of writing-conversation and drifting record up to its editing and publishing'). 日本思想 *Journal of Japanese Thought* 26: 69–98.

Ito, K. [伊藤維典] (Ed.). (1764). 問槎餘響 ('Resonances after meeting Chosŏn envoys'). Kyōto: Heian Shorin. Vol. 1 & 2 retrieved May 30, 2021, from www.digital.archives.go.jp/DAS/meta/listPhoto?LANG=default&BID=F1000000000000044173&ID=M2015062314252752613&TYPE=&NO=; www.digital.archives.go.jp/DAS/meta/listPhoto?LANG=default&BID=F1000000000000044173&ID=M2015062314254252614&TYPE=&NO=.

Jang, J.-Y. [張眞熀] (2017). 癸未通信使 筆談의 東아시아的 意味 ('Significance of brush-talk of 1763 Chosŏn missions to Japan from an East Asian perspective'). Paju, Korea: Bogosa.

Koo, J.-H. [具智賢] (2006). 1763 癸未通信使 使行文學 研究 ('Studies on Tongsinsa travel literature in 1763'). Seoul: Bogosa.

Koo, J.-H. [具智賢] (2011). 1763年 筆談唱和를 通해 본 朝鮮과 日本의 詩文唱和 認識 變化 ('Change in the perception of *Shimunchanghwa* of Chosŏn and Japan as seen through the *Pildamchanghwa* of 1763'). 東아시아文化研究 *Journal of East Asian cultures* 49: 65–88.

Li, D. C. S. (2020). Writing-mediated interaction face-to-face: Sinitic brushtalk (漢文筆談) as an age-old lingua-cultural practice in premodern East Asian cross-border communication. *China and Asia* 2(2): 193–233.

Matsuzaki. Kankai. [松崎観海] (1748). 來庭集 ('A record of meetings with Chosŏn envoys'). Unpublished manuscript. 日本國立公文書館 (National Archives of Japan). Retrieved May 30. 2021. from www.digital.archives.go.jp/DAS/meta/listPhoto?LANG =default&BID=F1000000000000044157&ID=&TYPE=&NO=.
Matsuzaki. Kōdō. [松崎慊堂] (1811/2018). 接鮮瘖語 ('Silent conversation with Chosŏn people'). In L.-W. Wang [王連旺] (Ed.). 朝鮮通信使筆談文獻研究 ('Studies of brush-talk documents by Chosŏn envoys') (pp. 119–305). Shanghai: Shanghai Jiaotong University Press.
Miyase. R. [宮瀬龍門] (1748). 鴻臚傾蓋集 ('A collection of brush-talk records of casual meetings at a tavern'). Edo: Nishimuraya Genroku.
Shin. R.-S. [신로사] (2011). 1811年 辛未通信使行과 朝日 文化 交流: 筆談·唱酬를 中心으로 (Sinmi-Tongsinsa in 1811 and Joseon-Japan Culture Exchange). Unpublished PhD thesis. Department of East-Asian Studies. Sungkyunkwan University. Korea.
Sin. K.-S. [辛基秀] & Nakao. H. [仲尾宏]. (Eds.). (1993–94). 大系朝鮮通信使 – 善隣と友好の記錄 1–8 ('A compilation of the records of Chosŏn missions to Japan – A record of good-neighborly relations and friendship'). Tokyo: Akashi Shoten.
Taira. no Shunkei [平俊卿] (1764). 賓館唱和集 ('A record of poetic improvisation at a lodge'). Kyoto: Kyoto Shoshi.
Takahashi. M. [高橋昌彦] (2007). 朝鮮通信使唱和集目錄稿(一) ('A catalogue of the collection of poetic improvisation of Chosŏn missions to Japan. 1'). 福岡大學研究部論集A The Bulletin of Central Research Institute Fukuoka University Series A, Humanities 6(8): 17–35.
Takahashi. M. [高橋昌彦] (2009). 朝鮮通信使唱和集目錄稿(二) ('A catalogue of the collection of poetic improvisation of Chosŏn missions to Japan. 2'). 福岡大學研究部論集A The Bulletin of Central Research Institute Fukuoka University Series A, Humanities 9(1): 21–40.
Taki. K. et al. [瀧鶴臺等] (1765). 長門癸甲問槎 ('Chosŏn envoys who visited Nagato in 1763–1764'). Nagato [長門]: Meirinkan [明倫館]. Tokyo Metropolitan Central Library.
Toby. R. (1991). *State and diplomacy in early modern Japan: Asia in the development of the Tokugawa Bakufu*. Stanford. CA: Stanford University Press.
Toby. R. (1991/2013). 日本 近世의 '鎖國'이라는 外交 ('"Sakoku" as diplomacy in early modern Japan') (Y.-J. Huh [許恩珠]. Trans.). Seoul: Ch'anghae.
Toriyama. S. [鳥山崧岳] (1764). 寶曆甲申朝鮮人贈答錄 ('A record of poetry exchange in 1764'). Unpublished manuscript. Fukui Municipal Library. Japan: Fukui-jō. Retrieved May 30. 2021. from https://lib.city.fukui.fukui.jp/archives/ko2.htm.
Watanabe. H. [渡辺浩] (1985). 近世日本社會と宋學 ('Early modern Japanese society and Neo-Confucian idealist philosophy'). Tokyo: University of Tokyo Press.
Watanabe. H. [渡辺浩] (1985/2007). 朱子學과 近世日本社會 ('Neo-Confucian idealist philosophy and early modern Japanese society') (H.-K. Pak [朴鴻圭]. Trans.). Seoul: Yemun Sŏwŏn.
Wŏn. C.-K. [元重擧] (1764). 乘槎錄 ('Journal of travel by sea'). Unpublished manuscript. Seoul: Korea University.
Yi. H.-S. [李慧淳] (1995). 朝鮮通信使의 文學 ('The literature of Chosŏn t'ongshinsa'). Seoul: Ewha Womans University Press.
Yi. H.-W. [李曉源] (2017). 通信使와 徂徠學派의 交流 樣相과 그 意味-文明과 武威의 錯綜과 衝突. 그리고 疏通의 可能性 ('The aspect of exchange and its meaning between T'ongsinsa (通信使) and Soraigakuha (徂徠學派) in the eighteenth century: Collision and combination between civilization and military prestige. and the possibility of communication'). 韓國文化 (Korean Culture) 77: 19–47.
Yi. W.-S. [李元植] (1991). 朝鮮通信使 ('Chosŏn t'ongsinsa'). Seoul: Minumsa.

Part 3
Script-specific communication in Sinitic
Significance for historical pragmatics, cultural anthropology, and East Asian studies

12 Sociocultural functions of Chinese characters and writing

Transnational brush-talk encounters in mid-nineteenth- and early-twentieth-century East Asia

Reijiro Aoyama

Introduction

When asked about the purpose of writing, our immediate answer is likely going to be reading. We learn both at the same time early on in our education and it is hard not to think about one without the other. A text is written to be read primarily for its linguistic value, making comprehension a key criterion in examining literacy as the original function of writing. The more we think about various types of texts, however, the more we realize that the relationship between writing and language is not always as clear-cut as when it is viewed only through the prism of legible literacy. Written characters are not mere tools of language-based communication, something that can be observed in a contemporary context when we think of Chinese character tattoos on people who do not read Chinese or when we leaf through the pages of Japanese lifestyle magazines routinely featuring paragraphs interspersed with English and French phrases inserted in the headings. Going back in time to societies' early applications of writing, written symbols were often used for their talismanic power, such as the sinogram-like marks on earthenware pottery from the Yayoi 弥生 (c. 300 BCE – 250 CE) and Tomb 古墳 (c. 250–600 CE) periods in Japan, whose role likely involved warding off evil or bringing good fortune (Hirakawa 1999). Earlier still, the original function of oracle bone script as it emerged in China during the late Shang Dynasty (c. 1200–1050 BCE) was to facilitate pyromantic divination (Keightley 1996: 71–72, 2006: 185–191). Examples like these underscore that the value of written characters – whether logographic or phonographic – has been aesthetically appreciated in the art form of calligraphy or typography in many locales throughout history, or, as in many early societies, that written symbols held magical power over people through their ritualistic functions. In China, where the handwriting of powerful individuals has been historically endowed with special honor and significance, calligraphy could be harnessed for political ends given its augmented magical and ideological effect on people, as demonstrated by Richard Curt Kraus (1991) in his exploration of the relationship between this art form and Chinese politics. Kraus even argues

DOI: 10.4324/9781003048176-15

284 *Reijiro Aoyama*

that the belief in the mysterious power of sinograms in China continued into modern times and was reflected in the superstitions surrounding written objects and writing tools. He references anecdotes according to which Zhou Jianren 周建人 (1888–1984) had to burn any papers bearing sinograms in big iron basins rather than ordinary stoves as a gesture of respect, and Zhou's brother, the great modern writer Lu Xun 魯迅 (1881–1936), helped their father drink a dose of old writing ink as remedy for bleeding (Kraus 1991: 4–5).

While the use of sinograms originated in China, it is hard to overstate their overwhelming influence on the linguistic and cultural landscape of neighboring societies including Japan. Following their introduction in Japan as early as the first century of our era, they were first used to write Chinese as a foreign language, but in time became adapted to allow residents of the Japanese archipelago to express their own spoken language in a written form for the first time. They have continued in this function until this day and constitute one component of the modern Japanese mixed-script writing system along with the two *kana* syllabaries whose origins, too, can be traced back to Chinese characters. Just like their Chinese neighbors, the Japanese developed a complex and emotional relationship with the characters, ranging at various historical times from profound reverence to outspoken advocacy for abolition of the logographic script as an obstacle to the advancement of universal literacy (Gottlieb 1995).

Drawing on David Lurie's (2011) concept of *alegible* texts, this chapter explores Japanese interactions with writing in the mid-nineteenth and early twentieth century to shed light on the various ways in which different social groups simultaneously used sinograms in sometimes radically distinctive ways. I focus on transnational encounters conducted via brush-talk to outline the class of relations to sinograms and sinogram-based texts that did not necessarily involve reading in the conventional sense and argue that such non-linguistic meaning-making functions of Sinitic writing – including the action of writing and the production of written objects – formed an essential component of Japanese literacy accorded by the sociocultural conditions of Sinographic East Asia or the Sinographic cosmopolis (King 2015).[1]

Heterogeneous values of *alegible* texts

Chinese characters are logograms that record the Chinese language, with each character or sinogram corresponding to one morpheme or meaningful unit in the language.[2] They developed as a means of writing the Chinese language starting as early as the late Shang (Norman 1988: 77; Handel 2019b). For centuries, the

---

1 In this chapter I generally use 'Sinograms' and 'Sinitic' when referring to historical transnational use of Chinese characters and Literary Chinese as distinct from contemporary use of Chinese characters in China and *kanji* in Japan. For terminological differences between Sinitic and Literary Chinese, see Kornicki (2018: 19) and Handel (2019a).
2 While this is generally true, some exceptions exist, for example, 蝴 as in 蝴蝶 (unlike 蝶, which can be used on its own), and 琵琶.

characters functioned as a vehicle of content-based communicative practice essential to transmitting ideas and storing information, facilitating what is commonly understood as literacy; however, the earliest known artifacts inscribed with the characters' ancestral scripts were not necessarily produced for their normative literacy values. As previously noted, the original function of oracle bone script, a script ancestral to all subsequent forms of Chinese characters, was for fortune telling rituals (Keightley 1985).

Chinese characters were also used to record non-Chinese languages including Korean, Vietnamese, Zhuang 僮族/壯族, Khitan 契丹, and Jurchen 女真, and have remained a key component of the Japanese writing system. While the exact time when sinograms arrived in the Japanese archipelago is unclear, coins and mirrors carrying short inscriptions in Chinese script were found inside tombs dating from as early as the first century BCE.[3] The subsequent reception of sinograms in the archipelago during the period from their arrival to the seventh century when domestic literacies emerged has been a major topic of scholarly speculation centered on the relationship between the inscribed artifacts and the production of writing.

In his book *Realms of Literacy: Early Japan and the History of Writing*, Lurie (2011) considers whether the Japanese attached the same meanings to objects inscribed with Chinese characters as when these writings circulated in the Chinese contexts. With this query, he questions the privileged role of 'comprehension' as the only criterion for examining the uses of writing. He illustrates his point by citing a passage from the classic in the genre of anthropological memoir, *Tristes Tropiques*, written by Claude Lévi-Strauss (1973/1955) and recounting the anthropologist's encounter with the illiterate Nambikwara people in the Amazon basin. When the Nambikwara chief sees Lévi-Strauss writing, he too makes a show of drawing wavy lines on the sheets of paper in front of the villagers, acting as if the meaning of those lines is understood by Lévi-Strauss. The anthropologist deems this behavior as a farce aimed primarily at boosting the chief's image and authority in the eyes of his people. To Lurie, the irony of this interpretation of the historical significance of the advent of writing in illiterate societies derives from the presumed relationship between writing and its political meaning, which could only be possible if both parties in the incident subscribed to the inherent transparency and institutional dimension of writing. While Lévi-Strauss focuses on the power of literates over illiterates regardless of whether the 'literate' person understands the text or just pretends to do so, Lurie sees the possibility of resistance in actions that do not regard writing from the perspective of a transparent relationship, that is, considering texts only as either legible or illegible. Instead of viewing the incident through the lens of domination exerted by means of a written word, Lurie interprets

---

3 These objects are the earliest known evidence of the presence of writing in the Japanese archipelago. Japanese had not produced any known indigenous writing before the arrival of Chinese characters.

the Nambikwara chief's tactful use of *opaque* 'writing' as an expedient way to maintain independence from his interlocutor. As far as the chief did not read French, he was free from Lévi-Strauss's writing and the accompanying textual and linguistic apparatus of the colonizing power. In fact, he was free from any writing including his own drawing (pretend-writing) of wavy lines, as he did not regard any writing through the narrow dichotomy of legible and illegible texts. Drawing on William Harris's (1989) criticism of Lévi-Strauss's hypothesis that the primary function of written communication is to facilitate slavery, Lurie sheds light on the possibility of mental, economic, and political independence in the actions of illiterate people by recognizing the value of their opaque relations with writing. He makes a case for the importance of writing that cannot be interpreted as a literacy event, that is, to be read and understood via the conventional relationship between written form (*signifiant*) and linguistic meaning (*signifié*). When a person in a pre-literate society comes to learn about the existence of writing, s/he does not instinctively recognize the essential meaning of writing as a matter of course and does not immediately enter into a relationship with the literate colonizer as an illiterate subject who strives to decipher the meaning of a text and grasp its linguistic functions. Rather, such a person might maintain her/his independence by treating writing as opaque outside of the dichotomy of legibility and illegibility while recognizing other socially grounded values of writing such as decorative, aesthetic, magical, talismanic, and so forth.

In the history of Japan's contact with Chinese writing, inscribed objects played an important role in mediating the tributary relationship between the early Japanese chiefdoms and the Chinese court. However, they did so regardless of the specific content or 'legible' political meanings they carried.[4] One example involves the record of the mid-third century (238 CE) diplomatic communication between the Wei 魏 emperor Cao Rui 曹叡 (206–239) and the Wa 倭 queen Himiko 卑弥呼 (170–248) described in the last chapter of the 'Book of Wei' 魏書, which is the first part of the 'Records of the Three Kingdoms' 三國志. Along with biographies of other ethnic groups inhabiting Chinese periphery regions such as Wuwan 烏丸, Xianbei 鮮卑, and Dongyi 東夷, the record provides an account of the characteristics of Wajin 倭人 or Japanese people and describes the tributary relationship between the Wei court and the queen of the Wa who briefly unified the various regional chiefdoms under the proto-Japanese federation of Yamatai 邪馬台, recounting the diplomatic exchanges involving envoys, tributes and written communications. Regarding the early encounters with Chinese writing via written objects and Japan's adaptation of sinograms in the Yayoi period, Lurie poses a fundamental question of whether Chinese characters were regarded as 'true', that is, legible writing or merely talismanic marks by Himiko and her officials. The following line in the *Records of the Three Kingdoms* mentioning an exchange of

---

[4] These objects were usually seals, swords, and mirrors.

written texts has often been interpreted as evidence that Japanese people read and wrote sinograms.

傳送文書賜遺之物詣女王 不得差錯 (Chen 1964: 856)

[The official] sends the documents and bestowed items to the Queen, so it is impossible to tamper with them.

(Lurie 2011: 76)

Against that reading, Lurie argues that the Japanese in the Yamatai federation 邪馬台國 regarded the documents as artifacts not writing. Since the word 賜 'bestow' is used appropriately only if the gifts flow from the Chinese court but not the other way around, it can be interpreted that the Japanese only received the documents. This does not automatically preclude that the Japanese queen and her officials could read the documents and were able to understand the linguistic meanings of sinograms. It does however allow us to surmise that for the queen, the documents and other written objects received from the Kingdom of Wei at the very least served as artifacts that helped enhance her magical power and political authority independently of the linguistic meanings they carried. In other words, the significance of these objects for Himiko did not necessarily derive from the 'true' meaning of the writings they featured but from her independent re-appropriation and re-purposing of the inscriptions towards readings that presumably deviated from the tributary power relationship they were originally meant to acknowledge.

Using various examples pertaining to Japan's early accommodation and responses to sinograms such as the one involving queen Himiko as mentioned earlier, Lurie theorizes the context in which people relate to texts outside the narrow dichotomy of legibility and illegibility and conceptualizes as *alegible* the specific relations to texts developed by early adaptors in which the potential linguistic content of texts is not necessarily considered essential. The alegible texts are sets of graphs that are seen but not necessarily read. In the ancient Japanese archipelago, alegible texts such as the documents bearing sinograms were often used to enhance the power and authority of the owner. Whether texts were read or unread is hard to establish as well as less significant than the effects the writings conferred on the recipients. Lurie writes:

> We should note that the readability of a text was simply not the major issue in the contexts in which those artifacts were being produced and employed. The role of the 'unread' at this early stage in the history of Japanese writing draws attention to the continuing importance of this class of relations to texts, even in contexts that also involve widespread acts of reading in the familiar sense. Such coexistence, which occurs worldwide in both premodern and modern contexts, involves familiar phenomena such as the use of graphs in amulets or logos, the magical power or social cachet of illegible inscriptions (whether in ancient books or on contemporary T-shirts and

tattoos), and the aesthetic dimensions of writing considered as calligraphy or typography.

(Lurie 2011: 3)

This passage not only reminds us of the dual values people have assigned to texts across time and space – the linguistic and non-linguistic meanings we ascribe to written words – but also underscores that sometimes our relationship with a text can be ambiguous and opaque. In some contexts, Chinese characters function as non-linguistic symbols, for example, when they first arrived in the ancient Japanese archipelago inscribed on shell ornaments around the first century BCE. Although it is impossible to know with certainty what their 'readers' made of the marks, we can assume they were valued as ritual objects and symbols of social distinction, political authority, and magical power rather than being regarded in the narrow sense of writing that conveys linguistic meaning. In modern times Chinese characters generally operate as purely linguistic tools intended to deliver ideas and store information, just as how we use them when we read a newspaper or write emails. In alegible contexts in which sinogram-based texts were not simply defined as something to be read or to be 'unread' based on a modern, normative sense of literacy, the two functions intersected, operating simultaneously and fluidly side by side while reflecting the heterogeneous mix of the 'readers' differing relationships with Chinese characters. Sometimes sinograms were assigned with strictly linguistic or non-linguistic values and sometimes with varying degrees of both depending on the person and other context-specific concerns. For instance, as a form of visual art, Chinese calligraphy conveys both aesthetic and semantic meanings; an illiterate viewer at the very least may be able to appreciate the former, while a literate one may understand either, or both. By the same token, identical texts and written objects can be valued differently by different users depending on their class, gender, occupation, sociocultural dispositions and so on, as well as their collective consciousness as members of a given social group, be it a tribe, ethnolinguistic group or a transnational community of people bound together by a specific sociocultural framework such as Confucian literati in premodern East Asia. To recall Lévi-Strauss's encounter with the Nambikwara people in the Amazon basin, the illiterate village chief used his own imagination of how social existence ought to be played out to establish a sociocultural relationship with writing, albeit not necessarily the kind that conformed to the paradigm espoused by Lévi-Strauss. As Lurie observes in his commentary on the incident, whether through his writing-pretense performance the chief sought to pursue social distinction, political authority, magical power over his fellow illiterates or independence from his literate guest remains a moot point. Similarly, how Chinese writing – in terms of both written text and the act of writing – was treated and valued in premodern and modern Japan would depend on the sense-making processes underpinning the collective imaginary of non-Chinese receivers and users of sinograms. While the linguistic meanings attached to texts were relatively straightforward, the non-linguistic values of sinograms to the Japanese users varied from political to religious and aesthetic to commercial depending on the alegible contexts in which these writings were received and the social imaginaries that enabled and legitimized the sense-making practices of the recipients.

In what follows, I will use the concept of alegible texts to explore the tacit richness of opaque writing functions that are discernible from specific brush-talk encounters between East Asian users of sinograms in Japan during the nineteenth and early twentieth centuries. Events related to two historical contexts will be examined, one being historic trade negotiations between the USA and Japan in 1854 featuring the participation of the Chinese businessman/interpreter Luo Sen, the other being Japanese encounters with Vietnamese independence activists seeking assistance from Japan in 1905. My discussion will focus on various ways in which literate and 'illiterate' Japanese users assigned sociocultural values to the production of Sinographic writing based on the shifting relationship between legible and alegible meanings it conveyed to the readers/writers and/or spectators.

Role of Sinitic writing in the 1854 USA-Japan negotiations

Tao Demin (2005), a historian of modern Sino-Japanese relations, points out the often-forgotten historical fact that two foreign languages, Chinese and Dutch, played an essential role in early USA-Japan diplomacy. He elaborates the circumstances which saw Luo Sen 羅森, a Hong Kong-based Chinese businessman, join in 1854 the pivotal American expedition to Japan, which marked a turning point in the country's history. The trading treaty extracted from the Tokugawa shogunate by the American side through their use of gunboat diplomacy ended 220 years of Japan's self-imposed seclusion and forced it to open the country's ports to American merchant ships and rescue stranded American seamen. As it turns out, Luo Sen's role in that critical moment of history and his contribution to American diplomacy was quite substantial. A bilingual speaker of Cantonese and English – the latter acquired through his trading business – he did not know Japanese. This did not, however, stop him from successfully conducting 'conversations' with Japanese officials and connecting with ordinary Japanese people directly via writing enacted by Sinitic brush-talk. In fact, Luo Sen's ability to converse with Japanese officials in brush-talk using erudite expressions in elegant calligraphy helped to resolve many of the underlying tensions and allay suspicions between the two negotiating sides during the early stage of the talks.

How did Luo Sen, by all accounts an ordinary, if educated, Cantonese merchant in his thirties, become implicated in historical events of such great importance? It had much to do with Japan's political reticence and the peculiar linguistic ecologies of Sinographic East Asia. Due to restrictive isolationist policies, the linguistic expertise of the Japanese side was severely circumscribed (Aoyama 2020), forcing Commodore Matthew C. Perry (1794–1858), the American commander of the expedition, to conduct the negotiations in either Dutch or Chinese. While the talks during his first trip to Japan in 1853 were largely facilitated in Dutch via Dutch-speaking interpreters provided by both sides, for the second trip in 1854 Perry decided to make heavier use of Chinese. The man he chose to assist him both times as chief interpreter for the Chinese language was a fellow American, Christian missionary Samuel Wells Williams (1812–1884), who had spent decades in China and was regarded among Western orientalists at the time as an expert not only on China but also on Japan (Turner 1851). Although he possessed a high level of communicative competence in Chinese, Williams was fully aware that the task would require either elegant Chinese writing skills or good knowledge of colloquial Japanese, neither of which was his forte. Having decided to enroll an educated Chinese interpreter to serve as his assistant during the second voyage, he recruited Luo Sen in Shanghai. We can only speculate what moved the Cantonese businessman to take up the position when most other eligible Chinese fellows would prefer to focus on advancing their careers through more conventional means of civil service, but it appears that his decision may have been partially motivated by discontent with the Qing court, which had failed to acknowledge his contribution in suppressing the Taiping Rebellion (Luo 1856: 400; Tao 2005). Williams and Luo had quickly developed a congenial and productive working relationship, with Luo translating documents and taking dictation from Williams. Of his decision to bring Luo Sen onboard as the diplomatic dealings advanced between 1853 and 1854 Williams wrote:

> Heretofore, most of my taking having been in a small way and on unimportant matters, if I bungled't was not so much consequence; but now the affair is serious, so I bring Lo[5] into considerable service to make one language help the other, and thereby avoid many mistakes.
> (Williams 1889: 219)

Luo's contribution to the fruitful result of the expedition was not, however, limited to his secretarial skills deployed behind the scenes; his ability to carry on face-to-face communication with the Japanese officials via brush-talk was just as – if not more – important. Returning to Japan in 1854, after they presented the letter from President Millard Fillmore requesting the opening of political and commercial relations between the two countries a year earlier, Americans felt a deep sense of suspicion on the Japanese part. In his diary of the expedition, Luo Sen reports seeing a fleet of more than a hundred Japanese vessels anchored near the shore of Yokohama in Edo Bay and a military camp on land deployed by the shogunate in preparation for possible conflicts. To complicate the matters, Dutch-speaking interpreters from the Japanese side were not always available to participate in the meetings; on such occasions, the Chinese language – which was Williams's preferred language for documentation – was used as an official medium of communication. Despite very limited direct interaction between the Chinese and the Japanese during the preceding 200 years, Sinitic writing proved to be an ineluctable and indispensable link connecting the two nations that could be brought to bear on the spot to facilitate communication using brush, ink, and

---

5 Lo is an alternative romanization of Luo.

paper, without the need for a single word to be uttered in speech. Because the same sinograms were pronounced differently by the Chinese and the Japanese they were mutually unintelligible if read out loud, yet none of it mattered in written communication. Luo Sen's advantage over Williams as a Chinese literatus intimately familiar with the cultural and intellectual resources of the Chinese literary canons enabled him to use Sinitic with greater freedom in order to express and play with various meanings accessible to those who, like him, were educated in the same tradition – in this case, the Japanese commissioners and dignitaries involved in the diplomatic negotiations. As attested by Williams in his diary, Luo Sen 'gets on admirably with the natives; he is indeed the most learned Chinaman they have ever seen' and the Japanese feel 'delight in showing off to him their attainments in Chinese' (Williams 1889: 219).

The momentous nature of the events was only matched by the tremendous extent of distrust and intimidation tactics involved on both sides. In a diplomatically charged situation in which the negotiating parties had no recourse to a common spoken language, the option to resort to brush-talk offered invaluable assistance that effected dual merit. First, at the level of linguistic content facilitated by the morphographic nature of Sinitic, it allowed the interlocutors to convey their messages to one another (Li 2020; Li et al. 2020). Even though the Japanese side did not speak any Chinese, the writing-mediated 'conversation' could still take place using brush, ink, and paper and produce a certain measure of linguistic meanings readily legible to both sides. In the hands of literati with erudite knowledge of Sinitic classics and canons rooted in a shared intellectual tradition, the range of meanings that could be yielded and mutually recognized by the educated interlocutors would expand immeasurably. What is more, the sense-making processes employed in brush-talk were not operating only in relation to the potential legible meanings of the produced text; what mattered more was the symbolic value of shared Sinitic writing that allowed the interlocutors to recognize and acknowledge each other as members of the same cultural sphere or community. Luo Sen's ability to compose erudite phrases when engaging in brush-talk with the Japanese officials, therefore, helped more than just to overcome a language barrier; in a way it also allowed him to transcend the cultural and political apprehensions that had accrued between the Chinese and Japanese as a result of their lack of direct contact for over 200 years. As an immediate effect, his agility and literary flair in Sinitic brush-talk provided the wherewithal to earn goodwill from the Japanese side and helped to allay latent suspicion of the samurai officials and extenuate some of the tension that inevitably afflicted the initial negotiations (Tsu 2010; Tao 2005). Not only was face-to-face, back-and-forth writing instrumental in helping the parties to instantly grasp one another's intentions and clarify misunderstandings but it also aided Luo Sen in creating a relaxed atmosphere during the talks and forging rapport and personal connections with the Japanese hosts.

It was a standard practice for educated literati of Sinitic to use brush-talk to exchange poetic verses, which Luo Sen did many times during his interaction with the Japanese scholar-officials. On one occasion Luo and the Japanese officials shared in amazement at how well they could communicate with the help of just brush, ink, and paper[6]:

> On the same day, Wau-che-choo, of Shan-pun, asked me to inscribe a fan for him, and presented to me the four following lines:
>
> 'Say not our meeting here was all of chance;
> To you we owe the treaty and our peace.
> From far the strangers came, their language strange,
> 'Twas well we had your pencil and your tongue.'
> (Luo 1856: 402)
>
> 橫濱相遇豈無因
> 和議皆安仰賴君
> 遠方駃舌今朝會
> 幸覩同文對語人
> (Luo 1854–55: 590 (129))

Rhapsodic interactions such as these give us a vivid idea of the Japanese hosts' delight and recognition of Luo Sen's participation in the negotiations which was largely attendant on Sinitic writing. Unlike colloquial speech, direct communication via brush-talk provided a much better means of signaling erudition and cultural credentials required to prove one's worth as a fully-fledged member of a mutually shared realm of intellectual tradition and civilized learning across Sinographic East Asia. Likewise, exchanging poetry, inscribing handheld fans and gifting of writing tools typified time-honored attitudes which developed as an important ingredient of Chinese literacy and functioned as another kind of meaning-making device within a sociocultural framework sanctioned by Sinitic writing. Thus, by exchanging poetic verses, Luo Sen and his Japanese partners engaged in a centuries-old cultural practice that enabled them to forge a high level of intimacy and trust, both being crucial dispositions towards building consensus.

Symbolic power of sinogram inscriptions on handheld fans

The extensive use of brush-talk was not just a feature of Luo Sen's primary undertaking in Japan as an interpreter for the American side. He was just as likely to turn to brush and ink when meeting with Japanese people in a private capacity beyond his official business. While strolling around the port of Shimoda 下田

---

6 Luo Sen's notes from his visit to Japan were translated by Samuel Williams into English and first published on 11 September 1854 in *Overland Register and Price Current of Hong Kong*. They were later included as appendix in the official record of Perry's mission published in 1856: https://books.google.com.hk/books?id=OD08AQAAIAAJ. Luo's 'Journal of a Visit to Japan' 日本日記 in the Chinese original was published separately in Nov. and Dec. 1854 and Jan. 1855 issues of 'Chinese Serial' 遐邇貫珍 in Hong Kong. There are significant differences between the two versions.

one time he was approached by two Buddhist monks who asked him to write something for them, to which he responded by inscribing a phrase 'encircling peaks, girdling waters' 峰回水繞 in reference to the surrounding scenery. The pair reciprocated with a poem,

> "Here in our little cells we sit,
> Bound our inkstones the white clouds meet,
> Mere dust to us is gold so rare,
> The future gives us not a care.
> (Luo 1856: 404)

> 一丈方庵玉座同
> 寸餘硯石白雲通
> 黃金畢竟塵中物
> 不省明朝炊米空
> (Luo 1854–55: 591(128))

It can be postulated that the Japanese monks saw the encounter with Luo Sen as a miraculous moment worthy of commemoration in the spirit of Buddhist philosophical thought. A chance encounter with strangers from foreign lands became a spiritually inspiring juncture that transcended space and time and brought the two sides together through the act of writing. In fact, such incidents happened frequently enough that Luo Sen wrote:

> As the Japanese for two hundred years have had no intercourse with foreigners, and have seen none, excepting the few Chinese and Dutch who carry on the trade at Naga-saki, I found myself quite an object of interest; and as they set a great value on Chinese characters and compositions, whenever I went to the hall of reception many of them were sure to ask me to write on fans for them. The fans which I inscribed during a month while we were at Yokuhama could not be fewer than five hundred.
> (Luo 1856: 401)

Even after Luo Sen's official engagement in the negotiations between the Americans and Japanese came to an end in June 1854, he continued to interact with Japanese people on various occasions (Tao 2005: 106–108, Williams 1910: 209). In every port at which he disembarked during the course of his entire sojourn in the country – including Yokohama, Shimoda, and Hakodate 函館 – he received scores of requests from the local public to inscribe Chinese characters and verses on their fans. Since a person's chance of meeting a foreigner at that time was close to zero, the excitement of coming face to face with someone from outside the Japanese territory was likely overwhelming, both for the educated and uneducated folk. We can only speculate how many of the people who approached Luo Sen for fan inscriptions were literate enough to comprehend the 'true' meaning of the writing he inscribed for them, but it is safe to assume that many in fact did not read Sinitic. All the same, the requests kept coming through wherever Luo went and the locals were clearly keen on having their fans inscribed with sinograms. Indeed, as evidenced in the aforementioned passage from his diary, the enthusiasm and curiosity towards Luo Sen displayed by the Japanese in Yokohama were not dictated simply by the fact that he was a foreigner but specifically because he could produce Sinitic writing on their fans, which were held nationwide as socio-culturally prestigious and therefore good to have.

The custom of inscribing handheld fans goes back to the Heian 平安 period (794–1185), when court aristocrats began using fans made of cypress wood for writing down poetry and recording the order of ceremonial events alongside their original function of creating an airflow for cooling one down (Casal 1960). The nobles traditionally gave and received inscribed fans adorned with their poems and drawings (Park 2016). Later on, when folding fans developed into ones made of bamboo and paper, they grew more decorative and became fashionable items carried casually around by the wealthy class. With the commercialization of foldable fans (Davies 2019) in the Edo period (1603–1867), the custom of inscribing poetry and drawings on fans was able to spread among ordinary people. A once-in-a-lifetime event of coming face-to-face with a foreigner – particularly one who could produce Sinitic writing – deserved to be cherished and commemorated, and an inscription on one's fan provided for a perfect memento.

Both Luo's and Williams's diaries contain many mentions of the Japanese commoners' keen interest in obtaining Sinographic inscriptions on their fans. Williams, for example, observed:

> he [Luo Sen] turns a graceful verse or two for them [the Japanese] upon a fan; of these he has written, I should think, more than half a thousand since coming to Japan.
>
> (Williams 1889: 219)

Conversely, there appear to be no references in the relevant historical records to any requests for English fan inscriptions directed at the American navy officials. It was always sinograms and Chinese verses that were sought out by the Japanese receivers. What is strikingly interesting here, however, is that the power of sinograms was not limited to educated literati but applied equally to commoners with no or limited literacy. The Japanese, both literate and illiterate folk – including the many women who rarely received formal education and thus could not be expected to be able to decode the lexical meanings of the sinograms[7] – each set value on Sinitic writing in their own way. Accordingly, the examples discussed in this section attest to the diversity and richness of non-linguistic meanings attached by the readers (scholar-officials, Buddhist monks) and onlookers (literate and illiterate fan inscription enthusiasts) of Chinese characters to writing. The functions performed by sinograms and Sinitic writing here should thus be interpreted as

---

7 According to Dore (1964), female literacy rate in late Edo was around 15%.

partly alegible and aesthetically loaded with symbolism associated with literacy in Literary Sinitic.

While the normative literacy level of the Japanese officials who crossed paths with Luo Sen was presumably rather high, the same cannot be easily estimated of the women seeking out his fan inscriptions. In any case, it is beside the point whether any of Luo's writings were read by either group for their linguistic content – as is indeed the feature of alegible contexts. Rather, the significance of brush-talk events discussed within this section relates to Sinitic writing's unique potential for enabling sense-making practices that do not unduly privilege the linguistic function of literacy and remain open to a variety of opaque readings which are rooted in a collective centuries-old cultural imaginary within Sinographic East Asia. The shared sociocultural meanings and symbolic values embodied in Sinitic writing meant that the Japanese from all walks of life were able to create an instant kinship with Luo Sen, despite having been instilled with mistrust towards foreigners as a matter of official policy and given the fact that exposure to non-Japanese speaking people had been extremely limited.

Brush-talk as a preferred mode of communication in the early 1900s

Did the power of Sinitic writing as a means that facilitated transnational encounters in premodern Japan extend into the twentieth century? In the early 1900s, Japan was a very different country compared with the time of the Perry expeditions. In the decades that followed Luo Sen's mission it embraced modernity and opened its doors to foreign goods, knowledge, and residents. By the 1900s, ninety percent of school-age population was enrolled in elementary public education, learning the national language, so basic literacy and knowledge of sinograms was comparatively more widespread (Rubinger 2007).[8] Given the transformed landscape of regional hierarchies and notions of collective belonging informed by Japan's radical makeover, what functions and meanings did Sinitic writing generate for its users in the early 1900s? This is possibly one of the last times we see interactional brush-talk in action as an attested mode of transnational communication in face-to-face encounters between Japanese and non-Japanese members of Sinographic East Asia. This section turns to Phan Bội Châu 潘佩珠 (1867–1940), a prominent leader of the Vietnamese revolution and independence movement and a foreign sojourner in early-twentieth-century Japan, and the transnational interactions with the people he encountered during his 1905 politically intriguing visit to Japan.

One of the most widely respected figures in Vietnam's modern history, Phan Bội Châu is known for initiating the struggle against the French colonial rule and organizing Đông-Du Movement 東遊運動 or Go East Movement, which

---

8 For example, three-quarters of Japanese males of 20 years of age possessed elementary level of literacy in 1905, while 10% were illiterate (Saitō 2012).

encouraged young Vietnamese revolutionaries seeking to rise against the French domination to pursue education and training in Japan. As founder and representative of the Vietnam's Association for Modernization 維新會, Phan himself left his homeland in 1905, heading first to China and on to Japan in search of political collaboration, military assistance, and financial aid for Vietnam's independence movement. Born to a poor Confucian scholar, he began studying Chinese classics at the age of five and sat in the civil service examinations. Despite lacking proficiency in spoken Chinese, he had extensive knowledge of Sinitic and was well acquainted with Confucian thought and Chinese poetry. In the context of his venture to Japan Phan wrote the following in reference to his linguistic skills:

> The most awkward thing was that I did not understand Japanese and was not well versed in Chinese; brush-conversation and talking by gesture were very troublesome (筆談手語煩累滋多). What a great shame for a diplomat!
> (Phan 1999/1926: 84)

Based on what we know about his training and the fact that he succeeded in conducting multiple successful brush-talk interactions throughout his trip, Phan's self-professed weakness in Chinese composition appears to be an exaggeration. In Hong Kong he conducted a fruitful face-to-face interaction in writing with Feng Chih-you 馮自由, the editor of the *Journal of China* 中國日報, delineating his plan for an anti-French uprising in Vietnam and soliciting leads on possible collaborators sympathetic to his cause within the Qing government (Phan 1999/1926: 82). On the ship from Hong Kong to Shanghai, Phan managed to obtain the Japanese address of the Chinese scholar and reformist Liang Qichao 梁啟超 (1873–1929) by 'brush-talking' with another passenger, a Chinese student named Chou Chun 周椿, and on the train from Kobe to Yokohama, he made friends with a student from Hunan surnamed Chao 趙, who was in Japan to study the Japanese language. Of Chao's dedicated assistance during the journey, Phan wrote:

> He never minded the trouble he took and did not expect any compensation; this is a really fine quality of people of a great nation. Then again, my Chinese composition may have helped too (大國民之美質誠然哉.亦漢文之介也).
> (Phan 1999/1926: 84)

Phan's Sino-Vietnamese pronunciation and the students' Chinese pronunciation of the sinograms produced in the course of these conversations were mutually unintelligible (DeFrancis 1977: 161–162), but like what happened to Luo Sen half a century earlier in Japan, the literati could rely on brush-talk as a convenient and efficient means of exchanging practical information in the absence of interpreters. As Phan proceeds along his journey and arrives in Yokohama, he writes:

> I then got off the train and went to the gate of the station. My luggage was nowhere in sight. I stood there helplessly for a long time, until a Japanese

wearing a white cap and a sword came up to me. I took a small notebook out of my pocket. He wrote the question: 'Why don't you leave?' I answered: 'I cannot find my luggage.' He wrote: 'I have paid for a reservation at the inn for you. Your luggage will be sent there'.

(Phan 1999/1926: 85)

Spotting a foreign traveler, the railway guard figured that speaking to him in Japanese would not be of much use, but the visitor's East Asian appearance made him instead reach for a pen – in an instinctive decision to give brush-talk a try. It may not be a coincidence for a train guard to deploy this mode of communication spontaneously in 1905 Yokohama. After China's unexpected defeat in the First Sino-Japanese War in 1895, Japan became a popular destination for Chinese students pursuing overseas education in liberal arts and modern sciences, not least because of the country's relative affordability compared with the cost of overseas study in the west (Harrell 1992: 77–78) and, in fact, thanks to the shared script (Vogel 2019: 132–149). In 1905 more than eight thousand Chinese students were enrolled in various courses in Japan (Sanetō 1960); many of them would have passed through the Yokohama station early on in their Japanese sojourn, before they had a chance to learn Japanese. Even though we have no way of knowing the precise literacy level of the Japanese train guard who approached Phan Bội Châu in the Yokohama station, his readiness to assist a disoriented foreigner through writing suggests that their interaction was not an isolated case and that brush-talk indeed must have functioned as a standard practice of transnational communication between the increasing numbers of foreign travelers and Japanese railway staff, at least in train stations with a high volume of foreign passengers.

Not being able to speak Japanese, Phan Bội Châu relied extensively on brush-talk in both mundane matters and diplomatic encounters of a high order. Just like when one may turn to a translation app on one's mobile phone when traveling abroad in the 2020s, Phan carried with him a pen and a notebook which he would procure whenever he had to 'talk' to a Japanese local or someone from China. When he visited Liang Qichao at his home in Yokohama, the first part of their conversation was assisted by Tăng Bạt Hổ 曾拔虎 (1856–1906), Phan's Vietnamese travel companion who spoke some Cantonese and translated orally for Phan and Liang. This got them only so far, however, and every time the conversation turned to a more intricate or momentous subject, the two scholars would resort to brush-talk to clarify their intentions and record their ideas in written form. For educated literati such as Phan and Liang, brush-talk was thus not at all an inferior substitute for a spoken language – something that perhaps may have been the case in more quotidian interactions such as the encounter in the railway station. At the most basic level, it permitted the speakers to bypass the interpreter whose assistance could potentially alter or dilute the speakers' intended meanings. Additionally, since writing proceeds at an inherently slower pace than speaking, it further empowered the speakers to convey their thoughts in a measured and deliberate manner, which in turn facilitated firsthand comprehension of the interlocutors' perspective and intent – a direct meeting of the minds so to speak. As we have learned from the interaction between Luo Sen and his Japanese interlocutors, this function of brush-talk played an important role in negotiating multiple layers of complex meaning-making within the sociocultural ecologies shaped by the partly shared Sinitic canons. Even though Phan and Liang's conversation focused entirely on the pan-Asian anti-colonial movement, their use of brush-talk was a way of conveying ideological camaraderie, a profound connection which in all likelihood would go well beyond the literal meanings of the written words they exchanged on the spot and back to the complicated and opaque literacy values attached to writing by the literati class of the Sinoghrapic cosmopolis. During his stay in Japan, Phan also met twice with Sun Yat-sen 孫逸仙 (1866–1925), leader of the Chinese republican movement, at his home in Yokohama. Likewise, they discussed matters related to the revolutionary fronts in Vietnam and China and communicated in brush-talk, with Sun promptly bringing out brush and paper on Phan's arrival (Phan 1999/1926: 101). Their first meeting lasted four hours, from eight in the evening until midnight, and covered a wide range of delicate topics including their different takes on constitutional monarchy and the democratic republican system, including the question of which revolution, Chinese or Vietnamese, should be achieved first. This further shows us the wide range of complex subjects that could be effectively addressed via brush-talk in the skillful hands of solidly trained literati in Sinitic.

Sinitic as a semantic and semiotic interface at a historic transcultural meeting

Through the introduction of Liang Qichao, Phan met the influential elder Japanese statesmen Okuma Shigenobu 大隈重信 (1838–1922) and Inukai Tsuyoshi 犬養毅 (1855–1932) at a gathering in Inukai's home, an occasion which provides us with additional interesting insights into the functions of brush-talk as a mode of communication and a vehicle of linguistic and non-linguistic meaning-making among the East Asian literati of Sinitic. The four men spent the entire afternoon discussing politics including plans to bring Prince Cường Để 彊柢 (1882–1951), the heir of the Nguyễn dynasty 阮朝 (1802–1945), out of Vietnam to secure the royal family's endorsement for the anti-colonial movement, ideas for uniting Vietnamese intellectuals and organizing a revolutionary party, and the difficult position of the sympathetic Japanese political leaders who were wary of provoking a direct confrontation with France if they were to support Vietnam. All conversations were almost entirely writing-mediated and took place without interpreting. At a more practical level, the disinclination toward speech was dictated by the fact that between the three first languages represented in the group – Vietnamese, Chinese, and Japanese – none was spoken by all parties. It appears that only Liang Qichao had the option of communicating orally with the Japanese interlocutors if we assume that his Japanese proficiency was adequate to the task. This should be a reasonable expectation given his lengthy stay in Japan – he had fled China to Japan seven years earlier – and the fact that he had composed a Japanese textbook for his countrymen (Kotajima 2008; Shen 2010).[9] Phan's account of the meeting, too, mentions that the three men, Liang, Inukai, and Okuma, spoke to each other in Japanese at one point (Phan 1999/1926: 88). Brush-talk, however, remained the principal mode of expression intended for readership and appreciation within the collective sphere, driven in part by the performative appeal of the physical act of writing itself.

One instructive example of such performative use of brush-talk in the meeting involved an act of 'poignant' writing by Liang, a deliberate gesture meant to underscore a moment of heightened emotion. After Phan laid out to everybody the details of Vietnam's predicament, Okuma made him an offer of subsistence and accommodation in Japan. Declining, Phan said that his reason for coming to Japan was to find relief for his fellow compatriots back home, not for himself. Moved by Phan's resolve and dedication, Liang wrote 'This man deserves great respect' 此人大可敬 (Phan 1999/1926: 256). As a speaker of Japanese, Liang could have said the same directly to Okuma and Inukai in Japanese – but we already know that the purpose of his message was not simply to convey linguistic information. That same message, if conveyed in spoken Japanese, would need to be translated to Phan in writing anyway. By contrast, apart from its all-inclusive audience function in that context, Sinitic writing helped cement solidarity and appeal for a shared sense of purpose performatively by seeking to drum up an intense emotional response from the interlocutors. By showing off his handwritten characters to Okuma and Inukai, Liang officially endorsed Phan as a person of outstanding character and sanctioned Phan's plea for help on his cause. Making a point of inscribing the relevant sinograms on paper and presenting them to interlocutors had its own, separate, ritualistic function which coincided with the 'actual' writing and reading – just as everybody was aware of what Liang's sinograms said they were even more acutely conscious of the symbolic meaning of his statement delivered in his solemn writing performance. We can therefore say that brush-talk here indexed socio-psychological influence, whereby the act of brushing sinograms was vested with a symbolic power that would otherwise be unattainable by their putative lexical equivalents in speech, or to put it more simply, where writing something endowed it with more power than simply verbalizing the same content. Thus, the brush-talkers utilized Sinitic as a semantic and semiotic interface which enabled them

---

9 Liang also traveled to Canada, Hawai'i, and Australia in 1899 and 1901, but Japan remained his primary home base from 1898–1912. The exact level of Liang's Japanese proficiency is unclear. After his arrival in Japan, Liang learned Japanese from a Chinese student Luo Pu who assisted him in the writing of a Japanese textbook for Chinese learners published in 1900: 和文漢読法 (Xia 1997; Kotajima 2008; Shen 2010). Luo Pu, who came to Japan before Liang, completed his language training at Tokyo Senmon Gakkō 東京專門學校 (currently Waseda University) which used western communicative language teaching methods (Kotajima 2008; Shen 2010; Chū 2017).

to channel linguistic meanings and symbolic messages side by side in complete abstraction of verbalized speech.[10]

Multi-layered functions of Sinitic writing

The material, semi-permanent record of brush-talk meant that even those who had not taken part in a conversation could gain access to its content at a later point provided they were shown the relevant sheets of writing. This is why Kashiwabara Buntarō 柏原文太郎 (1869–1936), an educator serving in the Japanese House of Representatives and one of the founders of East Asia Common Culture Academy (Tōa Dōbun Shoin 東亜同文書院), a pioneering institution in the field of Chinese studies, could offer his comments on the meeting after glancing through everyone's brush-talk inscriptions, even though he sat beside the other four men at the gathering without directly participating in the conversation. He wrote:

> Today, as I watched all of you, I felt as if I were reading a tale of the ancient heroes in a novel, since you are the first Vietnamese who has come to the Land of the Rising Sun to meet with our men in high positions.
> (Phan 1999/1926: 89)

Brush-talk, with its physical output, could thus help latecomers to join in the conversation and those who were never there to see what had been discussed, much like the function performed by modern-day meeting minutes, only richer in meaning because in addition to linguistic content it also provided a sense of the speakers' idiosyncratic handwriting and calligraphy. Furthermore, in a real sense, the semi-permanent record of brush-talk interaction had the potential to transcend time and space. Compared with a verbal summary, the handwritten materials resulting from international figures' brush conversation could lend far greater credibility of the Japanese leadership's undertaking to support foreign allies when revolutionaries like Phan Bội Châu returned home to persuade his compatriots and members of the Vietnamese royal family to join the anti-French movement (cf. 'a more prestigious and direct conduit for communication', Clements 2019: 305).

Not unlike Luo Sen fifty years earlier, Phan, too, ended up inscribing Chinese poetic verses on fans upon request, in a testament to the lasting symbolic power of sinograms and Chinese culture in Japan which stretched well into the early twentieth century. Towards the end of Phan's meeting with Liang Qichao and the

---

10 My intention here is not to argue that the sinograms convey messages directly to brush-talkers' minds, bypassing the speech sound (See 'the ideographic myth', DeFrancis 1984). In a silent conversation, as well as meanings, sinograms still represented speech sounds of the speakers' respective languages intersubjectively in individual speakers' minds (Li 2020; see also Li & Aoyama, this volume). The key to a successful communication in transcultural brush-talking, however, was to improvise sinograms interactively without vocalizing them.

Japanese statesmen, Inukai's wife Chiyoko 犬養千代子 (1866–1952) entered the room and asked Phan to write something on her fan as a way of commemorating the historical gathering of East Asia's distinguished political minds. Phan's deft inscription of a verse from the Book of Documents 書經 cleverly alluded to Chiyoko's role as devoted wife supporting her husband from the sidelines[11]:

> That the wind blows through all the Four Directions is thanks only to your great work.
>
> 四方風動 惟乃之休
>
> (Phan 1999/1926: 89)

Besides being a great resource on the role of brush-talk among the educated elite, Phan Bội Châu's autobiography affords us a glimpse into ordinary Japanese people's relationship with Sinitic writing in the early twentieth century. Lương Ngọc Quyến 梁玉眷, a young and destitute Vietnamese revolutionary who traveled to Japan to escape French surveillance and resided in Phan's lodging in Yokohama, was once forced to make the grueling trip to Tokyo on foot because he could not afford the Yokohama-Tokyo train fare.[12] The growing number of Vietnamese political activists taking refuge in Japan combined with limited funding meant that many had to go hungry and suffered from Japan's snowy winters, so one day Lương decided to seek assistance from Chinese students in Tokyo. Phan writes:

> He then walked all day long on an empty stomach to make his way from Yokohama to Tokyo. That night he turned in to sleep in the doorway of a police station. The police questioned him in Japanese. In a state of blank incomprehension, he did not know what to answer. When they made a search, they found his pockets to be empty. They suspected him of being feeble-minded. When brush-conversation began, however, then at last it emerged that he was a young man from our country [Vietnam]. The Japanese police were astonished, and supplied him with the money to go back to Yokohama by train.
>
> (Phan 1999/1926: 97)

Lương's shabby appearance and lack of Japanese language skills flagged him as suspect to Japanese police; however, as soon as he proved himself to be literate in Sinitic the policemen's distrust was instantly dispelled and they recognized him as a respectable person. Knowing sinograms not only allowed Lương to explain his circumstances through brush-talk but also earned him confidence and goodwill on the part of the Japanese policemen who in turn ended up paying for his

---

11 Inukai Chiyoko later became the chairwoman of Seiwakai 清和会, the Association for Women's Suffrage (Uemura 2011).

12 Yokohama and Tokyo are approximately 35 kilometers apart.

train fare. It makes us wonder if writing in a European language would produce a similar effect, at least as far as proving one's upstanding stature goes since the leery policemen would not be able to comprehend the actual content of the scribbled text in this case. By 1905 Japanese attitudes toward foreign cultural elements began to shift in favor of English, so it is conceivable that European writing could be recognized as prestigious because of its modern symbolic connotations. Nevertheless, the historical record of Phan Bội Châu's visit to Japan presented earlier strongly suggests that the symbolic affordance or currency of Sinitic writing among all classes of the Japanese society remained relevant well into the early twentieth century (Nguyễn & Nguyễn 2020).

Conclusion

Following sinograms' arrival in the Japanese archipelago during the Yayoi period they were not only regarded as a vehicle of advanced thought and technology but in fact as writing itself, with native Japanese scripts appropriating sinograms for their phonetic value beginning to emerge only in the fifth century (*man'yōgana* 万葉仮名).[13] The notion of Sinitic writing as a vector of cultural and technological legitimacy endured in Japan well into the early twentieth century and shaped Japanese people's relationship with linguistic and non-linguistic functions of literacy throughout the intervening period.

As a logographic script, Sinitic may have had an advantage over phonographic *kana* scripts insofar as individual sinograms were mostly morphographic with a more or less well-defined meaning beyond speech sounds, something that semi-literate and literate users of sinograms alike would be quite cognizant of. Another factor influencing the symbolic status of sinograms in premodern Japan was related to diglossia, that is, hierarchical functional division between the written and spoken language, privileging Sinitic as a 'high' language variety which was common across the whole of Sinographic East Asia. These features of Sinitic were of particular significance in transnational encounters since they allowed for the transmission of meaning via visual forms of the 'sacred language' (Anderson 2006), intersubjectively without the need for working out how the relevant sinograms corresponded to sounds.

As it happens, contemporary Japan continues to be a particularly rich field demonstrating the ways in which foreign written words often become appropriated for their symbolic status, usually in advertising. Jan Blommaert, for instance, refers to the power of French words for the Japanese consumers who do not read the language to explain how written symbols change their meanings and functions, depending on who reads them, from linguistic signs to emblematic ones in transnational contexts (Blommaert 2010: 28–30). His concept of indexicality

---

13 Man'yōgana employs sinograms to represent Japanese language phonetically. The two Japanese phonographic scripts: square form *katakana* 片仮名 and cursive form *hiragana* 平仮名, were developed in the ninth century.

highlights the sociocultural function of language and emphasizes the need to think of language semiotically rather than linguistically at a time when human languages move across the globe, no longer tied to stable and resident communities (Blommaert 2010: 181). Two transcultural settings discussed in this chapter illustrated how mid-nineteenth- and early twentieth-century Chinese and Vietnamese speakers gained the goodwill of literate and non-literate Japanese public through inscribing handheld fans and showing off their writings performatively in a ceremonious manner. It was the multi-layered functions of Sinitic writing that enabled amiable, intellectual, and poetic exchanges of various kinds, in addition to the symbolic power of sinograms that motivated locals to communicate with foreigners without a shared spoken language.

In her article conceptualizing brush-talk as the lingua franca of East Asian diplomatic encounters in the Edo period, Rebekah Clements draws our attention to a scroll painting attributed to Hanabusa Itchō 英一蝶 (1652–1724) depicting Japanese townsman asking a Korean envoy on horseback to inscribe for him an autograph in Sinitic (Clements 2019: 300–302; see Figure 12.1). The scene portrays an event from an early eighteenth-century Chosŏn embassy parade, with a Japanese townsman extending a large piece of paper to the Korean representative who is writing with a brush.

As previously mentioned, Edo period's seclusion policies made it exceedingly hard for Japanese samurais and common folk alike to interact with foreigners outside the port of Nagasaki. In virtually all cities Korean envoys passed they would draw crowds of Confucian scholars and feudal domain retainers eager to quench their thirst for knowledge and achieve recognition outside the archipelago. Plentiful brush-talk records produced during these encounters attest to Japanese intellectuals' passion for learning Korean customs and history, advanced medical knowledge, and the latest situation of Chinese academia (Trambaiolo 2014). For example, Sin Yu-han 申維翰 (1681–1752), secretary of the 1719 Chosŏn embassy, remarks that he stayed up until dawn drawing calligraphy for the Japanese visitors, while Wŏn Chung-kŏ 元重擧 (1719–1790), secretary to the Vice-Envoy of the 1764 embassy, mentions that he inscribed 'two thousand' verses of poetry as tokens of exchange during his three- to four-month stay in Japan (Tenri Central Library 1988; see also Jang, this volume). Japanese curiosity about Korean envoys was not limited to educated classes, but – as Hanabusa's work clearly demonstrates – also extended to merchant class townspeople, reflecting widespread enthusiasm for Sinitic writing in time of increasing literacy rates among wealthier merchants and peasants bolstered by the burgeoning commercial print industry in the Edo period (Clements 2015; Rubinger 2007; Suzuki 2017). We have no way of knowing what the townsman's precise motive was when he requested a Sinitic autograph from the passing Korean envoys. It could have been intellectual curiosity about the meaning of the line(s) he anticipated to receive, aesthetic appreciation of the writing's visual aspect if he were to display the calligraphy like a piece of art, or expectation of a commercial gain if he planned to sell the autograph for a price afterward, or any combination of these. Furthermore, the townsman's literacy level is similarly uncertain, leaving us to speculate if he

304 *Reijiro Aoyama*

Figure 12.1 Chōsen no kozōzu 朝鮮小童図 or 'Calligraphy of a Korean boy'.
Source: Courtesy of Osaka Museum of History[14]

14 According to the curator at the Osaka Museum of History the depicted scroll painting could be a copy of the original artwork by Hanabusa (author's personal correspondence). 'Hanabusa Itchō's Picture Book' 英一蝶画譜, a collection of the artist's drawings, contains a work with a nearly identical composition (see National Diet Library Digital Collection 2021 at https://dl.ndl.go.jp/info:ndljp/pid/2554324/17). In the drawing, pails with water are clearly visible to the side of the main scene as is the ink stone held up by the footman, which implies that the townsman was well prepared to take advantage of the encounter with the Korean visitors rather than it being a chance meeting.

had the ability to read the inscription in a conventional sense or was drawn to its prestige-laden symbolic meanings.

Whatever the case may be, Lurie's (2011) concept of alegible texts helps broaden our focus beyond these hierarchies of different degrees of literacy to a more contextualized overview of writing as a socially embedded cultural practice. As early as the beginning of the eighteenth century, a Japanese townsman had the good sense to stop a foreigner from Korea and ask him to inscribe sinograms on a sheet of paper. Even if he was not able to decipher the linguistic meaning of the inscription himself, at the very least he knew that Korean guests and his own society's educated elite deferred to the same venerated script, rendering the inscription now in his hand a valuable commodity and/or cultural artifact admired and desired by many Japanese or even foreigners. His interaction with writing was thus shaped by a collective imagination extending beyond Japan to all of Sinographic East Asia where sinograms were looked upon as a symbol of affinities between people who did not necessarily speak the same language and ascribed heterogeneous – legible and alegible – values to texts based on the social contexts in which those texts were read and/or spectated. The main goal of this chapter is to show that the departure from what we tend to view as the core, that is, the content-driven function of writing, was an essential feature of literacy in Sinographic East Asia. What is more, the symbolic functions of sinograms over and above their lexical meanings apprehended by literate beholders, applied in equal measure to educated and illiterate classes of the Japanese society between the mid-1850s to early 1900s.

As evidenced in the analysis of the Chinese-Japanese and Vietnamese-Japanese brush-talk encounters discussed in this chapter, the role of face-to-face writing was rarely just about facilitating reading. In such transnational scenarios, sinograms functioned as 'the desirable' (Kluckhohn 1951: 395), the symbol of value that influenced the selection from available modes of communication because of its rich potential to convey both linguistic and cultural meanings. As such, sinograms helped mediate collective life in the Sinographic cosmopolis by allowing strangers who did not share a spoken language to construct imaginary relations through interactive, face-to-face inscriptions. This is a less explored aspect of brush-talk which serves to underline the difference between this mode of communication and other forms of inscription in premodern Japan whose users rarely held a global view of writing from a cross-border transcultural perspective.

References

Anderson, B. (2006). *Imagined communities: Reflections on the origin and spread of nationalism*. London: Verso.

Aoyama, R. (2020). Writing-mediated interaction face-to-face: Sinitic brushtalk in the Japanese missions' transnational encounters with foreigners during the mid-nineteenth century. *China and Asia* 2(2): 234–269.

Blommaert, J. (2010). *The sociolinguistics of globalization*. Cambridge: Cambridge University Press.

Casal, U. A. (1960). The lore of the Japanese fan. *Monumenta Nipponica* 16(1/2): 53–117.
Chen, S. [陳壽] (1964). 三國志 ('Records of the three kingdoms'). Peking: Zhonghua Book Company (Original work published during late 3rd century).
Chū, G.-K. [仲玉花] (2017). 梁啓超の翻訳活動について ('About Liang Qichao's translation activity'). *Wakumon* 32: 45–56.
Clements, R. (2015). *A cultural history of translation in early modern Japan*. Cambridge: Cambridge University Press.
Clements, R. (2019). Brush talk as the 'lingua franca' of diplomacy in Japanese-Korean encounters, c. 1600–1868. *The Historical Journal* 62(2): 289–309.
Davies, H. (2019). Fanology: Hand-fans in the prehistory of mobile devices. *Mobile Media & Communication* 7(3): 303–321.
DeFrancis, J. (1977). *Colonialism and language policy in Viet Nam*. The Hague: Mouton.
DeFrancis, J. (1984). *The Chinese language: Fact and fantasy*. Honolulu: University of Hawai'i Press.
Dore, R. (1964). *Education in Tokugawa Japan*. Berkeley: University of California Press.
Gottlieb, N. (1995). *Kanji politics: Language policy and Japanese script*. London: Routledge.
Handel, Z. (2019a) Review of Kornicki, Peter F., *Languages, scripts, and Chinese texts in East Asia*. H-Asia, H-Net Reviews. August, 2019. Retrieved May 19, 2021, from https://networks.h-net.org/node/22055/reviews/4572501/handel-kornicki-languages-scripts-and-chinese-texts-east-asia
Handel, Z. (2019b). *Sinography: The borrowing and adaptation of the Chinese script*. Leiden & Boston: Brill.
Harrell, P. (1992). *Sowing the seeds of change: Chinese students, Japanese teachers, 1895–1905*. Stanford, CA: Stanford University Press.
Harris, W. V. (1989). *Ancient literacy*. Cambridge, MA: Harvard University Press.
Hirakawa, M. [平川南] (1999). 日本最古の文字 ('Japan's oldest script'). In K. Takamatsu (Ed.), *Kojiki no Genzai* ('Records of ancient matters now') (pp. 3–36). Tokyo: Kasama Shoin.
Keightley, D. N. (1985). *Sources of Shang history: The oracle-bone inscriptions of Bronze Age China*. Berkeley, CA: University of California Press.
Keightley, D. N. (1996). Art, ancestors, and the origins of writing in China. *Representations* 56: 68–95.
Keightley, D. N. (2006). Marks and labels: Early writing in Neolithic and Shang China. In M. T. Stark (Ed.), *Archaeology of Asia* (pp. 177–201). Oxford: Blackwell Publishing.
King, R. (2015). Ditching 'diglossia': Describing ecologies of the spoken and inscribed in pre-modern Korea. *Sungkyun Journal of East Asian Studies* 15(1): 1–19.
Kluckhohn, C. (1951). Values and value-orientations in the theory of action. In T. Parsons & E. A. Shils (Eds.), *Toward a General Theory of Action* (pp. 388–433). Cambridge, MA: Harvard University Press.
Kornicki, P. F. (2018). *Languages, scripts, and Chinese texts in East Asia*. Oxford: Oxford University Press.
Kotajima, Y. [古田島洋介] (2008). 梁啓超『和文漢読法』(盧本)簡注——復文を説いた日本語速習書 ('Liang Qichao's *Hewen handufa* or *How to learn Japanese through Chinese* with a bibliographical introduction and brief notes'). *Bulletin of Department of Japanese and Comparative Culture, Meisei University* 16: 29–64.
Kraus, R. C. (1991). *Brushes with power: Modern politics and the Chinese art of calligraphy*. Berkeley, CA: University of California Press.
Lévi-Strauss, C. (1973/1955). *Tristes Tropiques*. London: Cape.

Li, D. C. S. (2020). Writing-mediated interaction face-to-face: Sinitic brushtalk (漢文筆談) as an age-old lingua-cultural practice in premodern East Asian cross-border communication. *China and Asia* 2(2): 193–233.

Li, D. C. S., Aoyama, R., & Wong, T.-S. (2020). Silent conversation through brushtalk (筆談): The use of Sinitic as a scripta franca in early modern East Asia. *Global Chinese* 6(1): 1–24.

Luo, S. [羅森] (1854–1855). 日本日記 ('Journal of a Visit to Japan'). 遐邇貫珍 ('Chinese Serial'). November 1854 – January 1855 (three issues).

Luo, S. [A Native of China, pseud.]. (1856). *Journal of the Second Visit of Commodore Perry to Japan*. Washington, DC: A. O. P. Nicholson. Retrieved from https://books.google.com.hk/books?id=OD08AQAAIAAJ

Lurie, D. B. (2011). *Realms of literacy: Early Japan and the history of writing*. Cambridge, MA: Harvard University Press.

National Diet Library Digital Collection. (2021). 英一蝶画譜第三巻 ('Hanabusa Itchō's picture book') (vol. 3). Retrieved May 16, 2021, from https://dl.ndl.go.jp/info:ndljp/pid/2554324/17

Norman, J. (1988). *Chinese*. Cambridge: Cambridge University Press.

Nguyễn, H.-T., & Nguyễn, T.-C. [阮黃申、阮俊強] (2020). Sinitic brushtalk in Vietnam's anti-colonial struggle against France: Phan Bội Châu's silent conversations with influential Chinese and Japanese leaders in the 1900s. *China and Asia* 2(2): 270–293.

Park, Y.-M. [朴英美] (2016). 扇に書く和歌:『源氏物語』におけるその会話的機能をめぐって ('Poems written on fans: On the conversational function in *The Tale of Genji*'). *The 10th International Japanese Studies Consortium, Intercultural Studies and Japanese Studies* 12: 72–78. Tokyo: Ochanomizu University.

Phan, B.-C. [潘佩珠] (1999/1926). *Overturned chariot: The autobiography of Phan-Boi-Chau* (Vinh Sính & N. Wickenden, Trans.). Honolulu: University of Hawai'i Press.

Rubinger, R. (2007). *Popular literacy in early modern Japan*. Honolulu: University of Hawai'i Press.

Saitō, Y. [斉藤泰雄] (2012). 識字能力・識字率の歴史的推移: 日本の経験 ('Historical development of mass literacy in Japan'). *Journal of International Cooperation in Education* 15(1): 51–62.

Sanetō, K. [實藤惠秀] (1960). 中國人日本留学史 ('History of Chinese students studying in Japan'). Tokyo: Kuroshio Shuppan.

Shen, G. [沈国威] (2010). 日語難嗎？: 以近代初識日語的中國人為説 ('Is Japanese language difficult to learn? Examples of modern Chinese intellectuals'). *Institute of Oriental and Occidental Studies, Departmental Bulletin Paper* 43: 119–130. Osaka: Kansai University.

Suzuki, T. [鈴木俊幸] (2017). 江戸の読書熱—自学する読者と書籍流通 ('Edo period's reading fever: Self-studying readers and book distribution'). Tokyo: Heibonsha.

Tao, D.-M. (2005). Negotiating Language in the opening of Japan: Luo Sen's journal of Perry's 1854 expedition. *Nichibunken Japan Review* 17: 91–119.

Tenri Central Library [天理図書館] (1988). 朝鮮通信使と江戸時代の人々 ('Chosŏn envoys and the people of the Edo period'). Nara: Tenri University. Retrieved February 12, 2021, from www.tenri-u.ac.jp/inex/q3tncs0000137t13-att/q3tncs0000137t9t.pdf#search='筆談唱和'

Trambaiolo, D. (2014). Diplomatic journeys and medical brush talks: Eighteenth-century dialogues between Korean and Japanese medicine. In O. Gal & Y. Zheng (Eds.), *Motion and knowledge in the changing early modern world: Orbits, routes and vessels* (pp. 93–113). Dordrecht: Springer Verlag.

Tsu, T. Y. H. (2010). Japan's "Yellow Peril": The Chinese in imperial Japan and colonial Korea. *Japanese Studies* 30(2): 161–183.

Turner, W. W. (1851). Account of a Japanese romance. *Journal of the American Oriental Society* 2: 29–54.

Uemura, K. [植村和秀] (2011). 翻刻 塩原静『犬養木堂先生』『犬養千代子刀自』 ('Shizuka Shiobara's manuscripts remembering Prime Minister Tsuyoshi Inukai and his wife, Chiyoko Inukai'). *Bulletin of the Department of Law of the Kyoto Sangyo University* 45(1): 70–127.

Vogel, E. F. (2019). *China and Japan: Facing history*. Cambridge, MA: Harvard University Press.

Williams, S. W. (1889). *The life and letters of Samuel Wells Williams, LL.D.: Missionary, diplomatist, sinologue*. New York: GP Putnam's Sons.

Williams, S. W. (1910). *A journal of the perry expedition to Japan (1853–1854)*. Yokohama, Japan: Kelly & Walsh.

Xia, X. [夏曉虹] (1997). 梁啟超與日本明治文化 ('Liang Qichao and Japan's Meiji culture'). *Centre for Literature and Translation Occasional Paper Series No. 3*. Hong Kong: Lingnan University.

13 Discussion paper

Rebekah Clements

The chapters in this volume provide rich and fascinating evidence that brush-talk existed as a phenomenon in East Asia from some of the earliest written records until at least the first decades of the twentieth century. Brush-talk was a vital communication strategy, one which enabled the conveyance of semantic content in the absence of a shared spoken language. It occurred in diverse situations, from interactions between maritime officials and sailors who had drifted off course (Chapters 3 and 5), to diplomatic missions (Chapters 7–11), and even included the mundanities of getting the shopping done while traveling abroad (Chapters 4 and 12). This raises the question: what accounts for the vitality and longevity of brush-talk as a practice, and the preservation of brush-talk records down the centuries? Communication of semantic content in face-to-face meetings alone does not explain such careful preservation and reproduction of so many brush-talk records, and we must ask ourselves why people chose to use brush-talk when in many cases they had the option of relying on interpreters (compare Chapter 12).

We have surviving evidence that brush-talk records were reproduced in many different forms over the centuries. There were edited collections, such as the 'Ōkōchi documents' 大河內文書, discussed in Chapter 8 of this volume, which were compiled by the last daimyō of Takasaki domain, Ōkōchi Teruna 大河內輝声 (1848–1882), from written conversations between Chinese, Japanese, and Korean diplomats. There were anthologies containing the brushed poems resulting from diplomatic exchanges, such as that compiled by the Lê dynasty scholar, Phùng Khắc Khoan 馮克寬 (1528–1613): 'Collected poems from Mai Lĩnh's embassy to the efflorescence' (*Mai Lĩnh Sứ Hoa Thi Tập* 梅嶺使華詩集, 1597), which was regarded by later Vietnamese literati as having launched the genre of envoy poetry collections (Kelley 2005: 23–24); and 'Three generations chanting in harmony' (*Sansei shōwa* 三世唱和, 1764), edited by the Japanese Confucian scholar, Matsudaira Kunzan 松平君山 (1697–1783), which was published in woodblock print in Japan (Clements 2019: 297–298). There were also manuscripts preserved in a beautiful calligraphic hand, such as those which recorded discussions on Zen Buddhism and poetic exchanges between the powerful Japanese daimyō Yanagisawa Yoshiyasu 柳沢吉保 (1658–1714) and high-ranking Chinese monks, which Yoshiyasu had copied and presented to the Ōbaku Manpukuji temple 萬福寺 in Uji 宇治 near Kyoto (Lidin 2011: 7–9; Tsuji 1947: 251–252). These examples are by no means exhaustive of all the ways in which brush-talk records were preserved for posterity, but they offer a glimpse at the depth and breadth of the interactional phenomenon.

In addition to the preservation of brush-talk records, which suggests it had other meanings beyond the immediate concerns of the brush-talkers in action, in many cases brush-talk occurred despite the fact that there were interpreters present. These interpreters could have served as linguistic intermediaries if necessary. In Chapters 10 and 11, for example, the brushed exchanges between Japanese and Korean diplomats would have taken place in the presence of interpreters from Korea, as well as interpreters supplied by the Tsushima domain, the official intermediary between Tokugawa Japan and Chosŏn Korea (Sakai 2021). In chapter 7, Nguyễn and Nguyễn detail how communication through interpreters was the primary mode of communication in the Vietnamese-Qing diplomatic rite, but that envoys relied on brush-talk for private communications. Examples from other sources include eyewitness accounts of the meetings between the Japanese daimyō Yanagisawa Yoshiyasu and the Chinese abbots of Ōbaku Manpukuji temple, which record that interpreters were present but that Yoshiyasu and the abbots switched to brush-talk when they wished to converse on matters of importance, or 'discuss what was deep in their hearts' (Clements 2017: 611–612; Miyakawa 2007: 927). These patterns, which are common to encounters between representatives of various East Asian states, strongly suggest that as well as being a necessary expedient, brush-talk could also be a deliberate choice.

There was an important role accorded to brush-talk and a preference for written Sinitic over vernacular spoken languages, which may seem paradoxical to the modern observer used to oral communication. In Chapter 12 of this volume, Aoyama notes the reliance on written Sinitic by the Cantonese businessman, Luo Sen, who was selected to translate for the US-Japanese trade talks in the nineteenth century despite not being able to speak a word of Japanese. Aoyama shows that instead of being inconvenienced by his inability to speak Japanese, 'Luo Sen's ability to converse with Japanese officials in brush-talk using erudite expressions in elegant calligraphy helped to resolve many of the underlying tensions and allay suspicions between the two negotiating sides during the early stage of the talks' (p. 289)

The persistence of brush-talk despite the possibility of using interpreters, coupled with the careful preservation of brush-talk records for posterity, indicates that efficient communication of semantic content was not all that was at stake in the practice of brush-mediated conversations. When discussing the longevity of Sinitic script, Wiebke Denecke cautions against the assumption that '"efficiency" is the principal factor in the invention, cultural impact, or disappearance of scripts' (Denecke 2014: 212). Noting that efficiency is a fixation of modern language reformers who have a mission to expand mass literacy, Denecke draws on the work of Egyptologist John Baines, who shows that the use of several scripts carrying cultural prestige was common in many cultures of the ancient world, and notes that the goal of universal literacy is a relatively recent preoccupation (Baines 2008: 350). Denecke and Baines were mainly concerned with the question of script choice ('efficient' alphabetic scripts versus 'inefficient' logographic scripts), but lessons can be drawn by us here too in relation to oral versus written communication. Although in some instances the choice of brush-talk was undoubtedly driven by the need for efficiency (as in the ad hoc use of Sinitic by passengers on the Senzaimaru in order to conduct daily tasks, discussed in Chapter 4, for example), it is clear from the many cases pertaining to diplomatic encounters that efficiency was not the most important consideration. Other factors, such as the prestige of Sinitic literacy and the ability to bypass interpreters and engage directly with a foreign guest, were at play.

There are a variety of theoretical lenses that can be used to better understand this situation. Drawing upon Kluckhohn and Strodtbeck's (1961) theory of action, in Chapter 12, Aoyama notes that

> the role of face-to-face writing was rarely just about facilitating reading. In such transnational scenarios sinograms functioned as 'the desirable' . . . the symbol of value which influenced the selection from available modes of communication because of its rich potential to convey both linguistic and cultural meanings.
>
> (p. 305)

One of the earliest attempts to develop a cross-cultural theory of values, Kluckhohn-Strodtbeck's concept of the desirable allows us to understand Sinitic as a medium of collective life and experience in East Asia that afforded strangers without a shared language the opportunity to construct cordial relations.

Another source of insight into the complexities of brush-talk is the expanding field of diplomatic history, particularly that which pertains to the early modern period, from which many of the surviving examples of brush-talk come. The study of early modern diplomacy has shifted away from bureaucratic state-centric approaches to studies that consider the processes by which international relations were maintained, including the role of individual diplomats and monarchs, and their personal networks (Sowerby 2016). There is now a heightened awareness of the importance of interpersonal relations, and scholars have adopted an actor-centered approach (Tremml-Werner & Goetze 2019), which is particularly useful for understanding the significance of the interpersonal connection offered by brush-talk. Additionally, researchers have broadened their field of analysis to include diplomatic culture, such as diplomatic gifts, diplomatic ceremonial, and diplomatic hospitality, and to include actors other than official ambassadors (see, e.g., Sowerby & Hennings 2017), and these are precisely the contexts in which diplomatic brush-talk often occurred.

Understanding diplomacy as a sociopolitical activity undertaken not only by official ambassadors sheds light on why a cultural activity like brush-talk remained so important in East Asian diplomatic encounters. Brush-talk was not usually involved in the official ceremonies of a diplomatic mission. Furthermore, it was practiced both by official representatives, such as scribes and secretaries as well as by people who may be described as 'interested observers' including literati, medics, and even passers-by who sought brushed encounters with members of visiting embassies (Clements 2019). More research on this is needed in order to understand how practices differed between states and over time, but in the case of Japanese-Korean encounters during the seventeenth to eighteenth centuries, for example, the guides to official protocol did not mention brush-talk at all. The written documents with which protocol was most concerned were the official letters written in Sinitic from the Chosŏn sovereign, which each ambassador brought with him in a specially-designated palanquin in the diplomatic procession. When the Japanese shogun's Confucian teacher, Arai Hakuseki 新井白石 (1657–1725), wrote a review of the protocol for the meeting between the Chosŏn Korean representatives and the shogun in 1711, he went into great details about the timing and manner in which these documents were to be presented, opened, and finally read by the head of the shogunate's neo-Confucian academy (Ichishima 1905–1907 IV: 497–592). In contrast, there are no prescriptions for brush-talk in Hakuseki's protocol records, nor is there mention of it in the briefer and earlier record of the 1617 embassy composed by the neo-Confucian scholar and shogunal adviser Hayashi Razan (林羅山, 1583–1657), for example (Kyōto Shisekikai 1930: 248–250; Clements 2019: 302).

What we do know from other records, however, is that Razan and Hakuseki did in fact engage in brush-talk with Korean representatives (Clements 2019: 302–303). Such encounters usually took place at the temporary residence of the embassy, such as the Higashi Honganji temple 東本願寺 in Asakusa, Edo (Hayashi 1850/1912–1913 III: 286). They also occurred when the chance arose during official receptions, such as a brush conversation about music between Hakuseki and Korean representatives that took place during a break for musical entertainment at a reception for the Korean embassy in 1711 (Ichishima 1905–1907 IV: 721–724; see also Chapter 11). Other examples include brush-talk with Korean doctors, who traveled to Edo with the embassies, and Japanese physicians at rest stops along the route, for whom it was a precious opportunity to discuss medical topics with doctors from outside Japan (Trambaiolo 2014). In Chapter 7, Nguyễn and Nguyễn observe that in the case of Vietnamese-Qing interactions, brush-talk likewise took place sometimes randomly when opportunities arose during the embassy journey, and that brush-talk was not part of official ceremonies. What these and other examples contained in the chapters of the present volume show, is that brush-talk was often a 'diplomatic' activity, but one which was part of the unofficial culture of hosting diplomatic guests and which facilitated interpersonal relations between host and visitor, or afforded the opportunity for personal interaction with a foreign guest.

As a source of shared learning and literary allusion, written Sinitic glossed over language barriers in the East Asian Sinosphere and promoted the appearance of inter-personal and inter-state harmony in diplomatic encounters (Clements 2019). Because Sinitic is a logographic language, a Sinitic text may be read in Chinese, Japanese, Korean, Vietnamese, among other languages in which a reading tradition for Sinitic has developed. These reading traditions usually involved adding annotations to a Sinitic text, as a guide to local syntax and pronunciations.[1] The text could then be 'read' mentally or aloud in the local manner, producing a type of translation, one that was highly bound to the source (Wakabayashi 2005; Semizu 2006; Clements 2015: 104–114). As Peter Kornicki has noted, this meant there was a continuum between Sinitic and local languages, rather than a binary opposition (Kornicki 2018: 35; see also Lurie 2011). Language contact between Sinitic and other languages in East Asia also meant that Sinitic terms and structures as well as sinograms or Sinitic characters were part of the writing system of East Asian languages even for the vernacular, such that Sinitic was not foreign to Japanese, Koreans, or Vietnamese in the same way that a graphically and morphologically distinct language would have been. Kornicki notes:

> [W]e need to remember that Sinitic was not perceived to be a 'foreign language' until relatively late in the day: although Chinese may have thought differently, there are signs that 'ownership' of Sinitic was not so clear-cut in pre-modern East Asia, and that in the Qing dynasty, from the seventeenth to the nineteenth centuries, peripheral states even saw themselves as the preservers of the Sinitic tradition. In this sense, it is arguable that Sinitic, the cosmopolitan language of East Asia, was appropriated by neighbouring societies for their own use, thus attenuating its character as a cosmopolitan language of external origins.
>
> (Kornicki 2018: 41)

These features meant that written Sinitic was ideal for producing an appearance of harmony in East Asian diplomacy since each state could claim it as their own while at the same time sharing it with the others.

In addition to the appearance of harmony, however, brush-talk was also an opportunity for competition. Through demonstrations of literary skill, brushed encounters allowed participants to emphasize the claims of their state to its place in the civilized, East Asian world order. Exchanges of Sinitic poetry were vitally important in this context (see Chapters 5, 9, and 11). Although most of the case studies in this volume focus on writing-mediated brush conversations, as should be clear from the examples discussed earlier, poetry was an integral part of many brushed encounters, particularly those that took place in diplomatic contexts. This was not unique to East Asia. Literary composition was also integral to diplomatic practice from Europe to Islamicate Eurasia. As noted by Sowerby and Craigwood (2019: 4):

> Poems were exchanged within and alongside letters between princes in Islamicate Eurasia, while European queens might send poems to one another as gifts. Poems were written to celebrate important and unusual diplomatic

---

1 Unlike Japanese and Korean, Vietnamese is not an inflected language and so Vietnamese systems of glosses developed punctuation and pronunciation guides but not guides to syntactical rearrangement. For a comparison of glossing systems, see Kosukegawa (2014).

gifts: the giraffes that al-Mu'izz of Tunis and Lorenzo de Medici received from the Mamluk sultans were celebrated in verse. Meanwhile polemical verse could continue hostilities in the absence of open war . . . the prestige attached to poetry made it a useful vehicle for building cultural capital and, thereby, diplomatic benefit.

In East Asia, poetry had been a means of socializing among intellectuals in China since ancient times, and with the spread of Sinitic literacy to other parts of East Asia, Sinitic poetry with its practice of classical allusion was an important element of elite culture and elite education. Prior to the modern period, East Asian diplomacy was conducted by literati, monks, and classically trained court officials, and this in turn brought poetry into diplomatic exchanges (Murai 2009). It was conventional that diplomatic envoys recorded their impressions of their journey by composing Chinese poetry and exchanging poems en route with representatives of the country they were visiting. And at banquets which were given in honor of the visitors, poems appropriate to the occasion were composed, lauding the host sovereign with well-established poetic allusions from the storehouse of shared Sinitic culture (e.g., Morley 2019; Kelley 2005). The exchange of Sinitic poetry continued into the nineteenth century (Howland 1996).

In fact, not all poetry recorded from brushed encounters in early modern East Asian diplomacy was in Sinitic. In Japan, poetry composed in Classical Japanese was also an important marker of elite culture, and this influenced the nature of encounters between Japan and the Ryukyu Kingdom. In the years following the annexation of Ryukyu (modern-day Okinawa) by the Japanese domain of Satsuma in 1609, representatives of Ryukyu made regular trips to the shogunal capital of Edo (Miyagi 1982; cf. Chapter 6). There are numerous surviving records of classical Japanese *waka* 和歌 *poetry* exchanged between Ryukyuan ambassadors and their hosts in Japan, which have been compiled, much like the records of Sinitic poetry noted earlier (Ikemiya 1990). Although records of *waka* are not the Sinitic variety of brush-talk that this edited volume focuses upon, they constitute a written 'conversation' via poetic allusion and a shared storehouse of classical learning between Japan and Ryukyu.[2] They further demonstrate the role of poetry and literacy (in this case Japanese) in East Asian diplomatic encounters.

Returning to Sinitic, the cultural capital that accrued to men with skills in Chinese poetry was an important selection criterion when choosing members of a diplomatic mission. At the end of the sixteenth century, the Korean King Sŏnjo 宣祖 (r. 1567–1608) issued an order to ensure that only the most talented poets were chosen for the role of receiving Japanese visitors. His rationale was that 'if the talents of our men do not match theirs at times of exchange, we will be ridiculed in that country' (Murai 2009: 58). In Japan, the first collection of poetry by the shogun's Confucian teacher Arai Hakuseki contained forewords by the ambassador and secretary of mission to the 1682 embassy from the Chosŏn court to Japan. In a

---

2 For illustrations of Ryukyuan-Japanese and Ryukyuan-Korean Sinitic brush-talk, see Chapter 6.

testament to the cultural purchasing power of Sinitic poetry, Hakuseki acknowledged in his autobiography that it was thanks to these diplomatic endorsements that he was able to enter the prestigious Confucian academy of Kinoshita Jun'an 木下順庵 (1621–1698) and launch his career (Arai 1716/1979: 62–63).

In contrast with the cultural capital accruing from displays of brush-talk, oral interpreting was traditionally a low-status activity in East Asia. High-ranking officials thus had a preference for written rather than verbal communication. At the Chinese court, oral interpreting was the responsibility of lower-ranked functionaries known as 'tongue men' (*sheren* 舌人) (Cheung 2006: 36). In Korea, interpreters were excluded from the center of power, barred from taking the civil service examination that was the source of intellectual prestige and career progression at the Chosŏn court (Wang 2014). And in Japan, oral interpreting was handled by families of interpreters based in the port cities who were looked down upon for their lack of a proper (i.e., Sinitic) education (Sugimoto 1990: 72–76). Thus, there was little cultural incentive for diplomats to become fluent in the spoken languages of East Asia, which would have removed the need for brush-talk.

But what of the changes that occurred in the stature of Sinitic during the late nineteenth century – did this affect the status of brush-talk? After holding sway as the preeminent language of scholarship, religion, and literature since the eighth century, Sinitic began to fall out of favor in the late nineteenth century as the vernaculars were increasingly championed as national languages and began to dominate the field of text and print (Kornicki 2018: 26). Kornicki has written of an eventual 'dethronement' of Sinitic in the second half of the twentieth century, which saw the simplification of the traditional Chinese script, as in the case of the People's Republic of China, or its complete abandonment, as was the case of Vietnam (Kornicki 2018: 26). He notes that these developments affected not only East Asia, but even China itself, as from the late nineteenth century there was increasing pressure to replace Sinitic with a vernacular 'national language'. Although there were attempts by some intellectuals in Japan, Korea, and Vietnam to forge a common East Asian consciousness at the end of the nineteenth century and in the early twentieth by writing in Sinitic, this did not survive the Japanese annexation of Korea (Kornicki 2018: 300).

Despite these broad trends, the work of LIU Yuzhen (Chapter 9), Reijiro AOYAMA (Chapter 12), and WANG Baoping (Chapter 8) in this volume demonstrate that some pockets of Sinitic brush-talk survived into the twentieth century. In diplomatic contexts, brush-talk even seems to have outlived a shift away from using written literary Sinitic in favor of English in the composition of official diplomatic documents and in diplomatic negotiations. Alexis Dudden has shown how in the late nineteenth century, Japanese officials sought to take the language of diplomacy away from what they saw as Chinese control by redefining the meaning of Sinitic legal terms according to the norms of European international law, and eventually switched to using English in diplomatic negotiations. Dudden argues that the move away from Sinitic terms heralded an epistemic change in which the legitimizing language of power in East Asia was no longer Chinese but Western in origin (Dudden 1999, 2005). While this was clearly the case for the main negotiations and official documents, the chapters in this volume suggest that the cultural prestige of Sinitic and the written communication between individuals that it facilitated continued to be important in maintaining interpersonal relations in and around official ceremony and between people who were not the main actors.

This accords with the work of Douglas Howland, who has detailed how the practice of brush-talk, in the form of Sinitic poetic exchanges, continued to be a feature of East Asian diplomatic encounters well into the nineteenth century (Howland 1996: 43–68). The famous Chinese poet HUANG Zunxian 黃遵憲 (1848–1905) who served as secretary to the Qing legation in Tokyo from 1877 to 1882, often composed Sinitic poetry in the company of Japanese literati, contributing to the modern Japanese canon of Chinese poetry (*kanshi* 漢詩). In the opposite direction, Japanese literati composed Sinitic poems for another Chinese scholar-diplomat, YAO Wendong 姚文棟 (1852–1927), who was temporarily returning to China for family reasons, and these poems were later published in China. Howland has noted that at the personal level of friendly relations between scholars and officials from Japan and China, such exchanges served to include Japan within the sphere of Chinese civilization, emphasizing the shared cultural heritage of the two nations and smoothing relations (see also Fraleigh 2016). In Chapter 9, Liu shows that by exploiting the intellectual and emotional bond between brush-talkers, these nineteenth-century brushed encounters between Japanese poets and Chinese embassy staff could also be exploited for eliciting politically sensitive intelligence and national secrets.

Thus, brush-talk was part of a complex web of diplomatic culture, a cultural as well as a linguistic artifact. By focusing not only on ambassadors, but also on other actors, such as scribes, visiting scholars, and even passers-by, we can see that diplomatic practice, including brush-talk, extended far beyond the confines of official ceremony. Brush-talk was used to bypass interpreters and communicate semantic content directly between host and guest, and to create a harmonious atmosphere to smooth the running of the diplomatic mission. However, it could also be a site of conflict and competition, as skills in Sinitic were displayed in the interests of national prestige or used for espionage. These factors as well as the cultural capital that accrued through displays of brush-talk explain why the practice persisted for so long, and why so many brush-talk records were preserved for posterity.

References

Arai, H. [新井白石] (1716/1979). 折たく柴の記 ('Told round a brushwood fire: The autobiography of Arai Hakuseki') (J. Ackroyd, Trans.). Princeton, NJ: Princeton University Press.

Baines, J. (2008). Writing and its multiple disappearances. In J. Bains, J. Bennet & S. Houston (Eds.), *The disappearance of writing systems: Perspectives on literacy and communication* (pp. 347–362). London: Equinox.

Cheung, M. (2006). *An anthology of Chinese discourse on translation: From earliest times to the Buddhist project*. Manchester: St Jerome.

Clements, R. (2015). *A cultural history of translation in early modern Japan*. Cambridge: Cambridge University Press.

Clements, R. (2017). Speaking in tongues? Daimyo, Zen monks, and spoken Chinese in Japan, 1661–1711. *Journal of Asian Studies* 76(3): 603–626.

Clements, R. (2019). Brush talk as the 'lingua franca' of diplomacy in Japanese-Korean encounters, c. 1600–1868. *The Historical Journal* 62(2): 289–309.

Denecke, W. (2014). Worlds without translation: Premodern East Asia and the power of character scripts. In S. Bermann, & C. Porter (Eds.), *A companion to translation studies* (pp. 204–216). Chichester: Wiley Blackwell.

Dudden, A. (1999). Japan's engagement with international terms. In L. H. Liu (Ed.), *Tokens of exchange: The problem of translation in global circulations* (pp. 165–191). Durham, NC: Duke University Press.

Dudden, A. (2005). *Japan's colonization of Korea: Discourse and power*. Honolulu: University of Hawai'i Press.

Fraleigh, M. (2016). At the borders of Chinese literature: Poetic exchange in the nineteenth-century Sinosphere. In C. Rojas & A. Bachner (Eds.), *The Oxford handbook of modern Chinese literatures* (pp. 372–398). Oxford: Oxford University Press.

Hayashi, F. [林復斎] et al. (Eds.). (1850/1912–1913). 通航一覧 ('Record of sea voyages') (vols. 1–8). Tokyo: Kokusho Kankōkai.

Howland, D. (1996). *Borders of Chinese civilization: Geography and history at empire's end*. Durham, NC: Duke University Press.

Ichishima, K. [市島謙吉] (Ed.). (1905–1907). 新井白石全集 ('Complete writings of Arai Hakuseki') (vols. 1–6). Tokyo: Yoshikawa Han'shichi.

Ikemiya, M. [池宮正治] et al. (Eds.). (1990). 近世沖縄和歌集： 本文と研究 ('Early-modern Okinawan Waka poetry: Original texts and research'). Naha: Hirugisha.

Kelley, L. C. (2005). *Beyond the bronze pillars: Envoy poetry and the Sino-Vietnamese relationship*. Honolulu: University of Hawai'i Press.

Kluckhohn, F. R., & Strodtbeck, F. L. (1961). *Variations in value orientations*. Evanston, IL: Row Peterson.

Kornicki, P. (2018). *Languages, scripts, and Chinese texts in East Asia*. Oxford: Oxford University Press.

Kosukegawa, T. (2014). Explaining *kundoku* in the premodern Sinosphere. *Les dossiers de HEL [supplement électronique à la revue Histoire Epistémologie Langage]* 7: 1–20.

Kyōto Shisekikai [京都史蹟会] (Ed.). (1930). 林羅山文集 ('Collected writings of Hayashi Razan'). Osaka: Kōbunsha.

Lidin, O. (2011). Vernacular Chinese in Tokugawa Japan: The Inquiries of Ogyū Sorai. *Japonica Humboldtiana* 14: 5–36.

Lurie, D. B. (2011). *Realms of literacy: Early Japan and the history of writing*. Cambridge, MA: Harvard University Press.

Miyagi, E. [宮城栄昌] (1982). 琉球使者の江戸上り ('Ryukyuan ambassadors' journeys to Edo'). Tokyo: Daiichi Shobō.

Miyakawa, Y. [宮川葉子] (2007). 柳沢家の古典学（上）松蔭日記 ('Classical studies in the Yanagisawa household, vol. 1, diary of Matsukage'). Tokyo: Shintensha.

Morley, B. A. (2019). Poetry and diplomacy in early Heian Japan: The embassy of Wang Hyoryŏm from Parhae to the Kōnin court. *Journal of the American Oriental Society* 136(2): 343–369.

Murai, S. (2009). Poetry in Chinese as a diplomatic art in premodern East Asia (H. Wakabayashi & A. E. Goble, Trans.). In K. R. Robinson (Ed.), *Tools of culture: Japan's cultural, intellectual, medical, and technological contacts in East Asia, 1000s – 1500s* (pp. 49–70). Ann Arbor, MI: Association for Asian Studies.

Sakai, M. [酒井雅代] (2021). 近世日朝関係と対馬藩 ('Early-modern Japan-Korea relations and Tsushima domain'). Tokyo: Yoshikawa Kōbunkan.

Semizu, Y. (2006). Invisible translation: Reading Chinese texts in ancient Japan. In T. Hermans (Ed.), *Translating others* (2 vols., pp. 283–295). Manchester: St Jerome.

Sowerby, T. A. (2016). Early modern diplomatic history. *History Compass* 14: 441–456.

Sowerby, T. A., & Craigwood, J. (2019). Introduction: Literary and diplomatic cultures in the early modern world. In T. Sowerby & J. Craigwood (Eds.), *Cultures of diplomacy and literary writing in the early modern world* (pp. 4–21). Oxford: Oxford University Press.

Sowerby, T. A., & Hennings, J. (Eds.). (2017). *Practices of diplomacy in the early modern world c. 1410–1800*. London: Routledge.

Sugimoto, T. [杉本つとむ] (1990). 長崎通詞ものがたり—ことばと文化の翻訳者 ('Tales of the Nagasaki interpreters: Translators of language and culture'). Tokyo: Sōtakusha.

Trambaiolo, D. (2014). Diplomatic journeys and medical brush talks: Eighteenth-century dialogues between Korean and Japanese medicine. In O. Gal & Z. Yi (Eds.), *Motion and knowledge in the changing early modern world: Orbits, routes, and vessels* (pp. 93–113). Dordrecht: Springer.

Tremml-Werner, B., & Goetze, D. (2019). A Multitude of actors in early modern diplomacy. *Journal of Early Modern History* 23(5): 407–422.

Tsuji, Z. [辻善之助] (1947). 人物論叢 ('Collection of historical figures'). Tokyo: Yūzankaku.

Wakabayashi, J. (2005). Translation in the East Asian cultural sphere: Shared roots, divergent paths? In E. Hung & J. Wakabayashi (Eds.), *Asian translation traditions* (pp. 17–66). Manchester: St Jerome.

Wang, S. (2014). The sounds of our country: Interpreters, linguistic knowledge, and the politics of language in early Chosŏn Korea. In B. A. Elman (Ed.), *Rethinking East Asian languages, vernaculars, and literacies, 1000–1919* (pp. 58–62). Leiden: Brill.

Index

abjad script *see* script
'About the name Sairitsushi' 247
'A complete record of an embassy to the North' xxv, 36, 181–183, 186, 189–191, 194, 197
affordance xxiii, xxvii, 9, 11, 14, 37, 66, 92, 105–106, 193, 210, 212–213, 302
Ainu 133–134, 151
Akamatsu Hiromichi (1562–1600) 247
alphabet xvii–xviii, 8, 21, 25–26, 95, 127, 244
alphabetic xvii–xviii, 17, 26, 33–34, 114, 123, 311
alphabetic script *see* script
American xviii, xxi, 2, 16, 120, 123, 238, 289–290, 292–294
Anhui Province *see* province
Annam 15, 19, 24, 160, 181–186, 189–197, 217
'Annotation of the Asakusa library catalog' 250
anti-colonial xiv, 298; *see also* colonial
Arabic 8, 26, 31–32, 106, 113
Arai Hakuseki (1657–1725) xx, 131, 258, 266, 268–270, 275, 312, 314–315
'A record of drifting across the sea' 81, 132, 137–139, 150–151
art xix, 10, 203–4, 249, 288, 303; art forms 17, 54, 257, 283
auxiliary 2, 6, 97, 127

banquet 63, 78–79, 83, 134–135, 142, 209, 213–214, 225, 230, 270, 314
barbarian 10–12, 38, 58, 67, 72, 82, 122, 141, 185, 202, 243, 259–260, 272–274, 277
battle of writing 72–73, 263–265; *see also* brush battle
'Beads of poetic styles' 251
bilingual, 26–27, 48, 89, 99, 113, 131, 289

Black Ships xxi, 16
blog, blogger 2–3, 8
boat drifter 9, 13–14, 35–36, 49, 76–78, 80–81, 89–92, 98, 100, 103, 131–132, 150–151, 217
body language 209
'Book of Documents' 301
'Book of poetry' 183–184, 189–190, 250–251
'Book of Rites' 166, 269–270
borrowing 9, 26
British 82, 112, 119–120, 122
brothers xxii, 141, 197, 221
brush and ink 14, 39, 52, 66, 84, 89, 93, 105, 265, 292
brush-assisted compilation of information 100
brush(-assisted) conversation, 17, 61, 89, 95, 97–98, 106, 133, 160, 171
brush-assisted handwriting 244
brush-assisted interaction 105, 187
brush-assisted interpreter 51
brush-assisted interrogation 105
brush-assisted negotiations 51
brush battle 72–73, 263, 265, 276–277; *see also* battle of writing
brushed encounter 13, 15–16, 35, 46–47, 54, 64, 79, 112, 131, 120, 129, 131, 210, 212, 312–316
brush-talk: brush-talk involving boat drifters xxii, 9, 14, 76; brush-talk involving diplomatic envoys 9, 14, 35; brush-talk involving traveling literati 9, 35, 217; cultural brush-talk 37, 200–205, 300; drifting brush-talk, 9, 35, 81, 89, 93, 98, 104, 106; espionage brush-talk 12, 37, 200, 205–206, 218, 231–240; involuntary brush-talk 37, 200–201; two-sided account 130

320 Index

brush-talk manuscript 11–12, 48, 53, 130–131, 200, 205, 207–210, 215
brush-talk record xx–xxi, 13–16, 34–36, 46–51, 54–56, 58–66, 73–78, 80–84, 94, 99, 102, 104–105, 118, 129–134, 137, 154, 158–172, 185–186, 191–192, 204, 209–210, 220, 225–226, 228, 231, 234, 240–241, 247, 253, 257–259, 265–275, 303, 309–310, 316; 'Brush-talk at the feast' 131, 268–269; 'Brush-talk at Kanjŏng Alley' 16, 61–62; 'Brush-talk with Huding' 61–62, 130–131; 'Cluster of brush-talks with Korean visitors' 250; 'Collection of Chosŏn brush-talk' 133, 249, 251; 'Collection of Kyerim poetic exchange' 251–253, 255; 'Collection of the poetic exchange of seven poets' 252; 'Jehol diary' 61, 130
brush-talking 14, 16, 35, 38–39, 52–53, 64, 94–95, 98, 101–102, 105–106, 112, 116, 119, 121, 123, 151, 158, 160, 169, 189, 191, 193–194, 202, 207, 210, 212–213, 218, 228, 245, 252, 263, 296, 300
brush-talking process 16
Buddha 139–140, 149
Buddhism 20–22, 49, 51, 139–140, 144, 147, 164, 261; Zen Buddhism 309
Buddhist 22, 30, 69, 199, 244, 248, 293–294

calligraphy xix, 14, 22, 53–55, 122, 177, 194, 210, 257, 267, 283, 288–289, 300, 303–304, 310; calligraphic 54, 66, 80, 122, 194, 309; calligraphic scripts (see script); calligrapher 54
Cantonese xxi, xxvi, 6, 26, 29–30, 116, 243, 289–290, 297, 310
celestial capital 18, 20, 151, 181, 186, 194
Celestial Empire 57–58, 67, 145, 158, 187, 194
ceremonial (occasion) 258, 268, 271, 274, 294, 311
ceremony 7, 18, 59, 63–64, 74, 68, 156, 183–184, 197, 268, 271, 311–312, 316
center-peripheries 19–20; center 11–12, 18–20, 35, 47, 58, 259–260, 268, 277; peripheries 11, 18–20, 47, 58, 123, 217, 260, 268, 277, 286
center-periphery 11, 260
central efflorescence 38, 57, 73–74, 257–261, 268–277; efflorescence 58, 72, 141, 260, 309; reversal of efflorescence-barbarian relations 58, 260
chanting in harmony see socializing chanting
character scripts see script
Cheju (Island) xxi, 99–100, 102, 137, 145
chesulgwan ('official in charge of writing') 68, 75, 253–254, 262, 266–267
Chief-Envoy see envoy
Chinese characters 21, 26, 38, 46, 74, 111, 113, 134, 244, 248–9, 254, 283–288, 293–294
Chinese–Chinese social interaction 39
Chinese embassy 37, 83, 201–202, 205, 214, 219–221, 214, 225, 232, 237–241, 316
Chinese medicine 14, 254
Chinese script see script
Chinese World Order 19–20, 47, 257, 259; Sinocentric World Order 38
Ch'oe Pu (1454–1504) xxi, 35–36, 62, 81, 127, 132–133, 137–151
Chosŏn 20–21; Chosŏn boat drifter 13, 133–134; Chosŏn central efflorescence 259; Chosŏn *chesulgwan* 253, 267; Chosŏn embassy 303; Chosŏn dynasty 67, 78, 91, 99, 102, 268, 274; Chosŏn envoys (see envoy); Chosŏn government 37, 58, 72, 78, 128; Chosŏn king 81, 147, 245; Chosŏn Korea 20–21, 53, 57–58, 73, 81, 89–91, 104, 106, 130, 145, 151, 244, 246, 253, 258, 310; Chosŏn literati 62, 74, 138, 254, 264, 266–267, 270, 272–276; Chosŏn maritime official 81, 99, 101, 103, 132; Chosŏn mission 17–18, 60, 68, 74–75, 245, 259, 264, 269, 271, 273, 275; Chosŏn people xv, 74, 140, 266–267; Chosŏn poetry 264–265; Chosŏn seafarers 81, 135; 'Chosŏn Strategy' 228; Chosŏn *t'ongsinsa* 67–68, 72, 130, 258, 275; Chosŏn Vice-Envoy (see envoy); 'Little China' Chosŏn 260
Cho T'ae-ŏk (1675–1728) 71, 131, 268–269
Chữ Hán xxvi, 8, 25, 46, 128
chữ Nôm xxvi, 25
civil service examination 15, 21, 24, 37, 65, 113, 128, 132, 151, 166, 181, 183–184, 192–194, 197, 228, 249, 263–264, 268, 273–274, 315
classical canons 187, 215, 257
Classical (Chinese) xxi–xxiii, 9, 15, 17, 20–26, 30–37, 47–48, 51–52, 72, 83,

97, 101, 103, 105, 113–115, 121, 127, 151, 163–164, 167, 172, 187, 189–191, 197, 213, 215, 218–219, 223, 240–245, 247, 252, 255, 263, 314
clerical script *see* script
clothing (style) 22, 38, 60, 65, 74, 141, 184, 259, 268–271, 274
colonial 24–25, 295: *see also* anti-colonial
Confucian 15: Confucian attire 268, 272; Confucian civilization 257, 273, 275–277; Confucian canons 24, 254; Confucian classics 20, 27, 127–128, 156, 167, 170, 187, 189–190, 193, 248–249, 252–254, 260–261, 276–277; Confucian court music 222, 271, 273–274; Confucian culture 268, 271; Confucian doctor 253; Confucian education 156; Confucian heritage 268; Confucian ideologies 197; Confucian influence 24; Confucianism and Neo-Confucianism 49, 127, 140, 148–149, 164, 189, 194, 197, 243, 247–248, 250, 254, 259–261, 266, 272–277; Confucianist xx, 10, 15, 19, 38, 47, 57, 73, 122, 141, 204, 243–245, 247–249, 251–252, 254–255, 259, 268, 270, 276–277; Confucian learning xix; Confucian literati 288; Confucian official 247, 249, 253; Confucian order 277; Confucian philosophy 156, 259, 277; Confucian principles and practices 138, 276; Confucian rites and rituals 38, 156, 259, 269, 271–275; Confucian scholar 13, 24, 76, 82, 84, 96, 147, 192, 200, 209, 254, 259–261, 270, 296, 303, 309, 312; Confucian scholar-official 197; Confucian scholarship 190, 260, 277; Confucian state 140; Confucian studies 261, 277; Confucian-style social systems 276; Confucian teacher 312, 314; Confucian teachings 127, 140, 260, 270; Confucian Temple of Literature (Văn Miếu) 24; Confucian thoughts and knowledge 261, 296; Confucian values 38, 141, 156, 260, 274, 277; Confucian Way 140; Confucian works 247; Neo-Confucian academy 312, 315
contestation 38, 258–262, 268–272, 275
conversational routines xx, 187, 196
counsellor 55, 206–207, 219, 224, 227, 235, 241
couplet 64, 177, 184–185, 193–194, 230–231

cross-border (communication, interaction) xxii–xxiii, xxvi–xxvii, 1–3, 8–11, 17–18, 28, 34–39, 46–49, 64, 89, 113–118, 120–123, 128, 151, 196–197, 218, 231, 240, 305
cultural brush-talk *see* brush-talk
cultural capital 314–316
cultural superiority xxi, 10–11, 20, 38, 72, 257–260, 275–277
Cungtaplok 157–158, 160, 164–166, 169–171
Cyrillic script *see* script

delegation 60, 181–182, 184, 186–188, 189, 194–196, 228; Annam delegation 191, 194; Buddhist delegation 30
dialect xx, 26, 32, 39, 114, 116
diaries 13, 17, 36, 57–58, 136, 245, 294
diglossia 113, 302
diplomacy xix, xxvii, 16–18, 51, 91, 123, 128, 231–233, 240, 246–248, 289, 311–315
diplomat xx, xxii, 14, 38, 48, 53, 68, 196–197, 209, 220, 232, 255, 296, 309–311, 315–316
diplomatic xx–xxi, 9, 12–14, 16–18, 35–37, 47–54, 56–58, 63–72, 81–85, 91, 104, 123, 128–131, 139, 154, 160, 165, 169, 181–182, 189, 197, 207–208, 218–220, 232–235, 239–241
distressed seafarer *see* seafarer
dress (style) 197, 259, 268–270, 273–274
drifting brush-talk *see* brush-talk
drifting record xiii, 14, 35, 80–81, 85, 89, 102, 108, 132, 137
dual subordination 23, 155
dueling 38, 258, 261, 270–272, 275–277
Dutch xxi, 17, 32, 92, 112, 118–120, 123, 254, 289–290, 293

Early Mandarin *see* Mandarin
East Asian culture xix, 11, 40
Edo 13–14, 18–19, 37, 67–68, 72–73, 76–77, 91, 96, 106, 136, 157, 225, 243–246, 250–255
efflorescence *see* central efflorescence
emperor 11, 18–19, 24, 33, 49–50, 64, 80, 89, 91, 104, 141, 147–148, 154–155, 157–158, 169, 177, 185, 188, 191, 194, 199, 204, 206, 209, 219, 228, 233, 271, 273, 286
envoy xx, 9–16, 20–21, 35–38, 48–51, 56–69, 72–79, 82, 91, 128–131, 139–140, 145, 155–156, 158, 160,

169, 179, 181–190, 194–196, 205, 212, 217–218, 228–230, 232–236, 240, 243–255, 248, 257–277, 286, 303, 309–310, 314; Chief-Envoy xx, 60, 63, 68–69, 74–75, 181–186, 188, 195, 243, 250, 268–269; Chosŏn envoys xv, 10, 13, 38, 48–49, 57–59, 61–62, 64–66, 68, 72–76, 129–131, 158, 194, 217, 228, 246, 248–249, 257–276; Chosŏn Vice-Envoy xx, 73, 196, 268; 'Envoys to Peking' 15–16, 36, 56–59, 63, 233; 'envoy to probe the enemy' (t'amjŏksa) 248; north-bound envoy 49, 62–64, 79, 181–197; 'North-bound envoys' records' xxv, 36, 49, 62–64, 181, 190; Respond-cum-Return Envoy, 67; Third-Envoy 68, 247, 269–270; tribute envoys 67; Vice-Envoy xx, 36, 64, 68, 73, 75, 181, 187, 191, 195–196, 219, 221–2024/25, 232, 241, 243, 248–249, 268–269, 303
epigraph xix, xxiv, xxix
epistolary 32, 215
Erasmus 32–33
espionage 12, 37, 200, 205–206, 218, 231–240
espionage brush-talk *see* brush-talk
evidential research 190–191, 260, 274, 276

facial expression 8, 209
Family rites of Zhuzi 138, 141; *see also* Zhuzi studies
fans 17, 292–294, 300, 303
First Sino-Japanese War (1894–1895) 3, 8, 50, 215, 297
foreign Sinographic texts *see* Sinographic
'Four Books and Five Classics' 156, 247
France 25, 157, 298
French 24, 31, 33, 119, 283, 286, 295–296, 300–302
Fujian Province *see* province
Fujiwara Seika (1561–1619) 28, 51, 247, 250

Galileo xvii
genre 17, 23, 25, 36, 47–48, 58–59, 89, 121, 129, 134, 212–213, 215, 285, 309
geography xxi, xxiii, 10, 12, 21–22, 34, 81, 104, 137, 155, 158, 165, 185, 189–192, 194, 259
gesture 7–8, 176, 209, 267, 284, 296, 299
Ge Zhaoguang xix, 10–11, 217

gloss (glossing) 17, 21, 23, 27, 29, 31, 114, 214, 226, 273, 312–313
graphic units 26, 113
Guangdong Province *see* province
Guangxi Province *see* province
Guilin 184–186

Han (dynasty) xxi, 10–11, 18, 20–21, 24, 38, 163, 165, 189–190, 259, 262, 265, 269–271
Han Chinese xxiii, 65, 113–114, 259, 272, 277
hangŭl xxiii, 21, 127, 244
hanja xxvi, 8, 21, 46, 128
han schools (藩校) 252
hanshi 133, 221, 223–224, 261, 263
Hayashi Gahō (1618–1680) 249
Hayashi Hōkō (1644–1732) 249
Hayashi Jussai (1768–1841) 266–267
Hayashi Razan (1583–1657) 76, 209, 247, 250, 252, 260, 312
Heaven 11, 70, 141, 148, 260, 268; Son of Heaven 18, 165; tributes to heaven 10
heptasyllabic (octave, quatrain) 65, 122, 177, 202, 223, 226–227, 262
He Ruzhang *see* Qing legation to Japan
hiragana xxiii, 22, 30, 134, 302
hitsudan 3, 6, 9, 112, 115
hitsuwa 53
Hokkaido 35, 132–134, 136, 151
Hong Tae-yong (1731–1783) 16, 61–62
Honkoku Temple 250
honorific 36, 170–172
Hŏ Sŏng (1548–1612) 247
Huang Zunxian *see* Qing legation to Japan
Hubei Province *see* province
Hunan Province *see* province

identity xix, 15, 17, 34, 36, 57, 89, 92, 98, 103, 106, 127, 129, 131–135, 137, 139, 141, 144–146, 151, 155–156, 167, 214, 221, 233, 260–261, 277; cultural identities 47; mutual identities 62
idu, 21, 114, 244
illiteracy xviii
Im Kwang 任絖 (1579–1644) 70, 243, 250
Im Su-kan (1665–1721) 131, 268–269
Imjin War (1592–1598) 50, 68, 247, 257
improvisation 6–7, 17, 46–47, 54, 63–64, 66, 75, 79, 94, 105–106, 115, 124, 130–131, 158, 177, 186, 194, 202, 210, 212, 220–221, 230–231, 241, 261, 264, 300; literary improvisation 9, 17, 97, 218, 240, 263; poetic improvisation xx, 14, 35, 37–39, 59, 61–66, 75–80, 121,

137. 158. 186. 194. 196. 212. 220–222.
  223. 227. 230. 232. 240–241. 245. 249.
  257. 261. 263–266
imun 250
ink stone 92–93. 120–121. 135. 293. 304
Inō Jakusui (1655–1715) 253
inscription 38. 54. 285. 287. 292–295.
  300–301. 305
Institute of Sino-Nom Studies 57. 80. 182.
  189. 194
intelligibility (problem) xxvi. 5. 27. 34. 95.
  116. 212. 215
intelligible 8–9. 28. 33. 100. 106. 114.
  117–118. 146
interactional xxvii. 8. 10. 35. 37. 73. 115.
  117. 121. 169. 171–172. 206. 209–210.
  214–215. 250. 295. 310
interactively xxiv. xxvii. 2. 8. 17. 30. 34.
  39. 47–49. 60. 89. 94. 98. 106. 113. 118.
  122–123. 131–132. 136. 194. 199. 202.
  269. 300
intercultural (communication, exchange)
  46. 59. 94. 193. 211. 218. 220
interface: orthographic-phonetic interface
  8; Sinitic as semantic and semiotic
  interface 9. 298–299
international diplomacy xix. 16. 18. 51
interpreter xix–xxi. 14–16. 36. 38. 48–49.
  51–52. 59–60. 68. 89. 100–105.
  112–113. 120. 123. 160. 182. 185–188.
  221. 248. 253. 257. 289–290. 292.
  296–297. 309–311. 315–316
interpreting service 35. 103–105. 201
interrogation 14. 35. 76–78. 81. 98–105.
  131–132. 137–139. 144. 148
intersubjective *see* phonetic intersubjectivity
'Intimate Notes of Yōkōdō' 231–233.
  235–240
involuntary brush-talk *see* brush-talk
Ishikawa Jōzan (1583–1672) 250–251
Iteian Rotation 248

Japan 22–23
Japanese-flavored Sinitic 213–214
'Jehol diary' *see* brush-talk record
Jiangnan 77. 93. 147. 149. 151. 195
Jiangxi Province *see* province
journal xviii. xxv. 4. 48–49. 57. 59. 112.
  129. 134. 137. 148. 155. 248. 258. 265.
  268–269. 273. 277. 292. 296

kana xxiii. 4. 30. 98. 210. 284. 302
kanbun 4. 23. 111. 115. 156. 215. 219

kangaku 28. 94. 261
Kang Hang (1567–1618) 247
kanji xxiii. xxvi. 2. 4. 7–8. 22. 30. 46. 74.
  111–112. 128. 134. 161. 284
'Kanjŏng p'iltam' 16. 61–62
kanshi 205. 221. 316
katakana xxiii. 22. AG302
Kija 20. 142. 268
Kim Se-ryŏm (1593–1646) 243. 248–250
Koguryŏ xxi. 20. 142–144
Korea 20–21
Korean mission 15. 58. 247
Korean-Vietnamese exchange 64–66
Koryŏ 21. 67. 127. 139–140. 143. 247
Kume Village 24. 154. 156–157
Kumemura 24. 154
kundoku 4. 23. 94. 114. 156
kunten 23

Latin xvii. 31–34. 39. 106. 111. 113–114.
  243–244
legation *see* Qing legation to Japan
Lê Quý Đôn (1726–1784) xxii. 36. 64.
  181–197
letter of credence 67. 219. 245
lexico-grammatical xxiii. 36. 100. 106.
  113–114. 163–165. 171. 213. 215
Liang Qichao (1873–1929) 48. 50.
  296–298. 300
Liaodong (Peninsula) xxi–xxii. 3. 102.
  139. 142–143
Li Hongzhang 60–61. 91. 235. 237
Lim Key-zung 57. 59
lingua franca 7–9. 17. 31. 33–34. 111.
  115. 243. 258. 303
linguistic feature 31. 36. 46. 99–100. 115.
  153–154. 163–172. 209. 295. 302
Linhai County 81. 132
Li Shuchang *see* Qing legation to Japan
literacy xvii–xviii. 2. 4. 9. 24–28. 30.
  35–36. 47. 52. 82. 89. 91. 93. 95. 98.
  103–105. 114. 116–119. 123. 127. 132.
  150–151. 252. 283–286. 288. 292.
  294–295. 297–298. 302–303. 305.
  310–311. 314
literary improvisation *see* improvisation
Literary Sinitic xiii. 9. 12. 14. 17. 25.
  30–31. 33–34. 36–37. 83. 112–115.
  119. 122–123. 127. 135. 213. 220. 243.
  252. 255. 258. 295. 315
literati (of Sinitic) xx–xxiv. xxvii. 7.
  9–12. 15–17. 21. 24–25. 28. 30–31.
  35. 37–39. 49–53. 55. 62–65. 73. 77.

324 *Index*

79, 83–84, 87, 95, 99, 105, 112–115, 121–123, 127–132, 138, 142, 144–145, 150–152, 160, 163, 167, 171–172, 189, 196, 199, 212–215, 217–218, 220, 227–228, 243–245, 252–255, 257–277, 288, 291, 294, 296–298, 309, 312, 314, 316
'Little China' (Chosŏn) 15, 259–261, 258, 274
logographic script *see* script
Luo Sen xxi, 16, 289–296, 298, 300, 310

Maeda Tsunanori (1643–1724) 253
Manchu, 8, 57–58, 103, 246, 259–260, 268
Mandarin xx, xxiv, 5–6, 26, 29–30, 36, 101, 115–116, 119, 122, 156, 160, 164, 166–168, 171, 184, 187–188, 214, 243–244, 253; Early Mandarin 36, 164, 166–168, 171
man'yōgana 22, 302
maritime contacts 20
maritime country 24
maritime offices 104
maritime official xxi, 9, 14, 35, 49, 76–77, 81, 89–91, 93, 99, 103–106, 131–132, 136, 151, 309
maritime powers 157
maritime trade 154–155
maritime trading activities 76, 90
maritime traffic 46
Matsuzaki Kankai (1725–1776) 271–272
Matsuzaki Kōdō (1771–1844) 266–267, 275
Matteo Ricci xix, 12, 84
medical 13–15, 28, 38, 68, 253–254, 303, 312
medicine 2–3, 8, 10, 14, 25, 49, 90, 156, 230, 249, 254
Meiji 55, 200, 203, 219; Emperor Meiji (Meiji emperor) 157, 206, 219; Meiji era 53, 211, 221, 250; Meiji government 37, 232–235, 237–240; Meiji Japan 13, 21, 214, 241; Meiji officials 232; Meiji period 37, 200, 225, 240;Meiji reforms 52; Meiji regime 241; Meiji Restoration (1868–1912) 30, 233; Meiji Sinologists 204; post-Meiji vernacularization movement 30
Middle Chinese, 36, 164–167, 171
military 58, 67, 81; military action 236, 240; military affairs 50; military assistance 296; military base 51; military camp 290; military command 250; military confrontation 20, 240; military expansion 157; military officers 68, 132–133; military officials 132; military organization 119; military provisions 247; military prowess 58, 67, 72, 264–265; military reform 200; military support 155; military use 50; military venture 50
Min (Minnanhua) xxvi, 29–30
Ming 10–12, 21, 51, 58–59, 67, 259, 274; Ming army 51; Ming attire 269; Ming China 12, 23, 35–36, 50, 57, 81, 127, 131, 137, 140, 145, 151, 200, 233, 263; Ming Chinese 82, 118, 154, 200, 268; Ming-Chosŏn allied forces 250; Ming clothing style 65; Ming Confucianist 122; Ming Confucian scholar 13, 84, 259; Ming dynasty 10–12, 18, 28, 38, 46, 49, 57–59, 67, 77–78, 148, 190, 192, 233, 259, 264, 272, 274; Ming emperor(s) 24, 50, 141, 145, 154, 158, 233; Ming Empire 141; Ming (Chinese) envoys 51, 144; Ming era 274; Ming maritime officials 81; Ming-style writing 263; Ming tributaries (1587) 19; Ming tribute system 154; Ming troops 50
Ming and Qing dynasties 28, 46, 49, 57–58, 77
missions to Celestial Empire 57–58
missions to China 22, 58–59, 130, 253
'missions to Peking' 57–58, 67
missionary 12, 25, 81, 84, 119, 217, 290
mixed-script *see* script
'Miyajima Documents' xx, 12, 228, 231, 235, 241
Miyajima Seiichirō xx, 12, 37, 53–56, 204–206, 209, 217, 224–226, 228–241
modality of communication xxv, 2, 7, 10, 30, 47, 106, 117, 123
mode of communication x, xx, 48, 52, 61, 64, 76, 94, 98, 105, 118, 128, 151, 153, 160, 187, 196, 201–202, 215, 228, 244, 295, 297–298, 305, 310
monarchist xxiv
monk 10, 20, 22, 30, 51, 124, 133, 136, 143, 199, 209, 217, 244, 247–248, 250, 252, 257, 260, 265, 293–294, 309, 314
morphographic xxiii, 5, 8–9, 26, 29, 34, 39, 95, 105–106, 113, 123, 210, 212, 214, 244–245, 291, 302
morphographic hypothesis 34, 123
morphographic script *see* script
Murayama Tokujun (1832–1893) 250
music 38, 149, 189, 222–223, 228, 230, 260, 264, 268, 270–271, 273–274, 312

Nagasaki 35, 91–92, 94–96, 104–105, 112–113, 118, 219, 237, 253, 303
Nam Ok (1722–1770) 75, 266, 272, 277
Neo-Confucian academy *see* Confucian
Neo-Confucianism *see* Confucianism and Neo-Confucianism
Ningbo 19, 82, 90, 139, 145–146
Niwa Shōhaku (1691–1756) 253
Noma Seiken (1608–1676) 251
non-alphabetic script *see* script
non-phonographic xxiii, 5, 9, 34, 244
nonverbal (communication) 209–210
north-bound envoy *see* envoy
'North-bound envoys' records' *see* envoy
North Korea xxiii, 8, 21, 217

Ogyū Sorai (1666–1728) 262, 258–265, 270, 272, 275–276
Okajima Kanzan (1674–1728) 253
Okinawa xxvii, 12, 23–24, 90, 153–162, 217, 237, 314
'Ōkōchi Documents' xx, 11–12, 37, 48–49, 52–54, 199–200, 202, 204–205, 207, 211, 214, 231, 234, 241, 309
Ōkōchi Teruna 12, 17, 52–53, 202, 217, 221, 309
Old Chinese 36, 163–167, 171
oracle bone script *see* script
oral 60, 183, 311: oral communication 10, 17, 39, 227, 310: oral conversation 60: oral discussion 60: oral exchange 61: oral interpretation 105: oral interpreting 183, 315: oral talk 59: oral understanding problems 34
orthographic xxiii, 8, 97, 161
orthographic-phonetic interface *see* interface

Paekche 20, 142
painting xxvi, 52–53, 92, 119, 189, 193–194, 204, 220, 258, 267, 303–304
Pak Chi-wŏn (1737–1805) 61–62, 130
peerage (system) 157, 225
Peking-Hangzhou Grand Canal xxi, 81, 138, 149
pen-assisted conversation 1, 6, 8
pen-talk xxiv, 5–6, 9, 39, 50, 201, 215
pentasyllabic (quatrain, octave) 11, 230, 65–66, 204
peripheries *see* center-peripheries
Perry, Matthew C. xxi, 17, 289, 295
Phan Bội Châu (1867–1940) 295, 297, 300
phonetic 27, 30

phonetic inter-subjectivity xix, 8–9, 28, 35, 94–95, 106, 113, 115–117, 123, 212: inter-subjectively 95, 300, 302, 114, 116
phonetic scripts *see* script
phonographic script *see* script
phonetic adaptation 9, 30–31
phonetic intersubjectivity xix, 8, 9, 28, 35, 94–95, 106, 113–117, 123, 212, 300, 302
phonographic xxiii, 5, 9, 22, 26, 31, 34, 95, 106, 113, 123, 210, 244, 283, 302
Phùng Khắc Khoan (1528–1613), 15, 309
pinyin xxvi, 94
piracy, 67–69, 78, 146
pirate, 36, 81, 139, 146, 151, 155
poem 11, 15, 22, 30, 63–65, 75, 79–80, 122, 128, 133, 136–137, 144, 158, 165, 176–177, 185–186, 193–194, 197, 202, 204, 212, 220, 222–227, 230–231, 245–247, 249–251, 262, 264, 266–267, 293–294, 309, 313–314, 316
poet 128, 136–137, 223, 226, 230–231, 250–253, 257, 260, 263, 265, 267, 314, 316
poetic xix–xx, 9, 14–17, 25, 29, 34–39, 48, 54, 59, 61–64, 66, 73, 75–80, 97, 105, 118, 121, 129, 131–133, 135–137, 151, 154, 157–161, 171–172, 176–177, 194, 196, 211–212, 215, 218, 220–225, 227–228, 232, 240, 243, 245–246, 249–255, 257–258, 260–267, 276, 291–292, 300, 303, 309, 314–316
poetic improvisation *see* improvisation
poetry xix, 17, 24, 31, 48–49, 54–55, 57, 63, 66, 74, 83, 121, 129, 133, 135–137, 144, 184–185, 187, 189–190, 203, 205, 212, 220–224, 227, 231, 241, 243, 245–246, 250–251, 254, 261–269, 272, 275–276, 292, 294, 296, 303, 309, 313–316: Sinitic poetry 129, 221, 313–316
Portuguese 25, 82, 155, 199
pragmatics iii, xxiv, xxvii, 35, 154, 162, 169, 172, 214
primer 27–28, 114, 156, 168
private 206, 208: private accounts 131: private acquaintance 205: private affairs 207: private activities 59: private brush conversation 208: private capacity 35, 182, 195, 292: private collection 58, 250: private communications 310: private conversation 206: private documents 78: private encounters

38, 61; private friend 233; private interactions 128; private libraries 75; private life 208; private setting 210; private views 186; private words 206
pronoun xxi, 101, 103–104, 134, 164, 166, 170–171
pronounceable xxvi, 26, 29–30, 116
pronunciation xx, xxvi, 8–9, 21, 25–33, 94–95, 106, 113–117, 210, 244, 291, 296, 313
protocol 18, 76, 90–91, 92, 95, 99, 104, 258, 312
province 19, 50, 190; Anhui Province 182; Fujian Province 154; Guangdong Province 24; Guangxi Province 24, 182, 185–186; Hubei Province 28–29, 183–184, 186; Hunan Province 184, 186, 188, 190, 193–194, 296; Jiangxi Province 64, 183, 184; Shandong Province 93, 100–103; Zhejiang Province xxi, 35, 64, 137, 139, 146
Putonghua 29

Qin (dynasty) 24–25, 38, 262
Qing ambassador 55, 56, 229, 233–235, 238, 240
Qing China xxiv, 12, 20, 38, 57–58, 62–63, 65, 70, 89–91, 97, 99, 104–106, 111–112, 118–119, 122, 155, 170, 181, 190, 194, 197, 203–204, 207–209, 217–218, 220, 232–234, 238, 240–241, 261, 274
Qing Chinese 14, 17, 37, 49, 92, 117, 119–120, 188, 194–195, 201, 240
Qing court 52, 64, 153, 155–156, 186, 232–233, 240, 290
Qing dynasty 78, 83, 91, 97, 153, 190, 268, 313
Qing embassy 12, 51–52, 55, 208, 217, 219, 234
Qing emperor 80, 177, 228
Qing empire 122
Qing government 90, 112, 123, 155, 201, 206–207, 220, 238
Qing legation to Japan 49, 51, 54, 218–219, 240; He Ruzhang (1838–1891) 51, 53, 55, 201, 204, 207, 219–222, 227–229, 232–233, 240–241; Huang Zunxian (1848–1905) 12, 53, 55–56, 83, 205, 207–208, 219–223, 225–228, 230, 232, 235–236, 238–239, 241, 316; Li Shuchang (1837–1898), 54–56, 204–206, 209, 240; Shen Wenying (1833–1886) 53, 83, 232, 235, 237, 239, 241; Yao Wendong (1853–1929) 54, 56, 316; Zhang Sigui (1817–1888) 53, 219–220, 224, 241
Qing literati 62
Qing nation 4
Qing official 63, 232
Qing people 182, 237
Qing period 50, 89, 233
Qing regime 268
Qing scholar 189–191, 196, 276
quadrisyllabic (expression) 30, 96, 215
question and answer 89, 97, 99
Quốc ngữ xxiii, xxvi, 25

rapport 36, 38–39, 115, 151, 195–196, 291
record-keeping 9, 99, 112, 120
'Record of sea travel' 73, 248
'Record of the drifting ship' 132–137
'Records of the Border Defense Council of Chosŏn' 78, 99
repatriation (plan) 91, 104, 246, 257
Respond-cum-Return Envoy see envoy
reversal of efflorescence-barbarian relations see central efflorescence
revolutionary xxiv, 14, 296, 298, 300–301
rhyme 27, 64, 136, 177, 212, 222, 262
rhyming 64, 136–137, 194, 224, 226
Ri Sendatsu see Submission of the Chosŏn boat drifter Ri Sendatsu
rites and rituals 38, 59, 82, 259, 268–275
romanization, xxv–xxvi, 25, 29, 94, 290
Russian 26, 234
Ryukyu xxi, xxvii, 12, 14, 19, 23–24, 36, 47–49, 54, 64, 76, 84, 89–91, 153–177, 186, 206, 219, 231, 233–241; Ryukyu domain 23, 153, 157, 233, 236–237; Ryukan *hitsudan* xxvii, 154, 160–166, 169–171, 176–177; Ryukyu Islands, 90, 154, 199, 233; *Ryukyu-kan* 23, 160; Ryukyu Kingdom 12, 18, 20, 91, 114, 153–160, 169, 186, 217, 233, 240; Ryukyu residence 48, 154, 171, 177

samurai xxi, 35, 112, 123, 167, 225, 250, 261, 265, 268, 291
Sa'myŏngdang (1544–1610) 247–248
scholar-official xxii, 9, 12, 14–15, 31, 37, 48, 59, 63, 128, 136, 144, 149, 151, 160, 181, 183, 188, 191, 194, 196, 197, 205, 218, 220, 240, 271, 291, 294, 316
scholarship 14, 25, 39, 83, 190, 251, 260–261, 268, 276–277

script xviii, xxiii, xxv–xxvii, 8–9, 11, 17, 22, 25–26, 29, 114, 123, 285, 297, 302, 305, 310–311: abjad script 32: alphabetic script 33, 123: calligraphic scripts 80: character scripts 17: Chinese script 111, 285: clerical script 199: Cyrillic script 26: logographic script 33, 284, 302: mixed-script 30, 284: morphographic script 34, 113: non-alphabetic script 114, 123: oracle bone script 283, 285: phonetic scripts 22: phonographic script xxiii, 22, 85, 302: script-specific 17, 34, 123, 281: simplified script 29: Sinitic script 106, 212, 310: traditional script 29, 315
scripta franca xx, 9–10, 12, 14, 17, 34, 111, 115, 128, 218, 243–245, 255, 258
script-specific *see* script
seafarer: Chosŏn seafarers 81, 135: distressed seafarer 89–93, 96–98, 104–106
Sea of Japan 20, 89, 123, 218
second miracle xvii
semantic adaptation 9, 30–31
semantically stable 9, 118
semiotic (affordance, potential) xxiii, xxvii, 9, 11, 14, 37, 106, 193, 210, 212–213, 298–299
sentence-final particle xxi, 101, 103, 164
Senzaimaru 35, 112, 115, 117–120, 122–124, 311
Shandong Province *see* province
Shang (dynasty) 11, 20, 189, 268–270, 273, 283–284
Shanghai xxiv, xxix, 35, 55, 83, 111–113, 115–123, 290, 296
Shanghainese 30, 116
Shen Wenying *see* Qing legation to Japan
shipwreck 14, 35, 76, 91, 93–94, 96–99, 101, 104, 106, 132
shogun 69–71, 90, 99, 245, 247, 249, 271, 312, 314
shogunate 91–92, 94–95, 155–157, 209, 221, 225, 244, 246, 259, 261, 289–290, 312
Shōheizaka School 250
'*Shuowen Jiezi*' ('Explaining Graphs and Analyzing Characters') xiii
silent conversation iii, xxiii, 4, 7, 9–10, 14, 38–39, 46–47, 50, 64, 124, 151, 201, 209, 266, 300
Silla 20, 142
simplified script *see* script

sinicization 154, 156–157
sinicized 20, 24
Sinitic as semantic and semiotic interface *see* interface
Sinitic-based literary heritage 15, 196, 241
Sinitic poetry *see* poetry
Sinitic script *see* script
Sinocentric World Order *see* Chinese World Order
sinogram xviii, xxiii–xxvi, 5, 11, 22, 26–27, 31, 39, 47–48, 54, 89, 94, 116, 123–124, 161, 194, 199, 210, 215, 227–228, 231, 241, 244, 261–262, 283–284, 288, 292
Sinographic xvii–xix, 9–11, 47, 229, 289, 294: foreign Sinographic texts 11: Sinographic cosmopolis xviii, xxiii, 7, 9–12, 25, 30–31, 48, 160, 215, 218, 244, 276, 284, 305: Sinographic East Asia xxiii–xxiv, xxvii, 5, 8, 17, 20–21, 25, 27, 30–31, 34–35, 38–39, 46, 48, 62, 82–83, 106, 112, 114, 121, 128, 194, 196–197, 199–201, 212, 215, 217, 221, 228, 240, 257–259, 265, 276, 284, 289, 292, 295, 302, 305
Sino-Japanese cultural exchange 223
Sino-Japanese diplomacy 233
Sino-Japanese diplomatic relations 219–20
Sino-Japanese encounters 115
Sino-Japanese friendship 72
Sino-Japanese Friendship and Trade Treaty (1871) 51, 91, 218, 236
Sino-Japanese negotiations 219, 231–3, 235, 237, 240
Sino-Japanese relations 54, 111, 289
Sino-Japanese War (1894–1895) *see* First Sino-Japanese War (1894–1895)
Sino-Korean 21, 114
Sinosphere xx, 17–18, 28, 36, 46, 127, 139–141, 146, 150–151, 153, 167, 243–244, 249, 312
Sino-Vietnamese 24–25, 296
Sin Yu-han (1681–1752) 72–73, 264, 303
social exchange 63
socializing brushtalk 189, 232, 314
socializing chanting 15, 37, 54, 59, 62–63, 75, 189, 212, 215, 220, 232, 245, 291, 314: chanting in harmony 291
sociolinguistics xxiv, xxvii
Song (dynasty) 11, 27, 46, 59, 97, 128, 140, 166–167, 189–190, 199, 213, 222, 244, 262–264, 274
Sŏng Tae-chung (1732–1809) 75, 266, 272, 277

Son of Heaven *see* Heaven
Sorai school 259, 262–265, 270, 272, 275
Sorai studies 260–261, 275
sorobun 244
sound xviii–xix, 21–22, 26, 33, 116–117, 127, 141, 200, 209, 227, 262–263, 300, 302
South China Sea 24, 89–90
Southern Min xxvi
South Korea xxiii–xxiv, 8, 21, 68, 217
Sō Yoshinari (1604–1657) 246
speech xvii, xix–xx, xxiii, xxix, 1–2, 5, 7–8, 10, 26, 28, 30–31, 33–34, 36–39, 46–47, 49, 53, 60–61, 64, 89, 93–94, 101–103, 106, 113–114, 116–117, 123, 128, 133–134, 140–141, 147, 151, 154, 186–188, 196, 200–202, 206–207, 209–210, 212–213, 218, 220, 227, 257–258, 291–292, 299–300, 302
'Submission of the Chosŏn boat drifter Ri Sendatsu' 133–134
Sui (dynasty) 22, 67, 113, 142, 273
Sungkyunkwan University 59
Sun Yat-sen 14, 48, 50, 298
suzerain 18, 23, 47, 50, 57–58, 67, 138, 150, 271
symbolic (power, value) 18–19, 93, 267, 269, 276, 291–292, 295, 299–300, 302–303, 305
synchronous xxiv, 1–2, 8–9, 12, 32–34, 48, 51, 61, 94, 113, 122–123, 217
syntactic adaptation 30–31

Taiping Rebellion (1851–1865) 112, 119, 290
Taiwan xxvi, 5, 8, 23, 90, 153–154, 160, 162, 165, 170, 176–177, 233
Takeda Shun'an (1661–1745) 253
talents on horse 246
Tang (dynasty) xxiii, 10–11, 19, 22, 25, 27–28, 30, 46, 67, 72–73, 77, 81, 98, 128, 142, 251, 262–265, 273; Tang people 72–73; Tang (poem, poet) 226, 231, 265; Tang ships 77
Temple of Confucius 183
The Analects 190
Three Character Classic 156
Tokugawa 67, 70–71, 118, 155, 244, 247, 250, 259, 271
Tokugawa bakufu 245, 248
Tokugawa Confucians 273–274
Tokugawa court 73
Tokugawa General 67
Tokugawa government 72, 111–112

Tokugawa Japan 16, 23, 72, 89–91, 98–99, 104, 257–258, 277, 310
Tokugawa literati xx, 257
Tokugawan diplomacy 123
Tokugawa officials 14
Tokugawa period 15, 17, 73, 91, 275
Tokugawa Shogun 90
Tokugawa shogunate 91, 94, 209, 221, 225, 244, 246, 259, 289
t'ongsinsa xx, 38, 48, 66–69, 72–73, 75–76, 130–131, 212, 245–246, 249, 251, 254, 257–258, 260–277
topolect xxi, xxvi, 26–27, 30, 101, 105, 113–114, 116, 167
Toyotomi no Hideyoshi 50–51, 68, 70, 155, 247, 264
traditional script *see* script
transactional (communication) 8, 106, 115, 169, 171–172
transnational literary community 12, 25
travel diary xxvi, 16, 36, 136, 181–182
travel journal 57, 59, 129, 134, 137, 148, 258, 277
travelogue xxi, 9–10, 57, 61, 73, 81, 83, 129, 144, 150–151, 169; 'Travelogues to Peking' 48–49, 57–66, 129, 158
tributary (system) 12, 15, 18–20, 22–24, 47, 57–59, 67, 70, 91, 99, 139–140, 142, 145, 155, 158, 219, 231, 233–235, 240–241, 259, 271, 286–287; model tributary 18
tribute 10, 19, 62, 139, 158, 169, 176, 191, 223, 286; Tribute Embassies 19; tribute envoys 67; tribute goods 192; tribute items 18, 185; tribute journey 62; tribute mission 64; tribute rites and rituals 59; tribute ships 176; tributes to heaven (*see* Heaven); tribute system 19, 154; tribute-trading routes 91; tribute visits 181, 187
Tsushima xx, 14, 68, 70, 72, 244–246, 248–249, 257, 310
typhoon 23, 89, 104, 176

unintelligible xxvi, 11, 20, 24, 28, 105, 153, 291
universal Confucian civilization 121, 275–277, 284, 310

verbatim (record, transcript) 3–4, 35, 95, 97, 106, 112, 209–210
vernacular xxi, 21–23, 25–26, 31, 36, 47, 73, 84, 94–95, 100–101, 103, 105–106, 111, 113–114, 119, 128, 160, 164, 167,

172. 212–213. 215. 243–244. 310. 313.
315: vernacular Chinese 36. 103. 215:
vernacular literature 36. 167. 172
Vice-Envoy *see* envoy
Vietnam xix. xxiii–xxiv. 8. 15. 20. 24–26.
38. 49. 56–57. 62–64. 78–80. 84. 127.
181–182. 191. 194. 197. 217. 243–244.
295–296. 298–299. 301. 315
Vietnamese xxii–xxiv. xxvi. 2–3. 8–9.
11. 13–16. 24–26. 30–31. 36. 47. 57.
62–65. 78–79. 111. 181–182. 185.
187. 191. 197. 244. 285. 289. 295–298.
300–301. 303. 305. 309–310.
312–313
Vietnamese-Chinese 36. 79. 181. 191
Vietnamese-Korean exchange 64–66
Vietnam War (1955–1975) 2. 8. 25

waka 22. 314
Waseda University Library xxvi. 54–55.
158–159. 235
western 102. 222. 315: aggression 112;
Asia xvii: author name xxv: boat drifters
81: communicative language teaching
methods 299; countries: 49. 76: cultures
203: Europe 8: firearms 200: influence
47: missionaries. explorers. and
merchants 81: orientalists 290: paper
98: powers (maritime) xviii. 16. 20. 112.
157. 230: scholars/missionaries 12. 15:
scholarship 83: steamers 90: thoughts
47: vessels 23. 157: world 19
westerner 82. 111. 113. 118. 123.
203. 227
Williams. Samuel Wells xxi. 290–294

Wŏn Chung-kŏ (1719–1790) 75. 266.
272–273. 277. 303
writing-assisted conversation 244
writing-mediated (communication)
xxiii–xxiv. xxvii. 1. 3. 5–8. 32. 34–38.
46–50. 52. 66. 75–76. 81–82. 84. 105.
116. 123–124. 130. 151. 162. 171. 182.
186–187. 190. 193. 196–197. 199. 202.
208. 210–212. 215. 218. 220–221. 231.
257–258. 261. 265. 272. 276–277. 291.
298. 313
writing system xix. 8. 26. 113. 127. 244.
284–285. 313
Wu (dialect. topolect) 78. 113

Xu Shen (c. 58–148 CE) xviii

Yamagata Shūnan (1687–1752) 262
Yanagawa Shigeoki (1603–1684) 246
Yao Wendong *see* Qing legation to Japan
Yellow Sea 90. 99. 102
Yi Chi-hang (1647–?) 35–36. 132–137. 151
Yi Hyŏn (1654–?) 254. 262
Yin (dynasty) 147. 168–170
Yi Pong-hwan (1710–1770) 271–272
Yi Su-Kwang (1563–1629) 15. 158

Zen Buddhism *see* Buddhism
Zhang Sigui *see* Qing legation to Japan
Zhejiang Province *see* province
Zhu Shunshui 13. 84. 118. 259
Zhu Xi. 189. 244. 264
Zhuzi studies 138. 141. 258. 260–261.
269. 271–272. 274–275; *see also*
Family rites of Zhuzi

Printed in the United States
by Baker & Taylor Publisher Services